# Abingdon Pottery

Operating in Abingdon, Illinois, from 1934 to 1950, this company made vases, cookie jars, utility ware, and lamps. The sometimes used gold and decals to decorate their wares, and a decorated piece is worth about 25% more than the same shape with no decoration. Black, bronze, or red-glazed pieces are priced higher than those in other colors. See also Cookie Jars.

Ashtray, #510, donkey, black, scarce, 5½" dia ...............**95.00**
Bookends, #305, sea gulls, 6½", pr ....................................**60.00**
Bowl, #657, Contour ...........**22.00**
Candle holders, #126, Classic, white, 2", pr ..................**38.00**
Candle holders, #434, Fern Leaf, 5½x3", ea .......................**27.50**
Creamer & sugar bowl, #681 & #681, daisy ....................**30.00**
Figurine, #574, heron ..........**25.00**
Figurine, #661, swan, chartreuse, 3¾" .................................**35.00**
Jar, #301, Ming, turquoise, 7¼" ................................**80.00**
Mint compote, #568, pink, footed, 1942-47, 6" .....................**28.00**
Pitcher, #200, w/ice lip .........**30.00**

Tea tile, #. ☑
Vase, #104, Delta Classic, 10" .**28.00**
Vase, #315, Athena Classic, white, 1934-36, 9" ......................**38.00**
Vase, #550, fluted .................**26.00**
Vase, #599, quilted, white, 9" .**30.00**
Wall pocket, #375, double morning glory, white, 7¾" ......**45.00**
Window box, #498, Han, 14½" .**25.00**

# Advertising Collectibles

Since the late 1800s competition among manufacturers of retail products has produced multitudes of containers, signs, trays, and novelty items, each bearing a catchy slogan, colorful lithograph or some other type of ploy, all flagrantly intent upon catching the eye of the potential customer. In their day some were more successful than others, but now it's the advertising material itself rather than the product that rings up the big sales — to avid collectors and flea market shoppers, not the product's consumers! Condition plays a vital role in evaluating vintage advertising pieces. Our estimates are for items in at least near-mint condition, unless another condition code is present in the description. Try to

**Scroll bowl, ca 1941-1945, gold and decals on ivory, $45.00.**

5

be very objective when you assess wear and damage.

See also Ashtrays; Automobilia; Avon; Banks; Black Americana; Breweriana; Character and Promotional Drinking Glasses; Cigarette Lighters; Coca-Cola; Fast Food Collectibles; Gas Station Collectibles; Keen Kutter; Novelty Radios; Novelty Telephones; Pin-Back Buttons; Planters Peanuts; 7-Up. Refer to *Huxford's Collectible Advertising*; *Value Guide to Advertising Memorabilia* by B.J. Summers; *Zany Characters of the Ad World* by Mary Jane Lamphier; *Antique Tins* by Fred Dodge; and *Advertising Character Collectibles* by Warren Dotz. All are published by Collector Books.

### Ad Characters

Hundreds of easily recognizable characters have been created to represent a company or a particular product. These trademark personalities have been modeled as dolls, banks, cookie jars, and salt and pepper shakers; their faces adorn mugs, plates, tin containers, and scores of other items, and collectors love them all.

Aristocrat Tomato, talking alarm clock, Heinz, 1980s, 9½", NM ......................**150.00**
Aunt Jemima, puzzle, die-cut cardboard image, 4x5", EX ...............................**125.00**
Aunt Jemima & Uncle Mose, salt & pepper shakers, plastic, 1951, 5½", pr .................**35.00**
Beauregard w/bottle, rattle toy, plastic, Borden, 1950s, 5", EX ...............................**35.00**

Big Boy, bank, vinyl figure, Marriott, 1970s, 8", EX ........**20.00**
Big Boy, night light, vinyl figure, Marriott, 1970s, 7", NM ..**75.00**
Big Boy, PVC figure w/hamburger, Frisch's, 1980s, 2½", NM .**15.00**
Big Boy, salt & pepper shakers, ceramic, Marriott, 1950s, 4½", EX, pr ..................**125.00**
Blatz Baseball Players, display, 3 figures & 2 flags, 1968, 16", EX ...............................**150.00**
Blue Nun, display, vinyl figure, no base, 1974, 12", NM ......**35.00**
Blue Nun, display, vinyl figure, w/base, 1974, 12", NM ..**75.00**
Blue Nun, salt & pepper shakers, ceramic, 1970s, 4½", M, pr ...................................**125.00**
Bosco Rabbit, container, plastic figure, Bosco Chocolate, 1960s, 8", M ....................**20.00**
Bud Man, beer stein, ceramic figure, 1989, 8½", M ..........**30.00**
Bud Man, tab knob, vinyl figure, 1991, 9", M ....................**75.00**
Buster Brown & Tige, bank, red plastic ball, 1960s, 5", NM ................................**35.00**
Buster Brown & Tige, shoe tree, plastic, 4½", NM ............**35.00**

**Campbells Kid hotpad holder, painted plaster, 5¾", $10.00.**

# FleaMarket Trader

## Tenth
edition

Edited by
*Sharon & Bob Huxford*

**COLLECTOR BOOKS**
*A Division of Schroeder Publishing Co., Inc.*

The current values in this book should be used only as a guide. They are not intended to set prices, which vary from one section of the country to another. Auction prices as well as dealer prices vary greatly and are affected by condition as well as demand. Neither the Editors nor the Publisher assumes responsibility for any losses that might be incurred as a result of consulting this guide.

## *Searching for a Publisher?*

We are always looking for knowledgeable people considered to be experts within their fields. If you feel that there is a real need for a book on your collectible subject and have a large comprehensive collection, contact COLLECTOR BOOKS.

## *COVER INFORMATION*

Mr. Peanut, peanut butter maker, 12" tall, marked Mr. Peanut Standard Brands Inc., $25.00; *Country Gentleman* magazine, April 1943, $3.50; Vegetable bowl, 9½" diameter, violets in urn, no marks, $8.00; Pottery planter, 2 birds on pinecones, no marks, 8½x4", $10.00; Fostoria-American cereal bowls, $10.00; Postcard 3½x5½", loving thoughts, Germany, trademark 2136, $5.00; First Barbie horse, "Dancer," on stand, MIB, $75.00; G, $35.00; Pottery planter, elf and leaf, 5" tall, marked Made in Japan 39 in a circle, $12.00; Keen Kutter straight razor, 9¾" open, marked K17, ivory handle, $35.00; Shaving brush, 4½" tall x 1¼" diameter, marked sterilized 153 Rubberset trademark Made in U.S.A., $18.00; Pompeian Fragrance talcum tin, 6" tall, $8.00; McCoy planter with handle, white pottery, 7½" wide marked McCoy, $20.00.

Printed by IMAGE GRAPHICS, INC., Paducah, Kentucky

# INTRODUCTION

The Flea Market Trader is a unique price guide, geared specifically for the convenience of the flea market shopper. Several categories have been included that are not often found in general price guides, while others on antiques not usually seen at flea markets have been omitted. The new categories will serve to introduce you to collectibles that are currently coming on, the best and often the only source for which is the market place. As all of us who religiously pursue the circuits are aware, flea markets are the most exciting places in the world to shop; but unless you're well-informed on current values those 'really great' buys remain on the table. Like most pursuits in life, preparation has its own rewards; and it is our intention to provide you with the basic tool of education and awareness toward that end. But please bear in mind that the prices in this guide are meant to indicate only general values. Many factors determine actual selling prices; values vary from one region to another, dealers pay various wholesale prices for their wares, and your bargaining skill is important too.

We have organized our listings into general categories for easy use; if you have trouble locating an item, refer to the index. Unless another condition code is present in the description line, the values we have suggested reflect prices of items in mint condition. NM stands for minimal damage, VG indicates that the item will bring 40% to 60% of its mint price, and EX should be somewhere between the two. Glassware is assumed clear unless a color is noted. Only generally accepted abbreviations have been used.

This is our second full-color edition; we hope you enjoy the photos. We would like to take this opportunity to thank each author, dealer, and auction house who allowed us to use their photographs.

The Editors

# PHOTO CREDITS

*Black Collectibles Sold in America*, P. J. Gibbs

*Blue Willow, Identification & Value Guide*, Mary Frank Gaston

*Character Toys & Collectibles, First & Second Series*, David Longest

*Christmas Collectibles*, Margaret & Kenn Whitmyer

*Christmas Ornaments, Lights & Decorations*, George Johnson

*Collectible Glassware From the 40s, 50s & 60s*, Gene Florence

*Collecting Royal Haeger*, Lee Garmon & Doris Frizell

*Collector's Encyclopedia of American Dinnerware*, Jo Cunningham

*Collector's Encyclopedia of California Pottery*, Jack Chipman

*Collector's Encyclopedia of Children's Dishes*, Margaret & Kenn Whitmyer

*Collector's Encyclopedia of Cookie Jars*, Fred & Joyce Roerig

*Collector's Encyclopedia of Noritake*, Joan Van Patten

*Collector's Encyclopedia of Fiesta*, Sharon & Bob Huxford

*Collector's Encyclopedia of Geisha Girl Porcelain*, Elyce Litts

*Collector's Encyclopedia of Hall China*, Margaret & Kenn Whitmyer

*Collector's Encyclopedia of McCoy Pottery*, Sharon & Bob Huxford

*Collector's Encyclopedia of Niloak Pottery*, David Edwin Gifford

*Collector's Encyclopedia of Russel Wright Designs*, Ann Kerr

*Collector's Guide to Art Deco*, Mary Frank Gaston

*Collector's Guide to Novelty Radios*, Marty Bunis & Robert Breed

*Collector's Guide to Transistor Radios*, Marty & Sue Bunis

*Covered Animal Dishes*, Everett Grist

*Huxford's Collectible Advertising*, Sharon & Bob Huxford

*Illustrated Value Guide of Cookie Jars, An*, Ermagene Westfall

*Machine Made & Contemporary Marbles*, Everett Grist

*Modern Collector's Dolls, Sixth Series*, Pat Smith

*Modern Toys, American Toys, 1930–1980*, Linda Baker

*Purinton Pottery*, Susan Morris

*Royal Copley*, Leslie Wolfe (edited by Joe Devine)

*Salt & Pepper Shakers, Third Edition*, Helen Guarnaccia

*Sheet Music Reference & Price Guide*, Anna Marie Guiheen & Marie-Reine A. Pafik

*Teddy Bears, Annalee's & Steiff Animals*, Margaret Fox Mandel

*Shoes of Glass*, Libby Yalom

*Toys, Antiques & Collectibles*, David Longest

Campbell Kids, child's fork, engraved head above M-m-m Good, EX ..........................**5.00**

Campbell Kids, Christmas card, 15 kids, 1970, 3½x9", EX .....**15.00**

Campbell Kids, doll, girl, stuffed cloth, ca 1973, 15½", EX .**65.00**

Campbell Kids, salt & pepper shakers, plastic, 1950s, 4½", EX, pr ............................**35.00**

Cap 'N Crunch, coloring book, 1968, 8x10", EX .............**30.00**

Champ Man, PVC bendee, Champion Auto Stores, 1991, 6", M ...............................**15.00**

Charlie the Tuna, figural lamp, Star-Kist, 1970, missing shade, VG ......................**25.00**

Charlie the Tuna, squeeze toy, vinyl, Star-Kist, 1973, 7½", NM ................................**35.00**

Chuck E Cheese, bank, winking figural, plastic, 1980s, 5½", EX ..................................**10.00**

Colonel & Mrs Sanders, salt & pepper shakers, plastic busts, 4", NM .........................**100.00**

Colonel Sanders, bank, plastic figure w/cane, 1960s, 12½", EX ..................................**25.00**

Colonel Sanders, bank, plastic figure w/restaurant, 6", NM ......**45.00**

Colonel Sanders, night light, bisque, 1976, EX in box **70.00**

Count Chocula, painted vinyl figure, 1975, 8" ..................**35.00**

Cracker Jack Boy, window decal, lg, EX .............................**25.00**

Crayola Bear, stuffed plush, Crayola Graphics International, 1986, 6" ...........................**5.00**

Curad Taped Crusader, painted vinyl figure, Kendall-Futuro Co, 1975, 7½" .................**25.00**

Del Monte Pineapple, doll, plush, 1983, M ..........................**10.00**

Diaparene Baby, doll, vinyl, 1980, 5", NM ...........................**35.00**

Dino, bank, plastic figure, Sinclair Oil, 1960s, 4", NM .........**25.00**

Dino, vinyl inflatable toy, Sinclair Oil, 1960s, 12", NM .......**20.00**

Dutch Boy, display, pressed cardboard figure, 1950s, 15", EX .................................**90.00**

Elsie the Cow, bank, vinyl head, Borden, 1970s, 9", EX ...**75.00**

Elsie the Cow, Beulah & Beauregard, blotter, 1940s, 3½x6", EX ..................................**15.00**

Elsie the Cow, bowl, Elsie dancing in flowers, Cambridge, M ...**125.00**

**Elsie the Cow ceramic mug with gold trim, 3¼", from $65.00 to $75.00.**

Elsie the Cow, paperweight, shaped as milk carton picturing Elsie, G ....................**22.00**

Elsie the Cow, pendant, Elsie's face w/name, gold plastic...**6.00**

Elsie the Cow, postcard, Elsie's Cowdillac, color, NM .......**7.50**

Elsie the Cow, push puppet, wood & paper, Elsie moos, 1950s, 5", NM .........................**200.00**

Elsie the Cow, soap, Looking Glass, M in original holder .........................**145.00**

Elsie the Cow, tin, Borden's Instant Starlac, 5-qt .....**55.00**

Energizer Bunny, squeeze light, vinyl figure, 1991, 4½", NM ......................**10.00**

Ernie the Keebler Elf, squeeze toy, vinyl, 1974, 7", NM ........**15.00**

Eveready Cat, bank, plastic, 1970s, 6", M ...................**10.00**

Falls City Bottle Man, nodder, composition, 1970, 14", EX .**150.00**

Fisk Tire Boy, bank, white plastic figure, Uniroyal, 1970s, 8½", M ......./............................**125.00**

Gerber Baby, doll, rubber, sculpted hair, 1955, 12", EX ..........**45.00**

Good Humor Bar, squeeze toy, vinyl, 1975, 8", NM .....**250.00**

Hamm's Bear, bank, ceramic figure, 1980s, 11", M .........**25.00**

Hamm's Bear, salt & pepper shakers, ceramic, 1980s, 6", M, pr ..............................**25.00**

Handy Flame, salt & pepper shakers, ceramic, blue, 1950s, 4", EX, pr ......................**25.00**

Happy Foot, display, composition, McGregor, 1950s, 12", NM ...............................**400.00**

Hershey Bar, PVC bendee, 1980s, 4½", NM ...........................**7.00**

Hershey's Kiss, doll, plush, embroidered face, 8", EX....**8.00**

Hersheykin, holding a Mr Goodbar, PVC bendee, 2", NM......**5.00**

Hoover Housewife, nodder, ceramic, 1960s, 8", EX..**125.00**

Hush Puppies, bank, vinyl dog on base, 1970s, 8", EX+ .....**25.00**

ICEE Bear, bank, vinyl, ICEE Developers Inc, 1970s, 8", NM .................................**25.00**

Joe Camel, can cooler, vinyl head in sunglasses, 1991, 4", M ...**10.00**

Jolly Green Giant, squeeze toy, vinyl, 1975, 9½", NM ....**55.00**

KC Piston, nodder, papier-mache, 1960s, 7", NM ..............**125.00**

King Royal, bank, vinyl figure, Royal Gelatin, 1970s, 10", NM .................................**55.00**

Kool-Aid Man, mechanical bank, plastic, 1970s, 7", M ......**25.00**

Little Debbie, doll, porcelain, all original, MIB .................**40.00**

Little Miss Sunbeam, doll, plastic, M ...................................**125.00**

Little Oscar in Wienermobile, pull toy, plastic, 1950s, 4½", EX ....**150.00**

M&M's Candy Man, key chain, PVC figure, 1980s, 4", NM .........**3.00**

M&M's Candy Man, tree ornament/package lid, plastic, 1980s, 2½", NM ...............**2.00**

Mack Bulldog, figure, plastic, Mack Trucks, 1970s, 8", NM ................................**55.00**

**Magic Chef vinyl bank, 1980s, 7", NM, $10.00.**

Magic Chef, salt & pepper shakers, plastic, 1950s, 5", EX+, pr ....................................**35.00**

Magic Chef, vinyl figure, Magic Chef Inc, 1960s, 7½" .....**20.00**

Meow Mix Cat, pet toy, vinyl, Ralston Purina, 1976, 5", EX .........**25.00**

Michelin Man, vinyl figure, 1980s, 14", M .............................55.00

Mohawk Tommy, ceramic figure on base, Mohawk Carpets, 1960s, 6", EX+ .............350.00

Morton Salt Girl, mugs, pictures girl, 1964, MIB, set of 4...25.00

Mr Bubble, squeeze toy, vinyl figure, 1990, 8", NM ..........35.00

Mr Bubble Tub Pal, pink, blue & white vinyl, Airwick, 1990, 8" ................................35.00

Mr Clean, bottle, plastic figure, 1960s, 12", EX+ ...........150.00

Mr Clean, doll, vinyl, 1961, 8", NM ..............................100.00

Mr Zip, pull toy, plastic, US Postal Service, 1970s, 7½", NM ..............................125.00

Nipper the Dog, painted plaster figure, RCA Victor, 1980s, 4", NM ...............................35.00

Otto the Orkin Man, metal figure on base, 1960s, 4", NM .75.00

Pizza Hut Pete, bank, plastic, 1969, 7½", M ..................25.00

Poll Parrot, display, painted plaster parrot on perch, 1950s, 15", EX .........................200.00

Poppie Girl, doll, vinyl, jointed head, Pillsbury, 1972, 6", EX ...................................15.00

Poppie Girl, finger puppet, vinyl, Pillsbury, 3½", EX .........15.00

Poppin' Fresh, bank, ceramic, 1987, 7½", MIB ..............30.00

Poppin' Fresh, doll, painted cloth, Pillsbury, 14", EX ..........15.00

Poppin' Fresh, doll, vinyl, jointed head, Pillsbury, 7", EX ..12.00

Poppin' Fresh, salt & pepper shakers, ceramic, 1970s, 3½", EX, pr ...........................25.00

Punchy, game pieces, plastic, Hawaiian Punch, 1976, 3", M, set of 4 ...........................15.00

Quick Bunny, PVC figure, Nestle, 1991, 6", M ...............5.00

Quick Bunny, syrup container, Nestle, 1980s, 8½", M .....5.00

Raid Bug, windup toy, plastic, 1980s, 4", NM ...............35.00

Red Goose, bank, red plastic figure, 1960s, 5", NM ........15.00

Red Goose, plaster figure on base, 1940s, 5", EX ................20.00

**Reddy Kilowatt playing cards, double deck, dated 1951, EX+, $40.00.**

Reddy Kilowatt, bottle cap, Your Electric Servant, red & white plastic ..............................5.00

Reddy Kilowatt, coin, Light For Freedom...1879-1954, face on side ...................................8.00

Reddy Kilowatt, earrings, Your Favorite Pin-Up, screw type, pr .....................................12.00

Reddy Kilowatt, figure, glow-in-dark plastic, 1961, 6", from $100 to .........................125.00

Reddy Kilowatt, hot plate mat, face w/atoms on cardboard, 5½" dia ...........................15.00

Reddy Kilowatt, lighter, Florida Power & Light Co, Storm Master, metal ................25.00

Reddy Kilowatt, Magic Gripper, yellow rubber, 4½" dia, MIP ...............................10.00

Reddy Kilowatt, nodder, papier-mache cowboy, 1960s, 6½", EX+ ..............................250.00

Reddy Kilowatt, patch, face w/CIPS hard hat, Safety Club, 3" dia ......................**8.00**

Reddy Kilowatt, pin, The People's Choice, red & green on white, ¾" ......................**10.00**

Reddy Kilowatt, tie clip, For Better Living Tie In w/Reddy, 1953, MOC ...................**15.00**

Reddy Kilowatt, tie tack, face on pewter, round ................**16.00**

Scrubbing Bubble, bank, ceramic, 4½", MIB ........................**15.00**

Scrubbing Bubble, squeeze toy, vinyl, 1989, 3½", M .........**5.00**

**Snap! Crackle! Pop! push puppet, plastic, Kellogg's, 1984, 4", EX, ea. $15.00.**

Snap! Crackle! Pop!, squeeze toy, vinyl, 1975, 7½", EX, ea ..**20.00**

Sony Boy, doll, vinyl, Sony Corp, 1960s, 4", NM ..............**125.00**

Speedy Alka-Seltzer, bank, rubber, Canadian version, 1960s, 5½", EX ........................**175.00**

Speedy Alka-Seltzer, squeeze toy, vinyl figure, 1960s, 5½", EX ...............................**250.00**

Spuds MacKenzie, display light, polyethylene figure, 1980s, 15", NM ........................**100.00**

Squirt Boy, bank, ceramic figure, 1948, 8", EX+ ..............**150.00**

Squirt Boy, display, composition figure & bottle, 1947, 13", EX ...............................**400.00**

Tony the Tiger, squeeze toy, vinyl, Kellogg's, 1974, 7½", EX ...............................**30.00**

Toucan Sam, push puppet, plastic, Kellogg's Fruit Loops, 1984, 4", EX+ ..........................**15.00**

Trix Rabbit, squeeze toy, vinyl, General Mills, 1977, 9", EX+ ................................**25.00**

Twenty-Four Hour Bug, bank, vinyl, Pepto-Bismol, 1970s, 7", NM ...........................**35.00**

Wards Wise-Buy Owl, bank, metal, 1970s, 6", NM ....**25.00**

Westinghouse Tuff Guy, figure, composition & wood, 1940, 4", EX ...............................**125.00**

Westinghouse Tuff Guy, figure in chef's hat, plaster, 1952, 5½", EX ...............................**45.00**

Willie & Millie, salt & pepper shakers, plastic, 1950s, 3", EX, pr ...........................**15.00**

Wizard of O's, squeeze toy, vinyl, Franco-American, 1978, 7½" ......................**10.00**

Wrigley's Gum, squeeze toy, vinyl gum package, EX ..........**48.00**

**Door Plates**

Door push plates were generally used on screen doors of old general stores in a convenient spot where you would reach out to 'push' or 'pull' the door open. They carried a message to remind you to buy manufacturers' particular products. Many of the early (and the most desirable) push plates were made of porcelain, but other varieties were made of tin or celluloid. The average size of most push plates is 4" x 7" (although size may vary). Prices quoted are for push plates in very good to excellent condition; rarity is also considered. For further information we recommend contacting Edward Foley, who is listed in the Directory under Pennsylvania.

**Star Naphtha Washing Powder, porcelain, $125.00.**

Canada Dry Ginger Ale, tin .**40.00**
Colonial Is Good Bread, embossed & painted metal, 31½", EX  . .**110.00**
Crisco, porcelain .................**150.00**
Foley Kidney Pills, porcelain  .... **75.00**
King Cole Coffee & Tea (plain), porcelain ........................**70.00**
Reach for Sunbeam Bread, red, white & blue enameled metal, VG ................................**55.00**
Slipknot Rubber Heels, tin ..**30.00**
Tetley Tea, porcelain ...........**95.00**

**Miscellaneous**

Acorn Stoves & Ranges, trade card, 1881 calendar inside, VG ................................**16.00**
Angelus Marshmallows, tin, glass lid, round, EX ...............**55.00**
Ayer's Cherry Pectoral, trade card, girl & dove, EX .....**24.00**
Baker's Cocoa, cookie jar, glass, chocolate girl, 10", EX .**143.00**
Bayer Aspirin, sign, tin, Safe For Aches & Pains..., 15x18", VG+ ................................**50.00**

Beech-Nut Tobacco, sign, porcelain, pouch & product name, 11x22", VG .....................**60.00**
Berma Coffee, tin, screw lid, black & gold, 1-lb, EX .............**52.00**
Blue-Jay Corn Plasters, display, die-cut tin, Grandma, EX+ .**250.00**
Blue-Jay Corn Plasters, display, die-cut tin, Grandpa, VG ....**130.00**

**Boston Rubbers blotter, lady with umbrella, ca 1906, 6½x3¾", $8.00.**

Bubble Up, sign, tin, Kiss Of Lemon, Kiss Of Lime, 12x28", M ..**50.00**
Bull Durham Tobacco, trolley sign, bull image & product, 11x21", EX ...................**350.00**
Calumet Baking Powder, thermometer, wood, Best By Taste, 22", G+ .............**310.00**
CD Kenny Co, tip tray, litho tin, Thanksgiving Greetings, 5⅛" dia, EX ........................**240.00**
Chase & Sanborn Coffee, poster, men in New England grocery, 20x33", G ....................**150.00**
Cherry Smash, bottle topper, plastic, 2-sided, NM .............**10.00**

Chicken Dinner Candy, sign, waxed cardboard, Eat...5¢, 12x24", NM ...................**22.00**

Clabber Girl Baking Powder, grocer's notebook, 8x3¾", EX+ ...............................**12.00**

Dad's Root Beer, sign, die-cut cardboard, ½-gal bottle, EX+ ...............................**45.00**

Dan Patch Cut Plug, tin, slip lid, black & red on yellow, 3x4x6", EX ..................................**65.00**

Dills Cube Cut Tobacco, pocket tin, upright, VG+ ..........**45.00**

Dr AC Daniels, sign, embossed tin, white on black, 17½x28", EX ..................................**110.00**

Duke's Mixture, sign, porcelain, hand rolling cigarette, 8x5", G ....................................**110.00**

Eight O'Clock Coffee, bank, red w/gold logo, 4", NM .......**10.00**

Eskimo Pie, decal, Eskimo boy holding sign, Enjoy..., 16x9", EX ..................................**12.00**

Ex-Lax, thermometer, Millions Prefer, 36x8", EX ...........**90.00**

Fab Soap, sample box, full, 4x3x1", NM ....................**80.00**

Fatima Cigarettes, sign, cardboard, open pack, 20 for 5¢, 34x21", EX .....................**45.00**

Folger's Coffee, tin, key-wind lid, steamship, tall, VG .......**20.00**

Frostie Root Beer, sign, cardboard, billboard scene, 13x21", NM ....................**24.00**

Galt Teas, tin, slip lid, Rich Strong Flavor, VG .........**75.00**

General Electric Refrigerators, sugar bowl & shakers, milk glass, EX ........................**40.00**

Giant Salted Peanuts, tin, press lid, giant w/club, 10-lb, G ......**60.00**

Gold Dust Washing Powder, trade card, twins in tub, EX ...**28.00**

Green River Whiskey, sign, Black man & mule, 31x40",

VG ................................**175.00**

H&K Coffee, tin, man in turban, 1-lb, EX .........................**20.00**

Harley-Davidson, stein, high relief, pewter eagle on lid, 1983, MIB ....................**225.00**

Hi-Plane Tobacco, pocket tin, single prop, 4½x3", EX .......**55.00**

Hood's Sarsaparilla, puzzle, w/original box, G ...........**65.00**

**Hollywood Sani-Boot 'n Saddle Cream, box and contents, VG, $18.50.**

Invitation Coffee, tin, slip lid, 2-tone background, 1-lb, G .. **15.00**

Jergens Talcum Powder, tin, flat oval, shaker top, EX ....**100.00**

John Deere, pocket ledger, 1940, 70 pages, unused, EX ......**8.50**

John Deere, thermometer, 150th Anniversary, G ..............**45.00**

Johnson Baby Powder, sign, cardboard, baby on globe, 22x15", VG ..................................**80.00**

Kist Beverages, sign, cardboard hanger, bottle, 10x3", NM .. **20.00**

Lipton Tea, tin, tea pickers & buffalo, 5x4x4", EX ............75.00
Mail Pouch, thermometer, porcelain, Treat Yourself..., 38x8", VG ................................90.00
Mennen Baby Powder, tin, rose petals around baby's face, EX ................................15.00
Merrick's Thread, trade card, patriotic girl & baby, EX ........19.00
Monarch Tea, tin, lion & plantation, 4½x2½x2½", EX ....55.00
Nabisco, bowl, heavy ceramic, boy in slicker, 4½" dia, EX ...45.00
Nehi, bottle carrier, cardboard, Take Home ..., NM ........50.00
Nichol Kola, sign, embossed tin, bottle cap, 14x14½", NM .....40.00
NuGrape, calendar, 1957, complete, EX .........................25.00
Occident Flour, thermometer, embossed tin, red ground, 16", VG+ ........................50.00
Old Dutch Cleanser, swivel stickpin, can shape, EX ........27.00
Old Reliable Coffee, tin, key-wind, 1937, 1-lb, EX ................35.00
Orange-Crush, sign, embossed metal bottle cap, 1950s, 19" dia, EX ...........................80.00
Pabst Blue Ribbon, die-cut tin, Black porter & conductor, EX ..125.00

**Perl Sweeny Steel & Wood fan, 11", $9.00.**

Prudential, bank, glow-in-dark Rock of Gibralter, 1950s, 5x4x2", EX .....................18.00
Quaker Rolled White Oats, container, cardboard, 7½", EX ................................15.00
Red Seal Peanut Butter, pail, slip lid & bail, 1-lb, EX ......120.00
Remington UMC, poster, wild game, bullets & guns, 24x20", G ...............................125.00
Ritz Crackers, sign, paper, cracker box & salad, 1934, 10x14", EX .....................20.00
Royal Crown Cola, thermometer, embossed tin, pictures bottle, G ................................65.00
Runkel Bros Cocoa & Chocolate, trade card, maid pours tea, EX ................................32.00

**Schilling jar and bottle opener, $20.00; Coffee scoop, $10.00.**

Sherwin-Williams, display, painter dips brush in can, 22½x30", EX ..................25.00
Soapine, trade card, dog kissing horse, EX .....................13.00
Squirrel Peanut Butter, pail, slip lid & bail, 34-oz, EX ......80.00
Tiger Tobacco, lunch box, tin, red & black basket weave, EX ..65.00
Tums, thermometer, aluminum, Tums For The Tummy, 9", VG ................................20.00
Union Leader Tobacco, pocket tin, shows Uncle Sam, EX ...55.00
Velvet Night Talcum, tin, palm trees & sailboat, EX ......25.00

Warrenton Rum Cakes, tin, waiter carries turkey, 7" dia, EX ....................18.00
White Poppy Flour, pocket mirror, bag & poppies, oval, 2¾", EX ....................95.00
Zeno Chewing Gum, tin, Dutch graphics, 3x10x5", EX .150.00

# Airline Memorabilia

Collectors now seek nearly every item used by or made for commercial (i.e., non-military) airlines. The primary focus of interest are items actually used on the planes such as dishes, glassware, silver serving pieces and flatware, wings and badges worn by the crew, playing cards, and junior wings given to passengers. Timetables and large travel agency plane models are examples of advertising items which are also widely collected. Pre-war items are the most desirable, and items from before 1930 are quite rare. For further information we recommend contacting Mr. Dick Wallin, who is listed in the Directory under Illinois.

**Dinnerware, Air France, w/seahorse logo, Limoges, $35.00 each item.**

Booklet, TAT/Penn RR, 1929, EX ..............................125.00

Calendar, TWA, 1943, VG ....**75.00**
Carafe, American Airlines Captain's Flagship ..............**20.00**
Carafe, Pan Am, clear glass w/eagle & stars, NM .....**20.00**
Dishes, Air France, Limoges, ea pc ....................................**35.00**
Dishes, Delta, gold script, NM, ea pc ....................................**10.00**
Dishes, Northeast, Yellow Bird pattern, ea pc ................**20.00**
Menu, Pan Am, The President, 1960 ..............................**15.00**
Menu, TWA, collector series ..**5.00**
Silverware, AA Flagship, VG, ea pc ....................................**25.00**
Wings, TWA, Junior, metal, VG... **10.00**

# Akro Agate

This company operated in Clarksburg, West Virginia, from 1914 to 1951, manufacturing marbles, novelties, and children's dishes, for which they are best known. Though some were made in clear solid colors, their most popular, easy-to-identify lines were produced in a swirling opaque type of glass similar to that which was used in the production of their marbles. Their trademark was a flying eagle clutching marbles in his claws. Refer to *The Collector's Encyclopedia of Children's Dishes* by Margaret and Kenn Whitmyer (Collector Books) for more information.

Chiquita, creamer, green opaque, 1½" ..............................**5.00**
Chiquita, cup, opaque other than green, 1½" ....................**12.00**
Chiquita, sugar bowl (open), transparent green, 1½" .**12.50**
Chiquita, 16-pc boxed set, green opaque ..........................**50.00**

**Concentric Ring, 16-piece boxed set, transparent cobalt, from $300.00 to $350.00.**

Concentric Rib, creamer, opaque green or white, 1¼" .......**10.00**

Concentric Rib, cup, opaque colors other than green or white, 1¼" ...................................**8.00**

Concentric Rib, plate, opaque green or white, 3¼" .........**3.50**

Concentric Rib, saucer, opaque green or white, 2¾" .........**2.00**

Concentric Rib, 8-pc boxed set, opaques other than green or white .............................**30.00**

Concentric Ring, cereal bowl, opaque colors, 3⅜" .........**22.00**

Concentric Ring, creamer, transparent cobalt, 1⅜" .........**30.00**

Concentric Ring, plate, opaque colors, 4¼" ........................**6.50**

Concentric Ring, plate, transparent cobalt, 4¼" ...............**20.00**

Concentric Ring, saucer, marbleized blue, 3⅛" ...........**14.00**

Concentric Ring, sugar bowl, opaque colors, 1⅞" .........**25.00**

Concentric Ring, sugar bowl (open), marbleized blue, 1¼" ......**38.00**

Concentric Ring, 21-pc boxed set, opaque colors, from $300 to ........................**350.00**

Interior Panel, cereal bowl, lemonade & oxblood, 3⅜" .........**30.00**

Interior Panel, cereal bowl, marbleized red & white, 3⅜" .. **32.00**

Interior Panel, creamer, azure blue, 1¼" ........................**32.00**

Interior Panel, creamer, marbleized blue & white, 1¼" ............**27.00**

Interior Panel, creamer, pink lustre, 1¼" ..........................**27.00**

Interior Panel, creamer, transparent green, 1¼" ...............**15.00**

Interior Panel, pitcher, green lustre or transparent topaz, 2⅞" ...................................**15.00**

Interior Panel, plate, azure blue or opaque yellow, 4¼" ......**8.00**

Interior Panel, plate, marbleized green & white, 3¾" ........**10.00**

Interior Panel, plate, transparent green, 3¼" ........................**6.00**

Interior Panel, saucer, marbleized red & white, 2⅜" .............**8.00**

Interior Panel, sugar bowl (open), pink lustre, 1¼" .............**27.00**

Interior Panel, teapot, azure blue or yellow, 3⅜" ................**45.00**

Interior Panel, teapot, transparent topaz, 3¾" ................**32.00**

Interior Panel, 8-pc boxed set, azure blue or yellow ....**125.00**

Miss America, creamer, white w/decal, 1¼" ...................**55.00**

Miss America, cup, orange & white, 1⅝" ...................................**45.00**

Miss America, saucer, white, 3⅝" ...................................**15.00**

Miss America, sugar bowl (w/lid), forest green, 2" ..............**65.00**

Octagonal, cereal bowl, lemonade & oxblood, 3⅜" ...............**25.00**

Octagonal, creamer, dark blue, closed handle, 1½" .........**10.00**

Octagonal, creamer, dark green, blue or white, 1¼" .........**14.00**

Octagonal, pitcher, dark green, blue or white, 2¾" .........**18.00**

Octagonal, plate, lime green, 3⅜" ...................................**6.00**

Octagonal, plate, opaque colors, 4¼" ...................................**6.50**

Octagonal, saucer, light blue, 3⅜" ...................................**5.00**

Octagonal, saucer, opaque colors, 3⅜" ...................................**4.00**

Octagonal, sugar bowl (open), dark green, blue or white, 1¼" .**14.00**

Octagonal, 17-pc boxed set, lemonade & oxblood, from $290 to ........................**325.00**

**Powder jar, Scottie dog, blue, 6¼", $80.00.**

Raised Daisy, cup, blue, 1¾"... **45.00**

Raised Daisy, plate, blue, 3" .. **14.00**

Raised Daisy, saucer, yellow, 2½" .**10.00**

Raised Daisy, tumbler, beige, 2" ...................................**30.00**

Stacked Disc, creamer, opaque other than green or white, 1¼" ...................................**14.00**

Stacked Disc, cup, opaque other than green or white, 1¼"... **12.00**

Stacked Disc, plate, opaque green or white, 3¼" ...................**3.00**

Stacked Disc, sugar bowl (open), opaque green or white, 1¼" ......................**10.00**

Stacked Disc & Interior Panel, cereal bowl, opaque colors, 3⅜" ...................................**25.00**

Stacked Disc & Interior Panel, cereal bowl, transparent cobalt, 3⅜" .....................**28.00**

Stacked Disc & Interior Panel, creamer, transparent green, 1¼" ...................................**28.00**

Stacked Disc & Interior Panel, cup, marbleized blue, 1⅜" ......**40.00**

Stacked Disc & Interior Panel, pitcher, transparent green, 2⅞" ...................................**25.00**

Stacked Disc & Interior Panel, plate, transparent cobalt, 4¾" ...................................**15.00**

Stacked Disc & Interior Panel, saucer, transparent green, 3¼" ...................................**6.00**

Stacked Disc & Interior Panel, teapot, opaque colors, 3⅜" ........................**35.00**

Stacked Disc & Interior Panel, 8-pc boxed set, any opaque color........**75.00**

Stippled Band, creamer, transparent amber, 1½" ........................ **20.00**

Stippled Band, plate, transparent green, 3¼" ..........................**6.00**

Stippled Band, saucer, transparent azure, 3¼" ........................**12.00**

Stippled Band, sugar bowl (open), transparent amber, 1¼"...**30.00**

Stippled Band, sugar bowl (w/lid), transparent green, 1⅛"....**22.00**
Stippled Band, 8-pc boxed set, transparent amber .........**50.00**

## Miscellaneous

Ashtray, leaf shape, blue & white ...........................**9.00**
Ashtray, oxblood & white, 3" sq . ...........................**10.00**
Basket, green & white, 2 handles ...........................**36.00**
Bell, orange, #725 .............**225.00**
Bell, white............................**50.00**
Bowl, orange, tab handles, #321 .........................**25.00**
Candlesticks, yellow, 3¼", pr .....................**250.00**
Cornucopia, orange & white, #766 ...........................**18.00**
Cup & saucer, demitasse; beige or yellow............................**24.00**
Flowerpot, Banded Dart, yellow, #302 ...........................**50.00**
Flowerpot, Graduated Darts, green, 3" .......................**28.00**
Flowerpot, Graduated Darts, royal blue, #308 .........**100.00**
Flowerpot, Ribbed Top, black, #300F ...........................**20.00**
Flowerpot, Ribs & Flutes, ivory, #296 ...........................**12.00**
Flowerpot, Ribs & Flutes, orange & white, #297 .................**8.00**
Flowerpot, Ribs & Flutes, yellow, #305 ...........................**20.00**
Flowerpot, Stacked Disc, blue & white, 3" .......................**12.00**
Planter, blue & white, rectangular, #656 .......................**10.00**
Powder jar, apple shape, ivory. **400.00**
Powder jar, Colonial Lady, pink, 1939-42 .......................**55.00**
Powder jar, Mexicali, orange & white ............................**25.00**
Powder jar, Scotty Dog, deep pink ...........................**50.00**

Vase, Graduated Dart, blue, #312, 8¾" . ...............................**65.00**
Vase, Graduated Dart, orange & white, #312 ...................**65.00**
Vase, royal blue, tab handles, #317 .............................**30.00**

# Aladdin Lamps

Aladdin lamps have always been the most popular kerosene lamps around; they've been made since 1908 by the Mantle Lamp Company of America in over eighteen models and more than one hundred styles. During the 1930s to the 1950s, this company was a leading manufacturer of electric lamps as well. Many of the electrics are collectible; however, not everyone knows this, so many electric Aladdins turn up in shops, flea markets, and yard sales. The company is known today as Aladdin Industries Inc. of Nashville, Tennessee, and still makes kerosene mantle lamps in a wide variety of styles. Refer to *Aladdin — The Magic Name in Lamps; Aladdin Electric Lamps*; and *The Aladdin Kerosene Lamps and Electric Lamps Collector's Manuals and Price Guides*. All are written by our advisor, J.W. Courter, who is listed in the Directory under Kentucky. See also Clubs and Newsletters.

**G-195 Alacite electric table lamp, lighted base, 1940. Base, $45.00; Shade, $35.00; Finial, $20.00.**

#2060, electric, bridge lamp, EX .**140.00**
#3510, electric, wood floor lamp, NM ................................**175.00**
#3971, electric, floor lamp, with night light, VG ..............**95.00**
#4541, electric, torchere floor lamp, NM ....................**225.00**
B-101, kerosene, Corinthian, amber, EX ....................**115.00**
B-140, low boy table lamp, Model #21C, aluminum, NM ...**35.00**
B-30, kerosene, Simplicity, white, EX ..................................**85.00**
B-400, caboose lamp, Model C, aluminum, w/shade, EX ......**80.00**
B-53, kerosene, Washington Drape, clear, EX .............**70.00**
B-75, kerosene, Tall Lincoln Drape, scalloped foot, Alacite, M .**395.00**
BL-1983, kerosene, student lamp replica, Model #23, brass, NM ................................**500.00**
C-164, kerosene, glass quilted shelf lamp, Brazil, EX ...**65.00**
C-6100, kerosene, Colonial shelf lamp, EX .........................**30.00**
C-6175, kerosene, 75th-anniversary shelf lamp, white, NM ....**90.00**
G-16, electric, figure, Alacite, NM ...............................**450.00**
G-190, electric, table lamp w/shade, EX ...................**75.00**
G-355C, electric, Hopalong Cassidy gun wall lamp, Alacite, w/decal, NM ................**425.00**
G-36, electric, boudoir, Alacite, NM ................................**70.00**
G-376, electric, Urn, Alacite, NM ................................**90.00**
G-50, electric, powder dish lamp, w/shade, EX .................**425.00**
M-350, electric, metal wall lamp, VG ..................................**20.00**
Model #11, kerosene, table lamp, nickel, NM ...................**110.00**
Model #23, kerosene, Short Lincoln Drape, amber, undated, NM ................................**80.00**

Model #5, kerosene, table lamp, nickel, EX ....................**150.00**
Model #7, kerosene, table lamp, brass, EX ....................**220.00**
Short Lincoln Drape, 1980, ruby, NM ................................**100.00**
Short Lincoln Drape, 1987, cobalt, NM ................................**120.00**
TV-384, electric, ceramic TV lamp, shell form, NM ....**50.00**

# Aluminum

From the late 1930s until early in the 1950s, kitchenwares and household items were often crafted of aluminum, usually with relief-molded fruit or flowers on a hammered background. Today many find that these diversified items make an interesting collection. Especially desirable are those examples marked with the manufacturer's backstamp or the designer's signature.

You've probably also begun to see the anodized (colored) aluminum pitchers, tumblers, sherbet holders, etc., that were popular in the late fifties, early sixties. All of a sudden, they're everywhere, and with a wide range in asking prices. Tumblers in good condition with very little wear seem to be about $2.00 to $3.00 each. The pitchers are fairly common and shouldn't be worth much more than about $12.00.

Our advisor for this category is Danny Woodard, author of *Hammered Aluminum, Hand Wrought Collectibles, Hammered Aluminum, Hand Wrought Aluminum Book II*, and publisher of *The Aluminist*, a newsletter printed six times a year. Her address is in the Directory under

Texas. See also Clubs and Newsletters.

Ashtray, 3-rest, daisy, Everlast, 6" dia ..................................**20.00**
Bowl, mixed blossoms, scalloped & fluted rim, Warranted, 2½x11" dia .....................**20.00**
Bread tray, tulip, flower & ribbon handles, Rodney Kent, oval, 8x13" ..............................**25.00**
Cake stand, shield band, serrated rim, Wilson Metal, 8x12" dia .......................**15.00**
Candlesticks, handled saucers w/sockets, beaded rim, unmarked, pr ................**30.00**
Candy dish, dogwood & butterfly, Arthur Armour ..............**65.00**
Candy dish, pine cones, coiled handle, unmarked, 6" sq .**5.00**
Casserole, fruit & floral lid, circular handles, Cromwell, 3x7" dia ..................................**10.00**
Casserole, rose w/petal & leaf finial, World Hand Forged, 4x8" dia ..........................**15.00**
Coaster, sailboat framed by rope design, fluted edge, unmarked, 3¾" ................**8.00**
Compote, wild rose, serrated rim, Continental, 5x5" dia ....**20.00**

**Continental Silver Co. electric coffee urn in the chrysanthemum pattern, $85.00; Coaster set, $25.00 to $35.00.**

Hurricane lamps, grape & leaf, handled, Everlast, 3" bases, pr .....................................**40.00**
Ice bucket, hammered, mushroom & leaf finial, Everlast, 7x9" dia ..................................**25.00**
Magazine rack, gold anodized, world map, Arthur Armour ........................**150.00**
Measuring cups, anodized, Colorcraft, set of 4 ....................**4.00**
Napkin holder, thistle, crimped edge, unmarked, 4x6x2" **15.00**
Pitcher, wild rose, serrated rim, ear handle, Continental, 8x6" dia ..................................**45.00**
Punch bowl, tray & ladle, Fleur-de-lis, Wendell August Forge ...........................**350.00**
Salad bowl w/servers, tulip, Rodney Kent ........................**55.00**
Sandwich tray, hammered, iris, fluted rim, unmarked, oval, 10x12" ...........................**15.00**
Sandwich tray, stylized cactus, plain rim, Kensington, 12" dia ..................................**35.00**
Saucepan, floral lid, acorn finial, twisted handle, unmarked, 9" dia ..................................**30.00**
Serving tray, iris, Continental....**55.00**
Silent butler, flower, serrated rim, twisted handle, Buenilum, 7" dia ..................................**20.00**
Smoking stand, removable ashtray, Wendell August Forge .**175.00**
Snack tray, flying quail, scalloped rim, Wendell August Forge, oval, 7x9" ......................**60.00**
Spoon rest, anodized, heart shape, Colorcraft ........................**3.00**
Teakettle, anodized, maroon-red, Regal, M ........................**30.00**
Tidbit tray, grape & cable, loop handle, Designed Aluminum, 6" ......................**10.00**
Tray, bamboo, 2-tier, Everlast, 9x10" dia ......................**35.00**

Tray, hammered, rose, applied embossed handles, Continental, 13x18" ......................**35.00**

Tumbler, anodized, flared rim, 3¼" ....................................**3.00**

Tumbler, chrysanthemum, w/foot, Continental ....................**15.00**

Wastebasket, Clayton Sheasley, Coach & Four ..............**250.00**

Water pitcher, anodized, Bascal, 12½" ..............................**12.00**

## Animal Dishes with Covers

Popular novelties for part of this century as well as the last, figural animal dishes were made by many well-known glasshouses in milk glass, slag, colored opaque, or clear glass. These are preferred by today's collectors, though the English earthenware versions are highly collectible in their own right. Many on the market today are reproductions. Beware! Refer to *Covered Animal Dishes* by Everett Grist (Collector Books) for more information.

Bambi, powder jar, pink, Jeannette Glass, 1950s .........**20.00**

Bird on jar, milk glass, Avon .**10.00**

Bull's head, mustard jar, opalescent milk glass, ladle gone, Atterbury .....................**175.00**

Chick on top of egg w/gold features, milk glass, unmarked, 6½" ..............**65.00**

Deer on fallen tree base, clear, used as condiment by Flaccus ................................**155.00**

Dog on wide-rib base, amber, attributed to Belmont Glass, 7" long ............................**65.00**

Dolphin, white, sawtooth rim, Kemple reproduction ....**75.00**

Dolphin on sauce dish, milk glass, attributed to Westmoreland, 7" long ..........................**100.00**

**Dog on wide-rib base, amber, Westmoreland, $65.00; Swan on knobby basketweave base, amber, marked Patent Appl'd For, attributed to Belmont Glassworks, 7" long, $165.00.**

Donkey, powder jar, clear, unmarked ......................15.00

Duck, soap dish, clear w/painted bill ..................................15.00

Duck, swimming, milk glass, Vallerysthal, 5" ..............75.00

Duck on wavy base, milk glass, Westmoreland, 8" long ..65.00

Elephant, standing, clear, unmarked, 9" long .........25.00

Entwined fish w/shell finial, milk glass, lacy round base, Atterbury ............................200.00

Fish on collared base, frosted glass, Central Glass ....150.00

Fish on ribbed base, milk glass, attributed to Fostoria, 8½" long ..............................165.00

Hen, straight-headed, clear, Imperial, sm ...........................25.00

Hen, straight-headed, milk glass, Indiana Glass ................15.00

Hen on basketweave base, milk glass, Westmoreland, 3" .10.00

Hen on wide-rib base, blue with white face, Westmoreland Specialty ........................65.00

Hen w/chicks on basketweave base, any color, Hazel Atlas ....35.00

Hen w/chicks on split-rib base, milk glass, McKee, 5½" long ..............................165.00

Jack rabbit, clear, attributed to Vallerysthal ..................150.00

Knobby-back turtle, clear, LG Wright reproduction .....35.00

Knobby-back turtle, milk glass, unmarked .....................100.00

Lamb on picket base, milk glass, unmarked ......................95.00

Lamb on split-rib base, milk glass, McKee, 5½" long ..........185.00

Little Hen, milk glass, Hazel Atlas, sm .........................15.00

Rabbit, full figure w/glass eyes, milk glass, Atterbury, 9" long .300.00

Rat on stippled egg, pink, Vallerysthal ..............................175.00

Robin on pedestal base, milk glass, Westmoreland .....35.00

Rooster, standing, clear, attributed to LE Smith ..........45.00

Rooster on wide-rib base, blue, w/white head, 5½" long .70.00

Snail on strawberry, milk glass, Vallerysthal, 5¼" .........120.00

Swan on basketweave base, clear, attributed to Belmont Glass, 7" long ..........................125.00

Swan w/raised wings on lacy base, milk glass, attributed to Atterbury ......................225.00

Turkey, standing, milk glass, LE Smith ...........................130.00

Turkey on split-rib base, milk glass, McKee, 5½" ........110.00

# Appliances

Old electric appliances are collected for nostalgic reasons as well as for their unique appearance and engineering. Especially interesting are early irons, fans, vacuum cleaners, and toasters. Examples with Art Deco styling often bring high prices at today's auctions and flea markets. But remember, condition is important. Be sure they're reasonably clean and in excellent working condition before paying listed prices.

Electric coffee urn in the Cattail pattern by Hall China, 13", $95.00.

Beater, Vidrio, cobalt blue glass bottom ............................**110.00**
Blender, Waring, chrome base, heavy glass jar, EX .......**45.00**
Coffeepot, Westinghouse, #CM-81, nickel w/Bakelite handles, 14" ..................................**25.00**
Deep fryer, Fryite, EX ..........**12.50**
Egg cooker, Hankscraft, #599, china base, 1920s ..........**35.00**
Fan, Star Rite, #431 .............**75.00**
Fan, Westinghouse, 10" brass blade & cage .................**145.00**
Hot plate, Universal Thermax, wood handle, 1920s .......**25.00**
Iron, IWANTU, natural gas, double-point ..........................**45.00**
Iron, Proctor, Never Lift, 2-prong ............................**100.00**
Juicer, Chicago Electric, glass reamer top, 9" .................**12.50**
Mixer, Hamilton Beach, Seville yellow, complete ..........**150.00**
Percolator, Manning Bowman, #K336 .............................**50.00**
Popcorn popper, metal w/glass lid marked Fire-King, electric .**35.00**
Popcorn popper, Monarch Teenie Weenie, EX .....................**55.00**
Teakettle, Mirro, internal heating element, 1930s, 4-qt ......**22.00**
Toaster, Kenmore, 2-slice, chrome, 1940s ..............................**25.00**
Toaster, Proctor #1405 .........**85.00**
Toaster, Sun Chief #680 .......**25.00**
Toaster, Universal #E-944 ...**65.00**
Vacuum cleaner, Davis Sweep-O-Matic, brown Bakelite housing, ca 1942 ...................**98.00**
Vacuum cleaner, Hamilton Beach Beating-Brush Cleaner, ca 1930 ..............................**68.00**
Vacuum cleaner, National, Harvey Stone Sales, 1900s, 52", VG ..................................**80.00**
Waffle iron, Berstead, chrome w/Bakelite handles & feet, 1930s ..............................**35.00**

Washing machine, Minier Mfg Co, General Electric motor, ca 1924, EX ......................**165.00**
Washing machine, Pastime, Maytag, early, minimum value ............................**150.00**
Whipper, Knapp Monarch, chrome motor housing, 1930s, 7" .....................................**22.00**
Whipper/beater, Challenger, 1930s, MIB ....................**35.00**

# Ashtrays

Even though the general public seems to be down on smoking, ashtrays themselves are beginning to be noticed favorably by collectors, who perhaps view them as an 'endangered species'! Some of the more desirable examples are those with embossed or intaglio designs, applied decorations, added figures of animals or people, Art Deco stying, an interesting advertising message, and an easily recognizable manufacturer's mark. See also Advertising; Coca-Cola; 7-Up; Clubs and Newsletters.

Brass, crumber pan form w/painted hinged lid, early 1950s, 3" long ................**15.00**
Brass lamp, holds cigarette, tray base, 1950s, 8½x4½" .....**25.00**
Chrome, stylized birds w/beak holders, round base, 1930s, 2¼x6" dia .......................**20.00**
Chrome w/black enamel trim, 7" long ...............................**12.00**
Evans, 2-pc set, chrome egg-shape holder+round tray, rope & leaf trim ........................**32.00**
Glass, black, 4 corner rests, 4½" sq ......................................**8.00**
Glass, blue base w/chrome sailboat, marked FD Co, 5" dia .....**60.00**

**Deco-style dog figure attached to ashtray base, heavy metal, hallmarked, 5½x6½", $100.00.**

Glass, red, white & blue Cadillac shield logo, EX ............**30.00**

Harry Davis Molding, chrome standing nude on round black Bakelite, 5" ....................**40.00**

Japan, metal garden scene, w/built-in holder, lighter & music box ......................**45.00**

Lady's profile, painted ceramic, Japan, 6" ........................**28.00**

Snufferett Executive, Ekstrand Mfg, cobalt-glazed ceramic 4½" dia ..........................**40.00**

### Tire Ashtrays

Tire ashtrays were sometimes issued as souvenirs of world's fairs or as part of an advertising promotion by a tire manufacturer. Though most inserts are clear glass, occasionally you'll find a colored one or one made of tin. The tires themselves are usually black, though other colors turn up once in awhile too. Our tire ashtray advisor is Jeff McVey; he is listed in the Directory under Idaho. You'll also find information on how to order his new book, *Tire Ashtray Collector's Guide,* which we recommend for further study.

Armstrong Miracle SD Rhino Flex, clear imprinted insert .....**25.00**

BF Goodrich Comp T/A high performance tire, clear imprinted insert ................**30.00**

Brunswick Balloon 33x6.00-21, amber Brunswick Tires insert ...........................**75.00**

Cooper Cobra Radial GT 75th Anniversary, clear imprinted insert ...........................**25.00**

Dayton Thorobred Heavy Duty Six Ply 7.50-18 or 7x50-17, D on insert ........................**80.00**

Dunlop Gold Seal 78 Twin Belt, clear imprinted insert ...**30.00**

Falls Evergreen Tube That Sentenced Air..., Weller Pottery insert ...........................**175.00**

Firestone plastic tire, red & black plastic insert .................**20.00**

Firestone 13.0/24.0-13 Formula 1 Super Sports GP (Spain), metal insert ...................**75.00**

General Streamline Jumbo, green or clear embossed insert ... **70.00**

Goodrich Silvertown Heavy Duty Cord 36x6, green embossed insert .............................**40.00**

Goodyear Balloon All Weather 33x6.00, amber or green disc wheel insert ...................**80.00**

Goodyear Flight Eagle airplane tire, clear imprinted insert ...........................**45.00**

Goodyear 3-T Power Cushion 3-T, clear imprinted insert ...**30.00**

Kelly Springfield Tom Cat non-pneumatic truck tire, clear insert ...........................**100.00**

Mohawk Cord Balloon 33x6.00 For 21x5 Rim, green disc wheel insert ..................**90.00**

**Pennsylvania Gold Standard Balloon Tires, 33x6.00 6-ply cord, M, $60.00.**

Pennsylvania Vacuum Cup 34x4 or 33x5, 1-pc colored glass ..**200.00**

Pirelli Cinturato (Italy), clear imprinted insert ............**35.00**

US Royal Master Tempered US Rubber, marbelized embossed insert ...........................**75.00**

# Autographs

Autographs of famous people from every walk of life are of interest to students of philography, as it is referred to by those who enjoy this hobby. Values hinge on many things — rarity of the signature and content of the signed material are major considerations. Autographs of contemporary sports figures or entertainers often sell at $10.00 to $15.00 for small signed photos. Beware of forgeries. If you are unsure, ask established dealers to help you.

Adjani, Isabelle; signature on 4x6" color photo .............**15.00**

Agar, John; signature 8x10" black & white photo ................**15.00**

Allen, Steve; signature on 8x7" black & white photo ......**15.00**

Amsterdam, Morey; inscribed & signed 8x10" black & white photo ............................**20.00**

Andrews, Harry; signature on 8x10" black & white photo ...........................**10.00**

Asner, Ed; inscribed & signed on 8x10" black & white photo ...........................**15.00**

Aykroyd, Dan; inscribed & signed 8x10" color photo as Beldar ...........................**15.00**

Berry, Ken; signature on 8x10" black & white publicity photo, 1970s ...............................**15.00**

Bertinelli, Valerie; signature on 8x10" color photo ...........**12.00**

Bonet, Lisa; signature on 8x10" color photo .....................**35.00**

Borgnine, Ernest; signature on 8x10" black & white publicity still .................................**20.00**

Bowe, Riddick; signature on 8x10" color photo .....................**27.00**

Caine, Michael; signature on 8x10" color photo ...........**15.00**

Campbell, Glen; signature on 8x10" black & white photo, 1970s .**20.00**

Candy, John; signature on 8x10" black & white photo ......**20.00**

Carter, Jimmy; signature as President on card .................**35.00**

Cassidy, Shawn; signature on 8x10" black & white photo, late 1970s ......................**25.00**

Christie, Julie; signature on 8x10" color photo ....................**15.00**

**Chuck Conners as the Rifleman, signed 8x10" black and white photo, $65.00.**

Cotten, Joseph; signature on 8x10" black & white photo ........**30.00**

Curtis, Jamie Lee; signature on 8x10" photo, 1980s ........**20.00**

Curtis, Tony; signature on 8x10" color photo .....................**15.00**

Dixon, Jeanne; signature on typed letter .............................**14.00**

Douglas, Kirk; signature on 8x10" black & white photo ......**25.00**

Eisenhower, Mamie; signature on 5x7" color photo .............**45.00**

Ferrer, Jose; signature on 8x10" black & white photo ......**25.00**

Fleming, Rhonda; signature on 8x10" black & white publicity photo .............................**25.00**

Gould, Elliot; signature on 8x10" black & white publicity photo .............................**15.00**

Hamilton, George; signature on 8x10" black & white photo as Zorro .............................**20.00**

Harris, Richard; signature on 8x10" Man Called Horse publicity photo ....................**35.00**

Heston, Charleton; signature on 8x10" black & white publicity photo .............................**20.00**

Humphrey, Hubert H; signature on sheet of US memorandum .............................**30.00**

Hunter, Tab; signature on 8x10" black & white photo .....**20.00**

Joel, Billy; inscribed & signed 8x10" black & white photo .......**32.00**

**Johnny and June Carter Cash promo record *If I Were a Carpenter*, signatures on 3x5" cards, in frame, $45.00.**

Jourdan, Louis; signature on 8x10" black & white photo .......**25.00**

Keel, Howard; signature on 8x10" black & white photo ......**20.00**

Ketchum, Hank; signed Dennis the Mennace sketch on unlined 3x5" card ..........**37.00**

Lemmon, Jack; signature on 8x10" color photo ...........**12.00**

Marshall, Thurgood; signature on unlined 3x5" card ..........**35.00**

Meredith, Burgess; signature on 8x10" black & white photo, 1940s ..............................**25.00**

Mitchum, Robert; signature on 8x10" publicity photo, 1980s .......**15.00**

Moore, Roger; signature on 8x10" black & white photo as James Bond ...............................**35.00**

Nugent, Ted; inscribed & signed 8x10" black & white photo .............................**25.00**

O'Conner, Sandra Day; signature on 6x9" black & white photo ..............................**27.00**

Palmer, Betsy; signature on 8x10" black & white photo ......**15.00**

Patterson, Floyd; inscribed & signed photo ..................**22.00**

Poitier, Sidney; signature on 8x10" black & white photo .......**25.00**

Redford, Robert; signature on unlined 3x5" card ..........**27.00**

Ritter, John; inscribed & signed 8x10" black & white photo ..............................**15.00**

Rivers, Joan; inscribed & signed 8x10" black & white photo ..............................**12.50**

Rockefeller, Nelson; signature on 8x10" photo ...................**32.00**

Rogers, Ginger; inscribed & signed on 8x10" black & white photo ....................**27.00**

Savage, Fred; autographed note signed on back of 5x4" color portrait ..........................**23.00**

Schwarzenegger, Arnold; 8x6" color signed photo w/inscription ..................................**65.00**

Thomas, Clarence; Supreme Court Justice signature on card .**25.00**

Wallace, George; inscribed & signed 8x10" color photo ..............**25.00**

# Automobilia

Many are fascinated with vintage automobiles, but to own one of those 'classy chassis' is a luxury not all can afford! So instead they enjoy collecting related memorabilia such as advertising, owners' manuals, horns, emblems, and hood ornaments. The decade of the 1930s produced the items that are most in demand today, but the fifties models have their own band of devoted fans as well. Usually made of porcelain on cast iron, first-year license plates in hard-to-find excellent condition may bring as much as $200.00 for the pair. See also License Plates; Gas Station Collectibles; Tire Ashtrays.

Badge, visitor's; plastic w/Mercedes metal logo, 3¼x1", EX .....................................**45.00**

Bank, cardboard, pictures 4-door Chevy truck & bow tie logo, EX .....................................**20.00**

Blotter, Ford Trucks Last Longer lettered on logs in back of truck, VG ......................**40.00**

Book, Dodge, 1926 June Book Of Information, 128 pages, EX .....................................**35.00**

Booklet, Chevy II, 1964, 8 pages, 8x12", EX ..........................**5.00**

Booklet, Ford At The Fair, 1935, 28 pages, EX ..................**20.00**

Booklet, Mercury, 1956, black & white, 12 pages, 9x8", NM ...**8.00**

Booklet, Pontiac, 1964, 16 pages, NM ....................................**6.00**

Boyce Moto Meter, cast iron w/glass thermometer, Universal model, VG ..............**125.00**

**Brochure, 1957 Morris Minor 1000, EX, $18.00.**

Calendar, perpetual; brass, issued by Chrysler, 1962, turbine logo, EX .........................**25.00**

Catalog, Buick, 1911, black & white, 24 pages, 8½x11", EX ..................................**135.00**

Catalog, Corvair, 1960, color, 8 pages, 7x10", EX .............**6.00**

Cigar box, Syroco wood, Chevrolet, embossed, hinged lid, 3x12x9", EX .................**100.00**

Counter display, wood & glass, inserts of various cars, 1960, VG+ ...............................**50.00**

Foldout, Dodge, 1953, dealer stamped, unfolded: 21x31", NM ..................................**12.00**

Foldout, Kaiser, 1954, black & white, unfolded: 18½x24", VG .....................................**5.00**

Hat visor, cardboard, Chevrolet, 20 Years Sales Leadership, EX ......................................**5.00**

Hood emblem, Frazer, 1948, M ...**60.00**

Hood ornament, chrome & plastic, winged figure w/wheel in hand, EX .........................**80.00**

Key chain, Ford, tubular w/blue & white oval script logo, EX ....................................**20.00**

License plate topper, Chrysler-Plymouth Sales & Service, EX ....................................**25.00**

Magazine, Buick, May 1951, EX ......................................**5.00**

Magazine, Consumer Reports, annual auto issue, May 1955, 46 pages, NM ................**10.00**

Manual, owner's; Eldorado, 1979, EX ....................................**6.00**

Manual, owner's; Ford Falcon, 1964, G ..........................**8.00**

Manual, shop; Chrysler, 1941, 279 pages, EX .......................**30.00**

Pamphlet, Guide To General Motors, 1939 NY World's Fair, 4 pages, EX .............**4.00**

Pencil, Cadillac, 1920s, red, white & blue, pictures golfer, EX ......................**40.00**

Pin, Fiat, green, red, white & gold screw-back lapel, EX .....**50.00**

Pin, Stand By For The 1934 Chevrolet, EX ..................**8.00**

Pocketknife, Cadillac shield logo, made by Schrade USA, EX ....................................**60.00**

Salesman's award, pot metal, salesman on book, Chevrolet, 1940, EX ......................**125.00**

Screwdriver, Chevy bow tie logo, metal handle, EX ..........**25.00**

Sign, die-cut cardboard, tan & brown wood grain, Pontiac logo, VG .........................**10.00**

Sign, painted tin, Chevrolet Service, wood frame, 45x76", VG ...............................**190.00**

Sign, porcelain, Volkswagen logo above Service, 30x25", G+ ...............................**215.00**

Spoon, Ford, 1930s, Royal Stainless, script logo on handle, EX ....................................**8.00**

Tape measure, Royal Packard Co, St Paul-Minneapolis, blue & yellow, M .......................**85.00**

## Autumn Leaf

Autumn Leaf dinnerware was a product of the Hall China Company, who produced this extensive line from 1933 until 1978 for exclusive distribution by the Jewell Tea Company. The Libbey Glass Company made co-ordinating pitchers, tumblers and stemware. Metal, cloth, plastic, and paper items were also available. Today, though very rare pieces are expensive and a challenge to acquire, new collectors may easily reassemble an attractive, usable set at a reasonable price. Hall has produced special club pieces (for the NALCC) as well as some limited editions for an Ohio company, but these are well marked and easily identified as such. Refer to *The Collector's Encyclopedia of Hall China* by Margaret and Kenn Whitmyer (Collector Books) for more information.

Baker, oval, Fort Pitt ...........**90.00**
Bean pot, 2 handles, 2¼-qt ....**135.00**
Bowl, cereal; 6½" .................**10.00**
Bowl, fruit; 5½" .....................**6.00**
Bowl, salad ...........................**20.00**
Bowl, vegetable; oval, 10½" .**15.00**
Bowl, vegetable; round, 9" ...**90.00**
Bread box, metal ................**350.00**
Butter dish, regular, 1-lb ...**325.00**
Butter dish, regular, ¼-lb ..**150.00**
Cake plate, 9½" ...................**12.00**
Casserole/souffle, 10-oz ........**10.00**

Coaster, metal, 3⅛" ................**4.00**
Coffee maker, 9-cup, w/metal dripper, 8" ......................**35.00**
Cookie jar, Tootsie ..............**200.00**
Creamer, New Style ..............**8.00**
Creamer, Old Style, 4¼" ......**15.00**
Cup & saucer ..........................**8.00**
Cup & saucer, St Denis ........**22.00**
Custard cup ............................**4.00**
Fruit cake tin, metal ............**10.00**
Gravy boat ............................**18.00**
Hotpad, felt back, 7¼" ..........**15.00**
Pie baker, 9½" .......................**18.00**
Place mat, set of 8, MIP .....**325.00**
Plate, 10" ..............................**12.00**
Plate, 10" ..............................**12.00**
Plate, 6" .................................**4.00**
Plate, 8" .................................**8.00**
Plate, 9" ................................**10.00**
Platter, 11½" .........................**15.00**

**Teapot, Newport, 1930s, $175.00.**

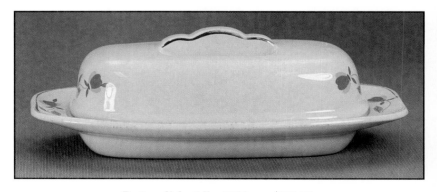

**Butter dish, ¼-lb., 8½" long, $150.00.**

Salt & pepper shakers, range, handles, pr ..................... **18.00**

Sugar bowl, New Style ......... **12.00**

Teapot, Aladdin .................... **38.00**

Teapot, Newport, dated 1978 ...**150.00**

Tidbit, 2-tier ......................... **75.00**

Vase, bud; 6" ........................ **175.00**

Warmer base, round ........... **110.00**

# Avon

Originally founded in 1886 under the title California Perfume Company, the firm became officially known as Avon Products Inc. in 1939. Among collectors they are best known not for their cosmetics and colognes but for their imaginative packaging and figural bottles. Avon offers something for almost everyone as such cross-collectibles including Fostoria, Wedgwood, commerative plates, Ceramarte steins, and hundreds of other quality items. Also sought are product samples, awards, magazine ads, jewelry, and catalogs. Their Cape Cod glassware has been sold in vast quantities since the seventies and is becoming a common sight at flea markets and antique malls. Our advisor for Avon is Tammy Rodrick, who is listed in the Directory under Illinois. See also Cape Cod by Avon.

1957-71, Wild Rose Bath Oil, full MIB .................................. **8.50**

1958-62, Persian Wood Perfumed Talc, red w/brass cap & trim, M ....**6.50**

1961-68, Lavender Powder Sachet, MIB .................. **15.00**

1962-63, Cotillion Beauty Dust, gold & white box w/plastic lid, M ............................. **18.50**

1964, Skin-So-Soft bottle w/tag, EX .................................... **6.00**

1964-65, Bay Rum After Shave, clear glass w/black cap, 4-oz, MIB ............................... **14.00**

1966, Avon Lady, ceramic figure, 1983, 8", NM ................. **55.00**

1966, Crystal Beauty Dust, glass powder dish, MIB .......... **25.00**

1966-68, Original Soap on a Rope, white w/embossed carriage, MIB ............................... **25.00**

**1971-73, station wagon decanter, 7¾" long, $10.00.**

1966-69, Regence Perfume, ½-oz, MIB ................................**15.00**

1967, Miss Lollypop Lip Pop, mirror top w/face on back, MIB ....**9.50**

1967-61, Cotillion Cream Sachet jar, pink, EX ....................**5.00**

1968-70, Splash & Spray Brocade, MIB ................................**20.00**

1969-71, Golf Bag decanter, black glass w/red clubs, VG ......**8.00**

1970-71, Dolphin & soap, MIB .**6.00**

1971, Avon Lady plate, MIB ...**10.00**

1971-75, Field Flowers Sachet, green ribbed glass w/purple cap, EX ............................**3.00**

1972, Avon Rose plate, MIB ...**10.00**

1972, Delft pitcher & bowl, blue glass ................................**10.00**

1972-75, Armoire decanter, white glass w/gold cap, EX .......**8.00**

1973-74, Courting Carriage decanter, clear glass, EX ...**5.00**

1974-75, Corncob Pipe decanter, amber glass w/black stem, VG ....................................**5.00**

1975-77, Baby Owl decanter, clear glass, 1-oz, EX .................**4.00**

1975-77, Bicentennial soap & plate, MIB ......................**5.00**

1976, Christmas plate, blue border, England, EX ...........**15.00**

# Azalea China

Manufactured by the Noritake Company from 1916 until the mid-thirties, Azalea dinnerware was given away as premiums to club members and home agents of the Larkin Company, a door-to-door agency who sold soap and other household products. Over the years, seventy chinaware items were offered as well as six pieces of matching handpainted crystal. Early pieces were signed with the blue 'rising sun'

Nippon trademark, followed by the Noritake M-in-wreath mark. Later the ware was marked Noritake, Azalea, Hand Painted, Japan.

Bonbon, #184, 6¼" ...............**50.00**

Bowl, oatmeal; #55, 5½" .......**28.00**

Bowl, vegetable; #101, oval, 10½" ...............................**60.00**

Butter chip, #312, 3¼" .......**145.00**

Cake plate, #10, 9¾" ...........**40.00**

Candy bowl, #185 ...............**195.00**

Casserole, #16 ...................**125.00**

Compote, #170 .....................**98.00**

Creamer & sugar bowl, #122 ...**158.00**

Creamer & sugar bowl, #7 ...**45.00**

Cruet, #190 ........................**195.00**

Egg cup, #120 ......................**60.00**

Mustard jar, #191 ................**60.00**

Pitcher, #100, 1-qt jug, 6", $195.00.

Plate, #8, 6½" ..........................**10.00**

Plate, cream soup; #363 .....**175.00**

Plate, dinner; #13, 9¾" .........**28.00**

Plate, soup; #19, 7⅛" ............**25.00**

Platter, #17, 14" ....................**60.00**

Platter, #311, 10¼" ...............**215.00**

Relish, #194, 7⅛" .................**85.00**

Relish, 4-part; #119, rare, 10" ...............................**150.00**

Salt & pepper shakers, bell form, #11, pr ............................**30.00**

Salt & pepper shakers, bulbous, #89, pr ............................**30.00**

Spoon holder, #189, 8" ........**115.00**

Teapot, #15 .........................**110.00**
Teapot, gold finial, #400 ....**495.00**
Toothpick holder, #192 .......**130.00**
Vase, fan form, footed, #187 .**185.00**
Whipped cream set, #3, 3-pc ...**38.50**

# Banks

After the Depression, everyone was aware that saving 'for a rainy day' would help during bad times. Children of the '40s, '50s, and '60s were given piggy banks in forms of favorite characters to reinforce the idea of saving. They were made to realize that by saving money they could buy that expensive bicycle or a toy they were particularly longing for. Many of the banks from this era were ceramic, and today these banks are popular again. They were made not only by American companies such as McCoy, American Bisque, Cardinal, Shawnee, Cleminson, etc., but many were imported from Japan and may bear the mark or label of Napco, Enesco, and Lefton.

The most popular (and expensive) type of older bank with today's collectors are the mechanicals, so called because of the antics they perform when a coin is deposited. Over three hundred models were produced between the Civil War period and the first World War. On some, arms wave, legs kick, or mouths open to swallow up the coin — amusing nonsense intended by the inventor to encourage and reward thriftiness.

The registering bank may have one or more slots and, as the name implies, tallys the amount of money it contains as each coin is deposited.

Many old banks have been reproduced — beware! Condition is important; look for good original paint and parts. Some of the banks listed here are identified by D for Davidson, M for Moore, and N for Norman, oft-used standard reference books. Our advisor for still, registering, and mechanical banks is Charlie Reynolds; he is listed in the Directory under Virginia. See also Advertising; Character Collectibles; Disney.

## Ceramic Figurals

**Snowman, American Bisque, $30.00.**

Baseball, All-Star, sm batting figure on top, Vandor paper label, 1991 .....................**30.00**
Child in Shoe, white, Twin Winton .................................**135.00**
Crocagator, Vandor in mold .**20.00**
Human Beans, This Is a Retired Human Bean, Enesco, 1981 ................**15.00**
Humpty Dumpty, American Bisque, 6" .....................**110.00**
Little Girl Pig, w/cold paint trim, American Bisque, 5¾" ...**25.00**

Monk, Twin Winton ..............**85.00**
Paddy Pig, white w/black trim &
    red hat, marked ABCO 1958
    USA ................................**25.00**
Pig, standing w/hands in pocket,
    lg bow at front, marked USA,
    5¼" ................................**28.00**
Pig Goody Bank, marked DeFor-
    est of California, 1965 .**150.00**
Sailor Elephant, Twin Winton ...**85.00**
Slot Machine, Fitz & Floyd ..**45.00**

## Mechanical Banks

Bear Hugging Tree Stump, D-30,
    cast iron, Judd, 1870-80, no
    trap, EX ......................**400.00**
Bird on Roof, cast iron, japanned
    or silver, Stevens, G .**1,250.00**
Boy on Trapeze, D-50, painted
    cast iron, J Barton Smith,
    1888, G .....................**1,500.00**
Charlie McCarthy, sitting w/legs
    crossed, pot metal, 1938, 5¾",
    M .................................**200.00**
Dapper Dan, D-145, tin, windup,
    Louis Marx & Co, ca 1920s,
    M .................................**600.00**
Magic Bank, D-311, cast iron,
    Stevens, G ..................**750.00**

**Magic Bank, J. & E. Stevens,
Patent 1876, EX, $1,300.00.**

Novelty Bank, cast iron, Stevens,
    VG+ ..............................**750.00**
Peg-leg Beggar, D-380, cast iron, HL
    Judd Co, ca 1880, G ......**850.00**
Pig in Highchair, D-390, nickel-
    plated cast iron, Stevens, ca
    1901, M ........................**500.00**
Presto Bank, D-397, cast iron,
    Kyser & Rex, key-lock trap,
    VG ...............................**250.00**
Punch & Judy, cast iron, Shep-
    herd Hardware, ca 1890,
    EX .............................**1,200.00**
Santa Claus at Chimney, D-428,
    cast iron, Sheperd Hardware,
    1889, G ........................**950.00**
Uncle Sam Bust, D-494, cast iron,
    EX ...............................**650.00**
Watch Dog Safe, D-560, cast iron,
    Stevens, ca 1890s, NM ..**450.00**

## Registering Banks

Astronaut Daily Dime, EX ...**20.00**
B&R Mfg 10¢ Register, NY,
    VG .................................**10.00**
Daily Dime Clown, VG .........**16.00**
Gem 10¢ Register, embossed
    eagle, EX ......................**20.00**
Honeycomb, C-105, 5¼", EX .**125.00**
Jr Cash, M-930, nickel-plated cast
    iron, worn, 4¼" .............**50.00**
Keep 'Em Rolling Dime Regis-
    ter, WWII tank, EX, ...**100.00**
Kettle 5¢ Register, painted nickel-
    plated cast iron, 3½" .....**20.00**
Snow White 10¢ Register, WDE,
    1938, EX ......................**160.00**
Spinning Wheel, tin litho w/2
    scenes, W Germany, square,
    4½", EX .........................**25.00**
Statue of Liberty, VG ...........**10.00**
Uncle Sam's 3-Coin, painted
    tin, Durable Toy & Novelty,
    EX ................................**38.00**
Wee Folks Money Box, tin litho,
    English, square, 5", EX .**50.00**
World Scope, VG ..................**32.00**

## Still Banks

**Mulligan Cop, A.C. Williams, ca 1910-1930, 6", NM, from $200.00 to $300.00.**

Apollo Globe & Rocket, M-800, pot metal, M ..................**70.00**
Bear w/Honey Pot, M-717, cast iron, 6½", EX ...............**120.00**
Begging Bear, M-715, cast iron, EX ...................................**75.00**
Calf, M-544, cast iron, black & white, VG ......................**65.00**
Covered Wagon, M-1599, cast iron, EX ..........................**45.00**
Cow, M-553, cast iron, EX ...**75.00**
Crown, M-1318, cast iron, EX ...**90.00**
Cutie Dog, M-414, painted cast iron, 1914, 3⅞", EX .....**150.00**
Duck on Tub, M-616, cast iron, 'Save for a Rainy Day,' 1930s, EX ................................**325.00**
Dutch Girl, M-16, cast iron, Grey Iron, G ..........................**450.00**
Elephant on Tub, M-484, cast iron, EX ........................**125.00**
Fox Head, M-1658, cast iron, black, M ..........................**40.00**
Goose, M-614, cast iron, 1920s, 3¾", EX ........................**175.00**

Indian Family, M-224, cast iron, G ..................................**850.00**
Newfoundland Dog, M-440, cast iron, 1930s, 3⅝", G ......**100.00**
Pirate Chest, M-928, lead, VG ...**45.00**
Queen's Doll House, M-1296, tin, EX ................................**50.00**

**Roper Stove, cast iron and sheet metal, Arcade, 1920s, 3¾x3¾", EX, $145.00.**

Scrappy, M-1623, cast iron, EX ................................**45.00**
Seated Rabbit, M-568, cast iron, 1910s, sm, EX ..............**325.00**
Seated Scottie Dog, M-428, cast iron, green, EX ............**325.00**
Toy Soldier, M-334, cast iron, M ..................................**45.00**
Treasure Chest, tin, orange, EX ................................**25.00**

## Barbed Wire

The collecting of antique barbed wires began in earnest about twenty-five years ago and today has grown into a national and international hobby. At the present time there are twelve State and Regional Collectors Associations and one National Society. See the Clubs and Newsletters section for relevant information.

Beginning with production of the first wire in 1868 and continuing into the early 1890s, many inventors vied for their share of a booming market that saw nearly every conceivable pattern introduced. In all, over 1,200 wires and variations were designed. It is these wires that today's collectors buy, sell, and trade at shows and conventions throughout the United States and via the mail. As in most other hobbies, scarcity and uniqueness go hand in hand in determining value.

Many museums across the country are finally recognizing antique barbed wires as the true historical items they are. More than the Winchester '73 and the windmill, barbed wire changed the once wide-open ranges of the Old West into civilized communities with established property lines.

Our advisor, John Mantz, is listed in the Directory under California. See the Clubs and Newsletters section for the address of the American Barbed Wire Collectors Society. Please note that prices are for wires made in the 19th century that are 18" in length. Pricing information is from *The Barbed Wire Collector*.

Allis's Buckthorn, 1881 ...........**25¢**
Brinkerhoff's XIT Ranch Wire, 1879, custom order ........**50.00**
Bronson's Link Wire, 1877 ...**15.00**
Burnell's Parallel, 1877 .........**3.00**
Dodge & Washburn's Bread Loaf Line, 1882 .....................**25.00**

Dodge's Rowel Wire, 1881, very rare ...............................**300.00**
Ellwood's Ribbon Wire, 1874, hard to find ...........................**250.00**
Ford's Link & Coil, 1885 ......**12.00**
Glidden's Three Line RR Wire, 1874, One Line Square .**10.00**
Glidden's UPPR Wire, 1874, custom order ..........................**50¢**
Glidden's Winner, 1874 (pattern for most modern wires) ....**10¢**
Guilleaume's Two Line, 1893 ...**50.00**
Haish's Walking Cane, 1975 ..**3.00**
Havenhill's Y-Barb, 1878 .......**1.00**
Hearst's Ranch, Copper Horse Wire, 1920(?) .................**10.00**
Hodge's Spur Rowel, 1887 .....**5.00**
Judson's Notched Ribbon, 1871 .............................**200.00**
Kelley's Diamond Point, 1868 ....**25¢**
Kelly's Pin Wire, 1868 ........**150.00**
Kelly's Single Line, 1868 .....**70.00**
Merrill's Buffalo Wire, 1876, very heavy ...............................**2.00**
Rose's Wooden Rail, 1873, very rare, per inch .................**20.00**

**Stubbe's Large Plate, $10.00. (Newly fenced-in cattle needed 'warning plates' to see the wires; John Stubbe patented two sizes in 1883. The large size has recently doubled in value; the smaller plate is scarcer and thus worth more.)**

Wilke's Double Staple Wire, 1879 ...............................**3.00**

# Barware

Gleaming with sophistication and style, vintage cocktail shakers are skyrocketing in value as the hot new collectible of the '90s. Young trend-setters are using this swank and practical objet d'art to serve their pre-dinner drinks. Form and function never had a better mix. The latest acquisition from America's classic Art Deco past is occasion enough for a party and a round of martinis.

In the 1920s it was prohibition that brought the cocktail hour and cocktail parties into the home. Today the high cost of dining out along with a more informed social awareness about alcohol consumption brings at-home cocktail parties back into fashion. Released across the country from after a half century of imprisonment in attics and china closets, these glass and chrome shaker sets have been recalled to life — recalled to hear the clank of ice cubes and to again become the symbol of elegance.

For further information we recommend our advisors, Arlene Lederman (listed in the Directory under New York) and Stephen Visakay (listed in the Directory under New Jersey).

Book, Grossman's Guide to Wines, Spirits & Beers, 1955, 427 pages ............................**10.00**
Book, Old Mr Boston...Bartender's Guide, hardcover, 1964, 8x5", EX .................**7.00**
Booklet, Put Life in Your Party, Southern Comfort, 10 pages, M ......................................**4.00**
Bottle, bar; Tear Drop, Duncan & Miller, 1935-55, 12", w/stopper .............................**125.00**
Cocktail napkin, linen w/rooster, 6x6" ................................**5.00**

Cocktail shaker, aluminum cylinder, 1933 World's Fair & recipes ...........................**95.00**
Cocktail shaker, chrome skyscraper with Bakelite top, Manning Bowman, 12" .............................**85.00**
Cocktail shaker, color rings on crystal, Hocking Glass, 1927-33 .................................**25.00**

**Cocktail shaker, lighthouse, silver-plated, marked Meriden SP Co., International, ca 1928, 14", $1,200.00.**

Photo courtesy Stephen Visakay.

Cocktail shaker, Rose Point, Cambridge, 1936-53, 46-oz, w/metal top ..................**150.00**
Cocktail shaker, ruby glass barbell w/silver band trim & metal top .......................**95.00**
Cocktail shaker, skyscraper style, Revere, ca 1936, 12¾x3½" dia ................**450.00**
Cocktail shaker, Sweet Ad-aline, crystal w/metal top, w/6 glasses ...........................**45.00**
Decanter, crystal, First Love, Duncan & Miller, 1937, 16-oz, w/stopper .....................**115.00**
Decanter, sherry; crystal, Orchid, Heisey, 1940-57, 1-pt ..**225.00**
Ice bucket, blue, Caprice, Cambridge, 1940s-57 .........**165.00**
Ice bucket, crystal, Navarre, Fostoria, 1937-80, 6" .........**145.00**

Pitcher, Manhattan; crystal, Candlewick, Imperial, 1936-48, 40-oz ...........................**225.00**
Pitcher, martini; chrome plate w/chrome spoon, Chase, 1936, 8¾" ................................**65.00**
Pitcher, martini; crystal, Canterbury, Duncan & Miller, 1937, 32-oz ..............................**40.00**

# Bauer

The Bauer Company moved from Kentucky to California in 1909, producing crocks, gardenware, and vases until after the Depression when they introduced their first line of dinnerware. From 1932 until the early 1960s, they successfully marketed several lines of solid-color wares that are today very collectible. Some of their most popular lines are Ring, Plain Ware, and Monterey Modern. Refer to *The Collector's Encyclopedia of California Pottery* by Jack Chipman for more information.

Bean pot, plain, all colors but black, no handle, 1-pt ...**45.00**
Bowl, beater; Ring, orange-red, dark blue or ivory, 1-qt .**75.00**
Bowl, fruit; Contempo, all colors, 5" ...................................**10.00**

Bowl, fruit; Monterey, white, 6" ..............................**22.00**
Bowl, mixing; Ring, black, #9, 1-gal ...............................**250.00**
Bowl, ramekin; La Linda, burgundy or dark brown ....**10.00**
Candlestick, Ring, orange-red or burgundy, spool shape, 2½" ................................**65.00**
Coffee server, Monterey, white, 8-cup ...............................**45.00**
Creamer, La Linda, burgundy or dark brown, new shape ...............**20.00**
Cup & saucer, Al Fresco, coffee brown or Dubonnet .......**18.00**
Cup & saucer, Monterey, white ...**40.00**
Gravy bowl, Ring, black .....**175.00**
Pitcher, La Linda, green or yellow, ice lip, 2-qt .....................**65.00**
Plate, Al Fresco, speckled, green or gray, 8" ........................**8.00**
Plate, Monterey, white, 9" ...**22.00**
Platter, Monterey Moderne, black, oval, 12" .........................**45.00**
Sherbet, Ring, orange-red, dark blue or burgundy ...........**50.00**
Sugar bowl, plain, black, with lid ...................................**85.00**
Tumbler, La Linda, green, yellow or turquoise, 8-oz ..........**15.00**
Tumbler, Ring, black, cylinder, no handle, 6-oz ...................**45.00**
Vase, Ring Gardenware, yellow, jade green or light blue, cylinder, 8" ..........................**75.00**

**Mixing bowls: #9 early Ring and Plain designs, either style, $40.00 to $50.00.**

# The Beatles

Beatles memorabilia is becoming increasingly popular with those who grew up in the '60s. Almost any item that could be produced with their pictures or logos were manufactured and sold by the thousands in department stores. Some have such a high collector value that they have been reproduced, beware! Refer to *The Beatles: A Reference and Value Guide* by Michael Stern, Barbara Crawford, and Hollis Lamon (Collector Books) for more information. Our advisor for this category is Bojo (Bob Gottuso), who is listed in the Directory under Pennsylvania.

Bambo plate, scene from Hard Day's Night, 12", M .......**75.00**
Banjo, plastic, Mastro, 22", EX ..............................**700.00**
Beach towel, Cannon, group in old-fashioned swim suits, NM ...............................**140.00**
Belt, various colors, multi-repeating faces in silver, NM ..**90.00**
Binder, vinyl, 3-ring, white w/group depicted, EX ..................**125.00**
Book, In His Own Write, John Lennon, paperback, Signet, 1965, EX .........................**15.00**
Bracelet, 5 charms, 4 Beatles+musical note, EX ...................**135.00**
Candy dish, Paul decal & gilt edge, Washington Pottery .....**165.00**
Cap, Ringo, various colors & materials, NM ..............**150.00**
Charms, oval plastic w/face, set of 4 different ......................**24.00**
Colorforms, instruments, stage & Beatles, NMIB ..............**325.00**
Coloring book, Saalfield, unused, NM ................................**80.00**
Commemorative coin, 1964 US Tour, MIP (sealed) .........**12.50**

Concert ticket, complete, minimum value ....................**40.00**
Concert ticket stub, minimum value ..............................**15.00**
Cup, fired-on decal, Washington Pottery ...........................**85.00**
Disk Go case, 45rpm record holder, plastic, EX .......**125.00**
Doll, inflatable, 13", set of 4, EX ................................**125.00**
Doll, vinyl, Paul or Ringo w/instrument, Remco, 4", ea .......**80.00**

**Drum, New Beat, with stand, sticks, etc., EX, $375.00.**

Harmonica, Hohner, NM in original box ..........................**90.00**
Headband, various colors, Better Wear Inc, MIP, ea ..........**45.00**
Lunch box, Yellow Submarine, EX ................................. **225.00**
Model, Ringo, Revell, EX in original box .........................**250.00**
Paint-By-Number Set, set of 4, complete, NM ..............**450.00**
Pencil case, yellow or gray, zipper top, by SPP, EX ...........**140.00**
Plate, fired-on decal on china, Washington Pottery ......**75.00**
Purse, cloth clutch type w/leather strap & pictures ..........**160.00**
Tablet, Vernon Royal, unused, NM ...............................**55.00**

**Wallet, EX, $150.00.**

# Beer Cans

If you can remember flat-top beer cans that had to be opened with those punch-type openers, chances are you were a high school or college-age student during the early 1930s. The cone-top with the bottle-cap lid was patented about 1935. It wasn't until the 1960s that the aluminum can with a pull-tab opener became commonplace. Even some of the latter are being collected today, and there are hundreds of brands and variations available. Many are worthless, and most are worth very little, but some have considerable value, and we've listed a few of those here. Just be sure to grade condition very carefully. No. 1: 'new,' rust-free; No. 2: only tiny dents or scratches, still rust-free; No. 3: only minor fading, scratching and rust; No. 4: all of the above, and more pronounced.

In the following listings, all cans are the 11- to 12-oz. size unless stated otherwise, and values are for cans in Grade 1 condition. Our advisor for this category is Steven Gordon; he is listed in the Directory under Maryland.

All American, flat top, white on blue ...............................**45.00**
Argonaut, flat top, stars on front ...........................**600.00**
Atlantic Ale, cone top, waiter on front ...........................**150.00**
Big Mac, flat top, Golden Gate bridge on front ...............**95.00**
Brockert Pale Ale, cone top ...**250.00**
Budweiser, flat top, gold w/eagle & stars ...........................**25.00**
Haa's Pilsner, cone top, red, black & gold ...........................**125.00**

JR Beer (from TV show, Dallas), pull tab ...........................**1.00**
M*A*S*H Beer, pull tab ........**1.00**
Metbrew Near Beer, pull top, stein on front ...................**1.00**
Miller Malt Liqueur, pull top, red w/gold eagle, 15-oz ..........**3.00**

**Old Crown Ale, Grade 2, $7.00.**

Rheingold, flat top, girl on front, Miss Rheingold Contest ...**375.00**
Turborg, pull top, gold w/red circle, 10-oz ..........................**8.00**
World's Fair Beer, pull tab, various colors ..........................**1.00**
007 Beer, pull tab, girl depicted on front ..............................**250.00**

# Bells

The earliest bells were probably connected with religion, since they have been traced to superstitions such as are evident in graves over 3,000 years old. Their purpose was to protect the dead, animals and humans alike, from evil spirits. As time passed, bells became more closely associated with Christianity, so we find them mentioned in the Bible. Other collectible bells include those that are silent or inanimate. These are shaped like bells but have no sound. Some of them are molds, paperweights, jewelry, banks, and smoke bells. Smoke bells are especially desired as they were used to keep the smoke off the ceiling during the days of kerosene lamps. Another type is a nodder figurine with an inside wire attached to the clapper so the head nods as the bell is rung. Originals of this type were brass and gave the sound of a bell. Modern nodders are usually china and are not shaken to produce sound. For further information we recommend our advisor (author of several books) Dorothy Malone Anthony, who is listed in the Directory under Kansas. See also Clubs and Newsletters.

**Glass with gold wash and jeweled flowers, Hungary, 6", $80.00.**

Brass, Queen Victoria, feet clappers, 3" ...........................**22.00**
Brass, St Peter's bell w/saucer, Italian, 6" ...................**325.00**
Brass, windmill, 5" ...............**25.00**
Bronze, Evangeline, Ballantyne, 1980 ............................**150.00**
China, Xmas 1988, Lladro .....**30.00**
China, pictorial, Royal Bayreuth ...........................**175.00**
Glass, Daisy & Button, custard, Fenton ...........................**15.00**
Glass, painted figure, Mary Gregory type, 4½" .................**37.00**
Metal, cowbell, decorated, Swiss, lg ....................................**70.00**
Metal, ice cream mold, bell shaped ...........................**27.00**
Pewter, crown handle, Norway, 4½" .................................**30.00**

Silverplate, leprechaun handle, Reed & Barton ..............**25.00**
Silverplate, Ring Around the Rosie, Hummel ..............**12.00**

**Nodders**

Brass, Chiantel Fondeur, Swiss, 1878 ..............................**25.00**
Brass, trolley car, ceiling mount ...........................**45.00**
China, embossed coral shells on bell body, Belleek ..........**65.00**
Glass, Queen's Lace, Bohemian ..............................**48.00**
Glass, smoke bell, milk glass w/blue edge ....................**45.00**
Glass, wedding, Pairpoint, 12" ................................**375.00**
Metal, hat button, China ...**150.00**
Metal, turtle, head & tail rings, Toledoware ..................**200.00**

Silverplate, caroler w/book, Reed
& Barton, 4½" ................**30.00**
Staffordshire, bone china, mod-
ern, 5" ...........................**23.00**

# Big Little Books

Probably everyone who is
now forty to sixty years of age
owned a few Big Little Books as a
child. Today these thick hand-
sized adventures bring prices
from $10.00 to $75.00 and
upwards. The first was published
in 1933 by Whitman Publishing
Company. Dick Tracy was the featured character. Kids of the early
fifties preferred the format of the
comic book, and Big Little Books
were gradually phased out. Stories about super heroes and Disney characters bring the highest
prices, especially those with an
early copyright. Our advisor for
this category is Ron Donnelly; he
is listed in the Directory under
Florida.

Adventures of Pete the Tramp,
#1082, VG .........................**8.00**
Alley Oop & Dinny, #763,
VG.................................**10.00**
Arizona Kid on Bandit Trail,
Whitman, 1936, EX ......**25.00**
Barney Baxter in Air w/Eagle
Squadron, Whitman, 1938,
VG .................................**15.00**
Beasts of Tarzan, 1937, EX .**40.00**
Big Chief Wahoo & the Lost
Pioneers, Whitman, 1938,
VG .................................**30.00**
Blondie, Baby Dumpling & All;
#1487A, 1941, NM ........**42.00**
Boss of the Chisholm Trail, #1153,
NM+ ..............................**34.00**
Buckskin & Bullets, Saalfield
#1135, 1938, EX ...........**30.00**

**Buck Rogers and the Plane-
toid Plot, 1936, EX, $95.00.**

Bullet Benton, Saalfield, 1938,
NM .................................**38.00**
Captain Easy, Soldier of Fortune;
#1128, EX ......................**19.00**
Captain Midnight & Sheik
Jomak Kahn, Whitman,
1946, NM ......................**75.00**
Chitty Chitty Bang Bang, Whit-
man #2025, 1968, NM .....**8.00**
Convoy Patrol, Thrilling US Navy
Story; Whitman, 1942, EX .**35.00**
Dan Dunn...& Border Smugglers,
#1481, 1938, EX ............**32.00**
Danger Trails in Africa, #1151,
EX ..................................**18.00**
Daniel Boone, World Syndicate,
1934, VG .......................**22.50**
Dick Tracy & the Boris Arson
Gang, #1163, EX+ .........**45.00**
Dickie Moore in Little Red School-
house, 1936, EX ...........**50.00**
Dirigible & the Disappearing Zep-
pelin, ZR90, #1464, VG .**15.00**
Donald Duck in America on
Parade, 1975, EX ...........**8.00**
Fighting Heroes, Battle for Free-
dom; #1401, EX .............**15.00**
Flame Boy & Indians' Secret,
#1464B, 1938, EX .........**35.00**
Flying the Sky Clipper w/Winsie
Atkins, 1936, EX+ .........**28.00**

Freckles & Lost Diamond Mine, Whitman, 1937, EX ......**17.50**
Gene Autry in the Law of the Range, #1453, EX .........**28.00**
In the Name of the Law, 1937, EX ................................ **28.00**

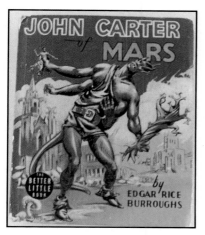

**John Carter of Mars, 1940, rare, NM, $150.00.**

Jungle Jim & Vampire Woman, #1139, 1937, EX .............**45.00**
Kazan in Revenge of North, Whitman, 1937, VG ..............**22.50**
Li'l Abner in New York, Al Capp, Whitman, 1936, EX ......**75.00**
Little Jimmy's Gold Hunt, #1087, VG ..................................**10.00**
Little Orphan Annie & Sandy, #716, 1933, VG ..............**50.00**
Lone Ranger, Menace of Murder Valley; #1465, VG .........**20.00**
Mickey Mouse the Mail Pilot, #731, 1933, VG ..............**30.00**
Pat Nelson Ace of Test Pilots, Whitman, 1937, G ........**15.00**
Pilot Pete Dive Bomber, #1466, 1941, VG .......................**24.00**
Popeye & Castor Oyl the Detective, 1941, G .................**20.00**
Red Barry Ace...Hero of Hour, #1157, 1935, EX ...........**35.00**

Red Ryder the Fighting Westerner, 1940, NM ...........**50.00**
Sequoia, #1161, movie edition, 1935, VG .......................**30.00**
Shadow & Living Death, #1430C, 1940, VG .......................**60.00**
Skippy, #761, VG+ ...............**18.00**
Story of Shirley Temple, Saalfield #1319, 1934, VG ...........**32.00**
Tailspin Tommy & Hooded Flyer, Whitman, 1937, EX ......**55.00**
Tailspin Tommy in the Famous Payroll Mystery, Whitman, #747, 1933, VG ..............**14.50**
Tarzan Twins, #770, 1935, VG ..................................**47.00**
Treasure Island, Jackie Cooper, #1141, VG .......................**10.00**
Treasure Island, Whitman, #720, 1933, VG .......................**35.00**
Up Dead Horse Canyon, Saalfield, 1940, VG .......................**12.50**

# Black Americana

This is a wide and varied field of collector interest. Advertising, toys, banks, sheet music, kitchenware items, movie items, and even the fine arts are areas that offer Black Americana buffs many opportunities to add to their collections. Caution! Because some pieces have become so valuable, reproductions abound. Watch for lots of new ceramic items, less detailed in both the modeling and the painting. Our advisor for this category is Judy Posner, who is listed in the Directory under Pennsylvania. Refer to these books for more information: *Black Collectibles Sold in America* by P.J. Gibbs, and *Black Dolls, An Identification and Value Guide, 1820-1991*, by Myla Perkins. (Both are published by Collector Books.)

**Figurine (double image), painted bisque, Germany, ca 1900-1920, 7", $135.00.**

Advertising mirror, Coats Thread We Never Fade, w/Black boy reproduction, M ...............**4.50**
Advertising mug for Robertson's, golliwog holding tennis racket, M .......................**65.00**
Advertising poster for Milwaukee Journal, Amos 'n' Andy, 11x14", EX ...................**350.00**
Advertising puzzle, Aunt Jemima for RT Davis Milling Co, 1800s, 4", NM ..............**125.00**
Advertising toast rack, 'Golly' for Robertson's Golden Shred, M ..................................**125.00**
Bell, chef figure in green pants & red shirt, glazed ceramic, 4", M ...................................**50.00**
Book, Little Black Sambo, Donohue, 1st edition, hardcover, 1919 .............................**125.00**
Book, Little Brown Koko's Pets & Playmates, 1959, 96-page, EX .................................**55.00**
Bottle opener, painted wood, boy in tie & baggy pants, Wal-Ope, 9", EX .....................**32.50**
Can label, Little Joe Vegetables, barefoot boy w/fishing rod, NM .................................**15.00**
Charm, full-figure Aunt Jemima, lead, reproduction .........**15.00**

Clock, Mammy figure holding pocket watch, American Pottery, 1940s, M ..............**350.00**
Cookie jar, Black chef holding red skillet, 1930s, 7½", EX ...**650.00**
Decanter, butler holding wine bottle, pottery, 1930s, 7½", EX ...............................**350.00**
Decanter, clown figure w/hand-painted features, terra cotta, 8½" .................................**70.00**
Figurine, Mammy in red dress, cast iron, 2½", NM .......**110.00**
Figurine, Uncle Mose type w/cane, painted wood, Syroco, 6", M .............................**65.00**
Greeting card, 'Jiminy Christmas,' Santa inside, 1930s, EX .................................**22.00**
Kitchen towel, shows 2 chefs, 'Two Many Cooks Spoil...,' 1930s, M ....................................**65.00**
Kitchen towels, embroidered pickaninny girls, 1930s, EX, set of 6 .....................................**95.00**
Magazine ad, Needlecraft, 1918, 'Cream of Wheat...' ........**25.00**
Match striker, nude girl in bathtub, wood, 1930s, EX ....**95.00**
Photo folder, 1939 Cotton Club souvenir, 8½x6½", EX ...**55.00**
Photograph, sepia image of matron, matte finish, Modern Photo Shop, EX .............**35.00**
Photograph, sepia image of woman in hat, Penn Park Photo Studio ..................**28.00**
Photograph, sepia image of 3 girls on doorstep w/puppy .....**35.00**
Pin, googly-eyed man, plastic, marked Taiwan, 3", EX ...**22.00**
Pin, winking girl, plastic, marked Taiwan, 3", EX ..............**22.00**
Planter, boy w/bunch of bananas, Japan, VG .....................**25.00**
Planter, girl beside watermelon, glazed ceramic, Intenco, 5", VG .................................**55.00**

Planter, girl in pink dress w/red hair bows near ear of corn, unmarked ......................**55.00**

Postcard, Blacks in watermelon field, Tampa FL, ca 1915, EX ................................**12.50**

Postcard, Blacks unloading banana boat, Mobile AL, color, EX ........................**10.00**

Postcard, Blacks w/turtles, Bogging for Terrapins, 1912, EX ...............................**12.50**

Postcard, Martin Luther King, I Have a Dream, dated 1968, EX ..................................**12.50**

Potholder rack, painted Mammy wearing dotted bandanna on wood, 10" .......................**18.00**

Premium coupon, Aunt Jemima Rag Doll Family, 1920s, 2¼x3½", NM ..................**65.00**

Range shakers, butler & maid figurals, pottery, 1930s, 4½", EX, pr ..........................**125.00**

Recipe booklet, 'A Recipe No Other Mammy Cook Could Equal,' 1928, EX ...........**70.00**

Recipe box, hard plastic, yellow, EX ................................**185.00**

Recipe cards, Aunt Jemima depicted, 1940s, complete w/envelope, M .............**225.00**

Salt & pepper shakers, Aunt Jemima & Uncle Moses, F&F Mold Co, EX, pr .............**28.00**

Salt & pepper shakers, little boy & palm tree, ceramic, EX, pr.....................................**55.00**

Salt & pepper shakers, Mammy figures, ivory pottery, rare, 4", EX, pr .........................**125.00**

Salt & pepper shakers, porter carrying suitcases, rare, 3½", EX, pr.....................................**125.00**

Salt & pepper shakers, Rastus & Eliza, painted wood souvenir, EX, pr ..........................**30.00**

Scatter pin, boy w/banjo, painted plastic, EX .......................**6.50**

Sewing emery, Aunt Dinah in bandanna, hand-painted features, 1913, M .............**175.00**

Spice jar, 'Cinnamon,' Aunt Jemima, F&F Mold & Die Co, EX .................................**45.00**

Spice rack, riverboat scene titled 'The Mississippi,' metal, rare, EX ...............................**395.00**

Spoon holder, chef in ivory outfit, chalkware, 7", MIB .......**95.00**

Sugar shaker, man w/top hat, porcelain & bisque, German, 4", M ...........................**225.00**

Toothpick holder, pickaninny figure in fancy garb, milk glass, 3", EX ...........................**155.00**

# Black Cats

This line of fancy felines was marketed mainly by the Shafford Company, although black cat lovers accept similarly modeled, shiny glazed kitties of other importing firms into their collections as well. Some of the more plentiful items maybe purchased for $15.00 to $35.00, while the Shafford cigarette lighter and the six-piece spice set in

**Salt and pepper shakers, 5", pr, from $45.00 to $55.00.**

**Shafford mugs, large, $40.00; small, with cat's head above rim, 3½",
$30.00; small, with cat's head below rim, 3½", $35.00.**

a wooden rack usually sell for more than $125.00. These values and the ones that follow are for items in mint paint, a very important consideration in determining a fair market price. Shafford items are often minus their white whiskers and eyebrows, and this type of loss should be reflected in your evaluation. An item in poor paint may be worth even less than half of given estimates. Note: Unless 'Shafford' is included in the descriptions, values are for cats that were imported by another company.

Ashtray, head form, open mouth, green eyes, Shafford .....**15.00**

Cigarette lighter, small cat standing by lamp with shade, book as base ............................**50.00**

Creamer & sugar bowl, heads are shakers, yellow eyes, Regal label ................................**50.00**

Creamer & sugar bowl, squatting sugar, upright creamer, Shafford ................................**45.00**

Cruet, slender form, gold collar & tie, tail handle ...............**12.00**

Cruets, oil & vinegar, he has 'O' eyes, she has 'V,' Shafford, pr.....................................**50.00**

Decanter, red polka dots, green eyes, head lifts off, 9", +6 shots ...............................**25.00**

Egg cup, footed, green eyes, Shafford ................................**25.00**

Planter, upright cat, green eyes, Shafford .........................**30.00**

Salt & pepper shakers, seated, 1 has head tilted, green eyes, Shafford 5", pr ...............**40.00**

Salt & pepper shakers, seated, 1 has head tilted, Shafford, 3¾", pr ..........................**25.00**

Shot tumbler, embossed cat face, green eyes, Shafford .....**20.00**

Spice rack, wireware face with green marble eyes, 4 hanging shakers, Shafford.........**150.00**

Stacking tea set, 'mamma' pot, 'kitty' creamer & sugar, yellow eyes .........................**50.00**

Teapot, ball-shaped body, green eyes, Shafford, 5¾" ........**45.00**

Teapot, panther-type face, squinty eyes, gold trim, 5" .........**20.00**

Utensil (fork, spoon or strainer), wood handle, Shafford, rare, ea ...................................**50.00**

Wall pocket, flattened, 'teapot' cat, Shafford, rare .........**85.00**

# Blue & White Stoneware

Collectors who appreciate the 'country look' especially enjoy decorating their homes with this attractive utility ware that was made by many American potteries from around the turn of the century until the mid-thirties. Examples with good mold lines and strong color fetch the highest prices. Condition is important, but bear in mind that this ware was used daily in busy households, and signs of normal wear are to be expected. Refer to *Blue and White Stoneware* by Kathryn McNerney (Collector Books) for more information.

Baker, Chain Link, flat button finial, 6½x7" dia .........**125.00**
Bowl, mixing; Diamond Point, 5½x10½" dia ...............**150.00**
Chamberpot, Fleur-de-Lis & Scrolls, original bail handle, 13" ...............................**225.00**
Cookie jar, Grooved Blue, 8x7¼" dia ...............................**130.00**
Crock, berry/cereal; Flying Bird, 2x4" dia .........................**90.00**
Crock, Boston Baked Beans, Swirl, embossed letters, acorn finial, 9" ....................**225.00**
Crock, Lard, Diffused Blue, snap-in bail ends, 5x5" dia ..**125.00**
Cup, custard; Fishscale, 5" ....**75.00**
Jar, mustard; Strawberry, marked Robinson Clay Pottery Co, 4" ..................................**135.00**
Measuring cup, Spearpoint & Flower Panels, top-spur handle, 6" ..........................**115.00**
Mug, Basketweave & Flower, bulbous bottom, rope handle, 5x3" dia ........................**115.00**
Mug, Flying Bird, ear-type handle, 5x3½" dia ...............**225.00**
Pitcher, Basketweave & Morning Glory, rope handle, 9" .**225.00**
Pitcher, Cherry Cluster & Basketweave, 10" .............**185.00**
Pitcher, Doe & Fawn .........**250.00**

Pitcher, Dutch Landscape, stenciled, tall ......................**200.00**
Pitcher, Grape Cluster in Shield, woodgrain body, 8" ......**225.00**
Pitcher, Grape Cluster on Trellis, 7" ................................**200.00**
Pitcher, Grape w/Rickrack, waffle background, 8" ............**150.00**
Pitcher, Iris, Quilted Diamond pattern below rim, 9" ...**225.00**
Pitcher, Stag & Pine Trees, spurred handle w/squared top, 9" ...........................**295.00**
Pitcher, Swan, curled top bands, beaded handle, 8½" .....**275.00**
Pitcher, Wildflower, stenciled, blue rim & ring ...........**250.00**

**Pitcher, Windmill and Bush, 9",** **$225.00.**

Planter, Diffused Blue, jug form, 4½" ................................**75.00**
Roaster, Wildflower, stenciled, 8½x12" dia, w/lid .........**195.00**
Soap dish, cat's head, 5½" ....**150.00**
Spittoon, Poinsettia & Basketweave, blue-glazed interior, 9" ...........................**175.00**
Toothbrush holder, Blue Band, rolled rim, 5½" ...............**90.00**
Toothpick holder, swan figure, 3¼" .................................**80.00**
Tumbler, Diffused Blue, 6" ......**75.00**

# Blue Ridge

Some of the most attractive American dinnerware made in the 20th century is Blue Ridge, produced by Southern Potteries of Erwin, Tennessee, from the late 1930s until 1956. More than four hundred patterns were hand painted on eight basic shapes. The Quimper-like peasant-decorated line is one of the most treasured and is valued at double the values listed below. For the very simple lines, subtract about 20%, and add 20% for more elaborate patterns. Refer to *Blue Ridge Dinnerware, Revised Third Edition,* by Betty and Bill Newbound (Collector Books) for more information.

**Pitcher, wisteria, rare pattern, 6", $145.00.**

Bowl, fruit; 5" .........................**4.00**
Bowl, salad; 10½" .................**45.00**
Bowl, vegetable; divided, round, 8" ....................................**15.00**
Box, Rose Step, china .........**100.00**
Casserole, w/lid ....................**40.00**
Coffeepot .............................**100.00**
Cup & saucer, after dinner; china .............................**30.00**
Cup & saucer, regular ..........**10.00**
Jug, syrup; w/lid ..................**80.00**
Pie baker .............................**28.00**

Pie plate, 7" ..........................**10.00**
Pitcher, Sculptured Fruit, china, lg .....................................**75.00**
Pitcher, Spiral, 7" .................**65.00**
Plate, aluminum edge, 12" ..**20.00**
Plate, dinner; 9½" .................**12.00**
Plate, Language of Flowers .**75.00**
Plate, novelty pattern, 6x6" .**45.00**
Plate, snack; divided ............**15.00**
Ramekin, w/lid, 5" ................**28.00**
Relish, china, heart shape ...**45.00**
Salad fork .............................**32.00**
Salt & pepper shakers, chickens, pr .....................................**95.00**
Salt & pepper shakers, mallards, pr ...................................**155.00**
Tea tile, round, 3" .................**25.00**
Teapot, Colonial shape .........**90.00**
Teapot, Woodcrest ..............**120.00**
Tidbit, 2-tier .......................**25.00**
Vase, china, ruffle top or tapered, ea .....................................**90.00**
Wall sconce ..........................**65.00**

# Bobbin' Head Dolls

Bobbin' head dolls made of papier-mache were produced in Japan during the 1960s until about 1972. They are about 7" tall, hand painted in bright colors, then varnished. Some represent sports teams and their mascots, and these are the most collectible. They've been made in countless variatons. If you want to learn more about them, we recommend *Bobbin' Head Dolls and Hartland Statues Price Guide* by our advisor, MinneMemories, listed in the Directory under Minnesota.

Type I, Baltimore Oriole, mascot, green diamond base, from $150 to .........................**200.00**
Type I, Minnesota Twin, boy head, blue square base, from $30 to .....................................**35.00**

Type II, NY Met, boy head, white square base, decal, from $260 to ................................**285.00**

Type III, Chicago Cub, mascot, white round base, 4½", from $300 to ........................**350.00**

Type IV, San Francisco Giant, boy head, round green base, from $50 to ...........................**70.00**

Type V, Cleveland Indian, Black head, round green base, from $515 to ........................**540.00**

**Type VI, Chicago White Sox, boy head, round gold base, from $50.00 to $60.00.**

Type VI, Kansas City Royal, boy head, round gold base, from $50 to ...........................**70.00**

Type VI, Seattle Pilot, boy head, decal, round gold base, from $200 to ........................**250.00**

Type VI, Washington Senator, boy head, round gold base, from $70 to ...........................**90.00**

Type VII, Clemente caricature, facsimile signature, rare, from $800 to ............**1,500.00**

Type VII, Mantle caricature, facsimile signature, from $600 to ...**650.00**

Type VIII, Little League, round green base, minature, minimum value ..................**100.00**

Type VIII, Little League Baseball, bank, early 1960s, minimum value ...........................**100.00**

Type VIII, Mr Met, round gold base, 1969, from $200 to ........**250.00**

Type VIII, Weirdos LA Dodger, white round base, minimum value ...........................**150.00**

**Football**

Type I, Baltimore Colt, square blue wood base, 1961-62, from $30 to ...................**40.00**

Type I, Pittsburgh Steeler, square gold wood base, from $100 to ................................**120.00**

Type II, Chicago Bear, NFL on black ceramic base, 1961, from $60 to ...................**80.00**

Type III, Detroit Lion, toes up, square base, 1962, from $45 .........**60.00**

Type IV, Dallas Cowboy, 00 on sleeve, round gold base, from $100 to ........................**130.00**

Type IV, NY Giant, 00 on sleeve, round gold base, from $25 to ................................**30.00**

Type V, Atlanta Falcon, merger series, round gold base, from $20 to ...........................**30.00**

Type V, Oakland Raider, merger series, round gold base, from $70 to ...........................**90.00**

Type VI, Boston Patriot, lg shoulder pads, baggy pants, from $300 to ........................**400.00**

Type VII, Buffalo Bill, ear pads, round gold base, from $100 to ................................**130.00**

Type VIII, NY Jet, AFL decal, round gold base, 1966-1967, from $60 to ...................**90.00**

Type XI, Spartans, player or mascot, 1962-68, any, from $75 to ................................**100.00**

**Other Sports**

Basketball, colored square base, 1961-1962, minimum value .....**150.00**

Basketball, Harlem Globetrotter, green/blue square base, minimum value ...................**150.00**
Basketball, Lil'dribbler, Black, late '60s-early '70s, minimum value ..............................**35.00**
Basketball, Lil'dribbler, white player, minimum value .**50.00**
Basketball, long hair & sideburns, round gold base, late 1960s ...........................**15.00**
Basketball, Seattle Sonics, Korea, late 1970s, from $3 to .....**4.00**
Hockey, Boston, realistic face, gold oval base, 1966-69, from $300 to .........................**400.00**
Hockey, Boston Bruin, boy head, colored square base, from $150 to .........................**250.00**
Hockey, Cleveland Crusader, boy head, square blue base, from $60 to .............................**80.00**
Hockey, Detroit Redwing, boy head, colored square base, from $50 to ....................**70.00**
Hockey, Toronto, realistic face, oval gold base, 1966-69, from $175 to .........................**225.00**

# Bookends

Made popular after the invention of the linotype, bookends of every type and material were produced in forms such as ships, animals, people, etc., and many people today find they make an interesting and diverse collection.

Basket of flowers, painted cast iron, 5½", pr ...................**65.00**
Black cat on book stack, shiny multicolor porcelain, Japan, 5", pr ..............................**40.00**
Cocker spaniel, gilt metal on white onyx base, pr .......**65.00**

**Girl with skirt held wide, painted metal on marble base, 5", pr, $67.50.**

Elephant on back legs, white w/black eyes on orange base, Japan, pr .......................**25.00**
Horse, rearing, bronze finish, Frankart, from $80 to .**110.00**
Horse head, stylized, Frankart, pr ...................................**120.00**
Indian head w/headdress, painted cast iron, 6½", pr, from $150 to ...................................**185.00**
Lady skier, multicolor matte porcelain, Japan, 6" ......**15.00**
Monk, seated w/book, brown painted chalkware, 5½", pr ...........................**35.00**
Nude w/arm stretched overhead, kneeling man at feet, Bronzemet, 8", pr ........**150.00**
Sailboat, Bronze Arts, 7", pr......................**200.00**
Sailor w/dog, Frankart, ca 1930s, pr ...................................**125.00**

# Bookmarks

Bookmarks have been around as long as books themselves, yet only recently has bookmark collecting been growing in popularity. Most collectors like modern ones as well as the antique; there is so much available that a person could establish a collection in a short time and on a limited budget. Many of the modern bookmarks from publishers and advertisers are free. Bookmarks are found in almost any material, brass, plastic, and paper to antique silk, silver, and celluloid (the latter three the hardest to come by and therefore the most highly prized). The old paper ones are still plentiful and modestly priced. Dated commemorative bookmarks, old or new, are the most popular with collectors. Our advisor for bookmarks is Joan L. Huegel, who is listed in the Directory under Pennsylvania. See also Clubs and Newsletters.

Acetate, Yellow Pages (phone book advertising), 1950s .**1.50**
Celluloid, hand-painted flowers, ribbon bow at top, 6" .......**4.00**
Celluloid, Welsbach Lights, 1901 calendar on back .............**8.00**
Needlework, Nearer My God...,Victorian, on ribbon ...............**5.00**
Paper, Bookmark for the Arts, came in book w/same name, 1930s, thin .......................**1.00**
Paper, Eagle Brand Condensed Milk, pretty girl, color print ...........................**3.00**
Paper, Green Lantern Restaurant in Halifax, 1930s, 8" ........**3.00**
Paper, Old Reliable Coffee, color print, early ......................**2.50**
Paper, pickle shape, Heinz, early 1900s ...........................**4.00**
Paper, plain, US Fidelity & Guaranty Co, calendar on back, 1940, 9" ...........................**2.00**
Paper, Smokey Bear w/fire prevention message, 1980s ...**50¢**
Silk woven, 1976 Bicentennial, w/tassel, set of 6 ..............**7.00**
Sterling silver, heart form, 1902, sm ..................................**50.00**

Sterling silver, Unger Brothers, early 1900s, 3½" .........**125.00**

# Bottle Openers

Figural bottle openers are models of animals, people, and various inanimate objects designed for the sole purpose of removing a bottle cap. To qualify as an example, the cap lifter must be part of the figure itself. Among the major producers of openers of this type were Wilton Products; John Wright, Inc.; L & L Favors; and Gadzik Sales. These and advertising openers are very collectible. Our advisor for this category is Charlie Reynolds; he is listed in the Directory under Virginia. The FBOC (Figural Bottle Opener Collectors) are listed under Clubs and Newsletters. (Numbers in listings refer to FOBC's guide.)

Beer drinker, F-406, cast iron, Iron Art ..........................**40.00**
Beer nail, F-234, steel, MIP .**60.00**
Buffalo Bill, N-509, bronze, wall mount, 1984, 5½x4½" ....**80.00**
Cowboy w/Guitar, F-28, painted hollow-cast metal, cactus between legs ................**350.00**
Crab, F-166, red, painted cast iron ................................**35.00**
Crescent Wrench, F-227, polished brass ............................**55.00**
Dachshund, F-84, brass, 5⅞"...**30.00**
False teeth, F-420, painted cast iron, wall mount ...........**95.00**
Fish, F-154, aluminum ........**20.00**
John Barleycorn, F-236, painted cast iron, opener located at heel .............................**250.00**
Lobster, F-167, red & black painted metal ................**35.00**
Lock, F-214, brass, 1961, 2½ ...**40.00**

**Parrot on perch, cast iron, 5¼",
NM, $55.00.**

Monkey, F-89, aluminum, 1976,
   2⅝" ................................**12.00**
Nude, F-171, brass, marked Copy-
   right Russwood 1946 ....**45.00**
Sea horse, F-140, brass, made in
   Canada ..........................**22.50**
Shovel, F-221, brass .............**24.00**
Signpost drunk, F-11, painted
   cast iron, 1 leg out, 1954,
   3⅞x2½" ............................**7.50**
Snake, F-144, steel, 1988, 5¼"
   long ...............................**20.00**
Squirrel, F-92, brown, painted
   cast iron, Wright .........**170.00**

# Bottles

Bottles have been used as containers for commercial products
since the late 1800s. Specimens
from as early as 1845 may still be
occasionally found today (watch for
a rough pontil to indicate this early
production date). Some of the most
collectible are bitters bottles, used
for 'medicine' that was mostly alcohol, a ploy to avoid paying the stiff
tax levied on liquor sales. Spirit
flasks from the 1800s were blown
in the mold and were often
designed to convey a historic, political, or symbolic message. Even
bottles from the 1900s are collectible, especially beer or pop bottles and commercial containers
from defunct bottlers. Refer to *Bottle Pricing Guide, Third Revised
Edition,* by Hugh Cleveland (Collector Books) for more information.

**Established 1845
Schroeder's Bit-
ters, Henry H.
Sufeldt & Co.,
Peoria, Ill, Sole
Owners, amber,
smooth base,
tooled lip, rare
with Peoria
embossing, 11½",
$325.00.**

Amour's Top Notch Brand,
   amethyst, 11¼" ................**5.00**
Baldwin's Celebrated Wines &
   Brandies, smoky, 11⅛" .**75.00**
Brigg's Tonic Pills, aqua, 2½" ... **4.00**
California Fig Syrup, clear, rect-
   angular, 7" .......................**2.00**
Caravan de France, Aubusson,
   clear, flat oval shape, 2¾",
   MIB ...............................**35.00**
Carnation Fresh Milk, amber, 1-
   qt .....................................**5.00**

Carter & Carter Ink, cobalt, applied mouth, original cap & label, 10" ......................**140.00**

Chalk's Petroid Cement, clear, 2¼" ................................**2.00**

Coffee & Spices Trade Mills Montreal, aqua, drum, 6½" ...**110.00**

Crystal Bottling Mineral Water, aqua, logo on diamond, applied top, 9" .................**7.50**

Dans la Nuit, Worth, blue ball form, w/stopper, 1¾" ....**110.00**

Dick's Ant Destroyer, clear, embossed lettering, 6" ..**20.00**

Doyles Hop Bitters, amber, 11¼" ...............................**25.00**

Dr J Blackman's Genuine Balsam, clear, 8-sided, 5½" ............**50.00**

Dr J Hostetter's Stomach Bitters, amber, open bubble, 9" ..**20.00**

Dr Tebbett's Hair Regenerator, gold-amber, tooled mouth, 7½" ...............................**40.00**

Dr Thomas Hall's California Pepsin Wine, amber, tooled mouth, 1880s ...............**220.00**

Dr Townsend's Sarsaparilla..., emerald green, applied mouth, 9⅜" ..................**110.00**

Eno's Fruit Salt, clear, rectangular ......................................**4.00**

Flaccus Bros Steer Head Catsup, smooth base, tooled mouth, stain, 9" ........................**350.00**

Foley's Kidney & Bladder Cure, amber, rectangular, 7½" ..**25.00**

Frostilla Fragrant Lotion, clear, 4½" ....................................**5.00**

George Bieler Sons Bourbon, yellow & green pottery, pear form, 6¾" ......................**60.00**

Golf's Bitters, clear, rectangular, 5½" ...............................**12.50**

Heaven Sent, Helena Rubenstein, frosted angel w/gold cap, 2½" .................................**55.00**

It's You, Elizabeth Arden, triangular w/gold label, 2", full, sealed .**88.00**

JG Godding Apothecaries Boston MA, cobalt, 6-sided, 5⅝" .**150.00**

Koken Barber Supply, Bay Rum w/florals on milk glass ..**125.00**

Loheide & Vorrath Wines & Liquors, orange-amber, smooth base, 11" ...........**70.00**

Merrell's Milk of Magnesia, blue, 8" .....................................**8.50**

Milkweed Cream, milk glass, 2½" .....................................**6.50**

Old Fiddle Kentucky Straight Whiskey, amber w/paper label, 10" ......................**35.00**

Owen Casey Eagle Soda Works Sac City, cobalt, smooth base, 7½" .................................**60.00**

Poison Tinct Iodine, skull & crossbones on cobalt, 2⅛" ......**70.00**

Quinine w/clovers, hand-painted milk glass, 1910, 8¾" .**175.00**

Romany Wine Bitters, aqua, rectangular, 6½" .................**40.00**

Schroeder's Bitters, Louisville KY, amber, 8¾" ..................**350.00**

Shriver's Oyster Ketchup, Baltimore, deep emerald green, 7½" .................................**575.00**

Stafford's Inks, Made in USA, cobalt, pour spout, 6" ....**25.00**

Swaim's Vermifuge Dysentery Cholera..., aqua, rolled mouth, 4" ......................**60.00**

Tornade, Revillon, scalloped side, gold label, 2¾", MIB ......**45.00**

Underwood Inks 32-Oz, cobalt, smooth base, stain, 1900s, 9⅞" ................................**70.00**

Vapo Cresolene Co, aqua, square, 3⅞" .................................**3.50**

W Braunewell Mustard, aqua, tooled mouth, pontil scar, 4¼" .................................**50.00**

Whittmore Shoe Polish, green, 5¼" .................................**6.00**

Wilson's Hair Colorer, bright blue-aqua, rectangular, rolled mouth, 5" ......................**135.00**

Wm Allen's Congress, emerald green, smooth base, applied mouth, 10" ...................**525.00**

Yarnall Brothers Pickles, clear w/6 sides, rolled mouth, 1890s, 13" ...................**400.00**

## Dairy

The storage and distribution of fluid milk in glass bottles became commonplace around the turn of the century. They were replaced by paper and plastic containers in the mid-1950s. Perhaps 5% of all US dairies are still using some glass, and glass bottles are still widely used in Mexico and some Canadian provinces.

Milk-packaging and distribution plants hauled trailer loads of glass bottles to dumping grounds during the conversion to the throw-away cartons now in general use. Because of this practice, milk bottles and jars are scarce today. Most collectors search for bottles from hometown dairies; some have completed a fifty-state collection in the three popular sizes.

Bottles from 1900 to 1920 had the name of the dairy, town, and state embossed in the glass. Nearly all of the bottles produced after this period had the copy painted and then pyro-glazed onto the surface of the bottle. This enabled the dairyman to use colors, pictures of his dairy farm or cows on the bottles. Collectors have been fortunate that there have been no serious attempts at this point to reproduce a particularly rare bottle! For further information we recommend contacting Mr. O.B. Lund, who is listed in the directory under Arizona.

Asgard Dairy, green pyro cow w/child, sq, ½-pt .............**8.00**

Avondale Farm Lurenburg MA, Direct From Farm..., orange pyro, 1-qt .........................**7.00**

Barlow Dairy, Sugar Grove PA, pyro, sq, 1-qt ...................**4.00**

Borden's, red pyro rectangle w/Elsie's head, sq, 1-qt, from $8 to ...............................**12.00**

Cloverdale Dairy, Chippewa Falls WI, cloverleaves, orange pyro, ½-pt .................................**3.00**

Cloverleaf Moderntop, Store Bottle..., red pyro, 1-qt .......**28.00**

Cloyed's Dairy Farm, pyro letters, ½-gal .............................**25.00**

Dairy Dale, Penn Reed Milk Co, Meyersdale PA, pyro letters, 1-qt ................................**18.00**

Danville Producers Dairy, Buy War Bonds & Stamps, pyro, 1-qt ................................**90.00**

Delwiche Farms, Green Bay, pyro baseball scene, 1-qt .......**28.00**

Diamond Farms, Salem NH, pyro, 10-oz ...............................**7.00**

Dublin Coop Dairies...(war slogan), red pyro, 1-qt .......**25.00**

Eastside Creamery Saratoga Springs NY, embossed name, 1-qt ...................................**8.00**

Estey's Farm Dairy, orange pyro, 1-qt ...................................**9.00**

Fischer's Dairy Farm, green pyro & embossed, 1-qt ...........**14.00**

Footman's Dairy, Food Fights Too..., orange pyro, squat, 1-qt ...................................**50.00**

Frates Dairy Inc, embossed name, ½-pt .................................**5.00**

Frederick's Farm Dairy, Conyham PA, brown pyro, cow on back, 1-pt ................................**18.00**

Gibb's Farm Dairy, Rochester MA, embossed name, 1-pt ......**6.00**

Goshen Dairy, embossed name, 1-qt .................................**20.00**

Helfand Dairy Products, red pyro, w/cap, 2x1¼" dia, NM ...**16.00**

Highlawn Farm, Lenox MA, embossed name, ½-pt ......**6.00**

Hood & Sons Boston, embossed name, 1-qt ........................**6.50**

Hygienic Dairy Co, red pyro lettering, ¼-pt ....................**12.00**

Ideal Farms, North Haledon NJ, pyro, wide mouth, 1-qt ..**18.00**

It's Hoods, orange pyro, sq, 1-qt .................................**5.00**

Liberty Natural Vitamin D Milk, Statue of Liberty, embossed name, 1-qt .....................**10.00**

Lueck Dairy, pyro, 1-pt .........**8.00**

Mangan's Guernsey Milk, embossed cow heads w/man's upper torso, 1-qt ............**28.00**

Maple City Dairy, Monmouth IL, war slogan, red pyro lettering, 1-qt ........................**65.00**

Monson Milk Company, Springfield, embossed name, ¼-pt ...........**24.00**

Morlen, baby's face on front, embossed, sq, 1-qt .........**45.00**

Mourer's Milk, Always Fresh, ...Buy US War Bonds, pyro, ½-pt ..............................**30.00**

Newsom's Pride Dairy, Milk the Champion of Drinks, black pyro, 1-pt .......................**30.00**

Pine State Dairy, Bangor ME, baby top, sq, 1-qt ...........**75.00**

Producers, embossed, sq, 1-qt ...**5.00**

Purity Milk Co, pyro, baby on back, 1-qt ......................**12.00**

Quality Dairy The Best..., Gloversville NY, pyro lettering, sq, 1-qt ....................**28.00**

Rojeck's Delicious Sour Cream, pyro, wide mouth .........**10.00**

Roosevelt Dairy, pyro, ½-gal ...**38.00**

Sun Valley Dairy, Highland Park IL, pyro on green, ½-gal .. **32.00**

Sunnymede Farm, Missouri Pacific Lines, red pyro, squat, ½-pt ..............................**22.00**

Store bottles: cream top with green pyro; grocer in red pyro, from $20.00 to $25.00 each.

University of Georgia, pyro, ca 1950, ½-pt ......................**12.50**

Wallas Dairy, New Castle PA, pyro, 1-gal .....................**30.00**

Walnut Crest Farm, Westbrook ME, pyro, 1-qt ...............**14.00**

Wauregan Dairy, It Whips, rhyme on back, 2-color, cream top, 1-pt ..................................**35.00**

Whiting Milk Companies, embossed, ½-pt ................**5.00**

Wilson Goat Farm, San Bernadino CA, pyro, ca 1950, 1-qt ..**30.00**

Woods Dairy Products, orange pyro lettering, double baby top, sq, 1-qt ....................**70.00**

## Soda Bottles With Applied Color Labels

This is an area of bottle collecting that has recently shown strong and sustained growth. Market prices have been climbing steadily. Refer to *The Official Guide to Collecting Applied Color Label Soda Bottles,* Volumes I and II, by Thomas Marsh for more information. Mr. Marsh is listed in the Directory under Ohio.

Photo courtesy Thomas Marsh.

**Walker's Root Beer, amber, Melrose MA, 7-oz. and 1-qt., $125.00 each; Tower Root Beer, amber, Charlestown MA, 7-oz. and 1-pt. 12-oz., $125.00 each.**

ABCB (convention bottle), Miami FL, 1955 ........................**75.00**
ABCB (convention bottle), Washington DC, 1957 ............**75.00**
Abenakis, green, 7-oz ...........**10.00**
All American, clear, 8-oz ......**15.00**
American, clear, 12-oz ..........**10.00**
Anita, clear, 12-oz .................**10.00**
Anton's, clear, 10-oz .............**10.00**
Ayer's, clear, 10-oz ................**10.00**
Badger State, clear, 7-oz ......**15.00**
Bald Mountain, clear, 7-oz ...**15.00**
Bell's, clear, 7-oz ...................**20.00**
Big Chief, clear, 8-oz, 10-oz or 12-oz ..............................**20.00**
Big Cola, clear, Birmingham AL, 13-oz ..............................**25.00**
Brown Cow, clear, Dyersburg TN, 8-oz ..................................**15.00**
Cow Boy, clear, Chicago, 6-oz ..**15.00**
Eight Ball, amber, Altoona PA, 1946, 7-oz ......................**75.00**
Neeco, amber, Boston MA, 1961, 6-oz ..................................**25.00**
Richardson, clear, 12-oz .......**10.00**
Ricky, green, 7-oz .................**10.00**
Roberson's, clear, 10-oz ........**10.00**
Rock Spring, clear, 10-oz ......**10.00**
Roxo, clear, 12-oz .................**25.00**
Royal Palm, clear, 6-oz .........**15.00**

Sahara Dry, clear or green, 7-oz .................................**20.00**
Solo, clear, 12-oz ..................**25.00**
Southern Maid, clear w/3-color label, 10-oz ...................**35.00**
Sparkle, clear, 7-oz ..............**10.00**
Spiffy, amber w/3-color label, 12-oz ............................**150.00**
Springtime, clear, 7-oz .........**20.00**
Sprite, green, 7-oz ...............**10.00**
White Lightnin', amber, FL, 1964, 10-oz ...........................**150.00**

# Boyd Crystal Art Glass

Since it was established in 1978, this small glasshouse located in Cambridge, Ohio, has bought molds from other companies as they went out of business, and they have designed many of their own as well. They may produce several limited runs of a particular shape in a number of the lovely colors of glass they themselves formulate, none of which are ever reissued. Of course, all of the glass is handmade, and each piece is marked with their 'B-in-diamond' logo. Most of the pieces we've listed are those you're more apt to find at flea markets, but some of the rarer items may be worth a great deal more. Our advisor for this category is Joyce Pringle who is listed in the Directory under Texas.

Airplane, Classic Black ........**15.00**
Aunt Shelia's Pin Dish, Daffodil .....................................**7.50**
Bird Toothpick, Light Rose ....**7.50**
Bow Slipper, Pocono Blue ....**17.50**
Brian Bunny, Cornsilk, 2" ...**10.00**
Candy Dish, Dawn ..............**25.00**
Chick Salt, Cardinal Red Carnival, 1" .............................**18.00**

Chick Salt, Crystal Satin, 1" ...**15.00**
Chicken, Cathedral Blue Slag,
 3" .....................................**15.00**
Chicken, Golden Delight, 3" ... **12.50**
Chicken, Violet Slate, 3" ......**15.00**
Colonial Lawrence, Vaseline ...**17.50**
Debbie Duckling, Alice Blue,
 1¼" ...................................**3.00**
Elephant Head Toothpick,
 Heather .........................**10.00**
Freddie the Clown, Dijon, 3" ....**9.00**
Fuzzy Bear, Sunflower Yellow..**11.00**
Grape Card Holder, Misty Vale..**7.50**
Gypsy Pot Toothpick, Cobalt ...**10.00**
Hand, Cobalt Carnival ...........**8.00**
Hand, Violet Slate ..................**7.00**
Heart & Lyre Cup Plate, Sand-
 piper .................................**3.50**
Hen, Rubina, 5" ...................**32.50**
JB Scottie Dog, September
 Swirl ...............................**16.00**
Joey Horse, Delphinium ......**12.50**
Joey Horse, Willow Blue ......**15.00**

**Lack Elephant, Alexandrite,
3½", $15.00.**

Logo Paperweight, Magic Mar-
 ble ...................................**7.50**
Louise, Chocolate .................**22.50**
Louise, Pippen Green ...........**12.50**
Louise Bell, Holiday Carnival..**17.50**
Lucky Unicorn, Ebony Satin ...**17.00**
Mini-vase, Cobalt .................**15.00**
Owl Bell, December Swirl ....**12.50**
Owl Bell, Snow, 4" .................**8.50**
Pooch, John's Surprise .........**15.00**
Pooch, Sunburst ...................**12.50**

Sammy the Squirrel, Classic
 Black Carnival ..............**10.00**
Suee Pig, Candyland Satin ..**12.50**
Tear Drop Wine, Persimmon .**7.50**
Tucker Car, Dijon .................**10.00**
Tucker Car, Patriot White ...**10.00**
Woodsie Owlet, Budding Pink...**7.50**
Zack Elephant, Lilac ...........**12.50**

# Brass

Brass, a non-rusting alloy of copper and zinc, was used as far back in civilization as the first century A.D. Items most often found today are from the 19th century, although even 20th-century examples are collectible, due to the simple fact that most are now obsolete. Even decorative brass from the 1950s has collector value. Refer to *Antique Brass and Copper* by Mary Frank Gaston (Collector Books) for more information.

Bowl, engraved floral, China, 10"
 dia .................................**75.00**
Chamberstick, brass handle, 19th
 century, 4½x5½" dia ......**75.00**

**Chamberstick, heart shaped,
English, 7", $220.00.**

Clock key, E Ingraham & Co Bris-
 tol Conn, 2" ......................**5.00**
Coffeepot, marked TKM, 5" ....**17.50**
Dipper, 4½" bowl, 13" long ...**75.00**
Fork, toasting; cast, British .**15.00**
Kettle, w/cast iron bail, American,
 1850s, 12x19" ..............**300.00**

Ladle, tasting; hand-wrought iron
handle w/hook, 11½" ........**65.00**
Letter holder, Bradley & Hub-
bard, 1920s, 3½x5" ........**65.00**
Letter opener, pierced work on
blade, gargoyle design han-
dle, 10" ...........................**40.00**
Playing card case, marked
Smoleroff Kard Pack, 1920s,
3½x2⅜" ...........................**25.00**
Sconce, embossed bird on branch,
English, 19x15" ...........**200.00**
Teakettle, oval w/goose-neck
spout, 1800's, 11½" ......**300.00**
Teakettle, wide flat handle,
American,1920s, 10" round
base ........................................**70.00**
Tray, stippled design, 1950s,
11x16" ...........................**65.00**
Wash boiler, marked Canco,
14x27" long ....................**80.00**
Water carafe, stylized, Maxwell
Phillips, 1950s, 8" .........**50.00**

# Brastoff, Sascha

One of the California designers whose work has become so collectible, Brastoff worked in a variety of mediums. Most of what
you'll encounter today are his
ceramic pieces, many decorated in
his signature style with fanciful
horses, Alaskan Eskimo scenes,
and figures of ballerinas. Some,
however, were decorated in simple
stripes with gold accents,
abstracts, or covered with textured gold. Shapes ranged from
flat plates and ashtrays to figurals. Besides the ceramic pieces,
he also worked with enamel on
copper to produce shallow bowls,
plaques, and ashtrays; grapes
were his preferred decoration, and
colors were vibrant. He also modeled figures and vases from a
material called resin. These pieces
are rarely encountered, and the
larger figures are becoming expensive; so are items signed with his
full name, indicating work done by
Brastoff himself, not his staff. For
more information we recommend
*The Collector's Encyclopedia of
California Pottery* by Jack Chipman and the *Collector's Encyclopedia of Sascha Brastoff* by Steve
Conti, A. DeWayne Bethany, and
Bill Seay. (Both are published by Collector Books.)

**Ashtray, ethnic man with gold
trim, 6", $25.00.**

Bowl, Alaska, w/native, 5¾" ... **60.00**
Bowl, geometric design, beige &
brown, oval, 3x9x5" .......**50.00**
Cigarette box, flowers, gold & sil-
ver on white, 1½x6x3" ...**85.00**
Dish, Alaska, polar bear, 3½" . .**25.00**
Figurine, horse, platinum on pink
matte, ca 1957, 10½" ...**188.00**
Figurine, poodle, satin-matt
crackle, 7x9" ................**155.00**
Mug, gold & white bird, 5" ...**45.00**
Mug, prancing horse moldeled as
handle ..........................**120.00**
Planter, floral design on light
blue, 4x5" ......................**50.00**
Plate, pink, gold lustre swirl, din-
ner size .........................**10.00**

Vase, abstract geometrics, color-
ful, 12" .........................**100.00**
Vase, abstract heads, 10" ...**160.00**
Vase, enamel & copper, 5" ....**65.00**

# Brayton Laguna

Located in Laguna Beach,
California, this small pottery is
especially noted for their amusing
Disney figurines and their children's series which were made
from the 1930s to the early 1950s.
Refer to *The Collector's Encyclopedia of California Pottery* by
Jack Chipman (Collector Books)
for more information.

Chess piece, Castle, in-mold
mark, 1946, 10½" ..........**45.00**
Creamer & sugar bowl, Gingham
Dog & Calico Cat ........**175.00**
Figurine, abstract man w/cat,
satin-matte black, 1957,
21" ..............................**215.00**
Figurine, baby on pillow ......**60.00**
Figurine, Black child w/flower
basket, early 40s .........**180.00**
Figurine, bull, purple .........**125.00**

Figurine, cow, purple ...........**95.00**
Figurine, Honeymoon, couple in
bathing suits .................**85.00**
Figurine, mule in harness,
7¼x10" ...........................**60.00**
Figurine, organ grinder & his
monkey ..........................**85.00**
Figurine, Pedro, w/serape & som-
brero, 6½" ......................**60.00**
Figurine, toucan, 11x12" ......**75.00**
Flower holder, Sally .............**30.00**
Mug, incised mark ...............**25.00**
Planter, girl holds apron wide,
opening between hands ...**65.00**
Planter, lady w/wolfhound, dated
1943 ..............................**64.00**
Teapot, peasant lady figural, circa
1930s ...........................**250.00**
Tile, cats on a roof, 4½" ........**95.00**

# Bread Plates

Bread plates were very popular during the last part of the
1800s. They were produced by
various companies, many of whom
sold their wares at the 1876
Philadelphia Centennial Exposition. Though they were also made

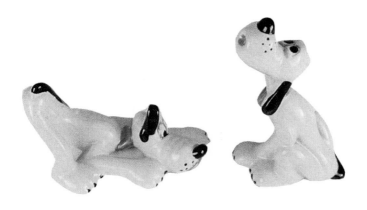

**Pluto, sniffing, 3¼x6", from $125.00 to $150.00; howling, 6", $175.00.**

in earthenware and metal, the most popular with collectors are the glass plates with embossed designs that convey a historical, political, or symbolic message.

Bates, L-375 .........................**65.00**
Bible, L-200 .........................**55.00**
Bishop, L-201 ....................**200.00**
Columbia, L-54 ..................**165.00**
Crying Baby .........................**50.00**
Diagonal Band ....................**28.00**
Egyptian, Cleopatra in center, 13" ...................................**55.00**
Flamingo Sword, L-209 .......**95.00**
Golden Rule, L-221 ..............**65.00**
Good Luck, 12" ....................**65.00**

**Grant, Let Us Have Peace, 10½", $90.00.**

Independence Hall, oval ......**95.00**
Jewel Band, Bread Is Staff of Life .................................**45.00**
Lord's Prayer ........................**40.00**
Lotus & Serpent ...................**55.00**
McKinley, Protection, L-333 ...**45.00**
Niagara Falls, milk glass, 2 American flags ..............**55.00**
Peabody, L-272 .....................**45.00**
Rock of Ages, milk glass center, F-569 ............................**175.00**
Scroll w/Flowers, 12" dia .....**35.00**
Shell & Tassel, oval ..............**55.00**
Three Presidents, In Remembrance, L-249 ................**95.00**
Wildflower, sq ......................**28.00**

# Breweriana

Beer can return collectors and antique advertising buffs as well enjoy looking for beer-related memorabilia such as tap knobs, beer trays, coasters, signs, and the like. While the smaller items of a more recent vintage are quite affordable, signs and trays from defunct breweries often bring three-digit prices. Condition is important in evaluating early advertising items of any type. See also Beer Cans.

Bar caddy, Piels Beer, full figures of Bert & Harry, 8½x8x3", EX ...................................**90.00**
Booklet, Duquesne Song Book, prince w/glass on cover, 1938, 12 pages .........................**10.00**
Bottle, Anheuser-Busch, light blue w/embossed logo, 9", VG ..................................**14.00**
Bottle, Ballantine's Beer, paper label, amber, 1-qt, 12" ...**12.50**
Bottle, Rettig Brewing Co Pottsville, PA, embossed, amber, 9¼" ......................**7.00**
Bottle, York Brewing Co, PA, embossed eagle & logo, crown top, 12-oz ......................**12.00**
Bottle crate, Alphen Brau, St Louis, wood, 1940s ........**15.00**
Bottle opener, Iroquois Beer, red plastic Indian boy figure, NM .................................**15.00**
Bottle opener, Schmidt's of Philadelphia, metal, 3⅜" ...**3.00**
Business card, G Crabtree for Wines..., aluminum, ca 1908, 3½x2" ...........................**30.00**
Clock, Glenlivet Scotch ........**17.50**
Cookbook, C Schmidt & Sons Brewing, Dainty Home Lunches, 1913, 8 pages ...**8.50**
Corkscrew, Anheuser-Busch, bottle form, nickel-plated brass, 2¾" ..................................**40.00**

Foam scraper, Krueger's Beer & Ale, red & white on blue, EX ...................................**15.00**

Ice bucket, Hamm's Beer, chrome finish w/red lettering, 5", EX ...................................**18.00**

Label, ABC Beer, U-type permit number, 1933-36, VG ....**10.00**

Label, High Grade Beer, Franz Bartl Brewing Co, preprohibition, EX ...........................**15.00**

Label, Humboldt Beer, eagle flying over stream, pre-1920, 11-oz, G ...........................**25.00**

Label, Legion Beer, Fitger Brewing Co, U-type permit number, 12-oz, EX ................**15.00**

**Mug, Schlitz, ceramic, fiesta scene, 6", $12.50.**

Pitcher, Indianapolis Brewing Co, ceramic, winged girl, ½-gal, VG ...............................**200.00**

Postcard, Drink Biograph Whiskey & See Moving Pictures, 1912 .......................**7.00**

Postcard, Pabst, aerial factory view, 1935, EX .................**3.50**

Sign, Akron Brewing Co, wood, factory image, 1930s-40s, 25x36" ...........................**375.00**

Sign, Ballantine Ale & Beer, cardboard, lady w/glass, EX ...**50.00**

Sign, Cook's Goldblume Beer & Ale, tin, tilted bottle, 8x19", NM ................................**55.00**

Sign, McGovern Beer, paper, mule & bottle, glass frame, 12x9", VG ................................**30.00**

Sign, Miller High Life Beer, glass, girl sitting on crescent moon, EX ................................**85.00**

Sign, Schlitz, embossed tin, bottle & label, 12x24", VG ....**125.00**

Soda jerk hat, Schlitz, brown on white, adjustable, 1974, EX ..................................**4.50**

Stein, Coors, 1988 Holiday, pictures brewery, 7", M .....**18.00**

Thermometer, Budweiser, pictures Spuds McKenzie, 12" dia, EX ...........................**12.50**

Tip tray, Adam Scheidt Brewing Co's Standard Beer, man w/glass, 4" dia .............**130.00**

Tip tray, Eagle Run Beer, boy riding eagle, 4¼" dia, VG .**150.00**

Tray, Columbia Beer, Bavarian man w/flagon, oval, 17x13½", G ...................................**220.00**

Tray, Haberle's Beer, eagle logo, green, red & white, VG .**45.00**

Tray, Olympia Beer, pictures lady on bottle, 13", VG ..........**20.00**

Tray, Pabst, sunburst logo surrounded by hops, 12" dia, G ...................................**35.00**

# Breyer Horses

Breyer collecting has grown in popularity throught the past several years. Though horses dominate the market, cattle and other farms animals, dogs, cats, and wildlife have also been produced, all with exacting details and lifelike coloration. They've been made since the early 1950s in both glossy and matte finishes.

(Earlier models were glossy, but from 1968 until the 1990s when both glossy and semi-gloss colors were revived for special runs, matte colors were preferred.) Breyer also manufactures dolls, tack, and accessories such as barns for their animals. Our advisor for this category is Carol Karbowiak Gilbert; she is listed in the Directory under Michigan.

Action American Appaloosa Stock Horse Foal, #238, 1987-88, EX ...................................**4.00**
Appaloosa Stock Horse Foal, #238, 1984-86, EX .........**15.00**
Appaloosa Stock Horse Stallion, #232, 1981-87, VG .........**16.00**
Arabian Family Stallion, gray points, 1973-95, EX .......**12.00**
Bear Cub, #308, 1967-73, EX ..**25.00**
Bear Mother, #306, 1967-73,EX..**35.00**
Bitsy Breyer & Quarter Horse Western Set, #105, 1983-87, EX ...................................**10.00**
Black Angus Bull, #72, 1960-78, 11x7", EX .......................**15.00**
Brahma Bull, #70, glossy, 1958-1995, EX .........................**30.00**
Jumping Horse 'Stonewall,' #300, jumping over wall, 1965-88, EX ...................................**29.00**
Kelso, #601, 1988, MIB ........**29.00**
Lady Phase, #40, 1976-85, EX...................................**25.00**
Legionario III Famous Andalusian, #68, 1982, MIB .....**25.00**
Lying Down Foal, #166, buckskin, 1966-74, EX ...................**35.00**
Man O' War, #47, 1967-1995, EX ...................................**16.00**
Old Timer, #205, gray gelding w/harness, blinders & hat, glossy, EX .......................**25.00**
Prancing Arabian Stallion, #812, light chestnut, 1988, MIB ...............................**31.00**

Proud Arabian Mare, #215, 1972-1988, EX ........................**22.00**

**'Steel Dust' Proud Arabian Mare, special run offered through the Breyer magazine *Just About Horses* in 1993, only 1,500 produced, $50.00.**

Suckling Foal, from set #3155, matte light chestnut, 1973-85, EX ...........................**23.00**
Texas Longhorn Bull, #75, 1961-1989 (there was no model in 1962), EX ......................**23.00**
Trakehner, #54, 1979-84, EX...**30.00**
Western Prancer, #115, 1961-63, EX ...................................**50.00**
Woodgrain Family Arabian Foal, #909, 1960-66, EX .........**75.00**
Yellow Mount, #51, 1970-87, EX......................................**30.00**

# Bubble Bath Containers

Figural bubble bath containers were popular in the 1960s and have become highly collectible today. The Colgate-Palmolive Company produced the widest variety called Soakies. Purex's Bubble Club characters were also popular. Most Soaky bottles came with detachable heads made of brittle plastic which cracked easily. Purex bottles were made of a softer plastic but lost their paint easier. Condition affects price considerably. The following prices are for containers in excellent to near-mint condition, unless noted otherwise.

Bambi, EX ............................**30.00**
Batman, Avon, MIB .............**25.00**
Cecil, Purex, green plastic, 9",
    NM ..................................**30.00**

Dick Tracy, Soaky, 10", NM, $35.00.

Deputy Dawg, 1963, 10", EX...**25.00**
Donald Duck, 1-pc version, 1960s,
    NM ..................................**20.00**
Dopey, 1963, 10", EX ............**25.00**
Elmer Fudd, 1963, hard plastic
    head, 9", VG ..................**25.00**
Goofy, 1963, 10", VG ............**15.00**
Linus, Avon, 1970s, 5", VG ..**17.00**
Mickey Mouse Bandleader, hard
    plastic head, 10", M ......**30.00**
Mousketeer Girl, 1960s, EX ...**20.00**

Mr Magoo, blue, VG .............**25.00**
Pebbles, Purex, 1963, name on
    base, 9", VG ...................**25.00**
Peter Potamus, Purex, M ....**25.00**
Popeye, hard plastic head, 10",
    EX .................................**30.00**
Porky Pig, 1963, 10", VG .....**20.00**
Rocky Squirrel, 1960s, M, from
    $25 to ............................**30.00**

**Smokey the Bear, Soaky, EX, 25.00.**

Speedy Gonzales, VG ...........**25.00**
Superman, w/cape, Avon, 1978,
    8", NM ............................**35.00**
Tennessee Tuxedo, 1963, 10",
    EX .................................**20.00**
Thumper, 1963, removable head,
    10", VG .........................**25.00**
Top Cat, 1963, 10", EX .........**30.00**
Tweety Bird, VG ..................**25.00**
Wendy Witch, EX ................**35.00**

# Cake Toppers

Cake toppers began to appear around the 1880s, made almost exclusively of sugar. During the 1900s toppers (bride and groom figures) were carved from wood and placed on plaster bases. A few single-mold toppers were made from poured lead. Bisque and porcelain also appeared around the same time. From the 1920s to the 1950s, the bisque and porcelain toppers became extremely popular. Celluloid kewpie-types made a brief appearance around the 1940-50 era as did those made of a chalk (plaster-of-Paris) substance. Kewpies and chalkware toppers were a spinoff from the heyday of amusement parks and carnivals when larger-scaled chalkware figures were awarded as prizes along a midway or arcade.

From the 1950s well into the 1970s, plastics were used nearly exclusively. Toppers took on a vacant, assembly-line appearance with no specific attention to detail or fashion. Around 1970 bisque returned, and plastic soon fell out of favor. About this same time grooms began appearing in various military dress — a reflection of the growing controversy surrounding the Vietnam War. Since the 1980s toppers have evolved into elegant and elaborate pieces, especially those from Royal Doulton and Lladro.

It should be noted here that toppers must not be confused with the bride/groom dolls of the same periods. While some smaller dolls could and did serve as toppers, they were usually too unbalanced to stay upright on a cake. The true topper consisted of a small bride and groom anchored to (or a part of) a round flat disk which made it extremely stable. Cake toppers never did double-duty as play items. Our advisor is Jeannie Greenfield, who is listed in the Directory under Pennsylvania.

Photo courtesy Jeannie Greenfield.

**Wood on plaster base, inscribed Good Luck, cloth flowers, 1890s, 8", $75.00.**

Bisque, Black couple waltzing, marked Lefton China, 1980s, 3" .....................................**20.00**

Bisque, cutie couple, jointed, crepe paper tux, Japan, 1930s, 3" ........................**40.00**

Bisque, Marine (or Army, etc) uniform, Wilton, 1960s, 4½" .**25.00**

Bisque, marked A196 & A197, incised Japan, 4½" ........**40.00**

Bisque, painted, cloth clothes, 1940s, 4" ........................**35.00**

Bisque, single mold, bride w/head band, marked Japan, 1920s, 3½" .................................**25.00**

Bisque, single mold, bride w/head band, unmarked, 1920s, 3½" .....................**25.00**

Celluloid, Kewpies, painted-on clothes, Japan, 1940s, fragile, 2½" .................................**35.00**

Chalk type, single mold, incised ACA on base, 1930s, 3½" .**25.00**

China, single mold, net veil & dress, unmarked, 1950s-60s, 6" ..................................**30.00**

German, she holds rosary w/cross, he wears tails & spats, 1920s, 1½" ..............................**20.00**

Lead, single mold, painted-on clothes, w/cloth flowers, 1900-20, 5" .............................**60.00**

Plaster, black, pink & white paint w/pearlized headdress, 1948, 5" ....................................**10.00**

Plastic, single mold, double-breasted jacket, unmarked, 1950s, 4" ......................**15.00**

# Candlewick

Candlewick was one of the all-time best-selling lines of The Imperial Glass Company of Bellaire, Ohio. It was produced from 1936 until the company closed in 1982. More than 741 items were made over the years; and though many are still easy to find today, some (such as the desk calendar, the chip and dip set, and the dresser set) are a challenge to collect. Candlewick is easily identified by its beaded stems, handles, and rims characteristic of the tufted needlework of our pioneer women for which it was named.

Ashtray, individual, #400/64 .**6.00**

Ashtray, sq, #400/653, 5¾" ...**37.50**

Bowl, divided, w/handles, #400/52, 6" dia ............................**22.00**

Bowl, heart, #400/49H, 9" ....**90.00**

Bowl, jelly, w/lid, #400/59, 5½" .**55.00**

Bowl, relish; #400/60, 7" ......**25.00**

Butter, beaded lid, #400/161, ¼-lb ............................**30.00**

Cake stand, low foot, 400/67D, 10" ...............................**50.00**

Calendar, desk; 1947 ..........**150.00**

Cigarette holder, beaded foot, #400/44, 3" .....................**40.00**

Coaster, w/spoon rest, #400/226 .................................**13.00**

Compote, 2-bead stem, #400/66B, 5½" ...............................**18.00**

Cruet, oil; w/handle, bulbous bottom, #400/275, 6-oz .......**55.00**

Cruet, vinegar; w/stopper, #400/121 ........................**65.00**

Cup, after dinner; #400/77 ...**17.50**

Cup, coffee; #400/37 .............**7.50**

**Dresser pieces: Powder box with etched stars, $135.00; Colognes, $75.00 each.**

Egg cup, beaded foot, #400/19 .**45.00**

Hurricane lamp, 2-pc candle base, #400/79 ........................**110.00**

Icer, seafood/fruit cocktail; 2-pc, 1-bead stem, #3800 .......**60.00**

Ladle, mayonnaise; #400/135, 6¼" ................................**10.00**

Marmalade, 4-pc, #400/89 ...**42.50**

Pitcher, plain, #400/424, 80-oz .**55.00**

Plate, #400/34, 4½" .................**6.00**

Plate, salad; #400/5D, 8" ........**9.00**

# Candy Containers

From 1876 until about 1960, figural glass candy containers of every shape and description were manufactured for the use of candy companies who filled them with tiny colored candy beads. When the candy was gone, kids used the containers as banks or toys. While many are common, some (such as Charlie Chaplin by L. E. Smith, Barney Google by the Barrel, Felix on the Pedestal, or the Rabbit Family) are hard to find and command prices in the $450.00 to $3,000.00 range. Refer to *The Compleat American Glass Candy Container Handbook* by Adele Bowden. Our advisor for this category is Doug Dezso, who is listed in the Directory under New Jersey. For the figural papier-mache candy containers, see Christmas; Halloween; etc.

**Automobile, Electric Runabout, #47, no closure, $60.00 (with closure $70.00.)**

Basket, #81, floral design ....**30.00**
Bear on Circus Tub, #83, original
    blades ...........................**375.00**
Chicken in Sagging Basket,
    #148 ............................**75.00**
Coal Car w/Tender, #170 ....**225.00**
Fairy Pups, #193 .................**75.00**
Felix by Barrel, #211, G
    paint ......................**750.00**
Ice Truck, #784, all original .**700.00**
Kiddies' Band, #314, com-
    plete ......................**275.00**
Lantern, #403, w/brass cap .**20.00**
Locomotive, #496, rectangular
    windows, w/closure .......**85.00**
Lynn Doll Nurser, #550 .......**32.00**
Peter Rabbit, #618 ..............**35.00**

**Liberty Bell, #85, blue, 4", $40.00.**

Rabbit in Eggshell, #608, gold
    paint ..............................**85.00**
Rabbit Nibbling Carrot, #609 .**35.00**
Rooster Crowing, #151, original
    paint ...........................**250.00**
Valise, #599 ........................**450.00**
Willy's Jeep Scout Car, #350 .**30.00**

## Cape Cod by Avon

Now that Avon is discontinuing their Cape Cod line, don't be surprised to see prices on the upward swing. They've been making this dark ruby red glassware since the seventies. In addition to the place settings (there are plates in three sizes, soup and dessert bowls, a cup and saucer, tumblers in two sizes, three different goblets, a mug, and a wine glass), there are many lovely accessory items as well. Among them you'll find a cake plate, a pitcher, a platter, a hurricane-type candle lamp, a butter dish, napkin rings, and a pie plate server. Note: Mint-in-box items are worth about 20% more than the same piece with no box.

Bell, marked Christmas 1979 on bottom, 6½" .....................**20.00**
Bowl, dessert; 1978-80, 5", MIB ...............................**10.00**
Bowl, serving; 1986, 8¾" ......**19.00**
Bowl, soup/cereal; 1991, 7½" **13.00**
Butter dish, ¼-lb, 1983-84, 7" long ................................**17.50**
Cake plate, footed, 1991, 3¼x10¾" dia, MIB .........................**50.00**
Candle holder, squat form, 1983-84, 3¾" dia, ea ................**6.50**

**Candlesticks, 8¾", $25.00 for the pair.**

Candy dish, footed, 1987, 3½x6" dia ...................................**12.00**
Creamer, footed, 1981-84, 4", .**7.00**
Cruet, 1975-80, 5-oz .............**10.00**
Cup, 1990, 3½", MIB ..............**9.00**
Decanter, w/stopper, 1977-80, 16-oz ...............................**15.00**
Dessert server, wedge-shaped stainless steel w/red plastic handle, 8" ......................**12.00**
Goblet, water; 1976-90, 6" .....**9.00**
Goblet, wine; 1992, 5¼" ..........**6.00**
Heart box, 1989, 4" wide, MIB .**13.00**
Mug, pedestal foot, 1982-84, 5" ...................................**10.00**
Napkin rings, set of 4, 1989 .**20.00**
Pie plate server, 1992, 11" ...**30.00**
Pitcher, water; footed, 1984, 8¼" ................................**30.00**

Plate, bread & butter; 1992, 5¾", MIB .................................**8.50**
Plate, dessert; 1980, 7½" ........**6.50**
Plate, dinner; 1982-83, 11" ..**14.00**
Platter, 1986, 10¾x13½", MIB .**24.00**
Salt & pepper shakers, marked May 1978, pr .................**12.00**
Sauce boat, footed, 1988, 8" long, MIB .................................**25.00**
Sugar bowl, footed, 1980-83, 3½" ................................**10.00**
Tidbit tray, 2-tier, brass handle, 1987, 9¾", MIB ..............**30.00**
Tumbler, footed, 1988, 3¾" .....**7.50**
Tumbler, straight-sided, 1990, 5½" ................................**8.50**
Vase, footed, 1985, 8" ...........**15.00**

# Carnival Chalkware

Chalkware statues of Kewpies, glamour girls, assorted dogs, horses, etc., were given to winners of carnival games from about 1910 until the 1950s. Today's collectors especially value those representing well-known personalities such as Disney characters and comic book heroes. Refer to *The Carnival Chalk Prize* by Tom Morris for more information. Mr. Morris is in the Directory under Oregon.

Bellhop, marked Jenkins, ca 1946, 13" ........................**45.00**
Buddy Lee, hand-painted pink chalk, unmarked, 1920s, 13½" ................................**85.00**
Charlie McCarthy, Copyright Dummy, Jenkins, 1938, 15" ...................................**75.00**
Donald Duck, 1934-50, 14" ..**75.00**
Girl, sitting in flower w/feet crossed, large eyes, ca 1920, 11" ..................................**120.00**
Horse w/English saddle, 11" .**35.00**

Kewpie Vamp, hand-painted, jointed arms, flapper hairdo, 1920s, 11" ....................**125.00**
Lone Ranger & Silver, ca 1938-50, 10½" ..............................**75.00**
Lotus Chinese Girl, Jenkins, 1924, 13¼" ...................**130.00**

**Mickey Mouse, no mark, circa 1930-35, rare, 8½", $175.00.**

Paul Revere, unmarked, ca 1935-45, 14½" .........................**35.00**
Sailor Girl, marked Copyright 1934, 14" ........................**65.00**
Scottish Lass, w/bagpipes, unmarked, 15" ...............**35.00**
Sugar, standing girl w/flowered hat, marked JY Jenkins, ca 1948, 13" ......................**120.00**
Tomboy, girl in pants, 1940, #1571, 14½" ...................**35.00**

# Carnival Glass

From about 1905 until the late 1920s, carnival glass was manufactured by several major American glasshouses in hundreds of designs and patterns. Its characteristic iridescent lustre was the result of coating the pressed glassware with a sodium solution before the final firing. Marigold, blue, green, and purple are the most common colors, though pastels were also used. Because it was mass-produced at reasonable prices, much of it was given away at carnivals. As a result, it came to be known as carnival glass. Refer to *The Standard Encyclopedia of Carnival Glass* by Bill Edwards (Collector Books) for more information.

**Garden Path bowl, amethyst, 8½", $85.00.**

Acorn Burrs, bowl, flat, marigold, Northwood, 5" ...............**30.00**
Acorn Burrs, tumbler, amethyst, Northwood .....................**80.00**
American, tumbler, marigold, Fostoria, rare .....................**95.00**
Apple Panels, sugar bowl (open), marigold, English ..........**35.00**
Arcs, compote, amethyst, Imperial .................................**90.00**
Autumn Acorns, bowl, marigold, Fenton, 8¼" ...................**55.00**
Banded Diamond & Fan, toothpick holder, marigold, English .........................**80.00**

Banded Grape, tumbler, blue, Fenton ..........................**50.00**
Banded Panels, sugar bowl, amethyst, Crystal .........**60.00**
Basketweave, bowl, green, open edge, Fenton, 5" ...........**55.00**
Beaded, hatpin, amethyst ....**45.00**
Beaded Cable, candy dish, marigold, Northwood ....**50.00**
Beaded Swirl, butter dish, blue, English ..........................**85.00**
Bells & Beads, bowl, amethyst, Dugan, 7½" ...................**90.00**
Bells & Beads, gravy boat, marigold, handled, Dugan ................**55.00**
Birds & Cherries, bonbon, blue, Fenton ..........................**65.00**
Birds & Cherries, compote, amethyst, Fenton ..........**60.00**
Blackberry Wreath, bowl, marigold, Millersburg, 5" ...............**50.00**
Blocks & Arches, pitcher, marigold, Crystal, rare .................**100.00**
Brocaded Summer Gardens, bonbon, pastel .....................**65.00**
Brocaded Summer Gardens, cake plate, pastel, center handle ........................**110.00**
Broken Arches, punch cup, marigold or amethyst, Imperial .................................**30.00**
Bubble Berry, shade, pastel .**75.00**
Butterflies, bonbon, blue, Fenton .................................**65.00**
Butterflies & Waratah, compote, marigold, Crystal, large ............................**120.00**
Butterfly, bonbon, amethyst, ribbed exterior, Northwood ..........................**250.00**
Butterfly & Berry, bowl, amethyst, footed, Fenton, 5" ...........**40.00**
Butterfly & Fern, tumbler, green, Fenton ..........................**85.00**
Buttermilk, Plain, goblet, green, Fenton ..........................**80.00**
Cane, compote, marigold, Imperial .................................**80.00**

Captive Rose, compote, green, Fenton ..........................**90.00**
Caroline, bowl, marigold, Dugan, 7"-10" ............................**70.00**
Checkerboard Bouquet, plate, amethyst, 8" ..................**85.00**
Checkers, ashtray, marigold .**47.00**
Cherry Chain, bonbon, green, Fenton ..........................**65.00**
Chrysanthemum, bowl, amethyst, footed, Fenton, 10" ........**75.00**
Cobblestones, bonbon, amethyst, Imperial .........................**75.00**
Cobblestones, bowl, marigold, Dugan, 9" .......................**65.00**
Concave Flute, vase, amethyst, Westmoreland ...............**65.00**
Cosmos & Cane, bowl, marigold, 5" .......................................**40.00**
Crackle, candy jar, marigold, Imperial .........................**30.00**
Cut Sprays, vase, marigold, 9" .............................**45.00**
Daisy & Plume, candy dish, blue, Northwood ...................**100.00**
Daisy Dear, bowl, peach opalescent, Dugan ...................**55.00**
Diamond & Daisy Cut, vase, marigold, US Glass, square, 10" .................................**125.00**
Diamond Lace, bowl, marigold, Imperial, 10"-11" ...........**65.00**
Double Star, tumbler, green, Cambridge, scarce ................**60.00**
Dragon's Tongue, shade, marigold, Fenton ..........................**40.00**
Dutch Twins, ashtray, marigold ......................**50.00**
Engraved Grapes, candy jar, marigold, Fenton ...........**85.00**
Feather & Heart, tumbler, marigold, Millersburg, scarce ...........**75.00**
Field Flower, tumbler, marigold, Imperial, scarce .............**35.00**
Floral & Wheat, bonbon, amethyst, stemmed, Dugan ............**45.00**
Flute, salt dip, marigold, footed, Northwood ...................**32.00**

Flute #3, toothpick holder, green, regular, Imperial ...........**75.00**

Fruit Salad, cup, peach opalescent, Westmoreland, rare ...............................**60.00**

Garland, rose bowl, amethyst, footed, Fenton ...............**70.00**

Georgia Belle, compote, green, footed, Dugan ................**85.00**

Golden Honeycomb, bonbon, marigold, Imperial ........**45.00**

Grape, bowl, fruit; amethyst, Imperial, 8¼" .................**60.00**

Grape, plate, marigold, footed, Fenton's Grape & Cable, 9" ...................................**145.00**

Grape, powder jar, marigold, Northwood's Grape & Cable ...........................**100.00**

Grape, tray, marigold, center handle, Imperial .................**45.00**

Grape Arbor, tumbler, marigold, Northwood .....................**45.00**

Heavy Diamond, creamer, marigold, Imperial ........**30.00**

Hex Base, candlesticks, marigold, pr .....................................**75.00**

Hobstar, cookie jar, marigold, Imperial .........................**65.00**

Hobstar & Arches, bowl, green, Imperial, 9" ...................**60.00**

Hobstar Flower, compote, amethyst, Northwood, scarce ...........................**65.00**

Holly, bowl, green, Fenton, 8"-10" ...............................**90.00**

Horses Heads, bowl, marigold, flat, Fenton, 7½" ............**75.00**

Illinois Daisy, cookie jar, marigold, English ..........**60.00**

Jack-in-the-Pulpit, vase, blue, Dugan ...........................**80.00**

Jewels, hat shape, amethyst, Imperial-Dugan .............**65.00**

Large Kangaroo, bowl, amethyst, Australian, 5" ................**65.00**

Lattice & Daisy, pitcher, marigold, Dugan .........................**225.00**

Leaf Chain, bonbon, blue, Fenton ...................................**50.00**

Long Prisms, hatpin, amethyst ......................**75.00**

Lustre Rose, butter dish, amethyst, Imperial .......**75.00**

Magnolia Drape, tumbler, marigold .........................**55.00**

Mayflower, bowl, pastel, 7½" .**50.00**

Melon Rib, powder jar, marigold, Imperial .........................**35.00**

Memphis, creamer or sugar bowl, amethyst, Northwood ...**70.00**

Northern Star, plate, marigold, Fenton, rare, 6½" ..........**90.00**

Northwood's Poppy, bowl, amethyst, 7"-8¾" .........**135.00**

Open Rose, bowl, blue, flat, Imperial, 9" ............................**50.00**

Optic & Buttons, salt cup, marigold, Imperial ........**50.00**

Orange Tree, mug, amethyst, Fenton, 2 sizes .............**80.00**

Oriental Poppy, tumbler, green, Northwood .....................**55.00**

Oval & Round, bowl, green, Imperial, 9" ............................**50.00**

Palm Beach, butter dish, marigold, US Glass .....**120.00**

Peacock & Dahlia, bowl, marigold, Fenton, 7½" ...................**50.00**

Peacock at the Fountain, tumbler, marigold, Northwood ....**40.00**

Pineapple, compote, marigold, English .........................**50.00**

Polo, ashtray, marigold ........**85.00**

Raindrops, bowl, amethyst, Dugan, 9" ......................**80.00**

Ribbed Swirl, tumbler, marigold ......................**60.00**

Rock Crystal, cup, amethyst, McKee ...........................**45.00**

Rose Bouquet, creamer, marigold .........................**60.00**

Rustic, vase, peach opalescent, Fenton, various sizes ....**75.00**

Singing Birds, tumbler, amethyst, Northwood .....................**75.00**

Smooth Panels, vase, marigold,
Imperial ........................**40.00**
Spring Basket, basket, marigold,
handled, Imperial, 5" ....**50.00**
Star Medallion, compote,
marigold, Imperial ........**45.00**
Sunray, compote, peach opales-
cent ...............................**55.00**
Ten Mums, tumbler, blue, Fenton,
rare ...............................**80.00**
Three Diamonds, vase, pastel,
Dugan, 6"-10" ................**60.00**
Tiny Hobnail, lamp, marigold .**110.00**
Tree Bark, candlesticks, marigold,
Imperial, 4½", pr ...........**30.00**
Tree Bark, pitcher, marigold, open
top, Imperial ..................**60.00**
US Diamond Block, compote,
peach opalescent, US Glass,
rare ...............................**90.00**
Waffle Block, parfait glass,
marigold, stemmed, Impe-
rial ...............................**30.00**
Waffle Block, sugar bowl,
marigold, Imperial ........**60.00**
Wide Panel, bowl, marigold,
Northwood-Fenton-Imperial,
9" ...................................**45.00**
Wide Panel, cup, marigold, Northwood-Fenton-Imperial ..**20.00**
Wide Rib, vase, green, Dugan .**70.00**

**Wild Rose syrup pitcher,
marigold, rare, $700.00.**

Windmill, bowl, marigold, Impe-
rial, 5" ...........................**20.00**
Windmill, tumbler, amethyst,
Imperial ........................**95.00**
Wreath of Roses, compote, green,
Fenton ...........................**50.00**
474, butter dish, green, Impe-
rial ...............................**125.00**

# Cat Collectibles

Cat lovers are often quite fer-
vent in their attachment to their
pets, and for many their passion
extends into the collecting field.
There is no shortage of items to
entice them to buy, be they figural
pieces, advertising signs, postcards, textiles, books, candy containers, or what have you. Mar-
bena Fyke has written an amusing and informative book called
*Collectible Cats, an Identification
and Value Guide.* If you're a cat
lover yourself, you're sure to enjoy
it. See also Black Cats.

Bank, Kilban cat w/red sneakers,
1979, 6½" .......................**22.50**
Cream pitcher, plain w/figural
handle, marked N in circle,
1940s, 10" ......................**15.00**
Figurine, bone china, marked
Germany, 1¾", from $10
to ...................................**12.00**
Figurine, brass, China, 2" ......**8.00**
Figurine, Cat Nap, bone china, Dan-
bury Mint, 1987, 4¾" ......**15.00**
Figurine, glass, marked Pilgrim
Glass 1975 on paper sticker,
4" ...................................**15.00**
Figurine, glass, Venetian, 1950s,
9½" ...............................**85.00**
Figurine, red glass, Viking, 1960,
6½", from $35 to ............**50.00**
Figurine, Ribby, painted bone china,
Beswick, England, 1951 ..**28.00**

**Measuring cup set, Japan, 3 pieces, $12.00.**

Figurine, Snowball, bisque w/glass eyes, Danbury Mint, 1988, 7½" .......................**75.00**

Night light, painted cast metal with bulb in tummy, 1940s, 5" ..**25.00**

Paperweight, black glass, Langham Glass House, England, 4¾" ................................**85.00**

Paperweight, Garfield, dated 1988 ................................**6.00**

Pendant, movable stylized figure w/jewel eyes, 1950s, 3" ..**10.00**

Pin, scatter type w/rhinestones, 1950s, from $7 to ...........**12.00**

Pin, w/Christmas packages, Avon, 1989 ................................**6.00**

Planter, 3 tiger kittens, creamware, unmarked, 1940s, 3¾x5" .**25.00**

Plate, painted china, Bradford Exchange, 1991, 9½" .....**29.00**

Plate, portrait on bone china, Liverpool Pottery, England, 1956, 6" ..........................**15.00**

Plate, Three Kittens, milk glass w/gold paint, ca 1900, from $35 to .............................**45.00**

Teapot, painted ceramic cat w/red fish spout, 1989, 5" ........**12.00**

Tile, signed Mimi Vang Olsen, Avon, 1991 .....................**15.00**

Tin, Droste Chocolates, 3 tiger kittens, 1920, 7x4½" .....**25.00**

Toothpick holder, lusterware, 1940s, 2" ........................**15.00**

TV lamp, Siamese cats, marked KROM, 1950s, 14", from $45 to ....................................**50.00**

Wall pocket, fiddler cat, painted lusterware, Japan, 1940s, 6½" .................................**28.00**

# Ceramic Arts Studio

Whether you're a collector of American pottery or not, chances are you'll like the distinctive styling of the figurines, salt and pepper shakers, and other novelty items made by the Ceramic Arts Studio of Madison, Wisconsin, from about 1938 until approximately 1952. They're not especially hard to find — a trip to any good flea market will usually produce one or several good buys of their shelf sitters or wall-hanging pairs. They're easily spotted, once you've seen a few examples; but if you're not sure, check for the trademark: the name of the company and its location.

Bank, Mrs Blankety Blank, 4½" .**95.00**

Figurine, angel w/candle, 5" .**42.00**

Figurine, bunny, 1¾" ...........**24.00**

Figurine, fawn, 4¼" .............**45.00**

Figurine, frog, 2" .................**20.00**

Figurine, harem girl sitting, 4½" .**35.00**

**Autumn Andy and Summer Sue,
$50.00 each.**

Figurine, Madonna w/Bible,
9½" ...........................**125.00**

Figurine, Panda w/hat, 2½" .**35.00**

Figurine, Promenade man &
woman, 7¾", pr ...........**145.00**

Figurine, Swedish dance couple,
7", pr ...........................**120.00**

Figurine, tortoise w/cane, 3¼" .**32.00**

Jug, Buddha ewer, 3½" ........**45.00**

Plaque, Grace & Greg, 9", pr .**80.00**

Plaque, Mermaid, 6" ...........**75.00**

Shakers, Butch & Billy (pups), 3",
2", pr .............................**95.00**

Shakers, Dutch boy & girl, 4", pr .**35.00**

Shakers, horse heads, 3¾", pr ..**45.00**

Shelf sitter, boy w/dog & girl
w/cat, 4¼", pr ...............**100.00**

Shelf sitter, collie mother, 5" .**40.00**

Shelf sitter, Fluffy, cat, white,
4¾" .................................**50.00**

Shelf sitter, Little Jack Horner,
4½" .................................**45.00**

Shelf sitter, Mexican boy & girl,
legs crossed, 5", pr ........**65.00**

Shelf sitter, Sun-Li & Sun-Lin
(chubby), 5½", pr ...........**48.00**

Vase, modern, square, 2" .....**20.00**

# Cereal Boxes

When buying real estate,
they say 'location, location, location.' When cereal box collecting

its 'character, character, character.' Look for Batman, Quisp,
Superman or Ninja Turtles — the
so-called 'Grain Gods' emblazoned
across the box. Dull adult and
health cereals such as Special K
or shredded wheat, unless they
have an exciting offer, aren't
worth picking up (too boring).
Stick to the cavity-blasting
presweets aimed at kids, like The
Jetsons, Froot Loops, or Trix. You
can hunt down the moldy
FrostyOs and Quake from childhood in old stores and pantries or
collect the new stuff at your
supermarket. Your local cereal
aisle — the grain ghetto — is
chock full of future bluechips, so
squeeze the moment! The big
question is: once you've gotten
your flaky treasures home, how
do you save the box? If you live
where pests (bugs or mice) aren't
a problem, display or store the
box unopened. Otherwise, eat its
contents, then pull out the bottom
flaps and flatten the package
along the fold lines. If you don't
want to flatten the box, empty it
by gently pulling out the bottom
flaps and removing the bag. Be
sure to save the prize inside,
called an inpack, if it has one;
they're potentially valuable too.
Prices are for cereal boxes that
are full or folded flat, in mint condition. For further information we
recommend *Cerealizing America,
The Unsweetened Story of American Breakfast Cereal,* by Scott
Bruce and Bill Crawford, and
*Cereal Box Bonanza* by Scott
Bruce. Scott (Mr. Cereal Box) is
our advisor for this category; he is
listed in the Directory under Massachusetts. See also Clubs and
Newsletters.

All Stars, Huckleberry Hound, w/flying wonder wheel, Kellogg's, 1963 ..................**350.00**

C-3PO's ..................................**50.00**

Capt'n Crunch, 1963, w/pirate ring inside, ..................**250.00**

Cheerios, Snoopy body sticker premium, 1986 ................**5.00**

Cheerios, Star Trek the Next Generation, 1987 ................**25.00**

Cheerios, Star Wars offer on back, 1977 ..............................**50.00**

Cocoa Krispies, Snagglepuss, trading cards on back, 1964, NM .**225.00**

Corn Flakes, Fernando Valenzuela, Kellogg's ..............**35.00**

Corn Flakes, Vanessa Williams, Kellogg's, 1984, NM ......**60.00**

Corn Flakes, Yogi Bear's 1st birthday, Kellogg's, 1960 ......**475.00**

Crispy Critters, Linus the Lionhearted, 1964 ..............**225.00**

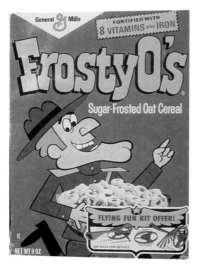

**Dudley Do-Right Frosty O's, 1970s, M, $450.00.**

Frosty-O's, Frosty-O's Bear, 1 Million Dollar Offer, 1961 .**125.00**

Fruit Loops, Toucan Sam, Oot-Fray, Oops-Lay slogan, 1963 .**135.00**

Fruity Pebbles, Bedrock dinosaur premium, 1991 ................**4.00**

Honey Smacks, The Banana Splits' Bingo w/toy train, Kellogg's, 1969 ..................**150.00**

King Vitamin, King cut-out mask on back, 1989 ..................**5.00**

Puffed Wheat, Sgt Preston & King, Quaker, 1956 ................**100.00**

Puffed Wheat, Shirley Temple, color photo, Quaker, 1930s .....**235.00**

Quake, Quaker, 1965 .........**350.00**

Rice Krispies, initial ring premium, Kellogg's, 1981 .....**6.00**

Sugar Crisp, Sugar Crisp Bear w/baseball trading card offer, 1965 ..............................**150.00**

Sugar Smacks, Quick Draw McDraw, Kellogg's, 1963 ..................**225.00**

Sugar Smacks, Quick Draw McGraw, $5 a Week for a Year, Kellogg's, 1963 ...**200.00**

Teenage Mutant Ninja Turtles, 3 trading cards on back, 1990 ............................**15.00**

Twinkles, Bullwinkle on back w/3-page story, General Mills, 1962 ..............................**350.00**

Wheat Puffs, Mickey Mouse figure, 1966, EX .................**15.00**

Wheaties, LA Lakers, 1987 .**40.00**

Wheaties, Lou Gehrig on front, 1992 ..............................**10.00**

Wheaties, Michael Jordan, General Mills, 1990 .............**50.00**

# Character and Promotional Glassware

Once routinely given away by fast-food restaurants and softdrink companies, these glasses have become very collectible; and though they're being snapped up by avid collectors everywhere, you'll still find there are bargains to be had.

The more expensive are those with Disney or Walter Lantz cartoon characters, super-heroes, sports greats, or personalities from Star Trek or the old movies. For more information refer to *The Collector's Guide to Cartoon and Promotional Drinking Glasses* by John Hervey (L-W Book Sales). See also Coca-Cola; Hires Root Beer; Pepsi-Cola; 7-Up.

Aquaman, Super Heroes Series, DC Comics/Pepsi, 1978, 6", from $8 to ...................**10.00**
Archie Bunker for President, green goblet w/portraits, Arby's .**10.00**
Bambi, Wonderful World of Disney, WDP/Pepsi .............**18.00**
Big Yella, Kellogg's, 1977 .......**8.00**
Boris & Natasha, PAT Ward/Pepsi, white letters, 16-oz ........**18.00**
Bugs Bunny, Warner Bros/Pepsi, Brockway, logo under name, 16-oz ...............................**10.00**
Captain Crook, McDonaldland Action Series, 1977 .........**5.00**
Christmas Carol, Subway/Pepsi, set of 4 ...........................**20.00**
Daisy Mae, Al Capp/Sneaky Pete's, 1975, 6¼", minimum value ...........................**35.00**

**Davy Crockett, Holiday Freeze, 7', $10.00.**

Detroit Tigers, Little Caesar's Pizza, 1984, any ..............**5.00**
Dinosaur, Monster March, Sea World/Pepsi/Pizza Hut, set of 4 ....................................**15.00**
Dinosaur, Tyrannosaurs Rex, Welch's, 1988, 10-oz, 4" ...**1.00**
Donald Duck, Picnic Series, WDP/Pepsi, 1979 .............**8.00**
Dudley Do-Right, PAT Ward/Pepsi, 16-oz ...............................**15.00**
Elsie the Cow, tall ................**45.00**
Empire Strikes Back, Burger King, 1980, 5⅞", any, from $3 to .....................................**5.00**
Endangered Species, Burger Chef, 1978, 5⅝", any, from $4 to .**7.00**
Ernest, Soft Batch Reminds Me of Cookies..., Keebler, 1984 ..**8.00**
Flintstones, face in base, Welch's, 4", any, from $6 to ...........**8.00**
Garfield, mug, It's Not a Pretty Life..., McDonald's, 1987 .**2.00**
Ghostbusters, w/No Ghost logo, 4" ......................................**5.00**
Gone for the Morning, mug, McDonald's .....................**3.00**
Great Muppet Caper, Miss Piggy, 1981, McDonald's, 5⅝" ....**3.00**
Holly Hobbie, Simple Pleasures, American Greetings, set of 6 ....................................**20.00**
Howard the Duck, Super Heroes, Marvel Comics/7 Eleven, 1977, 5½" ......................**20.00**
Howdy Doody, face in bottom, Welch's, 1950s, minimum value ...........................**12.50**
Incredible Hulk, Super Heroes Series, 7 Eleven/Pepsi, 1977 .............................**25.00**
Josie & The Pussycats, Hanna Barbera/Pepsi, 1977, 16-oz ...................................**25.00**
Jungle Book, Bagheera, WDP/Pepsi .............................**75.00**
Jungle Book, Mowgli, WDP/Pepsi, 1977, 16-oz ....................**60.00**

Keebler's, 135th Anniversary, 1988 ..................................**8.00**

Little Orphan Annie, Sunday Funnies Series, Pepsi .....**9.00**

Mickey's Christmas Carol, Disney/Coca-Cola, 6⅛", any .**10.00**

NFL, Browns, Mobil, double bands, 5½", any ...............**4.00**

NFL, Cowboys, Mobil, single bands, 5½", any ...............**6.00**

Noid, Avoid the Noid Sports Series, Domino's Pizza ....**4.00**

Paul Revere, Heritage Collector Series, Coca-Cola, 1976 ..**3.00**

Pierre the Bear, LK, 1978-79, set of 4 ..................................**12.00**

Pittsburgh Steelers, McDonald's, 1990, set of 4 .................**20.00**

Porky Pig, Warner Bros/Pepsi, Federal, white letters, 1973, 16-oz ..................................**6.00**

Rescuers, WDP/Pepsi, 1977, any, from $15 to ...................**20.00**

Robin, Super Heroes Moon Series, DC Comics/Pepsi, 1976 .**11.00**

Rocky Squirrel, PAT Ward/Pepsi, white or black letters, 16-oz ..................................**15.00**

Scooby Doo, Hanna-Barbera/Pepsi, 1977, 6¼", from $15 to ...**25.00**

Shakey's Pizza, Refill Me Free, Coca-Cola .........................**5.00**

Simon Bar Sinister, Leonardo TTV/Pepsi, 16-oz, 6¼" ....**15.00**

Sleeping Beauty, 1958, 5", set of 5 different .........................**70.00**

Star Trek, Captain James Kirk, Dr Pepper, 1976 .............**25.00**

Superman, breaking chains, Pepsi, 1978, 6" .................**7.00**

Superman the Movie, DC Comics/Pepsi, 1978, set of 6 ......**20.00**

Tasmanian Devil, Warner Bros/Pepsi, white letters, 16-oz ..............................**15.00**

Wile E Coyote, Warner Bros/Pepsi, Federal, 15-oz, from $8 to ..................................**10.00**

Winnie the Pooh for President, Sears ..............................**16.00**

Wizard of Id, Sir Rodney, Arby's, 1983 ...............................**10.00**

**Wizard of Oz, Scarecrow, wavy bottom, S&C Co., 5", $10.00 to $12.00.**

Wonder Woman, Super Heroes Series, DC Comics/Pepsi, 1978, 6¼" .........................**8.00**

101 Dalmatians, Wonderful World of Disney, WDP/Pepsi, from $10 to ..............................**12.00**

# Character Collectibles

One of the most active areas of collecting today is the field of character collectibles. Flea markets usually yield some of the more common items — toys, books, lunch boxes, children's dishes, and sheet music are for the most part quite readily found. Trade papers are also an excellent source. Often you will find even the rare and hard-to-find listed for sale. Disney characters, television personalities, and comic book heroes are among the most sought after.

One of our advisors for this category is Judy Posner, who is listed in the Directory under

Pennsylvania. Also refer to *Cartoon Friends of the Baby Boom Era* by Bill Bruegman, see the Directory under Ohio.

See also Advertising; Books; Bubble Bath Containers; Cereal Boxes; Character and Promotional Drinking Glasses; Character Watches and Clocks; Cookie Jars; Elvis Presley; Fast Foods; Games; Lunch Boxes; MAD Collectibles; Marilyn Monroe; Movie Memorabilia; Pencil Sharpeners; Puzzles; Radios; Star Trek; Star Wars; Shirley Temple; Telephones; The Three Stooges; Western Heroes; View-Master Reels and Packets.

Addams Family, coloring book, Saalfield, 1965, EX .......**55.00**
Addams Family, Thing bank, EX ................................**70.00**
Alice in Wonderland, doll, rooted blond hair, Sears, 9", EX .**45.00**
Baby Huey, hand puppet, 1950s, EX ..................................**30.00**
Banana Splits, chalkboard, Hasbro, 1969, 24x18", NM ..**45.00**
Barney Google, charm, full figure, silver finish, EX ............**18.00**
Batman, Batmobile license plates, 1966, VG .........................**28.00**
Batman, hand puppet, Ideal, 1965, MIB ......................**80.00**
Batman, night light, DC Comics/General Electric, 1978, 2½" dia, MIP ..........**4.00**
Batman & Robin, bookends, plaster, 1966, EX, pr, .........**100.00**
Beany & Cecil, jack-in-the-box, VG ................................**90.00**

## Betty Boop

Betty Boop was developed by the Fleischer Studios in 1930. All in all, there were about one hundred black and white cartoons produced during the decade of the thirties. Very few of these early cels remain today. Many of the cartoons were copied and colored in the sixties, and many of these cels are still available. Hoards of related items were marketed in the thirties, and many others were produced over the next forty years. During the eighties, still others were marketed. One of the leading companies in this resurgence of popularity was Vandor; they came out with dozens of different ceramic items. Another innovative company is Bright Ideas of San Francisco; they feature items ranging from playing cards to Christmas tree light sets. King Features still owns the copyright, and all items should carry the appropriate labeling. Our advisor for Betty Boop is Leo A. Mallette, who is listed in the Directory under California.

Bank, tin truck, 1988, MIB .**18.00**
Doll, celluloid, wind-up, Made in Japan, 7" .....................**400.00**
Doll, jointed vinyl, pink evening gown, M-Toy, 1986, 12", MIB ............................**22.00**
Doll, jointed wood, marked USA, 1932, 4½", EX ..............**120.00**
String holder, chalk, 1920s to 1930s, 10", EX .............**110.00**
Wall pocket, ceramic, Betty & Bimbo on front, 5½", EX .**90.00**

Beverly Hillbillies, doll, Ellie Mae Clampett, 12½", VG ......**75.00**
Bozo the Clown, figure, oak & rubber, 1950s, MIB .....**105.00**
Buck Rogers, pencil box, blue & red, VG .........................**30.00**
Bugs Bunny, bookends, Holiday Fair, 1970, EX ..............**70.00**

Bugs Bunny, planter, ceramic, Bugs beside wheelbarrow, WB, EX ...........................**45.00**

Bullwinkle, periscope, Laramie, 1970, MOC ...................**20.00**

## California Raisins

Photo courtesy Larry DeAngelo.

**Meet the Raisins 1st Edition, Banana White, marked Clamation-Applause, issued May 1989, M, $15.00.**

In the Fall of 1986, the California Raisins made their first commercials for television. In 1987 the PVC figurines were introduced. Initially there were four: a singer, two conga dancers, and a saxophone player. At this time Hardee's, the fast food restaurant, issued similar but smaller figures. Later that same year, Blue Surfboard (Horizontal), and three Bendees (which are about 5½" tall with flat pancake-style bodies) were issued for retail sale.

In 1988 twenty-one Raisins were made for sale in retail stores and in some cases used for promotional efforts in grocery stores: Blue Surfboard (vertical), Red Guitar, Lady Dancer, Blue/Green

Sunglasses, Guy Winking, Candy Cane, Santa Raisin, Bass Player, Drummer, Tambourine Lady (there were two styles), Lady Valentine, Male Valentine, Boy Singer, Girl Singer, Hip Guitar Player, Sax Player with Beret, and four Graduates. The Graduates are identical in design to the original four characters released in 1987 but stand on yellow pedestals and are attired with blue graduation caps and yellow tassels. Bass Player and the Drummer were initially distributed in grocery stores along with an application to join the California Raisin Fan Club located in Fresno, California. That same year, Hardee's issued six more: Blue Guitar, Trumpet Player, Roller Skater, Skateboard, Boom Box, and Yellow Surfboard. As was true with the 1987 line, the Hardee's characters were generally smaller than those produced for retail sales.

Eight more made their debut in 1989: Male in Beach Chair, Green Grunks with Surfboard, Hula Skirt, Girl Sitting on Sand, Piano Player, 'AC,' Mom, and Michael Raisin. That year the Raisins starred in two movies: *Meet the Raisins* and *The California Raisins — Sold Out*, and were joined in figurine production by five movie characters (their fruit and vegetable friends): Rudy Bagaman, Lick Broccoli, Banana White, Leonard Limabean, and Cecil Thyme.

The latest release of Raisins came in 1991 when Hardee's issued four more Raisins: Anita Break, Alotta Style, Buster, and Benny. All Raisins issued for retail sales and promotions in 1987 and 1988, including

Hardee's issues for those years, are dated with the year of production (usually on the bottom of one foot). Of those Raisins released for retail sale in 1989, only the Beach Scene characters are dated, and they are actually dated 1988. Hardee's Raisins, issued in 1991, are also undated.

In the last two years, California Raisins have become extremely popular collectible items and are quickly sold at flea markets and toy shows. On Friday, November 22, 1991, the California Raisins were enshrined in the Smithsonian Institution to the tune of *I Heard It Through the Grapevine.* We recommend *Schroeder's Collectible Toys, Antique to Modern,* for further information about the many miscellaneous items relating to California Raisins that are available. Listings are for loose items in mint condition, and all are marked CALRAB. Our advisor, Larry De Angelo, is listed in the Directory under Virginia.

**Meet the Raisins 2nd Edition, Mom (Lulu Arborman), marked CALRAB-Applause, issued September 1989, M, $95.00.**

Beach Theme Edition, girl sitting in sand w/boom box, green shoes, '88 ........................**15.00**
Beach Theme Issue, girl w/grass hula skirt, white gloves, 1988 ...............................**15.00**
Beach Theme Issue, male in beach chair, orange sandals & glasses, 1988 .................**17.00**
Beach Theme Issue, male in green trunks w/surfboard, white gloves, 1988 ...................**15.00**
Bendee, flat body, set of 3, M .**45.00**
Christmas Issue, Candy Cane Raisin, green glasses, red sneakers, 1988 ................**9.00**
Christmas Issue, Santa Hat, red cap & green sneakers, 1988 ...............................**9.00**
First Commercial Issue, Guitar, red guitar, 1988 ...............**8.00**
First Commercial Issue, Singer, w/microphone, 1988 ........**5.00**
First Commercial Issue, Sunglasses 1, eyes visible, 1988 ........**16.00**
First Commercial Issue, Sunglasses 2, can't see glasses, 1988 ..................................**6.00**
First Commercial Issue, Winky, hitchhiker pose, 1988 ......**6.00**
First Key Chains, Hands, hands up, thumbs at head, 1987 .**7.00**
First Key Chains, Microphone, right hand points up, 1987 ........**7.00**
First Key Chains, Saxophone, gold sax, no hat, 1987 .....**7.00**
First Key Chains, Sunglasses, orange glasses, fingers at face, 1987 ........................**7.00**
Graduate Key Chains, Hands, thumbs touch head, Applause, 1988 ..............**25.00**
Graduate Key Chains, Microphone, right hand points, Applause, 1988 ..............**25.00**
Graduate Key Chains, Saxophone, gold sax, Applause, 1988 ............................**25.00**

Graduate Key Chains, Sunglasses, fingers touch face, Applause, 1988 ..............**25.00**

Graduates First Commercial Issue, Conga Dancer, yellow base, 1988 ......................**35.00**

Graduates First Commercial Issue, Singer, yellow base, 1988 ..............................**35.00**

Graduates Post Raisin Bran Issue, Hands, yellow plastic base, 1988 ......................**35.00**

Graduates Post Raisin Bran Issue, Saxophone, yellow plastic base, 1988 .........**35.00**

Graduates Post Raisin Bran Issue, Sunglasses, yellow plastic base, '88 .............**35.00**

Hardee's 1st Promotion, Hands, thumbs touch head, 1987, sm ...................................**3.00**

Hardee's 1st Promotion, Microphone, right hand points up, 1987, sm ...........................**3.00**

Hardee's 1st Promotion, Saxophone, gold sax, no hat, 1987, sm ...................................**3.00**

Hardee's 1st Promotion, Sunglasses, orange glasses, 1987, sm ...................................**3.00**

Hardee's 2nd Promotion, Captain Toonz, blue boom box, Applause, 1988 ................**5.00**

Hardee's 2nd Promotion, FF Strings, blue guitar, Applause, 1988 ................**5.00**

Hardee's 2nd Promotion, Rollin' Rollo, w/hat marked H, Applause, 1988 ................**5.00**

Hardee's 2nd Promotion, SB Stuntz, yellow skateboard, Applause, 1988 ................**5.00**

Hardee's 2nd Promotion, Trumpy Trunote, w/trumpet, Applause, 1988 ................**5.00**

Hardee's 2nd Promotion, Waves Weaver, yellow surfboard, Applause, 1988 ................**5.00**

Hardee's 4th Promotion, Alotta Stile, w/shopping bags, Applause, 1992 ................**7.00**

Hardee's 4th Promotion, Anita Break, boom box, Applause, 1988 ..................................**7.00**

Hardee's 4th Promotion, Benny, bowling ball & bag, Applause, 1992 ..................................**7.00**

Hardee's 4th Promotion, Buster, w/skateboard, Applause, 1992 ..................................**7.00**

Meet the Raisins 1st Edition, Banana White, yellow dress, 1989 ................................**15.00**

Meet the Raisins 1st Edition, Lick Broccoli, red & orange guitar, 1989 ................................**15.00**

Meet the Raisins 1st Edition, Piano, red hair, blue piano, 1989 ................................**20.00**

Meet the Raisins 1st Edition, Rudy Bagaman, vegetable cigar, 1989 .....................**15.00**

Meet the Raisins 2nd Edition, AC, hand in 'low five' position, 1989 ................................**95.00**

Meet the Raisins 2nd Edition, Cecil Thyme, orange carrot-like, 1989 .......................**85.00**

Meet the Raisins 2nd Edition, Leonard Limabean, purple coat, 1989 .......................**85.00**

Meet the Raisins 2nd Edition, Mom, yellow hair, pink apron, 1989 ................................**95.00**

Post Raisin Bran Issue, Hands, hands point opposite ways, 1987 ..................................**4.00**

Post Raisin Bran Issue, Microphone, right hand makes fist, 1987 ..................................**4.00**

Post Raisin Bran Issue, Saxophone, inside sax painted black, 1987 ......................**4.00**

Post Raisin Bran Issue, Sunglasses, orange glasses, 1987 ..................................**4.00**

Sandwich Music Box, Hands, hands out to side, fingers point, 1987 .....................**25.00**

Sandwich Music Box, Microphone, both hands out as if to hug, 1987 ..............................**25.00**

Sandwich Music Box, Sunglasses, both hands out as if to hug, 1987 ..............................**25.00**

Second Commercial Issue, Bass Player, gray slippers, 1988, MIP .................................**20.00**

Second Commercial Issue, Drummer, black hat, yellow feather, 1988, MIP ........**20.00**

Second Commercial Issue, Ms Delicious, girl w/tambourine, 1988 ...............................**15.00**

Second Key Chains, Hip Band Hip Guitarist (Hendrix), w/headband, 1988 .........**25.00**

Second Key Chains, Hip Band Microphone-Female, yellow shoes, 1988 ....................**20.00**

Second Key Chains, Hip Band Microphone-Male, hand w/open palm, 1988 ........**20.00**

Second Key Chains, Hip Band Saxophone, black beret, blue eyelids, 1988 .................**20.00**

Special Edition, Michael, silver microphone, stud belt, Applause ........................**20.00**

Special Lovers Issue, Female, holding Be Mine heart, Applause, 1988 ................**8.00**

Special Lovers Issue, Male, holding I'm Yours heart, Applause, 1988 ................**8.00**

Special Raisin Club Issue, Tambourine Female, Applause, 1988 ..............................**15.00**

Third Commercial Issue, Hip Band Hip Guitarist (Hendrix), 1988 .....................**25.00**

Third Commercial Issue, Hip Band Microphone-Female, Applause, 1988 ................**9.00**

Third Commercial Issue, Hip Band Microphone-Male, Applause, 1988 ................**9.00**

Third Commercial Issue, Hip Band Saxophone, black beret, Applause, 1988 ..............**15.00**

Unknown Issue, Blue Surfboard (horizontal), not connected to foot, 1987 ......................**50.00**

Unknown Issue, Blue Surfboard (vertical), connected to right foot, 1988 ......................**35.00**

Captain Marvel, magic flute, MOC ..............................**55.00**

Captain Midnight, shake-up mug, 1957, EX ......................**85.00**

Casper, coloring book, 1960s, M .**22.00**

Casper, squeeze toy, Hungerford Plastic, late 1950s, EX ..**75.00**

**Casper the Ghost pull toy, wooden diecut with paper litho, American Pre-School/Harvey, 1962, NMIB, $125.00 to $150.00.**

Charlie McCarthy, hand puppet, composition head, cloth body, 1930, EX ........................**40.00**

Charlie McCarthy, spoon, Duchess Silver Plate, 1930s, NM ..**25.00**

Chucky, doll, 22", EX ...........**38.00**

Cool Ghoul, coloring book, 8 cut-out masks, 1964, M .......**60.00**

Daddy Warbucks, figure, hand-painted chalk, 6", EX ....**20.00**

Daffy Duck, doll, plush, 1971, NM ................................**15.00**

Dennis the Menace, night light, vinyl, 5x4", EX ..............**50.00**

## Dick Tracy

The most famous master detective of them all, Dick Tracy stood for law and order. Whether up against Boris Arson or the Spider Gang, he somehow always came out on top, teaching his young followers in no uncertain terms that 'Crime Does Not Pay.' Many companies parlayed his persona through hundreds of items for retail sales; and radio premiums such as badges, buttons, secret code books, and rings were free just for 'sending in.' In 1990 with the release of the movie, a new round of potential collectibles appeared. Our advisor is Larry Doucet, who is listed in the Directory under New York. He offers free appraisals to anyone who will send a long SASE and detailed descriptions or photographs.

**Note:** The ranges in the following suggested values reflect conditions varying from good (represented by the low side) to mint (represented by the high side).

Badge, Secret Service Patrol Lieutenant, 1939, from $50 to ..................................**150.00**

Book, Dick Tracy Ace Detective, hardcover, Whitman, 1943, from $10 to ....................**25.00**

Book, Junior Detective Punch-Out, Golden Press, 1962, from $20 to ....................**50.00**

Cartoon kit, Colorforms, 1962, minimum value ............**20.00**

Christmas light bulb, painted glass figure, 1940s, from $50 to ..................................**75.00**

Coloring book, Saalfield, 1946, from $20 to ....................**50.00**

Film strip viewer, Dick Tracy in Movie Style, Acme, 1948, from $50 to ..................**150.00**

Game, Master Detective, Selchow & Righter, 1961, from $30 to ..........................**100.00**

Hand puppet, Ideal, 1961, from $30 to ............................**60.00**

Premium, Secret Service Patrol Member Badge, Quaker, 1939, from $10 ..............**30.00**

Premium, 1933 Secret Code Book, Quaker, from $20 to ......**75.00**

Puzzle, The Bank Holdup, Jaymar, 1961, from $20 to ..**50.00**

2-Way wrist radios, Remco, 1950s, w/original box, from $50 to ..........................**150.00**

Photo courtesy Larry Doucet.

**Dick Tracy Candid Camera, Seymour Sales Co., early 1950s, 50mm, from $25.00 to $50.00.**

Elmer Fudd, coloring book, Watkins, 1962, NM .......**25.00**

ET, Colorforms, lg set, MIB .**25.00**

ET, kite, Spectra Star Kites, 1982, 42x26", MIP ...................**15.00**

Felix the Cat, bendee, Applause, 1988, 6", M ......................**6.00**

Felix the Cat, figure, celluloid, playing violin, 1920, 6", EX ..................................**55.00**

Flash Gordon, coloring book, some colored pages, 1952, EX+ .**28.00**

Flash Gordon, serving tray, litho tin w/action scene, 1979, 17½x13" .........................**12.00**

**Gumby Colorforms Play Set #16, Perma Toy Co., 1988, from $5.00 to $8.00.**

## Flintstones

Anyone alive today knows that Fred, Wilma, Barney, Betty, Pebbles, and Bamm Bamm lived in Bedrock, had a dinosaur for a pet, and preferred bowling over any other sport. The invention of Hanna-Barbera who introduced them all in 1959, they met with immediate, sustaining success,

and to date literally thousands of items featuring the Flintstone crew have been sold such as games, playing cards, pin-back buttons, cookie jar, puzzles, toys, dolls, T-shirts, etc., so today's collectors can build a large and varied collection of Flintstones memorabilia with ease.

Bank, Barney & Bamm Bamm, vinyl, 1971, 19", NM .....**18.00**

Bubble pipe, Bamm Bamm's head as bowl, Transogram, 1963, NM ...............................**14.00**

Camera, Fred's face as lens frame, uses Kodak 126 film, 1976, MOC ............................**32.00**

Coloring book, Whitman, 1960, 80 pages, 8x11", NM .........**24.00**

Costume, Fred, w/mask, Ben Cooper, 1973, EX ...........**35.00**

Dolls, Bamm Bamm & Pebbles, 12", in 16" plastic log cradle, M ..................................**325.00**

Figure, Dino, Bendy Co, 1961, 10", NM .........................**70.00**

Game, Flintstones Shooting Gallery, plastic, Marx, 1962, EX ...............................**225.00**

Game, Flintstones Brake Ball, Whitman, 1962, NM ...**125.00**

Gumball machine, Fred's head as dispenser, Hasbro, 1968, 10x5", NM ......................**60.00**

Night light, Barney, Electricord, 1979, MOC ......................**6.00**

Night light, plastic Fred, Snapit, 1964, 4", NM .................**18.00**

Pillow case, cotton cloth w/Fred at piano, 1960, NM ............**20.00**

Plate, Pebbles on Dino w/Bamm Bamm on pogo stick, Melmac, 8", EX ..............................**6.00**

Playset, Flintstones Kids Town of Bedrock, MIB ................**15.00**

Puppet, finger; Barney, Knickerbocker, 1972, EX ..............**4.00**

Puppet, hand; cloth & vinyl Bamm Bamm, Ideal, 1963, 12", NM ..........................**30.00**

Puppet, plastic Dino w/push-button base, Kohner, 4", M, from $25 to .............................**40.00**

Squeeze toy, Betty Rubble, Lanco, 1960s, 5", NM in EX package .........................**72.00**

Tray, litho tin scene at dinner table, 1979, 10¾", M .....**20.00**

Flip the Frog, coloring book, Saalfield, 1937, EX ..............**80.00**

Goofy on skate board, bendee, Gabriel, 1977, EX ..........**17.00**

Gumby, bendee, Applause, 1989, 5" .......................................**4.00**

Gumby, costume, Lakeside, 1965, any of 4, EX, ea .............**18.00**

Gumby, costume, silk w/glitter, 1968, EX ........................**35.00**

Gumby, drawing set, electronic, Lakeside, 1966, NM ......**50.00**

Gumby, figure, Super-Flex, Lakeside, 1965, 6", MOC .....**50.00**

Gumby, jeep, metal, windshield moves, rubber tires, Lakeside, 1966, EX ..............**70.00**

Heathcliff, bank, plastic, 1980s, VG ..................................**10.00**

Huckleberry Hound, bank, plastic, VG ...........................**20.00**

Huckleberry Hound, gloves, cotton, Boss Glove Co, 1959, MOC .............................**42.00**

Huckleberry Hound, wall plaque, plastic figure, 1960, 11", NM ........................**12.00**

Hulk, belt, Remco, 1978, NMIB ............................**10.00**

## I Dream of Jeannie

Barbara Eden played Jeannie in this comedy TV series from the 1960s. A cartoon version followed in the late seventies. Dolls, games, books, and many other items evolved on the retail level. Today her fans seek out such memorabilia, incredulous at the thought that many of their Jeannie treasures were made thirty years ago. Our advisor for this category is Richard Barnes; he is listed in the Directory under Utah.

Book, Still Dreaming of Jeannie, by Grandinetti, photos, minimum value ....................**20.00**

Comic book, Dell, 1966, only 2 issued, ea, from $20 to ..**60.00**

Costume, Jeannie w/blond hair, I Dream of Jeannie series, MIB ............................**150.00**

Costume, w/bright orange hair, cartoon series, Ben Cooper, MIB ...............................**35.00**

Decanter, smoked crystal genie bottle, Jim Beam, Christmas 1964 ...............................**35.00**

**Doll, Barbara Eden, rooted hair, sleep eyes, Libby, 20", M, $85.00.**

Doll, blue costume, Remco, 6", MIB, from $40 to ...........**60.00**

Doll, w/plastic genie bottle & playhouse, 18", MIB ....**365.00**

Game, Milton Bradley, 1966, MIB (sealed), minimum value ............................**100.00**

Jewelry set, plastic jade stones, cartoon series, 1977, from $10 to .....................................**20.00**

Magic Slate, w/drawing stylus, cartoon series, M, from $15 to .....................................**25.00**

Napkins, from 1977 cartoon series, MIP, up to ..........**10.00**

Paperback, I Dream of Jeannie, by Dennis Brewster, 1966, minimum value .............**50.00**


Ignatz, figure, jointed wood w/cloth tail, 6¼", EX ...**140.00**

Indiana Jones, playset, Streets of Cairo, Kenner, 1980s, MIB ...............................**32.00**

Jetsons, coloring book, Rand McNally, 1986, NM .........**6.00**

Jetsons, figure, PVC, Applause, any of 7 characters, MIP, ea ....**4.00**

Jiggs, figure, chalk, 8", EX ..**75.00**

Linus the Lionhearted, Colorforms, Post premium, 1965, 6x8", M ............................**45.00**

Little Mermaid, bendee, Just Toys, 2" to 6", 3-pc gift set, M .**10.00**

Lum & Abner, Family Almanac for 1937, Horlick's Malted, 32 pages, EX ........................**10.00**

Lurch, figure, vinyl, Filmways TV Productions, 1964, 5½", NM .................................**42.50**

Maggie, charm, full figure, silver finish, EX .......................**18.00**

Maggie & Jiggs, salt & pepper shakers, ceramic, w/stand, EX, pr ..........................**100.00**

Magilla Gorilla, doll, vinyl head, stuffed body, Ideal, M .**230.00**

Magilla Gorilla, hand puppet, Ideal, 1960s, VG ............**38.00**

Man from UNCLE, card game, EX ................................**25.00**

Mowgli, squeak toy, vinyl, Holland, 1967, 6", EX ........**20.00**

Mr Jinx, doll, plush w/vinyl face, cloth tag, 1959, EX ........**55.00**

Olive Oyl, charm, full figure, silver finish, EX ................**18.00**

Paddington Bear, bank, ceramic .......................**125.00**

## Peanuts

First introduced in 1950, the *Peanuts* comic strip has become the world's most widely read cartoon. It appears daily in about 2,200 newspapers. From that funny cartoon about kids (that readers of every age could easily relate to) has sprung an entertainment arsenal featuring movies, books, Broadway shows, toys, theme parks, etc. And surely as the day follows the night, there comes a bountiful harvest of *Peanuts* collectibles. If you want to collect, you should know that authenticity is important. To be authentic, the United Features Syndicate logo and copyright date must appear somewhere on the item. In most cases the copyright date simply indicates the date that the character and his pose as depicted on the item first appeared in the comic strip. Our advisor is Freddie Margolin; she is listed in the Directory under New York.

Bank, Baseball series, Schroeder, Determined, 1973, from $55 to ...................................**65.00**

Book, The Peanuts Philosophers, pop-up, Hallmark, 1972, from $55 to .............................**75.00**

Bullhorn, metal w/Head Beagle, Determined, 1970, from $8 to ...................................**10.00**

Card game, Snoopying Around, Hallmark, from $10 to ..**22.00**

Earrings, cloisonne Snoopy on pumpkin, Aviva, mid-1970s, from $10 to ....................**15.00**

Figure, PVC Snoopy as scout, Determined, early 1980s, from $2 to ........................**3.00**

Handkerchief, Snoopy kissing Lucy, Hallmark, early 1970s, from $3 to ........................**5.00**

Music box, Linus in the pumpkin patch, Anri, early 1970s, from $150 to .........................**200.00**

Nodder, Determined, 1976, 4", from $15 to ....................**35.00**

Nodder, Linus, Schroeder or Pig Pen, Lego, 1959, 5½", from $40 to .............................**65.00**

Nodder, Lucy, Snoopy or Charlie Brown, Lego, 1959, 5½", from $35 to .............................**60.00**

Ornament, Snoopy in kimono, Determined, ca 1977, from $15 to .............................**20.00**

Plate, Happy Mother's Day 1976, ceramic, Schmid, from $8 to ...............................**12.00**

Playset, Peanuts Kindegarten Rhythm, Chein, 1972, MIB, from $100 to ................**135.00**

Punching bag, Charlie Brown, Determined, early 1970s, 34", from $30 to ....................**50.00**

Trophy, Peppermint Patty w/You Are a Rare Gem, Aviva, from $2 to .................................**3.00**

Pixie & Dixie, gloves, cloth, blue graphics, Boss Glove Co, 1959, M ..........................**45.00**

Popeye, Auto-Magic Picture Gun, 6 films, complete, 1938, EX .....................**165.00**

Popeye, bank, vinyl...............**50.00**

Popeye, doll, stuffed body, rubber head & hands, 1983, 9" .**15.00**

**Popeye pencil box, 1934, $65.00.**

Popeye, tablet, sailor on deck w/Olive & Wimpy, 1929, NM ..........**18.00**

Porky Pig, car, diecast metal, Ertl, 1989, MIP ........................**5.00**

Quick Draw McGraw, wall plaque, plastic figure, 1960, 11", NM ...........................**12.00**

Raggedy Ann & Andy, Water 'n Color Paint Set, Larami, 1978, MOC ........................**6.00**

Rainbow Brite, bank, vinyl figure, 1983, MIB ......................**15.00**

Scooby Doo, gumball bank, plastic head, Hasbro, 1968, EX .**40.00**

Scrappy, bank, Charles Mintz, 1930s, 3½", EX .............**30.00**

Scrappy, Christmas lights, Mazda, EX .....................**95.00**

### Simpsons

A popular cartoon show since the late 1980s, the Simpsons are known for their satirical portrayals of the 'average' American family and their rude, often crude comments on life and society. Lisa, Marge, Maggie, Homer, and (last but not least) Bart have been portrayed on countless T-shirts, numerous posters, and a seemingly endless assortment of miscellaneous merchandise. Already they have a devoted following of collectors who want it all, a good example that sometimes (especially in the realm of toys and character collectibles) an item needn't be at all old to have some value.

Air mattress, inflatable, Mattel, 72x30" ..............................**8.00**

Bumper Sticker, Don't Have a Cow, Man!, NJ Croce, 9x3" .................................**1.00**

Christmas ornament, PVC figure w/candy cane, Presents, 3½" ....................................**3.50**

Doll, Bart, soft vinyl w/cloth clothes, Dan Dee, 16", M ..............**18.00**

Figure, Bart on skateboard, PVC, 1989 ................................**2.00**

Frisbee, Bart portrait on white plastic, Betras Plastics, M ...........................**3.00**

Key chain, Bart figure, Street Kids, 3", MIP ...................**4.50**

Stamper set, Rubber Stampede, set of 4 w/blue washable pad, M .....................................**4.00**

Tote bag, green nylon w/black nylon handles, Imaginings 3, 15x12x8" ........................**12.00**

## Smokey Bear

1994 was the 50th Anniversary of Smokey Bear, the spokesbear for the State Foresters, Ad Council, and US Forest Service. After ruling out other mascots (including Bambi), by 1944 it had been decided that a bear was best suited for the job, and Smokey was born. When a little cub was rescued from a fire in a New Mexico national forest in 1950, Smokey's role intensified. Over the years his appearance has evolved from one a little more menacing to the lovable bear we know today whose mission it is to instill the 'help prevent forest fires' motto in the minds of children, in the hope that they will become more responsible adults. For more information, we recommend *Smokey Bear, 20252, A*

*Biography* (20252 is Smokey's zip code), by William Clifford Lawter Jr. (Lindsay Smith publishers), and *Guardian of the Forest, The History of the Smokey Bear Program,* by Ellen Earnhardt Morrison (Morielle Press). Our advisor for this category is Glen Brady, who is listed in the Directory under Oregon.

**Smokey Bear cookie jar, 50th Birthday, limited edition (450 made), Treasure Craft by Don Winton, $150.00 to $175.00.**

Book, Big Golden Book, Story of Smokey Bear, 1971, G .....**8.00**

Cigarette snuffer, bust of Smokey, plastic w/magnet, 1960s, 1½", G ....................................**12.50**

Cigarette snuffer, Smokey's head, plastic w/suction cup, 3½", VG .................................**20.00**

Comic book, Dell, 4-Color #653, #1 (8 in series), Oct 1955, EX .................................**20.00**

Doll, Ideal, complete w/hat, badge & belt buckle, early 1960s, 18", VG .........................**55.00**

Doll, stuffed, Dakin, late 1970s, 10", M ...........................**25.00**
Little Golden Book & Record, 45 rpm, VG .........................**10.00**
Mug, milk glass, Help Keep Washington Clean, F in shield mark, 4", M ..................................**8.00**
Nodder, full figure Smokey, ceramic, no mark, 6", G .**65.00**
Pocket watch, Smokey on face, marked Bradley, 1976, VG ................**100.00**
Record, 33⅓ rpm, LP, Word D-707, Little Marcy Meets..., w/cover, VG ..................................**20.00**
Record, 78 rpm, Gene Autry, Smokey Bear Song, w/cover, VG ..................................**15.00**
Truck bank, Ertl #9124, 1913 Model T Van, #1 in series, 1989, M ..........................**40.00**

## Smurfs

A creation of Pierro 'Peyo' Culliford, the little blue Smurfs that we have all come to love have found their way to the collectibles market of today. There is a large number of items currently available at reasonable prices, though some, such as metal lunch boxes, cereal premiums and boxes, and promotional items and displays, are beginning to attract special interest. Because the Smurfs' 'birthplace' was in Belgium, many items are Euopean in nature. The values listed here are for items in mint condition. Those seeking further information may contact the Smurf Collectors' Club, listed in our Clubs and Newsletters section.

Barrettes, 1982, set of 2, MIP .**3.00**
Calendar, M, from $20 to .....**35.00**
Car, Burago, MIB, from $50 to .**75.00**

Figurine, pewter, M, from $15 to .....................................**35.00**
Figurine, USA issue, M, from $3 to .....................................**4.50**
Figurines, advertising, several, M, from $35 to .............**100.00**
Greeting card, Hallmark, M, from $5 to ................................**8.00**
Playset, Windmill, MIB .......**45.00**
Playsets, Super Super, MIB, different editions, from $25 to .................................**200.00**
Store displays, M, from $8 to .**40.00**
Toy, Space Traveler, 1978, MOC .........................**25.00**
Truck, lift; Hong Kong, MIB .**10.00**

Sneaky Pete, Magic Show, Remco, complete, 1950s, VG ...**125.00**
Snuffy Smith, charm, full figure, silver finish, EX ............**18.00**
Space Kidettes, magic slate, Watkins, 1968, M .........**35.00**
Spark Plug, pull toy, racer, King Features Syndicate, 1924, EX ...............................**500.00**
Superman, Color-By-Number Pencil Set, Hasbro, 1965, M ....................................**60.00**
Superman, slippers, DC Comics, 1967, child size, M ........**12.50**
Sweet Pea, charm, full figure, lead, silver finish, EX ...**18.00**
Terry & the Pirates, coloring book, 1946, VG ..............**10.00**
Tweety, bank, vinyl, 1 movable arm, swivel head, 6½", NM ......**25.00**
Tweety, figure, plastic, Sylvester's head as base, 6¼", NM ..**25.00**
Uncle Wiggly, figure, bisque, 4", EX ................................**18.00**
WC Fields, battery tester, 1974, MOC ..............................**15.00**
Yogi Bear, camera, plastic, 1960s, M .................................**90.00**
Yogi Bear, sticker book, 1964, M .................................**24.00**

# Character Watches and Clocks

Since the 1930s kids have enjoyed watches whose dials depicted their favorite cartoon character, western hero, or movie and TV personality. They're relatively scarce today (since they often met with abuse at the hands of their young owners) and as a result can be rather expensive to collect. The boxes they came in are even more hard to find and are often tagged with prices about equal to that of the watch they contained. Condition is of the utmost importance when evaluating a watch or clock such as these — watch for rust, fading, scratches, or other signs of wear that will sharply decrease their values. Refer to *Comic Character Clocks and Watches* (published by Books Americana) by our advisor, Howard S. Brenner, who is listed in the directory under New York.

**Dale Evans, Bradley, 1951, EX (NM box), $300.00.**

Alice in Wonderland, watch, Timex, 1958, EX ............**65.00**
Babe Ruth, watch, Exacta Time, baseball-shaped box, NM ........**800.00**
Batman, watch, Timex, 1978, EX ...............................**55.00**

Buck Rogers, pocket watch, Ingraham, etching ea side, 1935, EX ...............................**450.00**
Bugs Bunny, clock, alarm; talking, plastic, Janex, 1974, EX .**35.00**
Charlie McCarthy, clock, Gilbert, animated, 1938, EX .**1,500.00**
Charlie Tuna, clock, cube shape, 1972, VG ........................**30.00**
Davy Crockett, watch, US Time, came on powder horn, 1954, NM ...............................**275.00**
Dick Tracy, watch, New Haven, 1948, M ........................**175.00**
Dizzy Dean, watch, Everbrite Watch Co, 1935, EX ....**450.00**
Donald Duck, clock, Bayard, animated, 1964, NM ........**225.00**
Dopey, watch, Ingersoll, Mickey's birthday series, 1948, EX ........**250.00**
Hopalong Cassidy, clock, US Time, 1950, NM ..........**350.00**
Hopalong Cassidy, watch, US Time, saddle stand, 1950, NM ...............................**250.00**
Howdy Doody, watch, Patent Watch Co, animated eyes, 1954, EX ......................**200.00**
Little (Fiddler) Pig, watch, US Time, rare, 1947, NM .**350.00**
Mickey Mouse, clock, alarm; w/radio, Concept 2000, MIB ..........................**250.00**
Mickey Mouse, watch, electric, Timex, 1968, NM ........**175.00**
Mickey Mouse, watch, Ingersoll, 1933, NM ....................**275.00**
Orphan Annie, watch, New Haven, 1948, EX .........**125.00**
Pluto, clock, Bayard, animated head, 1964, EX ............**225.00**
Porky Pig, watch, Ingraham, square or round crystal, 1949, EX ...............................**125.00**
Puss 'n Boots, watch, Nuhope, 1949, NM ......................**75.00**
Robin, watch, Timex, 1978, MIB ........................**250.00**

Rocky Jones, watch, Ingraham, 1954, NM ......................**175.00**

Roy Rogers, clock, Ingraham, animated, 1951, EX ..........**145.00**

Smitty, watch, New Haven, 1935, EX .................................**175.00**

Smurf, clock, alarm; talks, MIB ...........................**95.00**

Smurf, wall clock, Bradley, looks like watch, 1982, M .......**15.00**

Snow White, watch, Ingersoll, 1939, NM ......................**175.00**

Superman, watch, Timex, 1976, M ....................................**75.00**

Woody Woodpecker, watch, Ingraham, 1950, NM ...........**145.00**

# Children's Books

Books were popular gifts for children in the latter 1800s; many were beautifully illustrated, some by notable artists such as Frances Brundage and Maxfield Parrish. From this century tales of Tarzan by Burroughs are very collectible as are those familiar childhood series books, for example, The Bobbsey Twins and Nancy Drew.

**Raggedy Ann Stories, Bobbs-Merrill Company, written and illustrated by Johnny Gruelle, copyright 1961, VG, $20.00.**

Adventures of Pinocchio, Macmillan, 1926, 399 pgs, VG ...............................**110.00**

Airport: Our Link to the Skies, Whitman Learn About Book #1704, VG ........................**5.00**

Alice's Adventure in Wonderland, Collins, 1951, 7 color plates, G ........................................**7.50**

Andersen's Fairy Tales, Viking, 1981, 1st edition, 155 pages, EX .................................**30.00**

Andy & the Acrobats, World Syndicate, 1931, dust jacket, VG .................................**10.00**

Anno's Counting Book, Crowell, 1st edition, 1977, unpaged, w/dust jacket .................**28.00**

Another Brownie Book, Appleton Century, 1941, 30th printing, 144 pages ......................**45.00**

At the Back of the North Wind, McKay, 1919, 1st edition, 342 pages, VG ......................**65.00**

Bed-Knob & Broomsticks, Harcourt Brace Jovanovich Book Club, EX ..........................**5.00**

Black Stallion's Filly, Random House, 1952, 309 pages, w/dust jacket .................**25.00**

Bobbsey Twins at Spruce Lake, Grosset & Dunlap, 1930, dust jacket, VG ......................**25.00**

Borrowers Afloat, Harcourt Brace, 1959, 1st edition, w/dust jacket, VG ......................**35.00**

Boy Emigrants, Scribners, 1900, Moran & Sheppard illustrations, VG ......................**35.00**

Buffalo Bill's Life Story, Holt Rinehart, 1966, Wyeth illustrations ............................**8.00**

Burgess Animal Book for Children, Little Brown, 1929, 353 pages, VG ......................**60.00**

Celery Stalks at Midnight, Atheneum, 1983, 1st edition, w/dust jacket .................**30.00**

Charlie & Great Glass Elevator, Knopf, 1972, 1st edition, dust jacket ............................**20.00**

Cinderella, Garden City, 1938, Weisgard illustrations, w/dust jacket ................**35.00**

Davy Crockett Frontier Hero, Coward McCann, 4th printing, EX ...........................**10.00**

Dorothy Dainty in the Country, Lothrop Lee Shepard, 1909, 1st edition ......................**15.00**

Dorothy on a Ranch, Chatterton, 1909, 1st edition, 260 pages, VG ...................................**15.00**

Dulac's Fairy Book, Fairy Tales of World Gallery, 1984, dust jacket, M ........................**25.00**

Eight Little Indians, Platt & Munk, 1935, G ...............**18.00**

Elegant Elephant, Rand McNally, 1st edition, w/dust jacket, VG .....................**75.00**

Fables of Aesop, Milner & Sowerby, ca 1870s, 296 pages, G ....................................**45.00**

Father Goose's Yearbook, Reilly & Britton, 1907, G .........**100.00**

Field & Forest Friends, FG Browne, 1913, 1st edition, 207 pages, VG ..............**25.00**

Five Little Peppers Midway, Grosset & Dunlap, 1962, VG ..**6.00**

Flicka, Ricka, Dicka & the Strawberries, Whitman, 8th printing, VG ...........................**18.00**

Flower Children, Volland, 1910, 19th edition, MT Ross illustrations, G .....................**35.00**

Friendly Bear, Doubleday, 1st edition, 1957, w/dust jacket, VG ...................................**20.00**

Ghost Parade, Judy Bolton #5, Grosset & Dunlap, 1933, dust jacket, VG .....................**30.00**

Girl Guides' Rules, Policy & Organization, Girl Guides, 1931, G .........................**15.00**

Green Sailors in the Caribbean, Hodder & Stoughton, 1958, VG .....................................**8.00**

Grimm Fairy Tales, Viking & Museum Modern Art, 1979, dust jacket, VG .............**30.00**

Hans Brinker, Winston, 1925, Clara Burd illustrations, 325 pages, VG ......................**30.00**

Hobby Horse Hill, Doubleday Doran, 1939, 270 pages, w/dust jacket, VG .........**30.00**

How Mr Dog Got Even, Harper, 1900, Hollow Tree Stories, 121 pages, G .................**15.00**

How's Inky?, Bobbs Merrill, 1943, signed, 135 pages, w/dust jacket, VG ......................**15.00**

How the Moon Began, Abelard-Schuman, 1971, Ardizzone illustrations, NM ..........**30.00**

Howdy Doody & the Monkey Tale, Whitman, 1953, unpaged, VG .................................**15.00**

Indian Sign Language, William Morrow, 1971, 13th printing, dust jacket ......................**6.00**

Insect Folk, Ginn, 1903, 1st edition, 204 pages, VG ........................**15.00**

Jane Withers & Hidden Room, Whitman, authorized edition, dust jacket .....................**10.00**

Joy Ride, William Morrow, 1974, 1st edition, EX ...............**10.00**

Land of Surprise, McLoughlin, 1938, unpaged, VG ........**40.00**

Life of Daniel Boone in Picture & Story, Cupples & Leon, 1934, G ......................................**6.00**

Little Book of Tribune Verse, Grosset & Dunlap, 1901, reprint, VG ....................**15.00**

Little Brown Bear, Platt & Munk, 1942, 52 pages, VG .......**18.00**

Little Brown Koko Has Fun, American Colortype, 2nd edition, 1945, VG ..............**55.00**

Little Hunchback Zia, Aldus Printers, 1955, limited edition, 33 pages ...............**25.00**

Little Lame Prince & His Traveling Cloak, Rand McNally, 1919, VG ........................**20.00**

Little Shepherd of Kingdom Come, Scribner, 1903, 1st edition, VG ..........................**50.00**

Little Stone House, Macmillan, 1944, 1st edition, w/dust jacket, VG ......................**40.00**

Madam Mary of the Zoo, Little Brown, 1899, 1st edition, 248 pages, VG .......................**25.00**

Maid of the Mountains, Hurst, 1906, 1st edition, girl w/bird on cover ..........................**16.00**

Mother Goose & Her Rhymes, Saalfield, 1915, 142 pages, G .....................................**50.00**

Mrs Mallard's Ducklings, Lothrop Lee & Shepard, 1946, 1st edition, VG ..........................**25.00**

Muffletumps, Holt Rinehart & Winston, 1966, 1st edition, w/dust jacket ................**22.50**

Mystery of the Desert Giant, Grosset & Dunlap, 1961, w/dust jacket, VG .........**35.00**

Mystery of the Stuttering Parrot, Collins, 1967, 1st ed., VG .**10.00**

National Velvet, William Morrow, 1935, EX .........................**7.50**

Oddkins: A Fable for All Ages, Warner, 1988, 1st printing, dust jacket .....................**25.00**

Once Upon a Monday, Volland, 1931, 1st edition, 39 pages, boxed, VG .......................**75.00**

Once Upon a Time, Viking, 1972, 1st edition, Rackham illustrations, VG ........................**25.00**

Patchwork Girl of Oz, Reilly, 1964, reprint, 341 pages, VG ..**18.00**

Penny Fiddle Poems for Children, Doubleday, 1960, w/dust jacket, VG ......................**20.00**

Peter Rabbit & the 2 Terrible Foxes, Altemus, ca 1925, 64 pages, VG ......................**25.00**

Pie & Patty-Pan, Frederick Warne, 1905, Beatrix Potter illustrations .................**100.00**

Pinocchio, Whitman, ca 1939, Disney illustrations, color wrappers, VG ........................**150.00**

Po-No-Kah: Indian Tale of Long Ago, Donohue, 1902, 1st edition, VG ..........................**20.00**

Pop-Up Book of Gnomes, Abrams, 1979, 1st edition, 12 pages, VG ....................................**18.00**

Pop-Up Little Orphan Annie & Jumbo the Circus Elephant, 1935, unpaged .............**300.00**

Prince Valiant in the Days of King Arthur, Treasure Book, 1954, VG ....................................**15.00**

Princess Goldenhair & the Wonderful Flowers, World Syndicate, 1932, VG ...............**40.00**

Rackham's Book of Pictures, Avenel, 1979, 1st edition, dust jacket, VG ..............**20.00**

Rainbow Round the World, Bobbs Merrill, 1954, 1st edition, EX ....................................**7.50**

Restless Robin, Houghton Mifflin, 1937, unpaged, w/dust jacket, VG ....................................**25.00**

Rover Boys at Big Bear Lake, Grosset & Dunlap, 1923, w/dust jacket, VG .........**25.00**

Roy Rogers & the Rimrod Renegades, Whitman, 1952, dust jacket, VG ......................**15.00**

Santa's Tuney Toy, Polygraphic Co of America, 1956 ..........**22.00**

Scott Burton on the Range, Appleton, 1920, 303 pgs, dust jacket .**22.00**

Secret Garden, Godine, 1987, 1st edition thus, 224 pages, dust jacket ...........................**25.00**

Secret of Pirate's Hill, Sampson Low, 1964, VG .................**7.50**

Silver Mace, Macmillan, 1956, 1st edition, Petersham illustrations, VG .........................**30.00**

Smoky the Cowhorse, Scribner, 1929, 17th printing, 310 pages, VG ......................**25.00**

Snow White & 7 Dwarfs, Rand McNally, 1937, Bess Livings illustrations ...................**15.00**

Steve Canyon Operation Eel Island, 1959, Grosset & Dunlap, dust jacket ..............**25.00**

Tales of Wells Fargo: Danger at Dry Creek, Golden Press, 1959, M ..........................**12.50**

Tillie the Toiler, Cupples & Leon, 1930, 10x10", EX ..........**60.00**

Tom Swift & the Cosmic Astronauts, Collins, no date, VG .........**12.50**

Tommy, Tilly & Mrs Tubbs; Jonathan Cape, 1937, London, 1st edition, VG ......**35.00**

Two Little Confederates, Scribner, 1888, 1st edition, 2nd printing, G .............................**45.00**

Uncle Wiggly & the Peppermint, Platt & Munk, 1939, EX .**18.00**

White Indian Boy, World, 1919, Pioneer Life Series, 222 pages, VG ......................**25.00**

**Rand McNally Junior Elf Books**

ABC Book, #694, 1955, EX .....**5.00**

Alexander Kitten, #8003, 1959, EX .....................................**3.00**

All Around the City, #8146, 1967, EX .....................................**4.00**

Animals at the Seashore, #8125, 1966, EX ...........................**5.00**

Animal's Boat Ride, #8124, 1966, EX .....................................**5.00**

Animal's Bus Ride, #8818, 1965, EX .....................................**3.00**

Animal Stories We Can Read, #8031, 1953, EX ...............**5.00**

Benjie Engie, #8008, 1950, illustrated by Eleanor Corwin, EX..........**5.00**

Big Helpers, #8047, 1953, EX.**4.00**

Big Red Apple, #8157, 1968, EX .....................................**3.00**

Bouncing Bear, #8054, 1945, illustrated by Tony Brice, EX.**8.00**

Captain Kitty, #8049, 1951, EX .....................................**3.00**

Child's Garden of Verses, #628, 1942, illustrated by Tony Brice, EX .........................**7.00**

Child's Garden of Verses, #8095, 1962, EX ...........................**5.00**

Cinderella, #8123, 1966, EX...**3.00**

Cock, the Mouse & the Little Red Hen, #8067, 1966, EX ......**4.00**

David & Nancy's Train Ride, #408, 1946, EX...............**15.00**

Disposal Truck, #8161, 1969, EX .....................................**3.00**

Doctor in the Zoo, #8171, 1971, EX .....................................**3.00**

Farm Animals, #8127, 1966, EX .....................................**3.00**

Feathered Friends, #8090, 1966, EX .....................................**3.00**

Fire Fighters, #8168, 1971, EX.**6.00**

Fireman Joe, #8006, 1959, EX.**5.00**

Foxy Squirrel in Garden, #121, 1933, illustrated by Frances Beem, VG.........................**7.00**

Friends of Jesus, #8022, 1954, illustrated by Janet Kennedy, EX .....................................**3.00**

Giant's Shoe, #8148, 1967, EX.**4.00**

Henny Penny, #8138, 1966, EX.**5.00**

House That Jack Built, #360, 1942, illustrated by Tony Brice, 64 pages, EX........**10.00**

House That Jack Built, #8055, 1942, illustrated by Tony Brice, EX .........................**8.00**

Humpty Dumpty, #674, 1954, EX .....................................**8.00**

Jolly Jingle Book, #8001, 1951, EX .....................................**4.00**

Little Fox, #8077, 1961, EX....**3.00**

Little Penguin #8057, 1960, EX .....................................**5.00**

Moth Is Born, #8154, 1967, EX.**3.00**

Mr Snitzel's Cookies, #8046, 1950, EX ....................................**9.00**

Mrs Hen Goes to Market, #8030, 1969, EX ...........................**8.00**

My Animal Picture Boom, #8025, 1959, EX ...........................**5.00**

My Toys, #8051, 1962, EX.......**7.00**

My Truck Book, #8062, 1960, EX ....................................**4.00**

Night Before Christmas, #8204, 1950, EX ...........................**5.00**

One, Two, Cock-A-Doodle-Doo, #384, 1944, 64-page, EX.**10.00**

Pinocchio, #272, 1939, 128 pages EX ................................**15.00**

Prayers for Little Children #227, 1944, illustrated by L. Patton, EX............................**10.00**

Runaway Airplane, #385, 1943, EX ................................**15.00**

See My Toys, #8092, 1947, illustrated by Tony Brice, EX.**8.00**

Snow White & Seven Dwarfs, #8028, 1959, illustrated by Irma Wilde, EX ................**5.00**

Story of Jesus, #164, 1936, 64 pages, EX........................**15.00**

Three Little Ducks, #8064, 1945, EX ....................................**4.00**

Three Little Kittens, #8108, 1964, EX ....................................**6.00**

Three Wishes, #415, 1955, EX ....................................**7.00**

Timmy Mouse, #8019, 1959, illustrated by Tony Brice, EX.**6.00**

Talk With Grandpa, #8126, 1967, EX ....................................**4.00**

## Whitman Tell-A-Tale Books

Bambi, #2548, 1972, sm, EX....**4.00**

Barbie & Skipper Go Camping, #2636, 1977, sm, EX ........**7.00**

Bedknobs & Broomsticks, #2541, 1971, sm, EX ....................**5.00**

Big & Little Are Not the Same, #2474-33, 1972, sm, EX ...**4.00**

Big Red Pajama Wagon, #2479, 1949, lg, EX ......................**8.00**

Billy Bunnyscoot the Lost Bunny, #888, 1948, sm, VG..........**6.00**

Boo Boo & the VIV, #2405, 1965, lg, EX ...............................**6.00**

Buffy & the New Girl, #2526, 1969, sm, EX ....................**7.00**

Bunny Button, #2526, 1953, sm, EX ....................................**6.00**

Captain Kangaroo's Picnic, 1959, sm, EX ...............................**7.00**

Children's Prayers, #822, Story Hour Series, 1945, sm, EX ....................................**7.00**

Circus Alphabet, #2505, 1954, sm, EX ....................................**7.00**

Clip Clop, #2569, 1958, sm, EX .**4.00**

Columbus the Exploring Burro, #826, 1951, sm, EX ..........**5.00**

Corky's Hiccups, #2428, 1968, lg, EX ....................................**5.00**

Daffy Duck, #2453-36, 1977, sm, EX ....................................**5.00**

Daktari, Judy & the Kitten, #2506, 1969, sm, EX ........**7.00**

Donald Duck, Bringing Up the Boys, #800, Story Hour Series, 1948, sm, EX......**30.00**

Donald Duck, Chip & Dale, #2407, 1954, sm, EX ........**5.00**

Donald Duck & the New Birdhouse, #2520, 1956, sm, EX...........**8.00**

Fat Albert & the Cosby Kids, #2598, 1975, sm, EX ........**7.00**

Fawn Baby, #2428, 1966, lg, EX ....................................**6.00**

Good Night, A Fuzzy Wuzzy Book, #2644, 1954, sm, VG ........**8.00**

Goofy & the Tiger Hunt, #2612, 1954, sm, EX ....................**7.00**

Huffin Puff Express, #2415, 1974, sm, EX ..............................**5.00**

Johnny Appleseed, #808, 1949, sm, EX ...........................**18.00**

Lady, #2552, 1954, sm, EX .....**7.00**

Land of the Lost, #2601, 1975, sm, EX ..............................**8.00**

Lassie, The Busy Morning, #2484, 1973, sm, EX ....................**5.00**

Lassie & the Cup Scout, #2503, 1966, sm, EX ..................**12.00**

Little Lulu Lucky Landlady, #2437, 1973, sm, EX ......**25.00**

Little Red Hen, #2431, 1953, sm, EX ....................................**5.00**

Mickey Mouse & the Really Neat Robot, #2475, 1970, sm, EX ......................................**5.00**

Mickey Mouse & the Second Wish, #2418, 1973, sm, EX.........**8.00**

Mother Goose, #2638, 1958, sm, EX ....................................**6.00**

My Father Can Fix Anything, #2424, 1965, lg, EX..........**6.00**

My Little Book About Our Flag, #2578, 1973, sm, EX ........**7.00**

Pink Panther Rides Again, #2401-3, 1976, sm, EX ................**6.00**

Raggedy Ann & Andy on the Farm, #2596, 1975, sm, EX ..........**6.00**

Rubbles & Bamm-Bamm, #2622, 1965, sm,VG .....................**8.00**

Snow White & Seven Dwarfs, #2533, 1957, sm, EX ........**5.00**

Story About Me, #2427, 1966, lg, EX ....................................**6.00**

Three Bears, #2551, 1955, sm, EX ...................................**10.00**

Tom & Jerry & the Toy Circus, #2545, 1953, sm, EX ......**10.00**

Tommy Tractor, #881, 1947, sm, EX ....................................**7.00**

Tweety, #2481, 1953, sm, EX.**10.00**

Tweety & Sylvester, Picnic Problems, #2537, 1970, sm, EX.**5.00**

Uncle Scrooge Rainbow Runaway, #2422, 1965, lg, EX.........**10.00**

Wally Gator, #2567, 1963, sm, EX ....................................**8.00**

Winnie the Pooh, #2526, 1974, sm, EX ..............................**3.00**

Wonderful Tony, #871, 1947, sm, EX ....................................**7.00**

Yogi Bear, No Picnic, #2461, 1961, lg, EX .............................**12.00**

**Wonder Books**

Though the first were a little larger, the Wonder Books printed since 1948 have all measured 6½" x 8". They've been distributed by Random House, Grosset & Dunlap, and Wonder Books Inc. They're becoming very collectible, especially those based on favorite TV and cartoon characters. Steve Santi's book *Collecting Little Golden Books* includes a section on Wonder Books as well. Steve is listed in the Directory under California.

Baby Huey Child's Book, 1960, 24 pages, NM ......................**15.00**

Casper the Friendly Ghost, #761, original price 39¢, M .....**12.50**

December Is for Christmas, #776, cover price 29¢, M .........**10.00**

Firemen & Fire Engines, #637, 1956, M ...........................**7.50**

Fred Flintstone: The Fix-It Man, #917, 1976, M .................**9.00**

Gandy Goose Book, 1957, 20 pages, NM .....................**10.00**

Giraffe Went to School, #551, original price 35¢, M .............**8.00**

Hans Christian Andersen's Fairy Tales, #599, 1976, M .......**4.00**

Heckle & Jeckle, 1957, 20 pages .............................**8.00**

Henny-Penny, #685, 1974, original price 49¢, M .............**5.00**

Huckleberry Hound: The Big Blooming Rosebush, #944, Deluxe Wonder Book ....**12.50**

Little Car That Wanted a Garage, #573, 1974, M .................**5.00**

Little Schoolhouse, #710, 1958, M ....................................**8.00**

Lonely Pony, #645, 1956, M ...**7.50**

Magic Bus, #516, original price 39¢, M .............................**9.00**

Night Before Christmas, #858, 1965, M ...........................**4.50**

Peter Pan, #597, original price 49¢, M ..............................**6.00**

Playful Little Dog, #562, original price 35¢, M .....................**8.50**

Popeye, #667, 1976, M ...........**6.00**

Popeye & the Haunted House, #500, 1980, 1st edition, M .........**15.00**

Surprise for Felix, 1959, 20 pages, NM ..................................**12.00**

What's for Breakfast, #846, original price 49¢, M ..............**6.00**

Who Goes There?, #779, 1975, original price 49¢, M .......**6.50**

Wizard of Oz, #543, 1977, M ..**6.00**

# Children's Dishes

In the late 1900s, glass companies introduced sets of small-scaled pressed glass dinnerware, many in the same pattern as their regular lines, others designed specifically for the little folks. Many were of clear glass, but milk glass, opalescent glass, and colors were also used. Not to be outdone, English ceramic firms as well as American potteries made both tea sets and fully acces-sorized dinnerware sets decorated with decals of nursery rhymes, animals, or characters from children's stories. Though popularly collected for some time, your favorite flea market may still yield some very nice examples of both types. Refer to *The Collector's Encyclopedia of Children's Dishes* by Margaret and Kenn Whitmyer (Collector Books) for more information.

## Ceramic

Bowl, Children Fishing, Noritake, 5⅞" ..................................**35.00**

Chamber pitcher & bowl, blue floral, English ..................**180.00**

Creamer, Blue Willow, England, 1⅝" ..................................**10.00**

Creamer, Kewpies, marked Copyright Mrs Rose O'Neill Wilson, Bavaria ..................**40.00**

Cup, Gumdrop Tree, Southern Potteries, 2¼" ...............**25.00**

Cup, Silhouette Children, Czechoslovakia, 1⅞" ........**7.00**

Cup & saucer, Merry Christmas, pink lustre, Germany ...**30.00**

**Blue Willow made by Ridgway's (English): Platter, $65.00; Gravy boat and underplate, $80.00; Plate, $25.00; Vegetable bowl with lid and underplate, $100.00. (The same items marked Japan would be worth about 40% less.)**

Gravy boat, Twin Flower, Flow Blue, 2½" ........................**75.00**

Mug, Blue Willow, Coalport, 2" ..**22.00**

Plate, Barnyard Scenes, Royal Winsor, 8" ........................**20.00**

Plate, Daffodil, Southern Potteries, 6" .............................**10.00**

Plate, Dimity, 3½" ..................**5.00**

Plate, Godey print, Salem China, 6¼" ....................................**5.00**

Plate, Happifats, Germany, 5¼" .**10.00**

Platter, Blue Marble, England, 4½" ....................................**40.00**

Platter, Flow Blue Dogwood, Minton, 5" ......................**45.00**

Rolling pin, Blue Onion, Germany, 8" .......................**300.00**

Saucer, Humphrey's Clock, Ridgway's England, 4" ............**3.50**

Saucer, St Nicholas, Germany, 4½" ....................................**4.50**

Sugar bowl (open), Mary Had a Little Lamb, Staffordshire, 1⅛" ...................................**8.50**

Teapot, Buster Brown, Germany, 5⅞" ...............................**160.00**

Teapot, Nursery Rhyme, Germany ..............................**32.00**

Teapot, Viktoria Pink Floral, Germany, 7" ........................**60.00**

## Glass

Bowl, Three Little Pigs, Hazel Atlas, 5¾" ......................**14.00**

Bread baker, Betty Jane, #256, crystal w/red trim, McKee Glass Co ........................**22.00**

Butter dish, Sweetheart, crystal, Cambridge, 2" ................**20.00**

Creamer, Bead & Scroll, crystal, United States Glass, 3" .**65.00**

Creamer, Cloud Band, crystal, Gillinder & Sons, 2½" ...**42.00**

Creamer, Colonial #2630, crystal, Cambridge, 2⅜" .............**16.00**

Creamer, Laurel, French ivory, McKee Glass Co, 2⅝" ....**20.00**

Creamer, Sawtooth Band #1225, red flashed, Heisey, 2½" .**70.00**

Mug, Circus Scenes, Hazel Atlas, 5¾" ..................................**8.50**

Mug, Space Scenes, Hazel Atlas, 3" ..................................**16.00**

Pitcher, Arched Panel, amber, Westmoreland, 3¾" .......**90.00**

Plate, Doric & Pansy, pink, Jeannette Glass, 5⅞" .............**8.00**

Plate, grill; Kidibake, blue, Fry Glass Co, 8" ..................**28.00**

Plate, Homepsun, pink, Jeannette Glass, 4½" ........................**8.50**

Punch cup, Nursery Rhyme, blue milk glass, US Glass, 1⅜" ..................................**42.00**

Reamer, white milk glass w/rabbit, 2 handles ................**90.00**

Saucer, Laurel, Scottie decal, McKee Glass, 4⅜" .........**15.00**

Spooner, Beaded Swirl, crystal, Westmoreland, 2¼" .......**35.00**

Sugar bowl, Braided Belt, crystal, Westmoreland, 3½" .....**100.00**

Sugar bowl, Fine Cut Star & Fan, crystal, Higbee, 3⅛" ......**28.00**

Sugar bowl (open), Little Tots, transparent green, England, 1⅛" ..................................**8.50**

Tumbler, Alphabet series, Hazel Atlas ..............................**12.00**

Tumbler, Davy Crockett, Hazel Atlas, 12-oz ....................**10.00**

Tumbler, Nearcut, crystal, Cambridge, 2" ........................**6.00**

# Christmas

No other holiday season is celebrated to the extravagant extent as Christmas, and vintage decorations provide a warmth and charm that none from today can match. Ornaments from before 1870 were imported from Dresden, Germany — usually made of cardboard and sparkled with tinsel trim. Later, blown glass ornaments were made there in literally thousands of shapes such as fruits and vegetables, clowns, Santas, angels, and animals. Kugles, heavy glass balls (though you'll sometimes find fruit and vegetable forms as well) were made from about 1820 to late in the century in sizes from very small up to 14". Early Santa figures are treasured, especially those in robes other than red. Figural bulbs from the '20s and '30s are popular, those that are character related in particular. Refer to *Christmas Collectibles, Second Edition*, by Margaret and Kenn Whitmyer, and *Christmas Ornaments, Lights & Decorations*, by George Johnson (both by Collector Books) for more information.

Bulb, bell shape w/embossed Santa face ......................**16.50**
Bulb, chick, milk glass w/multicolor paint, NM .............**55.00**
Bulb, Indian head, pink & orange, 2" ....................................**175.00**
Bulb, lantern, milk glass, Japan, VG paint, sm .................**12.00**
Bulb, little girl in green dress w/camera ......................**30.00**
Bulb, snowman, milk glass w/red hat & blue bag, 3" .........**20.00**
Bulb, snowman w/stick, 2¼" .**18.00**
Bulb, star w/face, milk glass, EX paint ..............................**15.00**
Bulb, woman in shoe, milk glass w/multicolor paint, NM .**125.00**
Candle clip, Santa in gold robe, embossed tin, 2½" .......**135.00**
Candy container, dwarf, cardboard w/glitter & painted face, 5" ..........................**45.00**
Candy container, house w/cotton Santa on cotton roof, marked Japan ............................**95.00**

Candy container, roasted turkey, brown composition, Germany, 3½" ..................................**55.00**
Candy container, Santa, papiermache, red coat & blue pants, 4" ....................................**130.00**
Candy container, Santa on house, cardboard w/cotton Santa, 3" ........................**70.00**
Candy container, Santa on snowball, papier-mache & cotton, 3½" ..................................**95.00**
Candy container, snowball, micacovered cardboard, Germany, 2½" ..................................**50.00**
Candy container, wreath, Dresden, 4¼" ......................**150.00**
Candy mold, Santa figure, tin, 3" ....................................**20.00**
Figure, fat laughing Santa on white base, plaster, Japan, 3" ....................................**35.00**
Figure, reindeer, standing, lead, Germany, 4½x3" long ....**25.00**
Figure, Santa on skis, bisque, Japan, 1¾" ....................**30.00**
Figure, Santa w/lantern, celluloid, 4½" ..................................**65.00**
Figurine, Santa w/green pack, bisque, Japan, 4½", EX .**50.00**
Garland, red oblong glass balls w/silver trim, 1920s, 153" ..................................**95.00**
Lamp, Santa holding tree between 2 candles, plastic ...........**28.00**
Lamp, wreath shape w/candle in center, cast iron, 8¾" .....**55.00**
Lights, Noma Bubble Lights, string of 12, EX, working .........**85.00**
Matchbook, Santa w/toys, 3¼x4¼" closed ............................**30.00**
Nativity set, cardboard litho, Concordia, 1950s, complete .**30.00**
Ornament, angel's head, diecut in spun glass circle, 2½", VG ..............................**65.00**
Ornament, apple, cotton, green & white, 1½" ....................**12.50**

Ornaments, blown Italian glass from the 1950s: Peter Pan and Spaceman, 6", $20.00 to $30.00 each.

Ornament, butterfly, red blown glass ...............................**65.00**

Ornament, candy cane, glass, red & silver, pre-1960, 6¼" long ...................................**8.50**

Ornament, clown, fat, multicolored & silvered blown glass, 3¼" .................................**50.00**

Ornament, dinner bell, blown glass, 4¼" .......................**22.50**

Ornament, flower, orange blown glass, 3" .........................**20.00**

Ornament, house w/turkey in front, blown glass, 1910-20, 3" ....................................**35.00**

Ornament, pear, blown glass, yellow w/red & pink shading, 1920, 3½" ......................**48.00**

Ornament, teapot, glass, red w/floral decoration, pre-1940 ..............................**15.00**

Ornament, turkey, silver, black & red blown glass, 1920s, 2½x2¼" ........................**150.00**

Ornament, 8-point star, free-blown glass, silver w/red & gold, 1910 ......................**10.00**

Pin, wreath shape w/bow & bell in center .............................**15.00**

Santa face, celluloid & cardboard, lights up, 1950s, 14" .....**55.00**

Santa Claus, Coca-Cola, circa 1960s, 17", M, $65.00 to $75.00. (Though the Black Santa is more desirable, they're also more common, so the value is about the same.)

Santa in sleigh w/2 reindeer, celluloid, Japan, 18", VG ...**45.00**

Trade card, Star Soap, Santa & reindeer, 1900s, 5x7" .....**20.00**

Tree, bottle brush type w/snow-covered bristles, 10" ......**12.50**

Tree, tinsel-type wire w/original ornaments & candles, 7½" ....................................**28.00**

Tree, vinyl, 1950s & later, 8" .**25.00**

Tree stand, metal pot in center, 8 series lamps, Noma, 1940s .........**85.00**

# Cigarette Lighters

Pocket lighters were invented sometime after 1908 and were at their peak from about 1925 to the 1930s. Dunhill, Zippo, Colibri, Ronson, Dupont, and Evans are some of the major manufacturers. An early Dunhill Unique model if found in its original box would be valued at hundreds of dollars. Quality metal and metal-plated lighters were made until the '50s to about 1960. About that time disposable lighters never needing a flint were introduced, causing a decline in sales of figurals, novelties, and high-quality lighters.

What makes a good lighter? — novelty of design, type of mechanism (flint and fuel, flint and gas, battery, etc.), and manufacturer (and whether or not the company is still in business). Most of the lighters listed here are from the 1930s. Sizes listed are approximate. For further information, we recommend *Collector's Guide to Cigarette Lighters, Identification and Values*, by James Flanagan (Collector Books).

**Camel Filters lighter modeled as a cigarette pack, EX, $12.00.**

Miniature, Aladdin, chrome w/lift arm, mother-of-pearl, '50s, ⅞", MIB ...........................**30.00**
Miniature, brass w/key chain, Pereline, 1950s, 1¼x1¼" .**7.00**
Miniature, chrome w/lift arm, flint wheel, Occupied Japan, 1948, ⅞" .........................**35.00**
Novelty, boat, Sarome, Swedish Chicago Line, painted chrome, 1960s, 1" ........................**10.00**
Novelty, camera w/flashlight, chrome & leather, Aurora, 1960, 2" ..........................**15.00**
Novelty, cannon, brass, Japan, 1938, 2½x5½" .................**20.00**
Novelty, glass bottle w/metal cap, Tribune Vermouth, 1950s, 5¼" ................................**10.00**
Novelty, Gremlin (seated figure), Aircraft, electric, 1930s, 4¼" .**50.00**

Novelty, pipe, brass, Occupied Japan, late 1940s, 2¾x4½" ............**40.00**
Novelty, saxophone, butane, Germany, 1990, 3½" ............**12.50**
Novelty, spark plug, Bosch of Germany, 1975, painted chrome, 3¼" ..................................**15.00**
Novelty, television, Swank, early 1960s, 2¾x3⅞" ...............**25.00**
Novelty, train engine, brass, early 1960s, 2¼x4¾" ...............**20.00**
Pocket, basketweave design on chrome, Regens, 1930s, 2⅛x1¼" ...........................**30.00**
Pocket, brass w/ostrich band, Evans, 1934, 2x1½", MIB..............**40.00**
Pocket, canister form, brass, Snap-A-Lite, mid-1910s, 2½x1" dia .......................**40.00**
Pocket, canister form, chrome, Austria, 1925, 2½x1¼" dia ....**40.00**
Pocket, chrome w/lift arm, mother-of-pearl inlay, Occupied Japan, 2" ................**60.00**
Pocket, coin style w/John Kennedy profile, mid-1960s, 1¼" dia ...........................**7.00**
Pocket, hammered chrome w/lift arm & case, Evans, 1930s, 3⅛" ..................................**40.00**
Pocket, pinup photo on chrome, Supreme, 1950s, 2x1⅝" .**15.00**
Pocket, plain chrome, Perfecto, 1930s, 2½x1½" ...............**25.00**
Pocket, Rosen-Nesor, Lake Shore Club of Chicago, 1950s, 1¾x2⅛" ...........................**10.00**
Pocket, torpedo shape, green plastic, late 1930s, 3⅛x⅝" dia ......**20.00**
Pocket, Twentycase, black w/chrome stripes, Ronson, 1935, 4¼", MIB ..............**45.00**
Pocket, Vu-Lighter, dice in clear plastic w/chrome top, Scripto, MIB ................................**10.00**
Pocket, Vu-Lighter, Scripto, pinup photo under plastic & chrome, '50s ...................**10.00**

Pocket, Zippo, Lucky Strike, painted girl logo, 1992, 2¼", MIB ...............................**20.00**

Pocket, Zippo, The Varga Girl 1935, pewter on chrome, 2¼", MIB ...............................**20.00**

Table, crystal, butane, Waterford, 1975, 3x3½" dia .............**50.00**

Table, decanter, silverplate, Ronson, 1936, 4½x2½" dia ...**40.00**

Table, Dunhill Silent Flame, chrome nude on plastic base, battery, 5" ......................**50.00**

Table, elephant, polished chrome, Ronson, 1935, 5", EX+ ..**90.00**

Table, lion, silverplate, 1935, 1¾x2⅜", NM .................**45.00**

Table, Miss Cutie (lower torso), gold plastic, Negbaur, 1950s, 4¾" ...............................**20.00**

Table, Nordic, marble & chrome, Ronson, 1955, 3½x2⅞" dia ...................**15.00**

Table, Oclette, black enameled chrome, Ronson, late 1940s, 3½" ...............................**50.00**

Table, rearing horse, chrome, butane, Japan, 1988, 7", NM ...............................**20.00**

# Cleminson

Hand-decorated Cleminson ware is only one type of the California-made novelty pottery that collectors have recently taken an interest in. Though nearly always marked, these items have a style that you'll quickly become acquainted with, and their distinctive glaze colors will be easy to spot. It was produced from the early 1940s until 1963.

Cleanser shaker, girl figure, 5 holes, w/card explaining use, 6½" ...............................**30.00**

Creamer & sugar bowl, Distlefink, pr .......................**24.00**

Egg cup, double; painted as lady w/spoon & apron, early .**25.00**

Hair receiver, girl w/folded hands, 2-pc ...............................**28.00**

Marmalade, green-dotted flowerpot base, strawberry finial lid ...............................**15.00**

Matchbox holder, wall hanging, white w/red cherries .....**32.00**

Pitcher, Gala Gray, 7" .........**22.00**

**Plate, fruit motif, 8", $9.50.**

Plate, rooster crowing, radiating yellow striped rim, 9½" .**22.00**

Ring holder, elephant w/head back & trunk up .............**45.00**

Ring holder, hand w/fingers spread, flower at wrist ..**45.00**

Salt shakers, Distlefink, pr .**16.00**

Spoon rest, white w/red cherries ...............................**18.00**

Toothpick holder, English Bobby ............................**18.00**

Wall pocket, coffeepot w/bail handle, Let's Have Another... ........**20.00**

Wall pocket, pink diaper ......**12.00**

# Clothes Sprinkler Bottles

From the time we first had irons, clothes were sprinkled with water before ironing for the best results. During the 1930s until the 1950s when the steam iron became a home staple, some of us merely took sprinkler tops and stuck them into bottles to accomplish this task, while the more imaginative enjoyed the bottles made in figural shapes and bought the ones they particularly liked. The most popular, of course, were the Chinese men marked 'Sprinkle Plenty.' Some bottles were made by American Bisque, Cleminson of California, and other famous figural pottery makers. Many were made in Japan for the export market. Note that all of the Chinese men listed here are inscribed 'Sprinkle Plenty.'

Cat w/marble eyes, American Bisque, 8", from $75 to ..................**95.00**

**Chinaman, Cardinal China, $28.00.**

Chinaman, red flowers w/black trim, Sprinkle Plenty ....**45.00**
Clothespin, 8" .......................**45.00**
Dutch boy or girl, 8", ea .......**75.00**
Elephant, red plastic ............**18.00**

**Flatiron shape with decal of girl at ironing board, from $35.00 to $45.00.**

Merry Maid, girl w/hands on hips, plastic, Made in USA ....**15.00**
Rooster, 10" ...........................**65.00**
Siamese cat ...........................**85.00**

# Coca-Cola

Since it was established in 1891, the Coca-Cola Company has issued a wide and varied scope of advertising memorabilia, creating what may well be the most popular field of specific product-related collectibles on today's market. Probably their best-known item is the rectangular Coke tray, issued since 1910. Many sell for several hundred dollars each. Before 1910 trays were round or oval. The 1904 tray featuring Lillian Nordica is valued at $2,350.00 in excellent condition. Most Coca-Cola buffs prefer to limit their collections to items made before 1970. Refer to *Collectible Coca-Cola Toy Trucks* by Gael de Courtivron, and *Goldstein's Coca-Cola Collectibles* by Sheldon Goldstein for more information. Both are published by Collector Books. Our advisors for this category are Craig and Donna Stifter; they are listed in the Directory under Illinois.

**Fan, circa 1950s, M, $30.00.**

Ashtray, metal, Coke Adds Life...,
1970s, 5x4", EX ...............**8.00**

Backpack, canvas, Enjoy Coca-
Cola, 1960s-70s, EX+ ......**7.00**

Bank, plastic, shaped as dispenser, 1980, NMIB ....**110.00**

Banner, Santa at tree w/gifts,
1972, 35x56", EX ..........**15.00**

Beach bag, mesh w/plastic lining,
Can't Beat The Feeling,
21x14", EX .......................**5.00**

Blotter, full-color image of 3 girls
behind fountain, 1944, 4x8",
EX ................................**13.00**

Blotter, shows lg bottle, Over 60
Million Sold..., NM .........**6.00**

Bottle carrier, aluminum w/lift
handle, 12-bottle, 1950s,
EX+ ..............................**50.00**

Bottle opener & cap catcher,
Sprite boy, NMIB ..........**15.00**

Bracelet, Rachel Welch, EX .**40.00**

Bumper sticker, Enjoy Coca-Cola,
Adds Life To Safe Driving,
unused ............................**5.00**

Calendar, 1980 Olympics, EX .**5.00**

Can, Play It Tops contest, 1980s,
EX ...................................**3.00**

Checkerboard, 2-sided, Chinese
checkers/plain checkers,
1930s-40s, VG+ .............**50.00**

Clock, giant pocket watch
w/chain, 1975, MIB .......**35.00**

**Bottle carrier, 6-bottle, aluminum, 1951, 7x8", $20.00 to $25.00.**

Clock, plastic, Things Go Better w/Coke, 16" square, G ...**10.00**

Cribbage board, w/instruction card, 1940s, EX+ ...........**25.00**

Domino set, Coke Is It, MIB ...**25.00**

Fan pull, 2-sided, Santa shape, Family Size, Serve Coca-Cola, EX .................................**20.00**

Fountain hat, white linen, red lettering, 1950s-60s, M .....**50.00**

Magazine ad, Ladies' Home Journal, farm girl, 1923, EX+ .**5.00**

Playing cards, wheat design, 1938, complete w/box, EX .......**75.00**

Playing cards, 1940s scenes, double deck, 1980, MIB ......**20.00**

Puzzle, 2-pc bent wire, The Pause That Refreshes, 1940s-50s, NM ................................**10.00**

Seltzer bottle, clear glass, straight-sided, incised lettering, EX ...........................**85.00**

Shot glass, Merry Christmas, 1986, EX ..........................**4.00**

Sign, cardboard, shows Bill Cosby, Have A Coke & A Smile, 32x66", EX .....................**25.00**

Sign, diecut cardboard, Santa & elves, 1960, 48x31", EX ..**30.00**

Sign, embossed tin, bottle & fishtail logo, 1958, 12x32", NM .**200.00**

Sign, paper, Santa w/bottle, Coke Adds Life..., 1976, 24x10", EX .................................**10.00**

Sign, tin, Coke bottle & fishtail logo, Enjoy..., 1960s, 12x32", VG ...............................**130.00**

Sign, tin button, red w/Drink Coca-Cola In Bottles, 1957, 12" dia, NM .................**180.00**

Syrup can, round w/red paper label, white lettering, 1-gal, 1940s, EX+ ...................**210.00**

Thermometer, plastic, Thirst Knows No Season, 12x4½", EX .................................**50.00**

Thermometer, tin bottle, 1958, 30", EX+ .........................**80.00**

Toy van, Corgi #437, 1978, 4¾" long, M in VG box .........**60.00**

Tray, food cart & fishtail logo, 1958, NM .......................**20.00**

Tray, ice skater seated on log, 1941, 13¼x10½", VG ...**110.00**

TV tray, harvest table w/bucket of Cokes & fiddle, 1961, EX .......................**50.00**

TV tray, party spread w/fondue & bottle, 1956, EX .............**20.00**

Whistle, wood, 1920s, NM ...**40.00**

Yo-yo, bottle-cap shape, EX .**15.00**

# Coin Glass

Coin Glass was originally produced in crystal, ruby, blue, emerald green, olive green, and amber. Lancaster Colony bought the Fostoria Company in the mid-1980s and is currently producing this line in crystal, green, blue, and red, but without frosted coins. (Beware — some people are sand blasting or satinizing the non-frosted coins!) The green and blue are 'off' enough to be pretty obvious, but the red is close. Here are some (probably not all) of the items currently in production: bowl, 8" diameter; bowl, 9" oval; candlesticks, 4½"; candy jar with lid, 6¼"; creamer and sugar bowl; footed comport; wedding bowl, 8¼". Know your dealer!

Emerald green is the most desired by collectors. You may also find some crystal pieces with gold-decorated coins. These will be valued at about double the price of plain crystal if the gold is not worn. Items with worn or faded gold seem to have little value. Our prices are for pieces with frosted coins. Numbers included in our descriptions were company-assigned stock numbers that collectors use as a means to distinguish variations in stems and shapes. For further information we recommend *Collectible Glassware from the 40s, 50s, & 60s,* published by Collector Books.

Ashtray, amber, #1372/114, 7½" ..............................**25.00**
Bowl, blue, #1372/199, footed, 8½" ..............................**85.00**
Bowl, nappy; amber, #1372/499, w/handle, 5⅜" ................**20.00**
Bowl, nappy; crystal, #1372/495, 4½" ..............................**18.00**
Bowl, ruby, #1372/179, 8" ....**45.00**
Cake salver, crystal, #1372/630, footed, 6½" ......................**90.00**
Candle holders, blue or ruby, #1372/316, 4½", pr ........**50.00**
Candy box, amber or olive, #1372/354, 4⅛", w/lid ....**30.00**
Creamer, blue or ruby, #1372/680 ......................**16.00**
Cruet, amber, #1372/531, 7-oz, w/stopper ......................**65.00**
Goblet, ruby, #1372/2, 10½-oz .**85.00**
Jelly dish, blue or ruby, #1372/ 448 ................................**25.00**
Pitcher, amber or olive, #1372/453, 32-oz, 6¼" ...**50.00**
Plate, crystal or olive, #1372/550, 8" ....................................**20.00**
Plate, ruby, #1372/550, 8" ....**40.00**
Punch cup, crystal, #1372/615 .**30.00**
Salt & pepper shakers, amber or olive, #1372/652, chrome tops, pr ....................................**30.00**
Salt & pepper shakers, blue or ruby, #1372/652, chrome tops, pr ....................................**45.00**
Sherbet, crystal, #1372/7, 9-oz, 5¼" ..............................**20.00**
Sugar bowl, blue or ruby, #1372/673, w/lid ............**45.00**
Tumbler, iced tea; crystal, #1372/58, 14-oz, 5¼" .....**30.00**

**Wedding bowl, emerald green, #1372/162, with lid, $125.00.**

Vase, bud; green, #1372/799, 8" ..................................**60.00**

## Compacts

Prior to World War I, the use of compacts was frowned upon. It was not until after the war when women became liberated and entered the work force that the use of cosmetics became acceptable. A compact became a necessity as a portable container for cosmetics and usually contained a puff and mirror. Compacts were made in many different styles, shapes, and motifs and from every type of natural and man-made material. The fine jewelry houses made compacts in all of the precious metals — some studded with precious stones. The most sought-after compacts today are those in the Art Deco style or made of plastic, figurals, and any that incorporate gadgets. Compacts that are combined with other accessories are also very desirable. Refer to *Ladies' Compacts of the 19th and 20th Centuries* (Wallace-Homestead Book Co.) and *Vintage Vanity Bags & Purses* and *Ladies' Compacts, An Identification Guide* (both published by Collector Books). All three are written by our advisor, Roselyn Gerson; she is listed in the Directory under New York. Another good reference is *The Collector's Encyclopedia of Compacts, Carryalls, and Face Powder Boxes* by Laura M. Mueller. See also Clubs and Newsletters.

Chrome, cookie form w/loop for chain ..............................**40.00**
EA Bliss, compact/bracelet, etched floral w/cutouts, minimum value ...................**250.00**
Elgin-American, Give Me Your Answer Do! on lid, blue enamel heart form ........**75.00**

**Elgin American, gold-tone with orange enamel floral, 3¼" wide, $24.00.**

Evans, gold-tone & mother-of-pearl compact/lipstick combination ...........................**35.00**

Flato, open umbrella on lid, fitted black faille case, minimum value ............................**125.00**
Girey Kamra-Pak vanity case, blue leather w/pink plastic top as camera ................**50.00**
Italy, 800 silver vermeil w/multi-color enamel swirls, 3" .**275.00**
Jonteel, repousse silver-plated octagon, finger-ring chain ................**70.00**
La Mode, vanity case, blue cloisonne on gold-tone w/metal mirror ..........................**100.00**
Miniature, red enamel on gold-tone bolster form ...........**25.00**
R&G, Nuwhite, green enamel fish-scale design compact, octagonal ......................**80.00**
Renard, clutch w/pull-up compact, sleeve lipstick, black & gold fabric .............................**45.00**
Rigaud, Mary Garden, embossed lady's profile on lid, brass, round ...............................**70.00**
Ronson, compact/cigarette lighter combination, brown enamel on gold-tone .................**125.00**
Rowenta, enameled petit-point, oval, sm ..........................**30.00**
Trio-ette, vanity case, molded plastic rose cameo as hand mirror ...........................**90.00**
Vanity box, black w/brass flip closure, double handles, miniature ................................**75.00**
Volupte, Swinglok, mother-of-pearl w/black faille case, compartments ....................**125.00**
Wadsworth, floral & butterflies on yellow enamel gold-tone fan form ...............................**80.00**
Wilardy Original, Stardust Bag, envelope closure, swing handle ................................**325.00**
Zell Fifth Avenue, poodle w/red cabochon gems & lipstick on gold-tone .......................**95.00**

# Cookbooks

Advertising cookbooks, those by well-known personalities, and figural diecuts are among the more readily-available examples on today's market. Cookbooks written prior to 1874 are the most valuable; they often sell for $200.00 and up. Refer to *A Guide to Cookbook Collecting* by Colonel Bob Allen and *The Price Guide to Cookbook and Recipe Leaflets* by Linda Dickinson for more information. (Both books are published by Collector Books.)

**Calumet Reliable Recipes, 32 pages, 9x5", VG, $4.00.**

Better Homes & Garden Lifetime Cookbook, 1935 .............**25.00**
Betty Crocker Cookbook, 1959, hardbound ....................**25.00**
Borden's Eagle Brand, 70 Magic Recipes ...........................**12.00**
Cake Secrets, Ingleheart, 1921 .**15.00**
Candy Making at Home, M Wright, 1920, 188 pages ..............**20.00**
Cooking for Two, J Hill, 1906, paperback ......................**18.00**
Easy Steps in Cooking, J Fryer, 1913 ..............................**35.00**

Farmer's Almanac Cookbook, 1965, 390 pages, paperback .......**3.00**
Fine Old Dixie Recipes, 1939 .**45.00**
Grand Rapids Cookbook, 1916, 260 pages, 2nd edition ..**12.00**
How To Cook a Wolf, Fisher, 1943 ..............................**12.00**
International Cookbook, Hardin, 1920 ..............................**20.00**
Let's Eat Out, Betty Crocker, 27 pages, leaflet ...................**2.00**
Little Daisy Salad Book, M Weber, 1923, 179 pages ...**2.00**
Martha Washington Cookbook, M Kimball, 1940 ..................**8.00**
Metropolitan Cookbook, 1918, 62 pages ..............................**6.00**
Microwave Cookbook, Betty Crocker, 1981, 288 pages .**8.00**
Modern Cooking, M Wilson, 1920, 409 pages ......................**15.00**
Mrs Allen's Cookbook, Allen, 1922, 724 pages .............**14.00**
Mrs Hill's Cookbook, 1881 ...**75.00**
Pillsbury Cookbook, 1911, 125 pages, paperback ...........**18.00**
President Cookbook, P Cannon, 1968, 545 pages, hardbound ...........................**15.50**
Secrets of Good Cooking, Sister St Mary, 1928, 309 pages ....**8.00**
Southern Cooking, Grosset, 1941 ..............................**20.00**

## Advertising

Armour & Co, Slices of Real Flavor, 1920s, G ....................**4.00**
Club Aluminum, The 1926 Recipe Book for Club Aluminum Ware, G ...........................**5.50**
Davis' Baking Formulas, Master Pattern Baking Formulas, 1940, EX ..........................**5.00**
General Motors, Your Frigidaire Recipes, 1937, 36 pages, VG .**5.00**
Heinz, figural pickle, paperback ...............................**5.00**

Hershey's Recipes, 1930 .........**8.00**
Knox Gelatin Recipes, 1914 .**10.00**
Knox Gelatin, Dainty Dishes, 1910, 2x2½", VG ..............**4.75**
Larkin Co, Good Things To Eat, 1909, 80 pages, VG .......**10.00**
Metro Life, Metropolitan Cookbook, 1948, 56 pages, VG .**5.00**
Pepsi-Cola Recipe Book, 1940, paperback ......................**12.00**
Pet Recipes, Pet Milk, 1930, 80 pages .................................**5.00**
Philadelphia Gas Co, Housewife's Gas Cooking Manual, 47 pages, VG ......................**16.50**
Royal Baking Powder, Royal Cookbook, 1925, 50 pages, VG ....................................**5.00**
Wesson Oil, For Making Good Things To Eat, 1927, EX .**5.00**
Westinghouse Electric, Meal Planning Guide, 1943, VG ...................................**5.00**
Worcester, The Worcester Salt Cookbook, 1933, 63 pages, VG ...................................**6.00**

## Jell-O

The Jell-O® Story: Peter Cooper dabbled with and patented a product which was 'set' with gelatin, a product that had been known in France since 1682. Peter Cooper's patent for an orange-flavored gelatin was granted in 1845 and was marketed from the 1890s through the early 1900s. Suffice it to say, it never did 'Jell' with the American public.

In 1897 Pearl B. Wait, a carpenter in Le Roy, New York, was formulating a cough remedy and laxative tea in his home. He experimented with gelatin and came up with a fruit-flavored dessert. His wife coined the name Jell-O®, and production began with four flavors: lemon, orange, raspberry, and strawberry.

Jell-O® is 'America's Most Famous Dessert.' In the infancy of advertising campaigns, this was the campaign slogan of a simple gelatin dessert that would one day become known around the world. The success story is the result of advertising and merchandising methods, new and different, having never before been employed. Well-groomed, well-trained and well-versed salesmen went out in 'spanking' rigs drawn by beautiful horses into the roads, byroads, fairs, country gatherings, church socials, and parties to advertise their product. Pictures, posters, and billboards over the American landscape as well as full-page ads in magazines carried Jell-O® with her delicious flavored product into American homes. For further information we recommend our advisor, Col. Bob Allen, listed in the Directory under Missouri.

**It's So Simple, Norman Rockwell illustrated, 1922, $20.00.**

A Calendar Year, Lucille Patterson Marsh illustrated, 1924 .**15.00**

Even If You Can't Cook, You Can Make a Jell-O Dessert, 1913 ........**35.00**

For Economy Use Jell-O, lady planning budget at table, 1920 .**20.00**

Jack & Mary's Jell-O Recipe Book, third edition, 1937 ........**15.00**

Jell-O & the Kewpies, Rose O'Neill illustrated, 1915, 4½x6" .**55.00**

Many Reasons for Jell-O, girl w/basket on hillside, Ball illustrated ......................**20.00**

Now Jell-O Tastes Twice As Good, 23 pages, 1934 ...............**15.00**

Recipes for Delicious Ice Cream, 1936 ...............................**15.00**

Save Money on Ice Cream, 7 pages, 1934 ....................**15.00**

Take This Short Cut to Delicious Ice Cream, 6 pages, 1929 ......**10.00**

The Charm of Jell-O, lady in green dress w/molded Jell-O on tray, 1926 ..................**25.00**

The Greater Jell-O Recipe Book, 1931 ..............................**15.00**

The Jell-O Girl Gives a Party, Rose O'Neill illustrated & signed ............................**55.00**

Thrifty Jell-O Recipes To Brighten Your Menus, 1931 ..............................**15.00**

Through the Menu w/Jell-O, Linn Ball illustrated, 1927 ....**15.00**

Tiktok & Nome King, 1934 ..**75.00**

Want Something Different?...; 23 pages, 1931 ....................**15.00**

What Mrs Dewey Did w/New Jell-O!, 1933, 20 pages, 4x6" .**15.00**

What You Can Do w/Jell-O, third printing, 1936 ..................**5.00**

# Cookie Cutters & Molds

Most of the very early cookie cutters were made from hand-cut tin, hand punched (for air to escape, if they were solid), and hand joined by soldering. A little later on, some were made with rolled handles and/or rolled tops. Machine-made cutters followed, made of tin, aluminum, and plastic. Prices often depend on age, rarity, design, size, composition, and the intricacy of the design. Our advisor is Rosemary Henry; she is listed in the Directory under Virginia. See also Clubs and Newsletters.

Be Mine Valentine Heart, plastic, 1977, 3", MIP ..................**4.00**

Charlie Brown w/ornament, plastic, Hallmark, 1972, M ..**10.00**

Christmas ball ornament, Joy, red soft plastic, Hallmark, 1979, 3", M ...............................**3.00**

Christmas tree, red plastic w/impression lines, Wilton, 1977, 5", M ......................**1.50**

Dove, painted pink, white & gold, Hallmark, 1978, 3½" .......**7.00**

Easter Bunny, plastic, Hallmark, early 1970s, 4½", M .........**5.00**

Easter egg w/chick, yellow plastic, Hallmark, 1980s, 3", M ..**3.00**

Friar Tuck, transparent green plastic, Robin Hood Flour, 1970s, 3½" ........................**5.00**

Girl Scout, white plastic w/impression lines, 1985, 4", M ....................................**1.50**

Lucy w/Christmas package, plastic, Hallmark, 1972, M ..**10.00**

Miss Piggy, plastic, ca 1979-80, M ....................................**8.00**

Mr Peanut tipping hat, transparent blue plastic, 1970s, 5", M ..............................**20.00**

Pennsylvania Dutch man's face, painted plastic w/impressions, '70s, 3" ..................**7.00**

Pilgrim, orange hard plastic, ca 1975, 3", M ..................**5.00**

**Trick or Treat Cookie Cutters, MIB, $65.00.**

Pillsbury Comicooky Cutter C, aluminum w/back, 1937, 4½" .**10.00**

Praying Angel, hard plastic, Hallmark, 1973, 4", M ............**5.00**

Praying angel, soft plastic, Hallmark, 1977, 4", M ............**3.00**

Reddy Kilowatt, transparent red plastic, 1970s, 3", M ........**6.00**

Ronald McDonald, red or yellow plastic, 1980, 3½" ............**2.00**

Santa w/Christmas sack, red plastic, Hallmark, ca 1979, 4", M ...**2.00**

Scooby Doo, hard plastic, Ambassador, ca 1979, M ............**5.00**

Shamrock, green hard plastic, 3", M .....................................**3.50**

Snoopy, Hi Sweetie, plastic, 1974, M .....................................**10.00**

Snoopy on House, hard plastic, 1970s, 8", MIP ................**7.00**

Snowman, green plastic w/cutout for hanger, Hallmark, ca 1977, 4" ...........................**3.00**

Snowman, white plastic, Ambassador, 1980s, M ...............**2.00**

Troll, aluminum w/back & self handle, Wrigley, 1965, 3", M .....................................**12.00**

Witch on Broom, orange plastic, Hallmark, 1976, 3½", M ..**3.00**

# Cookie Jars

The Nelson McCoy Pottery Co., Robinson Ransbottom Pottery Co., and the American Bisque Pottery Co., are three of the largest producers of cookie jars in the country. Many firms made them to a lesser extent. Today cookie jars are one of the most popular of modern collectibles. Figural jars are the most common (and the most valuable), made in an endless variety of subjects. Early jars from the 1920s and '30s were often decorated in 'cold paint' over the glaze. This type of color is easily removed — take care that you use very gentle cleaning methods. A damp cloth and a light touch is the safest approach.

For further information we recommend *The Collector's Encyclopedia of McCoy Pottery* by Sharon and Bob Huxford, *The Collector's Encyclopedia of Cookie Jars* by Joyce and Fred Roerig, *An Illustrated Value Guide to Cookie Jars* by Ermagene Westfall, (all published by Collector Books) and *McCoy Cookie Jars From the First to the Last* by Harold Nichols (self-published). Values are for jars in mint condition unless otherwise noted.

Ark, Treasure Craft, EX ......**35.00**

Avon Cookie Jar, Avon lady in door ...............................**70.00**

Baker, yellow, Red Wing, VG+ .**45.00**

Bantam Rooster, California Originals, NM ........................45.00
Basket Buns & Biscuits, marked INARCO Japan .............38.00
Bear, w/sweater & cookie, Avon, EX ...................................30.00
Bear, w/visor hat & bow, American Bisque, EX ..............80.00
Bear, white, Gilner, EX ........36.00
Birdhouse, Treasure Craft, EX ...................................45.00
Boy Head, sm biscuit jar w/rattan handles, Japan, EX .......30.00
Brown Bagger, Doranne of California, EX ......................30.00
Bunny, white, Brush, EX ...225.00
Bunny, w/cookie, Japan, M ..35.00
Cheshire Cat, Gustin/LA Potteries, EX ............................28.00
Chick, maroon checkered vest, American Bisque, EX ....65.00
Chipmunk, w/acorn, black & white stripes, DeForest of California ....................155.00
Churn Pitcher, American Bisque, EX ...................................18.00
Circus Horse, McCoy .........250.00
Circus Wagon, Enesco, 1980, EX ...................................38.00
Clown Head, Brush ............320.00
Coffee Grinder, McCoy .........45.00
Cookie Shack, Twin Winton, EX ...................................45.00
Cookie Time Clock, California Originals, EX .................45.00
Cookstove, McCo, .................50.00
Cookstove Mammy, Wisecarver, 1988 ............................225.00
Corn King, Shawnee, NM ..140.00
Dalmations in Rocking Chair, McCoy ..........................450.00
Dopey, Treasure Craft ..........80.00
Duck on Basketweave, McCoy .75.00
Elephant, Cumberland Ware, EX ...................................50.00
Elephant, Sierra Vista, EX ..95.00
Frog, Maurice of California, EX .............................65.00

Garbage Can, Doranne of California, EX ...........................28.00
Goldilocks, Regal China, EX .325.00
Grandfather Clock, McCoy ...85.00
Grandma's Cookies, Monmouth, Ill USA ...........................50.00
Granny, Treasure Craft, EX ..60.00
Gumball Machine, California Originals, NM ..............70.00
Hamm's Bear, McCoy .........225.00
Hen w/Chick on Back, Fredricksburg, EX .......................26.00
Hexagon Baker, Shawnee ....80.00

**Hi Diddle Diddle, Robinson-Ransbottom, marked RRP Co Roseville, Ohio #317, $375.00 to $400.00.**

Holstein Cow, Japan ...........60.00
Hound Dog, Doranne of California, EX ...........................32.00
Howdy Doody, Puritan, EX .565.00
Humpty Dumpty, Maddux ..300.00
Humpty Dumpty, peaked hat, Brush ..........................250.00
Ice Cream Cone, w/cherry on top, Japan, sm .....................22.50
Kissing Penguins, McCoy ....85.00
Kookie Kettle, black, McCoy ..35.00

Liberty Bell, House of Webster, EX ...................................**25.00**
Liberty Bell, McCoy .............**60.00**
Milk Can, Treasure Craft, EX **25.00**
Monk, McCoy .........................**45.00**
Monk, Twin Winton, EX ......**30.00**
Mother Goose, McCoy ........**150.00**
Old Churn, McCoy ...............**35.00**
Old-Fashioned Telephone, Cardinal, EX ............................**65.00**
Oreo Cookie, Doranne of California, EX ...........................**28.00**
Peter Pumpkin Eater, w/lock, Brush ...........................**275.00**
Pillsbury Dough Boy, 1988 ..**65.00**
Plaid Apron Mammy, Japan .**650.00**
Police Chief Bear, Twin Winton, EX ...................................**40.00**
Popeye Cylinder, McCoy ....**225.00**
Potbelly Stove, black, McCoy .**40.00**
Potbelly Stove, Hirsch, EX ..**30.00**
Quaker Oats, Regal China .**130.00**
Ring For Cookies Bell, American Bisque, EX .....................**35.00**
Sailor Duck, Made for JC Penney, MIB ................................**30.00**
Satchel, marked Kamenstein, EX ...................................**35.00**
Scarecrow, Royal Sealy, Japan .**28.00**
Scotty Dog, Metlox, EX ......**165.00**
Shedd's Spread Butter Tub, unmarked ......................**35.00**
Snacks Kettle, American Bisque, EX ...................................**65.00**
Snoopy on Doghouse, McCoy .**295.00**
Squirrel on Log, Brush ........**80.00**
Tigger, California Originals, EX ...............................**150.00**
Tony the Tiger, painted plastic, 1968, EX ........................**75.00**
Train Engine, Abingdon, EX .**135.00**
Upside Down Bear, panda, McCoy ...........................**75.00**
Victorian House, Treasure Craft, EX ...................................**35.00**
Walrus, Doranne of California .**38.00**
Wedding Jar, McCoy .........**110.00**
Wishing Well, McCoy ...........**45.00**

**Woody Woodpecker, marked Walter Lantz, 1967, from $750.00 to $1,000.00.**

Wren House, McCoy ...........**150.00**

**Yogi Bear, Hanna-Barbera Productions Inc., American Bisque, $500.00.**

## Corkscrews

Webster's dictionary defines a corksrew as an instrument consisting of a metal screw or helix with a sharp point and a traverse handle whose use is to draw corks from bottles. From early times this task was done by using the worm end of a flint-lock gun rod. The history of corkscrews dates back to the mid-1600s, when wine makers concluded that the best-aged wine was that stored in smaller containers, either stoneware or glass. Since plugs left unsealed were often damaged by rodents, corks were cut off flush with the bottle top and sealed with wax or a metal cover. Numerous models with handles of wood, ivory, bone, porcelain, silver, etc., have been patented through the years. Our advisor for this category is Paul P. Luchsinger; he is listed in the Directory under New York.

Anheuser Busch, nickel-plated bottle form, w/brass plate, dated 1897 ......................**50.00**

Carter's Ink, folding, Pat 1894 ..............................**12.50**

Cat figural, brass & steel, 1900s, 3¾" ...................................**55.00**

Champion, cast iron w/embossed vines overall, wood handle, bar mount ....................**125.00**

Elephant head, ivory handle w/glass eyes, sterling ferrule, 8" .....................................**65.00**

England, swivel-over collar, bronze finish on steel, VG ..................................**42.50**

English, The Utility, 1800s .**100.00**

France, double horn handle, octagonal frame .............**75.00**

France, Laurent Sibet Rockport, grapevine handle, EX ...**18.00**

Germany, Saks Fifth Ave, brass fish form, mid 1900s, 5½" ......**75.00**

Germany, spring over shaft, ca 1895, VG .........................**22.50**

Germany, swivel-over collar style, rubber ring on frame, 1950s .............................**25.00**

Italy, bar man figural, double-lever style, 10½" ............**48.00**

Italy, brass rack & pinion, 1920s, EX .................................**32.00**

Nifty, Vaughn of Chicago, folding worm & capper, sm .........**7.50**

Old Snifter, Senator Volstead, thermoplastic w/multicolor paint ............................**225.00**

Perpetual, double-threaded shaft, automatic reverse, unmarked ......................**75.00**

Plastic duplex (double worm), pic-nic type, modern ..............**5.00**

Rosewood handle, gilted shaft & worm, modern ...............**12.00**

Staghorn handle, marked sterling cap, 7½" .........................**65.00**

US, brass band on boar's tooth handle, 6", EX ..............**85.00**

US Clough Pat of 1904, crown cap lifter, advertising ..........**32.00**

Viking ship, nickel-plated cast iron, 3½x4¼" .................**35.00**

Weir's Pat 12804 25, Sept 1884, VG bronze finish .........**125.00**

# Cracker Jack

The name Cracker Jack was first used in 1896. The trademark as well as the slogan 'The more you eat, the more you want' were registered at that time. Prizes first appeared in Cracker Jack boxes in 1912. Prior to then, prizes or gifts could be sent for through catalogs. In 1910 coupons that could be redeemed for many gifts were inserted in the boxes.

The Cracker Jack boy and his dog, Bingo, came on the scene in 1916 and have remained one of the world's most well-known trademarks. Prizes themselves came in a variety of materials, from paper and tin to pot metal and plastic.

**Paper whistle, Blow For More, $45.00.**

The beauty of Cracker Jack prizes is that they depict what was happening in the world at the time they were made. All items listed are marked Cracker Jack. For further information we recommend our advisor, Phil Helley, listed in the Directory under Wisconsin.

Booklet, Cracker Jack in Switzerland, 1926, 4 pages, 1½x2½", VG ..................................**50.00**
Box, wax paper over cardboard, 1¼x3x6½", early 1900s, G .**160.00**
Box, 1930s, 1½x3x6½", VG .**100.00**
Donkey, cast metal, 1930s, 1" .**3.00**

Drawing book, 1930s, 8 pages w/tracing pages, 2½x3½", EX ......**77.00**
Gun, cast metal, 1930s, 1" .....**2.00**
Jar, glass with Angelus, w/tin lid .............................**500.00**
Lion, cast metal, 1930s, 1" .....**3.00**
Riddle card, G ........................**8.00**
Train car, cast metal, 1930s, 1" .**8.00**
Train engine, cast metal, 1930s, 1½" ..................................**8.00**

# Credit Cards

Credit items predate the 20th century and have been made from

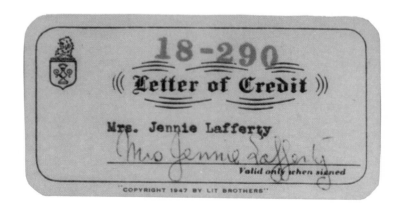

**Lit Brothers, Letter of Credit, copyright 1947, $85.00.**

various types of materials. Celluloid tokens and paper cards were among the earliest, followed by paper and metal plates with holders, metal tokens, and, finally, plastic cards. They have been issued by merchants, oil companies, the travel and entertainment industries, and banks to name the most common. Credit card collecting is one of the fastest growing hobbies today. By their very nature, credit cards and charge tokens were usually deliberately destroyed, making older credit items fiercely sought after. Our advisor, Walt Thompson, is listed in the Directory under Washington.

American Express Optima Gold Card, 1980s ...................**60.00**
American Express Violet Card, 1960s, M ......................**118.00**
American Oil Co National Credit Card, 1960 .....................**50.00**
Carte Blanche, plastic, 1966 .**28.00**
Carter Oil Co, paper, 1950s, NM ...................................**75.00**
Diner's Club Card, Sheraton Hotels Division, plastic .**36.00**
Diner's Club Credit Booklet, paper, early 1950s, M .**375.00**
Diner's Club Credit Card, plastic, 1960s ...............................**30.00**
ESSO, Humble Oil Refining Co National Card, 1964 .....**30.00**
Hilton Hotel Credit Card, paper, 1960s ...........................**18.00**
Husky Frontier Beeline, sample card, plastic ..................**10.00**
Midland Marine Bank, Visa ..**7.00**
Pennsylvania Railroad Pass, 1927 ...............................**9.00**
Pep Boys, Bencharge, caricatures ...........................**50.00**
Pioneer Hotel & Gamblin Hall, plastic ...........................**8.00**

Playboy Club Card, gold key, 1970 ...............................**12.00**
Playboy Club Card, metal, 1960s, M .....................................**43.00**
Prestige Dining Club Card, 1950s ...........................**14.00**
Sampson Oil Co, paper, 1925, EX ...............................**175.00**
Sears, paper & metal, 1940s .**57.00**
Silvermans Charge Coin, metal, rare ................................**50.00**
Sinclair Oil Co, paper, 1937 or 1938, M, ea ...................**85.00**
Sinclair Oil Co, paper, 1946, M..**52.00**
Stevens Hotel Charge Coin, metal ...........................**30.00**
Three Sisters Dress Shop, Paper, 3 portraits, Chicago IL, 1948, VG ................................**4.50**
Visa, 1981, M ........................**11.00**
Washington Mutual Cash Card, Visa, 1994 ......................**6.00**

# Cuff Links

Though you can still buy cuff links at very reasonable prices, if you want some of the better examples, be prepared to pay! What sets the 'special' cuff links apart from the others? Material, of course (some were made of actual coins, some are silver or solid gold), provenance (did they once belong to a famous personality?), presence of a well-known designer's mark, design and decoration, and special functions (in some pairs, one might be an actual watch, a working thermometer, or a compass). There are several specific areas that cuff link collections may be built around such as antique (pre-1900), non-precious (costume and fashion jewelry), 20th Century (1900-1940), specific subject (cars, animals, etc.), specific manufacturer,

Photo courtesy Gene Klompus.

**Cuff links, one containing a watch movement, from $125.00.**

precious metals or stones, material (wood, fabric, etc.), commemoratives, figural, closure type, sports, advertising, and sets (with tie bar, tie tac, etc.) Collectors view the diversity in cuff link designs as an apt barometer of the times — elaborate and colorful during periods of prosperity, small and simply styled when when our ecomony was depressed. For information on how to contact the National Cuff Link Society, see the Clubs and Newsletters section of our Directory. Our advisor for this category is Gene Klompus, society president, who is listed in the Directory under Illinois.

Anson, turquoise stone, w/tie bar, 1970, set ........................**25.00**
Dante, initial E form, w/tie tac, 1960, original box ..........**35.00**
Hickok, silver-tone antique car, 1950, original box ..........**45.00**
Kum-a-Part, separables, round, scrollwork w/mother-of-pearl, 1923, M ..........................**35.00**

Old Dutch Cleanser, enamel logo on sterling, 1905 .........**140.00**
Sheffield, gold-tone w/watch, 1950 .............................**125.00**
Simulated goldstone, 1953 ..**20.00**
Swank, changeable round color marble inserts, ca 1955 .**75.00**
Tintypes, man & woman in 14k gold w/filigree border, round, 1914 .............................**150.00**

### Other Accessories

Shirt studs, Acme, horseshoe form, 1920, set of 5 ......**100.00**
Shirt studs, button-pattern faces, mother-of-pearl, 1925, set of 4 ....................................**30.00**
Shirt studs, separable, elk heads, 1925, set of 4 .................**65.00**
Shirt studs, spring-release separables, 1930, set of 4, original card ................................**30.00**
Tie bar, Anson, gold-tone sabre, hinged wings for pierced tie, ca 1950 ..........................**65.00**
Tie bar, Anson, gold-tone w/photo panel, ca 1950 ...............**65.00**

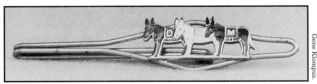

Photo courtesy Gene Klompus.

**Tie bar, Democratic donkeys, red, white, and blue enamel, $35.00 to $45.00.**

Tie bar, Hayward, silver-tone initial S on onyx-like inset, 1930 ..............................**35.00**
Tie bar, slide type w/movable dice, brass, 1940 ....................**55.00**
Tie bar, Swank, gold-tone telescopic pencil, ruled, ca 1953, 3¼" ...............................**35.00**

# Czechoslovakian Glass

Items marked Czechoslovakia are popular modern collectibles. Pottery, glassware, jewelry, etc., were produced there in abundance. Refer to *Czechoslovakian Glass and Collectibles* by Dale and Diane Barta and Helen M. Rose (Collector Books) for more information.

Perfume bottle, patterned white band on green-painted glass, 6", from $85.00 to $90.00.

Atomizer, cased, bright orange w/gold trim, 3" ..............**75.00**
Atomizer bottle, clear & frosted w/gold highlights, 4¾" ..**70.00**
Basket, cased, red w/applied jet rim & handle, ruffled, 6½" ...............................**80.00**
Bowl, cased, black w/red interior, 5" ....................................**85.00**
Bowl, cased, white w/applied maroon rim, ruffled, 6" .**135.00**
Candlestick, cased, varicolored, 8½" ..................................**80.00**
Candy dish, cased, red w/black design & knob, 7" ..........**95.00**
Candy dish, crystal w/frosted & enameled design, 7½" ...**85.00**
Decanter, clear w/hand-painted flowers, 10½" .................**60.00**
Honey pot, dark blue iridescent base & lid, enameled design, 5" ....................................**80.00**
Perfume bottle, black opaque base w/clear crystal stopper, 4½" ....................................**95.00**
Perfume bottle, crystal w/clear cut base & stopper, 5½" .......**85.00**

Pitcher, cased, mottled colors, applied cobalt handle, 9" ............**125.00**
Pitcher, cased, red w/applied jet handle, 10⅛" ................**175.00**
Salt & pepper shakers, crystal hen & rooster w/blue heads, 3", pr ............................**45.00**
Toothpick holder, cased, orange w/black & green design, 2¼" ..................................**35.00**
Vase, cased, light blue w/pink interior, ruffled top, 6¾" ......**95.00**
Vase, cased, orange w/black applied serpentine design, 8" ......**90.00**
Vase, cased, orange w/multicolored design, satin finish, 9½" ..................................**85.00**
Vase, cased, red & orange mottle, 4¼" ..................................**60.00**
Vase, cased, red w/applied cobalt handles, 6" ....................**95.00**
Vase, cased, red w/applied jet rim & serpentine, ruffled, 6" .....**80.00**
Vase, cased, red w/mottling, jet rim, 7" ............................**80.00**
Vase, cased, variegated pattern, 5½" ..................................**65.00**

Vase, cased, yellow & brown variegated, 3-footed pedestal base, 8" ...........................**95.00**
Vase, crystal w/blue variegated design, 8½" ..................**185.00**
Vase, crystal w/intaglio-cut design, ball form, 5" ......**80.00**

# Dakin

From about 1968 through the late 1970s, the R. Dakin Company produced a line of hollow vinyl advertising and comic characters licensed by Warner Brothers, Hanna-Barbera, and Disney as well as others. Some figures had molded-on clothing; some had felt clothes and accessory items. Inspiration for characters came from TV cartoon shows, comic strips, or special advertising promotions. Dakins were offered in different types of packaging. Those in colorful 'Cartoon Theatre' boxes command higher prices than those that came in clear plastic bags. Plush figures were also produced but the vinyl examples such as listed below are the most collectible. All are complete with clothes and accessories, and original tags are present unless otherwise noted.

For further information and more listings, we recommend *Schroeder's Collectible Toys, Antique to Modern.*

Bamm-Bamm, complete w/bone & hat, 8", NM.....................**35.00**
Bozo the Clown, Larry Harmon, 1974, MIP ......................**50.00**
Bugs Bunny, Warner Bros, 1976, MIB (cartoon theatre box) .**40.00**
Bullwinkle, 1976, MIB, from $60 to ....................................**75.00**

Deputy Dawg, Terrytoons, 1977, EX ..................................**40.00**
Dudley Do-Right, Jay Ward, 1976, MIB (cartoon theatre box) .**75.00**

**Elmer Fudd, vinyl with cloth attire, 8", VG, $25.00.**

Goofy Gram, Fox, 'Wanna See My Etching?,' 6", NM ..........**25.00**
Goofy Gram, Lion, 'Sorry You're Feeling Beastly,' EX ......**20.00**
Goofy Gram, Scotty Dog, vinyl w/cloth clothes, NM ......**35.00**
Lion in Cage, bank, 1971, EX .**25.00**

**Merlin the Magic Mouse, copyright 1974, EX+, $25.00.**

Mouse on Cheese Wedge, bank, 1971, EX ........................**25.00**
Oliver Hardy, MIP ...............**40.00**
Popeye, King Features, 1976, MIB (cartoon theatre box) .....**60.00**

Porky Pig, Warner Bros, 1976, MIB (cartoon theatre box) ......**40.00**

Speedy Gonzalez, Warner Bros, 1976, MIB (cartoon theatre box) .**50.00**

Sylvester, Warner Bros, 1976, 5¼", NM .........................**20.00**

Yosemite Sam, Warner Bros, 1976, MIP (fun farm bag) ........**40.00**

## Advertising

Hobo Joe, bank, 1977, EX ..**120.00**

Li'l Miss Just Rite, 1965, EX+ .**75.00**

Miss Liberty Belle, w/hat, 1975, M ......................................**75.00**

Quasar Robot, bank, '75, M .**175.00**

RCA's Nipper Santa Dog, MIP .**35.00**

Sambo's Tiger, 1974, EX+ ..**125.00**

Woodsy Owl, 1974, EX .........**60.00**

# Decanters

The James Beam Distilling Company produced its first ceramic whiskey decanter in 1953 and remained the only major producer of these decanters throughout the decade. By the late 1960s, other companies such as Ezra Brooks, Lionstone, and Cyrus Noble were also becoming involved in their production. Today these fancy liquor containers are attracting many collectors. Our advisors for decanters are Judy and Art Turner of Homestead Collectibles, who are listed in the Directory under Pennsylvania.

Beam, Automotive Series, Chevy Convertible, red, 1957 ..**95.00**

Beam, Automotive Series, Corvette, silver, 1963 ......................**69.00**

Beam, Automotive Series, Corvette, white, 1953 .....................**150.00**

Beam, Automotive Series, Corvette Pace Car, 1978 .............**195.00**

Beam, Automotive Series, Dodge Challenger, blue ..........**125.00**

Beam, Automotive Series, Ford Fire Pumper Truck, 1935 ........**59.00**

Beam, Automotive Series, Ford Mustang, red, 1964 .......**79.00**

Beam, Automotive Series, Train, Caboose, red ..................**65.00**

Beam, Automotive Series, Train, Lumber Car ...................**29.00**

Beam, Automotive Series, Woodie Wagon, 1929 ..................**65.00**

Beam, Casino Series, Golden Nugget, 1969 .................**49.00**

Beam, Casino Series, Horseshoe Club ................................**7.00**

Beam, Centennial Series, Colorado Springs ..................**5.00**

Beam, Centennial Series, St Louis Arch, 1967 ..........**10.00**

Beam, Convention Series, Harley Davidson Eagle ..........**250.00**

Jim Beam, elephant, 1960, $12.50.

Beam, Executive Series, Texas Rose, 1978 .....................**15.00**

Beam, Executive Series, Twin Doves, 1987 ...................**10.00**

Beam, Foreign Series, Australia, Tiger .............................**15.00**

Beam, Organization Series, Devil Dog ................................**19.00**

Beam, Organization Series, Shriner, Indiana .............**5.00**

Beam, People Series, Hank Williams Jr ....................**25.00**
Beam, People Series, Mr Goodwrench ...........................**29.00**
Beam, Sports Series, Clint Eastwood ...............................**15.00**
Beam, Trophy Series, Dog, Labrador ........................**29.00**
Beam, Trophy Series, Fish, Catfish ...............................**29.00**
Beam, Trophy Series, Fish, Walleye, 1987 .......................**14.00**
Beam, Trophy Series, Jackalope ...........................**10.00**
Beam, Trophy Series, Pheasant, 1961-1967 ......................**10.00**
Brooks, Automotive Series, Mustang Pace Car ................**25.00**
Brooks, Automotive Series, Tank ...............................**39.00**
Brooks, Chicago Fire ...........**25.00**
Brooks, Clydesdale ...............**15.00**
Brooks, VFW, 1974 .................**5.00**
Cyrus Noble, Gold Miner ...**325.00**
Double Springs, Automotive Series, Auburn ..............**15.00**
Double Springs, Automotive Series, Ford 1910 ..........**25.00**
Double Springs, Automotive Series, Rolls Royce ........**15.00**
Hoffman, Bear & Cub ..........**35.00**
Hoffman, Dog, Fox Terrier ...**15.00**
Hoffman, Georgia Bulldog ...**19.00**
Hoffman, Panda, mini ..........**12.00**
Hoffman, Stagecoach Driver .**19.00**
Hoffman, Wood Ducks .........**18.00**
LSU, Tiger #2 ......................**25.00**
McCormick, Daniel Boone ...**19.00**
McCormick, Elvis Aloha ....**150.00**
McCormick, Elvis Memories .**495.00**
McCormick, Jim Bowie ........**20.00**
McCormick, Muhammad Ali .**95.00**
McCormick, Paul Revere, mini .**10.00**
McCormick, Stonewall Jackson ...........................**65.00**
Michter, Canal Boat .............**15.00**
Michter, Daniel Boone Barn **15.00**
Michter, Texas Football .......**19.00**

OBR, Football Player, red ....**25.00**
Old Commonwealth, Fisherman ...........................**65.00**
Old Commonwealth, Yankee Doodle ...............................**15.00**
Old Mr Boston, Bart Star #15 .**45.00**
Pacesetter, Automotive Series, Tractor, Ford .................**65.00**
Ski Country, Animal Series, Bobcat ...............................**80.00**
Ski Country, Animal Series, Jaguar ........................**160.00**
Ski Country, Bird Series, Condor ...............................**74.00**
Ski Country, Christmas Series, Scrooge ..........................**79.00**
Ski Country, Fish Series, Rainbow Trout ...............................**65.00**
Ski Country, Rodeo Series, Bull Rider ...............................**75.00**
Wild Turkey, #4, Turkey & Eagle ...........................**85.00**
Wild Turkey, #9, Turkey & Bear Cubs ...............................**85.00**
Wild Turkey, Strutting Turkey, 1978 ...............................**25.00**
Wild Turkey, Turkey on a Log, 1972 ...........................**150.00**

# Degenhart

The 'D' in heart trademark indicates the product of the Crystal Art Glass factory, which operated in Cambridge, Ohio, from 1947 until the mid-1970s. It was operated by John and Elizabeth Degenhart who developed more than 145 distinctive colors to use in making their toothpick holders, figurines, bells, and other novelties. In general, slags and opaques should be valued at 15% to 20% above clear colors. See also Glass Shoes.

Baby Shoe Toothpick, Amberina ...........................**13.50**

Bicentennial Bell, 1776-1976, Light Pink ......................**10.00**

Bird Salt w/Cherry, Forest Green ...........................**17.50**

Bird Toothpick, Boyd Black .**32.50**

Colonial Bow Slipper, Amberina ...........................**22.50**

Colonial Drape Toothpick, Custard ................................**22.50**

Daisy & Button Salt Dip, Blue Bell ..................................**13.50**

Daisy & Button Toothpick, Sapphire Blue ......................**13.50**

Forget-Me-Not Toothpick, Amethyst .........................**13.50**

Great Seal of Ohio Cup Plate, Milk Blue .......................**10.00**

Gypsy Kettle Salt Dip, Amethyst ....................**13.50**

**Hand pin dish, Tomato, 5", $30.00.**

Hat Toothpick, Nile Green ...**17.50**

Heart & Lyre Cup Plate, Emerald Green ..............................**8.00**

Heart Toothpick, Royal Velvet **17.50**

Hen Covered Dish, Sapphire Blue 3" ....................................**17.50**

Michigan Beaded Oval Toothpick, Smoky Blue ...................**13.50**

Mini Pitcher, Crystal ...........**13.50**

Pooch, Sapphire Blue ...........**17.50**

Portrait Plate of Mrs Degenhart, Amber, 5" ......................**35.00**

Pottie Salt Dip, Crystal .......**10.00**

Robin Covered Dish, Lavender Blue, 5" ..........................**90.00**

Star & Moon Drop Salt Dip, Vaseline ..................................**13.50**

Stork & Peacock Child's Mug, Crystal ...........................**17.50**

Sunburst Wine Glass, Cobalt .**35.00**

Wise Ole Owl, Teal ..............**22.50**

# Depression Glass

Depression Glass, named for the era when it sold through dime stores or was given away as premiums, can be found in such varied colors as amber, green, pink, blue, red, yellow, white, and crystal. Mass-produced by many different companies in hundreds of patterns, Depression Glass is one of the most sought-after collectibles in the United States today. Refer to *The Pocket Guide to Depression Glass* by Gene Florence (Collector Books). See also Fire-King; Glass Knives; Jadite; Peach Lustre.

Adam, ashtray, pink, 4½" .....**27.00**

Adam, bowl, cereal; pink or green, 5¾" ................................**37.50**

Adam, cake plate, green, footed, 10" ................................**25.00**

Adam, platter, pink, 11¾" ....**25.00**

American Pioneer, cup, green .**12.00**

American Pioneer, ice bucket, green, 6" .........................**55.00**

American Pioneer, plate, pink, 6" .................................**12.50**

American Pioneer, plate, pink, 8" .................................**10.00**

American Pioneer, sugar bowl (open), green, 2¾" .........**22.00**

American Sweetheart, bowl, cereal; pink, 6" ..............**15.00**

American Sweetheart, creamer, pink, footed ....................**12.00**

American Sweetheart, plate, luncheon; monax, 9" ...........**10.00**

Anniversary, butter dish, crystal ................................**25.00**

Anniversary, cup, crystal .......**4.00**

Anniversary, plate, sandwich; pink, 12½" ......................**12.00**

Anniversary, plate, sherbet; pink, 6¼" ....................................**3.00**

Aunt Polly, bowl, berry; blue, 7⅞" ...................................**40.00**

Aunt Polly, candy dish, green, 2-handled, w/lid ................**60.00**

Aunt Polly, creamer, blue .....**45.00**

Aunt Polly, plate, luncheon; blue, 8" ....................................**18.00**

Avocado, bowl, relish; pink, footed, 6" .........................**23.00**

Avocado, cup, pink, footed ...**33.00**

Avocado, plate, luncheon; pink, 8" ....................................**17.00**

Beaded Block, plate, green, 7¾" sq ........................................**7.00**

Beaded Block, plate, dinner; green, 8¾" ......................**15.00**

Block Optic, bowl, berry; green, 4¼" .....................................**7.00**

Block Optic, candy jar, green, w/lid, 6¼" ........................**50.00**

Block Optic, ice bucket, pink .**40.00**

Block Optic, pitcher, green, 8½", 54-oz ...............................**38.00**

Block Optic, plate, dinner; green, 9" ....................................**20.00**

Block Optic, salt & pepper shakers, green, footed, pr .....**35.00**

Block Optic, sugar bowl (open), green or pink .................**12.50**

Bubble, bowl, fruit; blue, 4½" .**11.00**

Bubble, pitcher, red, w/ice lip, 64-oz ..............................**55.00**

Bubble, plate, dinner; crystal, 9½" .....................................**6.00**

Bubble, platter, crystal, oval, 12" .**9.00**

Bubble, tumbler, water; crystal, 9-oz ....................................**6.00**

Cameo, bowl, vegetable; yellow, oval, 10" .........................**35.00**

Cameo, candy jar, green, w/lid, 6½" ...............................**145.00**

Cameo, cup, green ................**13.50**

Cameo, plate, dinner; green, 9½" ....................................**16.00**

Cameo, plate, luncheon; green, 8" ....................................**10.00**

**Cameo 3-part divided relish, green, 7½", $27.50.**

Cameo, salt & pepper shakers, green, footed, pr ............**65.00**

Cameo, tumbler, juice; footed, 3-oz ................................**55.00**

Cherry Blossom, bowl, cereal; green, 5¾" ......................**35.00**

Cherry Blossom, plate, sherbet; green or pink, 6" .............**7.00**

Cherry Blossom, platter, pink, oval, 11" .........................**35.00**

Cherry Blossom, sugar bowl (open), green ..................**15.00**

Cherryberry, bowl, berry; green or pink, 4" ...........................**8.50**

Cherryberry, pitcher, green or pink, 7¾" ......................**150.00**

Cherryberry, sherbet, green or pink ...................................**9.00**

Circle, bowl, green or pink, 8" .**15.00**

Circle, plate, luncheon; green or pink, 8" .............................**4.00**

Circle, tumbler, water; green or pink, 8-oz .........................**9.00**

Colonial, bowl, berry; green, 4½" ....................................**15.00**

Colonial, butter dish, green .**55.00**

Colonial, plate, dinner; pink, 10" ....................................**45.00**

Colonial, tumbler, iced tea; pink, 12-oz ................................**42.00**

Colonial Block, bowl, green or pink, 4" .............................**6.50**

Colonial Block, butter dish, green or pink ...........................**45.00**

Colonial Block, pitcher, green or pink ................................**37.50**

Colonial Block, sherbet, green or pink ..................................**8.00**

Colonial Fluted, bowl, berry; green, 7½" ......................**16.00**

Colonial Fluted, plate, sherbet; green, 6" ...........................**2.00**

Columbia, bowl, cereal; 5" ...**15.00**

Columbia, cup, crystal ...........**8.50**

Columbia, plate, bread & butter; pink, 6" ...........................**14.00**

Columbia, plate, luncheon; crystal, 9½" ...........................**10.00**

Cube, candy jar, green, w/lid, 6½" ..................................**30.00**

Cube, cup, pink .....................**7.50**

Cube, pitcher, pink, 8¾", 45-oz ...................................**185.00**

Cube, plate, luncheon; green, 8" .**7.00**

Cube, tumbler, green, 4", 9-oz .**65.00**

Daisy, plate, dinner; amber, 9⅜" .**9.00**

Daisy, sugar bowl (open), crystal, footed ...............................**6.50**

Diamond Quilted, ice bucket, green ...............................**45.00**

Diamond Quilted, plate, sherbet; green, 6" ...........................**2.50**

Diamond Quilted, sherbet, green .**4.50**

Diana, tumbler, pink, 4", 10-oz .**35.00**

Dogwood, cake plate, pink, heavy solid foot, 13" .................**90.00**

Dogwood, cup, pink ..............**15.00**

Dogwood, plate, luncheon; green, 8" .......................................**8.00**

Doric, bowl, berry; green, 4½" .**8.00**

Doric, bowl, vegetable; pink, oval, 9" ....................................**25.00**

Doric, butter dish, pink ........**65.00**

Doric, candy dish, green, 3-part .**7.00**

Doric & Pansy, bowl, berry; pink, 4½" ....................................**8.00**

Doric & Pansy, plate, sherbet; pink, 6" ...........................**7.50**

English Hobnail, bowl, green or pink, 4½" .......................**10.00**

English Hobnail, candy dish, green or pink, cone-shaped, ½-lb .....**50.00**

English Hobnail, cup, green or pink ..................................**16.00**

English Hobnail, plate, green or pink, 8" ...........................**8.00**

English Hobnail, sherbet, green or pink ...........................**14.00**

Floragold, bowl, iridescent, sq, 4½" ..................................**5.50**

Floragold, butter dish, iridescent, oblong, ¼-lb ...................**24.00**

Floragold, cup, iridescent ......**6.00**

Floragold, plate, dinner; iridescent, 8½" .........................**35.00**

Floral, plate, dinner; green, 9" .**17.50**

Floral, plate, sherbet; green, 6" .**7.50**

Floral, tumbler, juice; green, footed, 4", 5-oz ...............**20.00**

Florentine No 1, ashtray, green, 5½" ..................................**22.00**

Florentine No 1, bowl, berry; yellow, 8½" .........................**27.00**

Florentine No 1, plate, grill; green, 10" ........................**10.00**

Florentine No 1, sugar bowl, yellow ...............................**13.00**

Florentine No 2, bowl, cream soup; yellow, 4¾" ...........**20.00**

Florentine No 2, cup, green ...**8.00**

Florentine No 2, plate, dinner; green or yellow, 10" .......**14.00**

Florentine No 2, tumbler, green, footed, 4", 5-oz ...............**14.00**

Forest Green, cup, .................**5.00**

Forest Green, plate, dinner; 10" .............................**27.50**

Forest Green, plate, salad; 6⅝" .**5.00**

Forest Green, tumbler, 10-oz .**7.00**

Fruits, bowl, berry; pink, 8" .**37.50**

Fruits, sherbet, green ...........**8.50**

Fruits, tumbler, juice; green, 3½" ..................................**20.00**

Georgian, creamer, green, footed, 3" ....................................**11.00**

Georgian, cup, green ..............**9.00**

Georgian, plate, dinner; green, 9" ....................................**25.00**

Heritage, bowl, fruit; crystal, 10½" ...............................**14.00**

Heritage, sugar bowl (open), crystal, footed .......................**20.00**

Hex Optic, cup, green or pink .**4.50**

Hex Optic, pitcher, green or pink, footed, 9", 48-oz .............**40.00**

Hex Optic, salt & pepper shakers, green or pink, pr ...........**26.00**

Hobnail, bowl, cereal; crystal, 5½" .................................**4.00**

Hobnail, plate, luncheon; crystal, 8½" .................................**3.50**

Hobnail, tumbler, water; crystal, 9-oz or 10-oz ....................**5.50**

Holiday, creamer, pink, footed .**8.00**

Holiday, cup, pink .................**7.00**

Holiday, plate, dinner; pink, 9" .**16.00**

Homespun, butter dish, pink .**55.00**

Homespun, sherbet, pink .....**16.00**

Indiana Custard, bowl, cereal; French ivory, 6½" ..........**20.00**

Indiana Custard, bowl, vegetable, French ivory, oval, 9½" .**27.50**

Indiana Custard, butter dish, French ivory .................**60.00**

Indiana Custard, plate, dinner; French ivory, 9¾" ..........**25.00**

Iris, bowl, berry; crystal, beaded edge, 4½" ........................**38.00**

Iris, bowl, soup; iridescent, 7½" ...............................**57.50**

**Iris butter dish, iridescent, $40.00.**

Iris, cup, crystal ...................**15.00**

Iris, plate, dinner; crystal, 9" .**50.00**

**Mayfair in blue: cup, $50.00; plate, round, off-center indent, 6½", $27.50.**

Iris, sherbet, crystal, footed, 4" ...................................**22.00**

Lace Edge, bowl, cereal; pink, 6⅜" .................................**17.50**

Lace Edge, compote, pink, 7" .**22.50**

Lace Edge, creamer, pink ....**22.00**

Lace Edge, cup, pink ............**22.00**

Lace Edge, plate, dinner; pink, 10½" ...............................**25.00**

Laurel, bowl, berry; French ivory, 5" .....................................**7.50**

Laurel, plate, salad; French ivory, 7½" .................................**10.00**

Laurel, salt & pepper shakers, French ivory, pr .............**45.00**

Lincoln Inn, ashtray, blue or red ...............................**17.50**

Lincoln Inn, bowl, cereal; blue or red, 6" ...........................**14.00**

Lincoln Inn, cup, blue or red .**17.50**

Lincoln Inn, plate, blue or red, 8" ...................................**12.50**

Madrid, butter dish, amber .**67.50**

Madrid, candlesticks, amber, pr ...............................**22.00**

Madrid, plate, dinner; amber or green, 10½" ....................**35.00**

Madrid, salt & pepper shakers, amber, footed, 3½", pr ...**65.00**

Madrid, sugar bowl (open), green ...............................**8.50**

Madrid, tumbler, green, 4¼", 9-oz ..............................**21.00**

Manhattan, bowl, berry; crystal, 7½" .................................**14.00**

Manhattan, candy dish, crystal, w/lid ...............................**37.50**

Manhattan, compote, crystal or pink, 5¾" .........................**30.00**

Manhattan, cup, crystal ......**17.50**

Manhattan, plate, dinner; crystal, 10" .................................**18.00**

Manhattan, plate, salad; crystal, 8½" .................................**14.00**

Manhattan, sherbet, pink ....**14.00**

Mayfair, bowl, cereal; pink, 5½" .**22.00**

Mayfair, cake plate, pink, footed ..........................**27.50**

Mayfair, candy dish, pink, w/lid ..........................**50.00**

Mayfair, goblet, water; pink, 5¾", 9-oz .................................**55.00**

Mayfair, plate, dinner; pink, 9½" ............................**47.50**

Mayfair, tumbler, juice; pink, 3½", 5-oz .................................**40.00**

Miss America, cake plate, pink, footed, 12" ......................**42.50**

Miss America, compote, pink, 5" .................................**25.00**

Miss America, creamer, pink, footed ..............................**17.50**

Miss America, plate, grill; pink, 10" .................................**22.50**

Moderntone, cup, cobalt .......**11.00**

Moderntone, plate, dinner; cobalt, 8⅞" .................................**17.50**

Moderntone, salt & pepper shakers, cobalt, pr ..................**40.00**

Moderntone, sherbet, cobalt .**13.00**

Moderntone, sugar bowl (open), cobalt ..............................**11.00**

Moonstone, bowl, dessert; opalescent, 5½" ..........................**9.50**

Moonstone, candle holders, opalescent, pr .................**17.50**

Moonstone, candy jar, opalescent, w/lid, 6" ..........................**25.00**

Moonstone, plate, luncheon; opalescent, 8" ................**15.00**

Moroccan Amethyst, candy dish, w/lid ...............................**30.00**

Moroccan Amethyst, cup, ......**5.00**

Moroccan Amethyst, ice bucket, 6" .................................**30.00**

Moroccan Amethyst, plate, salad; 7¼" ................................**7.00**

New Century, cup, green .......**6.50**

New Century, sherbet, green, 3" .**9.00**

New Century, sugar bowl, green, w/lid ..............................**23.00**

No 610 Pyramid, ice tub, pink .**75.00**

No 612 Horseshoe, bowl, vegetable; green, 8½" .........**20.00**

No 612 Horseshoe, cup, yellow .**12.00**

No 612 Horseshoe, sugar bowl (open), yellow ...............**16.00**

No 618 Pineapple & Floral, bowl, salad; crystal, 7" .............**2.00**

No 618 Pineapple & Floral, cup, amber .............................**9.00**

No 618 Pineapple & Floral, plate, dinner; amber, 9¼" ........**15.00**

No 622 Pretzel, cup, crystal ...**6.00**

No 622 Pretzel, plate, salad; crystal, 8¼" ...........................**6.00**

No 622 Pretzel, sugar bowl (open), crystal .............................**4.50**

Normandie, bowl, cereal; amber, 6½" .................................**15.00**

Normandie, cup, pink ............**9.00**

Normandie, plate, salad; amber, 7¾" ..................................**9.00**

Normandie, salt & pepper shakers, amber, pr ...............**48.00**

Old Cafe, cup & saucer, pink .**8.50**

Old Cafe, pitcher, pink, 80-oz .**90.00**

Patrician, bowl, berry; amber or green, 5" .........................**11.00**

Patrician, butter dish, amber .**85.00**

Patrician, plate, luncheon; amber, 9" .................................**12.00**

Petalware, creamer, monax, footed ..............................**6.00**

Petalware, plate, sherbet; pink or monax, 6" .........................**2.50**

Primo, cake plate, green or yellow, 3-footed, 10" ...................**20.00**

Primo, sherbet, green or yellow .**9.00**

Princess, ashtray, green, 4½" .**67.50**

Princess, cup, green or pink .**12.00**

Princess, plate, salad; pink, 8" .**13.00**

Princess, vase, pink, 8" ........**35.00**

Radiance, bowl, red or blue, crimped, 10" .................**37.50**

Radiance, comport, blue or red, 5" ..................................**27.50**

Radiance, cup, blue or red ...**16.00**

Raindrops, bowl, cereal; green, 6" ....................................**8.00**

Raindrops, cup, green ............**6.00**

Raindrops, saucer, green .......**1.50**

Raindrops, sugar bowl (open), green ................................**7.00**

Ribbon, candy dish, green, w/lid ............................**35.00**

Ribbon, cup, green ..................**5.00**

Ribbon, plate, luncheon; green, 8" ....................................**4.50**

Ribbon, salt & pepper shakers, green, pr .......................**27.50**

Rose Cameo, bowl, berry; green, 4½" ..................................**8.50**

Rose Cameo, plate, salad; green, 7" ..................................**11.00**

Rose Cameo, sherbet, green .**11.00**

Rosemary, bowl, cereal; amber, 6" ..................................**26.00**

Rosemary, cup, green .............**9.50**

Rosemary, plate, dinner; amber .**7.50**

Rosemary, sugar bowl (open), amber, footed ...................**8.50**

Rosemary, tumbler, amber, 4¼", 9-oz ...............................**28.00**

Roulette, cup, green ...............**6.50**

Roulette, plate, luncheon; green, 8½" ..................................**6.00**

Roulette, tumbler, water; pink, 4⅛", 9-oz ........................**20.00**

Round Robin, cup, green, footed .**5.00**

Round Robin, plate, luncheon; green, 8" ............................**4.00**

Round Robin, sugar bowl (open), iridescent ........................**6.00**

Royal Ruby, bowl, berry; 4¼" .**5.50**

Royal Ruby, creamer, footed .**9.00**

Royal Ruby, plate, dinner; 9".**11.00**

Royal Ruby, plate, luncheon; 7¾" ....................................**6.00**

Royal Ruby, sherbet, footed ...**8.00**

Royal Ruby, sugar bowl lid ..**10.00**

Royal Ruby, tumbler, juice .....**7.50**

Royal Ruby, vase, 6½" ............**8.00**

Sandwich (Hocking), bowl, berry; crystal, 4⅞" ......................**5.00**

Sandwich (Hocking), bowl, crystal, smooth or scalloped, 6½" ...**7.50**

Sandwich (Hocking), butter dish, crystal ............................**45.00**

Sandwich (Hocking), cup, crystal ................................**3.50**

Sandwich (Hocking), pitcher, juice; crystal, 6" .............**55.00**

Sandwich (Hocking), plate, dinner; crystal, 9" ...............**17.50**

Sandwich (Indiana), bowl, crystal, oval, 8" ............................**7.50**

Sandwich (Indiana), butter dish, crystal ............................**22.50**

Sandwich (Indiana), decanter, crystal, w/stopper ..................**22.50**

Sandwich (Indiana), plate, dinner; crystal, 10½" ....................**8.00**

Sandwich (Indiana), tumbler, water; crystal, footed, 8-oz ............**9.00**

Sharon, bowl, berry; pink, 8½" .**30.00**

Sharon, cake plate, pink, footed, 11½" ................................**40.00**

**Sharon salt and pepper shakers, pink, $47.50 for the pair.**

Sharon, sherbet, amber, footed .**12.00**

Spiral, bowl, berry; green, 8" .**12.50**

Spiral, cup & saucer, green ....**6.50**

Spiral, plate, luncheon; green, 8" ....................................**3.50**

Spiral, platter, green ............**25.00**

Spiral, salt & pepper shakers, green, pr ........................**32.50**

Strawberry, plate, sherbet; green or pink, 6" ........................**7.00**

Strawberry, sherbet, green or pink ...................................**7.50**

Sunflower, cake plate, pink, 10" .**15.00**

Sunflower, creamer, green ...**18.00**

Swirl, bowl, salad; ultramarine, 9" ...................................**27.50**

Swirl, candy dish, pink, w/lid .**95.00**

Swirl, tumbler, ultramarine, 5⅛", 13-oz ............................**100.00**

Tea Room, creamer, pink, 4" .**26.00**

Tea Room, ice bucket, green .**57.50**

Tea Room, plate, sherbet; pink, 6½" ..................................**30.00**

Twisted Optic, candlesticks, green or pink, 3", pr ................**18.00**

Twisted Optic, pitcher, green or pink, 64-oz .....................**30.00**

Twisted Optic, plate, luncheon; green or pink, 8" .............**3.50**

US Swirl, bowl, berry; pink, 4⅜" .**7.00**

US Swirl, creamer, pink ......**16.00**

US Swirl, sherbet, green, 3¼" .**5.00**

US Swirl, vase, green, 6½" ..**16.00**

Vitrock, bowl, cereal; white, 7½" .**6.00**

Vitrock, cup, white .................**3.50**

Vitrock, plate, luncheon; white, 8¾" ...................................**4.50**

Waterford, bowl, berry; crystal, 4¾" ...................................**6.50**

Waterford, plate, sherbet; pink, 6" .**6.00**

Waterford, sugar bowl lid, crystal, oval ...............................**5.00**

Windsor, bowl, vegetable; pink, oval, 9½" .........................**20.00**

Windsor, platter, crystal, oval, 11½" ..................................**7.00**

Windsor, relish platter, red, divided, 11½" ................**175.00**

# The Dionne Quintuplets

Scores of dolls, toys, books, and other types of memorabilia made to promote these famous quints are very collectible today. These five tiny girls were born in Canada in 1934, the first quintuplets ever delivered who survived for more than a few days after birth. King George V made them his wards and built them a private nursery near their parent's home where they remained until they were ten years old. The quints were used to promote products, appeared on countless magazine covers, and were otherwise commercialized, whereby, of course, they earned enormous sums of money for their once-poor parents. Today only three survive. Our advisor for this category is Jimmy Rodolfos; his is listed in the Directory under Massachusetts.

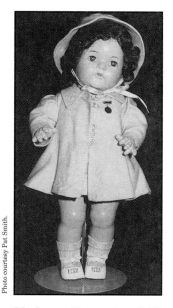

Photo courtesy Pat Smith.

**Madame Alexander doll, all original, in tagged clothes and coat, 20", $725.00 minimum value.**

Booklets, any, from $20 to ...**25.00**

Cup, china ...........................**45.00**
Game, Line Up the Quints ..**45.00**
Plate, china, 6" .....................**55.00**
Playing cards .......................**45.00**
Spoons, silverplate, set of 4, from
  $75 to ...........................**100.00**

# Disney Collectibles

Though there are lots of collectors for this facet of character-related memorabilia and the early examples are now fairly hard to find and expensive, items from the '50s to the present can easily be found on your flea market outings, and their prices are often very reasonable. For more information we recommend *The Collector's Encyclopedia of Disneyana* by Michael Stern and David Longest, *Stern's Guide to Disney Collectibles, First and Second Series,* and Longest's *Toys, Antique and Collectible.* Our advisor for this category is Judy Posner who is listed in the Directory under Pennsylvania. See also Bubble Bath Containers; Character Glasses; Character Watches and Clocks; Lunch Boxes; Pencil Sharpeners, Puzzles; View Masters.

Alice in Wonderland, mug, china,
  1970s, EX .......................**10.00**
Annette, coloring book, Whitman,
  1964, EX ........................**16.00**
Baby Flower, figure, American
  Pottery, 1940s, 3¼", rare size,
  M ..................................**80.00**
Bambi, ashtray, china, Goebel,
  1950s, 3x3½", EX ........**125.00**
Bambi, bank, ceramic, Leeds .**65.00**
Bambi, doll, Gund, 5x11x15",
  EX ................................**70.00**
Bambi, figure, ceramic, Evan K Shaw,
  1949, 4x6x8½", EX .........**150.00**

Bambi, planter, Leeds, 1940s,
  5x10x6", EX ..................**45.00**
Bambi & Flower, figure, Goebel,
  hand decorated, 5¼", M .**125.00**
Doc, paper mask, Denison, 1938,
  VG ................................**28.00**
Donald Duck, figure, jointed celluloid, long bill, 6", M .....**675.00**
Donald Duck, planter, as Santa,
  Leeds, 1950s, 6", EX ...**125.00**
Donald Duck, pull toy, on wooden
  cart, VG .......................**145.00**
Dopey, doll, original tag, Chad Valley, England, 1930s, EX .**200.00**

**Drinking cup, plastic,
hole for straw in lid, 6",
$25.00.**

Dumbo, doll, plush, Gund, 1950s,
  VG ................................**28.00**
Dumbo, figure, ceramic, Goebel,
  3½x4x4", EX, minimum
  value ...........................**400.00**
Dumbo, figure, painted plaster from
  mold kit, 1950s, 2½", EX .**15.00**
Dumbo, milk pitcher, Leeds, black
  & gold trim on ivory, 1940s,
  M ..................................**55.00**
Dumbo, salt & pepper shakers,
  ivory, ceramic, Leeds, 4", EX,
  pr ..................................**35.00**

Dumbo, squirt gun, 1960s, EX .8.00

Eeyore, squeeze toy, vinyl, Holland Hull, 1966, VG .20.00

Figaro, figure, china, Goebel, 1940s, 1½x2x2½", EX ..125.00

Figaro, figure, pressed wood, Multi Products, 2x2", EX .........65.00

Gepetto, figure, Twist & Flex, Marx, 1960s, EX ............55.00

Jessica (of Roger Rabbit), bendee, 1988, MOC ....................30.00

Jiminy Cricket, mug, plastic, 1960s, EX ......................10.00

Ludwig Von Drake, figural bank, by Dan Brechner, 6x5", NM .195.00

Mad Hatter, figure, Shaw pottery, EX ................................475.00

Mary Poppins, figure, china, 1964, 3x3½x8", EX ........35.00

Mary Poppins, hand puppet, Sweldin, 1960s, 11", EX .25.00

Mickey Mouse, bookends, composition, Determined, 1970, 6½", EX, pr ....................95.00

Mickey Mouse, bowl, Beetleware, Walt Disney Enterprises, 1930, EX ........................50.00

Mickey Mouse, figure, playing sax, bisque, Borgfeldt, 1930s, 4", EX ...........................125.00

Mickey Mouse, figure, Sun Rubber, 1949, EX .................25.00

Mickey Mouse, figure, Superflex, Lakeside, 1971, 2½", NM .20.00

Mickey Mouse, figure, Twist & Flex, Marx, 1960s, EX ..45.00

Mickey Mouse, figure, w/hat & cane, bisque, Borgfeldt, 1930s, EX ....................128.00

Mickey Mouse, locomotive, battery-op, tin & plastic, Japan, 1960, NM ....................150.00

Mickey Mouse, map, Disneyland, 1964, 30x45", EX ...........55.00

Mickey Mouse, mask, paper, Denison, 1930s, EX .......35.00

Mickey Mouse, napkin ring, Bakelite, EX .........................125.00

Mickey Mouse, pencil box, yellow & black graphics on green, 1930s, EX ......................95.00

Mickey Mouse, plate, 50th Birthday, Schmid, Limited Edition, MIB ................................95.00

Mickey Mouse, tray, 50th Birthday, Schmid, EX ............35.00

Mickey Mouse, TV night light, plastic, 1950, EX .........125.00

Mickey Mouse, viewer & film strips, Craftsman's Guild, 1940s, EX ......................95.00

Mickey Mouse & America on Parade, tray, litho tin, 1976, EX ................................35.00

Minnie Mouse, doll, Huff-N-Puff Inflatable Greeting, MIP .10.00

Minnie Mouse, doll, poseable, 1970s, 4", EX .................12.00

Minnie Mouse, hand puppet, Gund, 1970s, EX ...........25.00

**Mickey Mouse wooden rocker, 'Shoo Fly,' painted wood, 1950s, 31" long, EX, $150.00.**

Peter Pan, bookbag, canvas, 1952, EX ................................75.00

Pinocchio, bendee, Knickerbocker, 1960s, MIP ....................35.00

Pinocchio, doll, soft cloth, 1940s, 18", EX .........................180.00

Pinocchio, mask, Gillette premium, 1939, NM ...........25.00

Pluto, lamp, ceramic, Leeds, 1940, 6x4x4", EX ...................195.00

Pluto, nodder, M ..................95.00

Pluto, planter, ceramic w/cart, Leeds, NM ......................**65.00**

Pongo (101 Dalmatians), push puppet, Kohner, 1960s, EX ..**38.00**

Robin Hood, rub-on transfers, Letraset, 1970s, England, EX ................**6.00**

Sleeping Beauty, Colorforms Dress Designer, 1959, MIB .....**95.00**

Sleeping Beauty, figure, rubber, Dell, pastels, 1959, 6", EX ........**55.00**

Snow White, doll, composition head & body, Knickerbocker, EX ................................**260.00**

Snow White, night lite, Hankscraft, EX ..................**125.00**

Snow White, sand pail, tin litho, Ohio Art, 1938, EX ......**250.00**

Snow White & 7 Dwarfs, game, Parker Bros., 1938, EX ..**130.00**

Swamp Fox, board game, EX .**30.00**

Thumper, figure, brown, ceramic, 1 ear up, 1 down, Shaw, 1940s, 4", EX .................**65.00**

Thumper, planter, ceramic w/gold trim, Leeds, NM ............**65.00**

Tigger, squeeze toy, vinyl, Holland Hull, 1966, EX ...............**22.00**

Tinkerbell, bell, ceramic, Disneyland souvenir, 5", EX ..**185.00**

Tinkerbell, birthday candles, MIB ...............................**45.00**

Winnie the Pooh, bank, glazed china, 1964, EX .............**65.00**

Winnie the Pooh, bank, plastic figure, Sears, NM ...........**7.50**

Winnie the Pooh, bulletin board, 19x24", EX ....................**25.00**

Winnie the Pooh, crib mobile, colorful, 1964, EX .............**38.00**

Winnie the Pooh, nodder, plastic, 5½", EX ...........................**6.00**

# Dollhouse Furnishings

Collecting antique dollhouses and building new ones is a popular hobby with many today, and all who collect houses delight in furnishing them right down to the vase on the table and the scarf on the piano! Flea markets are a good source of dollhouse furnishings, especially those from the 1940s through the '60s made by Strombecker, Tootsietoy, Renwal, or the Petite Princess line by Ideal. Our advisor for this category is Marian Schmuhl; she is

**Boudoir chaise lounge, Ideal, MIB, $22.00.**

listed in the Directory under Massachusetts.

Birdcage, plastic on metal post, Commonwealth Plastics .**16.00**
Broom, plastic & straw, Irwin .**5.00**
Bucker, plastic w/wire handle, Irwin ...............................**4.00**
Buffet, brown, Marx, ½" scale .**3.00**
Buffet, brown, Renwal ...........**8.00**
Buffet, reddish-brown, Jaydon .**4.00**
Chair, folding; ivory & brown, Ideal ...............................**20.00**
Chair, kitchen; Mattel Littles, set of 4 ...................................**10.00**
Chair, lawn lounge; 2-color plastic, Ideal ...........................**12.00**
Chair, living room; green, Ideal .**5.00**
Chair, living room; red soft plastic, Marx, ¾" scale ...........**3.00**
Chair, rocking; pink & blue, Renwal ...............................**15.00**
Chaise lounge, Little Hostess .**14.00**
Chest of drawers, pink hard plastic, Marx, ¾" scale ...........**5.00**
China closet, pink, Superior, ¾" scale ...............................**3.00**
Clock, mantel; red, Renwal .**10.00**
Grandfather clock, brown, Plasco ...........................**14.00**
Hobby horse, pink, Best .........**6.00**
Hutch, cream, door opens, Renwal ...................................**7.00**
Kiddie cart, 3-color, Renwal #27 ...................................**40.00**
Lamppost & mailbox, red, Commonwealth Plastics .......**10.00**
Living room set, 5-pc on cardboard rug, Tootsietoy ....**65.00**
Mangle, white, Ideal, M .......**12.00**
Night stand, yellow or dark ivory, Marx, ½" scale .................**2.00**
Radio-phonograph, Renwal #18 ...................................**17.00**
Refrigerator, ivory & black, Renwal ...............................**14.00**
Refrigerator, red-handle, door opens, Renwal ...............**19.00**

Sofa, light blue w/brown base, Plasco ...............................**8.00**
Sofa, red, curved, Marx, ½" scale **4.00**
Stove, ivory hard plastic, Marx, ¾" scale ...........................**5.00**
Stove, Mattel Littles ............**15.00**
Stroller, blue or pink, Thomas .**5.00**
Swing, red, yellow & green, Acme ...........................**14.00**
Table, dining; red, Renwal ...**10.00**
Table, drop leaf; gate-leg style, w/2 drawers, Petite Princess, NMIB ...............................**17.50**
Table, folding; red or gold, Renwal #108 ...............................**12.00**
Table, kitchen; ivory, Ideal ....**6.00**
Telephone, w/cord & receiver, Renwal #28 ...................**24.00**
Television, Petite Princess ...**65.00**
Tommy horse, Acme ............**12.00**
Washing machine, door w/glass, Ideal ...............................**5.00**
Washing machine, wringer & lid, Renwal ........................**20.00**

# Dolls

Doll collecting is no doubt one of the most popular fields today. Antique as well as modern dolls are treasured, and limited edition or artists' dolls often bring prices in excess of several hundred dollars. Investment potential is considered excellent in all areas. Dolls have been made from many materials — early to middle 19th-century dolls were carved of wood, poured in wax, and molded in bisque or china. Primitive cloth dolls were sewn at home for the enjoyment of little girls when fancier dolls were unavailable. In this century from 1925 to about 1945, composition was used. Made of a mixture of sawdust, clay, fiber, and a binding agent, it was tough and durable. Modern dolls are usually made of vinyl or molded plastic.

Learn to check your intended purchases for damage which could jeopardize your investment. Bisque dolls may have breaks, hairlines, or eye chips; composition dolls may sometimes become crazed or cracked. Watch for ink or crayon marks on vinyl dolls. Original clothing is important, although on bisque dolls replacement costumes are acceptable as long as they are appropriately styled.

In the listings, values are for dolls in excellent condition unless another condition is noted in the line. They are priced 'mint in box' only when so indicated. Played-with, soiled dolls are worth from 50% to 75% less, depending on condition. Authority Pat Smith has written many wonderful books on the subject: *Patricia Smith's Doll Values, Antique to Modern; Modern Collector's Dolls* (seven in the series); *Vogue Ginny Dolls, Through the Years With Ginny;* and *Madame Alexander Collector's Dolls.* (All are published by Collector Books.) See also Holly Hobbie; Strawberry Shortcake; Trolls.

### American Character

In business by 1918, this company made both composition and plastic dolls, and many collectors count them among the most desirable American dolls ever made. Everything was of high quality, and the hard plastic dolls of the 1950s are much in demand. The company closed in 1968. All of their molds were sold to other companies. See also Betsy McCall; Tressy.

Miss Echo, plastic & vinyl, rooted hair, battery-operated, 29" ........**250.00**
Pittie Pat, vinyl, rooted hair, smile mouth, 1962-1963, 19½" ............................**200.00**
Sally Says, hard plastic & vinyl, talker, original clothes, 1965, 19" ................................**95.00**
Sweet Sue, hard plastic, original red ball gown, 14" .......**285.00**
Talking Marie, plastic & vinyl, battery-operated record player, 18" ......................**95.00**
Teeny Weeny Tiny Tears, vinyl, original clothes, 1964, 8½" .....**25.00**
Tiny Tears, hard plastic, sleep eyes, open mouth, 17", minimum value ...................**165.00**
Toni, vinyl, rooted hair & sleep eyes, mink-trimmed outfit, 1958, 10½" ...................**165.00**
Whimette, hard plastic & vinyl, red hair, replaced clothes, 1963, 18" ......................**35.00**
Whimsie, Miss Take, vinyl, rooted hair, 1960, 19" .............**100.00**

### Annalee

Annalee Davis Thorndike made her first commercially sold dolls in the late 1950s. Her dolls are characterized by their painted felt faces and the meticulous workmanship involved in their manufacture. Most are made entirely of felt, though Santas and rabbits may have flannel bodies. All are constructed around a wire framework that allows them to be positioned in imaginative action poses. Depending on age, rarity, appeal, and condition, some of the older dolls have increased in value more than ten times their original price. Refer to *Teddy Bears, Annalee's, and Steiff Animals* by Margaret Fox Mandel (Collector Books).

**Santa and Mrs. Mouse, ca 1970s, 7", $150.00 for the pair.**

Aerobic girl, all felt body, blue leotard, 1984, 10" .............**150.00**

Ballerina Bunny, tan felt w/pink net tutu, 1980, 7" ..........**85.00**

Ballerina Bunny, tan flannel w/blue polka dot tutu, 1979, 18" ..............................**200.00**

Clown, orange hair, pink & white outfit, 1984, 10" ...........**125.00**

Duck, lace-trimmed pink bonnet, Easter basket, ca 1985, lg, minimum value .............**85.00**

Monk, white fur beard, red robe, w/ski, 1970, 8½" ..........**175.00**

Rabbit in Easter crate, poseable body & limbs, 1978, 8" .**115.00**

Snowman, w/red scarf, black tophat & pipe, ca 1980s, #7505 on tag ................**100.00**

## Arranbee

Made during the 1930s through the '50s, these composition or plastic dolls will be marked either 'Arranbee,' 'R&B' (until 1961), or 'Made in USA - 210.'

Baby Kaye, celluloid over tin sleep eyes, composition & cloth, 14" ......................**250.00**

Dream Baby, composition, sleep eyes, red, white & blue romper, 11" ...................**175.00**

Nancy, composition, blond mohair wig, sleep eyes, 20", minimum value ...................**450.00**

Nancy Lee, hard plastic, pink party dress & shoes, MIB, minimum value ...........**475.00**

Nanette, hard plastic, garden dress w/parasol, 20" ....**375.00**

Nanette, hard plastic, walker, original outfit w/roller skates, 18" ...............................**325.00**

New Happy Tot, vinyl, molded hair, sleep eyes, redressed, 1955, 16" .......................**45.00**

Sunny Babe, composition & cloth, sleep eyes, smile mouth, ca 1937, lg .........................**300.00**

Susan, stuffed vinyl, brown wig, blue sleep eyes, original, 1952, 15" .........................**75.00**

## Barbie and Friends

Barbie has undergone some minor makeovers since 1959 — the first one had just white irises but no eye color. Today those early Barbies are almost impossible to find, but if you can find one in mint condition, she's worth about $2,500.00 — $1,000.00 more if the original box is with her. Refer to *The World of Barbie Dolls* and *The Wonder of Barbie, 1976 to 1986,* by Paris, Susan, and Carol Manos. Sibyl De Wein and Joan Ashabraner have written *The Collector's Encyclopedia of Barbie Dolls and Collectibles*; and *Barbie Fashion, Vol. I, 1959 to 1967,* by Sarah Sink Eames is also an excellent reference. Two recent releases to add to your library are *Barbie Exclusives* by Margo Rana, and *The Story of Barbie* by Kitturah B. Westenhouser. All these books are published by Collector Books.

Note: Values given for mint-in-the-box dolls will be from five to as much as seven times higher than the same doll in good, played-with condition.

Barbie, Gift Giving, pink & silver dress, 1985, MIB ...........**40.00**

Barbie, Happy Holidays 1989, white gown w/fur trim, MIB ...**125.00**

Barbie, Jewel Secret, long rooted blond hair, evening dress, 1986, MIB ......................**25.00**

Barbie, Kissing, press button at back, 1979, MIB, minimum value ...........................**50.00**

Barbie, Party Cruise, striped bodice & white skirt, 1986, MIB ...............................**35.00**

Barbie, Pool Side, yellow jacket w/red & blue sash, 1966, MIB ...............................**40.00**

Barbie, Sun Lovin' Malibu, 2-pc bathing suit, 1979, MIB .**12.00**

Barbie, Western Fun, pink & blue outfit, 1989, MIB ...........**20.00**

**Feelin' Groovy Barbie, with accessories, MIB, $200.00 minimum value.**

Ken, California Dream, beach outfit, 1987, MIB ...............**15.00**

Ken, Doctor, white lab coat & navy pants, 1987, MIB .**20.00**

Kevin, yellow & blue outfit, w/extra outfit, MIB .......**15.00**

Skipper, Babysitter, pink & white dot outfit, 1991, MIB ....**15.00**

Skipper, Homecoming Queen, white gown, 1988, MIB .**35.00**

Whitney, Perfume Pretty, reddish-brown hair, 1987, MIB ..**20.00**

## Betsy McCall

Tiny 8" Betsy McCall was manufactured by the American Character Doll Company from

1957 until 1963. She was made from fine quality hard plastic with a bisque-like finish and had hand-painted features. Betsy came with four hair colors — tosca, blond, red, and brown. She has blue sleep eyes, molded lashes, a winsome smile, and a fully-jointed body with bendable knees. On her back is an identification circle which reads ©McCall Corp. The basic doll could be purchased for $2.25 and wore a sheer chemise, white taffeta panties, nylon socks, and Maryjane-style shoes.

There were two different materials used for tiny Betsy's hair. The first was soft mohair sewn onto mesh. Later the rubber scullcap was rooted with saran which was more suitable for washing and combing.

Betsy McCall had an extensive wardrobe with nearly one hundred outfits, each of which could be purchased separately. They were made from wonderful fabrics such as velvet, felt, taffeta, and even real mink fur. Each ensemble came with the appropriate footware and was priced under $3.00. Since none of Betsy's clothing is tagged, it is often difficult to identify other than by its square snap closures (although these were used by other companies as well).

Betsy McCall is a highly collectible doll today but is still fairly easy to find at doll shows. The prices remain reasonable for this beautiful clothes horse and her many accessories. For further information we recommend our advisor, Marci Van Ausdall, who is listed in the Directory under California.

Doll, Horseman, MIB ...........**50.00**
Doll, nude, EX ......................**85.00**
Doll, w/#1 skating outfit, complete, 8", EX ................**145.00**
Doll, w/pink tissue & pamphlet, MIB, minimum value .**185.00**
Doll, with wrist tag, American Character, 14", all original ...........................**175.00**
Doll, w/wrist tag & curlers, Ideal, 14", all original ............**150.00**
Figurine, porcelain, Rothschild, MIB ...............................**25.00**
Magazine paper doll sheet, McCall's, May 1951, 1st issue of Betsy ..........................**10.00**
Outfit, April Showers rain gear, MIP, from $35 to ...........**40.00**
Outfit, Prom Time, pink or blue formal, for 8" or 14" doll, EX, ea ...................................**35.00**
Pamphlet, original ...............**15.00**
Playset, Betsy McCall Fashion Designer Studio ..........**250.00**

Photo courtesy of Leslie Robinson.

**Betsy McCall, Sunday Best outfit, complete, 1959, EX, $50.00.**

## Cabbage Patch

Special editions have been issued by Babyland General Hospital, Cleveland, Georgia, since 1978, and many of these are now valued at more than $500.00. But of the many varieties of retail-level Coleco dolls, few are worth more than they cost when new, simply because they were made in enormous quantities. We have listed a few exceptions below.

Babyland General, Christmas Edition, white hair, hand signed, 1980 ................**600.00**
Babyland General, E Bronze Edition, 1 of 15,000, 1979, minimum value ...................**600.00**
Babyland General, Ears Edition (preemie), 1982, minimum value ...........................**150.00**
Babyland General, Preemie Edition, 1 of 5,000, hand signed, 1980 ...........................**650.00**
Babyland General, Rose Edition, 1 of 40,000, 1984 .............**100.00**
Coleco, Black w/freckles, stamp signature, 1983, minimum value ...........................**175.00**
Coleco, brunette w/ponytail & single tooth, 1984-85, minimum value ...........................**165.00**
Coleco, Cornsilk Kid, from $30 to ..................................**50.00**
Coleco, freckled girl, gold hair, stamp signature, 1984, minimum value .....................**95.00**
Coleco, gray-eyed girl, blue stamp signature, 1985, minimum value ...........................**165.00**
Coleco, popcorn hair, green stamp signature, 1984, rare ..**200.00**
Coleco, powder scent, black stamp signature, 1983 .............**95.00**
Coleco, Splash Kid, from $30 to ..................................**50.00**

## Cameo

Best known for their Kewpie dolls, this company also made some wood-jointed character dolls with composition heads during the 1920s and '30s. Although most of the Kewpie molds had been sold to another company by then, the few that were retained by the company were used during the 1970s to produce a line of limited edition dolls. Kewpies marked 'S71' were actually made by Strombecker.

Baby Mine, vinyl & cloth, sleep eyes, 1962-64, 16" .......**100.00**
Kewpie, celluloid, jointed shoulders, marked Japan, 22" .......**500.00**
Kewpie, uses Miss Peep body & limbs, hinged joints, 18" .**265.00**
Miss Peep, vinyl w/pin-jointed shoulders & hips, 1960s, 15" ..................................**45.00**
Newborn Miss Peep, plastic & vinyl, regular 5-pc baby body, Black, 18" ......................**60.00**
Pete the Pup, composition head, segmented wood body & limbs, 8½" ....................**275.00**
Skootles, painted features on composition, 15", minimum value ...........................**600.00**

## Celebrity Dolls

Dolls that represent movie or TV personalities, fictional characters, or famous sports figures are very popular collectibles and can usually be found for well under $100.00. Mego, Horsman, Ideal, and Mattel are among the largest producers.

Angie Dickenson Policewoman, Horseman, jointed vinyl, 1976, 9" .........................**20.00**

Ann Margaret, Mattel, rooted hair, red suit & boots, 1966, 11½", M ...........................**30.00**

Diana & Prince of Wales, vinyl, rooted hair, Goldberg, 1983-84, set, M .......................**50.00**

Dolly Parton, plastic & vinyl, rooted hair, Eegee, 1987, 11½", MIB ......................**65.00**

Dorothy Hamill, Ideal, 1977, 11½", MIB (sealed) ........**75.00**

Emmet Kelly, Horsman, cloth & plastic, pull-string talker, 1978, 23" .........................**60.00**

Florence Griffith Joyner, LJN, jointed vinyl, 1989, 11½", MIB ...............................**28.00**

General Norman Schwarzkoph, In Time Productions, 1991, 7", MIB ...............................**32.00**

Groucho Marx, molded-on glasses, marked Effanbee/1983, 17" ................**45.00**

Lee Majors (Six-Million Dollar Man), Kenner, 1973, 13", M ....................................**60.00**

Madonna (Breathless Mahoney), molded gown w/feather boa, 1990, 14", M .................**15.00**

Marie Osmond, Mattel, rooted hair, glitzy skater outfit, 1966, 11½" .....................**45.00**

Marilyn Monroe, movie outfit, Tri-Star, 1982, 11½", MIB (sealed) .........................**75.00**

Michael Jackson, jointed vinyl, Thriller outfit, LJN, 1984, 11½" ...............................**40.00**

Pee-Wee Herman, cloth & vinyl, pull-string talker, Matchbox, 1987, 18" .......................**85.00**

Prince Charles, vinyl & cloth, suction cup hands, Korea, 12" ......**15.00**

Ronald Reagan, Horsman, plastic & vinyl, 1987, 17" ..........**65.00**

Sylvester Stallone (Lincoln Hawks), jointed plastic, Lewco, 1986 .**15.00**

Vanna White, vinyl, rooted hair, Home Shopping Club, 1990, 11½" ...............................**28.00**

Vivien Leigh, red gown w/feathers, World Dolls, 1967, 11½", M ....................................**40.00**

Warren Beatty (Dick Tracy), yellow trenchcoat, Playmate, 15", MIB .......................**15.00**

Winston Churchill, Great Moments in History, Effanbee, 1984, 15" ...............**45.00**

## Chatty Cathy

Made by Mattel, this is one of the most successful line of dolls

**Kiss, Mego, set of four, MIB, $500.00.**

135

ever made. She was introduced in the 1960s as either a blond or a brunette. By pulling a string on her back, Chatty Cathy could speak eleven phrases. During the next five years, Mattel added to the line with Chatty Baby, Tiny Chatty Baby, Tiny Chatty Brother, Charmin' Chatty, and Singing' Chatty. The dolls were taken off the market only to be brought out again in 1969. But the new dolls were smaller and had restyled faces, and they were not as well received. Our advisors for this category are Kathy and Don Lewis, authors of *Chatty Cathy Dolls, An Identification and Value Guide;* they are listed in the Directory under California.

Black Chatty Cathy, pageboy hair, 1962 ............................**450.00**
Black Tiny Chatty Baby ....**275.00**

**Chatty Cathy, blond, MIB, $250.00.**

Catty Cathy, porcelain, 1980, w/M box ...............................**700.00**
Chatty Baby, open speaker, brunette hair, blue eyes .**80.00**

Chatty Cathy, brunette hair, brown eyes ...................**140.00**
Singin' Chatty, blond hair ....**85.00**
Timey Tell, blond hair, blue eyes ...............................**55.00**
Tiny Chatty Baby, brunette hair, blue eyes ........................**80.00**

## Creata

Dolls with this mark were made by Creata International, Manhattan Beach, California, during the 1980s. Most were 12" Barbie-like dolls with lovely costumes and rooted hair.

Flower Princess Ballerina, vinyl, blond rooted hair, 1982, 11½" ..............................**25.00**
Peggy Sue Bobby Soxer, poodle skirt outfit, dated 1986, 11½" ..**38.00**
Teddy Girl, dark rooted hair, bend knees, dated 1986, 11½" .**30.00**
Today's Girl, Pony Gals series, star-painted eyes, vinyl, 1989, 6" .....................................**16.00**
1952 Bobby Soxer, vinyl, red athletic sweater, dated 1986, 11½" ...............................**30.00**

## Eegee

The Goldberger company made these dolls, Eegee (E.G.) being the initials of the company's founder. Dolls marked 'Made in China' were made in 1986. See also Celebrity Dolls.

Baby, all vinyl, inset eyes w/lashes, marked Eegee & China, 1986, 15" ............**30.00**
Charmer Bride, plastic & vinyl, marked 15 BB/Eegee/1984/4, 27", M ...........................**65.00**
Lester, cloth & plastic puppet, 1976, 26", missing glasses ........**45.00**

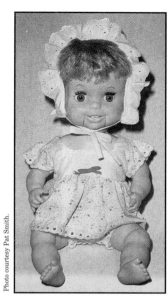

**Plastic and vinyl, sleep eyes, upper and lower teeth, lever on back of head makes mouth move, marked Eegee, 20", EX, $40.00.**

Little Debutante Bride, vinyl & plastic, sleep eyes, 14" ..**30.00**
Sue & Her Beauty Salon, vinyl w/rooted hair, marked 16BP, 17", M .............................**18.00**
Walking Annette, Black, vinyl w/rooted hair, ca 1980s, 31" ................................**75.00**

## Effanbee

This company has been in business since 1910, continually producing high quality dolls, some of all composition, some composition and cloth, and a few in plastic and vinyl. In excellent condition, some of the older dolls often bring $300.00 and up.

Baby Liza, all vinyl w/1 leg bent, 1980, 9½" .......................**30.00**

Colonial Prosperity, Historical Series, 1711 costume, 14" .........**600.00**
Jezebel, Grand Dames Series, 1980, 15" .......................**75.00**
Kim, One World Collection, plastic & vinyl, rooted hair, 1980, 11½" ..............................**45.00**
King Ferdinand, New World Collection, rooted hair, 1989, 16", M ....................................**85.00**
Little Lady Majorette, composition, human-hair wig, sleep eyes, 15" .......................**350.00**
Mother Goose, plastic & vinyl, sleep eyes, 1984-87, 11½" .........**35.00**
Patsy, all composition, mohair wig, sleep eyes, ca 1933, 14" .**365.00**
Patsy, composition w/cloth body, open mouth, original dress w/button ......................**365.00**
Patsy Baby Babyette, all composition, lg sleep eyes, 9", M .**245.00**
Patsyette Baby, all composition, sleep eyes, caracul wig, 9", M w/tag ...........................**265.00**
Portrait doll, composition, sleep eyes, all original, 11", minimum value ....................**95.00**
Queen of Hearts, plastic & vinyl, sleep eyes, 1984, 11½" ...**35.00**
Rosemary Walk Talk, mohair wig, original print dress, 1925, 21" ..............................**265.00**
Skippy, composition w/painted features, original hat w/pin, 14" ...............................**465.00**

## Eugene

Dolls marked Eugene have been made during the last ten years. Some have sleep eyes with lashes, some have a puppet mouth with a pull string in the back, and all are well dressed and of good quality. In 1990 they had a line of 11" Desert Storm dolls that were imported from China.

Ballerina, plastic & vinyl, sleep eyes, rooted hair, 1987, 13" ......**24.00**

Happy Birthday Baby, cloth & vinyl, sleep eyes, 1987, 12" .......**20.00**

Old Fashioned Girl, vinyl w/cloth body, painted features, 1986, 16" ..................................**30.00**

Paratrooper, Desert Shield Series, vinyl, molded hair, 1990, 11", MIB ..............................**28.00**

Satin 'n Lace, cloth & vinyl, sleep eyes, blond rooted hair, 1987, 18" ..................................**22.00**

Suzie Sez, vinyl hands & head, cloth body, lever mouth, 1987, 18" ..................................**35.00**

## Fisher-Price

Since the mid-1970s, this well-known American toy company has been making a variety of dolls. Many have vinyl heads, rooted hair, and cloth bodies. Most are marked and dated.

Baby Ann, cloth & vinyl, painted features, 1979, 17" ........**45.00**

Baby's First Doll, pink & white checked cloth, yarn hair, ca 1975, 12" ......................**50.00**

Baby Soft Sounds, cloth & vinyl, rooted hair, battery voice box, 16" ..................................**38.00**

Honey, cloth body, vinyl hands & head w/molded hair, 1975, 12" ..................................**40.00**

Kermit the Frog, green felt w/plastic eyes, 1976, 18", MIB ..............................**28.00**

Muffy, Fisher-Price Kids, cloth & vinyl, rooted hair, 1978, 8" ..................................**28.00**

My Bathing Baby, vinyl, sleep eyes, rooted hair, 1982, 14½" ..**30.00**

My Friend Becky, rooted red hair, ballerina outfit, 1983, 16", MIB ..............................**40.00**

**My Friend Becky, vinyl head and limbs, white cloth body, marked Fisher-Price, 1987, 16", $42.00.**

My Friend Jenny, vinyl w/white cloth body, rooted hair, 1978, 16" ..................................**45.00**

## Galoob

The Lewis Galoob Toy company produced many series of action figures and dolls, some of which were made in China. Look for the tag, most of which are dated.

Magic Diaper Babies, turn color in water, 1991, 2½", set of 5, MIP ..............................**10.00**

Pretty Cut & Grow, vinyl w/painted features, yarn hair, 1980, 13" ......................**32.00**

Punky Brewster, plastic & vinyl, rooted hair, 1984, 18", MIB .............**38.00**

Snap Happy Out in Space, flat plastic w/rooted hair, 1989, 3", MIP ..........................**18.00**

So Playful Penny, jointed elbows & knees, inset eyes, 1990, 13" .....................................**38.00**

Talking Mr T, plastic & vinyl, hands hold tools, 1983, 12", MIB ................................**38.00**

Walking Baby & Walker, painted vinyl, battery-operated, 1988, 6½" ....................................**30.00**

## Hasbro

Some of these dolls sold extremely well on the retail level during the 1980s — you probably remember the 'Real Baby' dolls. They came in two versions, one awake, the other asleep. They were so realistic that even grown-up girls had them on their Christmas lists! See also Jem and GI Joe.

Bathing Beauty, vinyl & plastic, rooted hair, round eyes, 1972, 14", M .............................**30.00**

Brenda, plastic & vinyl, blond rooted hair w/tiara, 1989, 17½", MIB ......................**45.00**

Dance 'n Romance Maxie, rooted blond hair w/grow feature, 1987, 11½" ....................**30.00**

Marissa, plastic & vinyl, long dark rooted hair, 1989, 17½" ..**30.00**

My Buddy, cloth body & limbs, painted vinyl head, 1985, 24" ...................................**35.00**

Sleeping Real Baby, inset eyes & lashes, bunny suit, 1984, 20" ...................................**40.00**

Sparky Dreamer, yellow rooted hair, star-form glasses, 1986, 5½", M ............................**15.00**

## Horsman

During the 1930s, this company produced composition dolls of the highest quality. Today many of their dolls are vinyl. Hard plastic dolls marked '170,' are also Horsmans. They are best known for their 'Hee-Bee,' 'She-Bee,' and 'Patsy' dolls.

Ballerina, vinyl, rooted hair, gold tutu, replaced slippers, 1958, 10" ...................................**35.00**

Chubby Baby, composition & cloth, flirty eyes, ca 1946, 22" ...............................**125.00**

Photo courtesy Pat Smith.

**Emmet Kelly, pull-string talker, cloth and plastic, marked Horman, 1978, 23", EX, $60.00.**

He-Bee, jointed composition, 1925, 10½", minimum value .**525.00**

Lavender Ballerina, sleep eyes w/painted lashes, 1982, 8", M ...................................**20.00**

Mary Poppins w/Michael & Jane, plastic & vinyl, 1960s, set of 3, MIB .........................**165.00**

Nadia Ballerina, plastic & vinyl, blond rooted hair, 1987, 11½" ...............................**20.00**

Randy, plastic & vinyl, sleep eyes, rooted hair, ca 1980, 12", MIB ................................**25.00**
Willie Talk, vinyl, cloth & plastic, pull string mouth, 1978, 23" ....**50.00**

## Ideal

For more than eighty years, this company produced quality dolls that were easily affordable by the average American family. Their 'Shirley Temple' and 'Toni' dolls were highly successful. They're also the company who made 'Miss Revlon,' 'Betsy Wetsy,' and 'Tiny Tears.' For more information, see *Collector's Guide to Ideal Dolls* by Judith Izen. See also Shirley Temple; Celebrity Dolls; Tammy.

Baby Big Eyes, vinyl, sleep eyes, rooted hair, 1954-59, 23", MIB ................................**60.00**
Baby Crissy, vinyl, grow hair, sleep eyes, redressed, 1973-76, 24" ............................**35.00**
Baby Sees All, vinyl & cloth, press tummy & eyes move, 1981, 13" ..................................**30.00**
Betsy Wetsy, rubber, pink organdy dress & booties, 1937, 11", MIB ................................**85.00**
Betty Jane, jointed composition, mohair wig, sleep eyes, 1940-43, 14" ..........................**185.00**
Bibsy, vinyl, rooted blond hair, blue sleep eyes, ca 1970, 23", MIB ................................**35.00**
Black Movin' Groovin' Crissy, vinyl, grow hair, 1971, 17½" .....**40.00**
Blessed Event, soft vinyl w/oil-cloth body, 1950, 21", M w/blanket ....................**100.00**
Cream Puff, vinyl, coo voice, yellow dress & bonnet, 1959-62, 21" ..................................**85.00**

Dodi, vinyl & plastic, long rooted hair, felt outfit, 1964, 9", M .......**40.00**
Ducky Deluxe, rubber head w/soft fontanel, 1932-1939, 11", MIB ................................**65.00**
Lolly, hard plastic walker, sleep eyes, redressed, 1951-59, 9½" ...**20.00**

**Magic Flesh vinyl-head doll with Saran wig, marked Ideal/16"=16, EX, $85.00.**

Miss Revlon, jointed vinyl & plastic, pierced ears, 1956-59, 20", MIB ..............................**150.00**
Pretty Curls, soft vinyl, rooted hair, 1981-82, 12½", w/styling set ..................................**20.00**
Saucy Sue, composition head & limbs, says 'mama,' flirty eyes, 14" ......................**100.00**
Saucy Walker, vinyl, rooted hair, print dress & pinafore, 1960, 32" ..............................**250.00**
Snuggles, vinyl & cloth, rooted hair, w/blanket, 1978-81, 12½" .**25.00**
Tammy, vinyl & plastic, rooted hair, teen style, 1962, 12" .......**40.00**
Thumbelina, vinyl, molded hair, mama voice, 1982-85, 18", MIB ................................**30.00**

Tiny Kissy, pull hands together & lips pucker, 1963-68, 16", MIB ...............................**80.00**

Tiny Tears, vinyl, glassene eyes, rooted hair, 1982-85, 14", MIB ...............................**30.00**

Tiny Tears, vinyl, rooted hair, glassene eyes, long gown, 1984, 14" ........................**20.00**

Tiny Thumbelina, vinyl & cloth, rooted hair, key-wind, 1962-68, 14", M ......................**30.00**

Toddler, jointed composition, chubby body, dress & coat, 1940, 17", M ................**150.00**

Trilby, vinyl, 3-faced w/turning knob on head, 1951, 18¾", M ..................................**65.00**

### Jem Dolls and Accessories

The glamorous life of Jem mesmerized little girls who watched her Saturday morning cartoons, and she was a natural as a fashion doll. In 1985 Hasbro introduced the Jem line of 12" dolls representing her, the rock stars from Jem's musical group, the Holograms, and other members of the cast, including Rio, the only boy, who was Jem's road manager and Jerrica's boyfriend.

Production was discontinued in 1987. Each doll was posable, jointed at the waist, heads, and wrists, so that they could be positioned at will with their musical instruments and other accessory items. Their clothing, their makeup, and their hairdos were wonderfully exotic, and their faces were beautifully molded. Our values are given for mint-in-box dolls. All loose dolls are valued at about $8.00 each.

Aja, blue hair, w/accessories, complete, MIB ......................**40.00**

Ashley, curly bond hair, w/stand, 11", MIB ........................**20.00**

Banee, waist-length straight black hair, w/stand, complete, MIB ...............................**30.00**

Clash, straight purple hair, complete, MIB ......................**40.00**

Danse, pink & blond hair, invents dance routines, MIB .....**40.00**

Jem Roadster, AM/FM radio in trunk (working), scarce, EX .....**150.00**

Jem Soundstage, Starlight House #17, from $40 to ............**50.00**

Jem/Jerrica, Glitter & Gold, complete w/accessories, MIB .**50.00**

Jetta, black hair w/silver streaks, complete, MIB ..............**40.00**

Krissie, dark skin w/dark brown curly hair, w/stand, 11", MIB ......**20.00**

Pizazz, chartreuse hair, complete, MIB ...............................**40.00**

Raya, pink hair, complete, MIB ...............................**40.00**

Rio, Glitter & Gold, complete, 12½", MIB .....................**50.00**

Rio (Jem's road manager and Jerrica's boyfriend), Hasbro, 1986, 12½", MIB, $50.00.

Roxy, blond hair, complete, MIB ...............................**40.00**
Shana, purple hair, complete, MIB ...............................**40.00**
Stormer, curly blue hair, complete, MIB .......................**40.00**
Video, band member who makes audio tapes, MIB ...........**40.00**

## Kenner

This company's dolls range from the 12" jointed teenage glamour dolls to the tiny 3" 'Mini-Kins' with the snap-on changeable clothing and synthetic 'hair' ponytails. (Value for the latter: doll only, $7.00; doll with one outfit, $12.00; complete set, $65.00.) See also Strawberry Shortcake.

Baby Teefoam, vinyl w/painted features, cries, 1978, 13" .....**42.00**
Baby Won't Let Go, plastic & vinyl, rooted hair, 1977, 17", M .**25.00**
Black Cover Girl Dana, marked 56 on head, 1978, 12½", M .**35.00**
Darci Cover Girl, vinyl, rooted hair, 1978, 12½", MIB ...**35.00**
Nancy Nonsense, plastic & vinyl, pull-string talker, 17" .......**40.00**
Precious Hugs, stuffed plush, rooted hair, inset eyes, 1985, 18" ...................................**42.00**
Sweet Cookie, 1972, 18" .......**30.00**
Tickles & Gigget, vinyl, rooted hair, marked 1986 Hallmark, 6", set .............................**25.00**

## Liddle Kiddles

Produced by Mattel between 1966 and 1971, Liddle Kiddle dolls and accessories were designed to suggest the typical 'little kid' in the typical neighborhood. These dolls can be found in sizes ranging from ¾" to 4", all with posable bodies and rooted hair that can be restyled. Later, two more series were designed that represented storybook and nursery rhyme characters. The animal kingdom was represented by the Animiddles and Zoolery Jewelry Kiddles. There was even a set of extraterrestrials. And lastly, in 1979 Sweet Treets dolls were marketed.

Our values are for items that are mint on card or mint in box undless otherwise noted. Deduct 25% for dolls complete with accessories but with the box or card missing, and 75% if no accessories are included, but the doll itself is dressed. For further information and more listings, we recommend *Schroeder's Collectible Toys, Antique to Modern.* Our advisor, Cindy Sabulis, is listed in the Directory under Connecticut.

Animiddles, tiger, lion, mouse or deer, 2", ea .....................**45.00**
Bracelet or ring, any doll in bracelet w/chain or ring, ea ..........**25.00**
Carring case, w/clear plastic window, 8 compartments, 10½x14½" .......................**20.00**
Carrying case, round or rectangular, 5x7½", ea .................**40.00**
Cherry Blossom Skediddle, Oriental doll w/green parasol .**60.00**
Chitty Chitty Bang Bang Kiddles, set of 4, w/stands, minimum value ...........................**200.00**
Doll, Babe Biddle, girl in blue scarf, dress, red jacket & yellow car ...........................**55.00**
Doll, Calamity Jiddle, cowgirl w/rocking horse .............**70.00**
Doll, Florence Niddle, nurse w/baby in blanket & stroller .......**45.00**
Doll, Peter Paniddle, Peter Pan costume w/accessories, minimum value ...................**150.00**

Doll, Rah Rah Skediddle, cheer-
leader w/yellow & orange
paper pom-poms ............**50.00**
Kolognes, any doll in plastic bubble cologne bottle w/chain,
ea ...................................**30.00**
Locket, any doll in plastic bubble
locket w/chain, ea ..........**25.00**
Lunch box, minimum value .**150.00**

**Kosmic Kiddle, Greeny Meeny
with spaceship, 2½", MIB, $200.00.**

Paper dolls, uncut, M ...........**20.00**
Skediddle Kiddle, any doll w/rid-
ing toy .............................**45.00**
Skediddle Kiddle, any doll
w/snap-on walker ..........**35.00**

**Tea Party Kiddle, Lady Crimson,
M in enclosed plastic case, $100.00.**

Teacup Kiddle, doll w/teacup &
saucer, enclosed in plastic
case, ea ........................**100.00**

Thermos, minimum value ...**25.00**
Zoolery Kiddle, lion, monkey, bear
or panther, ¾", minimum
value, ea ......................**175.00**

# Mattel

Though most famous, of course,
for Barbie and her friends, the Mattel company also made celebrity
dolls, lots of other action figures (the
Major Matt Mason line and She-Ra,
Princess of Power, for example), and
in more recent years, 'Baby Tenderlove' and 'P.J. Sparkles.' See also
Barbie; Liddle Kiddles.

Baby Cries for You, vinyl &
stuffed cloth, pull string,
1979, 14", VG ................**25.00**
Baby Love Notes, plays tunes
when hands & feet are
pressed, 1974, 10" .........**15.00**
Baby Pat-A-Cake, cloth & vinyl,
rooted hair, w/potty chair,
1981, 16" .......................**18.00**
Baby Rose Tenderlove, plastic &
vinyl, 1988, 15", w/layette,
MIB ...............................**24.00**
Baby White Star Rose, christen-
ing gown, 1976, 4", w/cradle,
M ...................................**20.00**
Crawling Baby, plastic & vinyl,
key wind, 1984, 15", M .**18.00**
Dimples, plastic & vinyl, short
chubby legs, dotted pinafore,
1988, 13" .......................**18.00**
Hush Lil' Baby, vinyl, rooted hair,
red dress & white shoes,
1976, 14" .......................**28.00**
Lavender Lace Rose, rooted blond
hair, 1976, 4", w/fancy
stroller, M .....................**20.00**
Ms Giddie Yup, Gorgeous Crea-
tures Series, rooted hair,
1979, 7½", M .................**25.00**
My Child, stuffed flannel, stitched
fingers, 1985, 15" .........**22.00**

Pedal Pretty, cloth body w/face mask, yarn hair, w/trike, 1973, 15" .........................**35.00**

PJ Sparkles, plastic & vinyl, light-up hair bow & heart, 1988, 15" .........................**26.00**

Rainbow Brite, vinyl & cloth, yarn hair, 1983, 18" ................**30.00**

Twinkle Sprite, vinyl & stuffed plush, red feet & hands, 1983, 11", M .............................**10.00**

Yawning Beans, vinyl & cloth, painted eyes, rooted hair, 1970, 10" .........................**12.00**

## Mego

When you think of Mego, you think of action figures and celebrity dolls, but they also made lots of 'baby dolls,' such as we've listed here. For action figures and celebrity dolls, see *Schroeder's Collectible Toys, Antique to Modern.*

Baby Sez So, plastic & vinyl, rooted hair, battery operated, 1976, 16" .........................**30.00**

Kelly, sleep eyes, open/closed mouth, battery-operated, 1980, 17½" ......................**14.00**

Lady Linda, tenon-jointed arms, turn waist, side-part hair, 1978, 18" .........................**45.00**

Maddie Mod, plastic body & legs, vinyl head & arms, 1974, 11½", M .............................**6.00**

Prince Charming, Puppet Love Series, cloth w/vinyl head, 1977, 6", MIP ..................**5.00**

## Remco

The plastic and vinyl dolls made by Remco during the 1960s and '70s are gaining popularity with collectors today. Many have mechanical features that were activated either by a button on their back or batteries.

Baby Crawl-a-Long, 1967, 20".**15.00**

Baby Glad, 1966, 14" ...........**20.00**

Baby Grow-a-Tooth, 1969, 14" .**25.00**

Baby Laugh-a-Lot, 1970, 16" **20.00**

Baby Stroll-a-Long, 1966, 15" .**15.00**

Baby This 'n That, vinyl, press toes for action, 1976, 13", NM .................................**38.00**

Brown Eye Billy, plastic & vinyl, sleep eyes, 1970s, 14", MIB .......**30.00**

Lindalee, cloth & vinyl, 1970, 10" ................................**25.00**

Orphan Annie, plastic & vinyl, 1967, 15" .........................**35.00**

Proud Family, Mother may appear pregnant, 1978, set of 3, M ................................**45.00**

Rainbow, fashion type, 1979, 8½", w/makeup & fashion center, MIB ................................**60.00**

Sweet April, vinyl, 1971, 5½" .**10.00**

Yes-No Baby, plastic & vinyl, button on back moves head, 1978, 14", NM ...............**29.00**

## Shirley Temple

The public's fascination with Shirley was more than enough reason for toy companies to literally deluge the market with merchandise of all types decorated with her likeness. Dolls were a big part of that market, and the earlier composition dolls in excellent conditon are often priced at $600.00 and higher on today's market. Many were made by the Ideal Company, who in the 1950s also issued a line made of vinyl.

Bisque, painted w/molded hair, Japan, 6" .....................**250.00**

Composition, Bright Eyes, cotton dress, 1934, all original, 18" .................................**750.00**
Composition, flirty eyes, cotton dress, all original, 1934, 15" .....**700.00**

**Shirley Temple, all composition, Ideal, 1934, 16", EX, $675.00.**

Vinyl, dressed as Cinderella, 1961, 15" .......................**325.00**
Vinyl, Ideal, 1961, 12", w/original box ................................**200.00**

Vinyl, red polka dot dress, 1973, 16" .................................**125.00**
Vinyl, 1950s, all original, 15" .**325.00**

## Tammy

In 1962 the Ideal Novelty & Toy Company introduced their teenage Tammy doll. Slightly pudgy and not quite as sophisticated-looking as some of the teen fashion dolls on the market at the time, Tammy's innocent charm captivated consumers. Her extensive wardrobe and numerous accessories added to her popularity with children. Tammy had everything including a car, a house, and a catamaran. In addition, a large number of companies obtained licenses to issue products using the 'Tammy' name. Everything from paper dolls to nurse's kits were made with Tammy's image on them. Tammy's success was not confined to the United States. She was also successful in Canada and in several European countries. Doll values listed here are

Photo courtesy Cindy Sabulis.

**Tammy by Ideal in various hair colors and styles, straight legs, $40.00.**

for mint-in-box examples. (Loose dolls are generally about half mint-in-box value as they are relatively common.) Values for other items are for mint-condition items without their original packaging. (Items other than dolls with their original packaging or in less-than-mint condition would then vary up or down accordingly.) Our advisor, Cindy Sabulis, is listed in the Directory under Connecticut.

Accessory package, from $10 to .....................................**20.00**
Carrying case, any, from $10 to .....................................**25.00**
Doll, Black Tammy .............**200.00**
Doll, Bud ...........................**300.00**
Doll, Dodi ...........................**65.00**
Doll, Glamour Misty ............**90.00**
Doll, Grown-Up Tammy .......**55.00**
Doll, Patty, Montgomery Ward's Exclusive ......................**125.00**
Doll, Pepper ...........................**40.00**
Doll, Pepper, slim body, 1965 .**50.00**
Doll, Pepper, w/orange hair .**65.00**
Doll, Pos'n Dodi ....................**75.00**
Doll, Pos'n Pepper ................**45.00**
Doll, Pos'n Pete ....................**80.00**
Doll, Pos'n Salty ...................**80.00**
Doll, Pos'n Tammy & Her Phone Booth ............................**65.00**
Doll, Tammy, straight legs ...**40.00**
Doll, Tammy's Mom or Dad, ea .....................................**45.00**
Doll, Ted ...............................**45.00**
Game ....................................**20.00**
Outfit, MIB, from $25 to ......**65.00**
Outfit, MOC, from $10 to .....**20.00**
Record ...................................**20.00**
Storybook, from $10 to .........**20.00**
Tammy's Car, minimum value .**75.00**
Tammy's Catamaran ..........**150.00**
Tammy's Ideal House, minimum value ............................**100.00**
Tea set ................................**150.00**

## Tressy

American Character's Tressy doll was produced in this country from 1963 to 1967. The unique thing about this 11½" fashion doll was that her hair 'grew' by pushing a button on her stomach. Tressy also had a 9" little sister named Cricket. These two dolls had numerous fashions and accessories produced for them. Never-removed-from box Tressy and Cricket items are rare; so unless indicated, values listed are for loose, mint items. Never-removed-from box items are worth at least double the loose value. For further information we recommend our advisor, Cindy Sabulis, listed in the Directory under Connecticut.

Carrying case, Cricket .........**25.00**
Carrying case, Tressy ...........**20.00**
Doll, Cricket .........................**20.00**
Doll, Mary Makeup ..............**15.00**
Doll, Pre-Teen Tressy ..........**50.00**
Doll, Tressy ...........................**15.00**
Doll, Tressy w/Magic Makeup Face ...............................**20.00**
Gift package, w/doll & clothing, MIB minimum value ..**100.00**
Hair accessory package, MIB (sealed) ..........................**20.00**
Hair or cosmetic accessory kit, minimum value .............**50.00**
Outfit, MIB (sealed), any, minimum value .....................**40.00**
Outfit, MOC (sealed), any ....**20.00**
Pattern, Tressy doll clothes, M .**6.00**
Tressy Apartment ..............**150.00**
Tressy Beauty Salon ..........**125.00**
Tressy Hair Dryer ................**40.00**
Tressy Millinery .................**150.00**

## Uneeda

Uneeda dolls generally date from the 1960s and '70s; they

were made of vinyl and plastic, and many had cloth bodies. Most are marked and dated.

Baby Bee, sleep eyes, rooted hair, open mouth/nurser, 1984 ..**10.00**
Fairy Princess, extra joint at wrist & waist, ballerina outfit, 32" ..........................**145.00**
Jennifer, vinyl, sleep eyes, rooted hair, bridal outfit, 1972-73, 14" ..................................**27.00**
Plummie Splash, painted vinyl, molded hair, flat face, 1974, 13" ..................................**14.00**
Stella Walker, rooted hair, sleep eyes, pink organdy dress, 1960, 34" ........................**95.00**
Tummy the Pudgy Pixie, painted features, rooted hair, 1972, 9½" .................................**18.00**

## Vogue

This is the company that made the 'Ginny' doll famous. She was first made in composition during the late 1940s, and if you could find her in mint condition, she'd bring about $450.00 on today's market. (Played with and in relatively sad condition, she's still worth about $90.00.) Ginnys from the 1950s were made of rigid vinyl. The last Ginny came out in 1969. Tonka bought the rights in 1973, but the dolls they produced sold poorly. After a series of other owners, Dakin purchased the rights in 1986 and began producing a vinyl doll that resembled the 1950-style Ginny very closely.

Baby Wide Eyes, plastic & vinyl, sleep eyes, 1975-1982, 11" .........**30.00**
Brickette, mod red hair, sleep eyes, pinafore dress, 1978-79, 16" ..................................**95.00**

Photo courtesy Pat Smith.

**Ginny, hard plastic, 8", #99, #100, #101, $265.00 each, minimum value.**

Ginny, vinyl, sleep eyes, rooted hair, red coat & hat, 1984, 8" ....................................**50.00**
Ginny Baby, vinyl, painted features & molded hair, early '50s, 8" .........................**265.00**
Littlest Angel, plastic & vinyl, red rooted hair, 1965, 15", MIB ...............................**30.00**
Mary Jane, composition, pink dress w/blue coat & hat, 1947, 14" ......................**345.00**
My Baby, sleep eyes, open mouth, original pink dress & shoes, 12", M ...........................**22.00**
Polish Ginny, vinyl, sleep eyes, rooted hair, traditional dress, 1965 ..............................**50.00**
Toodles, composition, Uncle Sam outfit, ca '40s, 8", minimum value ...........................**295.00**

# Door Knockers

Though many of the door knockers you'll see on the market today are of the painted cast-iron

147

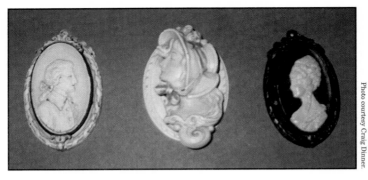

**Colonial man, marked WS in triangle, Pat Apld For, 4⅜x2½",
$150.00; Victorian lady, #615, 3⅞x2⅞", $345.00; Colonial woman,
Waverly Studio, Wilmette Ill, 4⅜x2½", $150.00.**

variety (similar in design to doorstop figures), they're also found in brass and other metals. Most are modeled as people, animals, and birds; and baskets of flowers are common. All items listed are cast iron unless noted. Prices shown are suggested for examples in excellent condition without damage and with original paint. For further information we recommend our advisor, Craig Dinner, listed in the Directory under New York.

Butterfly, multicolor w/pink rose, cream & purple backplate, 3½" ...............................**115.00**

Cardinal, female w/berries on branch, cream & green backplate, 5x3" ...................**180.00**

Cardinal, red w/black details, w/berries & branch, oval backplate, 5" ................**195.00**

Castle, cream w/3 flags, green trees & blue sky, white backplate, 4x3" ...................**165.00**

Cottage, white w/peaked red roof, 2 chimneys & trees on cream, 3½" ...............................**285.00**

Flower basket, multicolor, 3-color backplate, marked Hubley #205, 4x2" .....................**95.00**

Flower basket, pink & blue in white basket w/yellow ribbon, 4x2½" .............................**95.00**

Flower basket w/blue bow, multicolor, cream backplate, 4x3" ................................**65.00**

Ivy in basket, shaded green & yellow, white backplate, 4¼x2½" .........................**125.00**

Morning Glory, single purple-blue flower w/bud, leaf backplate, 3x3" .............................**210.00**

Owl, yellow, brown, white, & black, cream & green backplate, 4¾x3" .................**175.00**

Parrot, pink, blue & yellow, holding branch, cream & green backplate .....................**100.00**

Peacock, multicolor spread feathers, black body, white backplate, 3x3" ...................**300.00**

Red-headed woodpecker, pink flowers w/leaves & brown tree backplate .............**100.00**

Rooster w/branch, red, yellow & brown, oval cream & green backplate .....................**160.00**

Ship, gold w/details, oval backplate w/blue waves, 4x2¾" ....**130.00**

Snow Owl, white w/black details, cream & green backplate, 4¾x3" ...........................**200.00**

# Doorstops

Doorstops, once called door porters, were popular from the Civil War period until after 1930. They were used to prop the doors open during the hot summer months so that the cooler air could circulate. Though some were made of brass, wood, and chalk, cast iron was by far the most preferred material, usually molded in amusing figurals — dogs, flower baskets, frogs, etc. Hubley was one of the largest producers. Refer to *Doorstops, Identification and Values,* by Jeanne Bertoia (Collector Books) for more information. Beware of reproductions!

**Flower Basket, painted cast iron, $100.00 to $125.00.**

Amish Man, full-figure solid casting, 8½x3¾", EX ..........**200.00**

Bird Dog, National Foundry, flat casting, 6x11¾", EX ....**180.00**

Boston Terrier, Hubley, full-figure hollow casting, 10x10", EX .................................**85.00**

Boxer, Hubley, full-figure hollow casting, 8½x9", EX ......**275.00**

Boy w/Bear, Albany Foundry, full-figure solid casting, 5x3½", EX ................................**160.00**

Buddha, full-figure hollow casting, 7x5¾", G ..............**200.00**

Cat by Flower, flat casting, 5x6¼", EX .................................**125.00**

Colonial Dame, Hubley, flat casting, 8x4½", EX .............**200.00**

Colonial Pilgrim, flat casting, 8¾x5", VG ....................**350.00**

Doll on Base, full-figure solid casting, 5½", G ..............**90.00**

Dutch Girl, Hubley, flat casting, 9¼x5½", EX .................**175.00**

French Girl, Hubley, flat casting, 9¼x5½", G ....................**195.00**

German Shepherd, Hubley, full-figure hollow casting, 9¾x13", EX .................................**135.00**

Hunchback Cat, Hubley, full-figure hollow casting, 11x7½", EX .................................**135.00**

Lighthouse, flat casting, 14x9¼", EX .................................**160.00**

Monkey on Barrel, Taylor Cook No 3 1930, flat casting, 8", VG ..............................**300.00**

Owl, Hubley, flat casting, 10x4½", EX ..............................**200.00**

Peacock, flat casting, 6¼x6¼", EX ..............................**165.00**

Pelican on Dock, Albany Foundry, flat casting, 8x7¼", EX .**225.00**

Persian Cat, Hubley, full-figure hollow casting, 8½x6½", VG .**150.00**

Poppies & Cornflowers, Hubley, flat casting, 7¼x6½", EX .....**120.00**

Putting Golfer, Hubley, flat casting, 8⅜x7", G ...............**275.00**

Rabbit by Fence, Albany Foundry, flat casting, 7x8⅛", EX .**325.00**

Saddled Horse, full-figure hollow casting, 10x11½", EX ..**200.00**

Soldier, Albany Foundry, flat casting, 9½x5", EX .............**200.00**

Vase, full-figure hollow casting,
12x8", EX ..................**180.00**
Whistling Boy, full-figure hollow
casting w/rubber knobs, 10",
EX ..............................**350.00**
Woman Holding Hat, full-figure solid
casting, 6x4⅛", VG ........**160.00**
Yawning Child, full-figure hollow
casting, 9x5", EX .........**275.00**

# Egg Cups

For generations Europeans
and Americans ate their eggs
from an egg cup. A soft-boiled egg
was put in the cup and the shell
gently tapped so that the top
third could be removed and the
egg consumed. Some egg cups
were double-ended; the end that
was not in use became the base.
The smaller end was for a boiled
egg that was eaten from the shell
and the larger for eggs (either
poached or boiled) that were to be
eaten by 'toast dunkers,' a per-
fectly acceptable social practice at
this time.

Today's collectors find
ceramic figural egg cups make
very interesting collectibles. The
majority are shaped like chickens
(hens and roosters), ducks, and
birds; those in the shapes of other
animals, people, or characters are
highly prized. Our advisor for this
category is Joan George, who is
listed in the Directory under New
Jersey. See also Clubs and
Newsletters.

Blue Willow, Norcrest, 2" .......**6.00**
Chick, French Opalex, 2¼" ....**8.00**
Chick, milk glass w/red trim, West-
moreland #602, 3½" .......**15.00**
Chick w/cup on back, tan lustre,
Japan, 2½" ....................**15.00**

**Boy, marked Occupied Japan,
2⅜", $12.00.**

Girl bunny standing w/egg cup
flower, multicolor, Japan,
3" ...................................**15.00**
Goose, multicolor matte glaze,
Japan, 2½" .....................**15.00**
Milk glass, 3 cups w/center metal
handle, 4¼" dia ..............**35.00**
Pelican, tan lustre cup, multicolor
shiny glaze, Japan, 2¼" ..**15.00**

# Egg Timers

Figural egg timers were produced primarily during the 1930s
and 1940s and were made mainly
in Japan or Germany; some are
marked accordingly. Figures
range from storybook characters
(Oliver Twist) to animals and little people dressed in native costume. Another type of timer was
the tableau or scenic timer. These
are about the same height as a
figural timer but depict a person
in a setting such as a kitchen or
before a fireplace. The glass sand
tube was usually located at the
side of the scene.

A timer may no longer have
its original sand tube, but it can

be recognized by the hole that goes through the back of the figure or the stub of a hand. In the case of the tableau timer, the hole may be very small, making this style more difficult to spot, once the tube is gone. Most timers are made of ceramic (china or bisque), but some are cast iron or wood. Timers can be detailed or quite plain. Listings below are for timers completely intact with their sand tubes. Our advisor is Jeannie Greenfield; she is listed in the Directory under Pennsylvania.

Photo courtesy Jeannie Greenfield.

**Chimney Sweep, German, from $25.00 to $35.00; Maid, German, timer in left hand, $25.00.**

Clown, timer under right arm, Japan, 4½" .....................**10.00**
Little girl w/timer standing behind, wood, unmarked, 4" .........**5.00**
Lucite, commemorative of JFK on clear block, 3x3x¾" .........**5.00**
Owl, timer sits in nearby pouch, marked Goebel #81503, 1960s, 3½x3" .................**45.00**
Pilgrim scene, ceramic, Swansea, England, 3½x3x1" .........**15.00**
Rooster, timer through mouth to back of head, Germany, 3" ........**25.00**
Sailor/skipper, nautical clothes, timer in right hand, unmarked, 3" .................**15.00**

Sea gull, cast iron w/timer outside of bird, unmarked, 3½" .**15.00**
Windmill, yellow w/4th blade as timer, 4" .........................**15.00**
Woman in long gown silhouette, litho tin w/timer riveted to center .............................**25.00**

# Elvis Presley

The King of Rock 'n Roll, the greatest entertainer of all time (and not many would disagree with that), Elvis remains just as popular today as he was in the height of his career. In just the past few months, values for Elvis collectibles have skyrocketed. The early items marked 'Elvis Presley Enterprises' bearing a 1956 or 1957 date are the most valuable. Paper goods such as magazines, menus from Las Vagas hotels, ticket stubs, etc., make up a large part of any Elvis collection and are much less expensive. His records were sold in abundance, so unless you find an original Sun label (some are worth $500.00), a colored vinyl or a promotional cut, or EPs and LPs in wonderful condition, don't pay much! The picture sleeves are usually worth much more than the record itself!

Our advisor is Rosalind Cranor, author of *Elvis Collectibles* and *Best of Elvis Collectibles* (Overmountain Press); see the Directory under Virginia for ordering information.

Balloon, advertising Kid Galahad movie, w/cardboard feet ..**50.00**
Belt buckle, name & guitar in relief on brass, belt missing ...**195.00**
Bolo tie, framed photo, ca 1956, M .................................**250.00**

Book, Films & Career..., Citadel Press, 1st edition, 1976 .**20.00**

Book, The Elvis Presley Trivia Quiz Book, 1978, softcover, EX ...............................**7.50**

Bracelet, dog tag on chain, original card, M ...................**27.50**

Complimentary plastic bag, Las Vegas Hilton, 1970 ........**30.00**

**Doll, Graceland, plastic and vinyl, 1984, any one of six different outfits, MIB, each, $75.00.**

Drinking glass, standing pose w/guitar, heavy gold overlay, 1956 .............................**225.00**

Fan club membership card, photo w/member's name, 1950s, G ........................**32.00**

Gum card wrapper, Donruss, 1978, NM, from $4 to ......**5.00**

Hankerchief, song titles & portrait border, 1956, any of 3 prints, ea ......................**460.00**

Hawaiian lei, w/color portrait disc pennant, Blue Hawaii promotion ..............................**150.00**

Herald, Double Trouble, Metro-Goldwyn-Mayer, 1967 ...**15.00**

Herald, Loving You, 2-color .**45.00**

Insert card, Girls Girls Girls, Paramount, 1962, 14x36" .**40.00**

Insert card, Jailhouse Rock, 36x14" ..........................**275.00**

License plate, blue, green & white metal, 1987, 6x12", M .....**7.00**

Lipstick, facsimile signature on tube, Hound Dog Orange .......**245.00**

Lobby card, GI Blues, Paramount, 1960, 11x14", set of 8 ..**225.00**

Lobby photo, King Creole, 22x28" ........................**225.00**

Magazine, Let It Rock, December, 1973, London, England .**15.00**

Mug, Hal Wallis' GI Blues w/facsimile signature on clear glass, unmarked .........**225.00**

Pen, From Elvis & the Colonel .**25.00**

Perfume, Teddy Bear Eau de Parfum, copyright 1957, original box ..............................**250.00**

Photo, in gold lame suit, blue guitar border, promotional, 1957, 8x10" ............................**50.00**

Picture, from paint-by-number set, painted, 1956, 7x9½" ...**125.00**

Pin-back, Elvis for President, celluloid, unmarked, late '50s, 3⅜" ....**80.00**

Pin-back, Elvis Solid Gold 1954-1974, fan club issue ......**25.00**

Pin-back, Elvis the Spirit of '76, photo center, Mark Pack Inc MI .................................**20.00**

Pin-back, gold record w/portrait center, late 1950s, ⅞" ....**50.00**

Pin-back, I'm a Kissin' Cousin, red & white, LA Stamp Co, 2¼" .**90.00**

Pin-back, I Want Elvis for Xmas, green on white, 3⅜" ....**105.00**

Pin-back, National Fan Club/RCA Records, pink & black .**140.00**

Pocket mirror, portrait w/block letters, England, 1960s .**35.00**

Poster, Change of Habit, NBC Universal, 1969, 41x21" .......**45.00**

Poster, Follow That Dream, United Artists, 1962, 41x27" .....**80.00**

Poster, Frankie & Johnny, United Artists, 1966, 81x41" ....**85.00**

Poster, Harum Scarum, Metro-Goldwyn-Mayer, 1965, 27x41" ...........................**50.00**

Poster, It Happened at World's Fair, Metro-Goldwyn-Mayer, 1963, 27x41" .................**75.00**

Poster, Loving You, Paramount, 1-sheet ...........................**325.00**

Poster, Spinout, Metro-Goldwyn-Mayer, 1966, 27x41" .....**50.00**

Pressbook, Flaming Star, 20th-Century Fox, 1960 ........**50.00**

Pressbook, Fun in Acapulco, Paramount, 1963 ..........**30.00**

Pressbook, Tickle Me, Allied Artists, 1965 ..................**30.00**

Pressbook, Viva Las Vegas, Metro-Goldwyn-Mayer, 1964 ..............................**45.00**

Promotional folder, Tickle Me, w/feathers ......................**65.00**

Puzzle, black & white photo, fan club issue, 1970s, 8x10" .**18.00**

Puzzle, Whitman Publishing UK Ltd, ca 1974, 224-piece, 18½x13" .........................**22.00**

Scrapbook, holds guitar & stands on record, copyright 1956, 12x14" ...........................**500.00**

Song book, for Emenee guitar, sm photo on cover ...............**80.00**

Standee, Easy Come Easy Go, Paramount, 1967 ..........**75.00**

Still photo, Blue Hawaii, color, Paramount, 1961, 8x10" .**17.00**

Still photo, Roustabout, color, Paramount, 1964, 8x10", ea .....................................**10.00**

Sweater clip, dog tags w/chain, EX ...............................**160.00**

Trailer, Girl Happy, Metro-Goldwyn-Mayer, 1965 ...........**45.00**

Trailer, Wild in the Country, 20th-Century Fox, 1961 ........**55.00**

Wallet, standing pose w/record & song titles on red ground, M ..................................**480.00**

Window card, Kid Galahad, United Artists, 1962, 22x14" ......**40.00**

Window card, Paradise Hawaiian Style, Paramount, 1966, 14x22" ...........................**30.00**

# Enesco Kitchen Accessories

Enesco is an importing company based in Elk Grove, Illinois. They're distributors of ceramic novelties made for them in Japan. During the 1960s, they sold a line of novelties originally called 'Mother-in-the Kitchen.' Today's collectors refer to them as 'Kitchen Prayer Ladies.' Ranging from large items such as canisters and cookie jars to toothpick holders and small picture frames, the line was fairly extensive. Some of the pieces are very hard to find, and those with blue dresses are much more scarce than those in pink. For a complete listing and current values, contact our advisor, April Tvorak, who is listed in the Directory under Colorado.

Another Enesco line destined to become very collectible is called 'Kitchen Independence.' It features George Washington with the Declaration of Independence scroll held at his side, and Betsy Ross wearing a blue dress and holding a large flag.

Both lines are pictured in *The Collector's Encyclopedia of Cookie Jars, Volume 1 and 2*, by Joyce and Fred Roerig.

### Kitchen Independence

Egg timer, George Washington .**50.00**

**Kitchen Independence cookie jar, Betsy Ross, $200.00; Kitchen Prayer Lady, blue, $400.00.**

Napkin holder, George Washington ...................................**20.00**

Salt & pepper shakers, George Washington & Betsy Ross, pr ...................................**22.00**

Spoon holder, Betsy Ross .....**15.00**

### Kitchen Prayer Ladies

Bell, blue ...............................**55.00**

Bell, pink ..............................**35.00**

Canister set, blue, 4-pc (Flour, Sugar, Coffee & Tea) ...**650.00**

Canister set, pink, 4-pc (Flour, Sugar, Coffee & Tea) ...**450.00**

Cookie jar, pink, 10½" ........**200.00**

Napkin holder, blue, 6½" .....**30.00**

Napkin holder, pink, 6½" .....**24.00**

Picture frame, blue .............**60.00**

Picture frame, pink .............**50.00**

Salt & pepper shakers, blue, 4", pr ....................................**18.00**

Salt & pepper shakers, pink, 4", pr, from $10 to ...............**12.00**

Scissors holder, blue, wall mount, minimum value .............**65.00**

Scissors holder, pink, wall mount, minimum value .............**45.00**

Soap dish/scouring pad holder, blue, 5½" ........................**35.00**

Soap dish/scouring pad holder, pink, 5½" ........................**20.00**

Spoon holder, blue, flat ........**50.00**

Spoon holder, pink, flat ........**38.00**

Tea set, blue, 3-pc, minimum value ...........................**200.00**

Tea set, pink, 3-pc, minimum value ...........................**150.00**

Toothpick holder, pink or blue, 4½", from $15 to ............**20.00**

## Farm Collectibles

As you drive through the country, you'll notice a trend toward more older decorations around homes and farmsteads. While making the outdoor scene nicer to view, the old pieces of horse-drawn machinery, wheels, fencing and other items also depict bits of rural history.

Items collectors look for include actual scale models and toy tractors; tractor, seed or other advertising items and giveaways; tools related to milking, blacksmithing, or other farming activities; windmills, weathervanes and

**Curry/tail comb for grooming horses, $15.00.**

lightening rod balls; and many other miscellaneous antiques and collectibles. For further information we recommend our advisor, Gary Van Hoozer, listed in the Directory under Missouri. See also Clubs and Newsletters for information about *Farm Antiques News*.

Bridle bit, workhorse, 2 swivel rings in center, NM .........**7.00**
Calf weaner, metal, hangs over nose to prevent sucking, EX ..................................**12.00**
Cream separator, Economy on nameplate, missing bowl, gears stuck ....................**25.00**
Dinner bell, uncracked, complete ..........................**175.00**
Egg crate, unpainted boards **.25.00**
Hay hook, blacksmith-made w/fancy iron handle ......**15.00**
Horse collar, leather, large, EX **.45.00**
Implement seat, cast iron w/stem, unmarked .......................**12.00**
Kettle, cast iron, lg, no cracks, from $175 to ................**225.00**
Milk can, w/original top, no dents or rust, EX ......................**20.00**
Pedal tractor, resembling '40s-'60s model, any, from $275 to **.450.00**
Sack stitcher, working condition w/most original chrome plating ...................................**12.00**
Scythe, factory-made w/wood handle, little rust ................**14.00**

Scythe, home-manufactured with rustic handle .................**18.00**
Toy tractor, Farmall Model H, Ertl, ca 1966 ...................**75.00**
Toy tractor, Fordson, cast iron, ca 1935, original ..............**550.00**
Watch fob, Minneapolis-Moline or others, authentic, ea, from $40 to .............................**75.00**
Wood auger, iron bit w/wood handle ..................................**12.00**
Wrench, Maytag in raised letters on handle, multi-jaws both ends, EX .......................**75.00**
Wrench, Model A era w/Ford logo on handle, open-ended, sm ....**7.00**
Wrench, multi-size jaws, Midland Mfg in raised letters on handle ..................................**40.00**

# Fast-Food Collectibles

Everyone is familiar with the kiddie meals offered by fast-food restaurants, but perhaps you didn't realize that the toys tucked inside are quickly becoming some of the hottest new fun collectibles on today's market. Played-with items are plentiful at garage sales for nearly nothing, but it's best if they're still in the packages they originally came out in. The ones to concentrate on are Barbies, the old familiar Disney characters,

Photo courtesy Pat and Bill Poe.

**Burger King, Beauty and the Beast, 1991, Belle and the Beast, $4.00 each ($5.00 mint in package): Cogsworth and Chip, $6.00 each ($7.00 mint in package).**

and those that tie in with the big blockbuster kids' movies. Collectors look for the boxes the meals came in, too, and even the display signs that the restaurants promote each series with are valuable. The toys don't have to be old to be collectible.

Our values are for toys that are still in the original packaging. A loose example is worth about 20% to 25% less than one still sealed. Our advisors for this category are Joyce and Terry Losonsky, authors of a book on McDonald's® premiums who are listed in the directory under Maryland, and (for restaurants other than McDonald's) Bill and Pat Poe (see Florida). See also Character and Promotional Drinking Glasses.

Burger King, Aladdin, 1992, any ..............................**4.00**
Burger King, Beach Party, 1994, any ..................................**3.00**
Burger King, Bonkers, 1993, any except Disney Adventure Magazine .........................**3.00**
Burger King, Crayola Coloring Mystery Sets, any of 6, ea .......**4.00**
Burger King, Dino Crawlers, 1994, any of 5 ..................**3.00**

Burger King, Glow-in-the-Dark Troll Patrol, 1993, any of 4 .........**3.00**
Burger King, Go-Go Gadget Gizmos, 1991, any of 4 ..........**4.00**
Burger King, Goof Troop Bowlers, 1992, any of 4 ..................**3.00**
Burger King, Lion King, 1994, any of 7 ............................**4.00**
Burger King, Little Mermaid, 1993, any of 4 ..................**4.00**
Burger King, Mickey's Toontown w/Diarama, 1993, any of 4 ................................**6.00**
Burger King, Save the Animals, 1993, any of 4 .................**4.00**
Burger King, Teenage Mutant Ninja Turtles Bike Gear, 1993, any of 5 ..................**3.00**
Burger King, Z-Bots w/Pogs, 1994, any of 5 ..................**4.00**
Dairy Queen, Rock-a-Doodle, 1992, any of 4 .................**7.00**
Denney's, Adventure Seekers, 1993, any ........................**3.00**
Denney's, Flintstones, Fred & Wilma (together in bag), plush, 1989 .....................**8.00**
Denney's, Flintstones Dino-Racers, 1991, any of 5 ...........**4.00**
Denney's, Jetson's Planets, 1992, any of 5 ............................**4.00**
Denney's, Jetsons Go Back to School, 1992, any of 4 .....**3.00**

Hardee's, Days of Thunder Racers, 1990, any .................**5.00**

Hardee's, Dinosaur in My Pocket, 1993, any of 4 ..................**3.00**

Hardee's, Eureka Castle Stampers, 1994, any of 4 .........**3.00**

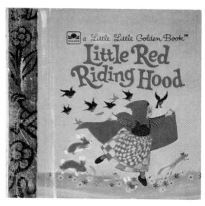

**Hardee's, Little Golden Book, M, $5.00.**

Hardee's, Micro Super Soakers, 1994, any of 4 ..................**3.00**

Hardee's, Muppet Christmas Carol (finger puppets), 1993, any of 4 ............................**3.00**

Hardee's, Nicktoons Cruisers, 1994, any of 8 ..................**3.00**

Hardee's, Swan Princess, 1994, any of 6 ...........................**4.00**

International House of Pancakes, Pancake Kids, 1992, any of 4 ...........................**5.00**

Long John Silver, Map Activities, 1991, any .........................**4.00**

Long John Silver, Treasure Trolls (pencil toppers), 1992, any of 4 .....**3.00**

McDonald's, Animaniacs, 1994, any of 8 (no under three) ..**1.50**

McDonald's, Astrosniks, 1985, any of 11, from $7 to .....**15.00**

McDonald's, Bambi, 1988, any of 4 (no under three), from $2 to ......**3.00**

McDonald's, Barnyard/Old McDonald's Farm, 1986, any of 7, from $15 to ............**20.00**

McDonald's, Batman, 1992, any of 4 .......................................**2.00**

McDonald's, Berenstain Bears, 1987, any of 4 (no under three) .............................**4.00**

McDonald's, Cabbage Patch Kids/Tonka, 1994, any of 8 ......**1.50**

McDonald's, Crazy Vehicles, 1991, any of 4, from $2.50 to ....**3.50**

McDonald's, Dink the Little Dinosaur, any of 6, from $10 to .....................................**15.00**

McDonald's, Disney Favorites, 1987, any of 4, from $3 to .**5.00**

McDonald's, Duck Tales I, 1988, any of 5, from $2 to .........**3.00**

McDonald's, Dukes of Hazzard, 1982, any of 4, from $25 to ........**40.00**

McDonald's, Flintstone Kids, 1987, any of 4 (no under three) .............................**12.00**

McDonald's, Fun w/Food, 1989, any of 4, from $5 to .........**7.00**

McDonald's, Garfield, 1989, any of 4 (no under three), from $2 to .....................................**3.00**

McDonald's, Going Places/Hot Wheels, 1983, any of 4, from $7 to ..............................**10.00**

McDonald's, Good Sports, 1984, any of 6, from $4 to .........**7.00**

McDonald's, Jungle Book, 1990, any of 4 (no under three), from $2 to ........................**3.00**

McDonald's, Lego Building Sets, 1986, any of 6, from $4 to .**6.00**

McDonald's, Little Engineer, 1987, any of 5 (no under three) ..............................**6.00**

McDonald's, Little Mermaid, 1989, any of 4, from $3 to ..........**5.00**

McDonald's, Matchbox Super GT, 1988, any of 16, from $8 to ...................................**10.00**

McDonald's, Michael Jordan windup time clock, M ......**4.00**

McDonald's, Mickey & Friends/Epcot Center, 1994, any of 8 .........**1.50**

**Wendy's, 1990, Alien Mix-up Characters, M (no package), $2.00 to $3.00 each.**

McDonald's, Muppet Workshop, 1995, any of 4 (no under three) ...............................**1.00**

McDonald's, New Archies, 1988, any of 6, from $6 to .......**10.00**

McDonald's, Oliver & Company, 1988, any of 4, from $2 to .**3.00**

McDonald's, Olympic Sports (puzzles), 1984, any of 5, from $20 to ....................................**25.00**

McDonald's, Play-Doh, 1983, any of 5, from $15 to ............**20.00**

McDonald's, Raggedy Ann & Andy, 1989, any of 4, from $6 to ....................................**8.00**

McDonald's, Runaway Robots, 1987, any of 6, from $6 to .........**15.00**

McDonald's, Super Looney Tunes, 1991, any of 4 (no under three) ...............................**2.00**

McDonald's, Tale Spin, 1990, any of 4 (no under three) .......**1.50**

McDonald's, Turbo Macs, any of 4, from $4 to ........................**7.00**

McDonald's, Yo, Yogi!, 1992, any of 4, from $3 to ................**4.00**

McDonald's, Young Astronauts, 1992, any of 4 (no under three) ...............................**1.50**

Pizza Hut, Beauty & the Beast (hand puppets), 1992, any of 4 .......................................**5.00**

Pizza Hut, Eureka's Castle (hand puppets), 1990, any of 3 ..**5.00**

Roy Rogers, Gator Tales, 1989, any of 3 ...........................**8.00**

Sonic, Brown Bag Kids, 1993, on skis, snowboard or tube, ea ....................................**5.00**

Taco Bell, Busy World of Richard Scarry, Lowly Worm or Huckle Cat, ea .................**8.00**

Wendy's, Cybercycles, 1994, any of 4 ......................................**4.00**

Wendy's, Endangered Animals, 1993, any ..........................**2.00**

Wendy's, Mighty Mouse, 1989, any ....................................**4.00**

Wendy's, Speed Writers, 1991, any ....................................**4.00**

Wendy's, Yogi Bear & Friends, 1990, any ..........................**4.00**

White Castle, Bow Biters, 1989, any ....................................**5.00**

White Castle, Camp White Castle, 1990, any ..........................**4.00**

White Castle, Castle Meal Friends, 1989, any of 6 ...**5.00**

# Fenton

The Fenton glass company, organized in 1906 in Martin's Ferry, Ohio, is noted for their fine art glass. Over one hundred thirty patterns of carnival glass were made in their earlier years (see Carnival Glass), but even items from the past twenty-five years of production (Hobnail, Burmese, and the various colored 'crest' lines) have collector value.

Aqua Crest, pitcher, 7" .........**67.50**

Beaded Melon, creamer, milk glass, 4" ..........................**24.00**

Bicentennial, bell, Patriot, red .**52.50**

Bicentennial, plate, Patriot, milk glass ...............................**15.00**

Coin Dot, bowl, blue opalescent, 10" ...............................**90.00**

Coin Dot, creamer, cranberry opalescent, 4" ................**55.00**

Daisy & Button, bell, Lime Sherbet ...............................**22.00**

Daisy & Button, bonbon, French opalescent, 5" ................**15.00**

Daisy & Button, vase, milk glass, footed fan form, 10" .......**35.00**

Diamond Optic, vase, blue opalescent, flared, 8½" ............**50.00**

Dolphin, bowl, console; jade green, handles, oval, footed, 10½" ...............................**110.00**

Dolphin, candy box, Velva Rose, w/lid ...............................**37.50**

Emerald Crest, compote ......**35.00**

Gold Crest, bowl, 6" .............**10.00**

Hobnail, basket, blue opalescent, 4" ...................................**50.00**

Hobnail, basket, peachblow, shallow, 5½" .........................**45.00**

Hobnail, bonbon, blue opalescent, 6" ...................................**36.00**

Hobnail, bonbon, yellow opalescent, 5½" .........................**30.00**

Hobnail, bowl, cranberry opalescent, double-crimped, footed, 11" ...............................**67.50**

Hobnail, candle holders, topaz opalescent, squat, pr .....**48.00**

Hobnail, candy jar, milk glass, footed, 9" .......................**37.50**

Hobnail, cruet, blue opalescent, 4" ...................................**32.00**

Hobnail, epergne, pink pastel .**65.00**

Hobnail, fan vase, blue opalescent, footed, 6" ..............**32.00**

Hobnail, jam set, cranberry opalescent, w/lid & spoon ........**45.00**

Hobnail, lamp, fairy; blue opalescent, 2-pc ......................**18.00**

Hobnail, salt & pepper shakers, French opalescent, flat base, pr ...................................**45.00**

Hobnail, tumbler, green, 4¼" .**27.50**

Hobnail, vase, bud; topaz opalescent, footed, 8" ..............**42.50**

Hobnail, vase, bud; yellow opalescent, footed ....................**40.00**

Hobnail, vase, green opalescent, 4" ...................................**20.00**

Hobnail, vase, peachblow, 6" ..**72.50**

Jade Green, sugar bowl .......**18.00**

Jade Green, vase, straight sides, 8" ...................................**35.00**

Orange Tree, candlesticks, cream satin, pr .........................**37.50**

Orange Tree, jelly compote, crystal ...............................**20.00**

Pekin Blue, candle holders, 3", pr ...................................**65.00**

**Poppy basket in rose satin, 9", from $50.00 to $65.00.**

Silver Crest, basket, 7½" .....**36.00**

Silver Crest, bowl, salad; 9½" .**60.00**

Silver Crest, cake plate, pedestal foot, low, 13" dia ............**35.00**

Silver Crest, candle holders, saucer base, 3¾", pr ......**55.00**

Silver Crest, compote, ruffled & crimped, 8½" ..................**17.50**

Silver Crest, plate, 10¾" ......**30.00**

# Fiesta

Since it was discontinued by Homer Laughlin in 1973, Fiesta has become one of the most popular collectibles on the market. Values have continued to climb until some of the more hard-to-find items now sell for several hundred dollars each. In 1986 HLC reintroduced a line of new Fiesta that buyers should be aware of. To date these colors have been used: cobalt (darker than the original), rose (a strong pink), black, white, apricot (very pale), yellow (a light creamy tone), turquoise, (country) blue, seamist (a light mint green), and lilac. Persimmon is the new color for 1995. When old molds were used, the mark will be the same, if it is a molded-in mark such as on pitchers, sugar bowls, etc. The ink stamp differs from the old — now all the letters are upper case.

'Original colors' in the listings indicates values for three of the original six colors — light green, turquoise, and yellow. Refer to *The Collector's Encyclopedia of Fiesta* by Sharon and Bob Huxford (Collector Books) for more information. See also Clubs and Newsletters.

Ashtray, original colors ........**38.00**
Bowl, cream soup; '50s colors .**60.00**
Bowl, cream soup; red, cobalt or ivory ..............................**48.00**
Bowl, fruit; '50s colors, 4¾" .**28.00**
Bowl, individual salad; med green, 7½" ......................**80.00**
Bowl, nappy; original colors, 8½" ..............................**30.00**
Bowl, nappy; red, cobalt or ivory, 9½" ..................................**50.00**
Bowl, salad; original colors, footed, lg ...................................**190.00**
Candle holders, bulbous, original colors, pr ........................**70.00**
Casserole, original colors ...**110.00**
Coffeepot, original colors ...**135.00**
Compote, sweets; original colors ..............................**48.00**
Compote, sweets; red, cobalt or ivory ..............................**65.00**
Creamer, '50s colors .............**26.00**
Creamer, med green .............**48.00**
Cup, demitasse; original colors .**50.00**
Egg cup, '50s colors ............**125.00**
Egg cup, original colors ........**40.00**
Mixing bowl, #1, original colors ..............................**90.00**

**Candle holders, tripod, in yellow, light green and turquoise, $325.00; in red, ivory and cobalt, $375.00 for the pair.**

Mixing bowl, #2, red, cobalt or ivory ...............................**80.00**
Mixing bowl, #3, red, cobalt or ivory ...............................**85.00**
Mixing bowl, #6, original colors ...........................**125.00**
Mug, Tom & Jerry; ivory w/gold letters ............................**60.00**
Mustard, original colors .....**125.00**
Pitcher, disk water; original colors ..................................**80.00**
Pitcher, ice; original colors ...**80.00**
Pitcher, jug, 2-pint, '50s colors .**95.00**
Plate, '50s colors, 9" .............**18.00**
Plate, calender; 1954 or 1955, 10" ................................**32.00**
Plate, chop; med green, 13" .**110.00**
Plate, chop; original colors, 15" .**35.00**
Plate, compartment; original colors, 10½" ......................**28.00**
Plate, deep; '50s colors .........**42.00**
Plate, med green, 10" ...........**80.00**
Plate, red, cobalt or ivory, 10" .**32.00**
Platter, med green ...............**90.00**
Sauce boat, original colors ...**32.00**
Saucer, med green .................**8.00**
Shakers, original colors, pr ..**17.00**
Sugar bowl, individual; yellow .**75.00**
Teapot, '50s colors ...............**35.00**
Teapot, med green ...............**50.00**
Tray, relish; mixed colors, no red ............................**185.00**
Tray, utility; original colors .**28.00**
Tumbler, juice; red, cobalt or ivory ..............................**32.00**
Tumbler, water; original colors .**45.00**
Vase, bud; original colors .....**50.00**

# Finch, Kay

From 1939 until 1963, Kay Finch and her husband, Braden, operated a small pottery in Corona Del Mar, California, where they produced figurines of animals, birds, and exotic couples as well as some dinnerware. Most items are marked. Refer to *The Collector's Encyclopedia of California Pottery* by Jack Chipman (Collector Books) for more information.

**Biddy hen, from $45.00 to $50.00.**

Figurine, Afghan, playing, #5555, sm ...............................**275.00**
Figurine, Butch & Biddy (rooster & hen), pr ......................**95.00**
Figurine, elephant, 5" ..........**75.00**
Figurine, Hannibal, angry cat, 10" ................................**185.00**
Figurine, Jeep & Peep (ducks), 4", pr ....................................**80.00**
Figurine, little blond girl in bl pinafore w/puffy sleeves, 5¼" ............**65.00**
Figurine, Polly, penguin, #467, 4¾" ...............................**120.00**
Figurine, poodle, 15" ..........**575.00**
Figurine, Sassy, pig, #611, 3½" .**25.00**
Figurine, set of angels, each w/different instrument, 3-pc .**175.00**
Mug, Missouri Mule .............**45.00**
Salt & pepper shakers, birds, blue & white, pr ....................**80.00**

# Fire-King Glass

From the 1930s to the '60s, Anchor Hocking produced a line

called Fire-King; various patterns and colors were used in its manufacture. Collectors are just beginning to reassemble sets, so prices are relatively low, except for some of the jadite pieces that are especially popular. Jadite is listed in its own category. Refer to *Collectible Glassware of the '40s, '50s, and '60s* by Gene Florence (Collector Books) for more information. We recommend our advisor April Tvorak, listed in the directory under Colorado. See also Jadite; Peach Lustre Glassware.

Alice, cup, white w/red trim, 8-oz, rare ...............................**15.00**

Alice, plate, white w/blue rim, 8½" ................................**16.00**

Anchorwhite, batter bowl, handpainted fruit, 7½" ..........**15.00**

Anchorwhite, dish, divided; handpainted florals, 11¾" oval .**7.50**

Anchorwhite Ovenware, cake pan, white, 8" sq ......................**6.50**

Anchorwhite Ovenware, pie pan, 9" .....................................**5.00**

Anniversary Rose, cup & saucer set ....................................**5.00**

Anniversary Rose, plate, dinner; 10" ....................................**5.50**

Beaded Rim, bowl, mixing; forest green, 4⅞" .........................**5.50**

Blue & Gold Floral, creamer, white w/wheat & floral decal ...............................**5.50**

Blue & Gold Floral, plate, salad; white w/wheat & floral decal, 7⅜" ....................................**5.00**

Bubble, bowl, cereal; white, 5¼" .**5.50**

Bubble, plate, dinner; crystal, 9¼" ....................................**5.00**

Bubble, plate, dinner; sapphire blue, 9¼" ........................**12.00**

Bubble, tumbler, juice; royal ruby, 6-oz ..................................**6.50**

Charm, bowl, salad; red, 7⅜" .**16.00**

Charm, cup & saucer set, forest green ................................**7.50**

Charm, plate, luncheon; azurite, 8⅜" ....................................**5.50**

Colonial Rim, bowl, mixing; white w/coral trim, 8½" ...........**15.00**

Fleurette, plate, salad; red & yellow floral decal, 7⅜" ........**3.50**

Game Birds, mug, white w/bird decal, 8-oz ........................**6.00**

Golden Anniversary, bowl, vegetable; flat swirl w/gold trim, late '50s ..................**6.00**

Golden Anniversary, platter, flat swirl w/wide gold trim, late 1950s ...............................**6.00**

Golden Shell, bowl, vegetable; deep swirl w/gold trim ....**6.00**

Golden Shell, platter, deep swirl w/gold trim ......................**6.00**

Gray Laurel, bowl, dessert; gray w/laurel band rim, 4⅞" ...**4.00**

Harvest, plate, dinner; white w/circle of grain sheafs, 10" .....**4.50**

Homestead, bowl, vegetable; orange & black decal, 8¼" ..........**12.00**

Homestead, cup, orange w/black indent base for stacking .**2.00**

Honeysuckle, creamer, white w/floral decal ...................**3.50**

Honeysuckle, platter, white w/floral decal, 9x12" ...............**9.00**

Ivory, bowl, mixing; no design, stacking set of 3 ............**18.00**

Ivory, cup & saucer set, no design .............................**5.50**

Ivory, plate, salad, no design, 7¾" ....................................**3.00**

Ivory Laurel, plate, dinner; ivory w/laurel band rim, 9" ......**6.50**

Ivory Ovenware, cake pan, no design, 9" .........................**6.00**

Ivory Swirl, cup & saucer set, no design .............................**3.00**

Ivory Swirl, plate, dinner, no design, 9" .........................**4.50**

Meadow Green, bowl, vegetable; white w/floral decal, 8¼" .**6.00**

Meadow Green, casserole, 1-qt, w/white knob lid ..............**5.00**

Milk White, plate, dinner; no design, 9" ........................**4.00**

**Modern Tulip, salt and pepper shakers, $15.00; Grease jar, $20.00.**

Pink Swirl, plate, dinner; no design, 9" ........................**6.00**

Pink Swirl, sugar bowl, no design, w/lid ................................**8.00**

Primrose, bowl, dessert; white w/red & pink floral decal, 4⅝" ....................................**3.50**

Primrose, cake pan, white w/pink & red floral decal, 8" sq ..**6.00**

Primrose, plate, dinner; white w/pink & red floral decal, 9" ......................................**5.50**

Ribbed, bowl, mixing; crystal, clear w/ribbed sides & band top, 6" ..............................**7.50**

Royal Ruby, bowl, vegetable, no design, 8" ........................**12.50**

Royal Ruby, cup & saucer set, no design ..............................**7.50**

Sapphire Blue Ovenware, baker, 5⅝" ....................................**4.50**

Sapphire Blue Ovenware, pie plate, 9" ............................**8.00**

Sheaf of Wheat, plate, dinner; clear w/wheat sheaves at rim, 9" ......................................**7.50**

Splash Proof, bowl, mixing; white, 4-qt ................................**15.00**

Sunrise, creamer, white swirl w/red band rim ................**5.50**

Sunrise, plate, dinner; white swirl w/red band rim, 9" ..........**6.50**

Swirl, bowl, mixing; ivory, 9" .**12.50**

Turquoise Blue, cup, no design, 8-oz ................................**3.50**

Turquoise Blue, egg plate, w/gold-trim rim ........................**16.00**

Wheat, baking pan, white w/wheat decal, 6½x10½" .**5.50**

Wheat, cup & saucer set, white w/wheat decal ..................**4.50**

Wheat, cup & snack plate set, white w/wheat decal .......**5.00**

White Swirl, plate, dinner; no design, 9" ........................**6.00**

# Fisher-Price

Since about 1930 the Fisher-Price Company has produced distinctive wooden toys covered with brightly colored lithographed paper. Plastic parts were first added in 1949. The most valuable Fisher-Price toys are those modeled after well-known Disney characters and have the Disney logo. A little edge wear and some paint dulling are normal to these well-loved toys and to be expected; pricing information reflects items that are in excellent played-with condition. Mint-in-box examples are extremely scarce. For further information we recommend *Fisher-Price, a Historical Rarity Value Guide*, by John J. Murray and Bruce R. Fox (Books Americana), and *Modern Toys, 1930-1980*, by Linda Baker (Collector Books). See also Dolls, and Clubs and Newsletters.

Allie Gator, #653, 1960 .......**100.00**

Barky Puppy, #103, 1931....**700.00**

Bunny Cart, #15, 1946..........**75.00**

Buzzy Bee, #325, 1950, 1st version ................................**40.00**

Cash Register, #972, 1960, w/3 wooden coins ..................**50.00**

Cry Baby Bear, #711, 1967 ...**40.00**

Dollhouse w/lights, #280, 1981, w/battery compartment & 7 outlets.............................**30.00**

Double-Screen TV Music Box, Hey Diddle Diddle, #196, 1964 ...............................**30.00**

Dr. Doodle, #132, 1958........**100.00**

Ducky Flip Flag, #175, 1964.**40.00**

Photo courtesy Doug Dezso.

**Goldilocks and the Three Bears Playhouse, #151, 1967, MIB $100.00.**

Humpty Dumpty Truck, #145, 1963 ................................**40.00**

Kicking Donkey, #175, 1937.**450.00**

Looky Chug-Chug, #161, 1949.**250.00**

Magnetic Chug-Chug, #168, 1964 ..............................**50.00**

Mother Goose, #164, 1964 ....**40.00**

Nifty Station Wagon, #234, removable roof, w/5 figures, 1960 ..............................**250.00**

Pick-Up & Peek Puzzles, #500, 1973-1986, any, ea .........**15.00**

Picture Disk Camera, #112, 1968, w/5 picture disks............**30.00**

Playful Puppy, #628, 1975 ....**25.00**

Pocket Radio, Yankee Doodle, #779, 1976 ......................**15.00**

Poodle Zilo, #739, 1962 .........**75.00**

Puzzle Puppy, #659, 1976, 8-pc take-apart & put together dog ...................................**15.00**

TV Radio, Farmer in the Dell, #166, 1963 ......................**20.00**

TV Radio, Ten Little Indians, #159, 1961................................**15.00**

Woodsey Bramble Beaver Book, #606, 1982, 32 pages......**20.00**

# Fishing Collectibles

Very much in evidence at flea markets these days, old fishing gear is becoming popular with collectors. Because the hobby is newly established, there are some very good buys to be found. Early 20th-century plugs were almost entirely carved from wood, sprayed with several layers of enamel, and finished off with glass eyes. Molded plastics were of a later origin. Some of the more collectible manufacturers are James Heddon, Shakespeare, Rhodes, and Pflueger. Our advisor for this category is Dave Hoover; he is listed in the Directory under Indiana.

Catalog, Creek Chub, 1947, 9x6", VG+ ...............................**85.00**

Catalog, Heddon, 1952, NM .**60.00**

Catalog, South Bend, 1948, 50 pages, 6¼x5¼", EX ........**25.00**

Decoy, Brown Trout by Carl Christenson, glass eyes, 4½", MIB ...............................**45.00**

Decoy, Northern Pike by Carl Christenson, #17, glass eyes, 5½", MIB ........................**35.00**

Fly reel, Horrocks-Ibbotson Mohawk #1106, EX .......**20.00**

Fly reel, Pflueger Medalist #1495, MIB ...............................**45.00**

Fly rod, Bug Eye Babbler, Tropical Bait Co, long single hook, NM ................................**85.00**

Fly rod, Creek Chub Floating Plunker, red, VG ...........**45.00**

Fly rod, Heddon Fuzzy Bug #75, yellow, bass size, EX ...**125.00**

Fly rod, Heddon Punkie Spook #980, NM ......................**85.00**

Lure, Best-O-Luck, MIB, $15.00.

Fly rod, South Bend Surf-Oreno, green scale, NM ............**50.00**

Lure, Arbogast Jitterbug, yellow plastic lip on green frog, EX .........................**20.00**

Lure, Arbogast Musky Jitterbug, wood, white w/red arrowhead, MIB ................................**20.00**

Lure, Bumble Bug, mechanical plastic, yellow w/black spots, MIB ................................**20.00**

Lure, Creek Chub Crawdad #400 series, tan, EX ...............**35.00**

Lure, Creek Chub Darter #2018, silver flash, MIB ...........**25.00**

Lure, Creek Chub Injured Minnow #1504, glass eyes, golden shiner, VG ......................**18.00**

Lure, Creek Chub Pikie #702, white w/red head, glass eyes, EX ..................................**20.00**

Lure, Creek Chub Plunker, rainbow w/glass eyes, EX ....**45.00**

Lure, Heddon Baby Crab Wiggler, pike finish, glass eyes, VG ..................................**25.00**

Lure, Heddon Crab Wiggler #1800, green crackleback, glass eyes, EX ...............**95.00**

Lure, Heddon Tadpolly #6000, green scale, glass eyes, EX ........**65.00**

Lure, Heddon Tiny Spook #310, red head, NM ...............**25.00**

Lure, Jenson Kicker, plastic, automatic kicking legs, NM .**20.00**

Lure, Martin Salmon, blue flash, MIB ................................**25.00**

Lure, Musky Sucker, gray w/black stripe, glass eyes, 4½", MIB .......................**35.00**

Lure, Paw Paw Wotta Frog, yellowish w/black splatter, NM ................................**70.00**

Lure, Pflueger Globe Baby, yellow w/gold spots, NM ...........**35.00**

Lure, Pflueger Wizzard, black & lightning flash, glass eyes, NM ................................**80.00**

Lure, Shakespeare Kingfish Wobbler #6535SF, silver flash, MIB ................................**75.00**

Lure, Shakespeare Mouse #6578T, wood, tiger stripes, MIB ................................**22.00**

Lure, South Bend Bass-Oreno, red, no eyes, EX ............**35.00**

Lure, South Bend Fish-O-Bite, plastic, white w/red arrow head, EX .......................**10.00**

Lure, Wilson Super Wobbler, cream & red flutes, EX .**40.00**

Plaque, Heddon Smallmouth Bass, wood, 10x5½", EX ..........**60.00**

Reel, Horrocks-Ibbotson Valiant #1909, model C, spin cast, EX ..................................**10.00**

Reel, JA Coxe #60, EX .........**35.00**

Reel, Langley Target #340, narrow spool, green w/silver target, VG ..........................**45.00**

Reel, Pflueger Akron #1895M,
jeweled, free spool, EX ..**25.00**
Reel, Pflueger Jupiter, spin cast,
star drag, EX ................**50.00**
Reel, Zebco #909, nickel, spin
cast, EX ........................**20.00**

# Flashlights

The flashlight was invented
in 1898 and has been produced by
the Eveready Company for these
past ninety-six years. Eveready
dominated the flashlight market
for most of this period, but more
than one hundred twenty-five
other U.S. flashlight companies
have come and gone to provide
competition along the way. Add to
that number over thirty-five
known foreign flashlight manufacturers, and you end up with
over one thousand different models of flashlights to collect. They
come in a wide variety of styles,
shapes and sizes. The flashlight
field includes tubular, lanterns,
figural, novelty, litho, etc. At present, over forty-five different categories of flashlights have been
identified as collectible. For further information we recommend
consulting the *Flashlight Collectors of America*, see Clubs and
Newsletters. Our advisor, Bill
Utley, is listed in the Directory
under California.

Bond, 1930, nickel-plated brass, 2
D cells, NM ....................**15.00**
Bright Star Pen Light, 2 AA cells,
NM ...................................**7.00**
Chase Vest Pocket, nickel-plated
hinged bottom, slide switch,
3", EX ............................**22.00**
Delta Buddy Flashlight Lantern,
1919, adjustable focus, 2 D
cells, VG ........................**10.00**
Eveready, Candle #1653, cast
metal base, painted candle, 2
C cells, VG .....................**28.00**

**Flashlights from the turn of the century. All are rare, no established values.**

Eveready, Candle #1654, Art Deco style, milk glass globe, 1932, EX+ .................................**32.00**

Eveready, Cigarette Case Vest Pocket Light #6992, 3 AA cells, 1914, EX ................**16.00**

Eveready, Lantern #4702, nickel, round, 1916, EX .............**29.00**

Eveready, Liberty Daylo Box Lantern #3661, gun-metal finish, 1919, EX+ ..........**25.00**

Eveready, Masterlite Table Model #2238, milk glass globe, 1935, EX+ .................................**32.00**

Eveready, Vest Pocket Light #6982, silverplated, 3 AA cells, 1912, EX ................**32.00**

Eveready, Wood Light, oak, black, 1911, VG+ ......................**55.00**

Eveready, 1904 Vest Pocket, nickel plate, ruby push-button switch, EX+ .............**18.00**

Eveready/Daylo #2631, nickel plated, bull's-eye lens, 2 D cells, 1917, VG ................**15.00**

Franco, Vest Pocket Light, green glass, button switch, EX+ .**20.00**

Jack Armstrong Light, black, 1 D cell, EX+ .........................**22.00**

Kwik-Lite, all nickel, unscrews at middle, 2 C cells, EX .....**12.00**

Ray-O-Vac, Sportsman, ribbed, 2 D cells, 1960, EX .............**7.00**

Seiss, Bike Light, 1 D cell, MIB ..........................**22.00**

# Florence Ceramics

Produced in California during the 1940s and '50s, these lovely figurines of beautiful ladies and handsome men have become items of much collector interest. Boxes, lamps, planters, and plaques were also made, but on a much smaller scale. Values are based on size, rarity, intricacy of design and decoration. Refer to *The*

*Collector's Encyclopedia of California Pottery* by Jack Chipman (Collector Books) for more information.

Betsy & David, gold & white, pr ............................**150.00**

Blue Boy ............................**300.00**

Camille, brown dress .........**165.00**

Charles, white w/gold trim, 8½" .**95.00**

Chinese boy & girl, gold & white, pr ..................................**150.00**

Chinese girl, black & white flowerpot ................................**50.00**

Choir Boy, 6" ........................**45.00**

Delores, green dress ...........**110.00**

Dutch girl, planter, green dress .**90.00**

Elaine, 6" ..............................**75.00**

**Elizabeth, 6x8", $275.00.**

Jim, 6¼" ...............................**70.00**

Lillian, tan dress .................**80.00**

Linda Lou, 8" ........................**95.00**

Memories, green & burgundy .**225.00**

Pat, yellow dress ...............**195.00**

Rhett ....................................**175.00**

Rose Marie, blue dress .......**175.00**

Sarah, gray, 7½" ..................**75.00**

Scarlett, green dress ............**75.00**

Sue, green dress ..................**75.00**

Wendy, planter, 6" ...............**50.00**

# Frankoma

Since 1933 the Frankoma Pottery Company has been producing dinnerware, novelty items, vases, etc. In 1965 they became the first American company to produce a line of collector plates. The body of the ware prior to 1954 was a honey tan that collector's refer to as 'Ada clay'. A brick red clay ('sapula') was used from then on, and this and the colors of the glazes help determine the period of production. Refer to *Frankoma Pottery, Value Guide and More*, by Susan N. Cox, our advisor for this category. She is listed in the Directory under California.

Ashtray, fish, 1962-76, #T-8, 7" **.20.00**
Bookends, Charger Horse, Ada clay, Black Onyx, #420, pr ....**195.00**
Bowl, 4-leaf clover, #223, 6" **.10.00**
Christmas card, 1965 ...........**60.00**
Christmas plate, 1968 ..........**65.00**
Cup, Lazybones, Clay Blue, 5-oz .................................**6.00**
Flower holder, elephant, #180 **.150.00**
Honey jar, Beehive, Ada clay, #803, 12-oz .....................**30.00**
Horseshoe, Ada clay, #167 .....**5.50**
Jug, Golda's Corn advertising, dated 1951 .....................**35.00**
Lazy Susan, Wagon Wheel, Woodland Moss, #94FC .........**65.00**
Mug, Wagon Wheel, Prairie Green, 12-oz ....................**4.50**
Mug, 1976 Bicentennial, Uncle Sam ................................**15.00**
Planter, mallard duck, Woodland Moss, 9½" .......................**12.00**
Salt & pepper shakers, milk cans, Sapulpa clay, pr .............**15.00**
Salt & pepper shakers, Plainsman, Onyx Black, sm, pr ........**11.00**
Salt & pepper shakers, Tepee, green, 3", pr ...................**12.50**
Sculpture, Circus Horse, red clay, Desert Gold ...................**75.00**
Sculpture, Swan, Rosetone, miniature ......................**50.00**

**Sculpture, Indian Bowl Maker, Ada clay, $90.00.**

Teapot, Mayan Aztec, red clay, Woodland Moss, 6-cup ..**17.50**
Trivet, Spanish Iron, 6" sq .........**12.00**
Vase, collector; V-10, Morning-Glory Blue, white interior, 11½" ..............................**40.00**
Vase, ringed cylinder, #72, 10½" ..........................**12.50**
Wall pocket, cowboy boot, white ..........................**10.00**

# Fruit Jars

Some of the earliest glass jars used for food preservation were blown, and corks were used for seals. During the 19th century, hundreds of manufacturers designed over 4,000 styles of fruit jars. Lids were held in place either by a wax seal, wire bail, or the later screw-on band. Jars were usually made in aqua or clear, though other colors were also used. Amber jars are popular with collectors, milk glass jars are rare, and cobalt and black glass jars often bring $3,000.00 and up if they can be found! Condition, age, scarcity and unusual features are also to be considered when evaluating old fruit jars.

Acme (on shield w/stars & stripes), clear, 1-qt ..........**1.50**
American (NAGCo), porcelain lined, aqua, rare, 1-qt ...**28.00**
Atlas EZ Seal, aqua, rare, 48-oz ...............................**15.00**
Atlas EZ Seal, blue, 1-qt ......**15.00**
Atlas EZ Seal, clear, ½-pt ......**4.00**
Atlas Strong Shoulder Mason, green, rare, 1-pt ............**20.00**
Ball Eclipse, wide mouth, clear, ½-gal ..............................**12.00**
Ball Ideal, blue, ½-gal ..........**12.00**
Ball Improved Mason's Patent 1858 (on 4 lines), aqua, 1-pt ...................................**20.00**
Ball Sanitary Sure Seal, blue, 1-qt ...................................**8.00**
Beechnut (Nut & Leaf), clear, no lid, ½-pt ...........................**6.00**
Canadian King (in shield), wide mouth, clear, rare, 1-qt .**24.00**
Clark's Peerless, aqua, 1-qt ...**8.00**
Decker's Victor Mason City Iowa, clear, 1-qt .......................**20.00**
Doolittle (block letters), sun-colored amethyst, rare, 1-qt ........**42.00**
Garden Queen, clear, 1-qt ......**8.00**
Gem, aqua, ½-gal .................**10.00**
Green Mountain CA Co (in circle), aqua, 1-qt ......................**15.00**
Hazel Atlas EZ Seal, light aqua, 1-qt .................................**12.00**
Keystone (Improved), aqua, 1-qt ...............................**18.00**
Klines Pat'd Oct 27 63 (on blown stopper), aqua, rare, 1-qt .......**120.00**
Mason CFJ Improved, aqua, midget ............................**20.00**
Mason's BGCO Improved, aqua, rare, 1-qt ........................**55.00**
Mason's Cross Improved, aqua, 1-pt ..................................**12.00**
Mason's Keystone Patent Nov 30th 1858, aqua, midget ........**30.00**

Mason's Patent Nov 30th 1858 S&R (on base), aqua, ½-gal ......**15.00**
Mason's 2 Patent Nov 30th 1858, aqua, ½-gal ....................**12.00**
Mason's 25 Patent Nov 30th 1858, aqua, 1-qt ......................**30.00**
Midland Mason, clear, 1-qt ....**6.00**
MJ Co (base), aqua, 1-qt ......**25.00**
Pine Deluxe, clear, 1-pt ..........**8.00**
Quick Seal, clear, 1-pt ............**2.50**
Safe Seal, clear, 1-pt ..............**3.00**
Standard (arched), aqua, 1-qt .**25.00**

**Sun/Trade Mark, aquamarine, pint, $135.00.**

Swayzee's Improved Mason, aqua, 1-pt ..................................**25.00**
Trademark Banner Registered (in banner), clear, 1-qt ........**10.00**
Trademark Keystone Registered, clear, 1-pt ........................**7.50**
Victory (in shield on milk glass lid), clear, 1-qt .................**8.00**
Whitney Mason Pat'd 1858, aqua, 1-qt .................................**20.00**

# Gambling Collectibles

By collecting gambling memorabilia, you can immerse yourself in gambling and still have the odds in your favor. Prices have risen steadily and future interest looks auspicious as countless hard-pressed government units look to legalized gambling as a painless revenue source.

In evaluating these items, add a premium for: (1) equipment rigged for cheating; (2) items bearing the name of an old-time gambling saloon or manufacturer, particularly of the American West (e.g., Will & Finck, San Francisco; Mason, Denver; Mason, San Francisco), as signed and named pieces are worth at least 50% more than unsigned ones; (3) items typically found in American gambling halls of the middle and late 19th century (parlor game items of whist, bezique, cribbage, bridge, pinochle, etc., are not as valuable as those of faro, poker, craps, roulette, etc.); and (4) gambling supply catalogs which are dated and have many large, colorful pages and good graphics.

Not listed here but of interest to many gambling collectors are a myriad of objects with gambling/playing card motifs: paintings and lithographs, ceramics, jewelry and charms, postcards, match safes, cigarette lighters, casino artifacts (ashtrays, swizzle sticks, etc.), souvenir spoons, tobacco tins, cigar box labels, song sheets, board games, etc. Values given here are for items in fine condition. Our advisor for this category is Robert Eisenstadt, who is listed in the Directory under New York.

Book, Fools of Fortune by John Philip Quinn, 1890, EX .**150.00**
Book, Foster's Practical Poker by RF Foster, 1905, EX ....**100.00**
Book, Official Rules of Card Games, Hoyle, US Playing Card Co, annual ............**10.00**
Card press, wooden box w/loose boards & threaded wooden dowel ..............................**75.00**
Card shuffler/dealer, automatic, 1940s, 5x5x5", common .**20.00**
Cardpress, mahogany w/petit point design, ca 1880 ..**275.00**
Catalog, Blue Book, KC Card Co, 50+ pages, 1930s-60s, any, from $20 to ....................**50.00**
Catalog, Club & Casino Equipment, HC Evans & Co, 1935, 64 pages, EX ................**150.00**
Chip, bone, plain, solid color, set of 100 .............................**15.00**
Chip, bone w/design or color border, 1mm thick, set of 100 .....**50.00**
Chip, bone w/engraving, 2-3mm thick, set of 100 .............**75.00**
Chip, casino; Castaways...Las Vegas, $25, green w/black & yellow, 1963 ...................**60.00**
Chip, Catalin or marbleized Bakelite, red, yellow & green, set of 100 .............................**30.00**
Chip, clay, embossed, inlaid or engraved, each, from $1 to .**3.00**
Chip, clay, plain, solid color, set of 100 ................................**10.00**
Chip, clay or metal, w/casino name, minimum value ....**3.00**
Chip, clay w/molded design, set of 100 ................................**15.00**
Chip, clay w/painted engraving, set of 100 ......................**25.00**
Chip, clay w/white plastic inlay, set of 100 ......................**30.00**
Chip, dealer; clay w/goat head in relief, ea .........................**50.00**
Chip, dealer; clay w/jackpot cup in relief, ea .........................**50.00**

Chip, plastic, wood or rubber, no design, set of 100 .............**5.00**
Chip, scrimshawed ivory, marked 5 or 25, ea ......................**30.00**
Chip, scrimshawed ivory w/concentric circle design ......**10.00**
Chip, scrimshawed ivory w/quatro or floral design, ea ........**25.00**
Chip rack, marbleized Bakelite, ice-block type, 3x4x7", no chips ...............................**75.00**
Chip rack, marbleized Bakelite, ice-block type, 3x4x7", w/200 chips .............................**150.00**
Chip rack, wood chest w/lid & pull-out rack, no chips, minimum value .....................**70.00**
Chip rack, wood Lazy Susan (carousel) type, cover, no chips ............**10.00**

**Clay chips, top: Stachelberg Cigars & Silver Age Rye Whiskey, ca 1900, lot of 31, $150.00; bottom: etched images of playing cards, horses, eagles & animals, ca 1900, lot of 66, $85.00.**

Counter, mother-of-pearl, etched, elliptical, 1½", 1mm thick .**4.00**
Counter, mother-of-pearl, relief carving, 2½", 3mm thick .**35.00**
Dice, ivory, ⅝", pr .................**55.00**
Dice, poker; celluloid, card symbols on sides, set of 5 ....**10.00**
Dice cage, felt-lined cardboard, thin wire & metal ..........**25.00**
Dice cage, hide drums, heavy chrome, 9x14" .............**300.00**
Dice cup, ivory ....................**100.00**
Dice cup, leather ..................**15.00**
Faro dealing box, metal, open top, spring for cards, minimum value ............................**200.00**
Faro layout, cloth attached to wood board, 40x16x1", minimum value ...................**375.00**
Keno goose, polished walnut bowl between posts, 13x24" ..**600.00**
Match safe, sterling w/engraved playing card etc, 1900s, from $100 to .........................**300.00**
Needlepoint card table cover w/gambling & card images, minimum value ...........**100.00**

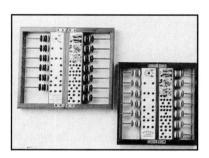

**Pharo casekeepers, one by Cowper Mfg., the second by Mason & Co., ca 1900, EX, from $450.00 to $500.00.**

Playing cards, faro; poker size w/sq edges, set of 52, minimum value......................**50.00**
Roulette pocket watch, 1 spinning hand, red & blk #s, 1900s, minimum value............**100.00**

171

Roulette wheel, black Bakelite wheel & bowl, 9" ...........**25.00**
Roulette wheel, 10" wood bowl w/wheel & simple design ..............**100.00**
Roulette wheel, 24" wood bowl w/elaborate inlays & veneer, chrome trim .................**600.00**

# Games

The ideal collectible game is one that combines playability (i.e., good strategy, interaction, surprise, etc.) with interesting graphics and unique components. Especially sought are the very old games from the 19th and early 20th centuries as well as those relating to early or popular TV shows and movies. As always, value depends on rarity and condition of the box and playing pieces. Our games advisor is Phil McEntee, who is listed in the Directory under Pennsylvania.

Air Trix, Milton Bradley, 1976, G+ .....................................**5.00**
Alien, Parker Brothers, 1979, EX ...............................**25.00**
All in the Family, Milton Bradley, 1972, EX .........................**20.00**
American Dream, Milton Bradley, 1972, VG ..........................**4.00**
Analysis, TransOgram, 1967, M ................................**10.00**
Baretta the Street Detective Game, Milton Bradley, 1976, VG .....................................**8.00**
Barnabas Collins, Milton Bradley, 1969, EX .........................**48.00**
Barney Miller & the 12th Precinct, Parker Brothers, 1977, VG ..........................**8.00**
Battlestar Galactica, Parker Brothers, 1970s, VG ......**15.00**
Beat the Clock, Milton Bradley, 1969, EX .........................**10.00**

Bionic Crisis Six Million-Dollar Man, Parker Brothers, 1976, VG .....................................**5.00**
Bird Watcher Game, Parker Brothers, 1958, MIB .....**48.00**
Black Beauty, TransOgram, 1958, EX ...................................**39.00**
Boake Carter's Star Reporter Game, Parker Brothers, 1937, VG+ .................................**60.00**
Bullwinkle Hide 'n Seek, Milton Bradley, 1961, EX .........**85.00**
Bullwinkle's Super Market Game, Whitman, 1970s, VG .....**45.00**
Captain Gallant, TransOgram, 1955, VG .......................**18.00**
Careers, Parker Brothers, 1965, EX ...................................**9.00**
Charlie Brown's All Stars, Parker Brothers, 1965, NM ......**16.00**
Charlie's Angels, Milton Bradley, 1977, EX .......................**18.00**
Chatty Games, Mattel, 1962, VG ..............................**26.00**
Checkered Game of Life, repro of original 1866 Milton Bradley, 1970, M .........................**12.50**
Cheyenne, Milton Bradley, 1958, G ....................................**10.00**
Chiclets Gum Village, Hasbro, 1969, M .........................**38.00**
Children's Hour, Parker Brothers, 1958, EX .........................**35.00**
Colombo Detective Game, Milton Bradley, 1973, VG ...........**8.00**
Crazy Clock, Ideal, 1964, EX .**35.00**
Creature Features Game of Horror, Athol Research Inc, 1975 ..**48.00**
Daniel Boone Trail Blazer, Milton Bradley, 1964, EX .........**57.00**
Dating Game, Hasbro, 1968, VG ..............................**5.50**
Dear Abby: A Game for Adults, Ideal, 1972, EX ...............**6.00**
Emergency Board Game, Milton Bradley, 1974, VG .........**22.00**
Family Feud, Milton Bradley, 1977, VG .........................**6.00**

**Munsters Card Game, Milton Bradley, #4531, 6x10", EX, $45.00.**

Felix the Cat, Milton Bradley, 1960, NM ........................**50.00**

Flintstones Brake Ball, Whitman, 1962, M ..........................**40.00**

Flying Nun, Milton Bradley, 1968, EX ..................................**55.00**

Game of the Stars, Milton Bradley, 1960, NM ........**18.00**

Gomer Pyle, TransOgram, 1960's, EX ..................................**45.00**

Great Escape, Ideal, 1967, EX .**35.00**

Gunsmoke, Lowell Toy Co, no date, EX ..........................**30.00**

Hardy Boys Mysteries, Universal Studios, 1977, NM ..........**7.50**

Hi Bid, 3M, 1969, EX ...........**12.00**

Hollywood Squares, Western, 1967, EX ........................**15.00**

Hot Wheels Wipe Out, Mattel, 1968, M ..........................**50.00**

HR Puf 'n stuf, Milton Bradley, 1971, EX ........................**38.00**

Huckleberry Hound, TransO-gram, 1961, EX .............**38.00**

Hungry Henry, Ideal, 1969, EX .**10.00**

I Dream of Jeannie, Milton Bradley, 1965, NM ........**44.00**

James Bond 007, Milton Bradley, 1964, EX ........................**26.00**

James Bond 007, Victory Game Co, NM ..........................**40.00**

King Kong, Milton Bradley, 1966, EX ..................................**40.00**

Know the Stars & Planets, Milton Bradley, 1960, M ..........**36.00**

Kukla & Ollie, Parker Brothers, 1962, NM ........................**60.00**

Let's Make a Deal, Ideal, 1970s, EX ..................................**15.00**

Lone Ranger, Milton Bradley, 1966, NM ......................**25.00**

Lost in Space, Milton Bradley, 1965, EX ........................**54.00**

Mary Poppins' Carousel Game, Parker Bros, VG ............**25.00**

McHale's Navy, TransOgram, 1962, EX ........................**45.00**

Men of Destiny: A Game of Our Presidents, Milton Bradley, 1956, VG ........................**12.50**

Milton the Monster, Milton Bradley, 1966, EX .........**40.00**

Mystery Date, Milton Bradley, 1965, EX ........................**40.00**

Navy Battle Game, Exclusive Playing Card Co, no date ......**50.00**

Newlyweds Game, Hasbro, 1967, M ..................................**15.00**

Perry Mason, TransOgram, 1959, EX ...................................**48.00**
Pink Panther, Milton Bradley, 1969, EX .........................**21.00**
Quick Draw McGraw Private Eye, Milton Bradley, 1960, EX .**20.00**
Rin Tin Tin, TransOgram, 1955, NM .................................**45.00**
Robinson Crusoe, Lowell, 1962, NM .................................**30.00**
Silly Safari, Topper, 1960, EX .**62.50**
Slap Trap, Ideal, 1967, VG ..**20.00**
Sorry, Parker Brothers, 1972, EX ...................................**10.00**
Stadium Checkers, Schaper, 1952, EX .................................**22.00**
Stars on Stripes Football Game, 1941, VG .........................**56.00**
State Capitols, Parker Brothers, 1966, VG ..........................**9.00**
Tank Battle Game, Milton Bradley, 1975, complete, NMIB .............................**38.00**
Time Tunnel, Ideal, 1966, NM .**135.00**
Touring, Parker Brothers, 1947 ............................**18.00**
Tripoly, Cadaco, 1965, EX ....**15.00**
Uncle Wiggly, Parker Brothers, 1967, NM .......................**25.00**

**Voyage to the Bottom of the Sea, Milton Bradley, #4538, VG, $40.00.**

Voyage to the Bottom of Sea, Milton Bradley, 1964, NM ..**65.00**
Wyatt Earp, TransOgram, 1958, EX ...................................**38.00**

# Gas Station Collectibles

From the invention of the automobile came the need for gas service stations, who sought customers through a wide variety of advertising methods. While this is a specialized area of advertising collecting, there is a wide scope of items available as well as crossover attraction to both automobilia and advertising collectors. For further information we recommend *Huxford's Collectible Advertising* by Sharon and Bob Huxford. Our advisor is Peter Capell, who is listed in the Directory under Illinois. See also Automobilia; Ashtrays.

Attendant's hat, Esso, black w/white, red & blue logo, VG .........**50.00**
Banner, canvas, Kendall Motor Oil, Change Now..., 1930s-40s, EX+ .....................**100.00**
Banner, canvas, lg Esso gas pump, The Gold Pump Is Here! 83x36", EX ...........**20.00**
Banner, plastic, shows lg Tiger, Put a Tiger In Your Tank!, 83x42", EX ...................**110.00**
Clock, dome atop display panel, Champion..., 1920-30, 14x26", VG ...............................**110.00**
Clock, plastic, Oilzum Motor Oil & Oilzum man, 16x16", EX+ ...........................**160.00**
Display, Anco Blades & Arms, features windshield wiper, 19x15", EX .....................**10.00**
Display, cardboard, 2-sided, X-Powder for Leaky Radiators, VG .................................**150.00**
Display, Permalube Oil, demonstrates need for oil change, 7x6", VG ........................**50.00**
Display cabinet, metal, glass front, Auto Lite Spark Plugs, 19x13", VG ....................**45.00**

Display rack, tin, Goodyear Tires, 1950s-60s, 25", NM ......**80.00**

Emblem, Mobil's red winged horse, porcelain, 36", EX+ ......**450.00**

Gas globe, orange & black Phillips 66 shield on white, 13½" dia, EX ................................**130.00**

Gas globe, red, white & blue Skelly Supreme on white, 13½" dia, EX ................**130.00**

Gas globe, white ribbed shell w/Shell lettered in red, late 1920s, EX ....................**350.00**

Gas nozzle, brass, McDonald, from $35 to ....................**50.00**

Gas pump, cast iron, milk glass globe, model #555, 65", EX+ ..............................**240.00**

Grease bucket, Red Giant Oil Co, no lid, 1930s-40s, 10-lb, 7", EX ................................**180.00**

Map holder, metal, Calso Gasoline Road Maps, 3-tier, 20x13", EX ..................................**95.00**

Map holder, painted metal, Gulf Tourgide (sic) Service, 18x9", VG ..................................**90.00**

Oil can, Gargoyle Mobiloil B, 1920-31, 5-gal, 14½", VG ........**70.00**

Oil can, Kendall Gear Lube, sm bail handle, 5-gal, 16x11" dia, VG ....................................**5.00**

Oil can, Veedol Motor Oil, Heavy Duty Plus, 1-qt, 5½x4" dia, EX+ ................................**40.00**

Oil can, w/handle & spout, Swingspout Measure Co, 1930s-50s, EX ................**40.00**

Salt & pepper shakers, AMLICO, 1960s, VG, pr ................**95.00**

Salt & pepper shakers, Esso, 1960s, VG, pr ................**25.00**

Sign, glass, Hastings Steel-Vent Piston Rings, 1935-45, 11x26½", VG ..................**35.00**

Sign, metal, vertical DELCO, battery below, 1940s-50s, 70x18½", EX ..................**35.00**

**Sign, Oilzum, painted metal, ca 1949, 10x16", EX+, $500.00 to $600.00.**

Sign, painted die-cut metal, 2-sided, Tydol man, 14x9¾", VG ................................**175.00**

Sign, porcelain, 2-sided, Phillips 66 shield, 1950s, 30x30", EX ................**145.00**

Sign, pump; die-cut porcelain, Ethyl Super 100, 1940, 12x11", EX ....................**95.00**

Sign, pump; elongated hexagon w/Sea Chief above Texaco star logo, EX ................**200.00**

Sign, pump; porcelain, shows the Sinclair dinosaur, 11" dia, G ..........................**250.00**

Sign, tin, man at GAS pump, vertical OILS above, 1950s, 30x12", VG ..................**400.00**

Spark plug service machine, metal, Champion, 40x14½x10½", VG ..............................**150.00**

Thermometer, Prestone Anti-Freeze, Set, Safe, Sure, 1950s, 36x9", VG ..........**95.00**

Tire gauge storage canister, Schrader, 1920-30, 15x6" dia, EX ..............................**160.00**

## Geisha Girl Porcelain

More than sixty-five different patterns of tea services were exported from Japan around the turn of the century, each depicting geishas going about the everyday activities of Japanese life. Mt. Fudji is often featured in the background. Geisha Girl Porcelain is a generic term collectors use to identify them all. Refer to *The Collector's Encyclopedia of Geisha Porcelain* by Elyce Litts (Collector Books) for more information.

Biscuit jar, Court Lady, cobalt, J#1 ...................................**65.00**
Bowl, berry; Boat Festival, cobalt, #35, individual ...............**10.00**
Bowl, Cherry Blossoms, red-orange edge, 7½" ...........**40.00**
Bowl, Pointing D, red-orange w/gold buds, 5¼" ...........**12.00**
Butter pat, Flower Gathering B, red-orange, 3¼" ...............**8.00**

**Cocoa pot, Lantern B, 9½", from $45.00 to $55.00.**

Cocoa pot, Parasol B: Torii & Parasol, cobalt w/gold, #16 ....**55.00**
Creamer, Long-Stemmed Peony, blue w/gold, slim, #20 ...**10.00**

Cup & saucer, AD; Torii & Parasol, red-orange w/gold, #19 ..**20.00**
Cup & saucer, chocolate; Garden Bench C, cobalt border .**15.00**
Cup & saucer, tea; Bamboo Trellis, red w/gold ...............**22.00**
Cup & saucer, tea; Flower Gathering A, blue w/gold lacing .**18.00**
Pin tray, Boat Dance, green w/gold lacing, 5x3" ........**14.00**
Plate, Bird Cage, red-orange w/gold, 6" ......................**12.00**
Plate, Checkerboard, cobalt, scalloped, 6½" ......................**20.00**
Plate, Fan A, red-orange, #19, 4¼" .................................**10.00**
Plate, Inside the Teahouse, apple green, swirl fluted, 8½" .**35.00**
Teapot, Kite A, brown w/gold ..**25.00**

# GI Joe

Toys are the big news of the nineties, as far as collectibles go, and GI Joe's vie for a spot near the top of many a collector's want list.

Introduced by Hasbro in 1964, 12" GI Joe dolls were offered in four basic packages: Action Soldier, Action Sailor, Action Marine, and Action Pilot. A Black figure was included in the line, and there were representatives of many nations as well. Talking dolls followed a few years later, and scores of accessory items such as vehicles, guns, uniforms, etc., were made to go with them all. Even though the line was discontinued in 1976, it was evident the market was still there, and kids were clamoring for more. So in 1982, Hasbro brought out the 'little' 3¾" GI Joe's, each with his own descriptive name. Sales were unprecedented. You'll find the small figures easy to find, but most of them are 'loose' and played with. Collectors prefer old store stock still in the original packaging; such examples are worth from two to four times more than those without the package.

**Sea Adventurer, flocked red hair and beard, NMIB, $150.00 to $170.00.**

## 12" Figures and Accessories

Air Police helmet, EX ...........**45.00**
Ammo pouch, US, EX .............**3.00**
Bazooka, EX .........................**20.00**
Billy club, EX .........................**5.00**
British gas mask, EX ...........**30.00**
Canteen & cover, Hasbro, EX .**16.00**
Cap, pilot, blue, EX .............**14.00**
Detonator, EX ........................**7.00**
Diver bouy, EX .......................**4.00**
Duffle bag, VG ........................**7.00**
Figure, Copter Rescue, blue flight suit, boots & camera, EX .**75.00**
Figure, Intruder Commander, #8050, M (EX card) .....**150.00**
Figure, Karate, #7372, M (EX box) ...............................**95.00**
Figure, Landing Signal Officer, #7626b, MOC ...............**112.00**
Figure, Marine Flame Thrower, complete w/accessories, EX ...................**185.00**
Figure, Scuba Diver, complete w/accessories, VG+ .....**175.00**

Figure, Talking Action Soldier, complete w/accessories, EX .**149.00**
Figure, Volcano Jumper, #7344, M (EX+ box) ........................**75.00**
First Aid Box, EX .................**12.00**
German holster, EX .............**10.00**
Ice Sabre, Artic Assault Vehicle, Hall of Fame, 1991, MIP .**15.00**
Knuckle knife, EX ..................**5.00**
Machete & scabbard, EX .......**9.00**
Medic crutch, EX ....................**8.00**
Paddle, black, EX ...................**6.00**
Rescue raft, green plastic pack, compass, 2-pc paddle, EX ......**35.00**

## 3¾" Figures and Accessories

**Adventure Team Action Pack, Flying Rescue, 1971, NMIB, $45.00.**

Battle Copter, w/Ace, blue, 1992, MIP ................................**10.00**
Cobra Jet ATV, 1985, MIP .....**8.00**
Figure, Alpine, 1985, MIP ...**37.00**
Figure, Barbecue, 1985, MIP .**36.00**
Figure, Beachhead, 1986, MIP .**33.00**
Figure, Capt Grid-Iron, 1990, MIP ................................**11.00**
Figure, Cobra FANG, w/accessories, 1983, EX ...........**10.00**
Figure, Flash, 1982, EX (original package) ........................**65.00**
Figure, Flint, 1985, M (NM package) ................................**45.00**
Figure, Heavy Duty, 1991, MIP .**10.00**
Figure, Knockdown, English, 1989, MIP ....................**22.00**
Figure, Mercer, 1990, MOC .**12.00**

Figure, Scoop, w/accessories, 1989, EX ..........................**6.00**

Figure, Swampmasher, 1988, M (NM package)..................**14.00**

Mudbuster, 1993, EX (original package) ..........................**8.00**

Night Boomer, Attack Jet, 1989, MIP ...............................**55.00**

Slugger (no driver), w/accessories, 1984, EX ........................**12.00**

Vector Jet, Battle Force 2000, 1987, MIP ......................**25.00**

# Glass Animals and Figurines

Nearly every glasshouse of note has at some point over the years produced these beautiful models, some of which double for vases, bookends, and flower frogs. Many were made during the 1930s through the '50s and '60s, and these are the most collectible. But you'll also be seeing brand new examples, and you need to study to know the difference. A good reference to help you sort them all out is *Glass Animals of the Depression Era* by Lee Garmon and Dick Spencer (Collector Books). See also Boyd.

Alley cat, ruby slag, Fenton, 11" ..............................**75.00**

American Eagle head, bookends, frosted crystal, Paden City, 7½", pr ........................**300.00**

Bashful Charlotte, crystal, Cambridge, 11½" ................**175.00**

Bird, dark medium blue, Viking, 1960s, 9½" .....................**25.00**

Bridge hound, dark emerald, Cambridge, 1¾" ............**30.00**

Bulldog, black w/rhinestone eyes, Westmoreland, ca 1910, 2½" ......................**35.00**

Bulldog, cobalt w/yellow eyes, red leather collar, Summit, 8½" ...............................**175.00**

Bunny, amber, New Martinsville, 1" .....................................**60.00**

Butterfly, candle holder, ruby carnival, Fenton, 1992 souvenir, 7½" ....................................**50.00**

Butterfly, light blue, Westmoreland, 2½" wingspread ...**22.00**

Cat, green, Viking, 1960s, 8" .**55.00**

Cat, light blue, Fostoria, 3¾" .**35.00**

Clydesdale, Ultra Blue, Imperial, 5½" ...............................**125.00**

Colt, balking, Horizon Blue, Imperial ................................**50.00**

Colt, kicking, crystal, Heisey, 1941-45, 4" ...................**195.00**

Colt, standing, crystal, Fostoria, 1940-43, 3⅞" ..................**45.00**

Dancing lady, flower frog, pink satin, New Martinsville, 1940s, 6¼" ....................**450.00**

Deer, sitting or standing, crystal or blue, Fostoria ............**45.00**

Donkey, custard, hand-painted daisies, Fenton, 1978, 4½" .**45.00**

Dove, head down, crystal, Duncan, 11½" long ............**175.00**

Draped lady, Dianthus (peachblo), satin finish, Cambridge, 8½" ...............................**125.00**

Duckling, standing, crystal, Heisey, 1947-49, 2½x1¾" long ...**150.00**

Elephant, caramel slag, Imperial, 4" .........................................**45.00**

Fish, candlesticks, crystal, Heisey, 1941-48, 5", pr ............**350.00**

Fish, red w/amberina tail & fins, Fenton, 2½" ...................**55.00**

Fish canape plate, teal, Imperial ...............................**25.00**

Frog, lemon, Fostoria, 1971-73, 1⅞" ...............................**35.00**

Goldfish, vertical, crystal, Fostoria, 1950-57, 4" ..............**95.00**

Goose, light blue, Paden City, ca 1940, 5" .........................**125.00**

Goose Girl, green or amber, LE Smith, 1950s, 6" ............**50.00**

Happiness bird, Fenton, 6½" long, depending on color, from $18 to ......................................**35.00**

Hen, crystal, New Martinsville, 5" ......................................**65.00**

Hen, milk glass, Imperial, 4½" .**35.00**

Heron, crystal, Cambridge, 12" ...........................**125.00**

Horse, bookend, rearing, black, LE Smith, 8", ea ............**65.00**

Horse, head up, crystal, New Martinsville, 8" .............**95.00**

Horse head, bookend, crystal, Heisey, 1937-55, 6⅞", ea ............**120.00**

Hunter/Woodsman, crystal w/sq base, New Martinsville, 7⅜" .............................**95.00**

Kemple rooster, head down, crystal, hollow base, KR Haley, 9½" ...................................**35.00**

Llama/sitting fawn, crystal, KR Haley, 6" .........................**20.00**

Madonna, frosted crystal, Heisey, 1942-56, 9" .....................**95.00**

Madonna prayer light, custard satin, Fenton, 1978, 6" ..**35.00**

Mallard, wings up, Horizon Blue, Imperial .........................**30.00**

Pelican, pink, Fostoria, commemorative 1991 ...................**55.00**

Penguin, crystal, Viking, 1960s, 7" ......................................**25.00**

**Tiffin, pheasant, in rare wisteria color, 7½", minimum value, $450.00.**

Pheasant, head turned, pale blue, Paden City, 12" ............**200.00**

Pheasant, paperweight, head down, crystal, Tiffin, 8¾x13" long ...............................**300.00**

Polar bear, topaz, Fostoria, 1935-36, 4⅝" ..........................**125.00**

Pony stallion, caramel slag, Imperial, 4" .............................**55.00**

Rabbit, amber, Viking, 1960s, 6½" ...................................**35.00**

Rabbit, paperweight, crystal, Heisey, 1941-46, 2¾x3¾" long .............................**150.00**

Robin, crystal, Westmoreland, no base, 3¼" long ................**20.00**

Rooster, Epic; avocado, Viking, 1960s, 9½" .....................**55.00**

Rooster, head down, crystal, Paden City, 8¾" .............**85.00**

Rooster, vase, crystal, Heisey, 1939-48, 6¼" ..................**85.00**

Rose lady, amber satin, Cambridge, 9¾" ...................**300.00**

Sassy Susie Cat, black w/painted trim, Tiffin, ca 1900, 11" .**175.00**

Scolding bird, Cathay Crystal, original issue, signed, Imperial, 5" ..........................**175.00**

Scottie dog, bookend, caramel slag, Imperial, 6½" ......**100.00**

September Morn Nymph, moonstone w/flower frog base, Fenton, 1928, 6" ................**135.00**

Sparrow, head down, crystal, LE Smith, 1950s, 3½" .........**15.00**

St Francis, silver mist, Fostoria, 1957-73, 13½" ..............**350.00**

Starfish, candle holders, almond, Westmoreland, 5" wide, pr .........................**30.00**

Swan, Crown Tuscan, Cambridge, 3" .....................................**50.00**

Swan, crystal, Cambridge, 3" .**25.00**

Swan, light emerald, Cambridge, 10" ..................................**125.00**

Swan, painted milk glass, LE Smith, ca 1930s, 8½" .....**45.00**

Swan, solid back, crystal, Duncan,
2¾x3" .............................**25.00**
Swan, 2-color sweetheart shape,
New Martinsville, 5", from
$15 to .............................**25.00**
Swordfish, crystal, Duncan,
5x3¼" ...........................**300.00**
Sylvan swan, crystal, Duncan,
10x11" wingspread ........**65.00**
Tiger, paperweight, jade green,
Imperial, 8" ...................**85.00**
Turtle, flower block w/7 holes, crystal,
Westmoreland, 4" long ......**55.00**

# Glass Knives

Glass fruit and cake knives,
which are generally between 7½"
and 9¼" long, were made in the
United States from about 1920 to
1950. Distribution was at its greatest in the late 1930s and early
1940s. Glass butter knives, which
are about 5" to 6½", were made in
Czechoslovakia. Colors of the fruit
and cake knives generally follow
Depression Glass dinnerware: crystal, light blue, light green, pink, and
more rarely amber, forest green,
and white (opal). The range of butter knife colors is even broader,
including bicolors with crystal.
Glass knives are frequently found
with hand-painted decorations.
Many were engraved with a name
and occasionally with a greeting.
Original boxes are frequently found
along with a paper insert extolling
the virtues of the knife and describ-
ing its care. As long as the original
knife shape is maintained and the
tip is not damaged, glass knives
with nicked or reground blades are
acceptable to collectors. Our advisor, Adrienne Escoe, is listed in the
Directory under California. See also
Clubs and Newsletters.

Aer-Flo, crystal, 7½" .............**25.00**
Aer-Flo, Forest Green, 7½" **200.00**
BK, pink, 9¼", min. value ..**150.00**
Block, green, 8¼" ..................**30.00**
Block, pink, 8¼" ..................**30.00**

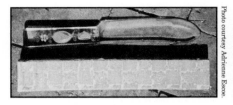

**Crystal with hand-painted lemons,
in original lemon-decorated box,
from $22.00 to $25.00.**

Dagger, crystal, 9¼" .............**75.00**
Dur-X, 3-leaf, blue, 8½" ........**22.50**
Dur-X, 3-leaf, pink, 8½" .......**20.00**
Dur-X, 5-Leaf, blue, 9⅜" ......**20.00**
Dur-X, 5-leaf, blue, 8½" ......**20.00**
Dur-X, 5-leaf, crystal, 8½" ...**12.00**
Plain handle, green, 8½" ......**30.00**
Plain handle, green, 9¼" ......**25.00**
Plain handle, pink, 9¼" ........**22.00**
Rose Spray, crystal, 8½", w/origi-
nal Christmas box .........**16.00**
Rose Spray, pink, 8½" ........**140.00**
Steel-ite, crystal, 8¼" ...........**16.00**
Stonex, green, 8¼" ...............**55.00**
Thumbguard (Westmoreland),
crystal, hand-painted flowers,
9¼" ................................**30.00**
Thumbguard (Westmoreland), crys-
tal, ribbed handle, 9¼" .**150.00**
Vitex (3-Star), blue, 8½" .......**20.00**
Vitex (3-Star), blue, 9¼" .......**20.00**
Vitex (3-Star), pink, 9¼", w/orig
box .................................**17.00**
Westmoreland, thumb guard, ribbed
handle, crystal, 9¼" .........**90.00**

# Glass Shoes

While many glass shoes were
made simply as whimseys, you'll
also find thimble holders, per-

fumes, inkwells, salts, candy containers, and bottles made to resemble shoes of many types. Our advisor for this category is Libby Yalom, author of *Shoes of Glass*; see the Directory under Maryland for information on how to order her book. See also Degenhart.

Baccarat, crystal, 1½" medallion design, 1956-70s, 3½x10" long ..............................**150.00**
Beads & wire, multicolor glass, ca 1900-20, 3" long .............**42.00**
Blue, horizontal ribbed bow, 1¾x4¾" long ..................**75.00**
Bottle, cat in shoe, milk glass, marked Souvenir..., ca 1900, 4" long ............................**49.00**
Bottle, cobalt, marked Adrien Maurin, 3 indented lace holes, 5¼" .**90.00**
Bottle, green man's shoe, horizontal ridges & laces, 2½x3½" ...**55.00**
Bottle, roller skate w/6 wheels, crystal, marked Depose, 2⅞" long ................................**75.00**
Cane/Chinese, blue, on toboggan, ca 1880s, 2¼x5⅛" long .**135.00**
Cane/Chinese, crystal, pointed toe, ca 1800s, 1¾x4¾" long ...**38.00**
Cuffed boot w/spur heel, black, thumbprint depression in sole, 4" long ..................**48.00**

Daisy, crystal, alligator on vamp & back, w/advertising, 5⅞" long ...............................**42.00**
Daisy & Button, amber, stippled spur, clear toe & heel, 3¾x3⅝" .**120.00**
Daisy & Button, apple green, 2½x4½x11¾" ................**130.00**
Daisy & Button, gold, open front, no holes, mesh sole, 5⅞" long ........................**45.00**
Daisy & Button, milk glass, solid heel, horizontal ribbed, hollow sole ..........................**40.00**
Diamond, crystal, plain front, vertical ribs at top edge, 7½" long ...............................**125.00**
Diamond, crystal, stippled bow & streamers, mesh sole, 5⅞" long ................................**39.00**
Diamond, green bootee, horizontal ribs, hollow sole, 2¼x4⅛" long ...............................**40.00**
Diamond Block, crystal, high-button roller skate w/12 buttons, 4¼" ................................**51.00**
Duncan, crystal or blue w/mesh sole, lg ..........................**45.00**
Duncan, vaseline w/Daisy & Button perfume bottle, medium ........................**75.00**
Dutch, crystal, 3 horizontal ribs on vamp, 3 buttons, 3⅛x7" long ...............................**45.00**

**Italian, red with metallic flakes and thread streaks, 2½x5⅝", $85.00.**

Finecut, laced up to bottom of finely stippled 'V,' diamond mesh sole ........................**45.00**

Frosted, baby w/gold painted laces, bow & florals, hollow sole, 2⅜" ..........................**30.00**

Frosted crystal, bow w/streamers to sole, 2⅝x5½" ...............**40.00**

High-button, crystal, horizontal ribs, hollow sole, solid heel, pr .....................................**95.00**

Milk glass, embossed flower & vine on sides, hollow sole, solid heel .........................**32.00**

Millefiore, frosted w/crystal heel & ruffled edge, elongated toe ...................................**60.00**

Spatter, dark red, white, green & yellow, crystal leaf & rigaree, 3" ...................................**100.00**

Spun glass, clear, 2¼x2" ......**15.00**

Stippled, crystal slipper, sm flat bow, 2½x4⅜" long ..........**20.00**

# Golf Collectibles

The scope of golf collectibles is so vast and varied that each enthusiast has his/her own unique perspective of the hobby. Not only do they seek the clubs, tees, bags and miscellaneous other items actually used on the greens, but many also appreciate artwork portraying golfers, games, advertising material, books, ceramics, bronzes, figurines — in short, anything related to the sport in about any way, shape, or form! Our advisor for this category is Pat Romano; he is listed in the Directory under New York. For more information we recommend *The Encyclopedia of Golf Collectibles* by John M. Olman and Morton W. Olman (Books Americana).

Autographed photo, Ben Hogan, from $100 to ................**150.00**

Autographed photo, Bobby Jones, from $350 to ...............**750.00**

Book, club history (depends on age & popularity), from $20 to ...................................**150.00**

Decanter, w/silver overlay of golfer in knickers, from $125 to ...................................**400.00**

Dinnerware, china w/painted golf scene, Royal Doulton, from $50 to ...........................**700.00**

Dish, baby's, Bunnykins, shows bunnies playing golf, from $125 to ..........................**175.00**

Golf ball, common mesh design, 1920-40s, from $5 to .....**20.00**

Golf ball, w/autograph, modern, from $10 to ....................**50.00**

Golf club, iron w/common wood shaft, from $10 to ..........**15.00**

Golf club, wood w/common wood shaft, from $20 to ..........**30.00**

Medal, from USGA or PGA Tournaments, 1930s-1950s, from $25 to ...........................**150.00**

Program, Master's Tournament, 1930s, from $125 to .....**200.00**

Program, US Open, 1930s, from $75 to ...........................**150.00**

Statue, bronze of famous golfer, depending on size, from $150 to ...............................**8,000.00**

# Graniteware

A collectible very much in demand by those who enjoy the 'country' look in antiques, graniteware (also called enameled ware) comes in a variety of colors, and color is one of the most important considerations when it comes to evaluation. Purple, brown, or green swirl pieces are generally higher than gray, white, or blue, though blues and blue-swirled examples are popular. Decorated pieces are unusual, as are salesman's samples and miniatures; and these also bring top prices. For more information refer to *The Collector's Encyclopedia of Granite Ware, Colors, Shapes, and Values, Vols I and II,* by Helen Greguire (Collector Books).

Ashtray, white, red & cream w/advertising for Whirlpool, 8" dia, NM ..................**155.00**

Bowl, blue & white splash mottle, black trim, 5¼" dia, M ..**60.00**

**Bowl, blue solid with advertising, 5½", VG, $85.00.**

Bowl, mixing; yellow & white swirl, black trim, 6x12¼" dia, NM ................................**40.00**

Bowl, mixing/serving; blue & white mottle, black trim, 10" dia, NM ........................**115.00**

Bread pan, lavender cobalt & white swirl, cobalt trim, oval, rare, G+ ......................**225.00**

Bread pan, light blue & white mottle, black trim, 9¾" long, G+ ...............................**395.00**

Chamber pot, large blue & white swirl, black trim & handle, 6½", EX ......................**255.00**

**Chamber pot, blue and white, 8" diameter, G, $150.00.**

Coaster, large blue & white swirl, cobalt trim, rare, 4" dia, M ..........................**275.00**

Coffeepot, blue & white swirl, black trim, handle & knob, 7½", M ..........................**425.00**

Colander, blue & white mottle, 2 handles, 3½x10" dia, G+ ........**295.00**

Cup, blue & white swirl, black trim, 1¾x4¼" dia, NM .**110.00**

Cup, child's, blue & white swirl, black trim & handle, 2x3" dia, G+ ..........................**175.00**

Cup, yellow & white swirl, black trim, 2x3⅛" dia, M ........**45.00**

Cup & saucer, blue & white splash-type mottle, black trim, G+ ........................**135.00**

Cup & saucer, gray & white mottle, labeled Pearl Enameled Ware, M ........................**125.00**

Egg plate, blue & white swirl, cobalt trim & handles, 9" dia, G+ ...............................**210.00**

Funnel, squatty shape, grayish blue & white mottle, black handle, NM ..................**165.00**

Match holder, green, marked Crawford Ranges, 4 molded feet, 1¼", NM ...............**115.00**

Measure, cobalt & white mottle, black trim & riveted handle, 3", G+ ...........................**365.00**

Mug, aqua & white swirl, cobalt trim, riveted handle, 5x4" dia, G+ ...............................**85.00**

Mug, brown & white swirl, riveted handle, miniature, G+ ..**465.00**

Pie plate, lavender blue & white mottle, black trim, 9⅞" dia, G+ ....................................**65.00**

Pie plate, red & white mottle, cobalt trim, 9¾" dia, NM .........**400.00**

Pitcher, water; aqua & white swirl, cobalt trim, 10¼", M ..................................**395.00**

Pitcher, water; blue & white swirl, black trim & handle, 9¾", G+ .........................**265.00**

Plate, light blue & white mottle, 9¾" dia, G+ ....................**65.00**

Platter, cobalt & white mottle, dark blue trim, oval, 16" long, G+ ................................**295.00**

Pudding pan, red & white swirl, cobalt trim, 3x8½" dia, G+ ........................**400.00**

Sauce pan, black & white swirl, black trim & handle, 5½", NM ...............................**255.00**

Sauce pan, cream w/green trim & handle, ribbed sides, 4x7½" dia, M .............................**60.00**

Soap dish, hanging; blue & white mottle, scalloped edge, 4x6", G ...................................**160.00**

Soup ladle, blue & white mottle, black riveted handle & trim, NM ................................**65.00**

Spoon, blue & white mottle, 15⅜" long, G+ .........................**75.00**

Spoon, gray mottle, marked Extra Agate Nickel-Steel Ware, 12" long, NM ........................**45.00**

Sugar bowl, squatty shape, gray mottle, 5⅛", G+ ...........**295.00**

Tea strainer, gray & white swirl, screened bottom, 4" dia, G+ ........................**165.00**

Tea strainer, red & white mottle, perforated bottom, 4" dia, G ............................**165.00**

Teakettle, blue & white swirl, black wooden bail handle & trim, 7", G+ .................**395.00**

Teakettle, light blue & white swirl, seamed body, wooden bail, 8", G+ ...................**170.00**

Teakettle, light gray mottle, riveted ears, wooden bail, 6½", G+ ...............................**195.00**

Teakettle, pink, black trim & handle, seamed body, 7¼", G+ ......**55.00**

Teapot, squatty shape, blue & white mottle, black trim, 5", NM ...............................**265.00**

Wash basin, child's, pink & white mottle, cobalt trim .......**395.00**

# Griswold

During the latter part of the 19th century, the Griswold company began to manufacture the finest cast-iron kitchenware items available at that time. Soon after they became established, they introduced a line of lightweight, cast-aluminum ware that revolutionized the industry. The company enjoyed many prosperous years until its closing in in the late 1950s. Look for these marks: Seldon Griswold, Griswold Mfg. Co., and Erie. Refer to *Griswold Cast Collectibles* by Bill and Denise Harned and *Griswold*, published by L-W Book Sales for more information.

Brownie cake pan, #9 ...........**90.00**
Cake mold, rabbit ..............**275.00**
Cornstick pan, #273 ...........**115.00**
Dutch oven, #10, Tite Top, large emblem .........................**75.00**
Dutch Oven, #8, Tite Top .....**38.00**
Golf ball pan, #14, 10⅜x7" .**115.00**
Griddle, #9, rectangular ....**125.00**
Muffin pan, #17 ....................**75.00**
Platter, #34 ...........................**20.00**
Roaster, #9 .........................**275.00**

Skillet, #0 ...........................**150.00**
Skillet, #10, large emblem, no
smoke ring ....................**70.00**
Skillet, #8, deep, w/lid .......**150.00**

**Tea-size corn stick pan #262,
marked Griswold, Erie, PA, U.S.A,
with original box, $150.00.**

Waffle iron, Heart & Star pat-
tern ...........................**160.00**
Wheat stick pan, #27 .........**185.00**

# Hall

Most famous for their extensive lines of teapots and colorful
dinnerwares, the Hall China

Company still operates in East
Liverpool, Ohio, where they were
established in 1903. Refer to *The
Collector's Encyclopedia of Hall
China* by Margaret and Kenn
Whitmeyer (Collector Books) for
more information. For listings of
Hall's most popular dinnerware
line, see Autumn Leaf. See also
Clubs and Newsletters.

Acacia, drip coffeepot, all china,
Radiance .....................**175.00**
Arizona, creamer, Eva Zeisel .**8.00**
Arizona, platter, Eva Zeisel,
17" ..............................**27.00**
Beauty, casserole, Thick Rim .**37.00**
Blue Blossom, bowl, Thick Rim,
8½" ................................**40.00**
Blue Blossom, cookie jar, Sun-
dial ...........................**290.00**
Blue Bouquet, bowl, cereal; D-
style, 6" .........................**11.00**
Blue Bouquet, plate, D-style,
9" ..............................**14.00**
Blue Bouquet, sugar bowl, Boston
style, w/lid, D-style .......**22.00**
Blue Garden, jug, loop handle .**110.00**

**Caprice, designed by Eva Zeisel: Serving bowl, $6.00; Dinner
plate, $5.00; Cup and saucer, $6.00.**

Blue Garden, water bottle, Zephyr style ..............................**225.00**

Bouquet, candlestick, Eva Zeisel, 4½", ea ............................**30.00**

Bouquet, egg cup, Eva Zeisel .**28.00**

Buckingham, onion soup, w/lid, Eva Zeisel .......................**30.00**

Cameo Rose, bowl, vegetable; w/lid ................................**45.00**

Cameo Rose, teapot, 8-cup ...**60.00**

Caprice, creamer, Eva Zeisel .**9.00**

Carrot/Golden Carrot, batter bowl, Five Band ............**65.00**

Clover/Golden Clover, casserole, Radiance ........................**42.00**

Crocus, bowl, flat soup; D-style, 8½" ..................................**22.00**

Crocus, plate, D-style, 8¼" .....**9.00**

Crocus, teapot, Boston shape, D-style ..........................**175.00**

Fantasy, coffeepot, Eva Zeisel, 6-cup ..............................**50.00**

Fantasy, creamer, floral decal, New York ........................**25.00**

Fantasy, gravy boat, Eva Zeisel ..........................**22.00**

Fantasy, sugar bowl, floral decal, w/lid ................................**37.00**

Fern, casserole, Eva Zeisel ..**25.00**

Fern, teapot, Eva Zeisel, 6-cup .**60.00**

Five Band, batter bowl, red or cobalt ..............................**55.00**

Five Band, syrup, colors other than red or cobalt ..........**50.00**

Flareware, bowl, Gold Lace, 6" .**7.00**

Flareware, casserole, Radial, 3-pt ..................................**8.00**

Frost Flowers, bowl, fruit; footed, lg ....................................**30.00**

Frost Flowers, sugar bowl, w/lid ............................**14.00**

Golden Glo, creamer, Boston .**12.00**

Golden Glo, mug, Irish coffee .**20.00**

Harlequin, bowl, vegetable; square, Eva Zeisel, 8¾" .**16.00**

Harlequin, egg cup, Eva Zeisel .**25.00**

Heather Rose, bowl, Flare shape, 7¾" ..................................**12.00**

Heather Rose, gravy boat, w/underplate .................**18.00**

Holiday, ladle, Eva Zeisel ....**13.00**

Holiday, salt & pepper shakers, Eva Zeisel, pr ................**17.00**

Meadow Flower, bowl, Thick Rim, 8½" ..................................**27.00**

Meadow Flower, Teapot, Streamline ................................**300.00**

Medallion, creamer, Lettuce ..**25.00**

Medallion, teapot, colors other than Lettuce or Ivory ..**110.00**

Monticello, bowl, vegetable; w/lid ..............................**32.00**

Monticello, sugar bowl, w/lid .**14.00**

Morning Glory, bowl, Thick Rim, 6" ....................................**13.00**

Morning Glory, teapot, Aladdin ...................**125.00**

Mount Vernon, creamer .........**9.00**

Mount Vernon, plate, 9¼" ......**6.50**

Mulberry, bowl, fruit; Eva Zeisel, 5¾" ....................................**5.00**

Mulberry, casserole, Eva Zeisel, 1¼-qt ..............................**32.00**

Mums, coffeepot, Medallion .**70.00**

Mums, salt & pepper shakers, handled, pr ...................**32.00**

Orange Poppy, bowl, cereal; 6" .**15.00**

Orange Poppy, bread box, metal ..........................**45.00**

Pastel Morning Glory, bowl, 9¼" ..................................**30.00**

Pastel Morning Glory, gravy boat ..............................**27.00**

Peach Blossom, cup & saucer, Eva Zeisel ..............................**9.50**

Peach Blossom, jug, Eva Zeisel, 3-qt ..................................**30.00**

Pert, bean pot, Chinese Red, tab handles .........................**50.00**

Pert, teapot, Cadet (blue), 3-cup ..............................**22.00**

Pinecone, butter dish, Tomorrow's Classic, Eva Zeisel ........**55.00**

Pinecone, plate, Eva Zeisel, 9¼" ....................................**8.50**

Primrose, cake plate ............**15.00**

Primrose, sugar bowl, w/lid **.14.00**
Radiance, bowl, ivory, 9" ......**11.00**
Radiance, salt & pepper shakers, canister style, red or cobalt, pr ....................................**50.00**
Red Poppy, bowl, soup; flat, 8½" ..............................**18.00**
Red Poppy, canister set, round, 5-pc ................................**40.00**
Red Poppy, plate, 9" .............**11.00**
Rose White, baker, French fluted ............................**30.00**
Rose White, creamer, Pert ...**14.00**
Royal Rose, custard, straight sides ................................**13.00**
Royal Rose, pitcher, ball jug, #3 ................................**50.00**
Serenade, bean pot, New England #4 ..................................**85.00**
Serenade, platter, 13¼" ........**22.00**
Serenade, teapot, New York .**110.00**
Silhouette, bowl, oval, D-style **.27.00**
Silhouette, creamer, Medallion ...........................**15.00**
Silhouette, plate, D-style, 8¼" **.8.50**
Spring, ashtray, Eva Zeisel ....**6.00**
Spring, ladle, Eva Zeisel ......**12.00**
Springtime, pitcher, ball jug #3 ................................**50.00**
Springtime, plate, D-style, 9" ..**9.50**
Sundial, coffeepot, red or cobalt, individual size ...............**50.00**
Sundial, teapot, colors other than red or cobalt, 6-cup ......**110.00**
Sunglow, ashtray, Eva Zeisel **.5.00**
Sunglow, cup & saucer, Eva Zeisel ...............................**7.00**
Teapot, Airflow, canary or turquoise, 8-cup ............**50.00**
Teapot, Aladdin, red or cobalt, oval opening ................**125.00**
Teapot, Albany, rose w/gold label ............................**65.00**
Teapot, Football, red or cobalt **.650.00**
Teapot, Hollywood, maroon, 6-cup ..................................**40.00**
Teapot, Manhattan, colors other than red or cobalt ..........**55.00**

**Teapot, Philadelphia, cobalt with gold decoration, 6½", $60.00 to $75.00.**

Teapot, New York, decal decoration, 3-cup ....................**130.00**
Teapot, Parade, canary ........**30.00**
Teapot, Streamline, red or cobalt ..........................**110.00**
Tulip, bowl, flat soup; D-style, 8½" ..................................**18.00**
Tulip, casserole, Thick Rim **.40.00**
Tulip, plate, D-style, 10" ......**25.00**
Wild Poppy, cookie jar, Five Band ...........................**225.00**
Wild Poppy, tea tile, 6" .........**50.00**
Wildfire, bowl, cereal; D-style, 6" ....................................**10.00**
Wildfire, cup & saucer, D-style **.16.50**
Yellow Rose, bowl, round vegetable; D-style, 9¼" .......**22.00**
Yellow Rose, creamer, Norse **.15.00**
Yellow Rose, plate, D-style, 9" **.9.00**

# Hallmark

Since 1973 the Hallmark Company has made Christmas ornaments some of which are today worth many times their original price. Our suggested values reflect the worth of those in mint condition and in their original boxes. Refer to *The Ornament Collector's Price Guide, Hallmark's Ornaments and Merry Miniatures,*

Photo courtesy Rosie Wells.

**Merry Miniatures, (#7) Kitten with green hat, 150 HPF-1013, 1978-81, $30.00; (#8) Turkey, gold with white dot in each eye, 150 TPF-12, 1978-79, $95.00; (#9) Pilgrim Boy with corn, TPF-1003, 1978-86, $32.00; (#10) Pilgrim Girl w/flowers, 150 TPF-1016, 1978-86, $30.00; (#11) Joy Elf, 150 XPF-1003, 1978, $120.00; (#12) Mrs. Snowman with purse, 150 XPF-23, 1978-79, $105.00.**

by our advisor, Rosie Wells, for more information. She is listed in the Directory under Illinois. See also Clubs and Newsletters.

A Christmas Carol Collection: Merry Carolers, QX 479-9, 1991 ...............................**55.00**

Baby's First Christmas, QX 551-2, 1993 ...............................**30.00**

Betsy Clark, XHD 110-2, 1973 .**135.00**

Brass Carousel, QLX 707-1, 1984 .............................**95.00**

Candy Apple Mouse, QX 470-5, 1985 .............................**55.00**

Candyville Express, QX 418-2, 1981 ...........................**100.00**

Checking It Twice, QX 158-4, 1980 ...........................**200.00**

Christmas Wonderland, QX 221-9, 1983 .............................**95.00**

Cowboy Snowman, QX 480-6, 1982 .............................**55.00**

Cycling Santa, QX 435-5, 1982 .......................**145.00**

Dad, QX 462-9, 1987 ...........**42.00**

Frosty Friends Third in Series, QX 452-3, 1982 ...........**265.00**

Frosty Friends: A Cool Yule, QX 137-4, 1980 .................**620.00**

Hallmark Merry Miniatures: Joy Elf, XPF 1003, 1978 ....**120.00**

Hallmark Merry Miniatures: Kitten, HPF 1013, 1978-81 ..**30.00**

Hallmark Merry Miniatures: Mrs Snowman, XPF 23, 1978-79 ........................**105.00**

Hallmark Merry Miniatures: Pilgrim Boy, TPF 1003, 1978-86 ........................**32.00**

Hallmark Merry Miniatures: Pilgrim Girl, TPF 1016, 1978-86 ...................................**30.00**

Hallmark Merry Miniatures: Turkey, TPF 12, white dot in eye, 1978-79 ..................**95.00**

Happy Holidays Kissing Ball, QX 225-1, 1976 .................**230.00**

Here Comes Santa: Santa's Motorcar, QX 155-9, 1979 .....**600.00**

Holiday Jingle Bell, QX 404-6, 1986 .............................**48.00**

Mary's Angels: Buttercup, QX 407-4, 1988 ...................**40.00**

Metro Express, QLX 727-5, 1989 ...........................**76.00**

Norman Rockwell, QX 106-1, 1974 ...............................**80.00**
Nostalgia Ornaments: Santa & Sleigh, QX 129-1, 1975 .**255.00**
Shuttlecraft Galileo, QLX 733-1, 1992 .............................**32.00**
Welcome Santa, QX 477-3, 1990 ...........................**30.00**

# Halloween

Halloween items are fast becoming the most popular holiday-related collectibles among today's collectors. Although originally linked to pagan rituals and superstitions, Halloween has long since evolved into a fun-filled event; and the masks, noisemakers, and jack-o'-lanterns of earlier years are great fun to look for. Our advisor for this category is Pamela E. Apkarian-Russell, the Halloween Queen; she is listed in the Directory under New Hampshire.

Book, Dennison Bogie ..........**35.00**
Box, Black children riding jelly bean on paper label, ca 1910, lg ...................................**400.00**

Box, orange children on black paper label on wood, ca 1910, sm ..................................**225.00**
Candlestick/sconce, litho tin, black cat on orange, ca 1940, pr ....................................**150.00**
Candy container, figural plastic black cat, Rosen Mfg, RI, 1950s .............................**30.00**
Candy container, mechanical witch eating cat, German, rare, 5½x5" ...............**1,800.00**
Candy container, orangy red cat stands on sm wood box, 1910, 2" .....................................**250.00**
Candy container, pumpkin-head witch, glass w/tin lid, 4¾", minimum value ...........**300.00**
Candy container, pumpkin policeman, glass w/metal lid, original paint ......................**300.00**
Clicker, tin, black owl on orange ground, USA ..................**15.00**
Costume, Cherry Merry Muffin, Collegeville, 1989, NM w/original box ..................**8.00**
Costume, ET the Extra-Terrestrial, Collegeville, 1982, MIB ..............................**15.00**
Costume, Lord Darth Vader, Ben Cooper, 1977, EX, w/original box ..................................**30.00**

**Cardboard party hat, 12" long, NM, $35.00.**

189

Costume, Princess Leia, Ben Cooper, 1981, original card, NM ...............................**25.00**

Costume, Spider Boy, Ben Cooper, 1979, MIB ......................**14.00**

Costume, Spiderman, Ben Cooper, 1972, MOC ....................**15.00**

Costume, Wendy the Witch, Ben Cooper, 1979, MIB ........**14.00**

Costume, 6 Million-Dollar Man, cloth, Ben Cooper, NM w/original box ............................**45.00**

Decoration, Jack-O'-Lantern face, paper & metal, wire handle, USA, 1902 ...................**400.00**

Decoration, Jack-O'-Lantern man, pulp paper, all orange, ca 1940, 12" ........................**75.00**

Doorstop, girl trick-or-treater, painted cast iron, ca 1900, original .....................**1,000.00**

Doorstop, girl trick-or-treater, painted cast iron, reproduction .................................**25.00**

Dress, orange & black crepe paper w/sewn-on bats & cats ..**28.00**

Funglasses, bat shaped, MOC .**35.00**

Jack-O'-Lantern, pulp paper, 1950s, 4½" ......................**40.00**

Lantern, black cat face, papiermache w/insert, 6" ......**120.00**

Lantern, glass pumpkin w/metal trim, battery operated, Japan, 1940s .................**35.00**

Lantern, glass pumpkin w/metal trim, battery operated, Japan, 1980s ...................**7.00**

Light bulb, painted glass Jack-O'-Lantern, fits Christmas string .............................**35.00**

Light bulb, painted milk glass skull, fits standard Christmas string .....................**40.00**

Lollypop holder, hard plastic figural, Rosen of RI, from $15 to ...................................**50.00**

Magazine paper doll, Halloween Betty Bonnet ................**15.00**

Noisemaker, plastic handle, Chein ...............................**6.00**

Noisemaker, tin litho tamborine, black cat on orange, USA, 1930s ..............................**35.00**

Noisemaker, tin shaker type, black cats & witches on orange, USA ..................**10.00**

Noisemaker, wood handle, Chein ...........................**20.00**

Pin, enameled pumpkin or lavender pewter, Barrel's Gift .**30.00**

Pinball machine, Haunted House, 3 levels w/music ..........**800.00**

Pitcher, Salem witch, Hampshire pottery .........................**500.00**

Postcard, real photo of Halloween party, 1920 ....................**22.00**

Postcard, Tuck Series #174, any of set of 12, ea ...................**12.00**

Postcard, Whitney, w/black cats ..**12.00**

Standee, black cat dressed as person, embossed cardboard, German, 20" .................**50.00**

Standee, Elvira for Coors beer, cardboard, 1991, life-size .....**100.00**

Store display, witch & cat w/Happy Halloween sign, papier-mache, 40" .......**375.00**

Tea set, Jack-O'-Lantern, miniature, 6-pc .....................**300.00**

# Harker

One of the oldest potteries in the East Liverpool, Ohio, area, the Harker company produced many lines of dinnerware from the late 1920s until it closed around 1970. Refer to *A Collector's Guide to Harker Pottery* by Neva W. Colbert (Collector Books) for more information.

Bowl, Colonial Lady, footed .**15.00**

Bowl, fruit; Chesterton (Teal), 5" ...................................**4.00**

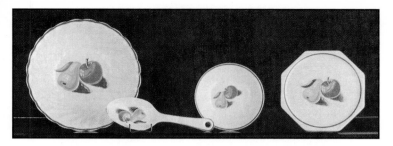

Red Apple II: Bowl, 9", $30.00; Spoon, $25.00; Sauce dish, $6.00; Hot plate, $28.00.

Bowl, mixing; Brim ..............**24.00**
Bowl, mixing; English Ivy ...**30.00**
Bowl, soup; Sea Fare, w/lid ...**8.00**

**Cameo Rose platter, 13", $12.50.**

Casserole, Amy .....................**18.00**
Cookie jar, Dainty Flower, Zephyr
   style ................................**32.50**
Cream & sugar bowl, Ivy .......**14.00**
Cream & sugar bowl, Newport .**5.00**
Cream & sugar bowl, Sweetheart
   Rose ...............................**13.00**
Creamer, Rosebud ..................**8.00**
Cup, Black-Eyed Susan .........**3.50**
Cup, Bouquet ..........................**4.00**
Cup & saucer, Stone China ....**4.00**
Custard, Jewel Weed .............**8.00**
Jug, Lisa, Regal style ...........**18.50**
Jug, Oriental Poppy, Regal style .**65.00**
Pie baker, Blue Grapes ........**15.00**
Pie baker, Dainty Flower .....**45.00**
Pie lifter, Delft ......................**14.00**
Plate, Alpine, 6" .....................**5.00**
Plate, chop; Chesterton (Yellow),
   lug handles, 10" .............**10.00**

Plate, dinner; Black-Eyed
   Susan ...........................**8.00**
Plate, dinner; Lemon Tree .....**8.00**
Plate, dinner; Teal Rose .........**8.00**
Plate, luncheon; Bamboo .......**8.00**
Plate, luncheon; Coronet, green or
   blue ...............................**7.00**
Plate, luncheon; Game Birds .**7.00**
Plate, luncheon; Ivy ..............**7.00**
Plate, luncheon; Windmill .....**7.00**
Platter, Carla, plain, oval, 12" .**7.00**
Platter, Pheasants, oval .......**22.50**
Platter, Wheat, Olympic style .**10.00**
Saucer, Heritance, 6" .............**2.00**
Spoon, Godey ........................**17.50**
Teapot, Amy ..........................**12.00**
Tidbit, Country Cousins, 1-tier .**5.00**
Tumbler, Green Blush, w/pink
   roses ...............................**12.50**

# Hartland

Hartland Plastics Inc. of Hartland, Wisconsin, produced a line of western and historic horsemen figures during the 1950s, which are now very collectible. Using a material called virgin acetate, they molded such well-known characters as Annie Oakley, Bret Maverick, Matt Dillon, and many others, which they painted with highest attention to detail. In addition to these, they made a line of sports greats as well as religious statues. See also Clubs and Newsletters.

**Babe Ruth, slightly discolored, replaced bat, EX+, $245.00.**

Brave Eagle w/horse, complete w/accessories, EX ........**135.00**
Buffalo Bill, w/horse & accessories, 9½", M, from $250 to ...**275.00**
Bullet, #700, EX+ .................**80.00**
Cochise, on semi-rearing pinto horse, complete, MIB ..**200.00**
Dale Evans & Buttermilk, w/original tag, 1950s, 9½", NM ......**200.00**
General Custer, w/horse & accessories, 9½", MIB ..........**200.00**
General George Washington, w/horse & accessories, 9½", MIB .............................**250.00**
Gil Favor, with horse, 5½", MOC .........................**60.00**
Horse, reddish brown w/white feet, 8" .............................**18.50**

Jim Hardie (Wells Fargo gunfighter), w/horse, 9½", EX .............**85.00**
Matt Dillon, w/horse, 5½", MOC, from $50 to ....................**85.00**
Paladin, w/horse, 5½", EX+ .**45.00**
Rifleman, w/horse, 5½", NM .**45.00**
Warren Spahn, off-white, EX+ ........................**175.00**
Wyatt Earp, w/horse & accessories, 9½", NM ...........**175.00**
Yogi Berra, full figure w/catcher's mask, NM ....................**325.00**

## Head Vases

Many of them Japanese imports, head vases were made

primarily for the florist trade. They were styled as children, teenagers, clowns, and famous people. There are heads of religious figures, Blacks, Orientals, and even some animals. One of the most common types are ladies wearing pearl earrings and necklaces. Refer to *Head Vases, Identification and Value Guide,* by Kathleen Cole (Collector Books) for more information.

Clown w/green top hat, lg red nose, ruffled collar, #9115, 6" ..**22.50**

Blond, w/feather hat, eyes closed, pearls, Inarco, #E-191/M/c, 5½" .................................**25.00**

Blond, w/hat, closed eyes, hand to face, lace collar, #2359, 6½" .................................**25.00**

Blond w/black hat w/gray bow, pearls, Napcoware, #C7496, 9½" .................................**50.00**

Blond w/bow right side of long hair, pearl earrings, green dress, 7" ........................**30.00**

Blond w/brown top hat, necklace, eyes closed, waving, 6½" .**25.00**

Blond w/green graduation hat & dress w/white collar, Shafford, 4½" ........................**20.00**

Blond w/hair pulled around front on left side, Inarco, #E6210, 6½" .................................**35.00**

Blond w/hat, eyes closed, hand to chin, necklace, Lefton's, #2251, 6" ........................**25.00**

Blond w/hat, eyes closed, hands to chin, pearls, Rubens, #495, 5¾" .................................**25.00**

Child w/polka-dot bow in hair, holds kitten, Enesco, 5½" .........**42.50**

Child w/wide-brimmed pink hat, lg shawl collar, gold trim, 3" ..........................**22.50**

Chinese lady w/white gold-trimmed hair, eyes closed, necklace, 6½" .................**25.00**

Chinese lady w/white headband, pink dress w/fan, gold lashes, 4¾" .................................**20.00**

Lady w/'60s flip hairdo, white collar, Inarco, #E2782, 6" ..**25.00**

Lady w/'60s flip hairdo w/bow, pearl necklace, Parma, #A172, 5½" .....................**20.00**

Lady w/curly white hair, low ruffle neckline w/bow, Relpo, #K1335, 8" .....................**35.00**

Lady w/green bow head band, hair on right side, Napcoware, #C8494, 7" ...........**30.00**

Lady w/hat, eyes closed, pearls, hand to face, Napco, #C3307C, 5½" ................**25.00**

Lady w/red phone to ear, white collar red trim, Nancy Pew, 6" .................................**25.00**

Lady yellow hat w/white bow, eyes closed, red hair, Japan, 5½" .................................**20.00**

**Little girl with umbrella, marked 'N,' 5", $55.00.**

# Hires

Did you know that Hires Root Beer was served to fairgoers at the Philadelphia Centennial in 1876? It was developed by Charles E. Hires, a druggist who experimented with roots and herbs to come up with the final recipe. The company originally chose the Hires boy as their logo, and if you'll study his attire, you can sometimes approximate a guess as to when an item he appears on was manufactured. Very early on he appeared in a dress, and from 1906 until 1914 it was a bathrobe. He sported a dinner jacket from 1915 until 1926. Most Hires memorabilia is still reasonably priced, but last year at auction the punch bowl (made by Mettlach) went for an unbelievable $20,000.00! Our advisors for this category are Donna and Craig Stifter; they're in the Directory under Illinois.

Booklet, Hires Puzzle Book of Unnatural History, 1910, 3¼x4", EX ......................**37.00**
Booklet, Legend of the Golden Chair, 1894, 20 pages, 3½x5", NM ................................**12.00**
Booklet, The Animals' Trip to Town, ca 1920s, 3½x5", NM ................................**16.00**
Bottle carrier, cardboard, Try 10-oz Bottles, Draft, NM ......**5.00**
Bottle topper, ...For Finer Flavors 5¢ lettered on flowers, 4x6", NM ................................**15.00**
Calendar, 1975, 8-pack & hand w/mug above full pad, M .**25.00**
Clock, glass lens, metal frame, Drink... on dot, numbered, round, EX ....................**275.00**
Decal, bottle cap, EX ............**10.00**

Display card, die-cut cardboard holds 3 bottles, 1930s, 9½x14", M ......................**25.00**
Dixie cup, waxed paper, 1960s, 4x3" dia, EX .....................**2.00**
Ice cream scoop, plastic, white w/lettering on handle, EX .......**10.00**
Menu board, tin, Drink... & bottle above chalkboard, 30x15", M ....................................**85.00**
Pocket mirror, Put Roses in Your Cheeks, gold border, oval, 2¾", EX ........................**225.00**
Puzzle book, EX ....................**35.00**
Sign, cardboard, Say! Drink... above farm boy, diagonal, 6x6", EX ......................**175.00**
Sign, cardboard stand-up, bottle & fireplace, 1940s, 18x12", EX ...................................**40.00**
Sign, embossed tin, Hires in Bottles, 1940s, 10x29½", NM .....**125.00**

**Sign, metal, 12x7", VG, $35.00.**

Sign, paper, icicles above Drink Real Oldtime... & mug, 14x11", M .......................**30.00**
Sign, paper, white, red & black, Drink Hires 5¢, 9x21", EX ..........**40.00**
Sign, tin, white on red, black & blue, R-J logo, 12" dia, M .........**90.00**
Syrup dispenser, counter clamp-on style, R-J label, 22", NM .....................**200.00**
Syrup dispenser, steel tank w/blue metal bracket, no top, 20", VG ..........................**80.00**
Thermometer, tin, Hires Root Beer, rounded ends, 17x5", EX+ ...............................**30.00**

Thermometer, tin bottle, 28",
EX ..............................**125.00**
Trade card, Drink Hires Root
Beer, Put Roses in Your
Cheeks, 1981, 3x5" ........**30.00**
Trade card, It's Time To Drink
Hires, EX .......................**20.00**

# Holly Hobbie and Friends

About 1970 a young home-
maker and mother, Holly Hobbie,
approached the American Greeting Company with some charming country-styled drawings of
children. Since that time over
four hundred items have been
made with almost all being
marked HH, H. Hobbie, or Holly
Hobbie. For further information
we recommend our advisor, Helen
McCale, listed in the Directory
under Missouri; see also Clubs
and Newsletters.

Book, The Art of Holly Hobbie, Ran-
dom House, 1986, EX .....**38.00**
Butter dish, Sharing Something
Good..., stoneware, 1980,
round ...............................**7.00**
Cake pan, half-figure Holly Hob-
bie, Wilton, 1975, w/booklet &
cookbook ........................**12.50**
Cup, Start Each Day in a Happy
Way, girl in blue, footed,
1973 .................................**7.00**
Cup, Today Can Be the Start of
Something Big, granite-
ware ................................**4.00**
Doll, marked Knickerbocker, 33",
MIB, minimum value ...**30.00**
Doll, marked Knickerbocker, 9",
MIB, minimum value ...**10.00**
Drinking glass, Holidays Are the
Happiest Days, Coke logo,
1978 .................................**2.00**

Figurine, girl on phone, porcelain, marked 600-HHF-20,
1974 ..............................**15.00**

Photo courtesy Helen McCale.

**Figurine, girl
with packages,
marked Deluxe
HHF 1, 1973,
$95.00.**

Figurine, Happy Hearts, girl
w/cat, Porcelain Miniatures
Series III ........................**12.50**
Figurine, One & Only, kneeling
ballerina, porcelain, minia-
ture ...............................**12.50**
Plate, Everyone Needs a Lazy
Day..., Classic Edition Series,
10" .................................**22.50**
Plate, For You Grandmother Just
Because You're Special, 4" .**5.00**
Plate, Friendship Makes the Rough
Road Smooth, 10" ...........**10.00**
Plate, It's a Star-Spangled Day..., Free-
dom Series, 1 of 6, 10" .......**15.00**
Plate, Kind & Good Is Mother-
hood, Mother's Day 1975,
10" .................................**10.00**
Plate, Love Is the Little Things You
Do, wavy edge, 1973, 7" ....**8.00**
Plate, Summer Is a Song Anyone
Can Sing, Four Seasons
Series, 6¼" .....................**25.00**
Tile, When You Fill Your Heart
w/Cheer, 1973, 6x6", w/wood
frame ...............................**5.00**
Tray, Holly & Heather in center,
painted metal, round ......**4.00**

Trinket box, Happiness Is..., girl w/cat, heart form, Made in Japan ..............................**6.50**

Vase, Happy Is the Home That Welcomes a Friend, ruffled top, 6" ..............................**6.00**

# Holt Howard

Ceramic novelty items marked Holt Howard are hot! From the late 1950s, collectors search for the pixie kitchenware items such as cruets, condiments, etc., all with flat, disk-like pixie heads for stoppers.In the sixties, the company designed and distributed a line of chickens — egg cups, napkin holders, salt and pepper shakers, etc. Items with a Christmas theme featuring Santa or angels, for instance, were sold from the '50s through the '70s, and you'll also find a line decorated with cats. Most pieces are not only marked but dated as well. Our advisor for this category is April Tvorak, listed in the Directory under Colorado.

Ashtray, wide-faced cat on plaid sq base, 4 corner rests, 1958 ....................**35.00**

Cookie jar, decorated w/embossed rooster ............................**80.00**

Cookie jar, Santa, 3-pc .......**145.00**

Egg cup, rooster figural .......**18.00**

Jar, Cherries, flat pixie head on lid w/cherry pick or spoon ...**45.00**

Jar, Honey, flat pixie head on brn stripes ............................**65.00**

Jar, Ketchup, flat tomato-head finial on lid, 1958 ..........**35.00**

Jar, Onions, flat onion-head finial on lid, 1958 ....................**35.00**

Napkin holder, rooster .........**12.00**

Salt & pepper shakers, decorated w/embossed rooster, pr .**20.00**

**Salt and pepper shaker set, marked, $25.00.**

Taper holder, Santa w/book, pr .**25.00**

# Homer Laughlin

Founded in 1871, the Homer Laughlin China Company continues today to be a leader in producing quality tablewares. Some of their earlier lines were made in large quantity and are well marked with the company name or HLC logo; collectors find them fun to use as well as to collect, since none are as yet very expensive. Refer to *The Collector's Encyclopedia of Homer Laughlin China* by Joanne Jasper and *The Collector's Encyclopedia of Fiesta* by Sharon and Bob Huxford (both published by Collector Books).

**Shapes: Republic 8" plate, Century 9" plate, Nautilus Eggshell cup, Liberty sugar bowl, Brittany sugar bowl, Debutante creamer.**

*Homer Laughlin China, An Identification Guide,* is another good reference; it is written by our advisor, Darlene Nossaman, who is in the Directory under Texas. See also Fiesta; Clubs and Newsletters.

## Blue Willow
**(1940s-50s pieces; prior years were made on a different shape)**

| | |
|---|---|
| Bowl, flat soup, 8" | **15.00** |
| Bowl, serving; oval or round | **30.00** |
| Bowl, 5" | **6.00** |
| Bowl, 5¾" | **8.00** |
| Casserole, w/lid | **45.00** |
| Creamer | **18.00** |
| Egg cup | **25.00** |
| Plate, 6¼" | **8.00** |
| Plate, 7¼" | **10.00** |
| Plate, 9¼" | **15.00** |
| Plate, 9¾" | **18.00** |
| Platter, 11" | **20.00** |
| Platter, 13" | **25.00** |
| Sauceboat | **30.00** |
| Saucer | **4.00** |
| Sugar bowl, w/lid | **20.00** |
| Teacup | **10.00** |
| Teapot | **75.00** |

**Blue Willow: Plate, 10", $18.00; Creamer, $18.00; Sugar bowl, $20.00.**

197

## Britanny Shape
### (available in Lady Alice, Emerald, Sylvan, and Hemlock)

Bowl, fruit; lg ...........................**5.00**
Bowl, fruit; sm ........................**3.00**
Bowl, rimmed soup ................**7.00**
Bowl, serving; round or oval .**10.00**
Casserole, w/lid ....................**30.00**
Creamer ...................................**8.00**
Egg cup ..................................**12.00**
Plate, chop; 13" dia ..............**20.00**
Plate, 10" ................................**8.00**
Plate, 6" ..................................**4.00**
Plate, 7" ..................................**5.00**
Plate, 8" ..................................**6.00**
Plate, 9" ..................................**8.00**
Platter, oval, 11" ...................**12.00**
Platter, oval, 13" ...................**14.00**
Sauce boat ............................**12.00**
Sauce boat liner .....................**8.00**
Saucer .....................................**3.00**
Sugar bowl, w/lid ..................**10.00**
Teacup ......................................**5.00**
Teacup, AD; w/saucer ...........**14.00**
Teapot ...................................**35.00**

## Century Shape
### (available in Briar Rose, Call Rose, Columbine, and English Garden)

Bowl, fruit; lg ...........................**7.00**
Bowl, fruit; sm ........................**5.00**
Bowl, serving .........................**15.00**
Bowl, soup ..............................**8.00**
Butter dish, w/lid .................**75.00**
Casserole, w/lid ....................**55.00**
Creamer ..................................**10.00**
Egg cup ..................................**18.00**
Plate, 10" ...............................**12.00**
Plate, 6" ..................................**5.00**
Plate, 7" ..................................**6.00**
Plate, 8" ..................................**8.00**
Plate, 9" ................................**10.00**
Platter, 11" ............................**15.00**
Platter, 13" ............................**20.00**
Sauce boat ............................**15.00**

Sauce boat, fast-stand ..........**20.00**
Saucer .....................................**3.00**
Sugar bowl, w/lid ..................**15.00**
Teacup ......................................**6.00**
Teacup, AD; w/saucer ...........**16.00**
Teapot ...................................**65.00**

## Debutante Shape
### (available in Blue Mist, Champagne, Gray Laurel, and Wild Grape)

Bowl, fruit; lg ...........................**6.00**
Bowl, fruit; sm ........................**4.00**
Bowl, serving .........................**12.00**
Bowl, soup ..............................**6.00**
Casserole, w/lid ....................**30.00**
Creamer ..................................**10.00**
Egg cup ..................................**12.00**
Plate, 10" ................................**8.00**
Plate, 6" ..................................**5.00**
Plate, 7" ..................................**5.00**
Plate, 9" ..................................**8.00**
Platter, 11" ............................**12.00**
Platter, 13" ............................**16.00**
Salt & pepper shakers, pr ....**12.00**
Sauce boat, fast-stand ..........**18.00**
Saucer .....................................**3.00**
Sugar bowl, w/lid ..................**12.00**
Teacup ......................................**5.00**
Teacup, AD; w/saucer ...........**14.00**
Teapot ...................................**35.00**

## Liberty Shape
### (available in Calirose, Dogwood, Greenbrier, and Statford)

Bowl, fruit; lg ...........................**5.00**
Bowl, fruit; sm ........................**3.00**
Bowl, serving .........................**12.00**
Bowl, soup ..............................**7.00**
Casserole, w/lid ....................**30.00**
Creamer ....................................**8.00**
Plate, 10" ................................**9.00**
Plate, 6" ..................................**4.00**
Plate, 7" ..................................**5.00**
Plate, 8" ..................................**7.00**
Plate, 9" ..................................**8.00**

| | |
|---|---|
| Platter, 11" | 12.00 |
| Platter, 13" | 14.00 |
| Sauce boat | 12.00 |
| Sauce boat liner | 7.00 |
| Saucer | 3.00 |
| Sugar bowl, w/lid | 12.00 |
| Teacup | 5.00 |
| Teapot | 35.00 |

**Nautilus Eggshell Shape
(available in Apple Blossom,
Nassau, Coronet, and Orchard)**

| | |
|---|---|
| Bowl, fruit; lg | 6.00 |
| Bowl, fruit; sm | 5.00 |
| Bowl, serving | 15.00 |
| Bowl, soup | 7.00 |
| Casserole, w/lid | 25.00 |
| Creamer | 10.00 |
| Plate, 10" | 9.00 |
| Plate, 6" | 4.00 |
| Plate, 7" | 5.00 |
| Plate, 8" sq | 7.00 |
| Plate, 9" | 8.00 |
| Platter, 11" | 15.00 |
| Platter, 13" | 18.00 |
| Salt & pepper shakers, pr | 12.00 |
| Sauce boat | 12.00 |
| Sauce boat, fast-stand | 18.00 |
| Sauce boat liner | 8.00 |
| Saucer | 3.00 |
| Sugar bowl, w/lid | 12.00 |
| Teacup | 5.00 |
| Teapot | 40.00 |

**Republic Shape
(available in Jean, Calais,
Priscilla, and Wayside)**

| | |
|---|---|
| Bowl, fruit; lg | 4.00 |
| Bowl, fruit; sm | 3.00 |
| Bowl, serving | 10.00 |
| Bowl, soup | 6.00 |
| Butter dish, w/lid | 30.00 |
| Casserole, w/lid | 25.00 |
| Creamer | 8.00 |
| Jug, 1-pt | 20.00 |
| Jug, 3½-pt | 30.00 |

| | |
|---|---|
| Plate, 10" | 9.00 |
| Plate, 6" | 4.00 |
| Plate, 7" | 5.00 |
| Plate, 8" | 7.00 |
| Plate, 9" | 8.00 |
| Platter, 11" | 14.00 |
| Platter, 13" | 16.00 |
| Sauce boat | 12.00 |
| Sauce boat liner | 6.00 |
| Saucer | 3.00 |
| Sugar bowl, w/lid | 12.00 |
| Teacup | 5.00 |
| Teacup, AD; w/saucer | 16.00 |
| Teapot | 35.00 |

# Hull

Established in Zanesville, Ohio, in 1905, Hull manufactured stoneware, florist ware, art pottery, and tile until about 1935, when they began to produce the lines of pastel matt-glazed artware which are today very collectible. The pottery was destroyed by flood and fire in 1950. The factory was rebuilt and equipped with the most modern machinery which they soon discovered was not geared to duplicate the matt glazes. As a result, new lines — Parchment and Pine, and Ebb Tide, for examples — were introduced in a glossy finish. During the forties and into the fifties, their kitchenware and novelty lines were very successful. Refer to *Robert's Ultimate Encyclopedia of Hull Pottery* and *The Companion Guide*, both by Brenda Roberts (Walsworth Publishing), for more information. Brenda also has authored a third book, *The Collector's Encyclopedia of Hull Pottery* which is published by Collector Books.

Banded Ware, casserole, green band on cream, w/lid, #113, 7½" ..................**95.00**

Bank, Corky Pig, cork in nose, pink & blue on cream, 5" ........**75.00**

Bank, dinosaur, premium for Sinclair Oil Co, early 1960s, 7" ...................................**215.00**

Bank, pig, Tawny Ridge (warm tan), #196, 6" .................**32.00**

Bow-Knot, cornucopia, pink & turquoise, #B-5, 7½" ...**175.00**

**Bow-Knot ewer, B-1-5½", $165.00.**

Bow-Knot, wall pocket, pitcher form, turquoise & blue, #B-26, 6" ...........................**225.00**

Butterfly, creamer, embossed motif on cream, #B-19, 5" ........**55.00**

Butterfly, lavabo, glossy; original metal hanger, #B-24/B-25, 16" .........................**180.00**

Butterfly, vase, #B-14, 3-footed, 10½x6" ..........................**85.00**

Butterfly, vase, embossed motif on cream, 3-footed, #B-14, 10½" ...............................**85.00**

Calla Lily, vase, floral on blue matt, sm handles, unmarked, 9½" ...............................**250.00**

Camellia, basket, floral on shaded pastels, handle, #142, 6¼" ................................**325.00**

Early Art, Alpine tankard, blended brown glaze, #492, 9½" ................................**275.00**

Early Art, vase, streaky red-brown on turquoise, stoneware, #32, 7" .........**80.00**

Heartland, bowl, soup/salad; brown heart stamp, yellow rim, 8" ..............................**5.00**

Heartland, creamer, brown heart stamp, yellow trim, 4¾" .**22.00**

Iris, candle holder, florals on pink to blue, #411, 5", ea .......**65.00**

Lustreware, console bowl, yellow, unmarked, 10" .............**120.00**

Lustreware, flower frog, blue, unmarked, 4½" ..............**20.00**

Magnolia, double cornucopia, glossy; floral on cream, #H-15, 12" ..........................**125.00**

Magnolia, teapot, matt; floral on yellow to dusty rose, #23, 6½" .............................**130.00**

Mirror Almond, creamer ......**12.00**

Mirror Almond, plate, dinner; 10" ..................................**8.00**

Mirror Almond, soup 'n sandwich set ...............................**20.00**

Mirror Almond, vinegar cruet, 5¾" ................................**15.00**

Mirror Brown, baker, oval, 10" .**15.00**

Mirror Brown, coffee mug, 3½" .**3.00**

Mirror Brown, cookie jar, Gingerbread Man, 12" ..............**85.00**

Mirror Brown, pitcher, ice lip .**24.00**

Mirror Brown, plate, dinner; 10½" ................................**6.00**

Mirror Brown, salt & pepper shakers, 3½", pr ..............**6.00**

Mirror Brown, spoon rest, Gingerbread Boy, 5" ....................**8.00**

Mirror Brown, vase, cylindrical, 6" ...................................**15.00**

Novelty, Daisy basket, floral on cream, blue handle, #70, 6½" .................................**45.00**

Novelty, Dancing Girl figurine, #955, 7" .........................**45.00**

**Mirror Brown: Creamer and sugar bowl, $25.00; Teapot, $32.00.**

Novelty, Mayfair leaf dish, yellow w/detailed veining, #86, 10" ..................................**30.00**

Novelty, rabbit planter, cream w/painted details, #952 USA, 4½" ................................**45.00**

Novelty, Siamese cat planter, opening in back, #63, 12" .......**75.00**

Novelty, Sun-Glow tea bell, rope handle, unmarked, 6¼" .**100.00**

Orange Tree, jardiniere, embossed decoration on cream, #546, 4" ..**40.00**

Rosella, cornucopia, floral on tan, #R-13, 8½" ...................**100.00**

Serenade, mug, birds on yellow, #S-22, 5½" ......................**55.00**

Serenade, vase, birds on light blue, #S-11, 10½" .........**105.00**

Sun-Glow, pitcher, floral on pink, w/Ice lip, #55, 7½" ..........**145.00**

Sun-Glow, vase, floral on pink, handles, #89, 5½" ..........**35.00**

Tangerine, bean pot, w/warmer, 9" ....................................**40.00**

**Novelty planter, cat with kitten, $100.00.**

Tangerine, Toast 'n Cereal tray & bowl, 9¾", 6½" ...............**24.00**

Tokay, cornucopia, pink grapes on green & Sweet Pink, #10, 11" ..................................**65.00**

Tokay, vase, pink grapes & green leaves on shaded ground, #8, 10" ..................................**95.00**

Tulip, flowerpot, multicolor tulips on blue, attached saucer, #116-33 .........................**110.00**

Tulip, jardiniere, tulips on gloss dark brown, stoneware, 10" ....**120.00**

Tulip, vase, bud; multicolor tulips on blue, #104-33, 6" .......**85.00**

Tuscany, basket, green grapes on Milk White, twig handle, #6, 8" .....................................**80.00**

Tuscany, basket, green vintage on Sweet Pink, #6, 8" .........**80.00**

Tuscany, ewer, green grapes on Milk White, #13, 12" ...**255.00**

Tuscany, leaf dish, green grapes on Sweet Pink, #19, 14" ......**50.00**

Wild Flower, vase, floral on pink to blue matt, handles, #51, 8½" ...............................**180.00**

Woodland, cornucopia, matt; floral on Dawn Rose to white, #W-10, 11" ...................**155.00**

Woodland, sugar bowl, glossy; floral on yellow, w/lid, #W-28, 3½" ..................................**30.00**

Woodland, vase, glossy; ivory, #W-1, 5½" ............................**45.00**

Woodland, vase, matt; Dawn Rose, ornate handles, #W-25, 12½" ..............................**485.00**

# Indiana Carnival Glass

Though this glass looks old, it really isn't. It's very reminiscent of old Northwood carnival glass with its grape clusters and detailed leaves and vines, but Indiana Glass Company introduced it in the '80s.

They made it in lustre colors of blue, marigold, and green. It's becoming very collectible, but prices are unstable at this point, simply because some dealers are unsure of its age and therefore its value. It you like it, now is the time to buy it!

Bowl, fruit; wide oval shape w/embossed grapes & vines, lg ......................................**22.50**

Butter dish, stick type, embossed grapes & vines ...............**18.00**

Candy dish, paneled cylinder w/embossed grapes & vines, w/lid, 7½" ......................**12.00**

Compote, embossed grapes & vines, 10x8½" ................**22.00**

Compote, jelly; thumbprint rim ..............................**9.00**

Covered dish, hen on nest ....**18.00**

Creamer & sugar bowl on tray, embossed grapes & vines .**15.00**

Egg plate, Press Cut design ..**12.00**

Goblet, water; embossed grapes ..........................**8.00**

Vase, red, Press Cut design, footed, 9" .......................**20.00**

**Pitcher, 10", $25.00; Tumbler, 5½", 10.00.**

# Insulators

After the telegraph was invented in 1844, insulators were

used to attach the transmission wires to the poles. With the coming of the telephone, their usefulness increased, and it is estimated that over 3,000 types were developed. Collectors today value some of them very highly — the threadless type, for example, often bring prices of several hundred dollars. Color, rarity, and age are all important factors to consider when evaluating insulators. Our advisor is Mike Bruner, who is listed in the Directory under Michigan.

Armstrong's No 14, clear .....**12.00**
Brookfield, aqua .....................**8.50**
Brookfield, New York, aqua ...**1.50**

**Clear 'Mickey Mouse' style from $18.00 to $22.50.**

Diamond, green ......................**3.00**
Diamond, pale lavender tint w/few milky wisps .........**13.00**
Hawley PA, USA, aqua, sm base chip .................................**2.50**
Hemingray 110, clear .............**5.00**
Hemingray 20, Made in USA, RDP, Hemingray blue .....**7.00**
Hemingray 20, ice blue w/lots of tiny bubbles ....................**3.00**

Hemingray 23, Hemi blue ...**10.00**
Hemingray 43, aqua, sm pings or chip ..................................**2.50**
Hemingray 518, spool, clear, bottom chip ..........................**2.00**
Hemingray 9, aqua, flare skirt ..**10.00**
Locke, dated, light aqua ......**35.00**
McLaughlin No 16, RDP, emerald green ................................**9.00**
McLaughlin No 19, light blue, shiny ...............................**10.00**
McLaughlin No 19, light green ..**5.00**
Pyrex 131, clear .....................**7.00**
Pyrex 662, carnival .............**10.00**
Star, green ............................**3.00**
Star, light aqua ....................**11.00**
W Brookfield, Dome embossed, light green .....................**20.00**
W Brookfield, New York, green ..........................**9.00**
W Brookfield, 45 Cliff St, NY, aqua ...............................**2.00**
W Brookfield, 45 Cliff St, 3 dates, aqua ...............................**5.00**

## Jadite

Many of today's kitchenware collectors have found the lovely green jadite glassware just as attractive today as it was to the homemakers of the forties through the mid-sixties. It was produced by the tons by several companies, Anchor Hocking and McKee were two of the larger producers, for both home and restaurant use. It was inexpensive then, and even today with all the collector demand, prices are still very reasonable. Refer to *Glassware of the '40s, '50s, and '60s* by Gene Florence (Collector Books) for more information. Our advisor April Tvorak, is listed in the Directory under Colorado.

## Dinnerware

Bowl, cereal; Jane Ray, Fire-King, 1945-63, 5⅞" ....................**9.00**

Bowl, cereal; Restaurant Ware, flanged rim, 1948-74, 8-oz, 6⅜" ....................................**9.00**

Bowl, cereal; Swirl, Fire-King, 1963-67, 5⅞" ....................**6.50**

Bowl, chili; Jane Ray, Fire-King, 1945-63, 5" ........................**3.25**

Bowl, dessert; Charm, Fire-King, 1950s, 4¾" ........................**5.00**

Bowl, dessert; Shell, Fire-King, 1963, 4¾" ..........................**3.50**

Bowl, nappy; Sheaf of Wheat, 1957-59, 4½" ..................**12.00**

Bowl, Restaurant Ware, Fire-King, 1948-74, 10-oz, 6" ..**7.00**

Bowl, sauce; Jane Ray, Fire-King ...............................**4.50**

Bowl, soup; Charm, Fire-King, 1950s, 6" ........................**15.00**

Bowl, soup; Jane Ray, Fire-King ...........................**14.00**

Bowl, vegetable; Jane Ray, Fire-King ...............................**14.00**

Bowl, vegetable; Shell, Fire-King, 8½" ....................................**7.50**

Bowl, vegetable; Swirl, Fire-King, 1963-67, 8¼" ..................**13.00**

Creamer, Charm, Fire-King, 1950s ................................**4.50**

Creamer, Jane Ray, Fire-King .**4.00**

Creamer, Shell, Fire-King, 1963 ..............................**4.25**

Cup, demitasse; Jane Ray, Fire-King ................................**20.00**

Cup, Jane Ray, Fire-King, 1945-63, 8-oz ..............................**3.00**

Cup, plain, Fire-King, 1954-56, 9-oz ..................................**5.00**

Cup, Restaurant Ware, Fire-King, 1948-74, 7-oz ....................**6.00**

Cup, Sheaf of Wheat, 1957-59, 6½" ..................................**12.00**

Cup, Swirl, Fire-King, 1963-67, 8-oz ..................................**4.25**

**Egg cup, double, 4", $15.00.**

Mug, Restaurant Ware, Fire-King, heavy, 1948-74, 7-oz .........**7.00**

Plate, bread & butter; Jane Ray, Fire-King, rare .............**20.00**

Plate, dinner; Restaurant Ware, Fire-King, 1948-74, 9" .....**7.25**

Plate, dinner; Shell, Fire-King, 1963, 10" ..........................**8.00**

Plate, luncheon; Charm, Fire-King, 1950s, 8⅜" .............**6.00**

Plate, pie; Restaurant Ware, Fire-King, 1948-74, 6¾" ..........**4.25**

Plate, plain, Fire-King, 1954-56, 9⅛" ..................................**8.00**

Plate, Restaurant Ware, Fire-King, oval, 1948-74, 11½" .........**16.00**

Plate, salad; Charm, Fire-King, 1950s, 6⅝" ........................**5.00**

Plate, salad; Jane Ray, Fire-King ...............................**5.00**

Plate, salad; Swirl, Fire-King, 1963-67, 7¾" ....................**5.50**

Plate, 5-compartment; Restaurant Ware, Fire-King, 1948-74, 9⅝" ..................................**10.50**

Platter, Jane Ray, Fire-King, 9x12" ...............................14.00

Platter, Swirl, Fire-King, 1963-67, 9x12" ...............................16.50

Saucer, Charm, Fire-King, 1950, 5⅜" ...................................1.50

Saucer, demitasse; Jane Ray, Fire-King, 1960s, 4½" ..........10.00

Saucer, Jane Ray, Fire-King, 1945-63, 5¾" .......................50

Saucer, Sheaf of Wheat, 1957-1959, 6" ...........................3.00

Saucer, Shell, Fire-King, 1963, 5¾" ...................................1.75

Sugar bowl, Charm, Fire-King, 1950s ...............................7.00

Sugar bowl, Jane Ray, Fire-King, 1945-63, w/lid, minimum value ...............................8.00

Tray, snack; Sheaf of Wheat, 1957-59, 7x10" ..............10.00

**Miscellaneous**

Ashtray, Fire-King, 1940-76, 4¼" ...................................7.00

Bowl, batter; plain, Fire-King, 1" band, 1950-70, 7½" ........15.00

Bowl, kitchen; ribbed, 1940s-50s, 6" ...................................10.00

Bowl, kitchen; ribbed, 1940s-50s, 9" ...................................18.00

Bowl, mixing; Beaded Rim, Fire-King, 1950-64, 8⅜" ..........9.00

Bowl, mixing; Colonial Rim, Fire-King, 1960-71, 8½" ........11.00

Bowl, mixing; Splash Proof, Fire-King, 1957-60, 3-qt, 8½" ...............................18.00

Bowl, mixing; Swedish Modern, Fire-King, 1954-58, 1-pt, 6¾" ...............................15.00

Bowl, mixing; Swirl, Fire-King, 1949-72, 6" .......................6.75

Bowl, mixing; Swirl, Fire-King, 1949-72, 8" ....................11.00

Butter dish, Fire-King, 1940s, w/clear lid, 2¾x6¾" .......25.00

Candy dish, Fire-King, flat, knob lid, 1950-58, 6¾" ...........11.00

Cup, Shell, Fire-King, 1960s, 3¼-oz ...............................4.00

Mug, shaving; Philbe design, heavy, 1942-67, 8-oz ........7.00

Skillet, w/1 spout, Fire-King, 1948-58, 6¼" ..................25.00

Tray, Sheaf of Wheat, Fire-King, 1940-76, 7x10" ...............11.00

# Jewelry

Today, anyone interested in buying gems will soon find out that the antique stones are the best values. Not only are prices from one-third to one-half less than on comparable new jewelry, but the craftsmanship and styling of modern-day pieces are lacking in comparison. Costume jewelry from all periods is popular, especially Art Nouveau and Art Deco examples. Signed pieces are particularly good, such as those by Miriam Haskell, Georg Jensen, David Anderson, and other well-known artists. See also Plastics.

Bracelet, Art Moderne, sterling interlocking open oval links, ⅜" wide ...........................30.00

Bracelet, bangle; gold-plated metal w/2 lion's heads ...22.50

Bracelet, bangle; Trifari, enamel stripes, hinged, ¾" wide 32.50

Bracelet, Bogoff, rhinestones form heart links, ½" wide ......30.00

Bracelet, Carnegie, gold-tone leaf links w/pearl & turquoise stones ...........................35.00

Bracelet, Emmons, rhodium chain w/3 black plastic squares, ca 1950 ...............................10.00

Bracelet, gilt-over-brass coiled asp w/garnet eyes, ca 1920 ..75.00

Bracelet, sterling w/3 rows of rhinestones, 1930s, ½" wide ....**90.00**
Bracelet, tennis; sterling w/red cabo-
chons & sterling balls .....**55.00**
Brooch, Sara Coventry, gold-
tone, seeds of wheat design,
1950 ...............................**10.00**
Brooch, sterling w/coral & turquoise
drops, ca 1920 .................**85.00**
Earrings, Alice, half-hoop, clip-on,
¾", pr .............................**15.00**
Earrings, Chr Dior (Christian
Dior), gold-plated shell, 1965,
pr ...................................**35.00**
Earrings, Eisenberg, blue &
pink imitation zircons,
1960s, pr .......................**65.00**
Earrings, Napier, gold-plated
twisted rope design, 1950s,
pr ...................................**15.00**
Earrings, sterling w/marcasites,
Art Deco style, 1⅛", pr ..**55.00**
Earrings, sterling w/4 sq aqua stones,
rhinestone border, pr .........**25.00**
Earrings, Weiss, gold-tone metal
w/amber faceted stones, 1965,
pr ...................................**35.00**
Earrings, 14k yellow gold, 7mm
pearl, pr .........................**40.00**
Earrings, 14k yellow gold w/blue
topaz studs, 7 carats, pr .**115.00**

**Dress clips, Eisenberg Originals,
rhinestones set in sterling, marked,
3", $600.00 to $750.00 for the pair.**

Hair pin, amber w/Art Deco
design, ca 1926 .............**65.00**

**Necklace and earrings, faux peri-
dots and rhinestones, marked Pat
Pend, $100.00 to $125.00 for the set.**

Necklace, amethyst quartz beads,
short ...............................**42.00**
Necklace, carnelian glass beads
on white metal w/brass open-
work ovals .....................**40.00**
Necklace, Christian Dior, 2
strands of pearls w/amethyst
in clasp, 25" ...................**95.00**
Necklace, faceted French jet beads,
Bohemian, 1920s ............**85.00**
Necklace, Peking glass beads,
Venetian, 1930s .............**75.00**
Necklace, purple cut glass beads
on gold-plated chain ......**22.50**
Necklace, wooden beads w/9
assembled multicolor wooden
drops .............................**30.00**
Necklace, yellow & amber cut
glass beads ....................**25.00**
Necklace, yellow-amber glass
cylinder beads w/clear spac-
ers, 54" ..........................**35.00**
Necklace, 3 gold-plated bows w/3
pink glass links on flat
chain ..............................**55.00**
Pendant, sterling apple on short
box-link chain, ¾" .........**27.50**
Pin, Brooks, gilt brass bird w/rhine-
stone accents, 1955-65 ....**75.00**
Pin, Coro, gold birds on sterling
branch w/cherries in frame,
2¼" ................................**40.00**

Pin, Coro, gold pelican on sterling, 1⅝" ..........................**45.00**

Pin, Coro, sterling wheel w/white stones at each end, 2½" .**35.00**

Pin, Eisenberg, Christmas tree w/multicolored rhinestones ........................**65.00**

Pin, Eisenberg, emerald green stone flower w/rhinestone accents ...........................**90.00**

Pin, gold-tone metal fish w/pink glass fins, 1½" ................**12.00**

Pin, silverplated kangaroo w/open body, rhinestone trim, 2" .**15.00**

Pin, silverplated rabbit w/green glass egg, rhinestone accents, 1¾" .................................**20.00**

Pin, 18k gold poodle in blue enamel sweater, orange enamel trim, 1" ...........**275.00**

Pin/earrings, Emmons, gold-tone w/faux pearls & blue rhinestones, 1960 ...................**45.00**

Ring, sterling, amethyst surrounded by double row of marcasites ......................**50.00**

Ring, yellow gold, cabochon garnet, 1920s ....................**175.00**

Ring, 12k yellow gold, oval w/15x11mm opal .........**350.00**

Ring, 14k yellow gold, gold florentine swirl w/6.6mm cultured pearl .............................**150.00**

Ring, 14k yellow gold wedding band w/7 round diamonds ......**500.00**

# Josef Originals

Josef Original figurines were designed by Muriel Joseph George of Arcadia, California, from 1946 until she retired in 1982. (The spelling Josef was a printer error in the first labels for Pitty Sing. The first retail sale and time did not permit them to correct it, so it remains 'Josef Originals.) They were made in California until the early 1960s, at which time George Good (Muriel's representative and soon-to-be partner) convinced her to go to Japan to remain competitive in the marketplace. All figures produced in Japan were made to her exact specifications, and the quality continued to be very high. After she retired, her partner, George Good, retained the Josef name and produced figurines until 1985 (she still designed some things for him) when he sold the company to Applause who continues to make Josef Originals, though limited in number and not of the same quality. Examples listed below are from the period of the 1940s through the 1980s (before Muriel's retirement) when the girls had all black eyes and a glossy finish and animals were done in a semigloss. More recent figures have brown-red eyes, and the animals may have a flocked finish. Prices are for figurines in perfect condition; one with repair or damage is not considered collectible. Caution: we have found figurines that have Josef labels, but are not Josef Originals. All Josef Originals are marked with an oval sticker, either with the California or Japan designation, and all (except the animals) carry either an incised or ink-stamped mark, 'Josef Originals©.' Our advisors for this category are Jim and Kaye Whitaker (Eclectic Antiques), authors of *Josef Originals*; they are listed in the Directory under Washington.

Baby w/kitten, blue, pink or yellow, Japan, 3", ea ...........**25.00**

Bear Eating Honey, Japan, 4".**20.00**

Birthday Girl #1, blue & white gown, black eyes, Japan..**25.00**

Birthday Girl #16, blue gown, black eyes, Japan...........**30.00**

Birthstone Doll, February, lavender gown, purple stone, Japan..............................**18.00**

Christmas Lady Music Box, fur collar, Japan, 6½", from $75 to......................................**85.00**

Dinner Belle, blue gown, holding plate, California, 3"........**27.00**

Doll of the Month, w/birthstone, California, 3¼"...............**30.00**

**Duck family, Japan, 2" to 4", 3-piece set, from $48.00 to $58.00.**

Elephant, w/flower, Japan, 5".**30.00**

Frogs, green, various poses & sizes, ea..........................**12.00**

Girl at Piano, music box, pink gown, w/ponytail, Japan **75.00**

Jacques, pink suit & gray vest, California, 5¼"...............**50.00**

Ladybug, Japan, 2½"............**14.00**

Little International, France, pink, white & blue clothing, Japan, 4"......................**27.00**

Little International, Japan, pink kimono w/gold trim, Japan, 4".....................................**27.00**

Love's Rendezvous, aqua gown & hat, Japan, 9"...............**100.00**

Mice, semi-gloss, various poses & costumes, Japan, ea.......**15.00**

Ostrichs, mom & 2 chicks, Japan, set.....................**90.00**

**MaMa, carrying candle, California, 7¼", from $80.00 to $85.00.**

Rabbits, various poses, 3" to 5", ea.....................................**14.00**

School Belle, w/apple & book, yellow gown, Japan, 3½" ....**27.00**

Turtle, laying on side, Japan, 2"..................................**12.00**

# Keen Kutter

Watch for items marked Keen Kutter, a brand name used before the mid-1930s by E.C. Simmons Hardware Company. Not only are their products (household items, tools of all types, knives, etc.) collectible, but so are the advertising materials they distributed.

Axe, camp; K30 ....................**30.00**

Axe, Dayton pattern, KKD301, NM .................................**37.50**

**Puzzle, Keen Kutter logo, original box, EX, $1,500.00.**

Axe, house; KHA ................. **25.00**
Bit, auger; K3-20, any of 16 sizes, ea ..................................... **10.00**
Bit, reamer; KK115, NM ...... **15.00**
Bit brace, K10, 10" ............... **25.00**
Chisel, firmer; KSA8, 8-pc set .**150.00**
Drill, push; KK8, 9½", NM ..**30.00**
File, KM4 .............................. **15.00**
Glass cutter, diamond point, w/marked leather case ..**75.00**
Hammer, brick; KKB15, 24-oz, NM .................................. **40.00**
Hatchet, claw; KKBC1, NM ..**30.00**
Hatchet, lathing; KKBAL1, NM ............................. **30.00**
Knife, butcher; K160, 6", w/origi-nal box .......................... **50.00**
Knife, pocket; EC Simmons, equal end, cocobola handle, 2-blade, 3¼" .............................. **45.00**
Knife, pocket; #218, peanut, ivory-type handle, 2-blade, 2⅞" .**25.00**
Marking gauge, K26 ........... **25.00**
Pipe cutter, K2, 3 wheel pattern, ¼"-2", NM ...................... **80.00**
Plane, block; K65, 7" ........... **30.00**
Plane, fore; K6C, 18" ........... **40.00**
Plane, jack; K26, 15" ........... **50.00**
Plane, jointer; KK8, smooth bot-tom, 24", NM ................. **70.00**

Pliers, combination; K160 ...**25.00**
Plumb bob, K60 .................... **45.00**
Rule, 6-fold, K503, 36" ........**50.00**
Saw, back; K44 ..................... **30.00**
Saw, compass; K95 .............. **30.00**
Saw set, K195 ...................... **25.00**
Square, carpenter's, K3, steel, 24" ................................ **25.00**
Staple puller, K700 ............. **25.00**
Weed cutter, KWCS-K, NM .**38.00**
Wrench, monkey; KB6, 6" ....**50.00**

# Kentucky Derby Glasses

Kentucky Derby glasses are the official souvenir glasses sold filled with mint juleps on Derby Day. The first glass (1938), picturing a black horse within a black and white rose garland and the Churchill Downs stadium in the background, is said to have either been given away as a souvenir or used for drinks among the elite at the Downs. This glass, the 1939, and two glasses said to have been used in 1940 are worth thousands and are nearly impossi-ble to find at any price. Our advisor, Betty Hornback, is listed in the Directory under Kentucky.

1940s, aluminum ............... **400.00**
1940s, plastic Beetleware, from $2,500 to ................... **3,500.00**
1945, short ......................... **800.00**
1945, tall ........................... **300.00**
1948 ................................... **125.00**
1949 ................................... **125.00**
1950 ................................... **300.00**
1951 ................................... **375.00**
1952, Gold Cup .................. **125.00**
1953 ..................................... **85.00**
1954 ................................... **100.00**
1955 ..................................... **85.00**
1956, from $150 to ............. **250.00**
1957 ..................................... **75.00**
1958, Gold Bar .................. **150.00**

1958, Iron Liege ...............**150.00**
1959 ...............................**70.00**

**1960, $65.00.**

1961 ...................................**85.00**
1962 ...................................**60.00**
1963-65, ea .........................**40.00**
1966-67, ea .........................**35.00**
1968 ...................................**38.00**
1969 ...................................**32.00**
1970 ...................................**45.00**
1971-72, ea .........................**28.00**
1973 ...................................**30.00**
1974, mistake ......................**16.00**
1974, regular .......................**14.00**
1975 .....................................**8.00**
1976 ...................................**12.00**
1976, plastic .......................**10.00**
1977 .....................................**7.50**
1978-79, ea .........................**10.00**
1980 ...................................**15.00**
1981 .....................................**8.00**
1982 .....................................**7.00**
1983 .....................................**7.00**
1984-85, ea ...........................**6.00**
1986 .....................................**7.00**

1986 ('85 copy) ...................**15.00**
1987-89, ea .........................**5.00**
1990 .....................................**4.00**
1991-94, ea ..........................**3.50**

# King's Crown

This is a pattern that's been around since the late 1800s, but what you're most apt to see on today's market is the later issues. Though Tiffin made it early, our values are for the glassware they produced from the forties through the sixties and the line made by Indiana Glass in the seventies. It was primarily made in crystal with ruby or cranberry flashing, but some pieces (from Indiana Glass) were made with gold and platinum flashing as well. Tiffin's tumblers are flared while Indiana's are not, and because Indiana's are much later and more easily found, they're worth only about half as much as Tiffin's. Refer to *Collectible Glassware from the '40s, '50s, and '60s* by Gene Florence (Collector Books) for more information.

**Plate, 10", $30.00.**

Bowl, flared, footed ..............**36.00**
Bowl, mayonnaise; 4" ...........**15.00**
Bowl, straight edge ..............**40.00**
Cake salver, footed, 12½" .....**60.00**
Candle holder, sherbet type .**22.50**

Creamer ...............................**20.00**
Cup .........................................**8.00**
Mayonnaise, 3-pc set ............**25.00**
Pitcher ...............................**100.00**
Plate, bread & butter; 5" ........**8.00**
Plate, party; 24" ..................**60.00**
Plate, salad; 7⅜" ..................**12.00**
Punch cup .............................**8.00**
Saucer ....................................**7.00**
Stem, claret; 4-oz .................**12.00**
Stem, wine; 2-oz .....................**7.50**
Sugar bowl ...........................**20.00**
Tumbler, water; 8½-oz ..........**12.00**
Vase, bud; 12¼" .....................**40.00**

# Kitchen Collectibles

From the early patented apple peelers, cherry pitters, and food choppers to the gadgets of the twenties through the forties, many collectors find special appeal in kitchen tools. Refer to *Kitchen Antiques, 1790-1940,* by Kathyrn McNerney and *Kitchen Glassware of the Depression Years* by Gene Florence for more information. Both are published by Collector Books.

**Beater jar, delphite bowl, from $60.00 to $70.00.**

Apple peeler, Goodell, cast iron, 1898, complete ..............**70.00**
Baker, Skokie green, oval, McKee, 7x5" ................................**15.00**
Bean slicer, Vaughns ............**35.00**
Beater, Chicago, electric, w/jadite bowl ................................**40.00**
Biscuit/doughnut cutter, aluminum w/wooden knob handle, 3¼x1¼" ....................**12.00**
Bisquit tin, Ivins Bakers of Good...1846, 5¼x5" sq ...**32.00**
Bottle, water; Duraglas, forest green ..............................**25.00**
Bowl, mixing; glass, green transparent, 9" ........................**18.00**
Cake mold, 2x8", tin, center tube, fluted & scalloped sides .**10.00**
Can opener, Never Slip, cast iron w/loop handles, Patent Nov 12, '02 ............................**14.00**
Canister, white clambroth, square w/rounded corners, metal lid, med ...............................**20.00**
Cherry seeder, cast iron, Enterprise ...............................**50.00**
Chopper, wood handle w/riveted curved metal blade, 5x6½" .**20.00**
Chopping knife, cast-steel blade, wishbone-shaped shaft, wood grip ...................................**45.00**
Churn, Dazey #30, 3-qt ........**80.00**
Churn, glass, unmarked, 1-qt .**195.00**
Churn, squared pressed glass, wooden paddles, cast-iron gears, 13½" ....................**45.00**
Corkscrew, steel w/chubby rosewood handle, ca 1920, 4½" ........**40.00**
Cornstick pan, cast iron, unmarked, 7 alternating ears ...........**40.00**
Doughnut mold, cast iron, Ace .**55.00**
Egg beater, tin w/iron handle, Peerless #2 ....................**32.50**
Egg beater/cream whip, Ladd..., NY, USA, rotary type, wooden handle ...........................**22.00**
Egg separator, advertising grocer, tin ...................................**12.50**

**Flour sifter, Hand-i-Sift, Made in US of A, $10.00.**

Flour sifter, tin & wire mesh, hand crank, wooden knob, 3½x3" .............................**15.00**

Grater, All In One, Pat Pend, ca 1940, 10⅝x4¼" ...............**25.00**

Grater, nutmeg; Bogar, ca 1896, EX ................................**110.00**

Grater, nutmeg; Edgar, tin & wood, Patent Nov 10, 1896 .......**90.00**

Grater, punched tin, half-circle shape ..............................**35.00**

Grinder, nut; Androck, glass bottom ................................**20.00**

Ice cube breaker, Lightning .**80.00**

Juicer, Handy Andy .............**35.00**

Kraut cutter, walnut w/iron blade, dark patina, 20x7¾" ......**50.00**

Ladle, amber glass, Fostoria .**22.50**

Ladle, cobalt glass, flat bottom .**18.00**

Lemon squeezer, cast iron, fluted bowl, 8" ..........................**20.00**

Lifter/tongs, heavy gauge metal, scissors type, 1930s-40s .**18.00**

Masher, heavy gauge wire, painted wood handle, 9¼" ...........**22.50**

Mayonnaise mixer, Wesson Oil .**75.00**

Measure, crystal, no handle, 4-cup ..................................**40.00**

Measure, custard glass, pitcher form, 4-cup ....................**30.00**

Mixer, Kwik Way ..................**30.00**

Muffin pan, cast iron, oval, Filley #6 ..................................**225.00**

Muffin pan, tin, 6 fluted cups in solid frame, EKCO, ca 1920s .............................**8.00**

Muffin/tea cake pan, cast iron, 11 sm pans in frame, 12½x8½" ........................**45.00**

Napkin holder, milk glass, Slendr-fold ...........................**48.00**

Pastry blender, nickeled iron prongs, painted wood handle, 9½" .................................**18.00**

Pie crimper, brass wheel w/wooden handle ...........**15.00**

Potato masher, heavy wire w/wood handle ...............**12.50**

Raisin seeder, cast iron, Crown .**75.00**

Refrigerator dish, pink glass, round, tab handles, w/lid ............**30.00**

Refrigerator dish, yellow opaque, 7¼" sq ...........................**35.00**

Rolling pin, white opaque, wooden handles, Imperial ..........**45.00**

Rolling pin, wooden, Munsing engraved on end ............**12.50**

Salad fork & spoon, all glass, clear w/pointed blue handles .............................**60.00**

Sifter, Androck, tin w/red bands, wood handle ..................**20.00**

Sifter, Necco, tin, 1-cup ........**12.50**

Sifter, 1-cup, rotary type, metal handle w/green wooden knob, NM ................................**10.00**

Skillet, cast iron, Wagner #3 .**30.00**

Spoon, mixing; Fidelity The Flour Supreme, opener end ....**10.00**

Vegetable slicer/cutter, fluted metal blade, wooden handle, 1900s, 9" ........................**15.00**

# Knife Rests

Several scholars feel that knife rests originated in Germany and France with usage spreading to England and later to America as travel between countries became more widespread. Knife rests have been documented from 1720 through 1839, and they're being made yet today by porcelain manufacturers and glasshouses to match their tableware patterns. Some of the present-day producers are located in France, Germany, and Poland.

Knife rests of pressed glass, cut crystal, porcelain, sterling silver, plated silver, wood, and bone have been collected for many years. Signed knife rests are especially desired. It was not until the Centennial Exhibition in Philadelphia in 1876 that the brilliant new cut glass rests, deeply faceted and shining like diamonds, appeared in shops by the hundreds. There were sets of twelve, eight, or six; some came boxed. Sizes of knife rests vary from 1¼" to 3¼" for individual knives and from 5" to 6" for carving knives. Glass knife rests were made in many colors such as purple, blue, green, vaseline, pink, and cranberry. It is important to note that prices may vary from one area of the country to another and from dealer to dealer. For further information we recommend our advisor, Beverly L. Ales, listed in the Directory under California. See also Clubs and Newsletters.

Art France, glass horse, pr ..**60.00**
Cut crystal, squash form .....**75.00**
Cut crystal, w/star on end of ball, 3" ....................................**65.00**
Cut crystal, 8-sided bar w/diamond cut on ball end, 5½" ........**45.00**
Imperial, milk glass, marked IG ............................**25.00**
Lalique France, marked, frosted ends ..............................**95.00**

Meissen, marked X w/sword logo on end, pr ....................**165.00**
Pressed glass, green, 3½", pr .**60.00**
Quimper, blue, registered 1883, HB, #797 ......................**75.00**

**Quimper knife rest, #499, 1950s, from $40.00 to $65.00; Quimper knife, from $25.00 to $35.00.**

Photo courtesy Beverly Ales.

Sabino, blue glass w/duck end .**35.00**
Silverplate, children hopping over stile ..............................**125.00**
Silverplate, squirrel w/lg bar on tail, Simpson Hall .......**195.00**
Waterford, marked, lg ..........**60.00**

# Law Enforcement

The field of law enforcement collectibles is very diverse and often highly specialized. This is a very difficult field for which to establish values as the hobby is still basically in its infancy, and there are vast differences of opinion.

The most common law enforcement collectible is the badge. This symbol of authority first made its appearance in the late 1840s and gained widespread use during the late 1800s to the early 1900s. Made in a variety of materials, the most common is nickel-plated brass. There are some examples constructed of sterling silver or gold that are sometimes embellished with gems. The price of these badges usually begins with the current market price of the precious metal

213

being used. Many badges will bear a hallmark or maker's name on the reverse. Beware! There are several companies and individuals who make reproduction badges! A good idea is to secure a copy of a reproduction catalog to protect yourself from individuals who try to sell these as originals.

Other popular law enforcement collectibles include photos, paper items such as posters, handcuffs, leg irons, uniforms, shoulder patches, and night sticks. Many collectors specialize in items from a specific era or location, which contributes to the wide diversity of values.

There are several books that offer information: *Badges of Law and Order* by George Virginies; the excellent work by Joe Goodson, *Old West Antiques and Collectibles*, and an outstanding new reference, *Badges of the U.S. Marshals*, by George Stumpf and Ray Sherrard. The field is also served well by the fine monthly newsletter, *Police Collector News*, published by Mike Bondarenko. Our advisor is Tony Perrin, who is listed in the Directory under Arkansas.

Badge, Chief of Police, Oklahoma City, 1955, gold filled ..**125.00**
Badge, Commissioner of Police-Fire, Chattanooga TN, 1911, gold .............................**450.00**
Badge, eagle atop shield, Sheriff Randolph Co AR, 1928 .**150.00**
Badge, police; crescent & star, El Paso TX ......................**450.00**
Badge, police; lg 6-point star, Chicago IL, 1910 .........**125.00**
Badge, Private Detective, sm 6-point star ..................**65.00**

Badge, sm eagle atop shield, current, Springdale AK ......**50.00**
Badge, stock; Circle Star, City Marshal, early .............**150.00**
Badge, stock; star, Deputy Sheriff, ca 1930s ........................**50.00**
Badge, 6-point star, St Joseph MO ..............................**250.00**
Bronze, bust of Deputy US Marshal, 8" ........................**175.00**
Daystick, turned rosewood ..**45.00**
Handcuffs & key, nickel plated, Iver-Johnson Mfg ..........**80.00**
Hat, City Marshal, dark blue pillbox style .......................**150.00**
Leg irons & key, nickel plated, Tower Mfg .....................**95.00**
Medal, shooting; Kansas City Police Dept, 1933 ..........**45.00**
Money clip w/NYPD badge, 10K gold ..............................**125.00**
Patch, US Marshal, for shoulder of uniform .......................**3.50**
Photo, cabinet, identified: M Logan, Memphis Police Lt, 1800s .**65.00**
Photo, City Marshal, TX, ca 1900 ...........................**100.00**
Photo, KY Peace Officers, ca 1900, 8x10" ..............................**40.00**
Photo, officer wearing Western-style hat, hand-colored, lg format ...............................**250.00**
Photo, SM NYPD, ca 1870 ...**65.00**
Photo, tintype, officer w/7-point star badge, 1800s ........**150.00**
Receipt, US Marshal, signed Montana Territory, 1800s ....**75.00**
Restraints, chain nippers w/T handles ..........................**25.00**
Reward postcards, Oklahoma State Penitentiary, 1928 ..........**10.00**
Reward poster, Leavenworth Penitentiary, escaped rustler, 1904 ..............................**125.00**
Reward poster, murder of 2 Denver policemen, 1899 ....**100.00**
Slapper, leather-covered weighted blackjack ........................**20.00**

# Lefton China

Since 1940 the Lefton China Co. has been importing and producing ceramic giftware which may be found in shops throughout the world. Because of the quality of the workmanship and the beauty of these items, they are sought after by collectors of today. Lefton pieces are usually marked with a fired-on trademark or a paper label found on the bottom of each piece. Our advisor is Loretta De Lozier, author of *Collector's Encyclopedia of Lefton China*; she is listed in the Directory under Iowa.

Box, #1365, Musical Hors d'oeuvres Christmas Tree, Green Holly ..............................**60.00**
Cake set, #1133, 7-pc .........**105.00**
Candy box, #1229, florals on white bisque, w/lid ........**58.00**

**Christmas tree music box, 8½", $35.00.**

Compote, #112, wheat design .**15.00**
Cup & saucer set, #936, girl's face ................................**25.00**
Decanter, #991, monk figural, 8½", w/6 mugs ..............**55.00**

Dish, #937, Americana, 3-compartment, 9" ..................**25.00**
Dish, bonbon; #2154, white w/pink roses, 2 compartments, 9" ..**22.00**
Figure, #462, lady, 6¼" .........**70.00**
Figure, #576, Bloomer Girl ..**48.00**

**Hand vase with double roses, 6½", $45.00.**

Head vase, #611, man, 6" .....**38.00**
Lantern, #2695, Green Holly, w/bracket .......................**75.00**
Lipstick holder, #903, 3½" ...**13.00**
Pitcher, #4870, Green Holly, 8¼" ..............................**30.00**
Planter, #2007, Madonna ....**28.00**
Planter, #5184, boot form, Green Holly, 3¼" .......................**12.00**
Planter, #5185, boot form, Green Holly, 4¾" .......................**20.00**
Plate, #3069, Green Heritage, 9" ................................**33.00**
Salt & pepper shakers, #1353, Green Holly, pr ..............**15.00**
Shoe, #1204, pink bisque, 4½" .**20.00**
Sleigh, #1346, Green Holly, 8" .**40.00**
Sleigh, #2637, Green Holly, 10½" ..............................**60.00**
Sleigh, #4621, Green Holly, 5" .**15.00**
Snack set, #2108, rose design .**12.00**
Spoon rest w/bluebird salt shaker, #151, 5½" .......................**16.00**
Sugar & creamer, #1355, Green Holly ..............................**30.00**

Teapot, #1357, Green Holly .**55.00**
Teapot, #279, 25th Anniversary
    w/silver trim .................**20.00**
Vase, #283, cornucopia form w/lily
    of the valley, 5½", pr ......**60.00**
Wall plaque, #1154, 4½" .......**14.00**
Wall plaque, #119, fruit design,
    8" .....................................**18.00**

# License Plates

Early porcelain license plates are treasured by collectors and often sell for more than $500.00 for the pair when found in excellent condition. The best examples are first-year plates from each state, but some of the more modern plates with special graphics are collectible too. Prices given below are for plates in good or better condition. Our advisor is Richard Diehl, who is listed in the Directory under Colorado.

Alaska, 1960 .........................**22.00**
Arizona, 1985 .........................**3.50**
California, 1934, G .............**12.50**
Connecticut, 1956 ..............**12.50**
Delaware, 1927 ...................**40.00**
Florida, 1958 ........................**10.50**
Georgia, 1991, peach .............**5.50**
Hawaii, 1981 ..........................**6.50**
Idaho, 1965 ............................**6.00**
Illinois, 1948, soybean .........**12.50**
Indiana, 1976, Bicentennial ..**4.50**
Iowa, 1934 .............................**8.50**
Kansas, 1942, sunflower ......**30.00**
Kentucky, 1989, horses ..........**6.50**
Louisiana, 1964/1965 .............**4.50**
Maine, 1990, lobster ...............**5.50**
Maryland, 1925 ....................**25.00**
Minnesota, 1983, graphic ......**2.50**
Montana, 1991 ......................**4.50**
Nebraska, 1941 ....................**25.00**
Nevada, 1969 .........................**8.50**
New Hampshire, 1920 .........**16.50**

New Jersey, 1929 .................**22.00**
New Mexico, 1992, cactus .....**3.50**
North Dakota, 1969 ..............**6.50**
Ohio, 1974 ..............................**2.25**
Oklahoma, 1928 ...................**30.00**
Oregon, 1991, tree .................**4.00**

Photo courtesy Richard Diehl.

**Pennsylvania: 1908, $200.00; 1909, $175.00; 1912, $50.00.**

Pennsylvania, 1942 ................**9.50**
Rhode Island, 1979 ..............**11.50**
South Carolina, 1969 ............**5.50**
South Dakota, 1950 ..............**7.00**
Utah, 1992, ski ......................**3.50**
Washington DC, 1952 ..........**20.00**

# Little Golden Books

Little Golden Books (a registered trademark of Western Publishing Company Inc.), introduced in October of 1942 were an overnight success. First published with a blue paper spine, the later spines were of gold foil. Parents and grandparents born in the '40s, '50s, and '60s are now trying to find the titles they had as children. From 1942 to the early 1970s, the books were numbered from 1 to 600, while books published later had no numerical order. Depending on where you find the book, prices can vary from 25¢ to $30.00 plus. The most expensive are those with dust jackets from the early '40s or books with paper dolls and activities. The three primary series of books are the Regular (1-600), Disney (1-140), and Activity (1-52).

Television influence became apparent in the '50s with stories like the Lone Ranger, Howdy Doody, Hopalong Cassidy, Gene Autry, and Rootie Kazootie. The '60s brought us Yogi Bear, Huckleberry Hound, Magilla Gorilla, and Quick Draw McGraw, to name a few. A TV Western title from the '50s is worth around $12.00 to $18.00. A Disney from 1942 to the early '60s will go for $8.00 to $15.00 (reprinted titles would be lower). Cartoon titles from the '60s would range from $6.00 to $12.00. Books with the blue spine or gold paper spine (not foil) can bring from $8.00 to $15.00. If you are lucky enough to own a book with a dust jacket, the jacket alone is worth $20.00 and up. Paper doll books are worth around $30.00 to $36.00. These values are meant only to give an idea of value and are for first editions in mint condition. Condition is very important when purchasing a book. You normally don't want to purchase a book with large tears, crayon or ink marks, or missing pages.

As with any collectible, a first edition is always going to bring the higher prices. To tell what edition you have on the 25¢ and 29¢ cover price books, look on the title page or the last page of the book. If it is not on the title page there will be a code of 1/ the alphabet on the bottom right corner of the last page. A is for a 1st edition, Z will refer to the twenty-sixth printing.

There isn't an easy way of determining the condition of a book. What is 'good' to one might be 'fair' to another. To find out more about Little Golden Books, we recommend *Collecting Little Golden Books* (published by Books Americana), a most informative book by our advisor, Steve Santi, who is listed in the Directory under California.

Animal Alphabet, #349, 1958, M ..................................**6.00**
Animals on the Farm, #573, 1968, M ......................................**4.00**
Baby Dear, #466, 1962, M ....**15.00**
Bambi, #D90, Disney, 1948, M .**8.00**
Ben & Me, #D37, Disney, 1954, M ..................................**12.00**
Bozo the Clown, #446, 1961, M .**10.00**
Bugs Bunny, #72, 1949, M ...**10.00**
Christmas Carols, #595, 1946, M ..................................**4.00**
Circus Boy, #290, 1957, M ...**15.00**
Cub Scouts, #5022, 1959, M .**20.00**

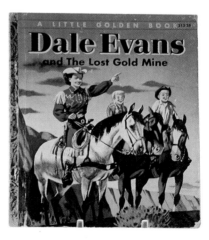

*Dale Evans and the Lost Gold Mine,* A Edition, EX, $12.00.

Daniel Boone, #256, 1956, M .**8.00**
Day at the Zoo, #88, 1949, M .**10.00**
Golden Goose, #200, 1954, M .**10.00**
Hansel & Gretel, #491, M ......**4.00**
Happy Days, #247, 1955, M ...**8.00**
Horses, #458, 1962, M ............**5.00**
Huckleberry Hound Builds a
    House, #376, 1959, M ...**10.00**
Indian, Indian; #149, 1952, M .**8.00**
Jack's Adventures, #308, 1958,
    M ....................................**8.00**
Jetsons, #500, 1962, M ........**20.00**
Let's Go Shopping, #33, 1948,
    M ..................................**10.00**
Let's Visit the Dentist, #599,
    1970, M ............................**5.00**
Love Bug, #D130, Disney, 1974,
    M ..................................**10.00**
Mary Poppins, #D113, Disney,
    1964, M ..........................**10.00**
Mickey Mouse's Picnic, #D15, Dis-
    ney, 1950, M ..................**12.00**
My Baby Brother, #279, 1956,
    M ..................................**18.00**
My Pets, #5027, 1959, M .....**12.00**
Never Pat a Bear, #105, 1972,
    M ....................................**4.00**
Nurse Nancy, #154, 1952, M .**25.00**
Our Puppy, #56, 1948, M .....**10.00**
Our World, #242, 1955, M ......**6.00**
Paper Dolls, #A3, Activity, 1951,
    M ..................................**25.00**
Pete's Dragon, #D137, 1977, M .**7.00**
Pinocchio & the Whale, #D101,
    Disney, 1961, M .............**15.00**
Plants & Animals, #5017, Giant,
    1958, M ..........................**12.00**
Play w/Me, #567, 1967, M ......**8.00**
Ruff & Reddy, #477, 1959, M .**8.00**
Sleeping Beauty, #D61, Disney,
    1957, M ..........................**12.00**
Steve Canyon, #356, 1959, M .**15.00**
Story of Jesus, #27, 1946, M .**12.00**
Three Little Kittens, #1, 1942,
    M ..................................**25.00**
Three Little Pigs, #544, 1973,
    M ....................................**4.00**
Tom & Jerry, #561, 1951, M ...**4.00**

***Puss in Boots***, **#359, 1959, EX $4.50.**

Twins, #227, 1955, M ...........**25.00**
Two Little Miners, #66, 1949,
    M ..................................**15.00**
Up in the Attic, #53, 1948, M ..**12.00**
Wiggles, #166, 1953, M ........**18.00**
Woody Woodpecker, Steps to Draw-
    ing; #372, 1959, M ..........**15.00**

# Little Red Riding Hood

This line of novelties and
kitchenwares has always com-
manded good prices on the collectibles market. Little Red
Riding Hood was produced
from 1943 to 1957; some items
were manufactured by the
Hull Pottery of Crooksville,
Ohio, who sent their white-
ware to the Royal China and
Novelty Company (a division of
Regal China) of Chicago, Illinois, to be decorated. But a
major part of the line was
actually made by the Regal
Company. For further information we recommend *Collecting
Hull Pottery's Little Red Riding Hood* by Mark Supnick (L-
W Book Sales).

Butter dish .........................**395.00**
Cookie jar, closed basket, mini-
　　mum value ..................**350.00**
Cookie jar, open basket, red
　　shoes ..........................**575.00**
Creamer, top pour, tab handle .**300.00**
Creamer & sugar bowl, side
　　pour ...........................**300.00**
Salt & pepper shakers, 3¼", pr .**125.00**
Spice jar, cinnamon, cloves,
　　nutmeg, or pepper, sq base,
　　ea ..............................**650.00**

Bowl, fruit; 5" .........................**5.00**
Bowl, mixing; 10" .................**75.00**
Bowl, salad ...........................**40.00**
Bowl, vegetable; 8½" ...........**10.00**
Butter dish ...........................**35.00**
Casserole, w/lid ....................**65.00**
Chop plate, 15" .....................**27.50**
Creamer ................................**6.00**
Cup ......................................**7.50**
Cup, demitasse ....................**35.00**
Egg cup ...............................**15.00**

**Teapot, 8½", $365.00.**

**Fruit juice tumblers, each from
$30.00 to $40.00; Fruit juice jug,
from $100.00 to $130.00.**

Pitcher, juice .........................**35.00**
Plate, 10" .............................**15.00**
Plate, 6" ...............................**4.00**
Plate, 9" ...............................**8.00**
Platter, 13" ...........................**15.00**
Salt & pepper shakers, pr ....**10.00**
Saucer ...................................**2.00**
Sugar bowl, w/lid .................**10.00**
Vase, bud; 2 styles, ea ........**200.00**

# Lu-Ray Pastels

Introduced in 1938 by Taylor, Smith, and Taylor of East
Liverpool, Ohio, Lu-Ray Pastels
is today a very sought-after line
of collectible American dinnerware. It was first made in these
solid colors: Windsor Blue, Surf
Green, Persian Cream, and
Sharon Pink. Chatham Gray was
introduced in 1948 and is today
priced higher than the other colors. For more information, we
recommend *Collector's Guide to
Lu-Ray Pastels* by Kathy and
Bill Meehan.

# Lunch Boxes

In the early years of this century, tobacco companies often packaged their products in tins that
could later be used for lunch boxes.
By the 1930s oval lunch boxes
designed to appeal to school children were produced. The rectangular shape that is now popular was

preferred in the 1950s. Character lunch boxes decorated with the faces of TV personalities, super heroes, Disney and cartoon characters are especially sought after by collectors today. Our values are for excellent condition lunch boxes only (without the thermos unless one is mentioned in the line). Refer to *Pictorial Price Guide to Vinyl and Plastic Lunch Boxes and Thermoses* and *Pictorial Price Guide to Metal Lunch Boxes and Thermoses* by Larry Aikens (L-W Book Sales) for more information. Our advisor is Terri Ivers; she is listed in the Directory under Oklahoma.

Barbie, Cool Time, pink plastic, 1989, w/white thermos & pink cup, EX .....................**2.00**
Battlestar Galactica, metal, 1978, w/thermos, EX ...............**29.00**
Beverly Hillbillies, metal, 1964, w/metal thermos, EX ....**88.00**
Bozostuffs, red plastic, 1988, w/thermos, EX ...............**20.00**
Care Bears, metal, 1983, w/thermos, EX ............................**5.00**
Chip 'n Dale Rescue Rangers, blue plastic, EX ...............**3.00**
Clash of the Titans, metal, 1981, EX ...................................**20.00**
Dick Tracy the Movie, Disney, plastic, w/thermos, EX ....**4.50**

**Disney Express, 1979, metal, with thermos, EX, $14.00.**

Disney School Bus, orange metal w/dome top, w/plastic thermos, VG+ ......................**29.00**

**Duck Tales, plastic, with thermos, M, $8.00.**

Dukes of Hazzard, metal, 1980, w/thermos, EX ...............**14.00**
Dynomutt, metal, 1976, NM .**28.00**
Evel Knievel, metal, 1974, NM ...........................**22.00**
Fall Guy, metal, 1981, EX ....**12.00**
Fraggle Rock, metal, 1984, NM .............................**16.00**
Go Bots, red plastic, 1984, w/thermos, EX ...........................**3.00**
Gremlins, metal, 1984, w/plastic thermos, EX .....................**8.00**
Harlem Globetrotters, metal, 1971, w/thermos, EX .................**32.00**
How the West Was Won, metal, 1978, VG+ ......................**29.00**
Jabber Jaw, Thermos, aqua plastic, 1977, EX ..................**22.00**
Life & Times of Grizzly Adams, dome top, 1977, VG .......**40.00**
Mickey & Donald, Aladdin, red plastic, VG+ .....................**2.00**
Mork & Mindy, metal, 1979, w/thermos, EX ...............**32.00**
Muppet Show, metal, 1978, EX .............................**14.00**
Muppets, metal w/Kermit on back, 1979, w/thermos, EX+ .....**9.00**
My Little Pony, blue plastic, Aladdin, w/thermos, EX+ .**4.00**

New Kids on the Block, orange plastic, 1990, w/thermos, EX ...............................**8.00**

Partridge Family, metal, 1971, NM ...............................**28.00**

Popples, metal, 1986, NM ......**5.00**

Real Ghostbusters, purple plastic, 1986, EX ...........................**3.00**

Return of the Jedi, plastic, 1983, w/plastic thermos, EX ...**18.00**

Satellite, American Thermos, 1958, VG ........................**35.00**

Sesame Street, metal, 1979, w/thermos, NM .............**19.00**

**Star Wars Return of the Jedi, 1983, metal, with thermos, EX, $18.00.**

Superman, metal, 1978, w/thermos, EX .........................**20.00**

**Thermos Bottles**

All Dogs Go to Heaven, 1989 .**7.00**

Batman (dark blue), Thermos, 1989 .................................**6.00**

Coco the Clown, Gary, 1970 .**20.00**

Disney World, Aladdin, Canada, 1974 ..............................**10.00**

Donny & Marie, plastic, 1976, EX ..................................**8.00**

Dream Boat, Feldo, 1960 .....**15.00**

Flintstone Kids, Thermos, 1987 .**5.00**

Fox & the Hound, plastic, Disney, 1981, NM ...........................**3.00**

Get Along Gang, Aladdin, 1983 .............................**8.00**

Gumby, Thermos, 1986 .........**9.00**

Howdy Doody, Thermos, 1977 .**22.00**

Kool-Aid Man, Thermos, 1986 .**10.00**

Mickey at City Zoo, Aladdin, 1985 ...............................**3.00**

Mighty Mouse, Thermos, 1979 .**20.00**

Pac-Man, plastic, 1980, EX ....**2.50**

Planet of the Apes, plastic, 1974, VG ...................................**7.00**

Popeye, King Seeley, 1964 ...**50.00**

Popples, plastic w/pink cup, 1986, EX ..................................**2.00**

Rainbow Brite, Thermos, 1983 .**5.00**

Rocketeer, Aladdin, 1990 .......**8.00**

Sesame Street, Aladdin, 1979 ..**6.00**

Six Million Dollar Man, plastic, 1974, VG+ ........................**6.00**

Sleeping Beauty, Aladdin, 1970 ...........................**70.00**

Tinkerbell, Aladdin, 1969 ....**90.00**

Wonder Woman, plastic, 1977, EX ..................................**15.00**

## MAD Collectibles

MAD, a hotly controversial and satirical publication that was first published in 1952, spoofed everything from advertising and politics to the latest movies and TV shows. Content bordered on a unique mix of lofty creativity, liberalism, and the ridiculous. A cult-like following has developed over the years. Eagerly sought are items relating to characters that were developed by the comic magazine, such as Alfred E. Neuman or Spy Vs Spy. Our advisor, Jim McClane, is listed in the Directory under New Jersey.

Bust, bisque, sold through MAD Magazine, early 1960s, 3¾" ...............**300.00**

Bust, bisque, sold through MAD Magazine, early 1960s, 5½" ...............................**400.00**

Calendar, any dated 1976 through 1981, ea ..........................**12.00**
Calendar, any dated 1989 through 1991, ea ..........................**10.00**
Campaign kits, 1960, 1964 or 1968 issue, complete, ea, from $125 up to ....................**275.00**
Charm bracelet, sold through MAD Magazine, ca late 1950s .**150.00**
Disguise kit, Imagineering Corp, 1987 ................................**20.00**
Game, Parker Brothers, board type, dated 1979 ............**10.00**
Game, Parker Brothers, card type, 1980 ......................**15.00**
Halloween costume, Mardi Gras style w/attached over-sized mask, no box ................**300.00**
Halloween costume, tuxedo style, plastic mask, Collegeville, 1960, MIB ....................**250.00**

**Mad 'Twists' Rock 'n Roll record album, 33⅓ rpm, M, $50.00.**

Necktie, Watson Brothers, 1992, M ....................................**35.00**
Pen, Spy Vs Spy, Applause, 1988, M ....................................**20.00**
Record, Fink Along With MAD, 33⅓ rpm, 1963, original sleeve, M ........................**60.00**
Record, MAD Twists, Rock 'n Roll, 33⅓ rpm 1962, original sleeve, VG......................**35.00**
Record, Musically MAD, 33⅓ rpm 1959, original sleeve, M .**50.00**

Squirt toy, any of 8 variations, Imagineering Corp, 1987, ea ................................**20.00**
Sunglasses, any of 4 versions, Imagineering Corp, 1989, ea ................................**30.00**
T-Shirt, various styles, 1980s, ea ................................**15.00**
T-Shirt, What Me Worry? I Read MAD!, late 1950s ........**400.00**
Watch, various styles, limited edition, Applause, 1988, ea .**65.00**
Watch, various styles, regular edition, Applause, 1988, ea .**25.00**

# Majolica

The type of majolica earthenware most often encountered was made during the 1880s and reached the height of its popularity in the Victorian period. It was produced abroad and in this country as well. It is usually vividly colored, and nature themes are the most common decorative devices. Animal and bird handles and finials and dimensional figures in high relief were used extensively. Refer to *The Collector's Encyclopedia of Majolica* by Mariann Katz-Marks (Collector Books) for more information.

Bowl, centerpiece; flower garlands w/wicker details, Wedgwood, 12" ................................**750.00**
Bowl, Dogwood, white blossoms on turquoise, branch feet, Geo Jones, 6" ......................**435.00**
Bowl, leafy cobalt border, turquoise interior, twig feet, 10½" ..............................**425.00**
Bowl, sauce; Daisy, embossed multicolored flowers form sides, 8¼" ......................**275.00**

Bread tray, Bamboo Fern, cobalt center, Wardle, 13" ......**150.00**

Butter dish, Basketweave & Bamboo, Banks & Thorley, 8" .........**300.00**

Cake stand, Leaf on Plate, low standard, 9" dia ...........**165.00**

Cheese keeper, Holly, berries & vines on brown, top hat form, 10½" .............................**485.00**

Cheese wedge, mottled colors, wheat sheaf figural handle, 5¾x9¾" .........................**185.00**

Compote, Morning Glory, Etruscan, footed, 8" dia ....**225.00**

Cuspidor, Sunflower, Etruscan, 7" .................................**600.00**

Leaf dish, pastel flowers on albino coloring, handle, 9½" .....**30.00**

Pitcher, Basketweave & Bamboo, lg leaves, Banks & Thorley, 8" ....................................**250.00**

Pitcher, Bird & Basketweave, brown & turquoise w/green, 8½" .....**145.00**

Pitcher, Butterfly & Floral, twig handle, cream size, 3½" .**70.00**

Pitcher, Dogwood & Lilacs, staved barrel form, 8" ..............**325.00**

Pitcher, ear-of-corn form w/stalk handle, Etruscan, 6" ....**350.00**

Pitcher, Fruit, on textured white body, brown handle, Clifton, 6½" ...............................**150.00**

Pitcher, Peas in Pod, on cream w/basketweave base, pewter top, 5½" ........................**275.00**

Pitcher, Pelican, 1 as body, 1 as handle, 9" ....................**900.00**

Plate, maple leaves on white, Etruscan, 9" ......................**135.00**

Plate, oyster; 5 lavender shells on cobalt w/seaweed, half-moon, 8" .................................**400.00**

Plate, Pineapple, 3 yellow pineapples on green, 9" ..........**165.00**

Plate, strawberries on blue, Etruscan, 9" ......................**245.00**

Plate, Wild Rose, flowers on white, eyelet handles, 8¾" ......**150.00**

**Pitcher, wild rose branch, 7", from $135.00 to $150.00.**

Platter, banana leaves on white w/turquoise border, 14" .**165.00**

Platter, Bird & Fan, sm rope handles, oval, 14" ..............**235.00**

Salt cellar, child holding small basket figural, Wedgwood, 5" ................................**435.00**

Sardine box, basket form w/fish forming lid, att Geo Jones, 8½" ..............................**375.00**

Shaving mug, Pansy, flowers on turquoise, lavender interior, Fielding .......................**150.00**

Teapot, chick on nest figural, twig handle, 6" ...................**235.00**

Teapot, Flying Crane, birds on white, bamboo handles, 6¾" ..........................**235.00**

Teapot, Strawberry & Bow, on blue basketweave, berry finial, 6" .......................**425.00**

# Maps

Maps can be collected in a variety of different categories. In addition to road maps and general political maps, there are railroad maps, airline and steamship maps, census maps, geological maps, military maps, and historical maps — to name but a few. There are also antique maps, some of which may be hundreds of years old. Some of these may carry price tags in the thousands of dollars. Occasionally one will turn up at a bargain price, but beware of reproductions which may be worth only pennies; and be careful of purchasing framed maps. Unfortunately many valuable antique maps have been ruined by being dry mounted before they were framed and this is not always evident until the frame is removed.

In the days before pump-yourself gas, oil companies used to hand out colorful, attractive, folding road maps for free! Today these maps are popular collectibles and often turn up for sale at flea markets, garage sales, and thrift shops. Folding road maps were also issued by various state highway departments, local chambers of commerce, and the American Auto Association. Like the oil company maps, these are collectible, too, and generally sell for about the same prices. The following guide shows what dealers typically charge for an oil company road map in excellent condition. For further information on map collecting, contact Charles Neuschafer, listed in the Directory under Florida. See also Clubs and Newsletters.

1916, Gulf, Pennsylvania ....**30.00**
1924, Amoco, Texas ..............**20.00**
1928, Standard, Middle Atlantic ...............................**20.00**
1930, Pure Oil, New York ....**10.00**
1933, Conoco, Idaho ............**10.00**
1936, Esso, New England ....**10.00**
1938, Phillips 66, Wyoming .**10.00**
1938, Texaco, New Mexico ...**10.00**
1940, White Rose, Kansas .....**8.00**
1942, Shell, Los Angeles ........**8.00**
1944, American, California ....**8.00**
1947, Co-Op, Missouri ...........**8.00**
1947, Conoco, Colorado .........**8.00**
1947, Sinclair, New England .**8.00**
1952, Humble Oil, Texas ........**6.00**
1953, Union 76, California ....**6.00**
1955, Skelly, Missouri ...........**6.00**
1956, Standard Oil, Chicago ..**6.00**
1960, Texaco, Montana ..........**5.00**
1965, Chevron, Iowa ..............**5.00**
1965, Citgo, Wisconsin ...........**5.00**

**1932, Sinclair, New York road map, $18.00.**

1972, Getty Oil, Pensylvania .**4.00**
1973, Deep Rock, Illinois .......**4.00**
1973, Exxon, New Jersey .......**4.00**
1977, Chevron, Los Angeles ..**4.00**
1987, Marathon, Tennessee ...**4.00**

## National Geographic Society Supplements

Maps published by the National Geographic Society as supplements to their magazines are also popular with collectors. Some representative examples are listed here.

# Marbles

Because there are so many kinds of marbles that interest today's collectors, we suggest you study a book on that specific subject such as one by Everett Grist, published by Collector Books. In addition to his earlier work on antique marbles, he has written a book on *Machine-Made and Contemporary Marbles* as well. His latest title is *Everett Grist's Big Book of Marbles*, which includes both antique and modern varieties. Remember that condition is extremely important. Naturally, chips occurred; and though some may be ground down and polished, the values of badly-chipped and repolished marbles are low.

In our listings, values are for marbles in the standard small size unless noted otherwise and in excellent to near-mint condition. Watch for reproductions of the comic character marbles. Repros have the design printed on a large area of plain white glass with color swirled through the back and sides.

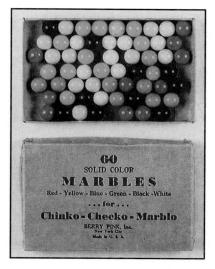

**Chinko-Checko-Marblo marbles, sixty in original box, $50.00.**

Agate, cornelian, oxblood .....**30.00**
Agate, lemonade w/oxblood .**80.00**
Agate, moss ...........................**1.00**
Agate, oxblood, brick w/white .**100.00**

Bennington, fancy, 1¾" ........**80.00**
Bennington, ¾" ........................**3.00**
Champion Jr (swirl) ...............**3.00**
Christmas Tree (red, green, & white swirl) ....................**60.00**
Comic, Emma .......................**85.00**
Comic, Kayo .......................**150.00**
Comic, Moon ......................**150.00**
Comic, Skeezix ...................**100.00**
Coral Swirl ...........................**30.00**
Corkscrew, lemonade ...........**25.00**
Corkscrew, lemonade w/sm line of oxblood ...........................**80.00**
Corkscrew, limeade .............**20.00**
Corkscrew, opaque ..............**15.00**
Corkscrew, transparent .......**20.00**
Corkscrew, tri-colored, Akro Agate ..............................**25.00**
Corkscrew, 2-color opaque ...**10.00**
Cornelian agate, Akro Agate .**35.00**
Cyclone (also called cobra or cleary) ..........................**400.00**
End of the Day, 1¾" .........**1,100.00**
Flame, Christensen Agate, from $150 to .........................**250.00**
Hurricane, Christensen Agate, from $75 to ..................**150.00**
Imperial ...............................**25.00**
Moonie, Akro Agate (opalescent) ..............................**3.00**
Opaque, striped ...................**40.00**
Opaque Swirl, ⅝" .................**35.00**
Rebel ....................................**60.00**
Sparkler, Akro Agate ..........**25.00**
Sulphide, child in chair, 1¾" .**600.00**
Sulphide, elephant, 1¾" .....**300.00**
Sulphide, rabbit, 1¾" .........**150.00**
Superman (red, blue, & gold swirl) ..............................**80.00**
Turkey, Christensen Agate ..**75.00**
9's, MF Christensen & Son (swirl forms '9') ........................**40.00**

# Mar-Crest Stoneware

The Western Stoneware Company of Monmouth, Illinois, made products for Marshall Burns, Division of Technicolor, a distributor from Chicago, with the Marshall Burns trademark: 'Mar-Crest.' The most collectible of these wares is a line of old-fashioned oven-proof stoneware with a warm brown finish, that includes a wide variety of items. The spelling Marcrest or MarCrest may also be found.

Bean pot, individual ...............**3.50**
Bean pot, lg .........................**25.00**
Bowl, cereal ...........................**4.50**
Bowl, French soup (open); individual ......................................**6.00**
Bowl, mixing; #1, 5" ...............**5.00**
Bowl, mixing; #2, 6" ...............**5.00**
Bowl, mixing; #3, 7" ...............**6.00**
Bowl, mixing; #4, 8¼" .............**7.50**
Bowl, mixing; #5, 9½" .............**9.00**
Bowl, vegetable; divided, oval .**10.00**
Carafe .................................**15.00**
Casserole, 8½", w/lid ............**15.00**
Casserole, 9", w/lid & warming stand ..............................**25.00**
Casserole warmer ...............**10.00**

Cookie jar, from $30.00 to $35.00; Snack plate, $7.00.

Creamer ..................................**6.00**
Cup & saucer ..........................**6.00**
Mug ........................................**3.50**
Pitcher, 6" ..............................**7.50**
Pitcher, 8" ............................**10.00**
Plate, dinner ..........................**4.50**
Salt & pepper shakers, pr ......**8.00**
Sugar bowl ..............................**7.00**

# Marilyn Monroe

The famous nude calendar shot by Tom Kelley in 1953 catapulted her to stardom, and by January of 1954, Marilyn had become 20th-Century Fox's biggest box-office attraction and Hollywood's leading sex goddess. Her hairstyle and wardrobe were imitated by women, and she was admired by men the world over. Some her best-remembered films include *How To Marry a Millionaire, The Seven Year Itch,* and *River of No Return,* Gable's last movie. But fame was short-lived and took its grim toll. In 1962 Marilyn was found dead in her apartment, an apparent suicide.

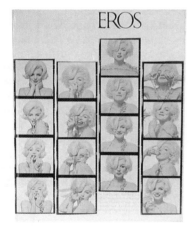

**Book, Eros, June 21, 1962; featuring photos by Bert Stern from Marilyn's last photo session, EX+, $125.00.**

Book, Let's Make Love, Bantam, softcover, 1st edition, 1960, EX ...............................**28.00**
Calendar top, A New Wrinkle, breasts exposed, 1953, 16x18", EX .....................**95.00**
Calendar top, nude pose against red ground, ca 1955, 16x20", EX ...................................**68.00**
Doll, jointed bisque, plays Diamonds Are Girl's Best Friend, 8½", M ............................**75.00**
Greeting card, dated 1974, NM ............................**9.00**
Greeting card, From Marilyn With Love, color, 1985, 6x9", M .**7.50**
Lobby card, Bus Stop, dancing pose, 20th-Century Fox, 1956, EX ................................**145.00**
Lobby card, Some Like It Hot, w/Tony Curtis, United Artists, 1959 ..............................**160.00**
Magazine, Collier's, 1956, July, EX .................................**15.00**
Magazine, Confidential, 1955, September, EX ..............**20.00**
Magazine, Eye, 1953, August, EX .................................**50.00**
Magazine, Hollywood Then & Now, 1987, EX .................**5.00**
Magazine, Modern Screen, 1953, October, EX ...................**20.00**
Magazine, Modern Screen, 1961, October, EX ...................**40.00**
Magazine, Modern Screen, 1962, November, EX ..............**10.00**
Magazine, Modern Screen, 1962, November, NM ..............**35.00**
Magazine, Movie Fan, 1954, July, EX .................................**65.00**
Magazine, Movie Mirror, 1957, May, EX .........................**20.00**
Magazine, Movie Mirror, 1961, October, NM ..................**60.00**
Magazine, Movie Screen Yearbook, 1957, EX ..............**65.00**
Magazine, Photoplay, 1953, February ........................**50.00**
Magazine, Picture Life, 1955, February, EX .................**35.00**
Magazine, Police Gazette, 1962, October, EX ...................**25.00**
Magazine, Reader's Digest, Oct. 1962, last interview before death .**17.50**

Magazine, Screen Stories, The 7 Year Itch, 1955, NM ......**68.00**

Magazine, Silver Screen, 1962, December, EX ................**35.00**

Magazine, Who's Who in Hollywood, 1955, EX ..............**25.00**

Magazine article, Photoplay, Sept 1955, 4-page, EX .............**8.00**

Playing cards, 52 cards+2 jokers, Photo Art, early '50s, VG .**85.00**

Postcard, bathing suit pose on beach, color, early 1950s, EX ..................................**3.50**

Postcard, in black negligee sitting on table, England, EX .....**8.00**

Poster, Monkey Business, 20th-Century Fox, 1952, 27x21", EX ................................**245.00**

Sheet music, River of No Return, 1954, EX ........................**22.50**

Window card, Love Nest, 20th-Century Fox, 1961, 14x16" ....................**255.00**

# Match Safes

The popularity of match safes started around 1850 and peaked in the early 1900s. These small containers were designed to safely carry matches on one's person. They were made from numerous materials including tin, brass, sterling, gold, tortoise shell and aluminum. They became a popular advertising media at the turn of the century. Most safes can be distinguished from other smalls by a rough striking surface. Match safes have been and are still being reproduced; there are many sterling reproductions currently on the market. Our advisor is George Sparacio, who is listed in the Directory under New Jersey.

Advertising, aluminum, Smoke Knukler's Old Standard Cigars, sm .....................**25.00**

Advertising, Cameron Steam Pumps, celluloid wrapped, 2½x1½", EX ...................**40.00**

Advertising, celluloid, Bankable, Warsaw IN, 2x2¼x⅛" ....**70.00**

Advertising, nickel plate, United Cigars in relief, 1⅝x2¼x¼" .**50.00**

Advertising, Pabst Beer both sides, brass, 2½x1½", EX ..........**55.00**

Advertising, Red Man motif, insert type w/plated brass, 2¾x1½" ...........................**50.00**

Advertising, Thorne's Whiskey, The Maze, plated brass, 2x1¼", EX ....................**135.00**

Advertising, United Hatters, Whitehead & Hoag, 2¾x1½", EX ................................**75.00**

Agate, cylindrical w/brass trim, 2⅝x1", EX ....................**165.00**

Anheuser Busch, eagle & A motif, plated brass, 2⅞x1⅝", EX .**92.00**

Art Nouveau, embossed florals on sterling, 2½x1⅝", EX .....**60.00**

Bicycle motif both sides, book form, gutta percha, 2x1½", EX ................................**155.00**

Checkers, red, white & black lithographed tin, 3x1½", VG ..............................**25.00**

Chinese dragon w/ball, brass, 2¾x1⅞", EX .................**225.00**

Circular, English sterling hallmarks, gold wash, w/ring, 1¾" dia ................................**95.00**

Cleopatra's needle, plated brass figural, 2¼x⅞x⅞", EX ........**275.00**

Columbus portrait, plated brass figural, 2⅝x1⅝", EX ......**17.00**

Dwarf w/beard on chamber pot, plated brass figural, 2⅞x1⅝", EX ................................**325.00**

English fob type, ring on side, sterling w/gold wash, 1¾x1¼", EX ................................**70.00**

High-relief gold filigree, ca 1925, 1¼x1½" ............................**20.00**

Krupp, w/3 connecting rings, silverplate, 2⅝x1⅝", EX ..**135.00**

Mail pouch, push-button release, brass, 2⅜x1¼", EX .......**115.00**

Marbles, Pat 1900 on bottom, plated brass, waterproof, 2¾x⅞", EX .....................**15.00**

Mother-of-pearl panels, nickel-plated brass, German, 2¾x1½", EX ...................**30.00**

Owl holding frog, plated brass figural, 2¾x1½", EX ........**450.00**

President Wilson/White House, celluloid wrapped, 2¾x1½", EX ..................................**78.00**

Privy w/man in top hat, brass, 2x¾x½" ..........................**235.00**

Rococo motif, sterling, 2¼x1½", EX .................................**55.00**

**Silver with jasper inlay, 1¾",** **$95.00.**

Snake, coiled brass figural w/glass eyes, 1¾x1⅜", EX .........**450.00**

# Matchcovers

Matchcover collecting is a relatively new hobby. Trying to get officially organized at the 1939 New York World's Fair, six lonely matchcover collectors scoured the fairgrounds for every matchcover they could find. The fair produced quite an assortment. Over three hundred different styles are now known, including those made for this fair and others, restaurants, hotels, banks, services, and businesses in the New York area.

Matchcover clubs grew from small gatherings of the dedicated, mostly from the northeastern states — New York, New Jersey, Connecticut, and the New England states. At one time there were touted to be over a million matchcover collectors in this country, with many of them belonging to clubs. Those days are now gone, but many of the clubs remain. Only 4,000 or so collectors now belong to a club, but there are hundreds of thousands who collect matchcovers for fun and inexpensive recreation.

Information about matchcover collecting can be gained by joining America's foremost club, The American Matchcover Collecting Club (AMCC) (see Clubs and Newsletters). Dues are currently $18.00 yearly, and you receive *The Front Striker Bulletin* filled with matchcover information and values. For further information on pricing, *The Matchcover Collector's Price Guide, 1st Edition* ($16.95 + $3.25 shipping and handling), is available from our advisor and the club's director, Bill Retskin (listed in the Directory under North Carolina).

Note that only half the matchcovers ever produced are collectible. Of that 50%, less than 5% are worth more than a quarter. There are millions of valuable matchcovers in garages, attics, basements, and storerooms all over America. AMCC offers a

**Long Islanders, directions to football games, early 1940s, $15.00.**

complete appraisal service for estates and insurance purposes. Anyone writing for club or estate information will receive an immediate reply and several collectible matchcovers. Please include an SASE with your request.

Listed here are typical prices realized within the last twelve months from the Quarterly *Front Striker Bulletin* mail matchcover auction.

Key:

20S — 20 stick size
30S — 30 stick size
40S — 40 stick size
(B) — on the back
BS — striker on back
(F) — on the front
FB — full book
(F/B) — front and back
(I) — inside
(S) — saddle

Al Schacht, Clown Prince of Baseball, photo w/signature, spot striker ...........................**15.00**
Alligator, Parrot Jungle, Miami FL (F), Cockatoo, Flamingo Pond (B) ........................**45.00**
Canadian Pullmatch, silhouette of King & Queen, Made in England, 1937 ......................**12.00**
Club Cherry, Shioiri Machi, Tokosuke Te.148 (F/B), BS ...**12.00**
Disney/Pepsi, 751st Tank Battalion, elephant w/helmet in tank, No 1 ......................**13.00**

For President, Alfred E Smith, black & white photo (F/B), scarce ............................**27.50**
Girlie Single #132, Club Primadonna, Gardena CA (B), Reno NV (S), 40S .........**10.00**
Happy Birthday America, Nassau Bay Nat'l Bank, 30S, set of 12 cover ...............................**10.50**
Honolulu Barber Shop, 14 S Hotel St, Honolulu TH (F/B), #3 type mm .........................**14.00**
Make It a Democratic Year (B), Jimmy Carter photo (F), blank (S), BS ................**15.00**
Me for Yoo-Hoo, Yogi Berra photo (B), The Chocolate Drink... (F), FB ...........................**44.00**

**Mobilgas, Merry Christmas, $5.00.**

Redskins 1969 (not dated) Home Game Schedule w/ad (I), Jewelite, FS .........................**20.00**

Ronald Reagan, California's Governor, Vote...1970, w/photo (F), 5-20S ........................**8.00**

Royal Beer & Ale, Brewed & Bottled...Honolulu HI (B), type #2 mm ...........................**22.00**

WPEN Radio, Series B of 10, Smith-Allison-Brees-Farren..., 1956 .....................**17.00**

# McCoy

A popular collectible with flea market goers, McCoy pottery has been made in Roseville, Ohio, since 1910. They are most famous for their extensive line of figural cookie jars, more than two hundred in all. They also made amusing figural planters, etc., as well as dinnerware, and vases and pots for the florist trade. Though some pieces are unmarked, most bear one of several McCoy trademarks. Beware of reproductions made by a company in Tennessee who is using a very close facsimile of the old McCoy mark. They are making several cookie jars once produced by McCoy as well as other now-defunct potteries. Some of these (but by no means all) are now being dated with the number '93' below the mark.

Refer to *The Collector's Encylopedia of McCoy Pottery* by Sharon and Bob Huxford (Collector Books) for more information. These mark numbers refer to this book: #1) cojoined 'NM' over 'USA' — 1940-43; #4) 'M' with 'c' over right leg, 'C' with attached 'o,' 'Y' — 1940 to closing; #7) same as #4) with 'USA' below — 1939 to closing; #15) pitcher with 'MCP' below in square — Mt. Clemens trademark. See also Cookie Jars; Clubs and Newsletters.

Bank, Metz Brewing Co, Omaha NE, 2 sizes, from $55 to .**65.00**

Bank, piggy, mark #4, 1947 .**30.00**

Bank, Woodsy Owl, 1974 .....**65.00**

Basket, leaves & berries, mark #4, 1948 .........................**35.00**

Bowl, salad; El Rancho ......**165.00**

Creamer, dog figural, green, mark #4, 1950s ........................**70.00**

Decanter, astronaut, mark #15, Thomas 'n Sims Distillery, USA Dec 1968 ..............**70.00**

Lamp, panther, 1950s ..........**55.00**

Lamp base, horse .................**85.00**

Lamp base, 4 cherub faces ...**45.00**

Pitcher, elephant, mark #1, 1940s ..........................**125.00**

Planter, auto, mark #7, 1954 .**15.00**

Planter, baby cradle, mark #4 .**18.00**

**Planter, bird dog planter, 1954, $110.00.**

Planter, convertible auto, USA on tool chest, 1963 .............**20.00**

Planter, frog, mark #4, 1950 .**17.50**

Planter, goose w/cart, mark #4, 1943 ...............................**15.00**

Planter, hobby horse, mark #7, 1955 ...............................**25.00**

Planter, pelican, mark #1, 1941 ...........................**20.00**

Planter, poodle, mark #7, from $40 to ..............................**50.00**

Planter, stork w/basket, mark #7, 1956 ..............................**35.00**

Planter, swan, mark #7 ........**15.00**

Planter, wishing well, mark #7, 1950 ...............................**15.00**

Planter, 2 quail, mark #7, 1955 ...........................**40.00**
Planter, 5 Scotties, mark #4, 1949 ...............................**30.00**
Planter bookends, violin, mark #7, 1959, pr ....................**60.00**
Sombrero serve-all, El Rancho **350.00**
Spoon rest, butterfly, mark #7, 1953 ...............................**55.00**
Spoon rest, penguin shape, mark #7, 1953 .........................**60.00**
Strawberry jar, bird w/long tail, mark #4, 1950 ...............**20.00**

**Strawberry pot with bird, 8½",
$30.00.**

Tea set, Ivy, mark #7, 1950, 3-pc .................................**70.00**
Tea set, pine cone, mark #4, 1946, 3-pc ..............................**65.00**
Teapot, cat, 1971 ..................**70.00**
Vase, Blossomtime, 2 angular handles, mark #4, 1946 .......**20.00**
Vase, double grape clusters, mark #4, 1951 .........................**38.00**
Vase, English ivy, mark #7, 1953 ............................**35.00**
Vase, hand shape, mark #1, 1943 ............................**18.00**
Vase, hyacinth, mark #4, 1950 ........................**35.00**

Vase, sunflower, 1954 ...........**35.00**
Vase, swan, mark #4, 1946, 9" .**25.00**
Vase, Uncle Sam, mark #4, 1943 ............................**45.00**
Wall pocket, birdbath, mark #4, 1949 ...............................**35.00**
Wall pocket, grapes, 1953 ....**45.00**
Wall pocket, lily, mark #8, 1948 ...........................**40.00**
Wall pocket, lovebirds, mark #7, 1953 ...............................**45.00**
Wall pocket, orange, 1953 ....**35.00**
Wall pocket, umbrella, mark #7, 1955 ...............................**25.00**
Window box, pine cone, mark #4, 1945 ...............................**12.50**

# Metlox

Since the 1940s, the Metlox company of California has been producing dinnerware lines, cookie jars, and decorative items which today have become popular collectibles. Some of their most popular patterns are California Provincial (the dark green and burgundy rooster), Red Rooster (in red, orange, and brown), Homestead Provincial (dark green and burgundy farm scenes), and Colonial Homestead (farm scenes done in red, orange, and brown). See also Cookie Jars. For more information, refer to *Collector's Encyclopedia of Metlox Potteries* by Carl Gibbs, Jr.

California Ivy, bowl, vegetable; 11" .....................................**30.00**
California Ivy, bowl, 5" ...........**9.00**
California Ivy, casserole, w/lid .**60.00**
California Ivy, cup & saucer .**11.00**
California Ivy, plate, 10¼" ...**13.00**
California Ivy, plate, 6¼" .......**6.00**
California Ivy, platter, 13" ...**29.00**
California Provincial, cup & saucer ............................**16.00**

California Provincial, plate, 10" .............................**15.00**

California Provincial, plate, 6" .**7.50**

California Provincial, salt & pepper shakers, figural, pr .**48.00**

California Strawberry, bowl, salad; lg ..........................**55.00**

California Strawberry, butter dish w/lid................................**45.00**

California Strawberry, cup & saucer .............................**14.00**

California Strawberry, gravy boat ...............................**32.00**

California Strawberry, platter, oval, 11" .........................**30.00**

**Cock-a-Doodle-Do, Twin dip-biscuit basket, early 1960's, from $35.00 to $40.00.**

Homestead Provincial, butter dish w/lid................................**49.00**

Homestead Provincial, chop plate, 12" ...................................**55.00**

Homestead Provincial, coffeepot ..........................**95.00**

Homestead Provincial, creamer & sugar bowl ......................**45.00**

Homestead Provincial, mug, sm ..............................**22.00**

Homestead Provincial, plate, 10" ...............................**15.00**

Homestead Provincial, salt & pepper shakers, hen, pr ......**50.00**

Homestead Provincial, salt & pepper shakers, w/handle, pr .......**24.00**

Pepper Tree, cup & saucer ...**14.00**

Pepper Tree, plate, 10" .........**12.00**

Provincial Fruit, bowl, cereal; 7" .................................**13.00**

Provincial Fruit, plate, 7½" .**10.00**

Provincial Fruit, sugar bowl .**22.00**

Red Rooster Provincial, bowl, cereal ............................**14.00**

Red Rooster Provincial, bowl, vegetable; w/lid ..................**65.00**

Red Rooster Provincial, chop plate, 12" .......................**65.00**

Red Rooster Provincial, cup & saucer ...........................**15.00**

Red Rooster Provincial, gravy boat ...............................**35.00**

Red Rooster Provincial, platter, 11" ...................................**35.00**

Red Rooster Provincial, salt & pepper shakers, pr ........**22.00**

Sculptured Daisy, bowl, fruit; 6" .................................**10.00**

Sculptured Daisy, butter dish, ¼-lb, w/lid .....................**14.00**

Sculptured Daisy, casserole, w/lid .............................**45.00**

Sculptured Daisy, plate, dinner ............................**13.00**

Sculptured Daisy, sugar bowl, w/lid ..............................**24.00**

Sculptured Zinnia, cup & saucer .........................**14.00**

Sculptured Zinnia, plate, salad; 7½" .................................**10.00**

Woodland Gold, cup & saucer .**14.00**

Woodland Gold, plate, dinner .**13.00**

Woodland Gold, platter, 13" .**35.00**

# Milk Glass

Milk glass has been used since the 1700s to make tableware, lamps, and novelty items such as covered figural dishes and decorative wall plaques. Early examples were made with cryolite and ring with a clear bell tone when tapped. For more information, refer to *Collector's Encyclopedia of Milk Glass* by Betty and Bill Newbound. See also Animal Dishes; Westmoreland.

Axe, painted souvenir, 7" .....**15.00**
Bottle, cologne; bulbous base, narrow neck w/wide lip, floral stopper ...........................**25.00**
Bottle, New York World's Fair, 9", w/metal cap, from $20 to .**25.00**

**Bull's head mustard jar, original paint and tongue ladle (ladle very rare), $250.00.**

Cake stand, sq w/scalloped drape, footed, Indiana Glass, 1960-70, 7" ..............................**10.00**
Candy box, heart form w/3 sections, Consolidated, 1950s, 8½x7¼" ...........................**40.00**
Compote, 8-sided w/grapes, skim milk look, Anchor Hocking, 1960s-70s .........................**8.00**
Decanter, grape design, Imperial, 1950-58, 11½", w/8 wines ..**45.00**
Dish, swan w/open back, painted eye & beak, LE Smith, ca 1930, 9" ..........................**35.00**

Jar, apple w/shiny red & yellow paint, 1940-50, 3⅞" .......**10.00**
Jar, beehive shape for honey, pink, Jeannette, 1958-59, 4⅛" ................................**30.00**
Jar, ointment; paper label & tin lid, sm, from $5 to .........**10.00**
Jar, painted strawberry, 3¾" .**10.00**
Lamp, Mission Octagon, US Glass, ca 1912, 6½" .....**100.00**
Mug, child's; pyro nursery rhyme, Hazel Atlas, 1940s, from $4 to .....................................**6.00**
Pin tray, Helping Hand, painted flower at wrist, McKee, 5x2½" .............................**15.00**
Pin tray, Roses & Poppies w/lady's head, 6x3¼" ...................**25.00**
Plate, Columbus at center w/1492-1892 across chest, 9¾" .................................**40.00**
Plate, Flower & Scroll, unmarked, 8⅜" .................................**12.00**
Plate, painted windmill scene, lacy edge, 7" ...................**20.00**
Plate, Three Kittens, 7", from $30 to .....................................**35.00**
Salt, swan form, unmarked, ca 1960, 3⅞" ........................**15.00**
Toothpick holder, Daisy & Button top hat, 2¼", from $15 to .**20.00**
Vase, Regent, hand-painted pine cones & needles, Consolidated, 10" ........................**30.00**
Vase, Vintage Grape, footed, LE Smith, 1970s, 9" ............**15.00**

# Model Kits

The best-known producer of model kits today is Aurora. Collectors often pay astronomical prices for some of the character kits from the 1960s. Made popular by all the monster movies of that decade, ghouls like Vampirella, Frankenstein, and the Wolfman were eagerly built up by kids everywhere. But the majority of all model kits were vehicles, ranging from as small as 3" up to 24" long. Some of the larger model vehicle makers were AMT, MPC, and IMC. Condition is very important in assessing the value of a kit, with built-ups priced at about 50% lower than one still in the box. Other things factor into pricing as well — who is selling, who is buying and how badly they want it, locality, supply and demand.

Our Aurora models advisor is Bill Bruegman, author of *Aurora, History and Price Guide* (Cap'n Penny Productions, Inc). Other models are under the advisement of Gordy Dutt, author of *Collectible Figure Kits of the '50s, '60s, & '70s, Reference and Value Guide* (see Directory for ordering information). Both advisors are listed under Ohio. For more information and additional listings we recommend *Schroeder's Collectible Toys, Antique to Modern,* by Sharon and Bob Huxford. See also Clubs and Newsletters.

**1932 Chevrolet Coupe, Hubley, MIB, $40.00 to $50.00.**

Addar, Planet of Apes Stallion & Soldier, #107, 1/11 scale, 1974, MIB ......................**80.00**
Airfix, James Bond's Aston-Marton DB-5, 1/24 scale, 1966, MIB ............................**200.00**

AMT, Man From UNCLE Car, #912, 1/25 scale, 1967, MIB ...**200.00**
AMT, Munsters Drag-U-La, #905, 1/25 scale, 1965, MIB .**200.00**
Aurora, Addams Family House, built-up .........................**200.00**
Aurora, Batman, 1964, MIB .**200.00**
Aurora, Creature of the Black Lagoon, glow-in-the-dark, 1969, MIB ....................**100.00**
Aurora, Dr Jekyll, w/sq box, M ..............................**80.00**
Aurora, Dracula, glow-in-the-dark, 1969, MIB ............**75.00**
Aurora, Frankenstein, glow-in-the-dark, built-up ..........**45.00**
Aurora, Frankenstein, 1961, MIB ..............................**225.00**
Aurora, Godzilla, 1969, built-up, w/sq box .........................**85.00**
Aurora, Gruesome Goodies Monster Scene, MIB .............**72.50**
Aurora, James Bond, 1966, MIB ..........................**200.00**
Aurora, Lost in Space Robot, 1968, MIB ....................**750.00**
Aurora, Mummy, w/sq box, M .**80.00**
Aurora, Pendulum Monster Scene, MIB ....................**68.00**
Aurora, Phantom of the Opera, black plastic, 1963, MIB .........**275.00**
Aurora, Spiderman, Comic Scenes Series, 1974, MIB .........**47.50**
Aurora, The Incredible Hulk, Comic Scene Series, 1974, MIB ..............................**45.00**
Aurora, The Mummy, glow-in-the-dark, 1969, M ................**65.00**
Aurora, The Phantom, w/mask, built-up .........................**65.00**
Aurora, Witch, built-up ........**58.00**
Aurora, Wolfman, built-up ..**45.00**
Aurora, Zorro, 1965, MIB ..**225.00**
Bachmann, German Shepherd, #8005, 1/6 scale, 1960, MIB ............................**30.00**
Bachmann, Woodpecker, #9004, 1/1 scale, 1959, MIB ......**30.00**

Campbeltown Destroyer, Revell, 1971, sealed in original box, M, ....................................**35.00**
Hawk, Weird-Ohs Digger, #530, 1963, MIB ....................**100.00**
ITC, Lion, #3851, 1960, MIB .**35.00**
Lindberg, Big Wheeler, #277, 1965, built-up, EX, from $15 to ....................................**25.00**
Mego, King Kong/The Last Stand, #74040, 1976, MIB ........**40.00**
Monogram, Godzilla, #6300, 1978, built-up, EX, from $35 to .**45.00**
Monogram, Red Baron/Fokker Triplane, #5903, 1971, MIB ............................**40.00**
Monogram, Superman, #6301, 1/8 scale, 1974, w/decals, MIB .**45.00**
MPC, Dark Shadows Werewolf, #1552, 1969, MIB ........**200.00**
MPC, Darth Vader Action Bust, #1921, 1978, MIB ..........**50.00**
MPC, Dead Man's Raft, #5005, 1/12 scale, 1972-74, MIB ......**125.00**
Park Plastic, Born Losers Castro, #803, 1/10 scale, 1965, MIB ..............................**75.00**

**Planet of the Apes, Addar Products Corp., 1973, MIB, $40.00.**

Revell, Bonanza (Hoss, Little Joe & Ben), #1931, 1966, MIB .**125.00**
Revell, Fink-Eliminator, #1310, 1963-64, MIB ..............**175.00**
Revell, Flash Gordon & the Martian, #1450, 1/8 scale, 1965, MIB ..............................**200.00**
Revell, Gemini Astronaut, #1837, 1/6 scale, 1967, MIB ......**75.00**
Superior, The Seeing Eye, #3100, 2/1 scale, 1959-61, MIB .**35.00**

# Moon and Star

A reissue of Palace, an early pattern glass line, Moon and Star was developed for the market in the 1960s by Joseph Weishar of Island Mould and Machine Company (Wheeling, West Virginia). It was made by several companies. One of the largest producers was L.E. Smith of Mt. Pleasant, Pennsylvania; and L.G. Wright (who had their glassware made by Fostoria, Fenton, and Westmoreland) carried a wide assortment in their catalogs for many years. It is still being made on a very limited basis; but the most collectible pieces are those in red, blue, amber, and green — colors that are no longer in production. The values listed here are for pieces in red or blue. Amber and green prices (and crystal) should be 30% lower.

Ashtray, 10" ..........................**30.00**
Ashtray, 5½" ........................**12.00**
Banana bowl, 12" long .........**45.00**
Butter dish, 6x5½" ..............**50.00**
Candle holders, flared foot w/scalloped edge, 6", pr ..........**30.00**
Candy box, round body on short patterned foot, 6" .........**30.00**
Compote, raised stem on foot, 10x8" ..............................**50.00**

Compote, scalloped foot on stem, 4x8" ...............................**35.00**
Compote, scalloped rim, 7x10" .**40.00**
Console bowl, 8" ...................**25.00**
Creamer, raised foot w/scalloped edge, 5¾x3" ....................**30.00**
Creamer & sugar bowl, open, sm ...............................**20.00**
Cruet, 6¾" ............................**32.00**
Decanter, bulbous, ring foot, 32-oz, 12" .............................**50.00**

**Fairy lamp, ruby, $30.00 to $35.00.**

Goblet, water; 5¾" ................**12.00**
Goblet, wine; 4½" ...................**9.00**
Jelly dish, stemmed foot, 10½" .**45.00**
Nappy, allover pattern, crimped rim, 2¾x6" dia ...............**18.00**
Oil lamp, 12" .........................**65.00**
Plate, 8" ...............................**25.00**
Relish bowl, 6 lg scallops form allover pattern, 1½x8" ..**12.00**
Relish dish, 1 plain handle, 2x8" ............................**18.00**
Salt & pepper shakers, metal tops, 2x4", pr ................**25.00**
Salt cellar, scalloped rim, sm flat foot ..................................**8.00**
Soap dish, oval, 2x6" ...........**12.00**

Spoonholder, straight sides, 6" .**30.00**
Sugar bowl, straight sides, scalloped foot, 8x4½" ..........**35.00**
Syrup, metal top, 4½x3½" ....**25.00**
Toothpick holder, scalloped rim, sm flat foot ...................**10.00**
Tumbler, iced tea; 11-oz, 5½" .**14.00**
Tumbler, juice; no pattern on flat rim or disk foot, 5-oz, 3½" ........**10.00**
Wine, 4½" ...............................**9.00**

# Mortens Studios

Animal models sold by Mortens Studios of Arizona during the 1940s are some of today's most interesting collectibles, especially among animal lovers. Hundreds of breeds of dogs, cats, and horses were produced from a plaster-type composition material constructed over a wire framework. They range in size from 2" up to about 7" and most are marked.

Afghan, tan & charcoal face, 7x7" ...............................**90.00**

**Boxer, 4", $55.00.**

Chow pup, lying down, tan & brown, 3x3" ....................**60.00**
Dachshund, standing, lg ......**80.00**
Dalmatian, #812, sm ...........**55.00**
English Setter, #848 ............**70.00**

German Sheperd pup, 3½x3½" .**40.00**
Great Dane, recumbent, black
    details on tan, 7½x6½" ..**80.00**
Persian cat ............................**50.00**
Pointer, sitting, ivory w/black
    spots, 4x4¾" ...................**70.00**
Springer Spaniel, 5" .............**70.00**

# Motion Lamps

Animated motion lamps were
popular from the 1920s to early
1960s. They are characterized by
action created by heat from a light
bulb which causes a cylinder to
revolve and create the illusion of
an animated scene. They were
most probably designed after the
burning candle type in early days
that rang bells and had hanging
designs. Some of the better-known
manufacturers were Econolite
Corp., Scene in Action Corp., and
L.A. Goodman Mfg. Company. As
with many collectible items, prices
are guided by condition, availabil-
ity, and collector demand which
seems to be more intense on the
west and east coasts, often result-
ing in higher prices there than in
the midwest. Values are given for
lamps in mint condition. Any
damage or flaws seriously reduce
the price. Advisors for this category are Jim and Kaye Whitaker
(Eclectic Antiques), listed in the
Directory under Washington.

Airplanes, Econolite, plastic,
    1958, 11", from $85 to .**125.00**
Antique Cars, Econolite, plastic,
    1957, 11", from $85 to .**125.00**
Bar Is Open, Visual Effects Inc,
    plastic, 1970, 13", minimum
    value .............................**30.00**
Christmas Tree, Econolite, paper,
    1951, 15", from $60 to ...**90.00**

Forest Fire, Econolite, plastic,
    1955, 11", from $60 to .**100.00**
Forest Fire, LA Goodman, plastic,
    1956, 11", from $65 to ...**95.00**

**Forest Fire, Roto-Vue Jr, 1940, 10",
$120.00.**

Fountain of Youth, Boy, Econolite,
    1950, 11", from $75 to .**115.00**
Marine Scene, Scene In Action, glass,
    1930s, from $100 to ........**175.00**
Merry-Go-Round, Econolite, Dis-
    ney, plastic, red, 1955, from
    $150 to .........................**225.00**
Merry-Go-Round, Econolite,
    Roto-Vue Jr, 1950, 10", from
    $90 to .........................**125.00**
Mill Scene, Econolite, plastic,
    1956, 11", from $75 to .**100.00**
Niagara Falls, Econolite, plastic,
    1955, 11", from $70 to ...**95.00**
Niagara Falls, LA Goodman, plastic,
    1957, 11", from $55 to ......**85.00**
Niagara Falls, Scene In Action,
    glass & metal, '30s, 10", from
    $100 to .........................**175.00**

Ocean Creatures, LA Goodman, plastic, 1955, 11", from $80 to ..................................**125.00**

Op-Art, Visual Effects Inc, plastic, 1970, minimum value ...**45.00**

Oriental Fantasy, LA Goodman, plastic, 1957, 11", from $75 to ..................................**115.00**

Santa & Reindeer, LA Goodman, plastic, 1957, 11", from $75 to ..................................**130.00**

Seattle World's Fair, Econolite, plastic, 1962, 11", from $80 to ..................................**125.00**

Ships, Rev-O-Lite, bronze & plastic, 1930s, 10", from $80 to ..................................**125.00**

Snow Scene w/Church, Econolite, plastic, 1957, 11", from $75 to ..................................**115.00**

Tropical Fish, Econolite, plastic, 1954, 11", from $55 to ...**70.00**

Water Skiers, Econolite, plastic, 1958, 11", from $100 to .**150.00**

# Movie Memorabilia

Vintage movies are meshed in our minds with fond memories of high school dates at drive-ins; of memorable performers like Vivian Leigh and Clarke Gable; of wonderful dancers like Rogers and Astaire; of terrifying monsters like Frankenstein and Daracula; of plush theatres, singing cowboys, and side-splitting comics. Posters, lobby cards, and souvenir booklets from those days before video stores, when Hollywood stars were epitomized as the ultimate in glamor and sophistication and movies were our number-one source of entertainment are highly collectible today — so are movie magazines, autographs, and any of the vast assortment of retail merchandise items that promote a particular performer or movie. Especially valuable are items from the twenties and thirties that have to do with such popular stars as Jean Harlow, Bella Lugosi, Carol Lumbard, and Gary Cooper. For further information we recommend our advisors, TVC Enterprises, listed in the Directory under Massachussetts. See also Autographs; Beatles; Character Clocks and Watches; Dolls, Celebrity; Elvis Presley; Games; Marilyn Monroe; Paper Dolls; Pin-back Buttons; Rock 'n Roll; Shirley Temple; Three Stooges; Western Heroes.

Photo courtesy Tom Morris.

**The Fred Astaire & Ginger Rogers Book, by Arlene Croce, 1972, $10.00.**

Ad card, Bob Hope in Beau James for Ever-Ready Razors, 10x7", NM ................................**12.00**

Ad card, Tess of the Storm Country, Mary Pickford, 1922, EX ......................**15.00**

Balloon, Muppet Babies, Kermit the Frog w/balloons, 17", M ........................**15.00**

Battery tester, WC Fields figural w/red bulb nose, 1974, original card ........................**15.00**

Candy box, Planet of the Apes, Phoenix Candy Co, 1967, NM ..................................**32.00**

Coloring book, Bette Davis, ca 1942, 10x15", VG ..........**40.00**

Coloring book, Rosemary Clooney, authorized edition, 11x12", NM ..................................**10.00**

Credit sheet, Yanks, Richard Gere, Universal, 1979, M ..........**1.00**

**Dalmatians, Buena Vista, 1961, 41x27", EX, $750.00.**

Dress pattern, Loretta Young, Advance Pattern Co, complete ..............**4.00**

Game, Scarlett O'Hara Marbles, Marietta Games, ca 1940, 6x8½", EX ......................**75.00**

Handout sheet, Kit Carson, John Hall, 1940s, 9x12", NM ...**2.00**

Handout sheet, Terrors on Horseback, Buster Crabbe, ca 1940s, 9x12", M ...............**2.00**

Herald, Gone With the Wind, ca 1941, 4 pages, 5¾x9", NM .**35.00**

Ice cream carton, Bing Crosby, color, dated 1954, 3x3x4", M ..................................**5.00**

Ice cream cup lid, Bob Hope in Son of Paleface, NM ........**4.25**

Ice cream cup lid, Gene Kelly, The Pirate, 1947, NM .............**3.50**

Insert card, Hanging Tree, Gary Cooper, 1959, 14x36", VG .**27.50**

Insert card, On a Clear Day, 14x22", VG .....................**20.00**

Instant marquee, White Hunter, Black Heart; Clint Eastwood, 1990, M ..........................**25.00**

Lithograph print, Jeans Dean, color, 8x10", M ...............**20.00**

Lobby card, Across the Atlantic, Monte Blue, ca 1925, 11x14", EX ...**15.00**

Lobby card, Beetlejuice, 11x14", M ......................................**3.50**

Lobby card, Cattle Queen of Montana, Barbara Stanwyck, ca 1954, 11x14" .....................**3.50**

Lobby card, Flying Tigers, John Wayne, Republic, color, 1942, 11x14" .............................**75.00**

Lobby card, Gun Talk, Johnny Mack Brown, Monogram, 11x14", set of 7 ..............**30.00**

Lobby card, Hell's Angels, Howard Hughs, 1940s, 11x14", EX .**40.00**

Lobby card, Monsignor, Christopher Reeve, set of 8, M ...**5.00**

Lobby card, Redwood Forest Trail, Rex Allen, Republic, 1950, set of 8 ..................................**35.00**

Lobby card, Sundown in Santa Fe, Rocky Lane, Republic, '48, 11x14", VG ......................**5.00**

Lobby card, The Thundering Herd, Lash LaRue, ca 1951, 11x14", set of 6 ..............**35.00**

Lobby card, True Grit, John Wayne, 1969, G .............................**30.00**

Lobby card, Where Were You When the Lights Went Out, Doris Day, 1968 ...............**3.50**

Magazine ad, Dennis O'Keefe, Van Heusen Shirts, 1954, 11x14", EX .......................**2.00**

Magazine ad, Rhonda Fleming, Lustre Creme Shampoo, 1955, 11x14", EX ........................**3.50**

Magazine ad, Susan Hayward, GE Radio, color, 1948, 11x14", EX ...................................**3.00**

Mug, Dr Zhivago, anniversary edition, MIB ....................**7.50**

Paint book, Judy Garland Fashion Paint Book, 1940s, 11x15", VG .....................**55.00**

Paint book, Zigfield Girl, Merrill #3465, 1941, 48 pages, 10x15", EX .....................**17.50**

Photo album, Grease, John Travolta, color photos, VG ....**7.00**

Plate, Cat on a Hot Tin Roof, Elizabeth Taylor, MIB .........**15.00**

Postcard, Errol Flynn, Warner Bros, ca mid-1940s, 3½x5½", EX .................................**15.00**

Postcard, Lauren Bacall, Warner Bros, ca mid-1940s, 3½x5½" ........................**12.00**

Postcard, Raiders of the Lost Ark, 1984, NM ..........................**5.00**

Postcard book, Close Encounters of the Third Kind, 1978, set of 48, M ..............................**15.00**

Poster, Africa Screams, United Artists, 1949, 41x27", EX+ .............**225.00**

Poster, Bedtime for Bonzo, Universal, 1951, 41x27", NM ..**350.00**

Poster, Dirty Harry, Warner Bros, 1971, 41x27", NM .......**250.00**

Poster, Giant, Warner Bros, 1956, 41x27", EX+ .................**300.00**

Poster, The Fighting Kentuckian, Republic, 1949, 36x41", VG+ ............................**100.00**

Poster, West Side Story, United Artists, 1961, 41x27", EX .............**285.00**

Poster, West Side Story, United Artists, 1961, 41x27", NM .............**300.00**

Pressbook, Hello Dolly, Barbara Streisand, 1970, 11 pages, NM .................................**15.00**

Pressbook, Hombre, Paul Newman, 1967, 12 pages, M .**10.00**

Pressbook, John Wayne, McQ, NM ................**15.00**

Pressbook, Stage to Thunder Rock, Barry Sullivan, ca 1963, 12x14", G ..............**8.50**

Pressbook, That Funny Feeling, Sandra Dee & Bobby Darin, 1965, M ..........................**10.00**

Pressbook, The Secret of the Nimh, EX .........................**2.00**

Pressbook, The Unforgiven, Clint Eastwood, 8 pages, NM .**25.00**

Presskit, Airplane II, Robert Hays, Paramount, 1980, 11 stills, M ..........................**25.00**

Presskit, Bladerunner, 21 stills, complete, M ...................**40.00**

Presskit, Risky Business, Tom Crews, 12 stills, complete, M ...............................**25.00**

Presskit, The Couch Trip, 14 stills, VG ....................**15.00**

Program, Dracula, Jean LeClerc, 7x12", VG ........................**3.00**

Program, Gone With the Wind, Rhett & Scarlett cover, 1939, 6x9½" .............................**30.00**

Program, Mutiny on the Bounty, Marlon Brando, EX .........**4.00**

Record, True Grit, John Wayne, 33⅓ rpm, VG .................**12.50**

Scarf, Little Women, black & white portraits on cotton, 1949, 23x27" ..................**35.00**

Script, Good Fellas, 1990, M .**20.00**

Sheet Music, A Night at the Opera, The Marx Bros, 1935, 9x12", NM ......................**20.00**

Souvenir book, King of Kings, NM ....................................**6.50**

Souvenir book, My Fair Lady, Audry Hepburn, 9x11", EX ...........**6.00**

Spoon, Norma Talmadge, Oneida, silverplated, ca 1925, 6", EX ...................**6.00**

Squirt gun, Planet of the Apes, ape's head, Apjac, 1967, MIP ................................**30.00**

Standee, Footloose, Kevin Bacon, Paramount, 1984, NM ..**45.00**

Standee, The First Power, Lou Diamond Phillips, Orion, 1990, M ............................**15.00**

Sticker book, My Fair Lady, Audrey Hepburn, ca 1964, 8½x11", EX .....................**12.50**

Still, Limehouse Blues, George Raft, black & white glossy, 1934, 8x10" .......................**5.00**

Still, Wings in the Dark, Myrna Loy, black & white glossy, 1934, 8x10" .......................**3.50**

Tablet, Betty Grable, ca 1950, 8x10½", EX .....................**3.00**

Tablet, John Wayne color photo, 1950, 8x10", M .............**25.00**

Tin container, Madeleine Carrol photo & Sunshine Co, ca 1940, 3", EX ...................**42.50**

Title card, Blondie Takes a Vacation, 1939, G .................**28.00**

Trailer, Batman, Michael Keaton, Warner Brothers, 1989, 35mm, M .......................**35.00**

Window card, Branded, Alan Ladd, 14x36", VG ..........**25.00**

Window card, North to Alaska, John Wayne, 14x22", EX ........**120.00**

# National Geographic Magazines

The National Geographic Magazine was first introduced in October 1888. There was only one issue that year, and together with the three published in 1889 make up Volume I, the most valuable group on the market. Volume I, No. 1, alone is worth about $12,000.00 in very good condition. A complete set of magazines from 1888 to the present is worth approximately $30,000.00 to $60,000.00, depending on condi-

tion, as condition and price are closely related. As time goes by, values of individual issues increase. The most sought-after years are pre-World War: 1888-1914. Still, some postwar recent issues command good prices. Be on the lookout for any in the following listing. Our advisor is Don Smith, who is listed in the Directory under Kentucky. Values are given for magazines in at least excellent condition.

| | |
|---|---|
| 1910–1915 | **8.00** |
| 1916–1920 | **7.50** |
| 1921–1925 | **7.00** |
| 1926–1930 | **6.75** |
| 1931–1935 | **6.50** |
| 1936–1940 | **6.25** |
| 1941–1945 | **5.75** |
| 1946–1950 | **5.25** |
| 1951–1955 | **4.75** |
| 1956–1960 | **4.50** |
| 1961–1965 | **4.25** |
| 1966–1970 | **4.00** |
| 1971–1975 | **3.75** |
| 1976–1980 | **3.25** |
| 1981–1985 | **2.75** |
| 1986–1990 | **2.50** |
| 1991– | **2.25** |

# Niloak

Produced in Arkansas by Charles Dean Hyten from the early 1900s until the mid-1940s, Niloak (the backward spelling of kaolin, a type of clay) takes many forms — figural planters, vases in both matt and glossy glazes, and novelty items of various types. The company's most famous product and the most collectible is their swirl or Mission Ware line. Clay in colors of brown, blue, cream, red, and buff are swirled within the mold, the finished product left unglazed on the outside to preserve the natural hues. Small vases are common; large pieces or unusual shapes and those with exceptional coloration are the most valuable. Refer to *The Collector's Encyclopedia of Niloak, A Reference and Value Guide,* by David Edwin Gifford (Collector Books) for more information.

Note: The terms '1st' and '2nd art mark' used in the listings refer to specific die-stamped trademarks. The earlier mark was used from 1910 to 1924, followed by the second, very similar mark used from then until the end of Mission Ware production. Letters with curving raised outlines were characteristic of both; the most obvious difference between the two was that on the first, the final upright line of the 'N' was thin with a solid club-like terminal.

Ashtray, second art mark, 1½x5" .........................**225.00**
Bean pot, Mission Ware, second art mark, 7¼" ..............**350.00**
Candlestick, Mission Ware, unmarked, 5¼" ...........**225.00**
Chamberstick, Mission Ware, first art mark, 4" .................**160.00**
Compote, Mission Ware, round sticker, 6x8¼" ..............**400.00**
Creamer, Castware, unmarked, 2½" .................................**30.00**
Figurine, Scottie Dog, Castware, unmarked, 3¾" ..............**50.00**
Flower bowl, Mission Ware, second art mark, 5¾x3" ...**170.00**
Gear shift knob, Mission Ware, unmarked, 2" ..............**250.00**
Inkwell, Mission Ware, 2½" .**165.00**
Lamp base, Mission Ware, Bull's-eye, open bottom, unmarked, 6½" ...............................**275.00**
Matchstick holder, Mission Ware, first art mark, 1½" ......**100.00**
Mug, Mission Ware, handled, 5½" .............................**325.00**

**Rooster, blue-green, 8½", $35.00; Pan on bowl, blue-green, 7½", $40.00.**

243

Pitcher, ball; Ozark Dawn II, block letters mark, 7¾" .**60.00**

Planter, bird shape, Castware, incised mark, 2¼" .........**20.00**

Planter, Mission Ware, first art mark, 4½" .....................**150.00**

Planter, moccasin shape, low relief mark, 1¾x5x2¼" ..**60.00**

Planter, squirrel shape, Castware, incised mark, 6" ............**25.00**

Stein, Mission Ware, first art mark, 4¼" ....................**250.00**

Vase, fan; Mission Ware, lg second art mark, 7¼" ..............**275.00**

Vase, violet; Mission Ware, first art mark, 3¼" ...............**175.00**

Wall pocket, Mission Ware, unmarked, 6" ...............**250.00**

# Nippon

In complying with American importation regulations, from 1891 to 1921 Japanese manufacturers marked their wares 'Nippon,' meaning Japan, to indicate country of origin. The term is today used to refer to the highly-decorated porcelain vases, bowls, chocolate pots, etc., that bear this term within their trademark. Many variations were used. Refer to *The Collector's Encyclopedia of Nippon Porcelain* (there are three volumes in the series) by Joan Van Patten (Collector Books) for more information.

Ashtray, Wedgwood, #2, 3" ..**325.00**

Bowl, swans on lake, cobalt w/gold, #4, 7" ...............**250.00**

Bowl, Wedgwood, cream on lavender, oval, handles, #2, 9½" .....**300.00**

Bowl, yellow florals, river scene beyond, gold handles, #2, 7¾" ...............................**110.00**

Candlestick, river scene, earth tones, #2, 6¼" ..............**135.00**

Candy dish, gold overlay on white, #4, 7" ...................**80.00**

Chocolate pot, iris on shaded brown, #4, 10" .............**300.00**

Cigarette box, roses on white gold, #2, 4½" .........................**225.00**

Compote, woodland scene, scalloped, footed, #2, 3½x6½" .........**200.00**

Creamer & sugar bowl, scenic with Wedgwood trim, #2, 5" .**235.00**

Cup & saucer, bouillon; blue bird & florals on white, 2 handles, #4 .....................................**50.00**

Dish, relish; Wedgwood, trimmed floral design, #2, 7½" ..**225.00**

Ferner, Egyptian decor, molded head handles, #2, 8½" .**275.00**

Ferner, silhouette figures, 6-sided, #2, 6¾" .........................**160.00**

Hair receiver, pink florals w/gold overlay on white, #4, 4½" .**75.00**

**Humidor, pagoda on beach scene, $175.00.**

Jar, potpourri; Wedgwood, #2, 5½" ...............................**375.00**

Jar, stream in the country, cobalt, #4, 5" ............................**250.00**

Lemon dish, gulls, blue on white, handles, #3, 5½" ............**35.00**

Matchbox holder, sampan scene, hanging, #2, 4½" .........**125.00**

Nut dish, Indian in canoe, 6-sided, handled, #2, 5½" ..........**150.00**

Pitcher, mountain & river scene on cobalt w/gold, #4, 6¾" ..**250.00**

Plaque, Doll Face pattern, #3, 6⅛" ...................................**75.00**

Plaque, lady's portrait reserve, ornate gold trim, #2, 10" .............**385.00**

Plaque, sampan scene, #2, 10½" .........................**200.00**

Plate, cobalt & gold, #2, 8½" .**150.00**

Plate, ships at sea, cobalt, #2, 8½" ................................**275.00**

Sugar shaker, floral w/gold, handled, #2, 3½" ...................**85.00**

Tea tile, windmill scene, 8-sided, #2, 5½" ...........................**65.00**

Vase, floral reserve, cobalt w/much gold, ring handles, #4, 7½" ...........................**255.00**

Vase, geishas in landscape, geometric border, handles, #4, 8" ....................................**175.00**

Vase, Gouda-style decoration, basket shaped, #2, 7" ........**160.00**

Vase, man on camel scene, angle handles, #2, 6" .............**160.00**

Vase, river scene, much gold overlay, long handles, #2, 7½" .....**275.00**

Vase, swan scene, upturned handles, #2, 6" ...................**150.00**

# Noritake

Since the early 1900s the Noritake China Company has been producing fine dinnerware, occasional pieces, and figural items decorated by hand in delicate florals, scenics, and wildlife studies. One of their most popular dinnerware lines, Azalea, is listed in its own category. Refer to *The Collector's Encyclopedia of Noritake* by Joan Van Patten (Collector Books) for more information.

Ashtray, red, butterfly & floral decor, red mark, 3½" dia .**70.00**

**Ashtray, lustre trim, Victorian lady in well, 4", $120.00 to $140.00.**

Bowl, bird & floral decor on yellow, ring handles, green mark, 11" dia ................**85.00**

Bowl, clover shape w/acorn decor on black, gold trim, green mark ...........................**120.00**

Bowl, desert scene w/camel, fancy gold handles, green mark, 8" wide ...............................**65.00**

Bowl, earth tones w/acorns in relief, green mark, 6¾" wide ...........................**100.00**

Bowl, red & blue flowers in relief, red mark, 7" dia ..........**135.00**

Bowl, shell form w/leaf & acorn design, red mark, 10" wide ....................**65.00**

Box, elephant w/howdah, gold highlights & finial, red mark, 6½" ...............................**350.00**

Box, figural clown w/head finial looking up, green mark, 5½" ...........................**285.00**

Candy dish, butterfly & floral decor, open handles, red mark, 9¼" ......................**50.00**

Candy dish, gold etched design, gold handles, backstamp, 6" long ...............................**85.00**

Candy dish, swirled colors w/gold trim & finial, red mark, 5¼" dia ................................**135.00**

Creamer & sugar bowl (open), floral decor on blues, green mark, 2½" ......................**50.00**
Creamer & sugar bowl (open), white to yellow, red mark, 2" ................................**50.00**
Dresser doll, lady w/fan, yellow dress, green mark, 5¾" .**285.00**
Flower frog, blue & yellow fish on orange base, red mark, 4½" .............................**235.00**
Honey jar, ribbed dome w/flowers & bees in relief, green mark, 4½" .................................**70.00**
Inkwell, southern belle in light blue dress, green mark, 4½" ............................**285.00**
Nappy, leaf shape, landscape scene, red mark, 6" wide ...........**65.00**
Nappy, leaf shape w/black loop handle, green mark, 7½" long ...............................**80.00**
Salt & pepper shakers, Niagara Falls souvenir, green mark, 3¼", pr ...........................**50.00**
Sauce dish, swan & dogwood tree on blue, gold trim, green mark, 3½" ......................**45.00**
Tray, flowers in relief on blue border, red mark, oval, 8" long ...............................**55.00**
Trivet, floral decor on striped ground, canted corners, green mark, 5" ..........................**65.00**
Vase, peacock on peach base, red mark, 5¼" ....................**100.00**

# Novelty Clocks

Small animated clocks with moving parts or pendulettes were made by Lux, Keebler, Westclox, and Columbia Time. Some were made of wood, others of china, Syroco (pressed wood), and plastic. Before electric-powered novelty clocks were first developed in the 1940s, they were all wind-up. Lux Manufacturing Co., the major producer of these clocks, was formed in 1912 and reached peak production of 3,000 clocks per day in 1930. Another company, Mastercrafter Novelty Clocks, first obtained a patent to produce their novelty animated clocks in the late 1940s. Their clocks were made of plastic and were electric powered. Prices of novelty clocks vary according to condition, rarity, and location of purchase. For further information we recommend contacting Carole Kaifer, who is listed in the Directory under North Carolina.

Photo courtesy Carole Kaifer.

**Clown with Seals, Lux Pendulette, $300.00.**

Lux, alarm, woman working, moving spinning wheel, ca 1950s .............................**65.00**
Lux, figural (cat, waiter, monk, etc), pressed wood, 6", from $150 to .........................**175.00**
Lux Pendulette, Beer Barrel Drinkers, non-animated, minimum value .................**350.00**
Lux Pendulette, Bluebird, animated, from $25 to ........**30.00**
Lux Pendulette, Bobbing Bird, animated, from $20 to ..**25.00**

Lux Pendulette, Boy Scout, non-animated, from $350 to ......**400.00**

Lux Pendulette, Checkered Borders, from $75 to .........**125.00**

Lux Pendulette, Cocker Spaniel, non-animated, from $300 to .............**350.00**

Lux Pendulette, Enchanted Forest, animated, from $100 to .**125.00**

Lux Pendulette, Hungry Dog, animated, from $350 to ....**375.00**

Lux Pendulette, Hunting Scene, non-animated, from $75 to ......**95.00**

Lux Pendulette, Lovebirds, animated, from $100 to ....**125.00**

Lux Pendulette, Rudolph, animated, from $100 to ....**125.00**

Lux Pendulette, Small Dove, non-animated, from $30 to ..**35.00**

Lux Pendulette, US Capitol, non-animated, from $325 to .**350.00**

Mastercrafter, Boy & Girl on Swing, animated, from $100 to ...................................**125.00**

Mastercrafter, Church w/Bell Ringer, animated, from $75 to ...................................**95.00**

Mastercrafter, Fireplace, animated, from $25 to ........**35.00**

Mastercrafter, Girl on Swing, animated, from $100 to ....**125.00**

Mastercrafter, Waterfall, animated, from $75 to ........**95.00**

Mi-Ken Pendulette, animal face w/moving eyes, Japan, from $25 to ............................**35.00**

Oswald, composition owl or dog, eyes move, Germany, from $250 to .........................**350.00**

Oswald, pressed wood owl or dog, eyes move, Germany, from $250 to .........................**350.00**

# Novelty Telephones

Novelty phones representing a well-known advertising or cartoon character are proving to be the focus of lots of collector activity — the more recognizable the character the better. Telephones modeled after a product container are collectible too, and with the intense interest currently being shown in anything advertising related, competition is sometimes stiff and values are rising. For further information we recommend *Schroeder's Collectible Toys* by Sharon and Bob Huxford.

**Batmobile Telephone Model BM-10, Columbia Telecommunication Group, Inc., DC Comics, 1990, MIB, $35.00. (See photo top of next page.)**

Ziggy, 1989, MIB ..................**75.00**
7-UP Can, NM......................**35.00**

# Nutcrackers

Of most interest to collectors are nutcrackers marked with patent information or those made in the form of an animal or bird. Many manufacturers chose the squirrel as a model for their nutcrackers; dogs were also popular. Cast iron examples are common, but brass, steel, and even wood was also used. Refer to *Ornamental and Figural Nutcrackers* by Judith A. Rittenhouse (Collector Books) for more information. Our advisor is Earl MacSorley; he is listed in the Directory under Connecticut. See also Clubs and Newsletters.

Beetle Bailey, EX+ ................**65.00**
Budweiser Beer Can .............**25.00**
Cabbage Patch Girl, Coleco, 1980s, EX ........................**95.00**
Charlie the Tuna, plastic, Star-Kist, 1980s, 10", MIB.....**50.00**
Crest Sparkle Man, Crest Toothpaste, 1980s, 11", M.......**45.00**
Garfield, reclining, lift receiver back & eyes open, MIB ..**60.00**
Heinz Ketchup Bottle, plastic, MIB..................................**65.00**
Mario Brothers, 1980s, MIB.**45.00**
Mickey Mouse, Unisonic, NM.**65.00**
Poppin' Fresh, plastic, 1980s, 14", M.....................................**90.00**
Punchy, plastic, Hawaiian Punch, 1980s, 11", M.................**150.00**
Raid Bug, plastic, 1980s, 9", MIB, from $125 to ..................**150.00**
Ronald McDonald, plastic, 1985, 10", NM...........................**95.00**

Alligator, painted aluminum, John Wright, 1960s .......**40.00**
Bearded elf, cast iron, 10" ..**285.00**
Big Ben, brass, English, 1900s ..**275.00**
Clamp-on style, cast iron, mechanical, marked Enterprise Pat 1914 ...............**30.00**
Clown (Pierrot), double-faced, brass, ca 1900, 5¼" ........**75.00**
Dog, black-painted cast iron, marked 24H on handle, ca 1900, 10½" .....................**65.00**
Dog, brass, 1930s, 3¾x9" .....**70.00**
Dog, cast iron w/tail handle, rectangular base, 13" ..........**95.00**
Dragon, cast iron, gold paint, 1900-10, 14" .................**275.00**
Duck head, wood, orange beak, glass eyes, early 1900s, 1½x8½" ........................**250.00**
Eagle head, cast iron, 1860s, 4⅛x10¾" ......................**125.00**
Elephant, cast iron, painted, 1920-30, 4¾x9¾" .........**150.00**

**Dogs, 9" long, circa 1927-30: rhodium-plated cast iron, $75.00; cast iron with paint traces, $75.00; brass, $85.00.**

Fish, olive wood, Greek, 1950s, 2¼x8" .............................**25.00**

Frog, wrought iron, glass eyes, Germany, 1800s, 6¼x8¾" ....**250.00**

Girl in hoop skirt, brass, marked MIE Pat App'd..., 1956, 3¾" ...................**125.00**

Home, cast iron, screws to table, long lever, 1800s ............**40.00**

Horse, cast iron, copper plating, English, 1930s, 4¼x7¼" .**175.00**

Lady's legs, flesh-painted cast iron, 1940s, 7" .............**110.00**

Lion, aluminum, on base, reproduction, 1900s, 5⅜x10" .**50.00**

Milford Saint Nicholas, wood, painted, 1900s, 15¾" ...**175.00**

Naughty Nellie, brass, unmarked, 6" ...................................**35.00**

Parrot, tail lever, multicolor-painted cast iron, 10" ....**75.00**

Pliers, engraved steel, crossover type, pointed handles, 5½" ............................**100.00**

Punch & Judy, full figure, brass, 5" ...................................**75.00**

Skull & cross bones, nickel-plated cast iron, English, 1928, 2x6" ...................**100.00**

Squirrel, bronze, 1920-30, 5¾x9⅜" .........................**200.00**

Squirrel on branch, bronze ..**25.00**

Standing Peasant, wood, painted, w/lever & tray, 1930s-40s .**225.00**

Whale, hand-wrought brass, marked HA PIND, 1900s, 1x6¼" ...........................**125.00**

Wolf's head, nickel-plated cast iron, marked Pat 1920, 4⅞x10" .........................**125.00**

## Occupied Japan

Items with the 'Occupied Japan' mark were made during the period from the end of World War II until April 1952. Porcelains, novelties, paper items, lamps, silverplate, lacquer ware, and dolls are some of the areas of exported goods that may bear this stamp. Because the Japanese were naturally resentful of the occupation, it is felt that only a small percentage of their wares were thus marked. Although you may find identical items marked simply 'Japan,' only those with the 'Occupied Japan' stamp are being collected. For more information we recommend the series of five books on Occupied

Japan collectibles written by Gene Florence for Collector Books. Items in our listings are ceramic unless another material is noted, and figurines are of average, small size.

Ashtray, cowboy hat form, copper-like metal, 3" wide ..........**8.00**
Ashtray, frog on lily pad ......**14.00**
Ashtray, Kentucky state map form ...............................**15.00**
Candy dish, leaf form, silvery metal ...............................**13.00**
Cigarette dispenser, piano form ...........................**25.00**
Clown, wearing coat, ruffles around neck, holds hat in front, 6¼" ........................**25.00**

**Colonial lady, gold trim, 6", $18.00.**

Cup & saucer, white w/floral design, gold handled, hexagon form ................................**17.50**
Figurine, bellboy, w/suitcases, Hummel-type, 4" ...........**20.00**
Figurine, boy feeding dog, Hummel-type, 8" ...................**38.00**

Figurine, boy w/saxophone, blue pants, red hair, 4⅝" .......**15.00**
Figurine, cat in a basket ......**18.00**
Figurine, cherubs, Triton, Trumpeter of the Sea, holds a seashell .**68.00**
Figurine, Colonial couple on base, man standing, lady on sofa w/cello .............................**38.00**
Figurine, Colonial group, couple dances, lady at spinet, 3¾x5" .............................**55.00**
Figurine, Colonial lady, seated, playing cello, 3¼" ..........**20.00**
Figurine, Colonial man leans against stump, lady holds book, 6", pr ....................**85.00**
Figurine, dog & hydrant, black & white dog, orange hydrant .**13.00**
Figurine, duck, humanoid type, relaxing ...........................**20.00**
Figurine, elephant sitting down, trunk in the air, white w/rose tones ...............................**12.00**
Figurine, frog playing accordion ...........................**20.00**
Figurine, frog playing blue drum ...........................**12.00**
Figurine, frog playing fiddle, 4½" ...............................**27.50**
Figurine, lady in pink dress w/fawn, 4½" ...................**18.00**
Figurine, lady in red jacket & gray skirt, w/Scottie dog, 4½" .**18.00**
Figurine, Mexican girl, wide skirt, lg sombrero, Ucago mark, 7½" ......................**40.00**
Figurine, Oriental girl w/long yellow kimono ....................**20.00**
Figurines, Colonial musicians, seated on stump, 5¼", pr .**75.00**
Figurines, Wise Monkeys, See, Speak, Hear No Evil, 3x2" ............**10.00**
Fishbowl ornament, lighthouse w/bridge leading to house, 2⅛x2½" ..........................**15.00**
Incense burner, Indian seated like Budda, wearing headdress, 3¾" .................................**25.00**

Jewelry box, crown form, red & white lid .........................**15.00**
Lamps, Wedgwood type, blue & white embossed lady .....**65.00**
Mug, barrel form, grapes on white w/blue borders, 4¼" .......**15.00**
Mug, beer; rabbit figural handle, shows house, equestrians & dogs ................................**35.00**
Mug, child's; 'Little Shaver' in gold, orchid lilacs, 3¼x3" .........**55.00**
Mug, silvery metal, embossed dragon, engraved 'Sue' ..**15.00**
Planter, boy by stump, 4½" ..**14.00**
Planter, puppy dog, 3½" .......**12.00**
Salt & pepper shakers, Dutch boy & girl, pr .........................**15.00**
Salt & pepper shakers, huggy bears, white w/red lips, eyes closed, pr .........................**22.50**
Salt & pepper shakers, Hummel-type girl & boy, pr .........**38.00**
Salt & pepper shakers, yellow birds, one head down, the other one up, pr .............**15.00**
Shelf sitters, boy & girl, wooden pegged bench, 6¾", 3-pc .**55.00**
Stein, dog figural handle, scene of people in carriage, 5½" .**55.00**
Stein, trio sitting at table drinking, brown w/blue background, 7½" ...................**55.00**
Tea canister, blue w/pink floral design ...........................**15.00**
Toby mug, skull face, white w/brown tones ...............**18.00**
Toby mug, smiling devil's head, gray beard & horns .......**38.00**
Toothpick holder, Dutch girl w/flower basket .............**18.00**
Tumbler, stoneware, rust w/gray & green leaves, 3½" .......**25.00**

# Old MacDonald's Farm

Made by the Regal China Co., items from this line of novelty ware designed around characters and animals from Old MacDonald's farm can often be found at flea markets and dinnerware shows. Values of some pieces are two to three times higher than a few years ago. The milk pitcher is especially hard to find. Our advisor for this category is Rick Spencer; he is listed in the Directory under Utah.

Butter dish, cow's head ......**225.00**

**Canister, large, $325.00.**

Cookie, jar, barn .................**275.00**
Creamer, rooster .................**110.00**
Grease jar, pig ....................**175.00**
Jar, spice; sm ......................**100.00**
Pitcher, milk .......................**400.00**
Salt & pepper shakers, boy & girl, pr ....................................**75.00**
Salt & pepper shakers, churn, pr ....................................**65.00**
Salt & pepper shakers, feed sacks, pr ..................................**165.00**
Sugar bowl, hen .................**125.00**
Teapot, duck's head ...........**250.00**

# Paper Dolls

Though the history paper dolls can be traced even farther back, by the late 1700s they were being mass produced. A century later, paper dolls were being used as an advertising medium by retail companies wishing to promote sales. But today the type most often encountered are in book form — the dolls on the cardboard covers, their wardrobe on the inside pages. These have been published since the 1920s. Celebrity and character-related dolls are the most popular with collectors, and condition is very important. If they have been cut out, even when they are still in fine condition and have all their original accessories, they're worth only about half as much as an uncut doll. In our listings, if no condition is given, values are for mint, uncut paper dolls.

**Annette, Whitman, #1971, 1964, 48 costumes and accessories, M, uncut, $45.00.**

Amy, Toy Factory, #109, 18-pc wardrobe ........................**35.00**

Antique French Dolls, Evergreen Press, PJ Rosamond, 1975, 3 dolls ...............................**35.00**
Baby Alive, Whitman, 1973 ...**5.00**
Bridal, Whitman, 1971, 2 dolls .**8.00**
Bridal Party, Whitman, #4723, 1968, 4 dolls, cut, complete, EX ...................................**9.00**
Bride & Groom, Whitman, 1979, 2 dolls, 23-pc wardrobe ......**6.00**
Cut Me Out, Abbott, #1358, 4 dolls ...................................**8.00**
Doll & Me, plus baby doll, Saalfield, 1969 ........................**5.00**
Dolls Across the Sea, Platt & Munk, 1965, 4 dolls, 14 outfits, cut .**8.00**
Dolls of the '30s, Evergreen Press, Janet Nason, 1976, 4 dolls .**35.00**
Dress Alike, Abbott, #1388, 3 dolls ...............................**15.00**
Effanbee Currier & Ives, Hobby House, 1979, 1 doll .........**8.00**
Family Affair, Whitman, #4767, 1968, 5 dolls, cut, complete, EX ...................................**20.00**
Goldilocks Story To Read, Whitman, 1972, 1 doll .............**5.00**
Jan & Dean, Built-Rite, 2 dolls .**9.00**
John Wayne, Dover, 1981 ....**10.00**
Judy Garland, Dover, 1982 ..**10.00**

**Lennon Sisters, Whitman, #1979, 1958, EX but cut, $20.00.**

Little Lulu & Tubby, Whitman, 1974, cut, complete, NM .**10.00**

Lydia, Whitman, #1970, 1977, 1 doll ..................................**10.00**

Mary Jane, 1972, complete w/magnets, VG ..............**15.00**

Mary Poppins, Whitman, 1973, 4 dolls ..............................**30.00**

Muppet Babies, 1984, 3 dolls .**10.00**

Newborn Baby Tender Love, Whitman/Mattel, 1973, 1 doll ..................................**8.00**

Peachy & Her Puppets, Whitman, #1966, 1974, 1 doll w/4 stick puppets ............................**7.00**

Raggedy Ann & Andy, Whitman, 1975, 2 dolls ....................**8.00**

Rudolph Valentino, Dover, 1979 ...........................**10.00**

Snow White & 7 Dwarfs, Whitman, #970, authorized edition, 1938, EX ..............**150.00**

Sunbeam, Saalfield, 1974, 6 dolls ...............................**5.00**

Sunny & Sue (toddlers), Abbott, #1387, 5 dolls ...............**15.00**

This Is Katie, Paper Doll w/Yarn Hair, Whitman, 1978, 8 outfits ....................................**10.00**

Tricia, w/White House, Saalfield, 1970, 1 doll ...................**25.00**

Vivien Leigh, Dover, 1979 ....**10.00**

Waltons, Whitman, 1975, 7 dolls, cut, complete, NM .........**20.00**

Welcome Back Kotter, Gabe Kotter, Toy Factory, 3 pages, 1976, 14" ........................**30.00**

### Magazine Paper Dolls

Children's Activities, Katje & Pieter of Holland, March 1937 ..................................**6.00**

Children's Play Mate, Little Boy Blue & Little Bo Peep, October 1941 ...........................**8.00**

Delineator, Margaret Butterick's Little Sister Betty, October

1913 ...............................**22.00**

Ladies' Home Journal, Cinderella, June 1913 ......................**14.00**

Life, Three Little Nixons, May 1970 ...............................**10.00**

McCall's, Jack & Jill, January 1921 ...............................**14.00**

McCall's, Pollykins Pudge, July 1919 ...............................**14.00**

National Doll World, Kewpie, November-December 1979 .**3.00**

Pictorial Review, Dolly Dingle, March 1927 ...................**15.00**

Pictorial Review, Dolly Dingle's Playmates, May 1929 ...**14.00**

Pictorial Review, Polly & Peter Pumpkin-Eater, October 1934 ...............................**9.00**

Wee Wisdom, Jean, May 1953 .**3.00**

Wee Wisdom, Wendy, July 1954 ...........................**3.00**

Woman's Home Companion, Goosey, Goosey, Gander, April 1921 ...............................**10.00**

Woman's Home Companion, Jackie Coogan, May 1925 .........**22.00**

Woman's Home Companion, Peter Pan, August 1925 .........**20.00**

## Paperback Books

Though published to some extent before the forties, most paperback book collectors prefer those printed from around 1940 until the late 1950s, and most organize their collections around a particular author, genre, publisher, or illustrator. Remember — (as is true with any type of ephemera) condition is extremely important. Unless noted otherwise, our values are given for books in near-fine condition. (Book dealers use the term 'fine' to indicate 'mint' condition). For more information and hundreds of values, refer to Huxford's Paperback Value Guide by Sharon and Bob Huxford (Collector Books).

Albert, Marvin H; Party Girl, Gold Medal 808, paperback original ..........................**20.00**

Anderson, Poul; The Golden Slave, Avon T388, 1960, 1st edition ............................**20.00**

Anthology, Beyond, Berkley G734, VG ....................................**4.00**

Asimov, Isaac; Currents of Space, Signet/Penguin 1082, VG .**4.50**

Bloch, Robert; Yours Truly, Jack the Ripper; Belmont 92-527, VG ...................................**10.00**

Blochman, Lawrence G; Wives To Burn, Dell 134, VG .........**6.00**

Block, Lawrence; Markham, Belmont 236, 1961, 1st edition, TV tie-in ........................**25.00**

Boyll, R; Darkman, Jove 10378, movie tie-in, VG ..............**4.50**

Brossard, Chandler; The Girls in Rome, Signet 1971, 1961 .**15.00**

Burroughs, Edgar R; Gods of Mars, Ballantine 702, VG ...........**5.00**

Burroughs, Edgar R; Mastermind of Mars, Ace F181, VG ....**4.50**

Cassiday, Bruce; Operation Goldkill, Award 211, 1967, TV tie-in ....................................**15.00**

Cerf, Bennett; Pocket Book of Jokes, Pocket 294, 1945, VG ......**20.00**

Chamberlain, William; Last Ride to Los Lobos, Gold Medal 1460, 1964 .....................**12.00**

Charteris, Leslie; The Saint & Mr Teal, Avon 629, VG ..........**5.00**

Chrispin, AC; Starbridge, Ace 78-329, 1st edition, signed .**12.00**

Christie, Agatha; Murder of Roger Ackroyd, Pocket 5, 11th printing, VG .............................**5.00**

Clarke, Arthur C; Expedition to Earth, Ballantine 52, VG ..**5.00**

Clinton, Jeff; The Fighting Buckaroo, Berkley G577, 1961, 1st edition ............................**12.00**

Coburn, Walt; Law Rides the Range, Popular Library 135, VG ....................................**4.50**

Colby, Robert; Run for the Money, Avon T430, paperback original, VG .............................**4.50**

Conroy, Albert; Mr Lucky, Dell B165, 1960, 1st edition, TV tie-in ............................**12.00**

Derleth, August; Not Long for This World, Ballantine 542, VG ....................................**4.50**

Doyle, Arthur C; Lost World, Pyramid 514, 2nd printing, movie tie-in ......................**4.00**

Dumas, Alexandre; Camille, Bantam 745, VG ....................**5.50**

Eden, Dorothy; Sleep in the Woods, Ace 76-971, VG ...**3.00**

Ellington, Richard; Shakedown, Bantam 1286, 1954, VG .**8.50**

Elwood, Roger; The Other Side of Tomorrow, Pyramid V3937, 1975, VG ..........................**3.50**

Farmer, Philip Jose; A Woman a Day, Beacon 291, 1960, 1st edition ............................**65.00**

Faulkner, William; Knight's Gambit, Signet 825, 1950, VG .**9.50**

Foley, Rae; Dangerous to Me, Dell 1770, 1974, VG ................**3.50**

Franklin, Max; Starsky & Hutch, Ballantine 24996, 1976, TV tie-in, VG ........................**5.00**

Gaines, William M; The Organization Mad, Signet S1795, 1960, VG ..........................**7.00**

Gardner, Erle S; Perry Mason & Case of Foot-Loose Doll, Pocket 6016 .....................**7.00**

Gersham, WL; Houdini, MacFadden 60-310, 3rd printing, VG ...**5.00**

Gilman, Dorothy; Unexpected Mrs Pollifax, Crest T1485, movie tie-in ......................**5.00**

Gruber, Frank; Whispering Master, Signet/Penguin 726, VG .**10.00**

Hamilton, Greg; So Eager To Please, Midwood 324, 1963, 1st edition ..................**20.00**

Hammett, Dashiell; Maltese Falcon, Pocket 268, 2nd printing, VG ..................................**5.00**

Hemingway, Ernest; Farewell to Arms, Bantam 1240, 5th printing, VG ..................**4.00**

Henry, O; Four Million, Pocket 65, 2nd printing, VG .............**5.00**

Hibbs, Ben; Great Stories of Saturday Evening Post, Bantam 555, VG ..........................**5.00**

Hitchcock, Alfred; Hold Your Breath, Dell 206, 1947, VG ...........**10.00**

Hodgson, William H; House on the Borderland, Ace D553, VG ..................................**4.00**

Irish, William; Six Times Death, Popular Library 137, VG .**10.00**

Jakes, John; The Last Magicians, Signet 3988, 1969, 1st edition ..................................**14.00**

James, Henry; Daisy Miller & Other Stories, Armed Services Edition T18 ............**8.00**

Johnston, William; Dr Kildare, Heart Has an Answer; Lancer 70-043, VG ......................**4.00**

Keene, Day; There Was a Crooked Man, Gold Medal 405, 1954 .....................**35.00**

Keene, James; Gunnison's Empire, Avon F169, 1963 .............**12.00**

Ketchum, Phil; Renegade Range, Monarch 256, paperback original, VG ..........................**4.00**

Keyes, Frances P; Queen Anne's Lace, Paperback Library 52-507, VG ............................**4.00**

Lutz, Giles A; Killer's Trail, Avon F174, 1963 .....................**12.00**

Maugham, W Somerset; Razor's Edge, Armed Service Editions Q31, VG ..........................**5.50**

Merril, Judith; Out of Bounds, Pyramid G499, 1960, 1st edition, VG .........................**16.00**

Metalious, Grace; Return to Peyton Place, Dell 7404, movie tie-in, VG .........................**4.00**

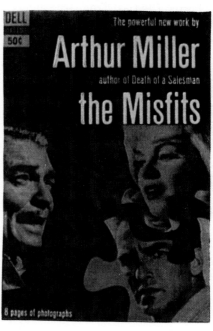

Miller, Arthur; *The Misfits*, Dell F-115, $20.00.

Milne, AA; Red House Mystery, Pocket 81, 8th printing, VG ...............................**5.00**

Morgan, John M; The Roman & the Slave Girl, Signet 1690, 1959 ..............................**20.00**

Morris, Janet & Chris; The Little Helliad, Baen 65-3666, 1988 ..............................**6.00**

Newman, Frank; Perma Crossword Puzzle Dictionary, Perma M4021, VG ...........**4.50**

O'Connor, The Monkees Go Mod, Popular 60-8046, 1967, VG .**7.50**

Partridge Family, Terror by Night #5, 1971, VG- ..................**5.00**

Pierson, LR; Roughly Speaking, Bart House 23, movie tie-in, VG ........................................**5.00**

Pohl, Frederik; Edge of the City, Ballantine 199, 1957, 1st edition ................................**70.00**

Portis, Charles; True Grit, Signet Q3761, 1959, VG .............**5.00**

Quarry, Nick; Trail of a Tramp, Gold Medal 824, 1958 ...**20.00**

Queen, Ellery; Tragedy of Y, Pocket 313, VG ................**4.50**

Raymond, A; Lion Men of Mongo, Avon 18515, Flash Gordon #1, VG ........................................**5.00**

Rico, Don; The Unmarried Ones, Beacon 713, 1964, 1st edition ................................**15.00**

Rosen, Victor; Dark Plunder, Lion LL11, 1955, 1st edition .**25.00**

Ryerson, Martin; Gun Fire at Big Needles, Vega W109, VG ..**8.00**

Sale, Richard; Lazarus #7, Harlequin 79, 1950, VG ..**50.00**

Schulman, Arnold; Hole in the Head, Gold Medal 891, movie tie-in, VG ..........................**4.50**

Scott, Sir Walter; Letters on Demonology & Witchcraft, Ace 14256, 1970 ..............**4.50**

Sheckley, Robert; Mindswap, Dell 5643, 1967 ......................**10.00**

Silas, AE; The Panorama Egg, Daw UE1395, 1978, VG ..**3.50**

Silverberg, Robert; Alpha 4, 1973, VG ........................................**3.50**

Simak, Clifford D; Time & Again, Ace 81000, VG ..................**3.50**

Simmons, Dan; Phases of Gravity, Bantam 27764, 1989, VG .**4.50**

Smith, General Holland M; Doomsday Wing, Monarch 388, VG ............................**4.00**

Smith, S; Ballad of the Running Man, Popular K48, movie tie-in, VG ..............................**4.00**

Spillane, Mickey; Me, Hood!; Signet/Penguin 3579, VG .**5.00**

Steinbeck, John; Once There Was a War, Bantam 2075, VG .**6.00**

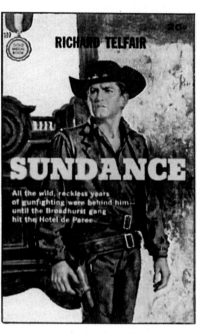

Telfair, Richard; *Sundance*, Gold Medal 999, 1960, TV tie-in, $5.00.

Tenn, William; Of All Possible Worlds, Ballantine 99, 1955, VG ....**12.00**

Tolkien, JRR; The Hobbit, Ballantine 01532, 1972, VG ......**2.50**

Vance, Jack; Space Opera, Pyramid 1140, 1967, 1st edition ...**20.00**

Verne, Jules; Journey to Center of Earth, Perma M4161, movie tie-in ................................**6.00**

Ward, Mary Jane; Snake Pit, Signet/Penguin 696, movie tie-in, VG ..........................**5.50**

Whittington, Harry; Charro!; Gold Medal 2063, movie tie-in reprint, VG ......................**4.00**

Wilson, Colin; The Space Vampires, Pocket 80916, 1977, VG ....................................**7.50**

Withers, J; Shuttered Room, Dell 7883, movie tie-in, VG ....**4.00**

Wormser, Richard; Thief of Baghdad; Dell First Edition B216, VG .................................. **4.50**

# Peach Lustre Glassware

Several dinnerware lines as well as baking dishes in white glassware with a lustrous gold fired-on finish sometimes called copper-tint was made by Fire-King from the early fifties through the mid-seventies. If you like it, now's the time to buy, since it's not yet widely collected. Refer to *Collectible Glassware of the '40s, '50s, and '60s* by Gene Florence (Collector Books) for more information. Our advisor for this category is April Tvorak; she is listed in the Directory under Colorado.

Bowl, dessert; Royal Lustre, 1976, 4¾" .................................. **3.50**
Bowl, soup; Lustre Shell, 1965-76, 6⅜" .................................. **5.50**
Bowl, soup; Peach Lustre, 1951-65, 7⅝" .......................... **5.50**

Bowl, vegetable; Peach Lustre, 1951-65, 8¼" .................... **8.50**
Bowl, vegetable; Royal Lustre, 1976, 8½" ...................... **12.00**
Creamer, Lustre Shell, 1965-76 .**4.50**
Creamer, Peach Lustre, footed, 1951-65 .......................... **4.50**
Cup, demitasse; Lustre Shell, 1965-76, 3½-oz ................ **5.00**
Cup, Peach Lustre, 1951-65, 8-oz .............................. **3.50**
Plate, dinner; Royal Lustre, 1976, 10" .................................. **5.50**
Plate, salad; Lustre Shell, 1965-76, 7¼" .......................... **3.50**
Plate, salad; Peach Lustre, 1951-65, 7¾" .......................... **4.50**
Platter, Lustre Shell, 1965-76, 9½x13" .......................... **6.50**
Platter, Royal Lustre, 1976, 9½x13" .......................... **6.50**
Saucer, demitasse; Lustre Shell, 1965-76, 4¾" .................... **3.00**
Saucer, Royal Lustre, 1976, 5¾" .**1.50**
Sugar bowl, Lustre Shell, 1965-76, w/lid .......................... **6.50**
Sugar bowl, Royal Lustre, 1976, w/lid .............................. **6.50**

**Dessert set, Leaf and Blossom, ca 1952, from $6.00 to $8.00.**

# Pencil Sharpeners

The whittling process of sharpening pencils with pocketknives was replaced by mechanical devices in the 1880s. By the turn of the century, many ingenious desk-type sharpeners had been developed. Small pencil sharpeners designed for the purse or pocket were produced in the 1890s. The typical design consisted of a small steel tube containing a cutting blade which could be adjusted by screws. Mass-produced novelty pencil sharpeners became popular in the late 1920s. The most detailed figurals were made in Germany. These German sharpeners that originally sold for less than a dollar are now considered highly collectible!

Disney and other character pencil sharpeners have been produced in Catalin, plastic, ceramic, and rubber. Novelty battery-operated pencil sharpeners can also be found. For over fifty years pencil sharpeners have been used as advertising giveaways — from Baker's Chocolate's and Coca-Cola's metal figurals to the plastic 'Marshmallow Man' distributed by McDonald's®. As long as we have pencils, new pencil sharpeners will be produced, much to the delight of collectors. Our advisor is Martha Hughes, who is listed in the Directory under California.

Airplane, red Bakelite w/US Army decal, EX .............. **45.00**
Batman, DC Comics/Hong Kong, 1981, 5", M ...................... **8.00**
Bugs Bunny figural, battery operated, Janex, 1975, VG ...**25.00**
Car, yellow & white plastic, ca 1950s, 2¾" ........................ **8.00**

Charley McCathy, Bakelite w/decal, 1¾" ................... **55.00**
Cinderella, portrait w/name at waist, Bakelite, round, scarce ............................ **65.00**
Donald Duck, painted portrait on Bakelite, round, scarce .**65.00**
Empire State Building, metal, marked USA, sm, EX ....**35.00**
Flintstones, painted character on hard plastic, 1983, 2½", set of 5 ..................................... **30.00**

**Goofy clinging to side, marked WDP, ca 1980, $20.00.**

Indian face, gold metal w/multicolor headdress, Occupied Japan, VG ...................... **55.00**
Lady, metal figural w/globe held overhead, Germany, ca 1920, 3", M ........................... **100.00**
Lone Ranger, bullet form, bread premium, M ................... **35.00**
Mickey Mouse, red Bakelite, 1930s, EX ...................... **80.00**
New York World's Fair Glove, plastic, dated 1961, MIB ......**22.00**
Pablo, Bakelite, EX .............. **35.00**
Pluto, Bakelite, EX .............. **35.00**

Robot, die-cast metal, Poppy, 3",
MIB ...............................**15.00**
Rocking horse, plastic w/hair tail,
marked Germany, EX ...**20.00**
Spiderman, colorful plastic figural,
Nasta, ca 1980, 4", MOC .**10.00**
Wolfman, gr plastic bust figural
on sharpener base, UP Co,
1960s, 3", M ...................**10.00**

# Pennsbury Pottery

From the 1950s through the
1970s, dinnerware and novelty
ware produced by the Pennsbury
company was sold through tourist
gift shops along the Pennsylvania
turnpike. Much of their ware is
decorated in an Amish theme. A
group of barber shop singers was
another popular design, and they
made a line of bird figures that
were very similar to Stangl's,
though much harder to find.

Ashtray, Outen the Light .....**20.00**
Bowl, grey, Fidelity Mutual,
7" .............................**40.00**
Bowl, Red Rooster, deep, 5½" .**14.00**
Butter dish, Lovebirds .........**28.50**
Butter dish, Red Rooster .....**25.00**
Casserole, Hex, w/lid, 9" ......**38.50**
Coaster, Horowitz ................**15.00**
Coffeepot, Folkart, 6-cup, 8½" .**48.50**
Cruet, Amish head, pr .......**100.00**
Cruet, Gay Nineties, pr .....**150.00**
Egg cup, Folkart ..................**20.00**
Figurine, wren, white, sm ...**75.00**
Mug, beer; Eagle, 5" ............**20.00**
Mug, pretzel; Amish, 5" .......**25.00**
Pitcher, Black Rooster, 4" ....**22.00**
Pitcher, Red Rooster, 7¼" .....**42.00**
Plaque, Papa's Half .............**30.00**
Plaque, Red Rooster, 7x5" ....**18.00**
Plate, Angel, Stumar ..........**30.00**
Plate, Hex, 8" .......................**18.00**
Sugar bowl, Hex ..................**20.00**
Sugar bowl, Red Rooster, w/lid .**18.00**
Tile, Eagle, 6" sq ..................**32.50**
Wall pocket, sailboat, 6½" sq .**50.00**

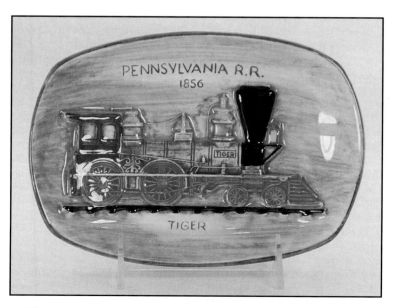

**Plaque, Pennsylvania R.R., 1856, 'Tiger,' from $38.00 to $42.00.**

# Pepsi-Cola

Pepsi-Cola has been around about as long as Coca-Cola, but since collectors are just now beginning to discover how fascinating this line of advertising memorabilia can be, its generally much less expensive. You'll be able to determine the approximate date your items were made by the style of logo they carry. The familiar oval was first used in the early 1940s, about the time the two 'dots' between the words were changed to one. But the double dots are used nowadays as well, especially on items designed to be reminiscent of the old ones — beware! The bottle cap logo was used from about 1943 until the early to mid-'60s with variations. For more information, refer to *Pepsi-Cola Collectibles* by Bill Vehling and Michael Hunt and *Introduction to Pepsi Collecting* by Bob Stoddard. Our advisors for this category are Craig and Donna Stifter, listed in the Directory under Illinois.

Blotter, Pepsi-Cola cap & girl serving 2 bottles, 1945, NM .**95.00**
Bottle opener, tin, bottle form, 1930s, 4", EX+ ...............**35.00**
Clock, light-up, white plastic bottle-cap form, 1950s, 12" dia, VG+ ..............................**160.00**
Game, checkers, wood Pepsi & Mountain Dew cans, 1970s, 14x14", NMIB .............**100.00**
Menu board, tin, Special Today, Hits The Spot, 1950s, 30x20", EX ................................**100.00**
Picnic cooler, metal, blue & white logo, 1950s, 12x18x9", EX+ .............................**70.00**
Salt & pepper shakers, swirl-type bottles, 1970s, 4", NM ...**40.00**

Sign, cardboard, party table, The Light Refreshment, 1950s, 20x18", G .......................**85.00**
Sign, stand-up, high-stepping Santa, Norman Rockwell, 1960s-70s, EX+ .............**60.00**
Soda jerk's hat, oilcloth, Drink...5¢, Worth A Dime, 1930s-40s, VG ...............**80.00**
Soda jerk's hat, paper, Have A Pepsi Day, 1970s, EX ......**4.00**

**Thermometer, metal frame with glass lens, 1951, 12" diameter, NM, $275.00.**

Thermometer, metal, Have A Pepsi & bottle cap, 1957, 27x7", NM ....................**135.00**
Thermometer, metal, Say Pepsi Please & bottle cap, 1967, 28", NM .........................**80.00**
Tip tray, black w/flower decor, 1950s, 5x7", G+ .............**30.00**
Tray, deep-dish, 3 bottles on ice, 1970s, 13" dia, EX .........**20.00**
Tray, Hits The Spot w/musical notes, 1940, 11x14", NM ..........**120.00**

# Pez Dispensers

Originally a breath mint targeted for smokers, by the fifties Pez had been diverted toward the kid's candy market, and to make sure the kids found them appealing, the company designed dispensers they'd be sure to like — many of them characters the kids could easily recognize. On today's collectible market, some of those dispensers bring astonishing prices!

Though early on collectors preferred the dispensers with no feet, today they concentrate on the character heads. Feet were added in 1987, so if you want your collection to be complete, you'll buy both styles. For further information and more listings, see *Schroeder's Collectible Toys, Antique to Modern*, by Sharon and Bob Huxford (Collector Books). Our values are for mint dispensers. Very few are worth collecting if they are damaged or have missing parts.

Angel, no feet, 1970s ............**25.00**
Barney Bear, no feet ............**35.00**
Baseball glove, no feet .......**150.00**
Batman, no feet, w/cape .....**120.00**
Batman, w/feet, black head & stem, from $1 to ..............**3.00**
Boy, w/feet, brown hair, from $3 to .....................................**8.00**
Bugs Bunny, w/feet ................**3.00**
Casper the Friendly Ghost, no feet .................................**70.00**
Cool Cat, w/feet ....................**30.00**
Donald Duck, w/feet, from $1 to ...................................**3.00**
Foghorn Leghorn, w/feet ......**35.00**
Football Player, no feet, red w/white helmet, from $75 to .........**95.00**
Fred Flintstone, w/feet, from $1 to ...........................................**3.00**
Garfield, w/feet, orange w/green hat & visor, from $1 to ....**3.00**
Gonzo, w/feet, from $1 to .......**3.00**
Joker, no feet, soft head .......**70.00**
King Louie, no feet ..............**35.00**
Merlin Mouse, w/feet ...........**10.00**
Monkey Sailor, no feet, from $25 to ....................................**35.00**

Mowgli, w/feet ......................**30.00**
Octopus, no feet, black .........**40.00**

**One-Eyed Monster, gorilla head, $35.00; Vamp (Erie Spectre Series), from $75.00 to $95.00.**

Panda, w/feet, whistle head ...**6.00**
Penguin, w/feet, whistle head .**6.00**
Pirate, no feet, from $25 to ..**40.00**
Pluto, no feet ........................**15.00**
Policeman, no feet ................**30.00**
Road Runner, w/feet ..............**6.00**

**Road Runner, $40.00; Uncle Sam, $70.00.**

Rudolph, no feet ....................**25.00**
Speedy Gonzales, w/feet ........**6.00**
Spike, w/feet ...........................**6.00**
Sylvester, w/feet .....................**5.00**
Wile E Coyote, w/feet ...........**25.00**
Woodstock, w/feet, from $1 to ..**3.00**
Zorro, no feet, w/logo ............**75.00**

# Pfaltzgraff Pottery

Since early in the 17th century, pottery has been produced in York County, Pennsylvania. The Pfaltz-graff Company that operates there today is the outgrowth of several of these small potteries. A changeover made in 1940 redirected their efforts toward making the dinner-ware lines for which they are now best known. Their earliest line, a glossy brown with a white frothy drip glaze around the rim, was called Gourmet Royal. Today collec-tors find an abundance of good examples and are working toward reassembling sets of their own. Vil-lage, another very successful line, is tan with a stencilled Pennsylvania Dutch-type floral design in brown.

Giftware consisting of ash-trays, mugs, bottle stoppers, a cookie jar, etc., all with comic char-acter faces were made in the 1940s. This line was called Mug-gsy, and it is also very collectible, with the mugs starting at about $35.00 each. For more informa-tion, refer to *The Collector's Ency-clopedia of American Dinnerware* by Jo Cunningham (Collector Books) and *Pfaltzgraff, America's Potter*, by David A. Walsh and Polly Stetler, published in conjunc-tion with the Historical Society of York County, York, Pennsylvania.

Gourmet Royale, bowl, cereal; 5½" ...................................**2.00**
Gourmet Royale, bowl, oval, #241, 7x10" ..............................**12.00**
Gourmet Royale, bowl, vegetable; divided ...........................**14.00**
Gourmet Royale, butter dish, ¼-lb, stick type ..................**12.00**
Gourmet Royale, casserole, round, w/lid ..............................**16.00**
Gourmet Royale, creamer, #24 .**5.00**
Gourmet Royale, cup ..............**2.00**
Gourmet Royale, gravy boat, w/twin spout, #426, lg ...**12.00**
Gourmet Royale, mug, #91 ....**3.00**
Gourmet Royale, pitcher, w/ice lip, #415 .........................**16.00**
Gourmet Royale, plate, dinner; 10" ...................................**4.00**
Gourmet Royale, plate, salad; 6¾" ...................................**1.50**

**Muggsy, Sleepy Sam mug, from $35.00 to $40.00; Handy Harry utility jar with lid, from $175.00 to $200.00.**

Gourmet Royale, salt & pepper shakers, pr ........................**4.50**
Gourmet Royale, saucer .........**1.50**
Gourmet Royale, sugar bowl, #22, w/lid ..................................**6.00**
Muggsy, ashtray .................**125.00**
Muggsy, canape holder, character face w/pierced lift-off hat .**95.00**
Muggsy, cigarette server ....**125.00**
Muggsy, clothes sprinkler bottle, Myrtle, black, from $200 to ......................**250.00**
Muggsy, clothes sprinkler bottle, Myrtle, white, from $125 to ......................**175.00**
Muggsy, cookie jar, character face, minimum value ...........**250.00**
Muggsy, jigger, w/handle, sm, from $40 to .....................**50.00**
Muggsy, mug, action figure (golfer, fisherman, etc), any, from $65 to .....................**80.00**
Muggsy, mug, Black action figure ...............................**125.00**
Muggsy, mug, character face, any, from $35 to .....................**40.00**
Muggsy, tumbler ...................**60.00**
Village, butter dish, ¼-lb .....**14.00**
Village, canister, set of 4 ......**85.00**
Village, creamer .....................**6.00**
Village, custard cup ................**4.50**
Village, mustard jar .............**10.00**
Village, plate, dinner; 10½" ...**6.00**
Village, platter, oval, 14" .....**10.00**
Village, sugar bowl .................**6.00**

# Photographica

Early cameras and the images they produced are today fascinating to many. The earliest type of image was the daguerreotype, made with the use of a copper plate and silver salts; ambrotypes followed, produced by the wet-plate process on glass negatives. Tin-types were from the same era as the ambrotype but were developed on japanned iron and were much more durable. Size, subject matter, esthetics, and condition help determine value. Stereo cards, viewing devices, albums, photographs, and advertising memorabilia featuring camera equipment are included in this area of collecting.

**Album, celluloid and cloth cover, gilded foredge, $110.00.**

Albumen, Civil War generals & staff, Mathew Brady, 3½x4½", NM ...............................**145.00**
Ambrotype, girl w/banana curls standing on chair, 6th plate, half case .........................**30.00**
Ambrotype, leather tanner w/tools & cowhide, 6th plate, half case ...............................**70.00**
Ambrotype, seated girl w/black dog in lap, 9th plate, +case ..**26.00**
Booklet, Historical...Account of Daguerrotype, 1969 reprint, EX ..................................**12.50**
Booklet, How To Make Good Pictures, Eastman Kodak, 12th edition, 1922 ...................**4.50**

**Camera, Voightlander Bessa 66, 1936-49, $40.00.**

Booklet, Velox Transparent Water Color Stamps, 1920s, 8 pages, G .......................................**5.00**

Bromide, banjo player, violinist & accordion player in group, 7x9", G ...........................**25.00**

Bromide, Commander Peary's ship Roosevelt, on 8x10" mount .**15.00**

Bromide, 6 cowboys on horseback, on 10x12" mount, NM ...**40.00**

Cabinet card, baby holding cast iron horse-drawn wagon, 3⅜x5⅛" ...........................**10.00**

Cabinet card, Che Mah Chinese dwarf standing on chair, VG .........**25.00**

Cabinet card, Col WF Cody Buffalo Bill in fancy outfit, Stacy, VG ................................**130.00**

Cabinet card, Grover Cleveland, side pose, VG ..................**10.00**

Cabinet card, Sara Bernhardt, sepia, late 1890s, 4x6½", EX .......**17.50**

Cabinet card, 2 sulky drivers & horses crossing finish line, VG ...................................**12.50**

Cabinet card, 3 sm girls in Victorian finery w/rocking horse, VG ...................................**12.50**

Cabinet card, 3 white kittens looking over draped chair, EX .................................**12.50**

Camera, Brownie 127, 1965-67, w/case, EX .....................**15.00**

Camera, Contaflex, 35mm, 1930s, w/leather case, EX ........**95.00**

Camera, Kodak Brownie Cresta, black plastic, box style, ca 1955, NM .......................**15.00**

Camera, Minolta A, 1955-57, EX ................................**45.00**

Camera, Polaroid Big Shot, fixed focus lens, 1971-75, M ..**15.00**

Camera, Ricoh Singlex, 35 mm, ca 1964-66, EX .................**110.00**

Camera, Sears Tower 37 by Mamiya, ca 1961, EX ....**65.00**

Camera, Zeiss Ikon Stereo Nettel, leather covered, 1927-30, VG ..............................**200.00**

Carte de visite, Anna Leake Thomson, armless lady on table, 1871, EX ..............**40.00**

Carte de visite, Bunker Hill Monument, ca 1875, VG ......**10.00**

Carte de visite, Kate Santley in theatrical dress, ca 1869, EX .**10.00**

Carte de visite, Major-General McPherson, EX .............**15.00**

Carte de visite, Mrs Rosina D Wood, Weight 615 Lbs, EX .........**12.50**

Carte de visite, postmortem of baby, marked Wilton NH, EX .................................**12.50**

Carte de visite, slave girl from New Orleans, dated 1864, EX ..................................**55.00**

Carte de visite, Tom Thumb & wife, black & white, EX .**15.00**

Carte de visite, View of Pagoda Anchorage, Foochow China, 1868, EX .........................**12.50**

Case, pressed paper & wood, eagle in flight atop shield, 6th plate, EX .........................**15.00**

Case, thermoplastic, geometric & scroll w/Union design, half plate, EX .......................**115.00**

Case, thermoplastic, starred shield w/draped flags, 9th plate, EX .........................**60.00**

Case, velvet w/metal back & frame, Halvorson Patent 1856, 9th plate ..............**90.00**

Daguerreotype, lady holding grandson's hand, 6th plate, +case, EX .......................**25.00**

Daguerreotype, seated stylish man, 6th plate, +Mead Brothers case ..........................**87.50**

Daguerreotype, teenage brother & sister, 6th plate, EX ......**15.00**

Daguerreotype, traditional husband & wife portrait, +case, EX ..................................**40.00**

Glass negative, drugstore window display, ca 1925, 8x10", NM .**180.00**

Magazine ad, Brownie camera w/6 Brownies, December 1900, 6x9", EX ...........................**7.50**

Photo album, leather, holds 50 carte de visites, dated 1863, 6x5¼" .............................**65.00**

Stereoview, bird's-eye view St Louis World's Fair, EX ..**10.00**

Stereoview, Palace of Trocadero, Paris Exhibition, Underwood, 1900, EX .......................**15.00**

Stereoview, Pan American Expo's fountains by night, #14493, 1901, EX .......................**17.50**

Stereoview, Rebel Fortifications, Atlanta GA, #3644, Anthony, ca 1864 ..............................**35.00**

Stereoviewer, gold embossed cardboard hood, complete, ca 1860s, EX ......................**30.00**

Tintype, house w/family group & sewing machine in yard, half plate, EX ........................**40.00**

Tintype, seated frontiersman w/Winchester rifle, 2½x3½", EX ..................................**90.00**

Tintype, seated girl w/large doll, 2½x4", EX ......................**15.00**

Tintype, standing cowboy w/shotgun, 6th plate, half case, EX ....**50.00**

Tintype, standing militiaman w/M1860 cavalry saber, 2¼x3½", EX ..................**90.00**

Tintype, 3 Indian War soldiers with beer bottles, 2½x3½", EX .**40.00**

# Pie Birds

What is a pie bird? It is a functional and decorative kitchen tool most commonly found in the shape of a bird. Other popular designs were elephants and black-faced bakers. Originally (in the 1800s) they were simple funnel-shaped vents used in England and Wales for meat pies. More recently, figural pie vents have been made as novelties.

The basic functions of the pie bird (vent, funnel, chimney, safe, steamer) are to raise the crust to prevent sogginess and to allow the steam to escape, thus preventing the filling from bubbling over onto the oven floor. Pie birds are now at the peak of their appeal and collectability. The new collector must be wary that there are new pie vents being sold by dealers (knowingly in many instances) as old or rare and at double or triple the original cost (which is usually under $10.00). Though most of the new ones can't really be called reproductions since they never existed before, there's a black bird that is a remake, and you'll see them everywhere. Here's how you can spot them: they'll have yellow beaks and protruding white-dotted eyes; but if they're on a white base and have an orange beak, they're old. Our advisor for this category is Lillian M. Cole, who is listed in the Directory under New Jersey.

**Songbird, blue, 4½", $22.50.**

Angel w/folded hands to front, white, England, 4" ........**50.00**
Benny the Baker, Cardinal China ...........................**65.00**
Bird, stoneware, NH pottery, new, 4¼" .................................**10.00**
Bird, white w/blue-dot eyes, Japan, new ......................**5.00**
Black Chef or Mammy, red, yellow & white outfit, Taiwan, 4½", ea ....................................**10.00**
Blackbird, white base, orange beak ................................**30.00**
Blackbird, yellow beak, white dot eyes, Japan, new .............**5.00**
Canary, yellow & pink .........**18.00**
Elephant ...............................**40.00**
Granny Pie Baker, Lorrie Design, Japan .............................**23.00**
Rooster, Blue Willow ............**20.00**
Rooster, multicolored, Cleminson ...............................**20.00**

# Pin-Back Buttons

Because most of the pinbacks prior to the 1920s were made of celluloid, collectors refer to them as 'cellos.' Many were issued in sets on related topics, Some advertising buttons had paper inserts on the back that identified the company or the product they were advertising. After the 1920s lithographed metal buttons were produced; they're now called 'lithos.' See also The Beatles; Elvis Presley; Marilyn Monroe; Political, Pin-Back Buttons.

Batman & Robin Society Charter Member, 3½" .................**12.50**
Batman Returns, set of 4, M .**8.00**
Be a Beatles Booster, all pictured, 1¾" .................................**9.50**
Big Top Pee Wee, M ................**2.00**

Charter Member Batman & Robin Society, 1966, 3⅜" .........**15.00**
Chief of Values, Pontiac Indianhead logo, ⅞", G ...............**2.00**
Comic Weekly Club, clown portrait, ca 1945, ⅞", NM .....**3.50**
Die Hard 2, M ...........................**.50**
Dynasty, Forsythe, Collins & Evans portraits, ca 1980, 3" ...............................**10.00**
Famous Monsters Fan Club, Phantom of the Opera ..**20.00**
Fantastic Four, Official Member Superhero Club, 1965, 3½" .............................**15.00**
Ferris Bueller's Day Off, Paramount, 1986, M .......**3.00**
Frigidaire, yellow & brown, 1941, EX ...................................**3.00**
General Douglas MacArthur, 1" ...............................**22.00**
Have a Good Summer, w/auto photo, 1972, VG ...............**3.00**
Heaven Can Wait, Warren Beatty, Paramount, 1978, M .......**5.00**
Holsum Bread, 2 parrots, 1930s, EX ...................................**12.00**
Hopalong Cassidy in Daily News, copyright 1950 William Boyd, 1¾" ...................................**9.50**
Huckleberry Hound for President, 1960, 3" ..........................**12.50**
I Am a Junior Celtics Rooter, Bob Lousy photo, 1984, MIP ..**55.00**
I Like Pat Boone w/photo on yellow ground, 1958,¾" dia, NM ...............................**10.00**
I Love Barbie, yellow on blue flasher type, 1970s, 2" ....**3.50**
I'm An A&P Salesman..., 1" dia, NM ...............................**14.00**
Invite the World, Expo '86, 2" .**5.00**
Kilroy Buy War Bonds, dated 1943, 1¼", EX .................**7.50**
Mickey Mantle in batting pose on blue, early, 1¾", EX .......**42.50**
Mickey Mouse, red, yellow & black, dated 1937, 1¼", NM .....**80.00**

Monkees, letters across guitar w/names, 1967, M ..........**7.00**
Monte Hale, Quaker Puffed Wheat Western Star, 1948, NM ..................................**7.00**
Mustang 20th Anniversary, 1984, 3", EX ..............................**5.00**

**Nudist Contest, ca 1930s, 2½", EX, $15.00.**

Official Superman Club, 1966, 3⅜", NM ...........................**7.50**
Quality Dairy Co St Louis, My Favorite Ice Cream, Hopalong photo ........................**8.50**
Reach for Stardom...Magazine 10¢, 1940s, 3¼", EX ........**8.00**
Read My Lips No New Taxes, Bush & Quayle, 1989, 3", M ..................................**6.00**
Reddy Kilowatt, 1950s, ⅞", NM ...........................**10.00**
Reggie Van Gleason the III, 1955, 1¼", complete w/ribbon & charm ...........................**40.00**
Replace Black on Black Crime w/Black on Black Love, 3", EX .................................**20.00**
Restless Gun, John Payne photo, dated 1958, 3½" .............**35.00**
Snow White & 7 Dwarfs, dated 1975, 3¼", EX .................**7.50**
Sugar Bowl Classic, St Mary's, 1946, red & black letters, EX ....**20.00**

Tales of Wells Fargo, Dale Robertson photo, ca late 1950s, 3½", EX ...................................**35.00**

The Fisher King, Robin Williams portrait, 1991, M .............**3.00**

Tim Holt, Quaker Puffed Wheat Western Star, 1948, EX ..**5.00**

Wagon Train, stars' photos, Dagostino, dated 1958, 3½" .....**35.00**

Winchester, lg W encircled by lettering, 1" dia, NM .........**33.00**

Write in Dick Gregory President, Peace & Freedom, 1968, 1½" ....................**20.00**

Yes! Let the Rabbit Eat Trix, red, white & blue, 2¼" ............**5.00**

Zorro & 7-Up, orange & black on white, Disney Productions, 1957, M ..........................**15.00**

## Pep Pins

In the late forties and into the fifties, some cereal companies packed a pin-back button in each box of their product. Quaker Puffed Oats offered a series of movie star pin-backs, but Kellogg's Pep Pins are probably the best known of all. There were eighty-six in all, so theoretically if you wanted the whole series, as Kellogg hoped you would, you'd have to buy at least that many boxes of their cereal. Pep pins came in five sets, the first in 1945, three more in 1946, and the last in 1947. They were printed with full-color lithographs of comic characters licensed by King Features and Famous Artists — Maggie and Jiggs, the Winkles, and Dogwood and Blondie, for instance. Superman, the only D.C. Comics character, was included in each set. Most Pep pins range in value from $10.00 to $15.00 in NM/M condition; any not mentioned in our listings fall into this range. The exceptions are evaluated below. Our advisor for Pep pins is Doug Dezso, listed under New Jersey in the Directory.

BO Plenty .............................**30.00**
Brenda Star ..........................**16.00**
Dick Tracy ...........................**30.00**
Felix the Cat ........................**75.00**
Flash Gordon .......................**30.00**
Herby, NM ...........................**7.00**
Jiggs .....................................**25.00**
Katzenjammer Kids, Fritz ...**14.00**
Maggie ................................**25.00**
Mama de Stross ....................**30.00**
Mama Katzanjammer ..........**25.00**
Orphan Annie .......................**25.00**
Pat Patten ...........................**10.00**

Photo courtesy Doug Dezso.

**Pep pin, Moon Mullins, $10.00.**

Popeye ..................................**30.00**
Smitty ...................................**6.00**
Smokey Stover .....................**10.00**
Superman .............................**35.00**
The Phantom .......................**75.00**
Tillie the Toiler ....................**15.00**
Winkles Twins .....................**75.00**

# Pinup Art

This is a relatively new area of collector interest, and nice examples such as calendars, magazines, playing cards, etc., by the more collectible artists are still easy to find and not terribly expensive. Collectors often center their attention on the work of one or more of their favorite artists. Some of the better known are Petty, Vargas, Ballantyne, Armstrong, DeVorss, Elvgren, Moran, and Phillips. Pinup art was popular from the '30s into the '50s, inspired by Hollywood and its glamorous leading ladies.

Blotter, Hello Everybody, Armstrong, 6x3", EX .............**10.00**
Blotter, What's Cooking, girl w/dog, Elvgren, 4x9", EX .**7.50**
Book, Esquire's Handbook for Hosts, Grosset & Dunlap, 1949, 6x10", EX .............**20.00**

**Calendar, 1947, illustrated by Elvgren, 12x8", M (with original mailer), $135.00.**
Calendar, Billy DeVorss, 1951, 16x33", EX .....................**30.00**
Calendar, Glamour Gal Proverb Calendar, 1957, 18½x13", complete ........................**55.00**
Calendar, Set To Go, Zoe Mozart, 1950, 11x23", NM ..........**32.50**
Calendar, True, Petty, 1947, EX .**48.00**
Calendar top, Armstrong, Girl of My Dreams, cardboard, 1925, 10x15" ...........................**30.00**

Cigarette lighter, Playboy, enameled letters & logo, ca '60s, 2x2" .................................**10.00**
Date book, Esquire, 1944-1945, 104 pages, 5¼x7", NM ....**5.00**
Drinking glass, bride decal, shows nude from back, gold trim, '40s, NM .........................**12.50**
Greeting card, Earl MacPherson, 17x24" .............................**12.50**
Magazine ad, Esquire, Petty, Jantzen swimwear, 1936, 14x10", EX .....................**10.00**
Magazine ad, Life, Petty, Airman Shirts, 1942, 4x9", M ....**50.00**
Magazine foldout, Esquire, Petty, nude in swing, 1941, NM .**32.50**
Mutoscope card, He's Safer Than a Wolf, Zoe Mozart, EX ...**7.50**
Mutoscope card, Stocking Up on Sugar, Earl Moran, M .....**7.50**
Photo card, Esquire, Hurrell Girls #8, set of 6, original mailer, EX .................................**37.50**
Playing cards, Esquire, Al Moore, original box, complete, EX ......................**55.00**
Playing cards, nude blond w/lg hat, Vargas, 1945, ea ......**2.50**
Print, A Beautiful Pair, blonde w/dogs, Walt Otte, 8x10", EX ................................**16.50**
Print, Betwitching, Billy DeVorss, 8x11", EX .......................**15.00**
Print, Cute Trick, Art Frahm, ca 1945, 5x6" ........................**6.00**
Print, Embarrassing Moments, Frahm, 8x10", EX .........**12.50**
Print, Flower Girl, Erbit, ca 1940s, 7x9", M .................**5.00**
Print, Peek-A-View, Elvgren, Louis Dow, ca 1940s, NM .........**12.50**
Print, Twinkle Toes, Armstrong, 4½x6", EX ......................**15.00**
Print, What Lines, blond w/phone & dog, Deckard, 5x6", EX .**5.00**
Print, Youth, Irene Patton, ca 1930s, 6½x8½", EX ........**15.00**

Sheet music, Yo-San, Armstrong,
EX ...................................**15.00**
Souvenir program, ice capades,
George Petty, 1964, 9x12",
EX ..................................**20.00**

# Planters

The years from about 1930 until the early 1970s was the era for figural ceramics. Planters were produced in every shape possible, and those designed in the forms of animals, birds, and children were preferred. Though many were imported from Japan, companies here in the United States made them as well. For more information refer to *American Bisque Collector's Guide With Prices* by Mary Jane Giacomini (Shiffer), and Collector's Guide to Made in Japan Ceramics by Carole Bess White (Collector Books). See also specific pottery companies such as McCoy, Shawnee, Cleminson, Royal Copley, etc.

Bird on lg blossom, unmarked,
5¾" ..................................**12.50**
Boy in fez w/2 lg yellow lustre
baskets, Japan, 4" .........**20.00**
Cat w/lg yarn ball, shiny multicolor
porcelain, Japan, 4¼" .....**10.00**
Cherub on swan boat, shiny white
w/black trim porcelain,
Japan, 3¼" ...................**15.00**
Cockatiel on stump, unmarked,
5" ....................................**12.50**
Davy Crockett 3 Years Old on
tree trunk, w/Davy & bear,
unmarked, 5" .................**50.00**

**Bear cubs around tree trunk, gold trim, unmarked American Bisque, 5x6", $20.00.**

Duck face on basketweave oval basket, unmarked, 3¼" ...**8.00**

Dutch girl w/lg wooden shoe, unmarked, 6" ...................**6.00**

Elephant, Art Deco style w/blue lustre, Japan, 3¼" .........**25.00**

Farmer pig w/ear of corn, unmarked, 6½" ................**6.00**

Goosey Gander, multicolor matte porcelain, Japan, 3½" ....**10.00**

Horse, reclining, pink, brown & cream, flat bottom w/wedges, 4½" ..................................**10.00**

Kitten & shoe, marked USA, 3½x6½" ...........................**14.00**

Man w/camel at oasis, multicolor & lustre porcelain, Japan, 2½" ..................................**10.00**

Musical frog trio w/lustre flower, Japan, 3" ........................**10.00**

Rabbit in log, unmarked, 5¾" **22.00**

Spaniel, sitting w/basket on back, marked USA, 5¾" ..........**22.50**

Stork w/cradle, marked USA, 6½" ..................................**8.00**

Three tiger kittens, creamware, unmarked, 3¾x5" ..........**25.00**

Tiger standing on barrel, multicolor matte porcelain, Japan, 5" .**10.00**

Yarn doll w/lg building block, unmarked, 5¾" ..............**18.00**

# Planters Peanuts

Since 1916 Mr. Peanut has represented the Planters Peanuts Company. Today he has his own fan club of collectors who specialize in this area of advertising memorabilia. More than fifteen styles of the glass display jars were made; the earliest was issued in 1926 and is referred to as the 'pennant' jar. The rarest of them all is the 'football' jar from the early thirties. Premiums such as glass and metal paperweights, pens, and pencils were distributed in the late 1930s; after the war, plastic items were offered.

Bag, plastic, filled w/marbles, 1950s ..............................**18.00**

Bookmark, cardboard, Mr Peanut, 1930s-50s .......................**15.00**

Coloring book, Presidents, 1977 ..**5.00**

Coloring book, 50 States, 1960s .**5.00**

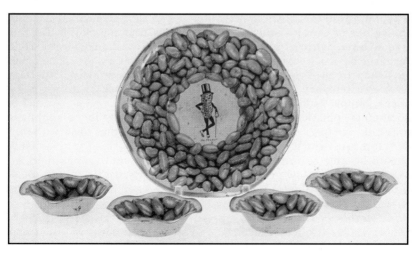

**Nut set, tin lithographed, largest: 6" dia, 5-piece set, EX, $25.00.**

Jar, Football, PLANTERS embossed on original lid ................**275.00**
Jar, Mixed Nuts, w/label & original tin lid, 1940s ...........**25.00**
Jar, Peanut Butter, w/label & original tin lid, 1950s ....**25.00**
Jar, round, frosted label, original knob-finial lid, 1950s ....**50.00**
Mug, plastic, Mr Peanut, 1-color, 1950s ................................**5.00**
Mug, plastic, Mr Peanut, 2-color, 1950s ..............................**10.00**
Nut grinder, litho tin w/peanuts & Mr Peanut, 1930s-60s, EX .**5.00**
Pin, tin, Mr Peanut, tab back, 1½" dia, NM ..........................**10.00**
Spoon, nut server, gold wash, Mr Peanut, NM ...................**10.00**
Tray, tin, oval, 1980s, M ......**20.00**
Whistle, plastic, police style ..**3.00**

# Plastic Collectibles

While early plastic items have long been a part of many areas of collecting interest (for instance, thermoplastic photo cases and jewelry), and over the past several years we have seen a tremendous acceleration in the values of Catalin and Bakelite items, there has only recently been a recent surge of interest in mid-century and later kitchenware items, appliances, lamps, radios, etc., made of common plastic. Because the market is just starting to develop, an informed shopper should be able to find excellent examples at very low prices. For information on plastic jewelry, refer to *Twentieth Century Fashionable Plastic Jewelry* by Lillian Baker (Collector Books). See also Kitchen Collectibles; Purses.

**Napkin holder, aqua, silhouettes of Spanish dancers, $28.00.**

Basket, Easter; solid color w/basketweave design, 1940-50s, lg .....................................**20.00**
Bed Lamp, pink w/metal decorations, light filter, 12x5" .**15.00**
Bottle, perfume; Lucite w/rose inclusion, w/atomizer ....**10.00**
Bracelet, bangle; 2-color Catalin stripes ...........................**70.00**
Bracelet, celluloid imitation tortoise w/inlaid rhinestones ........**40.00**
Bracelet, cuff; green marbled Bakelite, ¾" wide .........**32.00**
Buckle, latch type, 1-color, uncarved .....................................**5.00**
Buttons, card of 6, Scottie dog, fruit or carved floral figural ....**28.00**
Chopsticks, ivory, pr ...............**5.00**
Clock, electric w/alarm, Art Deco-styled black or brown Bakelite ....................................**65.00**
Crib toy, Tykie Toy, elephant or clown, Laolin head w/Catalin body, ea ..........................**60.00**
Dress clip, multicolor inlaid Art Deco design ...................**20.00**
Dresser set, ivory pearlescent or amberoid celluloid, 5-pc set ...............................**50.00**
Flatware, stainless w/1-color handle, 3-pc matched place setting .....................................**7.50**

Ice cream scoop, stainless w/red handle ........................**20.00**
Lamp base, red, amber & black, Art Deco design, 8" .......**44.00**
Letter opener, black & amber striped Art Deco design ..**20.00**
Mirror, dresser; ivoroid, oval bevel glass, 13" ......................**28.00**
Picture frame, ivoroid, easel back, rectangular, 2½" ............**12.00**

**Pin, American eagle, 2¾" wide, from $50.00 to $55.00.**

Pin, animal, resin wash w/glass eye, lg ..........................**110.00**
Pin, animal or vegetable, 1-color, lg ...................................**80.00**
Pin, yellow translucent Bakelite w/red flowers, 1½x1¼" ..**42.00**
Powder box, amber & green fluted cylinder, 4" ......................**60.00**
Shaving brush, red, green or amber, ea .......................**18.00**
Spoon, iced tea; chrome w/Catalin knob, 6-pc set ................**18.00**
Strainer, red, green or amber handle, 5" dia .........................**6.00**
Swizzle stick, baseball-bat shape, amber or red, ea ..............**4.00**

# Political Memorabilia

Pennants, posters, badges, pamphlets — in general, any-thing related to a presidential campaign or politicians — are being sought by collectors who have an interest in the political history of our country. Most valued are items from a particularly eventful period or those things having to do with an especially colorful personality. See also Matchcovers.

Balloon, Wallace for President, 1972, unused, M ..............**5.00**
Book, Every Man King, by Huey P Long, 1933, 1st edition, G .**57.00**
Book, Weep No More My Lady (Eleanor Roosevelt), 1950, 60 pages, EX ........................**17.50**
Clicker, Click Click With Dick, yellow litho tin, 1960, M ....**22.50**
Dollar token, Senator Goldwater, 1964 .................................**5.00**
Game, The Watergate Scandal, cards, boxed, VG ...........**10.00**
Key chain, President & Mrs Jimmy Carter photo, M ..............**20.00**
License plate, LBJ for the USA, red, white & blue, EX ...**25.00**
Medal, KKK Member in Good Standing, brass, EX ......**15.00**
Nodder, LBJ, vinyl, Remco, 1964, 4½", EX+ ........................**25.00**
Pamphlet, Dewey Gets Things Done, 16 pages, EX .........**6.00**
Pencil, Smith for President, 1928, figural plastic head, M ..**20.00**
Plate, Roosevelt & Little White House, Warm Springs, GA, 7" dia, EX ...........................**20.00**
Pocketknife, Carter & Mondale w/portraits, Barlow, M ..**20.00**
Postcard, George Bush, 41st President of the US, color, EX .**1.50**
Postcard, Nelson Rockefeller for President in '68, black & white, EX ........................**5.50**
Postcard, Roosevelt expedition to Africa, dated 1909, EX ..**22.50**

Poster, President Nixon...Protection of Environment..., 1972, 22x34" ..............................**20.00**

Program, Official 43rd Inauguration 1957, Eisenhower & Nixon portraits ..............**27.00**

Program, Truman inauguration, 1949, NM ........................**27.50**

Punching bag, George Bush caricature, 1988, EX ............**15.00**

Puppet, Jimmy Carter, 1970s, EX ..................................**18.00**

Ribbon, Remember the Maine, black letters on red, EX ..**25.00**

Sticker, Ike-Dick, red, white & blue, 5x5", M ...................**3.50**

Stickpin, McKinley enameled on metal, EX ........................**17.50**

T-Shirt, Come Home America, McGovern & Eagleton, 1972, M ....................................**35.00**

Tie bar, Vote Adlai in black & white letters, EX ...........**12.50**

Token, Senator Birch Bayh ....**4.00**

**Tray with William McKinley portrait, 17x12", VG, $70.00.**

Whistle, Whistle With Dick (lettered), blue on white tin litho, 1960 ..............................**24.00**

## J.F. Kennedy Memorabilia

Few would disagree that Kennedy was one of the most beloved presidents we've ever had. The tragedy of his assassination dealt a personal blow to each one of us, and it was extremely devastating to our country. Today collectors of JFK memorabilia continue to pay him tribute through their interest in the many items that were issued during his presidential campaigns or designed to commemorate him after his death. Our advisor for this category is Michael Engel; he is listed in the Directory under Massachusetts.

Board game, The Kennedys, EX in original box .............**250.00**

Campaign pamphlet, A New Leader for the '60s ........**15.00**

Campaign stamps, sheet of 100 .............................**20.00**

Face mask, JFK, plastic ......**30.00**

Magazine, Time, November 7, 1960, JFK on cover .......**10.00**

Matchbook, Congressman JF Kennedy ........................**80.00**

Pennant, red & white felt w/JFK color picture ...................**15.00**

Pin-back button, A Profile in Courage: Elect US Senator..., 1956 .............................**700.00**

Pin-back button, America Needs Kennedy & Johnson, 1960, 3½" ..................................**35.00**

Pin-back button, For President: John F Kennedy, 1960, 3½" .......**10.00**

Pin-back button, Youth for Kennedy, 1960, 4" .......**250.00**

Plate, multicolor JFK portrait w/gold rim, 9¼" .............**15.00**

Postcard, President Kennedy's Summer Home on Cape Cod .............................**10.00**

Poster, Leadership for the '60s, Kennedy & Johnson, 48x30" .......................**150.00**

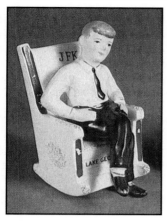

**Salt and pepper shakers, President Kennedy in his rocking chair, $25.00.**

Sash, Volunteers for Kennedy ..**200.00**
Scarf, silk w/JFK portrait, 30" .**25.00**
Sheet music, Kennedy Victory Song ...............................**40.00**
Tie bar, Kennedy '60 on silver PT-boat, MOC ......................**65.00**

## Pin-Back Buttons

Celluloid pin-back buttons ('cellos') were first widely used in the 1896 presidential campaign; before that time medals, ribbons, and badges of various kinds predominated. By the 1920s buttons with designs lithographed directly on metal ('lithos') became more common. The most attractive and interesting designs are found on 'classic' buttons made between 1900-15, and they (along with the plainer but very scarce buttons for presidential candidates of the 1920s) are also the most expensive.

Prices for political pin-back buttons have increased considerably in the last few years, more due to speculative buying and selling rather than inherent scarcity or unusual demand. It is still possible, however, to find quality collectible items at reasonable prices. In flea markets, recent buttons tend to be overpriced; the goal, as always, is to look for less familiar items that may be priced more reasonably.

Most collectors look for presidential items, but buttons for 'causes' (such as civil rights and peace) as well as 'locals' (governors, senators, etc.) are becoming increasingly popular as well. Picture buttons are the most desirable, especially the 'jugates' which show both presidential and vice-presidential candidates. Recently, 'coattail' items, featuring presidential and local candidates on the same button, have attracted a lot of interest. Most buttons issued since the 1964 campaign, with a few notable exceptions, should be in the range of $2.00 to $10.00. The listing here therefore concentrates on earlier items.

Condition is critical: cracks, scratches, spots, and brown stains ('foxing') seriously reduce the value of a button. Prices are for items in excellent condition. Reproductions are common; many are marked as such, but it takes some experience to tell the difference. The best reference book for political collectors is Edmund Sullivan's *Collecting Political Americana*, the second edition of which has been recently published. Our advisor is Michael Engel, who is listed in the Directory under Massachusetts.

1896, McKinley, portrait w/stars & stripes border, ⅞" ......**20.00**

1896, 16 to 1: Bryan/Sewall, blue, black & white, ⅞" ..........**40.00**

1900, Bryan-Stevenson, portraits, stars & stripes, 1¾" .......**65.00**

1908, For President: Debs (Socialist), red, white & black, ⅞" ....**150.00**

1912, (Theodore) Roosevelt the American, w/portrait, ⅞" .**45.00**

1912, For President: Woodrow Wilson 1912, black & white portrait, ⅞" ....................**40.00**

1920, For President: Warren G Harding, portrait w/red rim, ⅞" ..................................**15.00**

1924, Keep Coolidge, brown w/portrait, ⅞" ................**20.00**

**1928, Al Smith 'You Know Me,' extremely rare, large size, M, $650.00 to $800.00.**

1928, For President: Herbert C Hoover, w/portrait, 1¼" .**60.00**

1928, Smith for President, red, white & blue w/portrait, ⅞" ........**15.00**

1936, Landon for President, red, white & blue w/portrait, 1¼" ..............................**20.00**

1936, We Want FDR Again, red, white & blue, 2¼" ..........**25.00**

1940, He's Good Enough for My Buck: Roosevelt, w/portrait, ⅞" ..................................**20.00**

1940, No Third Term, red, white & blue, ⅞" ........................**5.00**

1940, Re-Elect Our President: FDR, black & white w/portrait, 1¼" ........................**20.00**

1944, Roosevelt-Truman, brown & white w/portraits, 1" ...**150.00**

1948, (Henry) Wallace: '48, black & white, 1¼" ..................**15.00**

1948, Dewey-Warren, portraits, ⅞" ....................................**35.00**

1948, Forward w/Pres Truman: No Retreat, red, white & blue, ⅞" ..........................**65.00**

1952, Forward w/Stevenson & Sparkman, multicolor w/portraits, 1¾" ......................**25.00**

1952, I Like Ike, red, white & blue, ⅞" ............................**2.00**

1952, Stevenson/President, red, white & blue w/portrait, 1¼" ..............................**15.00**

1960, The Winning Team: Nixon/Lodge, red, white & blue, 1½" ........................**5.00**

1964, A Choice Not an Echo: Goldwater/Miller, portraits, 3½" ................................**15.00**

1964, LBJ All the Way, black & white w/hat, 1½" ...........**15.00**

# Postcards

The first postcards were printed in Austria in 1869, but it was the Columbian Exposition in 1893 that started the postcard craze that swept the country for years to come. Today's collectors tend to specialize in cards of a particular theme or by a favorite illustrator. Among the famous artists whose work you may find are Rose O'Neill, Philip Boileau, Alphonse Mucha, and John Winsch. Many postcards are worth under $5.00. We have listed some of the more collectible varieties here. See also Black Americana; Movie Memorabilia; Political Memorabilia.

Advertising, American La France Fire Engine Co, Elmira, NY, color, EX ...........................**6.00**

Advertising, Anheuser-Busch Brewing Association, dated 1906 ...............................**28.00**

Advertising, Chevrolet w/Santa, 1934, color, G .................**10.00**

Advertising, hairstyling salon in hotel, chrome, ca 1950s, M .**4.00**

Advertising, Hamm Brewing Co, interior view, dated 1911, NM ...................................**17.50**

Advertising, M Rumley Co, Oil Pull Tractors harvesting in MN, color .........................**8.00**

Advertising, Mailomat, Pitney Bowes, ca 1943, VG .......**10.00**

Advertising, Nestles Food, cupid w/stork, 1910, color, EX .**15.00**

Advertising, United Bakery's Mother's Bread, movie star, sepia, EX ..........................**8.00**

Banana bark, hand-print scene, Hatian, ca 1969, EX ........**4.00**

Bon Voyage, Statue of Liberty in background, ca 1915, color photo, EX ........................**15.00**

Christy, Earl; lady's portrait, EX ...................................**3.50**

Clapsaddle, Halloween, black cat, EX ..................................**22.00**

Clapsaddle, Thanksgiving, International Art Series #1817, G .......................................**8.00**

Clapsaddle, 4th of July, International Art Series #4398, EX ...............................**15.00**

Comic, Dwig, Everytime series #182, embossed, Tuck, EX .**8.00**

Comic, Moon Mullens strip characters, color, dated 1942, EX ...................................**3.50**

**Decoration Day, copyright 1908, from $7.00 to $10.00.**

Easter, baby w/rabbit, embossed, Winsch, 1911, EX ............**6.00**

Exposition, Century of Progress 1933, RR Donnelley & Sons, EX ....................................**2.50**

Exposition, St Louis 1904, Social Economy Building, Cupples, color, EX .......................**12.00**

Foreign, Kronprinz Wilhelm, color photo, ca 1900, EX ........**10.00**

Foreign, store, Brandon, Manatoba Canada, black & white, ca 1915, EX .....................**6.00**

Foreign, Wohlfahrtskarte, Berlin, 1914 ...............................**17.00**

Halloween, Gabriel series, embossed, Frances Brundage, 1910, EX ........................**20.00**

Halloween, spooks & witches, Aleinmuller Art Co, embossed, EX .....................**25.00**

Halloween, witch in corn stalks, ca 1910, G ......................**12.00**

Hold-to-light, Easter 1906, angel, NY, EX ..........................**60.00**

Hold-to-light, WWI scene, EX .**25.00**

Leather, babies nursing from cow, ca 1905, EX ...................**12.50**

Linen, Fred Harvey, Jicarilla Apache Chief, AZ, ca 1940, M ......................................**5.00**

Linen, Remember Pearl Harbor, Kropp, 1943, VG ............**12.50**

New Year's, signed Lounsbury, embossed, M ....................**6.00**

Novelty, baby w/bottle, German-American Art Series #1025, embossed, G ......................**6.00**

Novelty, cupid & lady New Year w/silk clothes, embossed, EX ...................................**15.00**

Novelty, Little Old Man of the Woods, #70698, Detroit Publishers, G ........................**20.00**

Nude, The Young Bride's Christmas Gift, signed Neumont, ca 1912, EX .........................**12.00**

O'Neill, Kewpies w/umbrella, Gibson, G .............................**10.00**

Photo, Chief Bemidji, Bemidji MN, black & white w/tint, ca 1917, EX .........................**20.00**

Photo, Coney Island view, early, VG ..................................**2.00**

Photo, Echo Lake Lodge, interior view w/fireplace & rugs, 1930s ................................**8.50**

Photo, gas station, Churchtown PA, black & white, ca 1917 ......**6.00**

Photo, Hopi Indian snake priest, exterior view w/buildings, 1920s, EX .........................**4.50**

Photo, horse-drawn wagon delivering lumber, EX ...........**12.00**

Photo, Indian maiden, marked Gartner & Bender Publishing, VG ............................**10.00**

Photo, Kwataka Boys Dormitory, Albuquerque NM, 1914, EX .................................**8.00**

Photo, lumber camp, ca 1910, EX .................................**6.00**

Photo, Radio City Music Hall, 1949, M .........................**12.00**

Photo, roller coaster, Riverview Beach, Pennsville NJ, NM .**6.00**

Photo, Skagway AK, dog sled in front of store, VG ..........**15.00**

Photo, State Ferry, Mackinaw City MI, black & white, 1926 ..**15.00**

Photo, street scene, Philadelphia, black & white, 1907, EX .**15.00**

Photo, The Jersey Lily, Wench Series, England, ca 1905, NM ......**17.50**

Photo, Winnebago Indians at Bethesda Park, Waukesha WI, color, ca 1910 ............**8.00**

Photo, WWI US soldiers in France, black & white, EX ............**5.50**

Spurgin, You Are Just My Mark, Target series #262, color, EX ...................................**15.00**

Suffragette, I Don't Care If She Never Comes Back, #6, VG ............**7.50**

Suffragette, man at lady's restroom door, 1912, EX .................**15.00**

Tuck, Zeppelin, #406, embossed, ca 1910, EX ....................**25.00**

Veenfliet, Washington at Valley Forge, #5176b, Garre, embossed, EX ......................................**10.00**

**Girl on horseback, Germany, ca 1910, from $6.00 to $8.00.**

# Precious Moments

Little figurines with inspirational messages called Precious Moments were created by Samuel J. Butcher and are produced by Enesco Inc. in the Orient. They're sold through almost every gift store in the country, and some of the earlier, discontinued models are becoming very collectible. Refer to *Precious Collectibles*, a magazine published by Rosie Wells Enterprises Inc. for more information. Rosie is listed in our Directory under Illinois and again under Clubs and Newsletters.

Angel & Girl at Heaven's Gate, #101826, Olive Branch mark ..........................**120.00**
Angel w/Flashlight, #E-5637, no mark ...............................**95.00**
Baby Posing for Pictures, #E-2841, Cross mark ........**145.00**
Boy & Girl in Tub, #E-7165, Hourglass mark ..........**120.00**
Boy & Pig in Mud, #E-9259, Hourglass mark ..........**100.00**
Boy Holding Blue Bird, #E-7156R, Cedar Tree mark ..........**80.00**
Boy Holding Yellow Chick, #E-7156, Hourglass mark ..**110.00**
Boy Patching World, #E-1381R, G-Clef mark ...................**65.00**
Boy w/Piano, #12165, Dove mark ...........................**135.00**
Boy w/Teddy, #E-1372B, no mark ...........................**115.00**
Boy/Girl Indians in Canoe, #520772, Flower mark .**295.00**
Camel w/Wise Men, #E-5624, no mark, 3-pc set ..............**350.00**
Family/Thanksgiving, #109762, Cedar Tree mark .........**185.00**
Girl at Trunk w/Wedding Gown, #E-2828, Fish mark ......**95.00**

Girl Ironing, #E-9265, Hourglass mark .............................**115.00**
Girl Mailing Snowball, #112402, Cedar Tree mark .........**145.00**
Girl Sweeping Dirt Under Rug, #521779, Bow & Arrow mark ...........................**135.00**
Girl w/Bunny, #104531, Easter Seals, Cedar Tree mark, 9" ....**1,750.00**
Girl w/Fawn, #10048, Olive Branch mark ...............**110.00**
Girl w/Goose, #E-1374G, no mark ...........................**130.00**
Girl w/Piano, #12580, Olive Branch mark ...............**200.00**
Girl w/Puppies in cart, #E-1378, no mark .......................**850.00**
Grandma in Rocking Chair, #E-3109, no mark ...............**95.00**

**Jesus Is the Light, no mark, $115.00.**

Policeman, #12297, Dove mark .......................**120.00**
Three Kings, #E-5635, no mark, 3-pc set .......................**150.00**

Tracing in the Sand, #E-3113,
Cross mark ....................**35.00**

# Premiums

Since the radio shows of the
forties, product manufacturers
have offered premiums — rings,
decoders, watches, games, books,
and many other items — just for
mailing in boxtops or coupons. If
the premium wasn't free, the price
was minimal. Most of them were
easily broken, and as children we
had no qualms about throwing
them away, so few survive. Today
some of the earlier character-
related examples are bringing fantastic prices, though at present the
market is very volatile. For more
information and additional listings,
see *Schroeder's Collectible Toys,
Antique to Modern*, by Sharon and
Bob Huxford (Collector Books.)

Alvin & the Chipmunks, record,
Colgate Palmolive, 1963, M in
sleeve ..............................**30.00**
Amos & Andy, map, Pepsodent,
1935, w/mailer, M, from $60
to ...................................**75.00**

**Jack Armstrong Hike-A-Meter, 3"
diameter, EX, $24.00.**

Beechnut Gum, Yipes Stripes Col-
oring Book, 40 pages, 1961,
14x20", M ......................**35.00**
Boo Berry, toothbrush holder, blue
plastic, M .......................**20.00**
Cap'n Crunch, cereal bowl,
embossed plastic, M ......**25.00**
Cap'n Crunch, Oath of Allegiance,
1964, 8x10", NM .............**18.00**
Captain Marvel, Billy's Big Game
giveaway, Double-Bubble
Gum, M ..........................**80.00**
Captain Marvel, paint book, M .**75.00**
Captain Midnight, decoder, 1946,
EX, from $85 to .............**95.00**
Casper the Friendly Ghost, color-
ing book, American Dental
Assn, 1967 ......................**12.00**
Cisco Kid, badge, clip back, But-
ternut Bread, EX ..........**28.00**
Count Chocula, figurine, brown
plastic, 2¼", ca 1937, M ..**18.00**
Dell Comics, Jack & Beanstalk
Magic Bean Set, Miracle
Bowl Co, 1950s, M ........**35.00**
Freakies, cars, Ralston, 1974, set
of 7, MIB ......................**35.00**
Freakies, magnets, Ralston, 1970,
set of 6, M ......................**35.00**
Fruity Pebble's, change purse,
Hasbro, 1972, EX ...........**5.00**
Funny Face, iron-on patch, Pills-
bury, 1960s, 7x9", original
mailer, M ......................**15.00**
General Mills, Bullwinkle's How
To Have Fun Coloring Book,
1963, M ..........................**45.00**
General Mills, Fizzies Drink
Tablets, 1960s, MIP ......**55.00**
General Mills, Jet Plane, rubber-
band launcher, 1960s, 1",
MIP ...............................**18.00**
General Mills, Tennessee Tuxedo
& National Parks Coloring
Book, 1965 ......................**65.00**
Heinz 57, comic book, Capt Gal-
lant of Foreign Legion, 1955,
7x10", EX ......................**25.00**

**Little Orphan Annie and Sandy, Beetleware, Ovaltine premiums: Cup, 4", Mug, 3", from $15.00 to $25.00 each.**

Hopalong Cassidy, badge, black & silver w/photo, Bond Bread, 3", M ..............................**15.00**

Howdy Doody, flicker ring, Rice Honey's, M .....................**22.50**

Jack Armstrong, Explorer telescope, EX .......................**35.00**

Kellogg's, aircraft carrier w/2 launch rockets, 1950s, original mailer ....................**150.00**

Kellogg's, baking soda submarine, MIB .................................**17.50**

Kellogg's, Funny Jungleland, booklet, 1908, 6x8¼", VG ......**80.00**

Kellogg's, Story Book of Games #2, 1931, 8x10", EX .......**50.00**

Kool-Aid, canteen, green & clear plastic, marked F&F, 1960s, M ....................................**125.00**

Kool-Aid, Kooler Dispenser, logo on glass, 1961, 7½", MIB .....**38.00**

Kool-Aid, mug, figural grape cluster, EX ...........................**12.50**

Nehi, booklet, ca 1920s, 12 pages, EX ....................................**7.50**

OK's, Yogi the Bear swoppet, white plastic, ca 1960, NM ......**32.50**

Oscar Mayer, Hot Wheels car, figural hot dog, MIP ............**3.00**

Peter Pan Peanut Butter, coloring book, 1963, M ................**10.00**

Philip Morris Cigarette Co, Lucy's Notebook, 40 pages, 1954, 6x9", NM ........................**20.00**

Pop-Tarts, ballpoint pen, Secret Note, write & decode, 1980s, set of 2 .............................**2.00**

Popsicle, coin, movie star portrait on aluminum, 1930s, 1" dia ....**3.50**

Post Raisin Bran, badge, Ranch Foreman, M ...................**15.00**

Post's, Klicko the Climbing Monkey, paper, 1947, 6x7¾", NM .............................**22.50**

Post's, Tappin' Tom the Tap Dancer, paper, 1947, 6x7¾", M ...................................**25.00**

Post's, Zippo the Human Cannon Ball, paper, 1947, 6x7¾", EX .................................**22.50**

Quaker Oats, Treasure Island Cut-Out Coloring Book, w/crayons, MIP ............**20.00**

Quisp, Gyroscrambler, MIP .**35.00**

Red Barn Restaurants, trick-or-treat bag, paper w/handles, 1964, M ..........................**18.00**

Rin-Tin-Tin & Sergeant O'Hara, cloth patch, Nabisco, 1958, M ....................................**15.00**

Shadow, ink blotter, Blue Coal, NM ................................**30.00**

Sky King, ring, Navajo Treasure, EX ................................**150.00**

Straight Arrow, ring w/picture, EX ..................................**63.00**

Tootsie Rolls, game, Astronaut in Orbit, 1960s, MIP .........**25.00**

Trix, whistle, blue plastic, NM .**14.00**

Virginia Slims, telephone/note pad, Little Black Book, 1984, 2½x4" ..............................**3.50**

Wheaties, Hike-O-Meter, MIB .**35.00**

Wheaties, license plate, adhesive back, 1963, set of 6, M in mailer ............................**20.00**

Wonder Bread, Magic Tricks for Boys & Girls, dial wheel, 1946, 5x4" ..................................**22.50**

# Purinton

Popular among collectors due to its 'country' look, Purinton Pot-tery's dinnerware and kitchen items are easy to learn to recognize due to their bold yet simple designs, many of them of fruit and flowers, created with basic hand-applied colors on a creamy white gloss. For more information we recommend *Purinton Pottery, An Identification and Value Guide*, by Susan Morris (Collector Books).

Bowl, cereal; Apple, 5¼" ......**10.00**

Bowl, cereal; Pennsylvania Dutch, 5¼" ..................................**20.00**

Bowl, fruit; Intaglio, 12" ......**40.00**

Coffeepot, Fruit ....................**65.00**

Cup & saucer, Apple ............**15.00**

Cup & saucer, Maywood ......**20.00**

Honey jug, Ivy ......................**25.00**

Jug, Apple, Kent, 6¼" ..........**30.00**

Mug, Intaglio, 8-oz, 4" ..........**60.00**

Plate, Apple, 8½" ..................**20.00**

Plate, Normandy Plaid, 9¾" **15.00**

Plate, Pennsylvania Plaid, 12" .**30.00**

Salt & pepper shakers, Normandy Plaid, 4¼", pr .................**60.00**

Teapot, Apple, 2-cup ............**40.00**

Teapot, Ivy, 2-cup ................**45.00**

Teapot, Mountain Rose, 6-cup .**85.00**

Tumbler, Fruit, 5" ...............**20.00**

Tumbler, Sunflower, 12-oz, 5" .**30.00**

**Apple, sugar bowl, 5", $30.00; Creamer, 3½", $20.00.**

# Purses

From the late 1800s until well into the 1930s, beaded and metal mesh purses were popular fashion accessories. Flat envelope styles were favored in the twenties, and bags featuring tassels or fringe were also in vogue. Enameled mesh bags were popular in the late twenties and into the thirties, decorated in Art Deco designs with stripes, birds, or flowers. Whiting and Davis and the Mandalian Manufacturing Company were two of the most important manufacturers.

During the 1950s, purses made of Lucite or plastic of some other type became popular. These have lately become highly sought after, especially those with the label of a good manufacturer, an unusual shape, or in an especially vivid or hard-to-find color.

The following are base values. Worth-assessing factors such as condition, age, manufacturer, country of origin, rarity, attractiveness, quality of workmanship and design, weight (when considering silver), size of beads, and whether machine or handmade, must be taken into account. Listings are for purses in mint condition. Refer to *Antique Purses, A History, Identification, and Value Guide,* by Richard Holiner (Collector Books). Our advisor is Veronica Trainer; she is listed in the Directory under Ohio.

Chatelain purse, steel beads, 4x4", M ........................**120.00**
Cloth, metallic embroidery, France, 4x5", M .............**70.00**
Deco, enameled mesh, 3x6", M ..........................**175.00**

Finger ring purse, sterling silver, 3x4", M ........................**125.00**
Floral, fine glass beads, jeweled frame, 6½x10", M ........**475.00**
Floral, fine glass beads, sterling silver frame, 7x11", M .**550.00**
Floral, fine glass beads, 7x11", M ...............................**300.00**
Floral, medium glass beads, celluloid frame, 6½x12", M .**225.00**
Floral, steel beads in colors, jeweled frame, 7x12", M ...**500.00**
Geometrics, steel beads, 6x10", M ...............................**140.00**
Leather, hand tooled, 6x8", M .**150.00**
Leather, hand tooled, clutch type, Meeker, 5x9" .................**70.00**

**Lucite, octagonal shape in tortoise shell with amber lid, 6½" long, $110.00.**

Mandalian Mfg Co, enameled mesh, fringe bottom, 3½x7", M .................................**225.00**
Mandalian Mfg Co, enameled mesh, teardrop bottom, 4x7", M .................................**295.00**
Miser's stockings purse, lightly beaded w/steel beads, 2x12", M .................................**75.00**

Needlepoint, floral, jeweled frame, 7x6", M .............**400.00**

Nylon, yellow & brown drawstring bag, 1930s, 12x10", EX...**15.00**

Petit point, floral, jeweled frame, 7x6", M .........................**450.00**

Plastic, Lucite, box style, unmarked, M, from $40 to ..................**60.00**

Plastic beads, zipper, gate top, or flap closure, M, from $10 to .....**50.00**

Reticule, crochet, 5x10", M ..**40.00**

Reticule, fine beads, floral pattern, 6x10", M .............**200.00**

Reticule, medium beads, floral pattern, 8x11", M ........**120.00**

Rhinestones, France, 4x5", M .**80.00**

Rug pattern, fine glass beads, jeweled frame, 6½x11", M .**600.00**

Scenic or figural pattern, medium beads, 8x11", M ...........**450.00**

Scenic or figural pattern, steel beads, 7x12", M ...........**600.00**

**Sterling silver frame, fine bead floral, $450.00.**

Tam O'-Shanter coin purse, lightly beaded, 2x2", M .**75.00**

Tapestry, hand woven, sterling frame, 4x6", M .............**225.00**

Velvet, black w/pearlized stripes, mirror & comb, Ingber...**25.00**

Whiting & Davis, Dresden, enameled frame, fringe-cut bottom, 5x7", M ........................**200.00**

Whiting & Davis, fringe-cut bottom, enameled frame, 5x7", M ................................**225.00**

# Puzzles

Of most interest to collectors of vintage puzzles are those made of wood or plywood, especially the early hand-cut examples. Character-related examples and those representing a well-known personality or show from the early days of television are coming on strong right now, and values are steadily climbing in these areas.

**Broken Arrow, Sta-N-Place, Built Rite, M in torn box, $25.00.**

Addams Family, jigsaw, Milton Bradley, 1965, complete, EX ..............................**35.00**

Alien, jigsaw, HG #473, 1979, MIB ................................**75.00**

Archies, jigsaw, Whitman, 1972, complete, EX ..................**8.00**

Barbie's Rapunzel Little Theatre, frame tray, Golden, 1984, MIP ...................................**6.00**

Battle Star Galactica, jigsaw, 1978, 140-pc, complete, EX ........**8.00**

Beetle Bailey, jigsaw, Jaymar, 1963, 60-pc, NMIB ........**16.00**

Black Hole, frame tray, Whitman, 1979, complete, NM ........**5.00**

Bugs Bunny, frame tray, Jaymar, 1950s, complete, EX ......**30.00**

Captain Kangaroo, frame tray, Fairchild, 1971, MIP (sealed) ...........................**20.00**

Charlie's Angels, puzzle, HG, 1977, 150-pc, complete, EX ......**10.00**

Chitty-Chitty Bang-Bang, frame tray, Whitman #4529, 1968, complete, NM ................**20.00**

Disney on Parade, jigsaw, Springbok, 1973, EX .................**7.00**

Dracula, jigsaw, APC/Universal Studios, 100-pc, 1974, MIB ...**25.00**

Dukes of Hazzard, jigsaw, American, 11x17", 200-pc, complete, EX ..................................**10.00**

ET, jigsaw, Craft Master, 1982, complete, EX ...................**6.00**

Flintstones, frame tray, Warren, 1975, complete, NM ......**27.00**

Gabby Gator, frame tray, Preskool, 1963, complete, EX+ ......**10.00**

Green Hornet, frame tray, Whitman, 1960s, set of 4, 8x10", MIB ...............................**65.00**

Gremlins, frame tray, Golden, 1984, MIP ......................**10.00**

Happy Days, jigsaw, Fonz on motorcycle, MHG Toys, 14x10", 150-pc, EX ........**15.00**

How the West Was Won, jigsaw, HG Toys #493-01, 1978, MIB (sealed) ...........................**15.00**

Josie & the Pussycats, frame tray, set of 4, MIB ..................**50.00**

Love Boat, jigsaw, 1978, 150-pc, complete, EX .................**12.00**

Man From UNCLE, frame tray, Jaymar, 1965, 11x14", complete, NM ......................**45.00**

Mary Poppins, frame tray, Flying Kites, 1964, complete, EX .**10.00**

**Last Ray, plywood, 317 interlocking pieces, 1930s, 12x16", G-, $20.00.**

Maverick, frame tray, Whitman #4427, 1960, complete, NM ..................**30.00**

Michael Jackson, jigsaw, Colorforms, 500-pc, MIB (sealed) ......................**25.00**

Mickey Mouse, jigsaw, Parker Bros, 1950s, set of 4, EX, original box ..........................**45.00**

Mod Squad, jigsaw, Milton Bradley, 500-pc, NMIB .**40.00**

Mork & Mindy, jigsaw, Milton Bradley, 1978, 250-pc, complete, EX ..........................**8.00**

Munsters, jigsaw, Lily playing organ, Whitman, 1965, MIB ..............................**60.00**

Our Gang, jigsaw, Little Rascals in jalopy fire engine, complete, NM .....................**110.00**

Robin Hood, frame tray, Built-Rite, 1950s, complete, EX .......**20.00**

Roger Rabbit, jigsaw, Waddingtons, England, 500-pc, MIB ...........................**20.00**

Ruff & Ready, frame tray, Whitman, 1950s, complete, NM .......**25.00**

Sabrina the Teenage Witch (Archies), sliding tile, Roalex Co, MIP ..........................**12.50**

Space 1999, jigsaw, HG Toys, 150-pc, 1976, NMIB .............**20.00**

Spiderman leaping from building, Marvel Comics, 1980s, 11½x15", M .....................**3.00**

Winnie the Pooh w/Honey, frame tray, 10-pc, 1965, EX .....**15.00**

Zorro, frame tray, Whitman #4521, 1965, MIP (sealed) .........**40.00**

# Radios

Novelty radios have recently become attractive to collectors. Some carry an advertising message or are shaped like a product bottle, can or carton; others may be modeled after the likeness of a well-known cartoon character. It's sometimes hard to recognize the fact that they're actually radios. Prices listed here are for examples that are mint in the box. To learn more, we recommend *Collector's Guide to Novelty Radios* by Marty Bunis and Robert F. Breed (Collector Books.)

Transistor radios are also popular. First introduced in 1954, many feature space-age names and futuristic designs. Prices here are for complete, undamaged examples in at least very good condition. All are battery operated and AM unless noted otherwise. For further information, we recommend *Collector's Guide to Transistor Radios* by Marty and Sue Bunis (Collector Books). If you have vintage radios you need to evaluate, see *Collector's Guide to Antique Radios* (Bunis, Collector Books).

## Novelty

All Detergent, product box form w/soap logo, Hong Kong, 4¾x3½" ...........................**75.00**

Avon Skin-So-Soft, Avon, 1990, 7½x3", MIB ...................**35.00**

Baseball, Texas Rangers, Gatorade, 3½" dia .........**40.00**

Battery, Mallory Akaline Duracell, M ...........................**40.00**

Beetle, black & red plastic, British Registration Model HS-119, 3x4" .................**45.00**

Blinking Rabbit, LED flashing eyes, China, 6½" ............**25.00**

Bookcase desk, colonial design, Ami-Co Inc, 1974, 11½x4¾" ......**55.00**

Camcorder, Accent, tunes by turning lenses, China, 7x4½" .**50.00**

Campbell's Cup 2-Minute Soup Mix, China, 4¾x3½" ......**35.00**

**Pepsi, Hong Kong, 9½", $35.00.**

Care Bears, figure w/rainbow on
tummy, American Greetings,
1985, 5½" ......................**20.00**
Fabrege Brut For Men, bottle
form, Japan, 8x2½" .......**60.00**
Garfield, Music Is My Life, United
Features, 1978, 3x5" w/head-
phones ...........................**35.00**
Ghostbuster's Dancing Slimer,
Justin Toys/Columbia Pic-
tures, 1980s, 12" ............**30.00**
Guitar, plastic w/metal trim, Model 004,
Federal/Taiwan, 11½x4" .......**60.00**
Hair Dryer, AirWaves 2000, pis-
tol type, J&D Brush/China,
9½" .................................**50.00**

He-Man, Mattel/Nasta, 1984,
4¾x2¾" ...........................**35.00**
Incredible Hulk, Amico Inc, 1978,
7x5½" ..............................**75.00**
King Kong, stuffed cloth &
vinyl, Amico/Taiwan, 1986,
13x13" .........................**35.00**
Marlboro Cigarettes, Japan,
13x9" ............................**100.00**
Paul Masson's Burgundy, bottle
form, Hong Kong, 7x3½" .**50.00**
Polaroid 600 Plus, China, 5x4" .**30.00**
Scott Towels, 60 Years of Value,
Scott Paper Co, 1985 .....**60.00**
Shell X-100 10W30 Multigrade
Motor Oil, can form .......**40.00**
Spam, product tin form,
3⅜x3¾" .........................**50.00**
Sunkist Orange Fruit Drinks,
can form, Sunkist Growers
Inc ................................**35.00**
Tune-A-Lemon, realistic form,
braided strap handle, Hong
Kong, 6x4" .....................**35.00**
Washing Machine, Day's Ease
Home Products/Hong Kong,
4x2½" ............................**75.00**

**Transistor**

Admiral, 4P21, horizontal, 4 transistors, lg grill, chrome han-
dle, 1957 ........................**35.00**
Admiral, 528, horizontal, blue
leatherette, 6 transistors,
9x9½x3" .........................**35.00**
Ambassador, FM-10, vertical,
10 transistors, AM/FM,
1965 .............................**20.00**
Arvin, 65R29, vertical, 8 transistors, lg lower grill, crown
logo, 1965 ......................**15.00**
Arvin, 78R09, vertical, 8 transistors, telecoping antenna,
AM/FM, 1967 .................**10.00**
Channel Master, 6500, horizontal,
ivory, 6 transistors, pull-up
handle ...........................**25.00**

Columbia, vertical, gray, 4 transistors, circular grill, 1960 ...........................**30.00**

Continental, TR-682, vertical, plastic, 6 transisters, 1962, 4x2½" ...........................**35.00**

Deluxe, G-601, horizontal, plastic w/mother-of-pearl front, globe logo .................................**40.00**

Elgin, R-800, vertical, 10 transistors, lg lower perforated grill, 1964 ...............................**15.00**

**Emerson, 707, vertical, 8 transistors, USA, 1962, 4x2½x1¼", $40.00.**

Emerson, 849, horizontal, hourglass panel w/dials, 1955, 3½x5¾" .........................**150.00**

Emerson, 888 Titan, vertical, 8 transistors, off-center dials, 1963 ...............................**65.00**

General Electric, P740A, vertical, 8 transistors, lower grill, 1965 ...............................**15.00**

General Electric, 677, 5 transistors, 1956, 3x5½x1½" ..**125.00**

Hitachi, TH-831, vertical, plastic, solid state, lower grill, w/strap ...........................**20.00**

Kent, TR-605, vertical, 6 transistors, lg perforated grill, 1965 ...............................**15.00**

Lafayette, FS-204, vertical, 4 transistors, perforated grill, 1961 ...............................**30.00**

Lloyd's, TF-911, horizontal, 9 transistors, left grill, AM/FM, 1964 ...............................**20.00**

Magnavox, 2AM-70, vertical, 7 transistors, perforated grill, 1964 ...............................**30.00**

Majestic, Super 80, vertical, swing handle, 5¾x3½x1½" ............**25.00**

Motorola, L12G Power 8, horizontal, 6 transistors, 1960 ..**20.00**

Motorola, vertical, charcoal plastic, 8 transistors, 7x4½x2½" .....................**30.00**

Norelco, L1X75T/64R, horizontal, 7 transistors, perforated grill, 1960 ...............................**30.00**

Panasonic, T-100M, horizontal, 12 transistors, logo lower right, 1965 ...............................**25.00**

Philco, NT-807, horizontal, 8 transistors, perforated grill, 1965 ...............................**20.00**

Philco, T61-124, vertical, checkered grill, 4⅜x2⅝x1¼" ...**15.00**

RCA, T-1EH, vertical, 6 transistors, horizontal grill bars, 1959, 7" .........................**25.00**

RCA, 1-TP-1HE, vertical, 6 transistors, lattice grill, 1961, 4x2½" ...........................**20.00**

Realtone, TR-1820, 8 transistors, 1962, 4x2½x1¼" ..**25.00**

Sharp, BP-100, horizontal, 6 transistors, 1964, 2½x4½x1¼" .....**15.00**

Sharp, FX-110, vertical, 10 transistors, perforated grill, 1965 ...............................**15.00**

Sony, TR-610, vertical, 6 transistors, 1959, 4¼x2¾x1¼" .**100.00**

Star-Lite, DP-118, vertical, 6 transistors, lower lattice grill, 1965 ...............................**15.00**
Toshiba, 10TL-429F, 10 transistors, 1961, 6x9x2⅝" .......**30.00**
Valiant, AM1400 Hi Power, vertical, lower vertical-slot grill ............................**30.00**
Westinghouse, H-695-P8, horizontal, 8 transistors, 1959, 3x6x2" ...........................**35.00**
Zenith, Royal 2000, horizontal, 11 transistors, 1961, 10x11¾x5" ....................**50.00**
Zenith, Royal 50, vertical, lg upper front dial, 1962, 4x2¾x1½" ......................**30.00**

# Railroadiana

Memorabilia relating to the more than 175 different railway companies that once transversed this great country of ours comprises one of the largest and most popular areas of collecting today. Because the field is so varied, many collectors prefer to specialize. Lanterns, badges, advertising, dinnerware, silver, locks, and tools are only a sampling of the many types of relics they treasure. Some enjoy toy trains, prints showing old locomotives, or old timetables — in short, virtually anything that in any way represents the rapidly disappearing railway system is of value. Refer to *Railroad Collectibles, Third Revised Edition,* by Stanley L. Baker (Collector Books) for more information.

## Dinnerware

Ashtray, Great Northern, Mountains & Flowers, bottom stamped, 4" ....................**85.00**
Bowl, berry; Pullman, Indian Tree, top marked, 5½" .**100.00**
Bowl, berry; Union Pacific RR, Challenger, top logo ......**35.00**

**Plate, B&O Railroad, Lamberton China, 10", $290.00; Cup and saucer, B&O Railroad, The Philip E. Thomas 1938, $150.00.**

Bowl, bouillon; Pennsylvania RR, Purple Laurel ..............**25.00**

Bowl, cereal; Atchison Topeka & Santa Fe, Adobe, top logo, 6" ................................**50.00**

Bowl, soup; New York Central, Hudson, Haviland, back stamped, 8½" ................**75.00**

Bowl, vegetable; Canada Pacific, silverplate, w/lid, 7" ......**78.00**

Butter pat, Baltimore & Ohio, Centenary, Lamberton, back stamped ........................**75.00**

Butter pat, Delaware & Hudson, Canterbury ....................**35.00**

Butter pat, Missouri Pacific, Jefferson ............................**85.00**

Butter pat, Union Pacific, Blue & Gold ..............................**25.00**

Creamer, Canadian National, Mustard Gold, back stamped, 3¾" ..............................**25.00**

Cup & saucer, Canadian Pacific, bows & leaves design, back stamped ........................**85.00**

Cup & saucer, Dominion, logo on side ................................**95.00**

Cup & saucer, Southern RR, Piedmont, back stamped ......**45.00**

Fork, Seaboard Coast Line, silverplate, Zephyr ................**12.00**

Goblet, water; Union Pacific, white shield, stemmed, 5½" ............................**18.00**

Knife, butter; Great Northern, silverplate, Hutton ............**20.00**

Plate, Alaska RR, McKinley, top logo, 7½" ....................**350.00**

Plate, Baltimore & Ohio, Centenary, back stamped, 10½" .......**145.00**

Plate, Southern Pacific, Prairie Mountain Wildflowers, 9½" ..............**55.00**

Plate, Union Pacific, Challenger, top logo, 9½" ..................**65.00**

Plate, Western Pacific, Feather River, top logo, 5¼" .......**65.00**

Platter, Central & Northwestern, Rockford, back stamped, 8x12" ............................**110.00**

Platter, Illinois Central, Ruper, top logo, 9½x7" ..............**25.00**

Relish, Chicago Milwaukee St Paul & Pacific, Traveler, 4x9½" ............................**50.00**

Spoon, serving; Fred Harvey, silverplate, Albany, International ............................**18.00**

Sugar bowl, Amtrack, National ....................**32.00**

Teapot, New York Haven & Hartford, Platinum Blue, side logo, w/lid ....................**260.00**

Tumbler, water; New York Central, white logo, flanged base, 5" ....................................**10.00**

**Miscellaneous**

Apron, cook's; Union Pacific, Overland logo ................**10.00**

Blotter, Burlington Route, Glacier National Park, 4x9" ........**7.00**

Booklet, Northern Pacific, Storied Northwest, 1916, 11 pages ............................**10.00**

Calendar, Santa Fe, Grand Canyon, 1983, 24x14", VG .............**17.50**

Coat hanger, California Zephyr, wood ..............................**17.00**

**Commemorative coin, embossed locomotive, Oriental inscription, 1972, 2¼", MIB, $25.00.**

Globe, unmarked, clear, short .**20.00**
Globe, unmarked, green or red, 5½", ea ...........................**40.00**
Lamp, inspector's; Chicago Milwaukee St Paul & Pacific, clear lens, EX ................**65.00**
Lantern, Denver & Rio Grande Western, tin, sm ...........**88.00**
Lantern, Southern RR, Adlake Reliable, tall marked globe ..........**150.00**
Lock, Burlington Northern, Keline, steel, w/chain, EX ...........**15.00**
Lock, Philadelphia & Reading, Fraim, ornate cast brass, 1920, M ......................**265.00**
Menu, California Zephyr Italian Dinner, glossy card, 1950s, 6x7" ................................**10.00**
Napkin, Rock Island, 18" sq .**15.00**
Oil can, unmarked, long spout, unused, 30" ....................**36.00**
Pass booklet, Norfolk & Western, cardboard w/25 unused slips, 5" ....................................**25.00**
Switch key, Delaware & Hudson, Slaymaker ......................**32.00**
Switch key, Pennsylvania RR, Fraim, brass, knobby style, EX patina ......................**35.00**
Switch key, Seaboard, Adlake, brass ..............................**32.00**
Ticket, Clinchfield, cardboard, 2¼x1¼" .............................**3.00**
Timetable, Chicago Great Western, 1912, VG ................**40.00**
Timetable, Wabash, flag cover, 1954 .................................**5.00**
Towel, New York Central, red stripe on white cotton, 22x16" ..**20.00**

# Ramp Walkers

Ramp walkers date back to at least 1873 when Ives produced a cast-iron elephant walker. Wood and composite ramp walkers were made in Czechoslovakia and the USA from the 1920s through the 1940s. The most common were made by John Wilson of Watsontown, Pennsylvania. These sold worldwide and became known as 'Wilson Walkies.' Most are two-legged and stand approximately 4½" tall.

Plastic ramp walkers were manufactured primarily by the Louis Marx Co. from the 1950s through the early 1960s. The majority were produced in Hong Kong, but some were made in the USA and sold under the Marx logo or by the Charmore Co., a subsidiary of Marx.

The three common sizes are: 1) small premiums abut 1½" x 2"; 2) the more common medium size, 2¾" x 3"; and 3) large, approximately 4" x 5". Most of the smaller walkers were unpainted, while the medium and large sizes were hand or spray painted. Several of the walking types were sold with wooden or colorful tin lithographed ramps. Randy Welch is our advisor for ramp walkers; he is listed in the Directory under Maryland.

Baby Teen Toddler, plastic baby girl, Dolls Inc, lg ...........**30.00**
Bear, plastic, unmarked .......**15.00**
Boy walking behind girl, plastic, lg .....................................**45.00**
Cowboy riding horse, plastic w/metal legs, sm ...........**20.00**
Donald Duck w/wheelbarrow, Marx, NM .....................**20.00**
Dutch boy & girl, plastic ......**30.00**
Figaro the Cat w/ball, plastic .**25.00**
Goofy Grape, plastic, Kool-Aid .**60.00**
House Painters, European issue, EX+ ..............................**150.00**
Indian mother w/baby on travois .........................**75.00**

Mad Hatter & White Rabbit,
NM .............................**65.00**

**Mickey and Donald riding aligator, from $40.00 to $50.00.**

Mother Goose, NM ...............**55.00**
Native on zebra, Marx, NM .**25.00**
Spark Plug the Horse ........**175.00**
Top Cat & Bennie, EX ..........**42.00**

# Razor Blade Banks

In 1903 the safety razor was invented, making it easier for men to shave at home. But the old, used razor blades were troublesome, because for the next twenty-two years nobody knew what to do with them. In 1925 the first patent was filed for a razor blade bank, a container designed to hold old blades until it became full, in which event it was to be thrown away. Most razor blade banks are 3" or 4" tall, similar to a coin bank with a slot in the top but no outlet in the bottom to remove the old blades. These banks were produced from 1925 to 1950. Some were issued by men's toiletry companies and were often filled with shaving soap or cream. Many were made of tin and printed with an advertising message. An assortment of blade banks made from a variety of

materials — ceramic, wood, plastic, or metal — could also be purchased at five-and-dime stores. (Metal banks were mostly advertising giveaways as we previously mentioned.) Our advisor, David C. Giese, is listed in the Directory under Virginia.

**Barber, full figure, ceramic, 3",
$40.00.**

Advertising, Ever-Ready For Old
Blades, metal ................**65.00**
Advertising, Gem Record Shaves,
book form .......................**60.00**
Advertising, JB Williams, Safe for
Razor Blades, metal ......**65.00**
Advertising, JB Williams Co,
For New & Old Blades,
metal ...........................**60.00**
Advertising, Lamglois Shaving
Cream, metal ................**60.00**
Advertising, Listerine, Art Deco-
style ceramic frog ..........**25.00**
Advertising, Listerine, ceramic
donkey ..........................**35.00**
Advertising, Listerine, ceramic
elephant .......................**35.00**

Advertising, Listerine, glass jar, originally sold containing soap ................................**25.00**
Advertising, Mennen Lather Shave, metal ..................**60.00**
Advertising, Palmolive, metal .**60.00**
Advertising, Wardonia For Used Blades, plastic ...............**25.00**
Advertising, Williams Shaving Cream, metal .................**60.00**
Barber, ceramic bust ...........**60.00**
Barber, ceramic figure, 3" ....**55.00**
Barber, ceramic figure w/hand to chin, 4" ...........................**45.00**
Barber chair, ceramic, 4" .....**95.00**
Barber pole, ceramic w/face & metal arms .....................**40.00**
Barber pole, ceramic w/face & top hat ..................................**65.00**
Barber pole, ceramic w/red & white stripes ..................**30.00**
Brush handle, decorated w/blades, ceramic ..........**45.00**
Dandy Dan, plastic barber figure w/metal arms ................**30.00**
Frog, Used Blades on base ..**60.00**
Looie, holder w/bank ............**75.00**

Man, wood, vest unscrews to empty out blades ...........**55.00**
Mushroom, ceramic w/embossed shaving man at front ....**25.00**
Owl, ceramic, 4" ..................**65.00**
Policeman, cast iron, embossed figure at front ...............**65.00**
Soap dish, cast iron, doubles as blade bank .....................**75.00**
The Gay Blades, ceramic group of 4 singing barbers ..........**70.00**
Wall plate, brass ...................**20.00**

# Reamers

Though made for the simple task of extracting citrus juices, reamers may be found in fanciful figurals as well as the simple utilitarian styles. You may find wood, ceramic, or metal examples, but the most popular with collectors are those made of glass. Fry, Hazel Atlas, Hocking, Jeannette, and McKee are among the largest producers of the glass reamer, some of which (depending on color

**Clown reamer, ceramic, baby's, 4½", $70.00.**

**Jeanette, transparent ultramarine blue glass, footed boat shape, loop handle, ridged cone, $110.00.**

and rarity) may bring prices well into the hundreds of dollars. Refer to *Kitchen Glassware of the Depression Years* by Gene Florence (Collector Books) for more information.

Cambridge, crystal, ring handle ...............................**25.00**

Ceramic, baby's, chicks jumping rope, 2-pc .......................**55.00**

Ceramic, baby's, teapot shape, child on horse, Goebel .**110.00**

Ceramic, baby's orange, red & white, Japan ..................**50.00**

Ceramic, clown face, w/red lips, 2-pc ...............................**60.00**

Ceramic, duck figural cup w/reamer top, decal, Japan, 2¾" ...............................**85.00**

Ceramic, pelican figural, reamer on back, multicolor, Japan, 2¾" ...............................**125.00**

Federal Glass Co, amber, tab handle ...................................**12.50**

Foreign, crystal, embossed sword & hammer on tab handle ...**20.00**

Foreign, dark amber, tab handle ...............................**60.00**

Foreign, light transparent turquoise, tab handle ....**55.00**

Fry, crystal, tab handle ........**12.50**

Fry, vaseline, tab handle .....**45.00**

Hazel Atlas, cobalt, tab handle ...........................**235.00**

Hazel Atlas, fired-on red, ring handle, 2-cup .................**50.00**

Hazel Atlas, transparent pink, ring handle, 2-cup .......**120.00**

Hazel Atlas, transparent pink, tab handle, lg .................**30.00**

Hocking, green clambroth, tab handle ...........................**100.00**

Hocking, transparent green, tab handle ...........................**12.50**

Indiana Glass Co, transparent green, ring handle .........**35.00**

Indiana Glass Co, transparent pink, ring handle ..........**50.00**

Jeanette Glass Co, delphite blue, ring handle, sm ..............**60.00**

McKee, Sunkist, Chalaine blue, ring handle ...................**165.00**

McKee, Sunkist, custard, ring handle ...........................**30.00**

McKee, Sunkist, fired-on white, ring handle ....................**10.00**

McKee, Sunkist, opaque, ring handle ...........................**45.00**

McKee, Sunkist, transparent green, ring handle .........**45.00**

US Glass, frosted green, ring handle, 2-cup ........................**32.00**
Valencia, dark amber, unembossed ...........................**200.00**
Westmoreland, crystal w/oranges, flat loop handle .............**90.00**

# Records

Records that made it to the 'Top Ten' in their day are not always the records that are prized the highest by today's collectors, though they treasure those which best represent specific types of music: jazz, rhythm and blues, country and western, rock 'n roll, etc. Many search for those cut very early in the career of artists who later became superstars, records cut on rare or interesting labels, or those aimed at ethnic groups. A fast-growing area of related interest is picture sleeves for 45s. These are often worth more than the record itself, especially if they feature superstars from the fifties or early sixties.

Condition is very important. Record collectors tend to be very critical, so learn to watch for loss of gloss; holes, labels, or writing anywhere on the label; warping; and scratches.Unless otherwise noted, values are for records in like-new condition — showing little sign of wear, with a playing surface that retains much of its original shine, and having only a minimal amount of surface noise. To be collectible, a sleeve should have no tape, stickers, tears, or obvious damage.

Refer to *The American Premium Record Guide* by Les Docks for more information on extended play and 78 rpm records.

**Extended Play**

Ace, Johnny; Memorial Album, Duke 80 ...........................**40.00**
Beach Boys, Barbara Ann +3, PRO 2993 .......................**60.00**
Bell Notes, I've Had It, Time 100 ...............................**75.00**
Brown, Roy; Blues Boogie, King 254 ................................**50.00**
Brown, Ruth; Ruth Brown Sings, Atlantic 535 ....................**40.00**
Cash, Johnny; Country Boy, Sun 112 ................................**20.00**
Cash, Johnny; Sing's Hank Williams, Sun 111 .........**20.00**
Chantels, I Love You So, End 201 ................................**75.00**
Cline, Patsy; Come on In +3, Patsy Cline 11 ...............**20.00**
Cline, Patsy; Songs by Patsy Cline, Coral 81159 ........**50.00**
Clovers, Good Lovin', Atlantic 537 ................................**50.00**
Coasters, Rock 'n Roll with the Coasters, Atco 4501 ......**30.00**
Cockron, Eddie; Singin' to My Baby, Liberty 3061 ........**80.00**
Cooke, Sam; Another Saturday Night, RCA Victor 437 ..**50.00**
Crests, The Angels Listened In, Coed 101 ......................**100.00**
Crickets (w/Buddy Holly), The Chirping Crickets, Brunswick 71036 ...........................**100.00**
Crickets, The Crickets, Davis 211 ...............................**40.00**
Daley, Jimmy & the Ding-A-Lings; (no title) Decca 2431 ...........................**20.00**
Danny & The Juniors, At the Hop, ABC Paramount 11 .......**75.00**
Del Vikings, They Sing They Swing, Mercury 3362 ....**40.00**
Diddley, Bo; Bo Diddley, Chess 5125 ..............................**50.00**
Domino, Fats; Rockin' With Fats, Imperial 152 ..................**20.00**

Drifters, The Drifters Featuring Clyde McPhatter, Atlantic 534 ..................................**40.00**

Edwards, Tommy; It's All in the Game, MGM 1003 .........**30.00**

Everly Brothers, Rockin' With the Everly Brothers, Cadence 333 ...................................**30.00**

Fabian, Hold That Tiger, Chancellor 5003 ...........................**30.00**

Fireballs, Bulldog +3, Top Rank 1000 ...............................**75.00**

Five Satins, Toe the Aisle, Ember 101 ..................................**50.00**

Johnny Burnette Trio, Hits, Liberty 1011 ........................**50.00**

## Record Sleeves

AC/DC, Let's Get It Up, Atlantic 3894, VG+ .........................**4.50**

Allman Brothers Band, Straight From the Heart, Arista 0618, M ......................................**5.00**

Ames Brothers, Hello Amigos, RCA 7680, VG ................**11.00**

Arnold, Eddy; Tip of My Fingers, RCA 8869, VG ..................**7.50**

Bad Company, Rock 'n Roll Fantasy, Swan Song 70119, VG+ ................................**2.00**

Blues Brothers, Gimme Some Lovin', Atlantis 3666, VG .**4.00**

Boone, Pat; Sugar Moon, Dot 15750, VG .........................**7.50**

Bowie, David; Ashes to Ashes, RCA 12078, VG+ ..............**7.50**

Boyd, Jimmy; I Saw Mommy Kissing Santa Claus, Columbia 4-152, VG ......**19.00**

Buffett, Jimmy; Homemade Music, MCA 53360, EX+ .............**2.00**

Captain & Tennille, Shop Around, A&M 1817, EX+ ..............**4.00**

Carpenters, Rainy Days & Mondays, A&M 1260, VG ......**5.00**

Cheech & Chong, Earache My Eye, Ode 66102, VG ........**9.00**

Clapton, Eric; Forever Man, Warner 29081, VG ..........**2.00**

Creedence Clearwater Revival, Run Through the Jungle, Fantasy 641, M ...............**7.50**

Crosby, Stills & Nash, Wasted on the Way, Atlantic 3401, VG+ ....................................**5.00**

Daltrey, Roger; Free Me, Polydor 2105, EX+ ........................**5.00**

Dean, Jimmy; Dear Ivan, Columbia 42259, VG .......**6.00**

Eagles, Please Come Home for Christmas, Asylum 45555, EX+ ..................................**4.00**

Fleetwood Mac, Gypsy, Warner 29918, VG ........................**5.00**

Fogerty, Tom; Goodbye Media Man, Fantasy 661, VG+ ..**4.50**

Foreigner, Double Vision, Atlantic, #3514, EX .........**2.50**

Four Seasons, Patch of Blue, Philips, #40662, VG ......**10.00**

Fox, Charlie; All, Ambassador 219, VG+ ..........................**4.50**

Frampton, Peter; I'm in You, A&M 1941, VG ................**5.00**

Frey, Glenn; Smuggler's Blues, MCA 52651, EX+ ............**2.00**

Geils, J Band; Concealed Weapons, EMI 8242, VG .**2.00**

Go-Go's, Vacation, IRS 9907, EX+ ..................................**4.00**

Grand Funk, Walk Like a Man, Capitol 3760, VG+ ...........**4.50**

Greene, Lorne; Sand, RCA 8554, VG+ ..................................**9.00**

Jackson, Michael; Wanna Be Startin' Somethin', Epic 03914, VG ........................**4.00**

Jagger, Mick; Lucky in Love, Columbia 04893, EX+ .....**5.00**

James, Sonny; Don't Keep Me Hanging On, Capitol 2834, EX+ ..................................**6.00**

John, Elton; Candle in the Wind, MCA 53196, EX+ ............**4.00**

Lee, Brenda; I Wonder, Decca

31510, VG ......................**11.00**

Lennon, John; Mind Game, Apple 1868, VG ..........................**7.50**

Mathis, Johnny; Take the Time, Mercury 72432, VG .........**4.00**

Melloncamp, John Cougar; Rain on the Scarecrow, Riva 884 856, EX+ ..........................**2.00**

Mendes, Sergio; Fool on the Hill, A&M 961, VG ..................**4.00**

Mills, Hayley; Jeepers Creepers, Buena Vista 395, EX+ ..**12.00**

Monkees, Daydream Believer, Colgems 1012, VG .........**11.00**

Nicks, Stevie; Stand Back, Modern 99863, VG .................**5.00**

Osmond, Donny; Soldier of Love, Capitol 44369, VG ...........**1.50**

Palmer, Robert; Addicted to Love, Island 99570, EX+ ..........**2.00**

Rolling Stones, Start Me Up, RS 21003, VG+ ......................**4.50**

Sam the Sham & the Pharaohs, How Do You Catch a Girl, MGM 13649, VG .............**7.50**

Squier, Billy; She's a Runner, Capitol 5202, EX+ ...........**4.00**

Starr, Ringo; Wrack My Brain, Boardwalk 130, VG .........**4.00**

Tubb, Ernest; Thanks a Lot, Decca ED 2774, VG .........**6.00**

Vinton, Bobby; Clinging Vine, Epic 9705, VG+ ...............**4.50**

**Bobby Vinton, I Love How You Love Me, Epic BN26437, 1969, VG, $5.00.**

## Children's Records

Alice in Wonderland, I'm Late, Disney/Little Golden, ca 1950s, EX ......................**20.00**

Alice in Wonderland, 1950, 78 rpm, EX ..........................**22.00**

Bugs Bunny & Yosemite Sam, Little Golden, 1955, 78 rpm, EX ..................................**10.00**

Captain Kangaroo, CBS, 1956, 78 rpm, 12" sq sleeve, EX+ .**10.00**

Casper the Friendly Ghost, Wonderland, 1965, 33⅓ rpm, EX ......................**10.00**

Curious George Takes a Job, Scholastic, 1969, 33⅓ rpm, EX+ ................................**10.00**

Dennis the Menace, theme song, Golden, 1960, 78 rpm, NM .**10.00**

Doggie Daddy & Augie Doggie/ Story of Pinocchio, 1977, NM ..................................**4.00**

Flintstones Meet the Orchestra Family, Sunset, 1968, 33⅓ rpm, EX+ ......................**10.00**

Gene Autry's Western Classics, Columbia, 1947, 78 rpm, set of 4, EX ..........................**45.00**

Hokey Wolf and Ding-A-Ling/Snuffles/Cindy Bear, Golden, '61, 78 rpm, EX .....................**18.00**

Joke Along With Jimmy Nelson, Peter Pan, 1962, NM ....**20.00**

Ken Maynard Story Record, Tarzan on label, red plastic, 1940s, 78 rpm ................**20.00**

King Leonardo & His Short Subjects, Golden Record, 1961, 78 rpm, M ..........................**17.50**

Popeye the Sailor Man, Diplomat, 1960, 33⅓ rpm, EX+ .....**18.00**

Princess & the Pea, by The 3 Stooges, 1960, NM ........**12.50**

Punch & Judy, Twinkle Records, 1950s, M ......................**12.00**

Sergeant Preston & Case of the Orphan Dog, 78 rpm, EX .**10.00**

The Archies, 1968, 33⅓ rpm, EX ..................................**3.50**

Tom Corbett Space Cadet, RCA Victor, 1952 ....................**26.00**

Top Cat Starring As Robin Hood, HER Records, 1962, 33⅓ rpm, EX ..................................**20.00**

## LP Albums

Jack Paar's Favorites, Seeco, 1950s, EX+ ....................**10.00**

James Bond 007, Thunderball, United Artists, 1965, EX+ .........................**12.00**

Ring of Fire, Johnny Cash, Columbia, 1962, EX ......**20.00**

Route 66 & Other Great TV Themes, Capitol, 1962, EX+ ...........**18.00**

Saturday Night Live, Arista, 1976, NM .......................**22.00**

Shirley Jones & Jack Cassidy Record Album, Columbia, 1950s, EX+ ......................**8.00**

The James Dean Story, Capitol W881, 1957, NM ...........**25.00**

Wizard of Oz, MGM, 1960s, EX+ .............................**20.00**

## 45 rpms

Beatles, Hard Days Night/I Should Have Known Better, Capitol 5222, VG ...........**11.00**

Beatles, Let It Be/You Know My Name, Apple 2764, VG- ..**3.00**

Beatles, Yesterday/Act Naturally, Capitol 5498, VG ...........**11.00**

Chapin, Harry; Cat's in the Cradle/Vacancy, Elektra 45203, VG ....................................**3.25**

Charles, Ray; Go on Home/That's a Lie, ABC 11045, EX+ ...**6.00**

Chicago, Stay the Night/Only You, Warner 29306, VG+ ........**3.00**

Chordettes, Mr Sandman/I Don't Wanna See, Candence 1247, VG ..................................**3.50**

Clapton, Eric; I Shot the Sheriff/Give Me Strength, RSO 409, VG ..................**4.00**

Clark, Petula; I Know a Place/ Jack & John, Warner 5612, VG .....................................**4.00**

Cocker, Joe; Letter/Space Captain, A&M 1174, VG .......**3.50**

Coe, David Allen; Divers Do It Deeper, Columbia 10701, VG .....................................**2.50**

Cole, Nat King; Madrid/Give Me Your Love, Capitol 4125, VG ........**4.00**

Cole, Natalie; Pink Cadillac/I Wanna Be That Woman, EMI 50177, VG .........................**2.50**

Collins, Judy; Amazing Grace/ Nightingale 1, Elektra 45079, VG .....................................**3.00**

Collins, Phil; I Missed Again/I'm Not Moving, Atlantic 3790, VG+ ................................**27.50**

Como, Perry; I Think of You/El Condor Pass, RCA 1444, VG ....**2.50**

Cooke, Sam; You Send Me/Summertime, Keen 34013, VG .......**3.00**

Cooper, Alice; School's Out/Gutter Cat, Warner 7596, VG ....**4.00**

Cosby, Bill; Yes, Yes, Yes/Ben, Capitol 4258, VG+ ...........**4.50**

Costello, Elvis; Veronica/You're No Good, Warner 22981, VG .**2.50**

Craddock, Billy Crash; Walk Softly/She's About..., ABC/ Dot 17619, VG .................**3.00**

Cramer, Floyd; On the Rebound/ Mood Indigo, RCA 7840, VG ..................................**3.00**

Cream, Crossroads/Passing the Time, Atco 6646, VG .......**4.00**

Creedence Clearwater Revival, Lodi/Bad Moon Rising, Fantasy 622, VG ....................**3.50**

Croce, Jim; Operator/Rapid Roy, ABC 11336, VG ...............**3.00**

Crosby, Stills, Nash & Young, Woodstock/Helpless, Atlantic 2723, VG .......................**2.50**

Dave Clark Five, All Night Long/Try Too Hard, Epic 10004, VG .........................**8.00**

Hall, Tom T; Old Side of Town/Jesus on the Radio, RCA 11888, VG+ ..............**3.00**

Hall & Oakes, Maneater/One on One, RCA 13796, VG+ ....**3.00**

Hancock, Herbie; Rockit/Autodrive/Future Shock, Columbia 10050, VG .............**2.50**

Harris, Emmylou; Sweet Dreams/Armarillo, Reprise 1371, VG ...........................**4.00**

Harrison, George; This Is Love/Breath Away..., Dark Horse 27913, VG+ ...........**4.50**

Healey, Jeff Band; Angel Eyes/Confidence Man, Flashback 9956, EX+ ...............**3.25**

Heart, Magic Man/How Deep It Goes, Mushroom 7011, VG .............................**4.00**

Helms, Bobby; Love My Lady/Justa Little Lonesome, Decca 30557, VG+ ...........**4.50**

Henley, Don; I Can't Stand Still/Them & Us, Asylum 69931, VG ........................**2.50**

Jimi Hendricks Experience, Freedom/Angel, Reprise 1000, M ..........................**10.00**

Presley, Elvis; Crying In Chapel/I Believe in Man..., RCA 447-0643, VG ..........................**6.00**

Presley, Elvis; Love Me Tender/Anyway You Want Me, RCA 47-6643, VG ...**23.00**

Presley, Elvis; Surrender/Lonely War, RCA 447-0630, M ...**4.00**

Sam the Sham & the Pharaohs, Hair on My/Out Crowd, MGM 13581, VG ........................**4.00**

Scaggs Boz, Lowdown/Harbor Lights, Columbia 10367, VG ...........**2.50**

Seals & Croft, Summer Breeze/ East of Ginger Trees, Warner 7606, VG+ .......................**3.00**

Sedaka, Neil; All You Need/Candy Kisses, Elektra 45525, VG .**3.00**

Segar, Bob; Against the Wind, No Man's Land, Capitol 4863, VG+ .................................**3.00**

Shenandoah, Sunday in the South/Changes, Columbia 68892, VG .........................**2.00**

Sheppard, TG; Doncha?/Hunger for You, Columbia 05591, VG+ .................................**3.00**

Shore, Dinah; Salomes/Let Me Know, RCA 5176, VG ......**6.00**

## 78 rpms

Accedents, Wiggle, Wiggle, Brunswick 55100 ............**8.00**

Arkansas Woodchopper, Frankie and Johnny, Champion 45058 ...........................**10.00**

Anka, Paul; Diana, ABC Paramount 9831 ...................**20.00**

Barlow, Jerry; Just Thinking of You, Lyric 703 .................**6.00**

Berry, Chuck; Maybeline, Chess 1604 ...............................**15.00**

Billy & Lillie, La Dee Dah, Swan 4002 ...............................**20.00**

Bobby Darin (& the Jaybirds), Splish Splash, Alto 6117 .**25.00**

Buddy Young's Kentuckians, Fire On the Mountain, Superior 2519 ...............................**50.00**

Cadillacs, Speedo, Josie 785 ..**15.00**

Carr, Cathy; Ivory Tower, Fraternity 734 .........................**11.00**

Carson, Rosa Lee; The Drinker's Child, Okeh 45005 ........**12.00**

Cash, Johnny; I Walk the Line, Sun 241, VG+ ..............**12.50**

Champs, Tequila, Challenge 1016 ...........................**15.00**

Chantels, Maybe, End 1005 ..**20.00**

Charles, Ray; Rockhouse, Atlantic 2006 ...............................**20.00**

Checker, Chubby; The Class, Parkway 804, minumum value .**75.00**

Cherokee Ramblers, Back Up & Push, Decca 5402 ............**8.00**

Cleftones, You Baby You, Gee 1000 ...............................**10.00**

Cockran, Eddie; Sittin' in the Balcony, Liberty 55056 .......**30.00**

Diddley, Bo; Hush Your Mouth, Checker 896 ...................**15.00**

Dixie String Band, Dixie Waltz, Columbia 15273-D ........**15.00**

Doggett, Bill; Honky Tonk, King 4950 ...............................**12.00**

Frazier, Lee; The Ice Man Blues, Champion 16626 ...........**80.00**

**Gershwin, Elinore at the Piano, Rhapsody in Blue, Vogue R725, photo record, EX, $65.00.**

Goodson, Price; Lonesome Road Blues, Gennett 6154 .....**50.00**

Hackberry Ramblers, Cajun Crawl, Bluebird 2013 ....**12.00**

Hawkins & Puckett, Down in the Valley, Bluebird 5691 ....**15.00**

Hughey, Dan; Froggie Went A-Courtin' ...........................**10.00**

Justice, Dick; Henry Lee, Brunswick 367 ..............**20.00**

Locke, Rusty; Milk Cow Blues, TNT 1012 ........................**8.00**

Marshall, Charlie; The Old Hitchin' Rail, Vocalion 03045 ...........................**15.00**

Martin, Dan; The Cross-Eyed Butcher, Superior 2824 .**20.00**

McKinney Brothers, Old Uncle Joe, Champion 16830 ...**15.00**

McWinders, Odie; Down in Old Kentucky, Crown 3398 ..**30.00**

Miller, John; Highway Hobo, Superior 2839 ................**25.00**

Morris, Walter; Crazy Coon, Columbia 15079-D ........**15.00**

Mountain Dew Drop, Don't Love a Smiling Sweetheart, Okeh 456170 ............................**12.00**

New Arkansas Travelers, Handy Man, Victor 21288 .........**12.00**

Pavey, Phil; Bronco Bustin' Blues, Okeh 45308 ...................**12.00**

Pickell, Obed; Kitty Wells, Columbia 15141-D ........**12.00**

Potter & James, Down on the Farm, Supertone 9541 ..**75.00**

Price, Ray; Jealous Lies, Bullet 701 ...............................**50.00**

Regan, Walter; Moundsville Prisoner, Superior 2524 .......**40.00**

Rice, Edd; Cricket on the Hearth, Vocalion 5220 ................**15.00**

Roark, George; I Ain't a Bit Drunk, Columbia 15383-D .........**12.00**

Rodgers, Jessie; Rattlesnake Daddy, Bluebird 5839 ...**10.00**

Russell, Floyd; Coal Creek March, Supertone 9167 .............**10.00**

Scotty the Drifter, Gooseberry Pie, Decca 5296 ....................**10.00**

Short Brothers, Whistling Coon, Okeh 45206 ..................**15.00**

Smallwood, Lester; Cotton Mill Girl, Victor V40181 .......**60.00**

Steen, Joe; Railroad Jack, Champion 16258 .....................**15.00**

Stone, Jimmy; Midnight Boogie, Imperial 8137 ................**10.00**

Sweet Brothers, I Got a Bull Dog, Gennett 6620 .................**30.00**

Taylor & Bunch, Six Months Ain't Long, Supertone 9352 ...........................**12.00**

Texas Rhythm Boys; Benzedrine Blues, Royalty 600 ........**20.00**

Turner, Dave; That Old Covered Bridge, Supertone 9318 ..**12.00**
Val & Pete, Yodel Blues, Okeh 45225 ...............................**8.00**
Walsh, Dock; The East Bound Train, Columbia 15047-D ...........**15.00**
White, Reuben; Old Sefus Brown, Challenge 336 ...............**10.00**

# Red Wing

Taking their name from the location in Minnesota where they located in the late 1870s, the Red Wing Company produced a variety of wares, all of which are today considered noteworthy by pottery and dinnerware collectors. Their early stoneware lines, Cherry Band, and Sponge Band (Gray Line), are especially valuable and often fetch prices of several hundred dollars on today's market. Production of dinnerware began in the thirties and continued until the pottery closed in 1967. Some of their more popular lines — all of which were hand painted — were Bob White, Lexington, Tampico, Normandie, Capistrano, and Random Harvest. Commercial artware was also produced. Perhaps the ware most easily associated with Red Wing is their Brushware line, unique in its appearance and decoration. Cattails, rushes, florals, and similar nature subjects are 'carved' in relief on a stoneware-type body with a matt green wash its only finish.

We have listed only their very collectible dinnerware lines here; refer to *Red Wing Stoneware, An Identification and Value Guide,* and *Red Wing Collectibles,* both by Dan and Gail de Pasquale and Larry Peterson (Collector Books) for more information on stoneware. See also Clubs and Newsletters.

### Dinnerware

Blossomtime, cup & saucer, Concord shape .......................**5.00**

**Magnolia, tray, metal handle, $15.00.**

Blossomtime, plate, Concord shape, 7" ...........................**3.50**

Blossomtime, platter, Concord shape, 13¼" ....................**12.00**

Bob White, cup & saucer .....**20.00**

Bob White, hors d'ouevres bird ...........................**45.00**

Bob White, plate, 10½" ........**12.50**

Bob White, salt & pepper shakers, quail form, pr .................**40.00**

Bob White, teapot ................**70.00**

Capistrano, bowl, divided vegetable .............................**20.00**

Capistrano, plate, 6½" ............**5.00**

Damask, butter dish ............**15.00**

Frontenac, bowl, cereal ..........**5.50**

Frontenac, plate, 10" ..............**8.00**

Lotus, casserole, w/lid ..........**25.00**

Lotus, platter, oval, 13" ........**25.00**

Magnolia, bowl, fruit; 5¼" ......**5.00**

Magnolia, cup & saucer .......**10.00**

Magnolia, plate, 10" ..............**12.50**

Pompeii, cup & saucer ...........**8.00**

Random Harvest, cup & saucer .......................**15.00**

Round-Up, coffee mug ........**100.00**

Round-Up, creamer ..............**50.00**

Round-Up, salt & pepper shakers, pr ....................................**90.00**

Tampico, gravy boat w/attached underplate .....................**22.50**

Village Green, salt & pepper shakers, pr ....................**20.00**

Vintage, gravy boat .............**22.00**

# Rock 'n Roll

Concert posters, tour books, magazines, sheet music, and other items featuring Rock 'n Roll stars from the '50s up to the present are today being sought out by collectors who appreciate this type of music and like having these mementos of their favorite preformers around to enjoy. Our advisor for this category is Bojo

(Bob Guttuso); he is listed in the Directory under Pennsylvania. See also Beatles; Paperback Books; Elvis Presley; Records.

Bee Gees, jigsaw puzzle, 1979, 11x17", M (sealed) .........**19.00**

Bee Gees, phonograph .........**35.00**

Bee Gees, puffy stickers, 1979, set of 6 (any of 4 styles) ........**5.00**

Bo Didley, poster, Family Dog #92, 1967, VG ...............**25.00**

Boy George, wallet, blue nylon w/black trim, velcro closure, VG ....................................**3.50**

Charlatans w/Canned Heat, poster, San Francisco concert, 1967, EX ........................**50.00**

Culture Club, cup w/handle, Boy George & logo on white ground, 5¼" ...................**19.00**

Dave Clark Five, doll, w/names attached, Remco, set of 5, EX ..............................**285.00**

Dave Clark Five, jigsaw puzzle, Canadian, 1965, 180-pc, VG w/original box ..............**119.00**

**Dick Clark writing tablet, circa 1950s, EX, $12.00.**

Donny Osmond, nodder, NMIB .......................**25.00**

Fabian, pillow, printed stuffed cloth, 1950s, 11x11", EX .**65.00**

Gerry & Pacemakers, jigsaw puzzle, Canadian, 1965, 180-pc, VG w/box .....................**119.00**

Grateful Dead, poster, Family Dog #54, 22x14", EX .............**85.00**

Kiss, Colorforms, 1979, M ...**45.00**

Kiss, comb, various colors, Australia, ea ...........................**9.00**

Kiss, cup, plastic, 7-11/Majik .**20.00**

Kiss, guitar, plastic, 24", EX .**80.00**

Kiss, handkerchief, red w/Kiss logo, 21" ...........................**8.00**

Kiss, lapel pin, gold & black on sterling, 1977, 2¾", MOC .......**35.00**

Kiss, necklace, gold letters, gum machine item ....................**4.00**

Kiss, necklace, silver or gold 3-D logo, ea ...........................**10.00**

Led Zeppelin, poster, Oakland Stadium, July 1977, 23x18", NM .................................**62.50**

Monkees, arcade card, w/biography on back, 3½x5½" .......**7.00**

Monkees, backstage pass, 20th-Anniversary tour .............**7.00**

Monkees, charm bracelet, 1967, MIP .................................**25.00**

Monkees, finger puppet, Mickey, M w/original Sears box .**36.00**

Monkees, finger puppets, Mickey & Davey, Remco, NM in orig package ...........................**89.00**

Monkees, guitar, full-color cartoon graphics, Mattel, 20" .....**94.00**

Monkees, ring, chrome, flashes from 2 portraits to other 2, VG .**19.00**

Monkees, ring binder, vinyl, NM .............................**140.00**

Monkees, sunglasses, w/original tag ...................................**22.50**

Monkees, tambourine, 1967, original box, EX ....................**30.00**

Monkees, 45rpm record holder, vinyl, NM .....................**150.00**

New Kids on the Block, fashion plates, Hasbro, 1990, EX .**4.00**

New Kids on the Block, watch, digital, 1990, EX .............**8.00**

Pat Boone, bracelet, MOC ...**65.00**

Peter & Gordon, arcade card (vending machine), 1965-65, 3½x5½" .............................**6.00**

Rolling Stones, #1 Magazine, Crazy World of England's..., 1964, VG ......................**33.00**

Rolling Stones, key chain, lips, MIP .................................**8.00**

Rolling Stones, key ring, tongue card w/6 photos, 1983, MIP ........**9.00**

Rolling Stones, puffy stickers, 4 styles, 1983, any set of 6 .**4.00**

Rolling Stones, puzzle, Great Britain, 1960s, EX w/original box ...............................**250.00**

Rolling Stones, sticker, 1983, set of 8, MIP ........................**6.00**

The Police, puffy stickers, 1 style, set of 5, M ........................**5.00**

Van Halen, puffy stickers, 3 styles, any set of 5, 6 or 7 ............**5.00**

# Roselane Sparklers

A line of small figures with a soft shaded finish and luminous jewel eyes was produced during the late 1950s by the Roselane Pottery Company who operated in Pasadena, California, from the late 1930s until possibly the 1970s. The line was a huge success. Twenty-nine different models were made, including elephants, burrows, raccoons, fawns, dogs, cats, and fish. Not all pieces are marked, but some carry an incised 'Roselane Pasadena, Calif.,' or 'Calif. U.S.A'; others may have a paper label. Our advisor for this category, Lee Garmon, is listed in the Directory under Illinois.

Photo courtesy Lee Garmon.

**Elephant, jeweled headdress, either style, $12.00.**

Angelfish, pink jeweled eyes, California USA, 4½" ............**12.00**

Bulldog, jeweled eyes & collar, w/2 sm jewel-eyed pups ..**9.00**

Cat, blue jeweled eyes, amber collar, sitting, Calif USA, 6¾" ......**9.00**

Cat, slanted aqua jeweled eyes, pink collar, standing, #107, 5¼" ..................................**8.00**

Cocker spaniel, blue jeweled eyes, Roselane C in circle USA, 4½" ..................................**7.00**

Deer, pink jeweled eyes, standing, no mark, 5½" ..................**7.00**

Deer w/antlers, jeweled eyes & collar, standing, no mark, 4½" ..................................**8.00**

Elephant, jeweled eyes & head-piece, 6" .........................**12.00**

Kangaroo mother w/twins in pocket, amber jeweled eyes, from $20 to ....................**25.00**

Kitten, aqua jeweled eyes, sitting, 1¾" ..................................**2.00**

Modern owl, black w/gold trim, lg plastic eyes, 1960-70s, 5¼" ..............................**10.00**

Raccoon, yellow jeweled eyes, standing ..........................**8.00**

Siamese cat, blue jeweled eyes, recumbent .....................**12.00**

Siamese cat, jeweled eyes & collar, sitting, unmarked, 7" .....**12.00**

Spaniel dog, blue jeweled eyes, C in circle USA mark, 4½" .**7.00**

Whippet dog, amber jeweled eyes, sitting, marked Calif USA, 7½" ..................................**9.00**

# Rosemeade

Novelty items made by the Wapheton Pottery Company of North Dakota from 1941 to 1960 are beginning to attract collectors of American pottery. Though smaller items (salt and pepper shakers, figurines, trays, etc.) are readily found, the larger examples are scarce and can be very expensive. The name of the novelty ware, 'Rosemeade,' is indicated on the paper labels (many of which are still intact) or by the ink stamp. Our advisor for this category, Bryce L. Farnsworth, is listed in the Directory under North Dakota.

Ashtray, state, Minnesota shape ..........................35.00
Ashtray, state, Missouri shape ......................30.00
Ashtray, state, North Dakota shape ..............................40.00
Bank, fish ...........................420.00
Bookend, bear, single .........250.00
Figurine, elephants, miniature, pr ......................................65.00
Figurine, fighting cock, lg, pr .200.00
Figurine, skunk, miniature .17.50
Figurine, wolfhound, glossy black glaze ...............115.00
Flower frog, fish ....................22.50
Flower frog, pheasant ..........95.00
Lamp, TV; pheasant ...........550.00
Pitcher, ball shape ................27.50
Planter, pheasant ...............310.00
Salt & pepper shakers, Block-house, Fort Lincoln State Park, pr .......................210.00
Salt & pepper shakers, duckling, pr ......................................75.00
Salt & pepper shakers, elephant, pr ......................................55.00

Salt & pepper shakers, pheasant rooster, striding, pr .....155.00
Salt & pepper shakers, prairie dogs, pr ..........................42.50
Salt & pepper shakers, skunk, medium, pr ....................35.00
Salt & pepper shakers, turkey, lg, pr ....................................96.00
Spoon rest, cactus ...............42.50
Vase, doe figural, tall ..........45.00
Vase, swan figural ...............25.00

# Royal China

Several lines of the dinner-ware made by Royal China (Sebring, Ohio) are becoming very collectible, especially their Currier and Ives, decorated with scenes of early American life in blue on a white background, and their version of Blue Willow. Since the same blanks were used for all lines, they will all be the same size. Currier and Ives as well as

**Large pheasant figurine, rare, 14", $650.00.**

their Willow pattern was made in both blue and pink. (Pink Willow is not as easy to find as the blue nor as collectible.) For further information we recommend our advisor, BA Wellman, listed in the Directory under Massachusetts.

## Colonial Homestead

Bowl, fruit nappy; 5½" ...........**3.00**
Cake plate, tab handles, 10½" .**12.00**
Plate, bread & butter; 6" ........**1.50**
Plate, dinner; 10" ...................**4.00**
Plate, salad; rare, 7¼" ............**6.00**
Salt & pepper shakers, pr ....**12.00**

## Currier and Ives

Bowl, cereal; 6¼" ..................**12.00**
Bowl, fruit nappy; 5½" ...........**4.00**
Bowl, soup; flat, marked, 8¼" .**8.00**
Bowl, vegetable; 10" .............**20.00**
Calendar plate, ca 1970s-85,
  ea .............................**12.00**
Casserole, angle handles,
  w/lid .........................**65.00**
Chop plate, marked, 11" ......**20.00**

Creamer ..................................**6.00**
Cup & saucer ..........................**5.00**
Gravy boat ............................**13.00**
Pie plate, 10" ........................**15.00**
Plate, bread & butter; 6¼" .....**2.50**
Plate, dinner; 10" ...................**6.00**
Platter, oval, 13" ...................**28.00**
Salt & pepper shakers, pr ....**15.00**
Teapot ..................................**65.00**

## Memory Lane

Bowl, fruit nappy; 5½" ...........**3.00**
Bowl, soup; 8¼" ......................**7.50**
Bowl, vegetable; 10" .............**20.00**
Cake plate, w/handles ..........**12.00**
Chop plate, 12¼" ..................**20.00**
Creamer ..................................**6.00**
Plate, bread & butter; 6¼" .....**2.00**
Plate, luncheon; rare, 9¼" ......**8.00**
Plate, salad; 7¼" ....................**7.00**
Sugar bowl, w/lid ...................**9.00**

## Old Curiosity Shop

Bowl, fruit nappy; 5½" ...........**3.00**
Bowl, vegetable; 9¼" ............**18.00**
Cake plate, w/handles, 10¼" .**15.00**

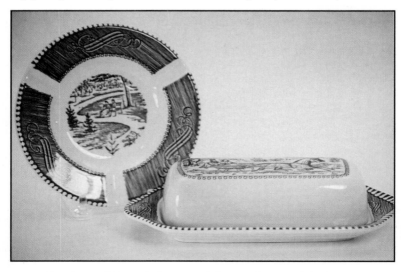

**Currier and Ives, Ashtray, 5½", $10.00; Butter dish, $25.00.**

**Memory Lane, Cup and saucer, $5.00; Ashtray, $10.00; Dinner plate, 10", $4.00.**

| | |
|---|---|
| Creamer | **6.00** |
| Cup & saucer | **5.00** |
| Plate, bread & butter; 6¼" | **2.50** |
| Plate, dinner; 10" | **4.00** |
| Sugar bowl, w/lid | **9.00** |

### Willow

| | |
|---|---|
| Bowl, fruit nappy; 5½" | **4.50** |
| Bowl, soup; 8¼" | **10.00** |
| Bowl, vegetable; 10" | **18.00** |
| Chop plate, 10" | **20.00** |
| Gravy boat | **15.00** |
| Plate, bread & butter; 6¼" | **2.00** |
| Plate, salad; 7¼" | **7.00** |

# Royal Copley

Produced by the Spaulding China Company of Sebring, Ohio, Royal Copley is a line of novelty planters, vases, ashtrays, and wall pockets modeled after appealing puppy dogs, lovely birds, innocent-eyed children, etc. The decoration is airbrushed and underglazed; the line is of good quality and is well received by today's pottery collectors. We recommend *Royal Copley, Books I and II,* by Leslie Wolfe, edited by Joe Devine (Collector Books). These books have been brought back by popular demand and include updated 1992 values. Our advisor, Joe Devine, is listed in the Directory under Iowa.

| | |
|---|---|
| Ashtray, leaf, 5" | **6.00** |
| Ashtray, mallard, paper label, 2" | **10.00** |
| Bank, pig, paper label or green stamp, 7½" | **45.00** |
| Figurine, Airedale, paper label, 6½" | **20.00** |
| Figurine, canary, paper label, 5½" | **35.00** |

**Bank, teddy bear, 7½", $65.00; Vase, white bear cub by tree stump, 7½", $50.00 minimum value.**

Figurine, Oriental boy holding jar, paper label, 7½" ............**15.00**

Figurine, sparrow, 5" ...........**15.00**

Figurine, titmouse on stump, full body, paper label, 8" ......**25.00**

Figurine, wren, paper label, 3½" .**18.00**

Lamp, cocker spaniel, 10" ....**65.00**

Pitcher, Pome Fruit, green stamp, 8" ....................................**26.00**

Planter, birdhouse w/bird, paper label, 8" ..........................**50.00**

Planter, Indian boy w/drum, paper label, 6½" .............**15.00**

Planter, Oriental boy w/basket on back, paper label, 8" ......**28.00**

Planter, wren on tree stump, paper label, 6¼" .............**18.00**

Plaque planter, fruit, embossed mark, 6¾" ......................**18.00**

Vase, goldfinch on stump, paper label, 6½" ......................**18.00**

Vase, Oriental-style dragons, footed, paper label, 5¼" ..**10.00**

Vase/planter, bird in flight, paper label, 7¼" ......................**20.00**

## Royal Haeger, Haeger

Manufactured in Dundee, Illinois, Haeger pottery has recently become the focus of much collector interest, especially the artware line and animal figures designed by Royal Hickman. These were produced from 1938 through the 1950s and are recognized by their strong lines and distinctive glazes. For further information consult *Collecting Royal Haegar* by Lee Garmon and Doris Frizzell (Collector Books). Ms. Garmon is listed in the Directory under Illinois.

Bookends, lion's head, R-700, 7½", ea ....................................**30.00**

Bowl, violin, R-293, 17" long .**30.00**

Candle holders, fish (single), R-183, 5", pr ......................**45.00**

Cornucopia, shell, R-298, 11" .**45.00**

Figurine, angelfish, head up, R-155, 5¼" ..........................**10.00**

Figurine, girl w/doe, R-411, 10½" .............................**40.00**

**Figurine, gypsy girl, R-1224, 16½", $150.00.**

Figurine, sitting cat, R-898, 6" ...............................**20.00**
Figurine, St Francis, R-1231, 10½" ...............................**25.00**
Figurine, wild goose, wings straight, F-17, 6½" ..........**8.00**
Flower block, leaping trout, R-169B, 7" .........................**30.00**
Gondola, no inserts, R-812, 15½" .............................**12.00**
Planter, greyhound, R-1331, 12" long ................................**35.00**
Planter, stag, R-1146, 5½" ...**15.00**
TV lamp/planter, greyhound, #6202, 13" long ..............**35.00**
Vase, ram's head, R-170, 11" .**35.00**
Vase, squid decor, 4-sided, footed, R-190, 8" ........................**30.00**

# Russel Wright Dinnerware

Dinnerware designed by one of America's top industrial engi-neers is today attracting the interest of many. Some of his more popular lines are American Modern, manufactured by the Steubenville Pottery Company (1939-59), and Iroquois, intro-duced in 1944. Refer to *The Collector's Encyclopedia of Russel Wright Designs* by Ann Kerr (Collector Books). Mrs. Kerr is listed in the Directory under Ohio.

**After-dinner coffeepot, Casual, lemon yellow, 4½", $100.00.**

Bowl, onion soup; Home Decora-tor, plastic, w/lid ............**24.00**
Bowl, soup; Meladur, plastic, 12-oz ...............................**9.00**
Bowl, vegetable; Highlight, Blue-berry, oval ......................**60.00**
Bowl, vegetable; Residental, oval, deep ...............................**13.00**
Butter dish, Iroquois Casual, aqua or brick red, restyled, ¼-lb .............................**250.00**
Casserole, Harker white Clover, clover decoration, w/lid, 2-qt .........**50.00**
Creamer & sugar bowl, American Modern, chartreuse, w/lid .**24.00**
Cup, Meladur, plastic, 7-oz ....**8.00**
Cup & saucer, AD; Iroquois Casual, canteloupe ......**125.00**
Cup & saucer, Knowles, 7½-oz .**20.00**
Dish set, child's, Ideal, complete in original box .............**150.00**
Gravy boat, spun aluminum .**125.00**
Gravy bowl, Iroquios Casual, oyster or charcoal, 12-oz, 5¼" ....**18.00**

Jug, water; Ideal Ware, lg ....**25.00**
Mug, Highlight, Citron ........**30.00**
Old-fashioned, double; American Modern ...........................**45.00**
Pitcher, Harker White Clover, clover decoration, w/lid, 2-qt ......**65.00**
Pitcher, water; sterling, 2-qt .**55.00**
Plate, dinner; American Modern, Glacier Blue, 10" ...........**20.00**
Plate, dinner; Home Decorator, plastic ..............................**5.00**
Plate, luncheon; sterling, 9" ..**7.00**
Salt & pepper shakers, Knowles, pr ....................................**24.00**
Teapot, American Modern, Seafoam, 6x10" ..............**75.00**
Tidbit tray, spun aluminum ..**85.00**
Tumbler, American Modern, 13-oz, 5" ....................................**30.00**
Tumbler, Flair ......................**15.00**
Tumbler, Imperial Flair, 14-oz ..**65.00**
Tumbler, juice; Iroquois Pinch, 6-oz ...............................**35.00**

# Salt Shakers

You'll probably see more salt and pepper shakers during your flea market forays than T-shirts and tube socks! Since the 1920s they've been popular souvenir items, and a considerable number has been issued by companies to advertise their products. These advertising shakers are always good, and along with miniature shakers (1½" or under) are some of the more valuable. Of course, those that have a crossover interest with other categories of collecting — Black Americana, Disney, Rosemeade, Shawnee, Ceramic Arts Studio, etc. — are often expensive as well. There are many good books on the market; among them are *Salt & Pepper Shakers, Identification & Values, Books I, II, III, and IV*, by Helene Guarnaccia; and *The Collector's Encyclopedia of Salt & Pepper Shakers* (there are two in the series), by Melva Davern (all published by Collector Books). See also Clubs and Newsletters; Advertising; Ceramic Arts Studio; Character Collectibles; Disney; Gas Station Collectibles; Shawnee; Scottie Dogs; Rosemeade.

Airflow trailer & streamline car, yellow & black ceramic, 1950s, pr ........................**15.00**
Airplanes, stand at angle, detailed metal, pr ..........**18.00**
Alligator, 1-pc w/holes at both ends, painted ceramic ...**12.00**
Bakelite ball form, yellow or green, pr, from $30 to ....**35.00**

**Fork and spoon people, $10.00 each pair pair.**

310

Ball canning jars, clear plastic w/rubber ring, wire bale handle, pr ...............................**5.00**

Bananas, painted ceramic, pr .**10.00**

Binoculars w/case, painted ceramic w/gold trim, pr .**15.00**

Bird on nest w/2 babies, mother is holder, ceramic, 3-pc .....**18.00**

Boston bull terriers, painted ceramic, pr .....................**12.00**

Butler & maid, windups, pr .**15.00**

Candlesticks, painted ceramic, pr, from $6 to .......................**10.00**

Carrot & pea people, doing housework, painted ceramic, pr **28.00**

Cat couple on couch, painted ceramic, pr .....................**12.00**

Cats, long stylized body & neck, ceramic, marked Napco, pr .**8.00**

Chickens, painted wood, Russia, pr .....................................**12.00**

Chickens, white w/red combs, painted ceramic, Japan, pr ................................**8.00**

Chimney sweeps, Goebel, pr .**30.00**

Church & priest, painted, pr .**15.00**

Coffeepot w/cup & saucer, painted ceramic, miniature, pr ..**22.50**

Cow & moon, painted ceramic, pr ...................................**15.00**

Cucumber people w/movable googly eyes, painted ceramic, pr ..**20.00**

Dog w/green collar & cartoon features, ceramic, pr ..........**12.00**

Donkey cart w/2 jugs, painted ceramic, 3-pc .................**10.00**

Donkeys, painted ceramic w/rhinestones along upper lip, pr .**8.00**

Easy chair & ottoman, painted ceramic, pr .....................**12.00**

English bulldog, realistic painted ceramic, pr .....................**15.00**

Flamingo & flower, painted ceramic, pr .....................**16.00**

Foxes w/top hats & canes, painted ceramic, pr .....................**12.00**

Frog sitting on crocodile, painted ceramic, Sigma, pr ........**45.00**

Galleon ships, lustre & painted ceramic, Japan, pr ........**12.50**

Giraffes, lavender w/gold bows, pr ...................................**10.00**

Goldilocks, painted ceramic, Relco, pr .........................**25.00**

Harlequins, roly-poly form, blue lustre, Japan, pr, from $35 to ...................................**50.00**

Jack & Jill, painted chalkware, 1940s, pr .........................**40.00**

Leopards, hand-painted bone china, Relco, pr .............**14.00**

Lions, ceramic w/fur trim, original Norcrest Furland tag, pr ...............................**14.00**

**Mermaids, either pair, $10.00.**

Little Miss Muffet & spider, painted ceramic, pr .......**30.00**

Mice couple, dressed as people, painted ceramic, pr .......**15.00**

Minnesota w/raised letters, state shape, Milford Pottery, pr ..**8.00**

Monkey resting on banana, painted ceramic, 2-pc ....**10.00**

Mother's Day, cylinder form painted bisque w/poem, pr ..............**8.00**

New Hampshire, metal w/enameled tourist attractions, Japan, pr ......................**12.00**

Peanut people, painted ceramic, pr .....................................**22.50**

Penguins, stylized, painted wood, pr ......................................**6.00**

Pigs, standing on hind legs, heavy silver-colored metal, pr .**15.00**

Pluto, painted ceramic, not authorized by Disney, pr ........**30.00**

Poodle on pillow, painted ceramic, Sarsaparilla, 1983, 2-pc ..**7.00**

Rainbow trout, painted ceramic, pr ......................................**8.00**

Record player & television, painted ceramic, pr .......**10.00**

Rocket ships, yellow & clear plastic, pr ................................**8.00**

Rolling pin & scoop, painted ceramic, pr .......................**6.00**

Seltzer bottles, white & gold painted ceramic, pr .........**7.00**

Sir George & dragon, painted ceramic, miniature, pr ..**30.00**

Space Needle, painted china, souvenirs, pr .......................**12.00**

Steamship w/double stacks, painted wood, 3-pc ........**12.00**

Stove & refrigerator, white ceramic w/red trim, 1940s, pr ...................................**12.00**

Swan, painted bone china, pr ..**8.00**

Telephone, red & green ceramic, 2-pc ...............................**20.00**

Toaster w/2 pop-up bread slice shakers, colored plastic, pr ...............................**15.00**

Turkeys, painted ceramic, Japan, pr ......................................**8.00**

**Tiny Power Mower, red and white plastic, MIB, $27.50.**

Valentine's Day heart, high gloss
glaze, 2-pc ........................**8.00**
Violin & accordion, painted
ceramic, miniature, pr ..**26.00**
Watering can w/garden poem,
painted ceramic, pr .........**8.00**
Watermelon slices, realistic
painted ceramic, pr .......**10.00**
Yale bulldog w/hat, white painted
ceramic, 2-pc .................**14.00**

## Schoop, Hedi

From the 1940s through
the '50s, Hedi Schoop managed
a small operation in North Hollywood, California, where she
produced novelty wares such as
figurines, lamps, and other
decorative items. Refer to *The
Collector's Encyclopedia of
California Pottery* by Jack
Chipman (Collector Books) for
more information.

Candle holder, mermaid holds 2
shell holders aloft, 13½" .**250.00**
Figurine, clown playing cello,
overglaze platinum, ca 1943,
12½" ............................**150.00**
Figurine, Dutch girl on green
base, 10" ........................**85.00**
Figurine, Josephine, in sarong,
holds bowl at hips, ca 1943,
13" ................................**125.00**
Figurine, lady in peach w/green
trim, basket on side, 13" .**95.00**
Figurine, Mexican lady, scarf over
hat, baskets on side, 12" .**75.00**
Figurine, Repose, kneeling lady
holds bowl, glossy tinted
bisque, 1949 ................**125.00**
Lamp, Colbert, lady figural
w/basket ea side, ca 1940,
11½" ............................**100.00**
Planter, lady reading book before
opening, 9" ....................**65.00**

**Josephine, holding small flower
bowl, ca 1943, 13", $125.00.**

Tray, King of Diamonds, in-mold
mark ..............................**65.00**
Vase, Maria, lady figural, 12½" .**85.00**
Vase/planter, lady in long gown
w/basket, applied flowers,
12½" ..............................**90.00**

## Scottie Dogs

An amazing array of Scottie
dog collectibles can be found in a
wide range of prices. Collectors
might choose to specialize in a
particular area, or they may
enjoy looking for everything from
bridge tallies to original portraits
or paintings. Most of the items

**Bookends, metal with brass finish, Frankart, $150.00 for the pair.**

are from the 1930s and 1940s, although you'll find Scottie items that were made both before and after those dates. Many were used for advertising purposes; others are simply novelties. Scottie collectors are among the most avid; many like to communicate with one another and gather to display their collections. There have been instances in which individuals and/or groups have shopped an area, leaving very little that was unique behind, causing first a shortage of merchandise and then an escalation of prices. For further information we recommend contacting Donna Palmer, who is listed in the Directory under Washington. She has been collecting, buying, and selling Scottie items for many years. See also Akro Agate; Clubs and Newsletters.

Advertising, blotter card, veterinary hospital ................**12.00**

Apron, hand-embroidered bows, garden & black Scotties on brown cloth ....................**25.00**
Ashtray, Buchanan's Black & White Scotch, bone china, Shelley .........................**125.00**

**Crumb brush in figural Scottie holder, 4¾", $16.00.**

Autograph book, painted Scottie w/leash on front wood cover ...........................**20.00**

Blotter card, 2 Scotties, advertising veterinary hospital .**12.00**

Book, Mac & Muff, John C Winston, ca 1951, illustrated cover & pgs ....................**38.00**

Bridge tallies, Scottie head on yellow strips, w/tassle, set of 4 .......................**16.00**

Cocktail shaker, facsimile of Check & Double Check on clear glass ......................**89.00**

Curtain tie backs, green metal, embossed gold Scottie profiles ................................**48.50**

Eraser, brown rubber full figure Scottie, sitting up ..........**18.00**

Figurine, black celluloid Scottie, standing, move tail & dog barks, sm ......................**24.00**

Handkerchief, gray w/black Scottie heads in each corner ..**9.00**

Magnets, black & white Hotsy & Totsy figures, marked Alunice USA, MIB ......................**65.00**

Padlock, brass, w/key, imprinted Scottie profile ................**49.00**

Pen stand & holder, marble base, metal sitting figure, ......**95.00**

Pincushion, pink taffeta, black & white china Scottie figures on top ...................................**87.00**

Print, Hide & Seek, original pen & ink, by Margaret Kirmse .**150.00**

Purse, child's; green plastic w/metal Scottie profile at side, EX ........................**65.00**

Salt & pepper shakers, painted black Scotties on milk glass, Tipp USA ......................**45.00**

Server, 4 chrome tiers, top tier supported by 3 Bakelite Scotties ..............................**165.00**

Thermometer, sitting black Scottie painted on white metal, EX .................................**45.00**

Tile, white w/sitting black Scottie .................................**16.50**

Wastebasket, silhouette of family w/leashed Scottie on pink metal ..............................**45.00**

# Scouting Collectibles

Founded in England in 1907 by Major General Lord Baden-Powell, scouting remains an important institution in the life of young boys and girls everywhere. Recently scouting-related memorabilia has attracted a following, and values of many items have escalated dramatically in the last few years. Early first edition handbooks often bring prices of $100.00 and more. Vintage uniforms are scarce and highly valued, and one of the rarer medals, the Life Saving Honor Medal, is worth several hundred dollars to collectors. Refer to *A Complete Guide to Scouting Collectibles* by Rolland J. Sayers for more information. Mr. Sayers is listed in the Directory under North Carolina.

Badge, Bobcat, 1932-40, crude clasp, EX ..........................**1.50**

Badge, First Class, cloth, kiwi twill ..................................**7.00**

Belt buckle, Max Silber, World Jamboree, bronze, 1981, EX ............................**100.00**

Bolo, National Jamboree, horseshoe form, silver/black tie, 1981, MIB ........................**7.50**

Book, Cub Scouting, Baden Powell, yellow cover, 1920, EX ...............................**22.00**

Book, Wolf Scouts, Gilwell, linen cover, 1930, EX .............**22.00**

Bookends, Girl Scouts, composition, 1940, pr .................**15.00**

Camera, Girl Scouts, Insta-Load, Kodak, 1968 ...................**15.00**

Canteen, flat w/khaki case, BSA symbol, EX ....................**10.00**

Coin, National Jamboree, aluminum, 1981, EX .............**3.00**

Coin, National Jamboree, bronze, 1969, EX ...........................**6.00**

Collar emblem, Girl Scouts, brass, 1918 ................................**10.00**

Cookie cutters, Girl Scouts, green handle, set .....................**20.00**

Cuff links, Baden Powell portrait on each, sterling silver, 19mm, EX ......................**35.00**

**Official First Aid Kit, Johnson & Johnson, EX, $15.00.**

Handbook, Merit Badge series, brown cover, 1920-32, EX .**9.00**

Knife, bone handle, 4-blade, insignia on shield, 1931-42, EX ...................................**24.00**

Mug, National Jamboree Commissary, red & white plastic, 1985, M .............................**3.00**

Paperweight, Tenderfoot, pewter, 3", VG ...............................**5.00**

Patch, Girl Scout Treasurer, green twill, 1937 ......................**10.00**

Patch, Paul Bunyan Axe, gauze back, VG .........................**4.00**

Pin, Community Service, GSA, green enamel, 1922-31, EX ...........................**75.00**

Pin, lapel; Episcopal God & Country, VG ...........................**10.00**

Pin, Maltise Cross, 4-point, Powell in center, 37mm, EX ......**85.00**

Pin-back button, Powell portrait, 23mm, EX ......................**30.00**

Pinewood Derby kit, Official Boy Scout, 1960, MIB .............**5.00**

Postcard, US, 1967 World Jamboree, embossed Baden Powell photo ..........................**2.00**

Scarf, lady's; National Jamboree logo, 1960, EX .................**7.00**

Tapestry, showing uniformed Baden Powell, 20x20" ...**40.00**

Toothbrush, National Jamboree, blue brush, white case, 1985, M ......................................**3.00**

Uniform & equipment checklist, National Jamboree, 1989, EX ................................**2.00**

Whistle, Official Girl Scouts of America, cylinder form, circa 1920s ............................**20.00**

Windshield scraper, Florida Sea Base, white & black plastic, VG ..................................**2.00**

Yearbook, Boy Scouts, 1923, VG .............................**20.00**

Yearbook, Boy Scouts, 1932, EX ...............................**9.00**

# 7-Up

Though it was originally touted to have medicinal qualities, by 1930 7-Up had been reformulated and was simply sold as a refreshing drink. The company who first made it was the Howdy

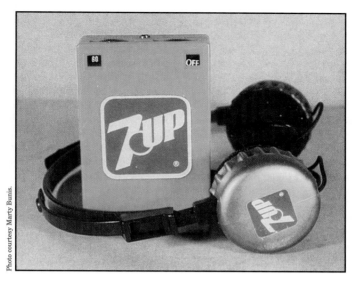

**Headphone radio, Made by Talbot Toys Inc, Hong Kong, 1983, from $35.00 to $50.00.**

Company. By 1940, its name had been changed to 7-Up, to correspond with the name of the soft drink. Collectors search for the signs, thermometers, point-of-sale items, etc., that carry the 7-Up slogans. Our advisors for this category are Craig and Donna Stifter, listed in Directory under Illinois. See also Character and Promotional Drinking Glasses; Novelty Telephones.

Bottle, green, 1968, 10-oz, EX .**7.00**
Bottle topper, die-cut cardboard, Dress Up The Dinner, EX .**4.00**
Bottle topper, die-cut cardboard, Easter Fresh Up, EX ......**8.00**
Bottle topper, die-cut cardboard, silhouetted leprechaun, 1954, NM ................................**10.00**
Calendar, lady in low-cut dress & flowers in hair, 1952, complete, NM .....................**200.00**
Clock, light-up, oak frame, Nothing Does It..., square, 16x16", NM ..............................**125.00**

Display, counter top, glass ice cube shape w/bottle, 9", EX ..**475.00**
Folding chair, tin, green & white striped seat, 1940s-50s, EX ......................**150.00**
Menu board, die-cut masonite, Fresh-Up With Lunch..., 12x21", EX+ ...................**70.00**
Menu board, tin, hand w/bottle & 7-Up above chalkboard, EX ................................**45.00**
Sign, cardboard, girl w/tennis racket & bottle, 1955, 11x21", EX ................................**30.00**
Sign, cardboard, plate & bottle, Beef Sandwich..., 1960, 10x17", EX+ ...................**10.00**
Sign, cardboard hanger, 2-sided, girl w/bottle, 1940s, 6" dia, NM ................................**25.00**
Sign, cardboard stand-up, family at beach, 1950, 12", NM ......**10.00**
Sign, cardboard stand-up, Fresh-Up Family, 1946, 12x9", NM ..**15.00**
Sign, cardboard stand-up, Santa w/bottle & sandwich, 1964, 24", NM ..........................**15.00**

*Photo courtesy Marty Bunis.*

Sign, drink rack; red on white, lg 7-Up logo, 12x19", EX ...**30.00**

Sign, tin flange, 2-sided, Fresh-Up left of 7-Up, 12x19", EX+ **.90.00**

Sign, vendor; plastic, metal frame, shows 2 cans, 12x24", EX ..................................**25.00**

Squeeze toy, Fresh-Up Freddie, vinyl, 1959, EX+ ..........**125.00**

Telephone, plastic, 7-Up Spot on black base, 1990, 12", M **.55.00**

Thermometer, plastic lens, metal frame, 1970s, round, 12" dia, NM ..................................**65.00**

Thermometer, porcelain, The Fresh-Up Family Drink, round ends, G ................**70.00**

## Sewing Items

Sewing notions from the 1800s and early 20th century, such as whimsical figural tape measures, beaded satin pincushions, blown glass darning eggs, and silver and gold thimbles are pleasant reminders of a bygone era — ladies' sewing circles, quilting bees, and beautifully handstitched finery. For further information we recommend (for figural pincushions) *Collector's Guide to Made in Japan Ceramics, Identification and Values,* by Carole Bess White; *Antique and Collectible Thimbles and Accessories*, by Averil Mathis; and *Toy and Miniature Sewing Machines, An Identification and Value Guide*, by Glenda Thomas (all published by Collector Books).

Emery, strawberry w/sterling top, unmarked ......................**80.00**

Gauge, knitting needle; celluloid, Good Shepard Yarns, 6½" **.12.50**

Guard, quilter's; leather, USA ..**2.00**

Mending kit, metal cylinder w/contents, Lydia Pinkham's, from $10 to ....................**12.00**

Mending kit, metal cylinder w/contents, WWI ...........**25.00**

**Tape measure, red plastic apple, USA, 2", MIB, $25.00.**

**Sewing cats, pincushions on backs, one has scissors 'eyeglasses,' one pull-out tape measure tongue, red clay, Japan, $20.00 each.**

Nanny pin, brass w/goldstone center, end unscrews, 2" ....**185.00**

Needle case, vegetable ivory .**40.00**

Needle threader, Prudential, mother w/child on handle .**3.50**

Net mender, celluloid, Linen Thread Co, 6½" ................**6.00**

Pincushion, turtle nodder, base metal w/glass eyes, Japan .**25.00**

Scissors, stork figural, base metal, 4" ....................................**20.00**

Skirt measure, marked In a Minit, Patented July 4, 1905 .............................**17.50**

Stiletto, sterling w/floral handle, adjustable ......................**50.00**

Tape measure, basket of flowers, painted celluloid, Germany ...........................**85.00**

Tatting shuttle, celluloid, Lady Pinkham, NM ................**85.00**

Tatting shuttle, French ivory, ca 1920, 2½", EX ................**20.00**

Tatting shuttle, sterling, marked Nussbaum & Hunold ....**75.00**

Thimble case, multicolor cloisonne cylinder, marked China ..**25.00**

Thimble case, sterling walnut form w/gold interior, Unger Bros .............................**150.00**

Thimble case, wood acorn form, unmarked ......................**60.00**

Thimble stand, bronze rooster, Austria .........................**30.00**

Tweezers, marked French Ivory, 6" ....................................**6.00**

### Figural Ceramic Pincushions

Boy w/bowtie & hat, orange, blue & white matte, Japan, 3" ...**25.00**

Boy w/mandolin, seated to left on shell form, multicolor, 2¾" ................................**8.00**

Calico dog w/lolling tongue & flower, shiny red, white & blue, 2¾" ........................**20.00**

Camel w/blue basket, white lustre & painted floral blanket, 3¼" ................................**15.00**

Clown in tub, blue & white lustre,
3" .....................................**25.00**
Dog cart, blue, tan & yellow lus-
tre, 3¼", from $20 to .....**28.00**
Dog w/book, shiny multicolor, 2¾",
from $20 to .....................**30.00**
Dog w/red ball, shiny multicolor,
2¾" ................................**12.00**
Duck, tan lustre, 2" ..............**10.00**
Elephant, shiny white w/applied
flowers, no mark, post-1960,
2¼" ...................................**5.00**
Girl w/big hat, standing before lg
trunk, orange & black matte,
4¼" .................................**25.00**
Girl w/lg rectangular basket,
shiny multicolor, 3¾", from
$18 to .............................**28.00**
Horse & carriage, shiny multi-
color & tan lustre, w/front
tray, 2¾" ........................**15.00**
Monkey, seated holding orange,
matte multicolor, 2¼" ....**12.00**
Radio dog, yellow & tan lustre,
3" .....................................**30.00**

## Thimbles

Advertising, aluminum, from $2
to ......................................**6.00**
Advertising, china, Franklin
Porcelain, USA, any ......**15.00**
Advertising, plastic, from $1 to .**4.00**
Advertising, sterling, unmarked,
from $25 to ....................**40.00**
Anri, painted girl w/lamb triplets
on wood, Italy ................**10.00**
Brass, Greek Key band, un-
marked ..........................**10.00**
Franklin Mint, china w/14k-gold
trim, First Ladies series,
any .................................**15.00**
Germany, enamel on sterling, 6-
point star mark .............**50.00**
Glass, clear w/painted florals,
unmarked ........................**8.00**
Goldsmith-Stern, 14k gold, anchor mark ....................**125.00**

Gorham, Norman Rockwell,
china, gold trim, any .....**15.00**
Ironstone, unmarked .............**3.00**
Ketcham & McDougall, ster-
ling, faceted rim, KMD
mark ...........................**30.00**
Plastic, adjustable, marked Pat
No 208047, USA ..............**2.00**
Simons, sterling, Chirstmas 1982,
shield mark ...................**45.00**
Simons, sterling, Greek Key band,
shield mark ...................**25.00**
Simons, sterling w/gold band .**40.00**
Souvenir, Grand Canyon Trea-
sured Keepsake, pewter,
MIB ...............................**10.00**
Souvenir, Korea, black leather .**3.50**
Souvenir, London, embossed scene
w/lady sewing, plastic .....**2.00**
Souvenir, Madrid Spain on
enameled black band on
brass, M .........................**5.50**
Sterns Bros, gold filled, double
anchor mark ..................**45.00**
Swan, Charles & Diana enamel portraits on sterling, 1981 ....**60.00**
Waite-Thresher, sterling silver,
waves on band, thimble in
star mark ......................**28.00**

## Toy Sewing Machines

Artcraft, Little Mother, ca 1940s,
8x4⅛x8¼", from $65 to ..**85.00**
Britains Petite Ltd of England,
Petite, battery-op, 1980s,
8¾x5x10" ......................**35.00**
Brother, Baby Brother, battery-op,
1960s-70s, 6½x4x8", from $75
to .................................**100.00**
Casige, Our Pet, gold scroll
design, pre-1945, 5x2x5",
from $100 to ................**135.00**
Casige, yellow flowers, pre-
WWII, 7½x4½x8" ........**85.00**
China, Colorstitch, manual or
battery-op, light, 1990s,
8x5x11¼" ......................**50.00**

China, Diana, plastic, battery or hand-op, 7x4½x9½", from $15 to ....................................**35.00**

China, Kittie #606, plastic, battery-op, 6½x4½x9", from $15 to ....................................**25.00**

China, Lovely Pony Sewing Machine, battery-op, 1990s, 6½x4½x9" ........................**10.00**

Delta Specialty, American Girl, 1930s-40s, 6x4x8¾", from $75 to ....................................**125.00**

Durham, Cabbage Patch Kids, battery-op, 1980s, 7x4½x9", from $25 to ....................**35.00**

England, Comet EMC, plastic on metal base, 7½x5½x9", from $75 to ..........................**100.00**

FW Muller, Model 0, sheet metal, pre-WWII, 5x2x4⅝", from $100 to ........................**150.00**

Gibraltar Mfg Co, Betsy Ross, 1950s, 6⅜x4x8", from $75 to .....**100.00**

Hasbro, Walt Disney's Alice in Wonderland Sewing Kit, from $45 to .............................**55.00**

Japan, Crystal, metal & plastic, manual or battery-op, 5x3½x7½" ........................**25.00**

Montgomery Ward, Signature Junior, electric, 1960s, 8x5x11" .....**40.00**

National, Busy Bee, 1920s, 6¼x3¾x8¾" ..................**150.00**

Sears, Model 49-1210, battery-op, 1960s-70s, 9x4½x10", from $30 to .............................**50.00**

Singer, Little Touch & Sew, 1960s-70s, 9x4½x10", from $30 to .............................**50.00**

Straco, Elect-O-Matic, belt driven, 1950s, 7½x4x8½", from $25 to ....................**50.00**

# Shawnee

The novelty planters, vases, cookie jars, salt and pepper shakers, and 'Corn' dinnerware made by the Shawnee Pottery of Ohio are attractive, fun to collect, and still available at reasonable

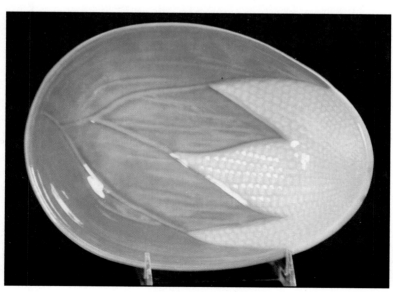

Bowl, Corn, #95, $35.00.

prices. The company operated from 1937 until 1961, marking their wares with 'Shawnee, U.S.A.,' and a number series, or 'Kenwood.' Refer to *The Collector's Guide to Shawnee Pottery,* by Janice and Duane Vanderbilt; *Shawnee Pottery, An Identification and Value Guide,* by Jim and Bev Mangus (both by Collector Books); and *Collecting Shawnee Pottery,* by Mark Supnick (L-W Book Sales) for more information. Note: Large shakers with decals and gold trim are very hard to find and have a minimum value of $225.00 for the pair. Our advisor for this category is Richard Spencer, listed in the Directory under Utah. See also Cookie Jars.

Ashtray, Valencia ................**17.00**
Bowl, mixing; Corn King, 6" ..**30.00**
Bowl, nesting; Snowflake, marked USA, 6" ..........................**15.00**

Casserole, French; Lobster, #902, 16-oz ...............................**25.00**
Cookie jar, Jo-Jo Clown, marked Shawnee 12, minimum value .........................**300.00**
Cookie jar, Mugsy, decals & gold trim, minimum value ..**550.00**
Creamer, elephant, gold trim & decals, marked Pat USA, from $150 to ................**175.00**
Creamer, Flower & Fern, marked USA ...............................**17.00**
Creamer, Puss 'n Boots, green & yellow, marked Shawnee 85, from $45 to ....................**55.00**
Creamer, Smiley, blue & yellow, marked Shawnee 86, from $50 to ...............................**60.00**
Figurine, Pekingese, w/sticker .**60.00**
Figurine, tumbling bear, gold trim & decals ......................**110.00**
Match holder, Fernware, marked USA ...............................**80.00**
Nappy, Valencia, 9½" ...........**17.00**
Pie plate, Valencia, 9" .........**22.00**

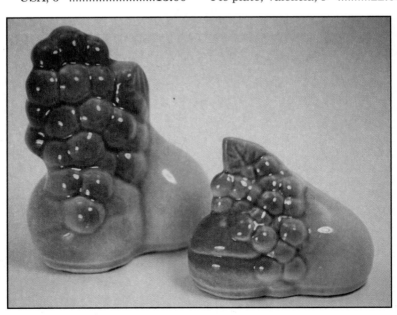

**Salt and pepper shakers, Fruit, large, $50.00 for the pair.**

Pitcher, Boy Blue, gold trim, marked Shawnee 46 ...**175.00**
Pitcher, chicken, marked Pat Chanticleer ....................**50.00**
Pitcher, Fernware, octagonal jug, marked USA ..................**50.00**
Pitcher, Pennsylvania Dutch, marked USA 64 .............**95.00**
Pitcher, Smiley, clover buds, marked Pat Smiley USA .............**175.00**
Planter, cat w/sax .................**40.00**
Planter, clown w/pot, marked USA 619 ........................**15.00**
Planter, fawn by stump, gold trim, marked USA 535 ...........**18.00**
Planter, Orientals ..................**6.00**
Planter, pony, curly mane & tail, marked Shawnee 506 ...**40.00**
Plate, Corn Queen, marked Shawnee 68, 10" ............**35.00**
Plate, Valencia, 10" ..............**15.00**
Salt & pepper shakers, Flower & Fern, lg, pr .....................**25.00**
Salt & pepper shakers, Pennsylvania Dutch, jug form, lg, pr .................................**55.00**
Salt & pepper shakers, Smiley, blue bib, lg, pr .............**100.00**
Salt & pepper shakers, Swiss boy & girl, gold trim, lg, pr ..**70.00**
Salt & pepper shakers, Winnie & Smiley, Clover Bud, sm, pr .................................**65.00**
Salt and pepper shakers, chef, gold trim, sm, pr, from $35 to ..**45.00**
Sugar bowl, Corn Line, #78, w/lid .............................**30.00**
Sugar bowl, Fruit, marked Shawnee 83 ...................**50.00**
Sugar bowl, Pennsylvania Dutch, tab handles, open ..........**80.00**
Teapot, Cottage, marked USA 7 ..............................**320.00**
Teapot, elephant, light green, gold trim, marked USA, from $200 to ..................................**225.00**
Teapot, Granny Ann, peach apron, marked USA ................**100.00**

Teapot, red flower, gold trim, marked USA ..................**60.00**
Teapot, sunflower, gold trim, marked USA ................**150.00**
Utility jar, white basketweave, green & gold trim, decals, w/lid ............................**100.00**

# Sheet Music

The most valuable examples of sheet music are those related to early transportation, ethnic themes, Disney characters, a particularly popular actor, singer, or composer, or with a cover illustration done by a well-known artist. Production of sheet music peaked during the 'Tin Pan Alley Days,' from the 1880s until the 1930s. Covers were made as attractive as possible to lure potential buyers, and today's collectors sometimes frame and hang them as they would a print. Flea markets are a good source for sheet music, and prices are usually very reasonable. Most are available for under $5.00. Some of the more valuable examples are listed here. Refer to *The Sheet Music Reference and Price Guide* (Collector Books) by Anna Marie Guiheen and Marie-Reine A. Pafik and *Collector's Guide to Sheet Music* by Debbie Dillon (L-W Book Sales) for more information.

All Alone, Irving Berlin, 1924 .**10.00**
All or Nothin', Rogers & Hammerstein II, from Oklahoma, 1943 ................................**8.00**
All Right, Louie, Drop the Gun; Arthur Godfrey photo .....**5.00**
Always, Irving Berlin, Deanna Durbin photo, 1925 .........**5.00**
An American in Paris, George Gershwin, 1929 ..............**5.00**

Ballad of the Green Berets, Sgt
Barry Sandler photo, 1966 .**5.00**
Buttons & Bows, Jane Russell &
Bob Hope, from Paleface,
1948 .................................**5.00**
Cheer Up Little Darlings, Morris
Manley, Little Mildred photo,
1917 ............................**15.00**
Chim Chim Cher-ee, Julie
Andrews & Dick Van Dyke
photo, 1963 ....................**10.00**

**Dapper Dan From Dixie Land,
$12.50.**

Dear Heart, Glenn Ford & Geral-
dine Page photo, 1964 .....**8.00**
Dixie Volunteers, Edgar Leslie &
Harry Ruby, Eddie Cantor
photo, 1917 ....................**20.00**
Do Nothin' Till You Hear From
Me, Frank Sinatra photo,
1943 ..............................**10.00**
Dream Dancing, Cole Porter,
from You'll Never Get Rich,
1941 ................................**5.00**
Good-Bye Boys, Black-faced Al
Jolson, from Honeymoon
Express, 1913 ................**35.00**
Harrigan, James Cagney & George
M Cohan photo, 1933 .....**15.00**
He Wears a Pair of Silver Wings,
Kay Kyser photo, 1941 ....**5.00**

Hello Dolly, Jerry Herman,
1963 ..............................**5.00**
How Much Is That Doggie in the
Window?, Patti Page photo,
1952 ..............................**10.00**
I Believe, Drake, Graham & Stillman,
Frankie Laine photo, 1952 ..**2.00**
I Can't Give You Anything But
Love, Jimmy McHugh photo,
1928 ..............................**10.00**
I Enjoy Being a Girl, Rodgers &
Hammerstein II, 1961 ....**5.00**
I Got Plenty O' Nuttin', from
Porgy & Bess, 1935 .......**10.00**

**I'll Sing You a Thousand Love
Songs, Clark Gable and Marion
Davies photo cover, $10.00.**

I Love the Way You Say Good-
night, Doris Day & Gene Nel-
son photo, 1951 ...............**5.00**
Jesse James, Jerry Livingston,
Eileen Barton photo, 1954 .**5.00**
King Cotton March, John Philip
Sousa, 1898 ...................**30.00**
Life Goes On, Theodorakis, Anthony
Quinn photo, 1966 ..............**5.00**
Love & Passion, Richard Gere
photo, from American Gigolo,
1980 ................................**3.00**

Malaguena, Marian Banks & Ernesto LeCuona, Connie Francis photo, 1954 ........**5.00**

Oh, Johnny! Oh Johnny! Oh!; Nora Bayes photo, 1917, G .....**10.00**

On the Sentimental Side, Bing Crosby & Mary Carlisle photo, 1938 ....................**10.00**

On the South Sea Isle, Irene Bordoni photo, 1916 ............**10.00**

Piccolino, Irving Berlin, Fred Astaire & Ginger Rogers photo, 1935 ....................**15.00**

Pleasant Moments Ragtime Waltz, Scott Joplin ........**50.00**

Red Sails in the Sunset, Kennedy & Williams, Ray Noble photo, 1935 ..............................**10.00**

Rollin' Stone, Mack Gordon, Perry Como photo, 1951 ............**3.00**

Route 66, Bob Troup, Nat King Cole photo, 1946 ..............**3.00**

Sam Johnson's Colored Cake Walk, Harrigan & Braham, 1883 ..............................**20.00**

Secret Love, Doris Day & Howard Keel photo, from Calamity Jane, 1953 ......................**5.00**

Sentimental Journey, Rose Marie photo, 1944 ......................**3.00**

Shall We Dance?, Gershwin, Fred Astaire & Ginger Rogers photo, 1937 ....................**10.00**

That's Amore, Dean Martin photo, 1953 ..............................**10.00**

There's No Place Like Home for the Holidays, Stillman & Allen, 1954 ......................**5.00**

They Are Fighting Over Liberty, Pershing & Washington photo, 1918 ....................**25.00**

They're on Their Way to Mexico, Irving Berlin, 1915 ........**15.00**

Till We Meet Again, Egan & Whiting, Frederick S Manning cover artist ............**15.00**

What Will I Tell My Heart, Bing Crosby photo, 1937 .......**10.00**

You Are My Lucky Star, from Broadway Melody of 1936, Jack Benny photo .........**10.00**

You'll Never Walk Alone, Rodgers & Hammerstein II, from Carousel, 1945 .................**3.00**

You're a Grand Old Flag, George M Cohan, James Cagney & Cohan photo .................**10.00**

You Were Meant for Me, from Broadway Melody, 1929 .**10.00**

Your Cheatin' Heart, Hank Williams photo, 1952 ......**3.00**

Zip-A-Dee-Doo-Dah, Wrubel & Gilbert, from Song of the South, 1946 ...................**10.00**

# Shell Pink Milk Glass

Made by the Jeannette Glass Company from 1957 until 1959, this line is made up of a variety of their best-selling shapes and patterns. The glassware has a satiny finish, and the color is the palest of peachbloom. Refer to *Collectible Glassware of the '40s, '50s, and '60s* by Gene Florence (Collector Books.)

**Candy dish, from $10.00 to $15.00.**

Bowl, Florentine, footed, 10" .**25.00**
Bowl, fruit; Gondola, 17½" ...**25.00**
Bowl, Holiday, footed, 10½" .**40.00**

Bowl, Lombardi, design at center, footed, 10⅞" ...................**40.00**
Bowl, Lombardi, plain center, footed, 10⅞" ...................**25.00**
Cake stand, Harp, 10" .........**30.00**
Candle holder, Eagle, footed, 5¼" .............................**65.00**
Candy dish, Florigold, footed, 5¼" .............................**20.00**
Compote, Windsor, 6" ...........**20.00**
Creamer, Baltimore Pear .....**14.00**
Goblet, water; Thumbprint, footed, 8-oz ....................**12.50**
Pitcher, Thumbprint, footed, 24-oz .............................**27.50**
Relish, Vineyard, octagonal, 4-part, 12" .................................**40.00**
Sherbet; Thumbprint, footed, 5-oz ...............................**10.00**
Sugar bowl, Baltimore Pear, footed ............................**10.00**
Tray, Harp, handles, 12½x9¾" .**50.00**
Tray, Venetian, 6-part, 16½" ..**30.00**
Tumbler, juice; Thumbprint, footed, 5-oz .......................**8.00**
Vase, 7" .................................**35.00**

# Shirley Temple Collectibles

Shirley Temple's impish charm began to allure movie-goers during the early 1930s. Many people have loved and admired her not only for the delightful talent she shared with the world as a child but for her adult accomplishments as well. Please consult *Shirley Temple Dolls and Collectibles,* by Patricia R. Smith (Collector Books); or *Shirley in the Magazines* (self published) by our advisor, Gen Jones, who is listed in the Directory under Massachusetts.

Book, Susannah of the Mounties, 1st Shirley Temple edition, 1936, EX ........................**15.00**

Book, The Little Colonel, Saal-field #1895, 4½x5", EX ..**25.00**
Booklet, Story of My Life, Paramount Theaters, 1934, 16 pages, 4x5" ..............**25.00**
Cigar band, photo, set of 7, M .**15.00**
Cigarette card, scene from Curly Top, Gallaher Ltd #33, M .**8.00**

**Coloring book, *This Is My Crayon Book,* Authorized Edition, Saalfield, 1935, NM, from $35.00 to $40.00.**

Fan, teen photo w/Royal Crown Cola, paper w/stick handle, 7", EX .............................**35.00**
Figurine, brown-speckled pottery, vintage, 6", EX ..............**45.00**
Figurine, carnival chalkware, sailor outfit, 1930s, VG .**65.00**
Hankerchief, Little Colonel in opposing corners, 1930s, M ...............................**30.00**
Herald, Baby Take a Bow, VG .**30.00**
Magazine, Popular Songs, Sept 1935, 36 pages, 8½x11½", EX .................................**25.00**
Magazine ad, Hope Chest, color, ca 1945, 10x14" .............**10.00**
Photo, black & white matte from newspaper supplement, 1936, 8x10", VG .......................**12.50**
Photo, tinted close-up, ca 1935, 8x10", EX .......................**10.00**
Plate, Poor Little Rich Girl, Nostalgia, MIB ...................**40.00**

Paper doll book, *Shirley Temple Dolls and Dresses,* Authorized Edition, $65.00.

Poster, Susannah of the Mounties, 27x41", G .....................**150.00**
Program, The Bachelor & the Bobby Soxer, 8-page, NM ............**14.00**
Sewing card, 1936, 4½x7", set of 12, original box, EX ......**60.00**
Sheet music, The Good Ship Lollipop, NM .......................**15.00**
Sheet music, When I'm With You, ca 1936, 6 pages, 9x12", EX ...............................**17.50**
Slipper box, authorized photo, ca 1930s, 10x6", EX ..........**75.00**
Song album, #2, dated 1936 ..**35.00**
Storybook, Shirley Temple, Saalfield, 1935, 108 pages, 7x9¼", VG .................................**20.00**
Storybook, The Story of Shirley Temple, Saalfield #1089, 1934, 5x5" .....................**30.00**
Toy, Bearly Temple teddy bear, NM ...............................**50.00**

# Shot Glasses

Shot glasses, old and new, represent a new area of interest to today's collectors and are relatively easy to find. Basic values are given for various categories of shot glasses in mint condition. These are general prices only. Glasses that are in less-than-mint condition will obviously be worth less than the price given here. Very rare and unique items will be worth more. Sample glasses and other individual, one-of-a-kind oddities are a bit harder to classify and really need to be evaluated on an individual basis. For more information we recommend *Shot Glasses: An American Tradition,* by our advisor for this category, Mark Pickvet. He is listed in the Directory under Michigan, and information about a newsletter is given in our Clubs and Newsletters section.

Glass, heavy equipment advertising, fired-on design, 2⅜", $4.00.

Aluminum ...............................**3.00**
Glass, barrel form ..................**6.00**
Glass, coated inside & out w/black enamel to look like porcelain .........................**4.00**
Glass, Culver 22k gold ...........**8.00**
Glass, cut, whiskey tumbler .**100.00**
Glass, Depression, clear, tall .**6.00**
Glass, Depression, in colors ...**8.00**

Glass, European, gold trim, round, sm ........................**3.00**
Glass, general ........................**3.00**
Glass, general, etched ............**7.50**
Glass, general, frosted ...........**3.00**
Glass, general, frosted, w/gold trim ................................**6.00**
Glass, general, w/gold trim ....**5.00**
Glass, iridized carnival-type .**50.00**
Glass, plain advertising .........**2.00**
Glass, pressed design, whiskey tumbler ..........................**75.00**
Glass, soda advertising ........**12.50**
Glass, square, w/design .........**7.50**
Glass, square, w/etching ......**10.00**
Glass, square, w/2-tone pewter design ...........................**13.00**

Glass, tourist, Taiwan ............**3.00**
Glass, tourist, turquoise & gold design ...............................**4.00**
Glass, w/pewter design, lg ...**10.00**
Glass, w/shield design in pewter .........................**10.00**
Porcelain, general .................**7.50**
Porcelain, tourist ....................**4.00**
Pre-prohibition whiskey sample glass ...............................**20.00**

# Silhouette Pictures

Silhouette pictures with the subject matter reverse painted on the glass (which is sometimes

Photo courtesy Shirley Mace.

**Benton, couple building snowman, full-color background, convex glass, 5x4", $25.00.**

curved) were popular dime-store items from the '20s until the '50s, and you'll often see them at flea markets and antique malls. Subjects range from animals and trees to children and courting couples, and some may incorporate an advertising message or perhaps a thermometer. Refer to *The Encyclopedia of Silhouette Collectibles on Glass* (Shadow Enterprises), by Shirley Mace for more information. She is listed in the Directory under New Mexico.

Benton, colonial gent playing violin, convex glass, 5x4" ...**20.00**
Benton, colonial lady playing piano, convex glass, 8x6" ..........**38.00**
Benton, colonial lady w/parasol, convex glass, 5x4" .........**18.00**
Benton, couple admiring swans, convex glass, marked R185-18, 5x4" ......................**14.00**
Benton, couple admiring swans, convex glass, marked R185-15, 5x4" ..........................**14.00**
Benton, couple building snowman, convex glass, full-color ground w/cabin, 5x4" ....**25.00**
Benton, couple ice skating w/full-color background, convex glass, 5x4" ......................**25.00**
Benton, couple in front of house, convex glass, 8x6" .........**40.00**
Benton, couple on bridge, convex glass, 8x6" ......................**40.00**
Benton, kitten watching bird, convex glass, 5x4" ...............**22.00**
Benton, romantic couple in garden, convex glass, full color, 5x4" ................................**20.00**
Benton, ship on choppy sea, convex glass, 5x4" ...............**20.00**
Buckbee-Brehm, 'May I See You Home?' flat glass, 1932, 6x4" ............................**20.00**
Buckbee-Brehm, 'The Hidden Pool,' plaster, 8x6" ..........**9.50**

Buckbee-Brehm, 'The Love Letter,' plaster, oval, 7x5" ....**7.50**
C&A Richards, 'John Alden,' flat glass, 4x4" ......................**22.00**
Deltex, 'Senorita,' flat glass, foil background, 1933, 10x8" .**32.00**
Fisher & Flowercraft, 'To My Mother,' flat glass, 7x4½" .**20.00**
Gleam O'Gold, 'Springtime of Life,' flat glass, 6x5" ......**28.00**
Newton, 'Days of Yore,' w/thermometer, full color, flat glass, 6x8" ................................**18.00**
Peter Watson, horse & rider jumping fence, convex glass, 5" dia ..............................**14.00**
Reliance, 'Colonial Girl,' flat glass, 4x4" ......................**16.50**
Reliance, 'Cosmos & Physalis,' flat glass, 12x9" .............**28.00**
Reliance, 'Lady Faire,' flat glass, 7x5" ................................**14.00**
Reliance, Little Red Riding Hood, flat glass, 10x8" .............**28.00**
Reliance, 'Old-Fashioned Garden,' flat glass, 11x7" .............**28.00**
Reliance, Swan Pond, flat glass, full color, 7x11" ..............**32.00**
Tinsel Art, Dutch couple, flat glass, full color, 11x9" ...**28.00**
West Coast Picture Co, 'Happy in Her Garden,' flat glass, 8x5½" ..............................**22.00**

# Skookum Dolls

Skookum Indian dolls were patented in 1914 by a Montana woman, Mary McAboy. The earliest dolls had corn-husk or dried apple heads, but the ones you're most likely to find are the later dolls with composition heads. Serious collectors avoid the plastic Skookums made in the 1940s. Skookum dolls are wrapped in Indian-style blankets, and the majority have eyes looking to their right. Those looking to their left or straight ahead are rarities. Our advisor for this category is Barry Friedman; he is listed in the Directory under California.

Chief w/felt leggings, 21" ...**185.00**
Female, braided hair, 6½" ....**15.00**
Female w/buckskin shirt, 18" .**150.00**
Female w/papoose, 12" .........**90.00**
Male, eyes looking left, 10" ..**125.00**
Male, Navajo Little Deer, 9",
    MIB ..............................**70.00**
Male, Skookum Bully Good
    Indian label on bottom of foot,
    10" ...................................**75.00**
Male, unusual white hair, 10" **100.00**
Male w/apple head, early, 10" .**65.00**
Male w/feather headdress,
    14" .........................**125.00**
Papoose, mailer type w/attached
    address card, 4" ..............**8.50**

# Snowdomes

The term snowdome refers broadly to any water-filled paperweight, but there are several distinctly different styles. Round glass globes which sit on a separate base have been made in a variety of shapes and materials and were first designed in the middle of the 19th century. Flea markets offer this type (which were made in America and Italy in the '30s and '40s) as well as newer ones which are produced today in Austria and the Orient.

Small plastic half-moons with blue backs often serve as souvenirs or Christmas toys. This style originated in West Germany in the 1950s. Dozens of other shapes followed, including round and square bottles, short and tall rectangles, cubes, and other simple shapes.

Figurals made of plastic were especially popular in the 1970s. Either the entire object was an unusual shape or a figure of an animal, mermaid, etc., was draped over a large plastic dome. Today snowdomes of this type are made of glass, ceramic, or artplas (very heavy plastic) in elaborate shapes. Some collectors buy all three styles while others specialize in only one type.

For further information we recommend contacting Nancy McMichael, author of *Snowdomes*, the first illustrated book on this subject, and editor of *Snow Biz*, the first newsletter and collector club. She is listed in the Directory under the District of Columbia. See also Clubs and Newsletters.

Advertising, Co name on base,
    oily liquid, 1950s, 2¾" glass
    globe ..............................**50.00**
Ashtray, Bakelite, glass globe
    w/scene, decaled base,
    1930s ..........................**55.00**
Award, oily liquid, black or brown
    base, ca 1950s, 2¾" glass
    globe ..............................**60.00**
Bank, all plastic, souvenir scene,
    sq base, slit at back .........**8.00**
Black subjects in glass globe,
    ceramic base .................**100.00**
Calendar, perpetual; all plastic,
    2 knobs either side of sq
    base ................................**8.00**
Cartoon character, plastic, sm .**10.00**
Christmas theme, plastic half-
    moon, sm .........................**5.00**
Commemorative (moon landing,
    etc), plastic bottle form .**25.00**
Disney character, plastic
    dome, marked Monogram,
    1960s .......................**30.00**

Disney character, styles other than above listing .........**12.00**

Figure, animal draped across lg plastic dome ...................**10.00**

Figure, animal w/water ball 'tummy,' 1970s ................**12.00**

Figure, cartoon character, plastic, 1970s .............................**50.00**

Figure, clown w/water ball 'tummy,' 1970s ................**30.00**

Figure, Indian w/water ball 'tummy,' 1970s ................**40.00**

Fraternal, oily liquid, glass globe on black base, flat sides, 1950s .............................**60.00**

Marx, copyrighted plastic half-moon, 1960s, set of 6, MIB ..........................**50.00**

Religious theme, saint in glass globe, decal on plastic base, 1930s .............................**40.00**

Roly-poly, Santa or snowman on top half of water compartment, 1970s ...................**20.00**

Saint or souvenir scene in glass atop shell base, Italy, 1940s ..........................**12.00**

Shakers, souvenir scene or place plaque inside, plastic, 1950s, ea ...................................**12.00**

Snowman, glass globe on plastic or ceramic base, 1940s ..**30.00**

Souvenir, glass w/bisque figure, Bakelite base, decal, 1940s ..........................**40.00**

Souvenir, glass w/bisque figure, ceramic base, decal, ca 1940s ...........................**40.00**

Souvenir, plastic, city, any shape ............................**7.00**

Souvenir, plastic, sm tourist attraction, any shape ......**8.00**

Souvenir, plastic, state, any shape ..............................**6.00**

Souvenir, plastic, television shape ..............................**7.00**

Souvenir, plastic, treasure chest shape ..............................**8.00**

World's Fair, glass w/bisque Trilon & Perisphere, 1939 .......**75.00**

World's Fair, plastic ball on red calendar base ................**20.00**

World's Fair, plastic half-moon shape ..............................**15.00**

Photo courtesy Nancy McMichael.

**Souvenir, small tourist attraction, any shape, $8.00; Perpetual calendar, all plastic, knob on either side of square base, $8.00.**

World War II general or serviceman, glass globe on ceramic base ...............................**50.00**

# Sports Collectibles

Memorabilia related to sports of any kind is attracting a following of collectors, many of which specialize in the particular sport that best holds their interests. See also Baseball Cards; Dolls, Celebrity; Golf Collectibles; Pin-Back Buttons; Sports Pins.

Beanie, World Series 1960 Pittsburgh, felt, rare .............**65.00**
Book, Guide to Best Fishing, 1948, dust jacket, NM .....**4.00**
Book, Ked's Handbook, baseball player cover, 1928, 48 pages, EX ..................................**12.50**
Book, Martin Basketball Storybook, Book Inc, 1952, dust jacket, NM ......................**5.00**
Book, 500 Miles To Go, 1961, Coward-McCann, 287 pages, dust jacket, VG .............**25.00**
Booklet, Official Softball Rules, 1935, 32 pages, EX ........**26.00**

Booklet, Tipps From Topps on How To Play Baseball, ca 1960s, NM ....................**25.00**
Candy box, Milwaukee Braves on baseball form box, 1958, NM .............................**185.00**
Cap, New York Yankees, ca 1979, M ....................................**12.00**
Comic book, Magnum Comics Vol 1 No 1, Mickey Mantle, 1991, 32 pages, M ....................**8.00**
Football, Joe Namath signature series, marked Franklin, M ..........**75.00**
Game, Eddy Arcaro Blue Grass Handicap Horse Race Game, Transogram, 1962 .........**40.00**
Game, Verne Gagne World Champion Wrestling, Gardner, 1950s, VG .....................................**50.00**
Glove & ball set, Eddie Yost, MIB .............................**85.00**
Handbook, NCAA Official Football Rules, 1967, VG .......**6.00**
Helmet, New York Jets, used in game ...........................**220.00**
Letter opener, golf ball w/celluloid blade, ca 1930s, 8", NM .**75.00**
Magazine ad, Johnny Bench & Shick razors, black & white, 1973, 11x5" ......................**3.00**
Magazine ad, Mickey Mantle & Armour Franks, 1967, 14x10", NM ...**12.50**

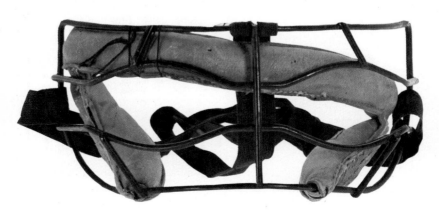

**Catcher's mask for girl, EX, $54.00.**

**Kellogg Sports Library, copyright 1934, EX, $16.00.**

Magazine ad, Ted Williams & Stan Musial for Chesterfields, 1947, 8x10", NM ...........**20.00**

Necktie rack, Over the Fence for TIE Score, wood, ca 1920s, 7x11" ..............................**35.00**

Pamphlet, How To Play Winning Football, 1930s, NM ......**45.00**

Pennant, Ali Vs Foreman, Fight of Century on red felt, NM ..**25.00**

Pennant, Chicago Bears, ca 1950, 28", M ............................**45.00**

Pennant, Indianapolis Motor Speedway May 1940 on yellow felt, M ......................**65.00**

Pennant, St Louis Browns & mascot on felt, 9" .................**45.00**

Photo, Carl Yastrzemski, 1960s, M ....................................**15.00**

Photo, Mike Tyson in boxing pose, 8x10", M .........................**12.50**

Place mat, Detroit Tiger World Series/Big Boy, 1984, EX .**5.00**

Postcard, Gaylord Perry, Atlanta Braves, real photo, 1970s, NM ................................**18.00**

Poster, Canseco & McGwire, The Bash Brothers, 1988, 24x36", EX ....................................**8.00**

Poster, Isiah Thomas Say No to Drugs, 18x24", M .........**10.00**

Poster, Ken Griffey Jr, The Next Generation, 1989, 24x36", EX ....................................**10.00**

Poster, New York Knicks, Crunch 'n Munch, 1985-1986, 36x24", M ....................................**12.50**

Poster, Nolan Ryan, Texas Heat, Costacos, 1990, 24x36", EX .................**10.00**

Poster, Welcome Home Dinner... NY Yankees..., April 18, 1958, 14x22" ..........................**60.00**

Price list, Golf Iron Heads...Clubs, Gibson Co, 1914, 1 page, 5x8", VG .........................**20.00**

Program, California Angels & NY Yankees, 1965, unscored, NM ...............................**12.50**

Program, Cleveland Browns & Indians, 1948, EX .........**20.00**

Program, New York Giants Vs Pittsburgh Steelers, 1962, M ...............................**35.00**

Program, Rutgers-Columbia, Baker Field, Sept 27, 1947, NM ...............................**17.50**

Program, Sonja Henie, 1952, EX ...........................**22.00**

Program, Tyson Vs Spinks, M .**55.00**

Ruler, Reds team color photo, ca 1970s, 12", M ................**35.00**

Switch plate, plastic dimensional football player's head, NM ......................**5.50**

T-shirt, San Francisco 49ers NFC Champions, printed cotton, 1987, M .........................**25.00**

Ticket, Penn Palestra, Ohio State Vs Penn, 1930, color, EX .**8.00**

Ticket Stub, Joe Louis Vs Lee Ramage, 1935, EX .........**22.50**

Wire photo, baseball, black & white, 1984, 8x10", EX ...**2.00**

Yearbook, Harlem Globetrotters Silver Anniversary, 1952, M ......................**35.00**

Yearbook, New York Giants Yearbook, 1954, M ................**95.00**

Yearbook, San Francisco Giants, 1967, M ..........................**75.00**

Yearbook, Topps Baseball Sticker 1982, EX ..........................**5.00**

# Sports Pins

Sports pins are given away by major league baseball sponsors at ballparks. Some sponsors such as Unocal and Chevron have a specific game night when a pin is given away to fans at the gate. The pin is then sold at participating stations while supplies last. Our advisor is Tony George, who is listed in the Directory under California.

A's, California Raisins, Rickey Henderson Night ...........**20.00**

A's, 1988, Unocal, set of 4 ....**40.00**

A's, 1994, Unocal, Stars of Tomorrow, set of 3 ......................**9.00**

Angels, 1992, Sport Mart/Rawlings (Nolan Ryan/4 No Hitters), set of 4 ..................**50.00**

Angels, 1994, Snapple, Dean Chance, Cy Young Award, 25th Anniversary ............**7.00**

Blue Jays, 1993, Domino's Pizza, World Series Trophy, Opening Day ..............................**20.00**

Braves, Chevron, NL Champions, set of 3 ..........................**18.00**

Braves, 1990, Coca-Cola, 25th Anniversary Season ......**10.00**

Braves, 1993, Chevron, Opening Day, Back to Back NL West Champs ..........................**8.00**

Brewers, 1988, Unocal, set of 4 ..............................**20.00**

Brewers, 1991, US Oil Co, set of 4 ......................................**24.00**

Cardinals, 1987 to 1990, Levi Strause, from $7 to .......**15.00**

Cardinals, 1991, Coca-Cola .**15.00**

Cardinals, 1992, Coca-Cola/ National, 100th Anniversary, set of 10 ........................**55.00**

**Cardinals, 1993, Coca-Cola, Rockies and Marlins, first series, set of three (only one shown), $35.00.**

Cardinals, 1994, Coca-Cola/ Quiktrip, NL Central Division ..............................**10.00**

Cubs, 1988, Unocal, set of 4 ..**18.00**

Cubs, 1990, Unocal, set of 4 ..**12.00**

Cubs, 1994, Builders Square, set of 2 ..................................**8.00**

Dodgers, 1987, Unocal, 25th Anniversary, set of 6 .....**18.00**

Dodgers, 1990, Unocal, United Way Centennial ..............**8.00**

Giants, 1989, Chevron, set of 3 ..............................**30.00**

Giants, 1990, Chevron, set of 4 ..............................**20.00**

Giants, 1991, Chevron, Hall of Fame inductees, set of 3 .**18.00**

Giants, 1993, Coca-Cola, Rockies/Marlins, first series, set of 3 ......................................**60.00**

Indians, 1988, Unocal, set of 4 ..............................**20.00**

Indians, 1989, Unocal, set of 4 ..............................**18.00**

Indians, 1991, Sunoco, Logo History, set of 5 ..................**25.00**

Indians, 1992, Sunoco, Historical Stadiums, set of 4 .........**20.00**

Indians, 1992, Sunoco, 60th Anniversary, set of 4 .....**20.00**

Mariners, 1988, Unocal, set of 4 ..................................**12.00**

Mariners, 1990, Red Apple Farms, set of 5 ...............**50.00**

Mariners, 1992, Chevron, Seattle Power Company, set of 5 ....................................**25.00**

Mariners, 1993, Dairy Queen, Award Winners, set of 5 ....................................**20.00**

Marlins, 1993, Bumble Bee Seafoods Inc., Inaugural Year ................................**75.00**

Mets, 1990, Sharp Electronics, World Series Championships, set of 4 ...........................**25.00**

Mets, 1993, Chemical Bank, First Games, Rockies/Marlins, set of 2 ...................................**10.00**

Mets, 1994, Chemical Bank, 25th Anniversary Themes, set of 5 ...........................**20.00**

Orioles, 1989, Toyota, World Series Titles, set of 3 .....**30.00**

Orioles, 1991, Toyota/Memorial Stadium Commission, set of 2 .....................................**25.00**

Orioles, 1993, Coca-Cola, All-Star Fan Fest .........................**10.00**

Padres, 1986, Great American Bank, Nate Clobert .......**10.00**

Padres, 1987, Great American Bank, Willie Mc-Covey .............................**12.00**

Padres, 1990, Vons/Coca-Cola, Gary Templeton ............**12.00**

Padres, 1992, Upper Deck, All-Star Fan Fest ..................**6.00**

Pirates, 1990, TCBY Yogurt, World Series Championships, set of 5 ...........................**40.00**

Pirates, 1991, Block Buster Video, Record Setters, set of 5 ....................................**35.00**

Pirates, 1992, Block Buster Video, Player Jerseys w/Numbers, set of 5 ...........................**25.00**

Pirates, 1994, Gatorade, All-Star Programs, set of 4 .........**20.00**

Rangers, 1990, Chevron, Ryan Records, set of 4 ............**20.00**

Rangers, 1993, Dr Pepper, Logo History & Ryan Farewell, set of 4 ................................**24.00**

Rockies, 1993, Coca-Cola/7-Eleven, First Games Played Vs NL, set of 13 .............**60.00**

Rockies, 1994, Coca-Cola, set of 7 ....................................**21.00**

Royals, 1989, Western Auto, Dated Logo, Brett & White, set of 3 ...........................**35.00**

Royals, 1990, Phillips 66, Dated Logo & Saberhagen, set of 2 .......................**20.00**

Royals, 1993, Phillips 66, 25th Anniversary, set of 2 .....**18.00**

Tigers, 1989, Unocal, set of 4 .**16.00**

Tigers, 1990, Unocal, set of 4 .**12.00**

Tigers, 1993, Little Caesars, World Series Highlights, set of 5 .................................**25.00**

Twins, 1989, Unocal, set of 4 .**16.00**

Twins, 1992, Gatorade, Tony Oliva .................................**12.00**

White Sox, 1989, Coca-Cola, Historical Events, set of 6 ..**35.00**

White Sox, 1990, Coca-Cola, Logo History, set of 5 .............**25.00**

White Sox, 1991, Scott Peterson Ballpark Franks, Hats, set of 4 .....................................**12.00**

White Sox, 1991, Unocal, set of 2 ....................................**8.00**

White Sox, 1992, Scott Peterson Ballpark Franks, Logos, set of 4 .................................**16.00**

White Sox, 1994, AFLAC, F Thomas, 1993 MVP .........**6.00**

White Sox, 1994, Unocal, 125th Anniversary of Baseball Logo ................................**5.00**

# Stangl

Originally known as the Fulper Pottery, the Stangl Company was founded in 1913 and until its closing in 1972 produced many lines of dinnerware as well as various types of artware. Birds modeled after the prints of Audubon were introduced in the early 1940s. More than one hundred different birds were produced, most of which are marked with 'Stangl' and a four-digit number to identify the species. Though a limited few continue to be produced, since 1976 they have been marked with the date of their production.

## Birds

Bird of Paradise, #3408 .....**100.00**
Blue Jay, #3715, w/peanut .**550.00**
Bluebird, #3276 ....................**88.00**
Broadbill Hummingbird, #3629 .**125.00**
Cardinal, #3444, pink, 6" .....**85.00**
Carolina Wren, #3590 ........**165.00**
Cerulean Warbler, #3456, 4½" .**65.00**
Chickadees, #3581 .............**225.00**
Cockatoo, #3584, 11⅜" .......**245.00**
Drinking Duck, #3250E .......**75.00**
Flying Duck, #3443, teal green .**350.00**
Golden Crown Kinglet, #3848 .**85.00**
Grey's Cardinal, #3596, 4¾" .**80.00**
Key West Quail Dove, #3454, 1 wing up ........................**275.00**
Oriole, #3402, 3¼" ................**60.00**
Painted Bunting, #3452 .......**90.00**
Rivoli Hummingbird, #3627, w/pink flowers .............**125.00**
Titmouse, #3592, 2½" ...........**55.00**
Wilson Warbler, #3597, yellow, 3½" ................................**50.00**
Wren, #3401 .........................**65.00**

## Dinnerware

Bowl, Festival, Terra Rose, deep, 11½" ...............................**75.00**
Bowl, fruit; Amber Glo, 5⅝" ...**8.00**
Bowl, fruit; Chicory ................**9.00**
Bowl, salad; Provinicial; 11" **35.00**
Butter dish, Provincial ........**35.00**
Celery tray, Blue Daisy ........**20.00**
Cream & sugar bowl, Prelude .**22.00**
Creamer, Country Garden ...**12.00**
Creamer & sugar bowl, Prelude ...........................**22.00**
Cup & saucer, Blueberry .....**12.00**
Cup & saucer, Country Life .**40.00**
Cup & saucer, Festival, Terra Rose .............................**15.00**
Cup & saucer, Provincial .....**12.50**
Mug, Golden Blossom ..........**20.00**
Pitcher, Apple Delight, 2-qt .**35.00**
Plate, Blueberry, 8" ..............**10.00**
Plate, Country Garden, 12½" .**40.00**
Plate, dinner; Fruit ..............**17.50**
Plate, First Love, 10" ...........**15.00**
Plate, Orchard Song, 8" .......**10.00**
Platter, Colonial, 12" ...........**26.00**

**Orchard Song, Salt and pepper shakers, $15.00 for the pair; Gravy boat, 9", $17.50.**

Teapot, Country Garden ......**65.00**
Teapot, Thistle ....................**55.00**

# Star Trek Collectibles

Star Trek has influenced American culture like no other show in the history of television. Gene Roddenberry introduced the Star Trek concept in 1964, and it has been gaining fans ever since. The longevity of the television show in syndication, the release of six major motion pictures, and the success of Star Trek the Next Generation television show have literally bridged two generations of loyal fans. This success has spawned thousands of clothing, ceramic, household, jewelry, and promotional items; calendars; plates; comics; coins; costumes; films; games; greeting and gum cards; party goods; magazines; models; posters; props; puzzles; records and tapes; school supplies; and a wide assortment of toys. Most of these still turn up at flea markets around the country, and all are very collectible. Double the value for an excellent condition item when the original box or packaging is present. For further information and more listings, see *Schroeder's Collectible Toys, Antique to Modern* (Collector Books).

Belt buckle, Paramount Pictures, 1979, M, from $6 to .......**10.00**
Book, Star Fleet Technical Manual, Ballantine, 1975, from $50 to .............................**75.00**
Book, The Enterprise Log, comic format, ca 1976, 224 pages, from $10 to ....................**15.00**
Book & record set, MIP (sealed), from $8 to ......................**12.00**

Calendar, The Next Generation, 1992, NM ........................**10.00**
Candy, Next Generation Photon Candies (jelly beans), New Age, 1991, MIB .............**45.00**
Decanter, Mr Spock bust, 1979, MIB, from $40 to ..........**60.00**
Figure, Captain Kirk, The Motion Picture, Mego, 3¾", EX ...**8.00**
Figure, Comander Riker, Galoob, 1988, 3¾", MIP, from $10 to ..........**12.00**
Figure, Dr McCoy, The Motion Picture, 3¾", EX .............**12.00**

**Figure, Lt. Uhura, Mego, MOC, $50.00.**

Figure, Mr Spock, Mego, 1974, 8", MIP, from $50 to ..........**60.00**
Figure, Mr Spock, PVC, Presents, 1992, 4", MIP ...................**4.00**
Figure, Scotty, Mego, 8", EX+ .**50.00**
Figure, Tasha Yar, Galoob, 1988, 3¾", MIP, from $20 to ...**25.00**
Figure, Troi, Playmates, MIP ..**25.00**
Game, Star Trek Trivia, 1985, MIB, from $35 to ..........**45.00**
Greeting card, ca 1970s, set of 6, MIP, from $8 to .............**12.00**
Gum cards, Impel, 1991, series 1, set of 160, from $18 to ..**20.00**
Key chain, Enterprise, Smithsonian exclusive issue, 1993, MIP .**10.00**
Kite, Enterprise on plastic, Hi-Flier, Delta style, 1992, 50", MIP ..................................**8.00**

Ornament, Next Generation Enterprise, Hallmark, 1993, MIB ................................**45.00**

Ornament, Starship USS Enterprise, Hallmark, 1991, MIB .....**350.00**

Paint set, The Motion Picture, Whitling, 1979, MIP .....**20.00**

Phaser, Official Starfleet Defensive Weapon, Playmates, 1992, MIB ......................**12.00**

Playset, Ferengi Fighter, Galoob, MIB, from $35 to ...........**50.00**

Program, International 1974 Convention, Mr Spock on cover, NM .................................**17.00**

**Record, 33⅓ rpm in original sleeve, Sytar, Power Records, FF-2296, from $10.00 to $15.00.**

Tablet, Kirk on cover, 1960s, NM .............................**38.00**

Vehicle, Klingon Warship, Star Trek II, #149, Corgi, MIP .........**20.00**

Vehicle, Next Generation spaceship set w/Borg ship, Galoob, 1993, MIP ......................**18.00**

Vehicle, USS Enterprise, Star Trek V, Ertl, 4½", MIP ..**20.00**

# Star Wars Collectibles

Capitalizing on the ever-popular space travel theme, the movie 'Star Wars' with its fantastic special effects was a mega box office hit of the late 1970s. A sequel called 'Empire Strikes Back' (1980) and a third adventure called 'Return of the Jedi' (1983) did just as well, and as a result, licensed merchandise flooded the market, much of it produced by the Kenner Company. Refer to *Modern Toys, American Toys 1930 to 1980,* by Linda Baker and *Schroeder's Collectible Toys, Antique to Modern,* (both by Collector Books) for more information. See also Halloween; Lunch Boxes.

**Figure, Han Solo, tri-logo card, 1983, MOC, $35.00.**

Blueprint, set of 15, 1977, M w/10x7½" plastic pouch, from $35 to ............................**50.00**

Book, coloring; Lando, Leia, Chewbacca & Han, Kenner, 1980, M ...........................**8.00**

Cake pan, Darth Vader, aluminum w/paper insert, 1980, M ...................................**12.00**

Clock, talking alarm; R2-D2 & C-3PO, MIB, from $75 to .**100.00**

Collector case, Darth Vader bust, black plastic, Kenner, EX .**15.00**

Figure, B-Wing Pilot, Power of the Force, 3¾", MOC ...........**12.00**

Figure, Chewbacca, Kenner, 1978-80, 15", NM, from $70 to .**90.00**

Figure, Klaatu, 3¾", MOC, from $12 to ..............**15.00**

Figure, Leia Organa, 1979, 11½", VG, from $30 to .............**50.00**

Figure, Rancor Monster, Kenner, 1983, 10", MIB ..............**35.00**

Game, Escape From Death Star, Kenner, 1977, NMIB .....**18.00**

Puzzle, Space Battle, Kenner, 1977, 500-pc, MIB .........**15.00**

Record Tote, Star Wars, EX .**12.00**

Salt & pepper shakers, Yoda figure, Sigma, ca 1977, pr, M ..............................**175.00**

Toothbrushes, Oral B, MIB .**10.00**

Vehicle, Endor Forest Ranger, Mini-Rigs, Kenner, NMIB ........**25.00**

Vehicle, Landspeeder, diecast, Kenner, EX ...................**30.00**

Vehicle, Millenium Falcon, diecast, Kenner, EX ......**30.00**

Vehicle, Millenium Falcon, Kenner, 1977, 23", NMIB ..**120.00**

Vehicle, Rebel Armored Snow Speeder, MIB ................**95.00**

Vehicle, Scout Walker, Kenner, 1982, complete, 11", EX .**15.00**

# Statue of Liberty Collectibles

For over one hundred years the Statue of Liberty has been the single object universally identified with our country. Hundreds of companies have adopted the name and symbol to represent their products, and Ms. Liberty's second century began with an outpouring of new, high-quality representations which accompanied her 1986 restoration. These included items such as ceramic pins, American-made Liberty statues, watches, knives, medals, prints, and scores of other objects adorned with Liberty's likeness.

Because of her wide appeal, so many varied products were made that flea market hunts result in exciting finds. Few collecting fields offer the opportunity for such diversity; some Liberty collectors have chosen to limit their searches to specific areas, such as postcards,

**Mug, Chewbacca, California Originals, 1977, 7", $60.00.**

Mug, Darth Vader, Sigma, MIB ..........................**28.00**

Night light, Chewbacca, 2½", MIP, from $5 to ......................**10.00**

Picture frame, C3-PO, ceramic, Sigma, 5x7", MIB ..........**25.00**

Playset, Droid Factory, Kenner, 1977, MIB ......................**75.00**

Playset, Ewok Village, Kenner, 1983, NMIB, from $65 to ...........**85.00**

Puzzle, Attack of the Sand People, Kenner, 1977, 140-pc, MIB ...............................**8.00**

medals, or ephemera. Our advisor is Mike Brooks, who is listed in the Directory under California.

**Figural thermometer, cast metal with copper patina, marked Made in USA, 5¾", $18.00.**

Letter opener, sterling, Germany, from $20 to ....................**30.00**
Mardi Gras doubloon, w/Liberty design, minimum value ..**1.00**
Pin-back button, Liberty Loan, minimum value ...............**5.00**
Plate, rolled edge, Rowland & Marsellus, from $75 to .**100.00**
Pocket watch, commemorative, quartz, 1986, w/papers, MIB .............................**50.00**

Poster, Lest I Perish, from $100 to ..................................**150.00**
Stereoview card, ca 1870s, from $75 to ...........................**125.00**
Thermometer, cast metal w/copper patina, marked Made in USA, 5¾" .......................**18.00**

## Strawberry Shortcake Collectibles

Strawberry Shortcake came onto the market around 1980 with a bang. The line included everything to attract small girls from swimsuits, bed linens, blankets, anklets, underclothing, coats, shoes, sleeping bags, dolls and accessories, games, toys, and delightful items to decorate their rooms. It was short lived, though, lasting only until near the middle of the decade. Our advisor is Geneva Addy; she is listed in the Directory under Iowa.

Balloons, Happy Birthday .....**2.00**
Bassinet, pink wicker on stand, 18x20" ............................**50.00**
Book, Crazy Baking Contest, hardcover .........................**6.00**
Book, The Winter That Wouldn't End, softcover, 8x11" .......**5.00**
Candy dish, strawberry form, porcelain w/gold trim, #50064, 5x6" ....................**8.00**
Canister, glass w/lid, 7" .........**6.00**
Carrying case, strawberry form, 12" ..................................**15.00**
Christmas lights, Strawberry Shortcake figurals, electric, 1 strand ..........................**10.00**
Clock, alarm; Big Ben type ..**30.00**
Doll, rag type, 18" ...............**30.00**
Dress pattern, girl's size 2-3-4 .**10.00**
Figurine, Strawberry Shortcake or friends, miniature, ea .**6.00**

**Big Berry Trolley, 1982, $20.00.**

**Doll, Apricot with Hopsalot, #43370, MIB, $20.00.**

Game, Win by a Whisker, cards .**3.50**
Halloween costume, w/mask, marked Age 8 ................**20.00**
Night light, strawberry form, battery operated ..................**12.00**
Record, I Love You or Splash Dance Party, 78 rpm, ea .**6.00**
Roller skates ..........................**20.00**
Soap dish, Strawberry Shortcake & Custard, floats .............**5.00**
Telephone pad ........................**3.00**
Tumbler, glass, 6" ...................**6.50**
Wastepaper basket .................**8.00**

## String Holders

Until the middle of this century, spools of string contained in devices designed for that purpose were a common sight in country grocery stores as well as many other businesses.

Today they're all collectible, with early examples of cast iron or wire and those with advertising the most desirable and valuable. Later figurals of chalkware or ceramics are also quite collectible.

Apple, litho tin, 2-pc, 4x4", EX ............................**75.00**
Apples & berries, painted chalkware, EX .........................**32.00**
Ball type, cast iron w/hinge, ca 1910, EX .......................**110.00**
Beehive, cast iron w/ornate wrapped rope design, Pat 1860 ...............................**95.00**
Bird, yellow on green string nest, ceramic ...........................**30.00**

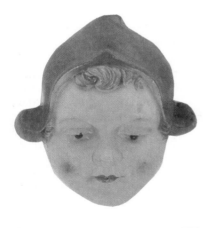

**Dutch girl, chalkware, 8", EX, $45.00.**
Court jester, painted plaster .**45.00**
Lady, Victorian dress, china .**30.00**
Lady in chair, ceramic, NM .**45.00**
Love bird, porcelain .............**30.00**
Sailor, eyes to side, w/pipe, chalkware ...............................**35.00**
Strawberry w/face, chalkware, EX ..................................**40.00**
Top hat w/face, painted chalkware, EX ........................**45.00**

# Sunday Comics

Sunday funnies in color have been issued continuously since 1896. Early comics included The Yellow Kid, Katzenjammer Kids, and Little Nemo. The '30s spawned Buck Rogers, Flash Gordon, Dick Tracy, and Superman. The pages of these and comic book through the '80s are actively collected by a growing number of fans. Our advisor is David H. Begin, who is listed in the Directory under California.

Alley Oop, 1934-38, per page .**4.00**
Alley Oop, 1944, half-page .....**1.00**
Any comics w/paper dolls, 1930s-50s, per page, ea, from $1 to ...................**10.00**
Buck Rogers, 1931, per page .**15.00**
Buck Rogers, 1952, complete year .........................**200.00**
Calvin & Hobbes, 1989, complete year ...............................**15.00**
Dick Tracy, 1932, per page ...**12.00**
Dick Tracy, 1943, full page ....**4.00**
Dick Tracy, 1952, complete year .........................**125.00**
Donald Duck, 1936, per page .**4.00**
Donald Duck, 1958, complete year ...............................**15.00**
Doonesbury, 1971, complete year ...........................**40.00**
Flash Gordon, 1934, complete year .........................**1,800.00**
Katzenjammer Kids, 1904, per page ...............................**10.00**
Katzenjammer Kids, 1925, per page ..................................**3.00**
Li'l Abner, 1949, complete year .........................**75.00**
Little Orphan Annie, 1942, full page ..................................**2.50**
Prince Valiant, 1940, per page .**6.00**
Prince Valiant, 1973, complete year ...............................**35.00**

Red Ryder, 1940, full page .....**4.00**
Tarzan, 1933, per page ...........**8.00**
Tarzan, 1990, complete year .**20.00**
The Phantom, 1940, complete
    year ..............................**225.00**
The Phantom, 1942, half-page ..**2.00**
Thimble Theatre w/Popeye, 1941,
    full page ..........................**4.00**

## Swanky Swigs

Swanky Swigs are the reusable glasses that originally contained Kraft cheese spreads. They came in various colors (light and dark blue, yellow, green, brown, black, and red) decorated with a mixture of different flowers (jonquils, corn flowers, posies, etc.). There was also a series called Carnival that utilized glass with allover color, however this series didn't stay in production very long as the contents couldn't be seen. Our advisor, Melvin Fountain, is listed in the Directory under Kansas.

Antique, from $2 to ................**3.00**
Bands, from $2 to ..................**3.00**
Bustlin' Betsy (Victorian), from $2
    to ......................................**3.00**
Carnival (Fiesta), from $4 to .**10.00**
Checkerboard, minimum value .**25.00**
Circles & Dots, from $3 to .....**5.00**
Flowers, from $2 to ...............**3.00**
Sailboats (Racing & Sailing), from
    $10 to .............................**15.00**
Special, Bicentennials, from $7
    to ...................................**15.00**
Special, Texas Centennial, mini-
    mum value .....................**10.00**

## Swatch Watches

Swatch watches, one of the hottest new collectibles in the United States, have been around since 1983 when a few nondescript watches were produced. Along the way something happened. They began to show up in unusual colors and original designs and became a sensation in Europe as fashion watches. Recently a Swatch watch brought

**Animal (Kiddie Kups) or Flowers, from $2.00 to $3.00 each.**

343

over $25,000.00 at auction. While this is not typical of Swatch values, it does add to the aura of Swatch, and it seems everyone must own one. Rare Swatches can still be found at garage sales and flea markets. Even the early models are now highly desirable.

Condition is extremely important. To bring the highest price, a watch must be brand new and never worn. While there is some interest in used Swatches, this market is better left to advanced collectors and experienced dealers. All Swatches are dated on the back. The first number is usually the year of manufacture. Example: 5123 — the 5 indicates 1985, the 12 the twelfth week of the year, and the 3 the third day of the week. Most Swatches are assigned a model number by the factory. These numbers do not appear on the watch.

Collector's clubs have been organized in many countries; some have as many as 20,000 members. In 1991 the first monthly Swatch magazine hit the stands in Italy, only to be completely sold out in less than one week. Refer to *Collector's Guide for Swatch Watches* published by W.B.S. Marketing, our advisors for this category. They are listed in the Directory under California.

Values are given for watches mint in box with guarantee papers. Used watches are worth about 50% less.

Ascot, GW 117, 1990, from $60 to ....................................**70.00**
Betty Lou, LN 111, 1990, from $30 to ............................**40.00**
Black Inlay, GB 145, 1991, from $50 to ............................**60.00**

Blue Bay, LK 106, 1987, from $40 to ....................................**50.00**
Blue Flamingo, GN 114, 1991, from $70 to ....................**80.00**

**Bondi Beach, Wipeout, GJ 102, 1989, Spring/ Summer, $110.00 mint in box.**

Casbah Rock, LN 105, 1989, from $70 to .............................**80.00**
Chelsea, LB 112, 1986, from $40 to ....................................**50.00**
Classique, GB 703, 1984, from $220 to .........................**250.00**
Cosmic Encounter, GS 102, 1986, from $230 to ................**310.00**

Crystal Surprise, GZ 126, 1994 ...........................**80.00**

Cunegonde, LK 149, 1994 ....**50.00**

Dark Vader, GK 110, 1988, from $110 to ...........................**130.00**

Follow Me, GJ 101, 1987, from $160 to ...........................**180.00**

GB 101, GB 101, 1983, from $360 to ...................................**390.00**

Godefroi, GK 174, 1994 ........**50.00**

Hypocampus, SDK 103, 1991, from $80 to ....................**90.00**

JFK, SCN 103, 1993, from $70 to ....................................**80.00**

Limelight II, LB 113, 1986, from $180 to ...........................**200.00**

Medusa, SDK 102, 1991, from $90 to ..................................**100.00**

Mint Drops, SDK 108/09, 1993, from $50 to ....................**60.00**

Pirelli, LM 102, 1984, from $220 to ...................................**250.00**

Polar Ice, LJ 104, 1992, from $30 to ....................................**40.00**

Roi Soleil, GZ 127, 1993, from $190 to ...........................**220.00**

Sixty Three Lui, GM 703, 1993, from $40 to ....................**50.00**

Snow Collage, LK 138, 1992, from $30 to ............................**40.00**

Soto, GB 109, 1986, from $130 to ...............................**150.00**

Tisane, GK 162, 1993, from $40 to ....................................**50.00**

Trevi, LB 117, 1987, from $60 to ....................................**70.00**

Tutti, GW 700, from $60 to ..**70.00**

Typesetter, GK 131, 1991, from $60 to ............................**70.00**

Variation, SLN 101, 1994 ....**50.00**

White Memphis, LW 102, from $180 to ...........................**210.00**

# Teapots

Tea drinking and the serving of 'afternoon tea' has enjoyed a resurgence of popularity in recent years, sparking an ever-growing interest in teapots. Though the first teapots were manufactured as far back as the late 16th century, early examples (including those from the 1700s and 1800s) can still sometimes be found in museums, and occasionally they will be offered for sale by the larger auction houses.

Almost every pottery and porcelain manufacturer in Europe, Asia and America has produced teapots. Most collectors start with a general collection of many different teapots until they finally isolate the specific type that holds the most appeal for them. Among the various collectible divisions of teapots are miniatures, doll or toy sets, those made by a certain manufacturer or with a particular style or type of decoration. Figural teapots are very popular. Many were made in Japan for the export market in the '50s and '60s, during their reconstruction period.

Two new books on teapots are available. *Teapots*, by our advisor, Tina M. Carter, (listed in the Directory under California), is a collector's guide to selecting, displaying, and researching modern and vintage teapots. *Novelty Teapots,* by Edward Bramah, is a coffee table-style book available in England from John Ives Bookseller, 5 Normanhurst Drive, Tickenham, Middlesex, TW1 1NA, England; because of the rate of exchange it's best ordered by charge card. See also Clubs and Newsletters.

**Ellgreave, Marked Div of Wood & Sons England, with florals, large, 4-cup, $30.00; small, 2-cup, $25.00.**

Aluminum, wicker on handle, marked Japan, 2-cup ......**6.00**

Beswick, various Dickens characters, NM ........................**45.00**

Brass w/hand decoration, lg bulbous base, marked India, 2-cup ..................................**14.00**

Brass w/hand decoration, slim handle & spout, footed base, 1-cup .............................**10.00**

British Royal Navy, brown, coralene, rope mark, NM .....**35.00**

Brown Betty, pottery, marked ALB, Made in England .**15.00**

Cottageware, marked Price Brothers, England, 6½" ..........**50.00**

Cube, Hall, British patent numbers, color other than red or cobalt .............................**18.00**

Cube, Hall, British patent numbers, red or cobalt, ea ....**22.00**

Cube, marked Staffordshire England, florals or scrolls, new .........**16.00**

Ironstone, marked w/wreath, Poland, 6-cup .................**10.00**

Japan, coralene, raised enamel dots & flowers, 2-cup ......**8.00**

Japan, coralene w/gold trim, marked, 6-cup, NM .......**11.00**

Japan, majolica, half-circle form, marked ..........................**14.00**

Japan, majolica, men at table w/ale, marked ................**15.00**

Milk glass, unmarked, w/lid, 1¼", +2 cups & saucers ...........**8.00**

Moss Rose, electric, marked Japan, 2-cup .................**14.00**

Moss Rose, marked Made in Japan, w/music box .......**30.00**

Novelty, airplane, SS Tea on side, ceramic w/gold trim, Fitz & Floyd .............................**48.00**

Novelty, cat, ceramic w/paw spout, tail handle, marked CMI, Japan ....................**30.00**

Novelty, cat, white china, marked China, 2-cup ..................**10.00**

Novelty, chef w/bee on nose, ceramic, Japan ..............**35.00**

Novelty, duck, ceramic w/frog on lid ..................................**25.00**

Novelty, elephant w/howdah, lustre ceramic, Japan ........**40.00**

Novelty, friar, ceramic, marked w/number, not Goebel ...**18.00**

Novelty, girl, ceramic, marked Red Wing ......................**49.00**

Novelty, Kilban Cat in white tuxedo, ceramic, Sigma .**85.00**

Novelty, lady's head, ceramic w/black hat lid, marked Japan .............................**25.00**

Novelty, Miss Cutie Pie, blue, pink or yellow, Japan, Napco, ea ..**35.00**

Novelty, orange w/face, ceramic, Florida, unmarked, 2-cup .**10.00**

**Spoons, demitasse; sterling with teapot finials, set of 4, $35.00.**

Novelty, pig, painted ceramic, marked #722 AK, German, 7½" ..................................**65.00**

Novelty, Santa holding cup, ceramic, marked Taiwan, 6-cup ..................................**14.00**

Novelty, Tom cat w/tie, ceramic, marked Takahashi, Japan ..............**45.00**

Novelty, tomato w/face, ceramic, marked Hand-Painted Japan ..........................**20.00**

Novelty, witch on broom, ceramic ........................**35.00**

Occupied Japan, florals, miniature, 1", NM .....................**4.00**

Souvenir, china w/gold trim, marked Made in Germany, NM ..................................**17.00**

Souvenir, marked Made in Japan, 2", +cup, saucer & stand **10.00**

Wade, spatter, octagonal, marked, VG ..................................**20.00**

### Related Items and Accessories

Caddy, marked EP Brass, Made in India, hinged lid, reproduction ..................................**15.00**

Caddy, silverplate, Godlinger, Paul Revere, 1991, reproduction ................................**18.00**

Cozy, quilted floral cloth, fits teapot ............................**14.00**

Dinner bell, ceramic w/gold teapot finial, Enesco, 1973 .......**25.00**

Infuser/strainer, ceramic egg shape w/chain, NM .......**12.00**

Infuser/strainer, chrome ball form w/red Bakelite finial .....**10.00**

Infuser/strainer, house shape w/TEA in design, chrome w/chain, '70s-80 ...............**6.00**

Infuser/strainer, teapot form, sterling, marked AMCraft, USA, w/saucer, MIB ...............**30.00**

Infuser/strainer, teapot w/etched design, silver w/chain, unmarked .....................**20.00**

Lemon dish, florals, thumb handle, English, saucer size ........**14.00**

Lemon dish, florals, thumb handle, Japan, saucer size ..**12.00**

Lemon dish, white, thumb handle, Hall China, saucer size .**10.00**

Salt & pepper shakers, plastic teapots w/holder, USA, ca 1960, pr .........................**18.00**

Scoop/measure, teapot form, marked Souvenir New Zealand, Exquisite ........**12.00**

Spoon holder, teapot form, brown pottery, wall-hanging style, Japan .............................**22.00**

Spoon measure, advertising JEE Tea ...................................**8.00**

Sugar tongs, silver, Victorian .**18.00**

Toast rack, silverplate, unmarked, Victorian .........................**35.00**

Wall pocket, teapot w/fruit design, ceramic, unmarked, lg ..**15.00**

Window-shade pull, Bakelite teapot form, unmarked, ca 1950 .................................**8.00**

Photo courtesy Margaret Fox Mandel and Kirk Stines.

# Teddy Bears and Related Collectibles

Only teddies made before the 1940s can be considered bona fide antiques, though character bears from more recent years are also quite collectible. The 'classic' bear is one made of mohair, straw stuffed, fully jointed, with long curving arms tapering at the paw and extending to the knees. He has very long skinny feet, felt pads on all paws, embroidered claws, a triangular, proportionately small head, a long pointed snout, embroidered nose and mouth, and a hump at the back of his neck. Related items and accessories are also eagerly sought by collectors. For more information, refer to *Teddy Bears and Steiff Animals* and *Teddy Bears, Annalees, and Steiff Animals*, both by Margaret Fox Mandel, as well as the *Collector's Guide to Miniature Teddy Bears, Identification and Values*, by Cynthia Powell (all published by Collector Books).

**Bear, American Panda, back and white mohair, plastic eyes, squeaker, ca 1940-50, $100.00.**

Bank, The Three Bears, yellow plastic, 3 slots in back, USA, 1950s, 4" .........................**30.00**

Bear, brown mohair, glass eyes, Knickerbocker, 1940s, 14", NM ...............................**250.00**

Bear, frosted mohair, open mouth, Hermann, 1940s, 21", NM .**65.00**

Bear, Gentle Ben, plush w/plastic eyes, felt tongue, Mattel, 1967, 17" .........................**55.00**

Bear, gold mohair, w/button, Steiff, 1950s, 13", M ....**665.00**

Bear, gold mohair over metal, fully jointed, Schuco, 2½", M ...............................**250.00**

Bear, Paddington, plush, rain outfit & boots, w/tag, Eden Toys, 1½" ...................................**8.00**

Bear, panda, acrylic over metal, plastic eyes, Weiss, 1970s, 2¾" ...................................**18.00**

Bear, plush, plastic eyes, black smile mouth, Knickerbocker, 1960s, 14" ......................**15.00**

Bear, white mohair, w/tag, Steiff, 1950s, 13", M ...............**875.00**

**Bear, mohair, cotton and straw stuffing, tagged Ideal Toy Corp, Hollis 23, NY, Made in Japan, ca 1950s, 12", $75.00.**

Book, The Teddy Bear That Prowled at Night, 1st edition, Gabriel, 1924 .................**75.00**

Buttonhook, silver w/figural handle, Birmingham, England, 1909 ...........................**275.00**

Christmas ornament, bear w/toy trunk, Lucy Rigg/Enesco, 1988, 1¾" ......................**35.00**

Cup, china w/gold trim, Joseph Horne Co Toy Store, England, 2¼" ................................**12.50**

Dish, tab handles for utensils, International Silver, 1930s, 7¼" .................................**65.00**

Figurine, Austrian crystal, Crystal Zoo, ¾" to 1¾", from $25 to ..................................**35.00**

Figurine, snow baby, bisque w/painted details, ca 1920, 1½" ..................................**50.00**

Perfume bottle, flocked plastic w/Max Factor bottle, 1960s-70s, 4½" .........................**25.00**

Plate, semi-porcelain w/decal, embossed ABC rim, Smith-Phillips, 7" .....................**55.00**

# The Three Stooges

A wide range of Three Stooges merchandise has been produced honoring the comedy trio of Moe, Larry and Curly over the last six decades. Starting with a set of beautifully crafted hand puppets in 1935 through a set of PVC Christmas ornaments in 1991, the Stooges' likenesses can be found on a wide array of products. Such items include bubble gum cards, finger puppets, comic books, records, beanies, school bags, flicker rings, vinyl punching bags, coloring books, 8mm films, and toys. For further information we recommend contacting our advisors, Soitenly Stooges Inc.; they are listed in the Directory under Illinois.

**Hand puppets, ceramic, 1935, set of 3, MIB, $200.00.**

Comic book, March of Comics, #292, 1966 .....................**10.00**

Finger puppet, Moe, Larry or Curly, 1959, ea ..............**10.00**

Flicker ring, Moe, Larry or Curly, 1960s, ea .........................**5.00**

Flying cane, 1959 ..................**30.00**
Moving Picture Machine, Pillsbury Farina, 1937 .......**150.00**
Poster, The Three Stooges Meet Hercules, 1961, 27x41" .**55.00**
Record, Curly Shuffle, Atlantic Records, 45 rpm, 1984 ....**5.00**
Rubber stamp set, 25-pc, 1974, w/original box ................**25.00**
Sticker, black & white, vending machine prize, 1977, set of 8 ....................................**5.00**
Watch, Bradley Time, 1985, ea ............................**25.00**

# Toothbrush Holders

Children's ceramic toothbrush holders represent one of today's popular collecting fields, with some of the character-related examples bringing $150.00 and up. Many were made in Japan before WWII. For a comprehensive look at toothbrush holders and current market values, we recommend *A Pictorial Guide to Toothbrush Holders* by Marilyn Cooper.

**Mickey Mouse, bisque, right arm jointed, late 1920s, 5", EX, $275.00.**

**Three Little Pigs, bisque, Japan, NM, $150.00.**

Baby Deer, Brush Teeth Daily, hanging, w/tray, 3 holes, Japan, 4" ........................**90.00**
Bear, hanging, w/tray, paw holds brush, Japan, 6", from $85 to ..........................**95.00**
Bell Hop w/Flowers, hanging, 1 hole, Japan, 5¼", from $65 to ..................................**75.00**
Bonzo, hanging, w/side tray, lustre, mouth holds brush, Germany, 3⅜" ..................................**130.00**
Cat, hanging, feet hold paste, 2 holes, Japan, 5¾", from $70 to ...................................**80.00**
Children in Auto, hanging, w/tray, 2 holes, Japan, 5", from $70 to ...................................**80.00**
Clown w/Mandolin, hanging, 1 hole, Japan, 6", from $80 to ...............................**90.00**
Cowboy w/Cactus, hanging, 3 holes, Japan, 5½", from $70 to ...................................**80.00**
Donkey, hanging, mane holds brush, 2 holes, Japan, 5¾", from $85 to ..................**100.00**
Halloween Policeman, hanging, feet hold paste, 1 hole, Japan, 5" ....................................**95.00**
Little Red Riding Hood, shaker top, Germany, 6¼", from $350 to ..................................**375.00**

Sailors on Anchor, hanging, w/tray, 2 holes, Japan, 5½", from $60 to .....................**70.00**
Siesta, hanging, w/tray, 1 hole, Japan, 6", from $80 to ...**90.00**
Skeezix, hanging, no tray, painted metal, 2 holes, marked from $150 to .........................**175.00**

# Toothpick Holders

Toothpick holders have been made in hundreds of patterns, in art glass, pattern glass, opalescent, and translucent glass of many colors, in novelty designs and figural forms. Today they are all popular collectibles, many relatively easy to find and usually affordable.

Acorn, peachblow, gold trim .**125.00**
Apollo .....................................**20.00**
Bird w/Basket, amber ..........**37.50**
Bubble Lattice, white opal .**115.00**
California ...............................**50.00**
Champion, green ..................**55.00**
Chutes & Ladders ................**22.00**
Columbian Coin, red coins .**200.00**
Cordova, green .....................**27.50**
Cordova, ruby stained ..........**40.00**
Daisy & Button, amberina, 3" .**200.00**
Dolphin, amber ....................**90.00**
Easter, green w/gold .............**85.00**
Empress, green w/gold .......**215.00**
Falcon Strawberry ...............**30.00**
Fine Cut, blue, hat shaped ..**30.00**
Frisco ....................................**70.00**
Gaelic, no gold .....................**24.00**
Geneva, custard ..................**135.00**
Harvard, ruby stained .........**45.00**
Holly .....................................**125.00**
Idyll, apple green .................**80.00**
Iris w/Meander, light blue ...**75.00**
Ivanhoe ................................**45.00**
Ladders & Diamonds ...........**30.00**
Mardi Gras ...........................**45.00**
Nester, blue ..........................**65.00**

Oregon ..................................**88.00**
Paddle Wheel .......................**45.00**
Pineapple & Fan, Heisey .....**75.00**
Priscilla ................................**40.00**
Prize ......................................**42.50**
Reverse Swirl, vaseline opal .**140.00**
Ribbed Spiral ........................**44.00**
Scalloped Panel, green .........**35.00**
Shoshone, ruby stained ......**115.00**
States ....................................**45.00**
Sunset, blue opaque .............**72.00**
Sylvan, clear w/gold .............**35.00**
Tennessee .............................**55.00**
Thumbnail ............................**30.00**
US Regal ...............................**24.00**
Vermont, green w/gold .........**65.00**
Wheeling Block ....................**45.00**

**Winged Scroll, Heisey, custard with gold trim, $195.00.**

# Toys

Toy collecting is a very popular hobby, and if purchases are wisely made, there is good potential for investment. Most of the battery-operated toys made from the forties through the sixties were made in Japan, even though some were distributed by American companies such as Linemar and Cragstan, who often sold them under their own names. Because of their complex mechanisms, few survive. Condition is very important in evaluating a battery-op, and the more complex their movements, the more they're worth.

Japanese wind-up toys are another fun and exciting field of toy collecting. The fascination with Japanese toys stems from their simplistic but exciting actions and bright and attractive colors. Many of the boxes that these toys came in are almost as attractive as the toys themselves!

Toys from the 1800s are rarely if ever found in mint condition but should at least be working and have all their original parts. Toys manufactured in the 20th century are evaluated more critically. Compared to one in mint condition, original box intact, even a slightly worn toy with no box may be worth only about half price. Character-related toys, space toys, toy trains, and toys from the sixties are among the most desirable. Several good books are available, if you want more information: *Modern Toys, American Toys 1930 to 1980,* by Linda Baker (Collector Books); *Collectible Male Action Figures,* by Paris and Susan Manos (Collector Books); *Collector's Guide to TootsieToys,* by David E. Richter (Collector Books); *Toys, Antique and Collectible,* and *Character Toys and Collectibles,* by David Longest (Collector Books); *Collecting Toys Soldiers, Collecting Toy Trains,* and *Collecting Toys,* by Richard O'Brien (Books Americana). For more information and additional listings, see *Schroeder's Collectible Toys, Antique to Modern* (Collector Books). See also Character Collectibles; Star Trek; Star Wars; Transformers.

## Battery Operated

Balloon Vendor, tin, cloth & vinyl, Japan, 1961, 11", EX w/original box ..........................**170.00**

Batmobile, bump-&-go action, lights & sounds, Taiwan, 11", NMIB ...........................**255.00**

Big John Chimpee Chief, Alps, 1960, MIB ....................**120.00**

Bouncing Army Jeep, 4 actions, MT, 1950s, NM ...........**125.00**

Brightlite Filling Station, litho tin, Marx, 9½", NM .....**525.00**

Busy Secretary, 7 actions, Linemar, 1950s, NM ..........**250.00**

Cat 'n Carrier, w/remote control, Cragstan, 1970, MIB ....**35.00**

Chippy the Chipmunk, Alps, 1950s, 12", MIB ..........**250.00**

Clang-Clang Locomotive, moves, lights & sounds, Marx, 1960s, 13", MIB ........................**78.00**

Cola Drinking Bear, 3 actions, Alps, 1950s, EX .............**65.00**

Cragstan Roulette Man, Japan, 1950s, NMIB ...............**275.00**

Dice Throwing Monkey, Alps, 1960, MIB ....................**100.00**

Diesel Locomotive, FYT/Taiwan, 1975, MIB ......................**40.00**

Friendly Bartender, Amico/Taiwan, 1970, MIB .............**25.00**

Golden Jubilee Car, 4 actions, TN, 1950s, NM ...................**185.00**

Happy Naughty Chimp, Daishin, 1960, MIB ....................**125.00**

Hoppity Hare, Alps, 1983, MIB ..........................**40.00**

Hot Rod Limousine, 4 actions, Alps, 1960s, NMIB ......**350.00**

James Bond Aston Martin DB5, working lights, Gilbert/Japan, 11", EX .............**200.00**

Jumbo the Bubble Blowing Elephant, Yonezawa, 1950, MIB .....**125.00**

Linus Lovable Lion, Illco/Hong Kong, 1970, MIB ...........**40.00**

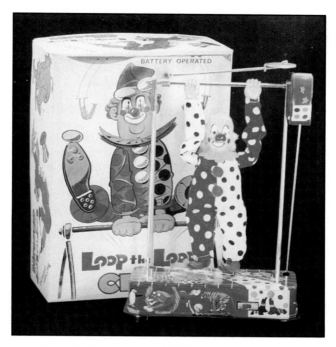

**Loop the Loop Clown, TN/Japan, MIB, $100.00.**

Mambo the Drumming Elephant, Alps, 1950, NM ...........**140.00**

Mickey Mouse on Big-Wheel, advances & sounds, Marx, NMIB ...........................**275.00**

Mickey the Drummer, tin w/cloth outfit, Japan, 1950s, 11½", NM ..............................**850.00**

Mightly Kong, plush over tin, Marx, 11½", MIB .........**650.00**

**Rusher Mach 1 Mustang, Japan, 1969, MIB, $125.00.**

Mother Goose, Cragstan/Japan, 1950, EX ......................**100.00**

Nosey the Sniffing Dog, Mego/ Japan, 1972, MIB ..........**50.00**

Nutty Mad Indian, 14", NMIB **95.00**

Phantom Raider, Ideal, 1963, NMIB ...........................**200.00**

Polar Bear, Alps, 1980, MIB .**60.00**

Reading Bear, 5 actions, Alps, 1950s, 9", EX ...............**175.00**

Russian Taxi, blue litho tin w/red interior, Ichiko, 9" ........**225.00**

Santa in Sleigh, litho tin & plastic, Modern Toys, 17", EX ............................**200.00**

Shaking Classic Car, Japan, 1960, MIB ..............................**125.00**

Snowmobile, w/remote control, Bandai, 9½", EX w/original box ................................**150.00**

Stunt Plane, TPS, 1960, NM .**175.00**

Twin Western Railroad Set, Wood-haven, 1950s, MIB ......**260.00**

Volkswagen Fire Chief Car, Illco, 1970, MIB ......................**50.00**

Worried Mother Duck, litho tin, Japan, 10", EX w/original box ................................**170.00**

Yo-Yo Car, lighted wheels, Japan, 9½", NMIB ...................**200.00**

## Friction

Antique Car, pink & black tin, Japan, 7½", VG w/original box ..................................**30.00**

Austin A50 Cambridge, white & maroon tin, Japan, 1950s, 8", non-working ................**200.00**

Avanti Coupe, tin, 1960s style, Bandai, 8", VG w/original box ................................**150.00**

Central Express Car, marked Super Express, TT/Japan, 6", MIB ..............................**100.00**

Central RR Train, wheels & con-nectors move, sounds, Japan, 8½", MIB ........................**95.00**

Champion Indy Racer #33, litho tin, rubber tires, Japan, 1950s, 4", NM ..............**110.00**

Circus Boat, litho tin & vinyl, KO/Japan, 7", NM w/original box ................................**140.00**

Convertible w/Donald Duck Driver, Linemar/WDP, 5", NM w/original box ..............**600.00**

Dino Ferrari, red tin w/plastic windows, YM/Japan, 11", EX+ ..............................**275.00**

Driving Pet #1, car moves & dog barks, Japan, 1950s, 7", MIB ............................**150.00**

Fast Freight Semi, Japan, 13", EX+ ..............................**70.00**

Flower Delivery Van, blue litho tin, Bandai, 12", non-work-ing, G ..........................**200.00**

Flying Fish Boat, red & green litho tin, Asahi/Japan, 11", VG ................................**50.00**

Future Car, advances & sounds, Meiko/Japan, 9", NMIB .**575.00**

Harley-Davidson Motorcycle, 3 pistons & wheels move, TN, 9", VG ..........................**150.00**

Highway Patrol Car (Plymouth), SY, 1950s, 8½", VG w/original box ................................**165.00**

Hurricane Racer, Midoriya Tokyo/Occupied Japan, 5", MIB ..............................**200.00**

Lincoln Wagon, Boat & Trailer, Olympic/Japan, NMIB .**270.00**

McDonnell Demon Navy Jet, white w/navy & red trim, Bandai, 7", NMIB .......**145.00**

Mighty Aircraft Carrier & Heli-copter, Cragstan, 9½", NMIB ........................**160.00**

Motorcycle w/Sidecar, sparks, SFA, 1930s, 4", EX, from $250 to ........................**275.00**

Navy Couger Jet, lever activated, w/6 rockets, Y/Japan, 8½", EX ...............................**180.00**

**Tom and Jerry Scooter, plastic, MGM, 1971, EX (EX box), $125.00.**

New Sports Car (experimental Toyota), ATC/Japan, 10", G w/original box ................**50.00**

Pan American Airlines Jet Plane, marked DC-8 on wings, H/Japan, NMIB .............**95.00**

Pluto Delivery Wagon, Linemar/ WDP, 6", EX+ ..............**388.00**

Porsche Formel II Micro-Racer, #1037, Schuco, 4", EX w/original box ..........................**110.00**

Record Racer, futuristic style, Bandai, 13", EX+ ........**400.00**

S-1011 Police Car, litho tin, Japan, 1952, 5", MIB ...**110.00**

Silver Jet Racer, litho tin & plastic, Japan, 10", NMIB ....**70.00**

Sparking Destroyer, TN/Japan, NMIB ...........................**175.00**

Super Electric Train, marked Super Express, K/Japan, 14", MIB ..............................**115.00**

Talking Police Car, Y/Japan, 1970, MIB ......................**60.00**

Thunderbolt Cap Firing Tank, fires & smokes, Frankonia, 1950s, 8", MIB .............**120.00**

Tom & Dick Hand Car, Japan, 6", MIB ..............................**125.00**

Trigger Action Plane, marked N38434 on wing, S&E, 8", NMIB ...........................**100.00**

Tumbling Monkey, plastic, Occupied Japan, 4", NMIB ...**45.00**

## Wind-Ups

Acrobat & Clown on Highbar, tin & celluloid, CK, 12", G w/original box ..........................**65.00**

Balky Mule, crazy actions, Marx, 1950s, 8", MIB, from $250 to ......................**350.00**

Bombo the Monk, monkey tumbles from palm tree, Unique Art, 10", EX ................**225.00**

Bubbling Boy, litho tin, 3 actions, San/Japan, 8", NMIB, from $175 to ........................**225.00**

Busy Mouse, litho tin, TPS/ Japan, 6x9" base, EX w/original box ........................**125.00**

Captain America, Marvel Comics/ Marx, 1968, 5½", MIB ..............................**95.00**

Circus Elephant on Tricycle, US Zone Germany, 8", NM, from $175 to ........................**225.00**

Cleo Clown Training the Dog, litho tin, TPS/Japan, 4½", NMIB ............................**350.00**

Dancing Couple, Occupied Japan, MIB ..............................**125.00**

Dancing Lassie, litho tin girl vibrates around, Lindstrom, 8", EX+ .........................**155.00**

Diving Submarine, w/2 3-D guns, Wolverine, 1940, EX ...**180.00**

Donald Duck, vibrates around as orange beak moves, Schuco, 6", EX ...........................**280.00**

Felix the Cat on Scooter, Nifty, 7½", VG ........................**750.00**

Go-Go Chimpee, Alps, 1960, MIB ...............................**75.00**

Gobbling Goose, pecks & lays golden eggs, Marx, 9", NMIB ....**200.00**

Gyro Cycle, plastic boy w/cloth arms on metal cycle, Tri-Ang, 8", EX ...........................**225.00**

Handcar, workmen pump yellow car, Strauss, EX+, from $250 to ...................................**300.00**

Harold Lloyd Bell, lever action, rings & face changes, Germany, 6½" ....................**210.00**

Hula-Hoop Monkey, Plaything/ Japan, 1950s, NMIB ...**100.00**

Humphrey Mobile, Wyandotte, 1950, 8½", EX ..............**550.00**

Jolly Pig, moves & clown pulls his tail, celluloid, Japan, 7", MIB ............................**165.00**

Jumpin' Jeep, crazy actions, Marx, 5½", MIB ...........**350.00**

Little Shoemaker Bear, Japan, 6", NMIB .............................**70.00**

Magic Arithmetical Dog w/Clown Trainer, German, 1950s, 7½", EX .................................**140.00**

Manrovier Tank, lever activated, sparking guns, Gescha, 8", NMIB .............................**165.00**

Mr Dan Coffee-Drinking Man, litho tin, TN/Japan, 1960s, MIB ..............................**125.00**

OHO Automobile, litho tin car w/driver, Lehmann, EX+, from $450 to ................**500.00**

Police Varianto 3040, Fernlenk Auto, Schuco, 4", MIB .**300.00**

Popeye on Tricycle, litho tin & celluloid, Linemar, 4", EX+ ......................**1,150.00**

**Speedy Boy Delivery Marx, 1930s, 10", M, $650.00.**

Rabbit w/Cymbals, Gunthermann, 9½", EX ............**375.00**

Reading Santa Claus, turns pages of book, Alps, 1950s, 7", MIB ........................**225.00**

Riding Cowboy, celluloid, TN/Occupied Japan, NMIB .........**175.00**

Rigi 900 Cable Car, Lehmann, 1950, complete w/figures, MIB ..............................**325.00**

Rocky Mountain Express, SE/Japan, 1950, MIB ..**115.00**

Rodeo Joe, cowboy in crazy car, Rico, 1950s, 4½", EX ...**350.00**

Santa on Tricycle, Suzuki, 1940, NM ................................**50.00**

Sea Wolf, peg-legged pirate circles & closes eyes, Alps, 7", EX+ .............................**165.00**

See-Saw Circus, Lewco Products, 1940s, VG, from $150 to .**200.00**

Strutting Parade Bear, litho tin & celluloid, Alps, 7", MIB .**120.00**

Tambourine Teddy, clothed plush bear sways, NGT/Japan, 7", MIB ..............................**140.00**

Tita the Hopping Monkey, litho tin & plush, Alps, 6", MIB .**120.00**

Transport Express Van, blue tin w/decals, Minic, 3½", NM .**80.00**

Walking Rabbit, Japan, 1960, EX .................................**30.00**

Zilotone, figure plays tunes w/3 interchangable disks, Wolverine, EX ........................**700.00**

# Transformers

It was in 1984 that transformers arrived on toy shelves in the United States. The original line was made up of only twenty-eight figures. Eighteen were cars that were known as the Autobots, the heroic warriors determined to put an end to the evil Deceptions. There were only ten Deceptions (evil robots) who could turn into such things as a jet or a handgun.

These original robots previously belonged to some of the Japanese series, for instance, Diaclone and Microman. (They had been produced by Takara in the 1970s.) Some did come to the U.S. and were licensed to Hasbro for the Transformer series. Not all were put into production, but the ones that were can be differentiated from their Transformer counterparts by color differences. (And toys from the original Diaclone series came with a small figure which could sit in the cockpit of jets or in the driver's seat of cars.)

It was from this beginning that the Transformer craze began. Immediately stores were flooded with children and collectors of all ages who were desperate to own one of these complex, attractively packaged, futuristic warriors. In truth, the excitement they generated was not just because of the toys themselves but was a result of the world of imagination and wonder that the Transformers represented.

The story of the Transformers and their epic adventures were told through several different comic books and animated series, as well as a highly successful movie. Through storytelling and complex characters, the Transformer series seethed with an excitement which the previous robot series had lacked.

This popularity was reflected internationally and eventually made its way back to Japan. In Japan the American Transformer animated series was translated into Japanese and inspired several parallel series there. Soon more of the Transformers themselves were being produced in Japan by Takara. These new Transformers were sold in the U.S. and continued in production until the fall of 1990, when the line was discontinued. While Hasbro service representatives referred to the Transformers as 'an exciting and integral line of toys,' they claimed that there was not enough interest being shown in them to continue their production in this country. Hasbro continued to make Transformers in Europe during this time, but for several years they were little more than fond memories in the hearts and minds of many fans. A few years ago, Hasbro announced their plans to reintroduce the line with Transformers: Generation 2. Transformers once again had their own comic book, and the old animated series was brought back in a revamped format. So far several new Transformers as well as recolored versions of the older ones have been released by Hasbro, and the size of the series continues to grow.

There is an extremely wide range of prices on Transformers due to the fact that they came in many different sizes. Prices given here are a representation for Transformers in unopened original boxes. One that has been opened or used is worth much less (about 25% to 75%), depending on whether it has all its parts (weapons, instruction book, tech specks, etc.) and what its condition is (whether decals are applied well or if it is worn). Our advisor is David Kolodny-Nagy, who is listed in the Directory under District of Columbia. See also Clubs and Newsletters.

**1986, Decepticon City Commander, TF1363, Galvatron, laser cannon, MIB (unopened), $60.00; As shown, used but complete, in VG box, $40.00.**

1984, Autobot Cars, TF1029 Rachet, ambulance ........**30.00**

1984, Autobot Commander, TF1053 Optimus Prime w/Roller, scout vehicle .**150.00**

1984, Decepticon Leader, TF1051 Megatron, Walther P-38 .**100.00**

1984, Minicars, TF1003 Bumblebee, red VW bug ............**25.00**

1985, Autobot Cars, TF1165 Red Alert, fire chief ..............**25.00**

1985, Constructicons, TF1133 Hook, crane ...................**15.00**

1985, Decepticon Jets, TF1189 Dirge, blue & yellow jet .**25.00**

1985, Deluxe Insecticons, TF1157 Barrage, boll weevil ......**45.00**

1985, Dinobots, TF1181 Sludge, brontosaurus .................**35.00**

1985, Minicars, TF1112 Windcharger, w/minispy ........**25.00**

1985, Minicars, TF1117 Seaspray, hovercraft ......................**10.00**

1986, Aerialbots, TF1267 Fireflight (3), Phantom ........**15.00**

1986, Aerialbots, TF1271 Silverbolt (5), Concorde ..........**35.00**

1986, Autobot Cars, TF1335 Kup, pickup truck ...................**30.00**

1986, Autobot City Commander, TF1369 STARS Control Center, mail-in ......................**60.00**

1986, Combaticons, TF1293 Vortex (4), helicopter ..........**12.00**

1986, Heroes, TF1329 Wreck-Gar, futuristic motorcycle .....**35.00**

1986, Minicars, TF1257 Hubcap, yellow race car ..............**15.00**

1986, Stunticons, TF1281 Drag Strip (4), Indy car ..........**10.00**

1986, Triple Changers, TF1323 Sandstorm, dune buggy/helicopter ............................**25.00**

1987, Duocons, TF1439 Flywheels, jet/tank .............**20.00**

1987, Headmaster Decepticons, TF1487 Mindwipe w/Vorath, bat ..................................**30.00**

1987, Monsterbots, TF1463 Doublecross, 2-headed dragon ...**25.00**

1987, Targetmaster Autobots, TF1455, Hot Rod w/Firebolt, race car/gun ...................**45.00**

1987, Technobots, TF1431 Lightspeed, race car w/decoy ..**15.00**

1987, Technobots, TF1435 Computron, gift set .............**90.00**

1987, Terrocons, TF1414 Rippersnapper, lizard w/decoy ..**15.00**

1987, Throttlebots, TF1402 Goldbug, VW bug w/decoy ....**15.00**

1988, Cassettes, TF1541 Grand Slam & Raindance, tank & jet .....**8.00**

1988, Firecons, TF1509 Flamefeather, monster bird ......**7.00**

1988, Powermaster Autobot Leader, TF1617 Optimus Prime w/HiQ .................**80.00**

1988, Pretender Beasts, TF1607 Snarler, boar w/shell .....**15.00**

1988, Pretender Vehicles, TF1611 Roadgrabber, purple jet w/shell ............................**30.00**

1988, Pretenders, TF1579 Cloudburst, jet w/shell ..........**25.00**

1988, Seacons, TF1515 Seawing (2), manta ray ................**10.00**

1988, Sparkbots, TF1503 Sizzle, funny car .........................**7.00**

1988, Tiggerbots, TF1529 Override, motorcycle .............**15.00**

1988, Tiggercons, TF1535 Windsweeper, B-1 bomber ..........**15.00**

1989, Legends/K-Mart Exclusives, TF1729 Jazz, Porsche ...**40.00**

1989, Mega Pretenders, TF1719 Thunderwing, jet w/shell .**25.00**

1989, Micromaster Stations, TF1673 Hot House, plane w/fire station .................**20.00**

1989, Micromaster Transports, TF1667 Roughstuff, military transport .......................**15.00**

1989, Micromasters Patrols, TF1661 Battle Patrol, set of 4 ....................................**10.00**

1989, Pretender Monsters, TF1693 Slog (6) ............**12.00**

1989, Pretenders, TF1705 Bludgeon, tank w/shell ........**30.00**

1989, TF1711 Grimlock, dinosaur w/shell ...........................**30.00**

1989, Ultra Pretenders, TF1725 Roadblock, tank w/figure & vehicle ............................**35.00**

1990, Action Masters, TF1783 Treadshot: Treadshot, Catgut (panther) .**15.00**

1990, Action Masters, TF1831 Megatron: Megatron, Neutro Fusion Tank ..................**60.00**

1990, Micromaster Combiners, TF1765 Constructor Squad, set of 6 ...........................**15.00**

1990, Micromasters Patrols, TF1755 Air Patrol, set of 4 ..............**7.00**

1992-93, Autobot Cars, TF1865 Sideswipe, black Countach ...................**20.00**

1992-93, Autobot Minicars, TF1885 Beachcomber, metallic dune buggy ...............**10.00**

1992-93, Color Change Transformers, TF1909 Drench .......**10.00**

1992-93, Constructicons, TF1853 Scavenger (2), orange version .......**7.00**

1992-93, Decepticon Jets, TF1875 Starscream, gray jet w/light .**25.00**

1992-93, Dinobots, TF1871 Slag, gray triceratops .............**30.00**

1992-93, Dinobots, TF1873 Snarl, red stegosaurus .............**25.00**

1992-93, Small Autobot Cars, TF1901 Windbreaker ......**7.00**

1992-93, Small Decepticon Jets, TF1891 Eagle Eye ...........**7.00**

1993, Laser Rod Transformers, TF1939 Volt ...................**15.00**

1994, Aerialbots, TF1915 Skydive (1), F-15 ...........................**7.00**

# Trolls

The first trolls to come to the United States were molded after a 1952 design by Marti and Helena Kuuskoski of Tampere, Finland. The first to be mass produced in America were molded from wood carvings made by Thomas Dam of Denmark. As the demand for these trolls increased, several U.S. manufacturers were licensed to produce them. The most noteworthy of these were Uneeda doll company's Wishnik line and Inga Dykin's Scandia House True Trolls. Thomas Dam continued to import his Dam Things line.

The troll craze from the '60s spawned many items other than dolls such as wall plaques, salt and pepper shakers, pins, squirt guns, rings, clay trolls, lamps, Halloween costumes, animals, lawn ornaments, coat racks, notebooks, folders, and even a car.

In the '70s, '80s, and '90s more new trolls were produced. While these trolls are collectible to some, the avid troll collector still prefers those produced in the '60s. Remember, trolls that receive top dollar must be in mint condition. Our advisor is Roger Inouye, who is listed in the Directory under California.

Bank, boy in felt jumper, any eye or hair color, 6", G .........**20.00**

Bank, glazed ceramic, marked Silvestre Bros Co, 1964, 18", M ................................**150.00**

Book, Wishnik Color & Play, Whitman/Uneeda Doll Co, 1966, rare, M ...............**100.00**

Carrying case, Wishnik, Niks & Naks inside label, Ideal, any color ...............................**20.00**

Carrying case, Wishnik, w/molded waterfall, M ..................**25.00**

Clown, yellow eyes, red nose, painted clothes, Dam, 1965, 5½" ..............................**250.00**

Cookie cutter, metal, Mills, 3½", very rare, M ....................**50.00**

Costume, Wishnik, Uneeda, MIB ............................**100.00**

Cow, brown hair, amber eyes, flesh tone, no bell, Dam Things, 5½" ..................**125.00**

Cow, brown hair, amber eyes, flesh tone w/bell, Dam Things, 5½" ..................**175.00**

Cow, marked Dam Things Est 1964, sm, M ....................**45.00**

**Dam boy in original felt clothes with shamrock, peach mohair sewn to head, brown eyes, sawdust filled, very rare, from $150.00 to $200.00.**

Dog astronaut w/shoes, mohair, Royalty Designs of Florida, 3½", M ............................**40.00**

Donkey, white hair & tail, amber eyes, marked Thomas Dam, 9", G ...............................**50.00**

Elephant, orange mohair, amber eyes, no bell, Dam Things, 1964, 5½" ....................**125.00**

Elephant, orange mohair, amber eyes, w/bell, Dam Things, 1964, 5½" ....................**175.00**

Finger puppet, Democrat donkey, any hair color, Dam Things, 1964, 3" ..........................**45.00**

Finger puppet, Republican elephant, any hair color, Dam, 1964, 3", M ....................**45.00**

Giraffe, amber eyes, gray hair, marked Thomas Dam, 12", G ........**125.00**

Greeting card, w/3" troll tied on, American Greeting, rare, 8" ..................................**100.00**

Handle bar grips, figural plastic, Sears, pr ......................**100.00**

House, vinyl w/cave furniture, Standard Plastics, w/handle, 12x8½" ..........................**20.00**

House (backward S), painted wood, unmarked, rare, 9x5½" ...**85.00**

Judge Wishnik, gray hair orange plastic eyes, w/gavel, Uneeda, 5½" .................................**30.00**

Lamp, Wishnik, 18", rare, complete ............................**250.00**

**Dam monkey, original clothing and hat, brown hair and eyes, marked Dam Things, very rare, from $200.00 to $300.00.**

Monkey, white hair, jointed neck, felt clothes, Shekter, 1966, 6" ..................................**40.00**

Moonitik, mohair body, rubber bird feet, shake eyes, Uneeda, rare, 18"........................**100.00**

Neanderthal, painted eyes, Bijou Toy, 1963, 7½" ................**32.00**

Nude, marked Dam, any eye or hair color, 3", G ................**8.00**

Outfit, MIP ............................**15.00**

Paper dolls, Wishnik, Whitman, 1964, M ...........................**65.00**

Pencil topper, astronaut, Scandia House, 1½", MIP ...........**45.00**

Pencil topper, bat w/feather hair, Relastic Stationary, set, MIP ......................**65.00**

Playset, troll village, Marx, MIB ...........................**300.00**

Salt & pepper shakers, boy & girl, painted clothes, 3½", pr .**150.00**

Photo courtesy Roger Inouye.

**Troll house, painted wood, unmarked, 11½", rare, from $100.00 to $150.00.**

Troll Trovelling Bag, plastic, marked Bunallan Inc, any color, 5x7", G .................**25.00**

# TV Guides

For most people, their *TV Guide* spends a week on top of their TV set or by the remote and then is discarded. But to collectors this weekly chronicle of TV history is highly revered. For many people, vintage *TV Guides* evoke happy feelings of the simpler days of youth. They also hunger for information on television shows not to be found in reference books. As with any type of ephemera, condition is very important. Some collectors prefer issues without address labels on the cover. Values are given for guides in fine to mint condition. Our advisor is Jeffrey M. Kadet, *TV Guide* Specialist, who is listed in the Directory under Illinois.

**1945, March 19-25, Groucho Marx cover, $35.00.**

1953, October 2-8, Red Skelton cover, Gene Autry article .**60.00**

1954, June 25-July 1, Howdy Doody & Buffalo Bob cover .......**150.00**

1955, December 10-16, Lucille Ball cover, Ding Dong School article ............................**95.00**

1956, May 26-June 1, Lawrence Welk & Alice Lon cover, Liberace article ....................**8.00**

1956, November 9-15, James Garner as Maverick cover, Robin Hood article ..................**50.00**

1957, April 27-May 3, Groucho Marx cover, Highway Patrol article ...........................**12.00**

1958, April 5-11, Gale Storm cover, Where Westerns Are Made article ..................**12.00**

1958, September 13-19, Lennon Sisters cover, Spike Jones article ..............................**8.00**

1959, August 22-28, I've Got a Secret cover, Johnny Carson article ..............................**7.00**

1959, June 13-19, Pat Boone cover, Joyce Brothers article ....**10.00**

1960, December 10-16, James Arness & Amanda Blake cover ...............................**18.00**

1960, March 12-18, Chuck Conners as The Rifleman cover .........................**37.00**

1961, January 14-20, Perry Como cover, Have Gun-Will Travel article ..............................**9.00**

1961, July 1-7, The Flintstones cover, Peggy Lee & Colt 45 articles ..........................**50.00**

1962, June 16-22, Dr Kildare cover, Paul Anka article ...........**10.00**

1962, November 10-16, Beverly Hillbillies cover, Stoney Burke article ................**50.00**

1963, April 6-12, 10th Anniversary Issue, Lucille Ball cover ...........................**60.00**

1964, November 21-27, Gomer Pyle cover, Edward Andrews article ..............................**8.00**

1965, August 21-27, Fess Parker as Daniel Boone cover .....**9.00**

1965, January 16-22, Bob Hope cover, Man From UNCLE article ..............................**7.00**

1965, November 27-December 3, Bob Crane cover, Green Acres article ...........................**26.00**

1966, January 1-7, Carol Channing, Ben Casey & LBJ articles ...................................**8.00**

1966, May 7-13, LBJ cover, My Three Sons article ...........**6.00**

1966, October 1-7, Vietnam War cover, Family Affair article .........................**15.00**

1967, June 10-16, Smothers Brothers cover, Time Tunnel article ...........................**27.00**

1967, March 4-10, William Shatner & Leonard Nimoy cover .........................**125.00**

1967, October 14-20, Johnny Carson cover, Star Trek Androids article ..............................**8.00**

1967, September 23-29, The Monkees cover, Barbara Eden article ..............................**48.00**

1968, November 9-15, Get Smart Wedding cover, James Garner article ..............................**18.00**

1969, May 17-23, Marlo Thomas cover, Ghost & Mrs Muir article ...................................**15.00**

1969, October 4-10, Bill Cosby cover, Sesame Street article ...................................**6.00**

1970, September 19-25, Mary Tyler Moore cover, Chad Everett article .................**8.00**

1971, January 23-29, Flip Wilson cover, Dark Shadows & Lassie articles .................**9.00**

1973, August 25-31, Buddy Ebsen as Barnaby Jones cover ..**4.00**

1974, November 4-10, John Wayne cover, Richard Nixon article ..............................**8.00**

1974, October 7-13, Bonanza cast cover, Mission: Impossible article ...........................**21.00**

1975, April 12-18, Cher cover, Barney Miller article ......**7.00**

1975, July 5-11, Tony Orlando & Dawn cover, Lucy & Lassie articles ............................**5.00**

1976, September 25-October 1, Charlie's Angels cover ..**35.00**

1977, October 22-28, Welcome Back Kotter cast cover, Rafferty article ......................**6.00**

1978, February 4-10, Love Boat cover, Carl Sagan article ..**5.00**

1979, October 18-24, Sophia Loren cover, Sneak Previews article ...............................**5.00**

1979, September 15-21, Robert Guillaume as Benson cover ...........................**4.00**

1981, March 7-13, Dukes of Hazzard cast cover ..............**10.00**

1982, August 28-September 3, Laverne & Shirley cover .......**5.00**

1982, December 11-17, Sally Struthers cover, Willard Scott article ...............................**3.00**

1982, May 8-14, Goldie Hawn cover, Capitol article .......**4.00**

1983, April 30-May 6, Tom Selleck cover .................................**5.00**

1983, June 18-24, Simon & Simon cast cover, Kathleen Beller article ...............................**5.00**

1984, August 25-31, Mike Hammer cast cover, Kim Ulrich article ...............................**4.00**

1985, December 21-27, Highway to Heaven cover, Hill St Blues article ...............................**6.00**

1986, April 5-11, Family Ties cast cover, Marlow Thomas article ...............................**6.00**

1986, May 10-16, Cheers cast cover, Susan Howard article ...............................**4.00**

1987, August 1-7, Young & the Restless cast cover, Equalizer article ...............................**3.00**

1988, May 21-27, Charles & Diana cover, Billy Cunningham article ......................**7.00**

1989, October 14-20, World Series cover, 8 Is Enough article .**3.00**

1990, November 10-16, Susan Lucci cover, Patty Duke & Cheers articles ...............**3.00**

1991, December 28-January 3, John Goodman cover, Star Trek article ......................**4.00**

1991, November 23-29, Madonna cover, M*A*S*H & MacGyver articles ...........................**5.00**

1992, April 25-May 1, Burt Reynolds cover, Last Cosby Show article ....................**3.00**

1993, July 3-9, Vanna White cover, Wynonna Judd article ...............................**3.00**

1994, November 19-25, ER cast cover, Law & Order article ........................**3.00**

# Universal

Located in Cambridge, Ohio, Universal Potteries Incorporated produced various lines of dinnerware from 1934 to the late 1950s, several of which are especially popular with collectors today. Refer to *The Collector's Encyclopedia of American Dinnerware* by Jo Cunningham (Collector Books) for more information.

Ballerina, bowl, cereal ...........**5.00**

Ballerina, creamer & sugar bowl ............................**20.00**

Ballerina, salt & pepper shakers, pr ....................................**12.00**

Calico Fruit, cup ....................**8.00**

Calico Fruit, platter ............**12.00**

Calico Fruit, utility shaker ..**12.00**

Cattail, bowl, berry; 5¼" ........**4.00**

Cattail, bowl, soup; 7¾" .........**7.00**

Cattail, cake lifter ...............**12.00**

Cattail, cup & saucer ...........**10.00**

Cattail, plate, 9" ..................**12.00**

**Mixed Fruit pattern, refrigerator jar with lid, 4", $10.00.**

Cattail, teapot ......................**20.00**
Red Poppy, pie plate ...............**8.00**
Zinnias, casserole .................**12.50**

# Valentines

One of the fastest-growing time frames of valentine cards today would be from the 1940s through the 1960s. These would include mechanical, penny, and boxed valentines. Valentines can cross over into many other collections today, such as Black memorabilia, advertising, transportation, cartoon characters, folk art, and so on.

Please keep these factors in mind when determining the value of your valentines: age, condition, size, category, and whether or not there is an artist's signature present. All of these were taken into consideration when the following valentines were priced. Also, it is important to remember that the East Coast tends to have a higher market value for them than the West Coast, due primarily to higher demand there. Our advisor for this category is Katherine Kreider, who is listed in the Directory under California.

In the listings that follow, HCPP stands for honeycomb paper puff, and MIG indicates valentines marked Made in Germany.

American Greeting, Black child on open-out, 1945-50s, 5¾x4½", NM ..................**10.00**
American Greeting, open-up w/elephant & plastic light bulb, 1950s .....................**10.00**
Car, litho w/children & dog inside, MIG, 1920s, 8½x6½", EX .**30.00**
Comic valentine, signed by Hugh Chennoweth, 1934, VG .**10.00**
G Carrington & Co, Chicago IL, goat, mechanical, 5½x4", NM ...............................**10.00**

G Carrington & Co, native American, mechanical, 1950s, VG .......**5.00**

H Fishlove & Co, plastic, wind-up heart, #522, 1958, NM ..**45.00**

Hall Bros, stand-up dog w/felt ears, 1940s, 8½x6¾", VG .**5.00**

Hallmark, Cinderella's coach, 1960, 9x7", VG .................**1.00**

Hallmark, musical, 1959, 9x7½", VG ...................................**15.00**

Hallmark, valentine booklet, 3-D, 4 pages, 1961, 9x7", NM .**8.00**

HCPP, gazebo w/children playing instruments, MIG, 1920s, 10½x8", NM .................**125.00**

HCPP, Wheel of Love, USA, 1920s, 9x5", NM ............**75.00**

Heart w/hand-painted wood clothespin, 1940s, 4½x3", EX .................................**15.00**

Little Boy Blue, mechanical litho, USA, 1930s, 10¾x7¾", NM ...............................**75.00**

Little Jack Horner, mechanical, Louis Kautz, USA, 1926, 6x3¾", NM ......................**40.00**

Little Lulu, 1950s, 4x4½", EX .**15.00**

Louis Kautz, cat, mechanical, stands w/tab, USA, 6¾x4", EX ..................................**15.00**

Louis Kautz, girl cooking heart at stove, litho, USA, 7½x6", EX..................................**15.00**

Mastiff w/child on back, litho, stands w/tab, MIG, 3¼x4⅛", NM..................................**10.00**

Mechanical, ballerina w/plastic eyes that roll, MIG, early 1920s, EX ......................**20.00**

Mechanical, bulldog, neck moves up & down, MIG, early 1920s, EX .................................**20.00**

Mechanical, dragonfly w/angel on back, stands w/tab, 7x5½", NM.................................**15.00**

Mechanical, Dutch lady, children pop in & out of wooden shoe, MIG, VG .........................**20.00**

Mechanical, fan w/kitten in center opens & closes, expands to 7", NM..................................**10.00**

Mechanical, stockbroker, stands w/tab, MIG, 1940s, 4¼x3¼", NM..................................**10.00**

Norcross, elephant, stands w/tab, 1940s, 11x7½", VG ...........**5.00**

Rolling pin, I'm Rolling in Dough, 4x½", VG...........................**5.00**

Rose, long stem, full bloom, 7½x5", EX.......................**10.00**

Rust Craft, dog w/felt ears, stands w/tab, 1946, 9½x7½", NM.**6.00**

Rust Craft, girl dressed for winter w/puppy, 1929, 4x4½", VG.**4.00**

Rust Craft, parasol, USA, 7x5", VG....................................**6.00**

Snow White & dwarfs baking pie, WD Enterprises, 1938, 5x4½", VG...................................**25.00**

Wiley Fox, mechanical, WDP, USA, 1938, 5x4½", VG...**25.00**

**Wimpy, 1939, NM, $25.00.**

Wizard of Oz, Lion, Loew's Inc, NM..................................**35.00**

3-D children w/sailboat & puppy, 1940s, 5½"x4, EX ...........**20.00**

3-D tennis court w/2 children playing tennis, 1920s, 7½x6", VG.....................................**25.00**

3-D train, Ambassador Cards, 1959, 7x9½", NM.............**25.00**

# Vernon Kilns

From 1931 until 1958, Vernon Kilns produced hundreds of lines of fine dinnerware that today's collectors enjoy reassembling. They retained the services of famous artists and designers such as Rockwell Kent and Walt Disney, who designed both dinnerware lines and novelty items. Examples of their work are at a premium.

Chintz, cup & saucer ............**17.00**
Chintz, plate, dinner; 10½" ..**15.00**
Dis'n Dot, teapot ..................**55.00**

Fantasia, plate, Nutcracker, 9" .............................**165.00**

Frontier Days, bowl, salad; 5½" .................................**20.00**

Gingham, bowl, divided vegetable; oval, 10" .............**25.00**

Gingham, bowl, fruit; 5½" ......**6.00**

Gingham, bowl, mixing; 5" ..**15.00**

Gingham, bowl, mixing; 9" ..**30.00**

Gingham, coffee carafe, 10-cup, from $30 to .....................**35.00**

Gingham, plate, bread & butter; 6½" ..................................**5.00**

Gingham, plate, luncheon; 9½" ..**10.00**

Gingham, teapot ..................**45.00**

Homespun, chop plate, 14" ..**40.00**

Homespun, egg cup ..............**18.00**

Homespun, plate, bread & butter; 6½" ..................................**5.00**

Homespun, plate, dinner; 10½" .**12.00**

May Flower, sugar bowl, w/lid .**15.00**

May Flower, teapot ..............**45.00**

Monterey, creamer ..............**12.00**

**Homespun, vegetable bowl, $15.00; Cup and saucer, $12.00; Tumbler, $15.00.**

Monterey, salt & pepper shakers,
pr .....................................**15.00**
Native California, bowl, rimmed
soup; 8" ...........................**15.00**
Native California, coffeepot, 8-
cup .................................**55.00**
Organdie, bowl, fruit; 5½" ......**6.00**
Organdie, plate, dinner; 10½" ..**15.00**
Organdie, plate, luncheon; 9½" .**9.00**
Organdie, teacup & saucer ..**10.00**
Organdie, teapot, from $35 to .**65.00**
Tam O'Shanter, bowl, divided veg-
etable ............................**30.00**
Tam O'Shanter, flowerpot, 3" .**25.00**
Tam O'Shanter, plate, 8½" .....**8.00**
Tam O'Shanter, platter, 12", from
$17 to ............................**25.00**
Tweed, plate, 6¼" ..................**5.00**

# View-Master Reels and Packets

View-Master, the invention of
William Gruber, was first introduced
to the public at the 1939-1940 New
York World's Fair and at the same
time at the Golden Gate Exposition
in California. Since then, thousands
of reels and packets have been produced on subjects as diverse as life
itself. Sawyers' View-Master even
made two different stereo cameras
for the general public, enabling people to make their own personal reels,
and then offered a stereo projector to
project the pictures they took on a
silver screen in full color 3-D.

View-Master has been owned
by five different companies: the
original Sawyers Company, G.A.F.
(in October 1966), View-Master
International (in 1981), Ideal Toy
Company, and Tyco Toy Company
(the present owners).

Unfortunately, after G.A.F.
sold View-Master in 1981, neither
View-Master International, Ideal,

nor Tyco Toy Company have had
any intention of making the products anything but toy items, selling mostly cartoons. This, of
course, has made the early non-
cartoon single reels and the three-
reel packets desirable items.

The earliest single reels from
1939-1945 were not white in color
but were originally dark blue with
a gold sticker in the center. They
came in attractive gold-colored
envelopes. Then they were made
in a blue and tan combination.
These early reels are more desirable as the print runs were low.

Most white single reels are
very common, as they were produced from 1946 through 1957
by the millions. There are exceptions, however, such as commercial reels promoting a product
and reels of obscure scenic
attractions, as these would have
had smaller print runs. In 1952
a European division of View-
Master was established in Belgium. Most reels and items made
there are more valuable to a collector, since they are hard to find
in this country.

In 1955 View-Master came
up with the novel idea of selling
packets of three reels in one colorful envelope with a picture or
photo on the front. Many times a
story booklet was included.
These became very popular, and
sales of single reels were slowly
discontinued. Most three-reel
packets are desirable, whether
Sawyers or G.A.F., as long as
they are in nice condition. Nearly
all viewers are common and have
little value except the very early
ones, such as the Model A and
Model B. These viewers had to be
opened to insert the reels. The

**Magazine ad showing Personal Stereo Camera; camera and case value: $100.00.**

blue and brown versions of the Model B are rare. Another desirable viewer is the Model D, which is the only focusing viewer that View-Master made. Condition is very important to the value of all View-Master items, as it is with most collectibles. Our advisor is Mr. Walter Sigg, who is listed in the Directory under New Jersey.

Camera, Mark II, w/case ...**100.00**
Camera, Personal Stereo, w/case ........................**100.00**
Close-up lens, for Personal Camera ...............................**100.00**
Film cutter, for cameras ....**100.00**
Packet, Addams Family or Munsters, 3-reel set ..............**50.00**
Packet, Belgium made, 3-reel set, from $4 to .....................**35.00**

Packet, miscellaneous subject, 3-reel set, from $3 to ........**50.00**
Packet, scenic, 3-reel set, from $1 to ....................................**25.00**
Packet, TV or movie, 3-reel set, from $2 to ......................**50.00**
Projector, Stereo-Matic 500 .**200.00**
Reel, Belgium made, from $1 to ...............................**10.00**
Reel, blue, from $2.50 to ......**10.00**
Reel, commercial, brand-name product (Coca-Cola, etc), from $5 to ..............................**50.00**
Reel, gold center, gold-colored package ..........................**10.00**
Reel, Sawyers, white, early, from 25¢ to ..............................**5.00**
Reel, 3-D movie preview (House of Wax, Kiss Me Kate, etc) .**50.00**
Viewer, Model B, blue or brown, ea .................................**100.00**
Viewer, Model D, focusing type .**30.00**

369

## Tru-View

Tru-Vue, a subsidiary of the Rock Island Bridge and Iron Works in Rock Island, Illinois, first introduced their product to the public at the 1933 Century of Progress Exposition in Chicago. With their popular black and white 3-D filmstrips and viewers, Tru-Vue quickly became the successor to the Stereoscope and stereocards of the 1800s and early 1900s. They made many stereo views of cities, national parks, scenic attractions and even some foreign countries. They produced children's stories, some that featured personalities and nightclubs, and many commercial and instructional filmstrips.

By the late 1940s, Sawyers' View-Master had become a very strong competitor. Their full-color 7-scene stereo reels were very pop-ular with the public and had cut into Tru-Vue's sales considerably. So it was a tempting offer when Sawyers made a bid to buy out the company in 1951. Sawyers needed Tru-Vue, not only to eliminate competition but because Tru-Vue owned the rights to photograph Disney characters and the Disneyland theme park in California.

After the take-over, Sawyers' View-Master continued to carry Tru-Vue products but stopped production of the 3-D filmstrips and viewers. Instead they adopted a new format with 7-scene 3-D cards and a new 3-D viewer. These were sold mainly in toy stores and today have little value. All of the pictures were on a cheaper 'Eastmancolor' slide film, and most of them have today faded into a magenta color. Many cards came apart, as the glue that was used tends to separate quite easily. The value of

**Tru-Vue 3-Dimension viewer, MIB, $5.00.**

these, therefore, is low. (Many cards were later remade as View-Master reels using the superior 'Kodachrome' film.) On the other hand, advertising literature, dealer displays, and items that were not meant to be sold to the public often have considerable collector value.

When G.A.F. bought View-Master in 1966, they gradually phased out the Tru-Vue format.

Card, from $1 to ......................**3.00**
Filmstrip, children's story, from $1 to ................................**3.00**
Filmstrip, commercial (promoting products), from $20 to ...**50.00**
Filmstrip, instructional, from $5 to ....................................**15.00**
Filmstrip, ocean liner ..........**15.00**
Filmstrip, personality (Sally Rand, Gypsy Rose Lee, etc), from $15 to ....................**20.00**
Filmstrip, scenic, from $1 to ..**5.00**
Filmstrip, World's Fair ..........**7.50**

# Wall Pockets

If you've been interested enough to notice, wall pockets are everywhere — easily found, relatively inexpensive, and very diversified. They were made in Japan, Czechoslovakia, and by many, many companies in the United States. Those made by companies best known for their art pottery (Weller, Roseville, etc.) are in a class of their own, but the novelty, just-for-fun wall pockets stand on their own merits. Examples with large, colorful birds or those with unusual modeling are usually the more desirable. There are three books we recommend for more information: *Collectors*

*Guide to Wall Pockets, Affordable and Other$*, by Marvin and Joy Gibson (L-W Books); *Collector's Encyclopedia of Wall Pockets* by Betty and Bill Newbound; *Wall Pockets of the Past* by Fredda Perkins; and *Collector's Guide to Made in Japan Ceramics* by Carole Bess White. (The last three are all published by Collector Books.) See also Cleminson; McCoy; Shawnee; other specific manufacturers.

**Sailboat, lustre, Japan, small, from $15.00 to $20.00; Masted ship, lustre, Japan, large, from $25.00 to $30.00.**

Blue Jay, flying against fruit, marked Fairyland Japan on paper label ....................**20.00**
Dutch boy w/buckets, painted porcelain, marked & incised Made in Japan ..............**20.00**
Florals, multicolor w/gold scroll handles, paper label, Japan ........................**15.00**
Fruit basket, painted porcelain, marked Enesco on silver label ..............................**15.00**
Grape cluster, clear glass, unmarked ......................**35.00**
Japanese lady standing near bamboo tree trunk, paper label, Japan ..................**20.00**

Lady in yellow hat, marked Napco Creation Japan on silver label ..............................**30.00**
Madonna, white porcelain, unmarked ......................**15.00**
Mexican woman, seated side view, white w/painted details, Japan ............................**15.00**
Parrot, on vase shape, maroon, gray & white porcelain w/gold, Germany ...........**60.00**
Parrot w/pink flowers, vase form, painted lustre, Japan ....**35.00**
Sunflower face, painted ceramic, sm ..................................**10.00**
Sunflower in sm decorated pot, incised Made in Japan ..**15.00**
Tulip bouquet, painted porcelain, incised Made in Japan ..**40.00**
Tulip on leaf, orange & green, marked USA, from $20 to .**25.00**
Violin w/pansies & cherries, Japan ............................**10.00**
White goose, blue waves at base, lustre, Japan .................**20.00**

Vase, lady with two vases, 11¼", from $40.00 to $50.00.

Shelf sitter, Oriental girl, marked, 9" ....................................**35.00**

Wall pocket, little girl with elbow resting on vase, 9¼", $35.00.

## Weil Ware

The figurines, wall pockets, and other decorative novelties made from the 1940s through the mid-1950s by Max Weil are among several similar types of California-made pottery that has today become the focus of much collector attention. Refer to *The Collector's Encyclopedia of California Pottery* by Jack Chipman (Collector Books) for more information.

Bowl, fruit; Malay Blossom, sq, from $8 to ......................**10.00**
Chop plate, Malay Bambu, 13" .**35.00**
Figurine, boy w/wheelbarrow, #4005 .............................**25.00**
Figurine, Buddy, boy, 7" .......**22.00**
Figurine, girl w/bowl, 11" ....**35.00**
Platter, Blossom, 13" ...........**22.00**

Vase, sailor boy w/bouquet, stamped mark, ca 1943, 11", from $45 to ...................**60.00**

# Western Collectibles

Items such as chaps, spurs, saddles, and lariats represent possibly the most colorful genre in the history of our country, and collectors, especially from the western states, find them fascinating. The romance of the Old West lives on through relics related to those bygone days of cowboys, Wild West shows, frontier sheriffs, and boom-town saloons. Our advisor, Barry Friedman, is listed in the Directory under California.

Bandana, red & white, ca 1920 ..........................**30.00**
Bedspread, Bates, cowboy pattern, twin size ...............**65.00**
Belt, bronco buster's, star designs .........................**60.00**
Bit, Crockett, port type ........**85.00**
Bit, Kelly Bros, heart decor .**70.00**
Blanket, cotton blend, cowboys, oil wells & cattle, ca 1940s .**85.00**
Blanket, cotton blend, steer-head & brands decor ..............**35.00**

Boot jack, figural iron beetle .**50.00**
Boots, Acme, inlaid uppers, 1940s, MIB .............................**150.00**
Boots, child's, horse-head decor .............................**35.00**
Bull whip, braided rawhide, 1930s ..........................**40.00**
Cabinet card, Oklahoma Territory, 2 cowboys ..............**60.00**
Carte de visite, John Fremont ..**45.00**
Chaps, batwings, very worn .**100.00**
Chaps, CP Shipley, black woolies, tooled billet ..................**550.00**
Chaps, fringed shotgun style, 1890s .........................**375.00**
Coat, buffalo skin, 1880s, NM .............................**425.00**
Cuffs, beaded, Indian-made, rare ............................**200.00**
Gauntlets, beaded Plateau style, 1930s .............................**95.00**
Hat, Resistol, stockman style .**80.00**
Hat, Stetson, Montana Peak .**240.00**
Holster, Buscadero style ....**190.00**
Holster, unmarked Mexican loop w/gun belt .....................**135.00**
Pin-back button, World Championship Rodeo, Denver, 1902 ..........................**18.00**
Program, Pendleton Round-Up, 1924 ..............................**22.00**
Quirt, horsehair, red & black .**85.00**
Rope, braided horsehair, EX .**75.00**

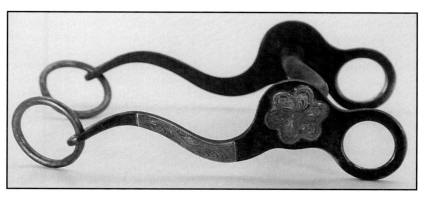

**Bit, Crockett & Renalde, from $85.00 to $95.00.**

Saddle, marked Heiser, ca 1925 .........................**285.00**
Saddle, single rig, high cantle, unmarked, ca 1900, EX .**500.00**
Saddlebags, hide out, G .......**90.00**
Spurs, Crockett, iron ............**48.00**
Spurs, Kelly Bros, silver inlay arrows & hearts, original leathers ........................**300.00**
Spurs, Mexican charro, silver inlay, G .........................**110.00**

## Western Heroes

Interest is very strong right now in western memorabilia — not only that, but the kids that listened so intently to those after-school radio episodes featuring one of the many cowboy stars that sparked the airways in the '50s are now some of today's more affluent collectors, able and wanting to search out and buy toys they had in their youth. Put those two factors together, and it's easy to see why these items are so popular. *Character Toys and Collectibles* by David Longest and *Schroeder's Collectible Toys, Antique to Modern,* by Sharon and Bob Huxford (both are Collector Books) have lots of good information on Western heroes. See also Character Watches; Movie Memorabilia.

Bat Masterson, Marshal; drinking glass, gold & white graphics, M .....................................**15.00**
Bobby Benson, book, The Lost Herd, Hecker-H-O Co premium, 1936, EX ............**25.00**
Bobby Benson, cereal bowl, red graphics on glass, ca 1930s, M .....................................**25.00**
Bonanza, book, coloring; Saalfield, 1965, 8x11", M ...............**20.00**

Bonanza, postcard, interior view Cartwright ranch house, NM ..................................**1.50**
Bonanza, puzzle, Milton Bradley, 1964, 125-pc, MIB .........**35.00**
Buffalo Bill, postcard, buckskin dress, dated 1952, EX .....**3.50**
Calamity Jane, postcard, sitting pose w/rifle, ca 1900, from $20 to .............................**40.00**
Cisco Kid, bandana, posed w/bucking bronco on gold satin ..**20.00**
Cisco Kid, bread label, 1950s, EX ..................................**20.00**
Cisco Kid & Pancho, mug, milk glass, 1950s, M ..............**35.00**
Custer, booklet, Nat'l Historical Monument Battlefield, 1949, from $20 .........................**30.00**
Daniel Boone, book, coloring; Fess Parker cover, 1964, 8x11", M ..................................**20.00**
Daniel Boone, paint & pencil by number, Standard Toykraft, 1964, MIB ......................**75.00**
Davy Crockett, book, comic; marked WDP, promoting Hudson Hornet, 1955 ....**20.00**
Davy Crockett, cereal bowl, brown graphics on ivory, 6¼", M ..................................**40.00**
Davy Crockett, cereal bowl, brown graphics on milk glass, Fire-King, M .........................**22.00**
Davy Crockett, drinking glass, Coonskin Congressman on clear, 5" .........................**15.00**
Davy Crockett, flashlight store display card, Bantam-Lite, 1950s, EX ....................**10.00**
Davy Crockett, flintlock pistol, Irwin, 1950s, 10", w/original tag .**36.00**
Davy Crockett, game, Disneyland's Official Indian Scouting, 1955, EX ...............**125.00**
Davy Crockett, gun, Auto-Magic Picture, Disney, ca 1955, MIB ............................**235.00**

Davy Crockett, hat, w/portrait & Ritchey's Milk, EX ........**65.00**

Davy Crockett, iron-on transfer, Alan Products, 1955, set of 12, MIP ...........................**7.00**

Davy Crockett, plaque, chalkware, Miller Studio, ca 1955, 7½" oval ........................**45.00**

Davy Crockett, plate, brown on ivory, Royal China, 1955, 9½", M ...................................**40.00**

Davy Crockett, Pony Express Bank, vinyl & cloth pouch form, MIP .....................**60.00**

Davy Crockett, powder horn, official issue, 1955, EX .......**65.00**

Davy Crockett, sheet music, Ballad of..., Disney, 1954, EX ....**35.00**

Davy Crockett, tie, portrait on brown, jewelled leather slide, EX ..................................**35.00**

Davy Crockett, tie clip & cuff link set, copper-colored metal, M ...................................**35.00**

Davy Crockett, wallet, 1950s, from $25 to ...................**40.00**

Gabby Hays, hat, black felt w/silver letters & drawstring tie, EX ..................................**58.00**

Gabby Hays, puzzle, frame-tray; NM ................................**15.00**

### Gene Autry

First breaking into show business as a recording star with Columbia Records, Gene went on to become on of Hollywood's most famous singing cowboys. From the late 1930s until the mid-'50s, he rode his wonder horse 'Champion' through almost ninety feature films. He did radio and TV as well, and naturally his fame spawned a wealth of memorabilia originally aimed at his young audiences, now grabbed up just as quickly by today's collectors.

Book, coloring; Chuck Wagon Chatter, from $25 to ......**40.00**

Book, Law of the Range, Big Little Book, 1939, VG ........**25.00**

Bread label, Schafer's Bread, ca 1950, EX .......................**20.00**

Cap pistol, Buzz Henry, 1950s, 7½", EX ........................**115.00**

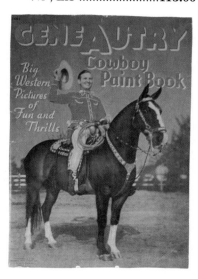

**Gene Autry paint book, Merrill Publishing #3484, dated 1940, from $40.00 to $65.00.**

Puzzle, frame-tray; Whitman, dated 1954, EX .............**37.50**

Ring, portrait, 1950s, EX+ ...**65.00**

Song book, 1950s, VG ..........**35.00**

Tablet, color photo w/facsimile signature, 1950s, 9x5½" .....**32.00**

Wallet, child's, colorful vinyl, original, from $20 to ...........**50.00**

### Hopalong Cassidy

One of the most popular western heroes of all time, Hoppy was the epitome of the highly moral, roll-model cowboys of radio and the silver screen that many of us grew up with in the '40s and '50s.

He was portrayed by Bill Boyd who personally endorsed more than 2,200 items targeting Hoppy's loyal followers. If you just happen to be a modern-day Hoppy aficionado, you'll want to read *Collector's Guide to Hopalong Cassidy Memorabilia* by Joseph J. Caro (L-W Book Sales).

Book, coloring; Abbott, 1951, EX ..................................**75.00**
Coaster, black on yellow, advertising honey, 4" dia ............**10.00**
Coaster, enameled metal, 1950s, 4" dia, set of 4, from $30 to .**50.00**
Game, Target Practice/Stagecoach Holdup, 1950, EX .........**135.00**
Milk bottle, 1950s, ½-gal, EX .**50.00**
Mug, red graphics on milk glass, 1950s, M ........................**32.50**
Napkins, Reed's, ca 1950, 32 in package, M ....................**36.00**
Pennant, felt, 1950s, 19", EX .**30.00**

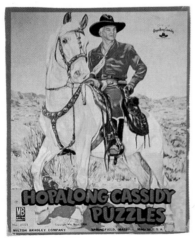

**Hopalong Cassidy puzzle, Milton Bradley, copyright William Boyd, 1950, set of 3, NMIB, $90.00.**

Tie tack, portrait in relief on metal, ca 1950, from $15 to ..............................**35.00**

Token, portrait, marked, 50¢, from $10 to ....................**20.00**
Wood-burning set, ca 1950, NMIB ..........................**150.00**

## The Lone Ranger

Recalling 'those thrilling days of yesteryear,' we can't help but remember the adventures of our hero, The Lone Ranger. He's been admired since that first radio show in 1933, and today's collectors seek a wide variety of his memorabilia; premiums, cereal boxes, and even carnival chalkware prizes are a few examples. Our advisors, Terry and Kay Klepey (listed in the Directory under Washington), have a newsletter, *The Silver Bullet*. See Clubs and Newsletters for more information.

Badge, bread premium, any of more than 15, ea, from $30 to ..................................**80.00**
Badge, shield form, secret compartment, EX, from $50 to ....**75.00**
Book, comic; Gold Key #19, G .**4.00**
Book, The Barbary Coast, Big Little Book, EX ..................**28.00**
Book, The Lone Ranger Outwits Crazy Cougar, Big Little Book, EX ........................**20.00**
Book, The Secret of Somber Cave, Big Little Book, VG .......**40.00**
Doll, Butch Cavendish, Gabriel #23623, NMIB ..............**40.00**
Doll, Tonto, Hamilton Gifts, #2869, w/stand, NM ......**22.50**
Doll, 1938, any of 3 sizes, ea, from $250 to ........................**400.00**
Figure, mounted on horse, Fleetwood, 3", MIP ................**20.00**
Figure, Tonto, colorful PVC, Hamilton Gifts, 4" ...........**6.00**
First Aid kit, ca 1938, box only, G ..................................**65.00**

**Lone Ranger Hi-Yo-o-o-o-o Silver game, Parker Brothers, dated 1956, complete in G box, $55.00.**

Game, Hi-Yo-o-o-o Silver, dated 1956, G .........................**55.00**

Game, The Legend of the Lone Ranger, Milton Bradley, 1980s, NM .....................**35.00**

Gun, ca 1980, from $20 up to ..**40.00**

Gun, squirt type, Masked Man, Durham .........................**15.00**

Hairbrush, decal & handle, with original box, from $40 to .................................**80.00**

Knife, 1-blade, Smoky Mountain Knife Works, EX ..............**9.00**

Mug, Lone Ranger & Tonto, Hamilton Gifts, M ...........**7.50**

Paperweight, silver bullet enclosed in clear plastic, Hamilton Gifts ..............**15.00**

Pin-back button, Silver Cup-Safety Scout, blue, original, NM .................................**55.00**

Pin-back button, Sunday Herald, portrait on Silver ..........**22.00**

Playset, Carson City Bank Robbery, Hubley #23641, EX .........**22.00**

Playset, Lone Ranger's Carson City, NM .........................**65.00**

Post-It pad, How Would The Lone Ranger Have Handled This? ca 1986, M ......................**6.00**

## Roy Rogers

Growing up during the Great Depression, Leonard Frank Sly was determined to make his mark in the entertainment industry. In 1938 after landing small roles in films featuring Gene Autry and others, Republic Studios (recognizing his talents) renamed their singing cowboy Roy Rogers and placed him in his first leading role in *Under Western Stars*. By 1943 he had become America's 'King of the Cowboys,' and his beloved horse, Trigger, was at the top with him. For further information about Roy and other singing cowboys, we recommend *Silver Screen Cowboys*; *Hollywood Cowboy Heroes*; *Roy Rogers, a Biography*; and *Singing Cowboy Stars*. All are written by our advisor, Robert W. Phillips, listed in the Directory under Oklahoma.

Alarm clock, w/Trigger, animated, Ingraham, 1952, 4½", from $225 to .........................**400.00**

Badge, Deputy Sheriff, Quaker/
Mother's Oats, 1950, from
$60 to ..............................**75.00**
Bedspread w/drapes & rug, che-
nille, Polly Prentiss, 1953,
from $100 to ................**300.00**
Book, Angel Unaware, by Dale
Evans, 1953, EX ............**10.00**
Book, coloring; Roy Rogers & Dale
Evans, Whitman, 1975, 8x11",
NM ...................................**16.00**
Book, Roy Rogers & Gopher Creek
Gunman, 1945, w/dust jacket,
from $15 .........................**25.00**
Book, Roy Rogers King of the
Cowboys, Better Little Book,
from $15 to ....................**50.00**
Book, Roy Rogers Paint Book, #1158,
cover, 1944, from $40 to ...**65.00**

Boots, child's, felted top w/fringe,
Goldberg, 1954, pr, from $100
to ...................................**140.00**
Boots, child's, Tex Tan Co, rubber
heels w/pull straps, minimum
value ............................**100.00**
Buckle, bust in relief on steel, 1950s,
3½x3⅞", minimum value .**75.00**
Camera, Herbert-George, Model
620 Snap Shot, early 1950s,
from $55 to ....................**95.00**
Crayon box, w/stencils & paper,
Sears #3G 4902, 1952, mini-
mum value .....................**55.00**
Cup, figural plastic bust
w/painted details, F&F Mold,
minimum value .............**40.00**
Game, 2 full-size horseshoes w/metal
stands, from $55 to ...........**85.00**

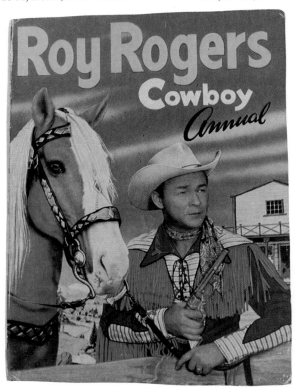

Photo courtesy Phillips Archives.

**Roy Rogers Cowboy Annual #6, British, 1956, from
$30.00 to $60.00.**

Guitar folio, Famous Music Co, ca 1954, 28 pages ..............**25.00**

Lobby card, The Wall Street Cowboy, color, 8x10", repro ....**5.00**

Magazine ad, Ladies' Home Journal, for Magic Chef, 1940, full-page ...............................**10.00**

Pencil, EX ..............................**7.50**

Pencil case, plastic, marked USA, 1950s, 8" ........................**35.00**

Pencil sharpener, round plastic w/photo, sm .....................**5.00**

Playset, Double R Bar Chuck Wagon Gear, plastic, 1950s, EX ................................**75.00**

Record, The Bible Tells Me So, Capital, 45 rpm, 1985, M .**7.50**

Record, The Night Before Christmas, 45 rpm, w/jacket, VG ........**25.00**

Slippers, MIB .....................**150.00**

Souvenir plate, Museum Victorville CA, 1970s, 7½" ..**35.00**

Stagecoach, plastic w/2 horses, Ideal, 8x13", VG ..........**125.00**

T-shirt, child's, Double R Bar Ranch, from $45 to ........**65.00**

Wallet, embossed leather, Toolcraft, ca 1950, from $45 to .......**65.00**

Yo-yo, plastic, ca 1940s, 2¼", M ...................................**15.00**

## Tom Mix

Cowboy film star Tom Mix reigned supreme on theater screens from 1909 to 1935. While at Fox Studios from 1918 to 1928, he earned $17,500.00 a week and turned out 85 features. He also starred with the Sells-Floto Circus from 1929 to 1931 and eventually had his own traveling circus from 1935 to 1938. To this day he remains the highest-paid circus performer in history.

Tom Mix is perhaps best remembered through the Tom Mix Ralston Straight Shooters radio program which ran from 1933 to 1950. During those years, the sponsor periodically offered premiums that could be obtained for a cereal boxtop, and eventually for a boxtop and 10 or 15¢. Today those original 148 premiums are highly-sought collectibles with prices ranging upwards to several hundred dollars each. Tom Mix premiums are regulated by supply and demand with prices being much higher on the East and West coasts.

Values are for items that are undamaged, complete, and in working condition. If accompanied by the original instruction sheet and mailing package, add another $25.00 to $50.00 to the price. For further information we recommend *The Tom Mix Book* by our advisor, M.G. 'Bud' Norris, listed in the Directory under Ohio.

Bandana, 1933 .....................**75.00**

Charm bracelet, 1940 ........**300.00**

Compass & magnifier, 1935 .**100.00**

Flashlight, bullet style, 1938 .**75.00**

Medal, captain's, 1941 .......**150.00**

Photo set, 1934 premium .....**70.00**

Pocketknife, 1939 .................**55.00**

Ring, magic-light tiger eye, 1950 ..........................**275.00**

Ring, signature, 1942 .........**135.00**

Ring, signet type, 1937 ......**150.00**

Rocket parachute, 1936 .......**80.00**

Wagon Train, book, comic; Dell #5, 1960, G .....................**2.00**

Wild Bill Hickok, gun, Leslie-Henry, 44 Cap Pistol, 1950s, 11", M ...........................**155.00**

Wild Bill Hickok, map, Treasure Guide, Kellogg's premium, lg, EX ...............................**55.00**

**Wild Bill Hickok comic book, Avon #26, Jan-Feb 1956, EX, $7.00.**

Wild Wild West, book, comic; Dell #7, VG+ ............................**7.00**

Wild Wild West, playset, Processed Plastic #1235, MIP ...........**7.50**

Wyatt Earp, badge, 6-point star, Wyatt Earp Entertainment, 1959, MIP ......................**15.00**

Wyatt Earp, color-by-number stencil set, NMIB ..........**28.00**

Wyatt Earp, coloring book, 1958, EX+ .................................**15.00**

Wyatt Earp, drinking glass, gold & white graphics, M .....**15.00**

Wyatt Earp, holsters (2), leather, 1950s, VG+ .....................**45.00**

Wyatt Earp, puzzle, Whitman, waist-length portrait, 1958, complete, NM .................**30.00**

Wyatt Earp, wallet, 1957, EX .**35.00**

Zorro, cap pistol, plastic, 1960s, EX .................................**35.00**

Zorro, display card, gumball machine ring premium, 1958, 3x3", M .........**40.00**

Zorro, hand puppet, Gund, 10", EX .................................**18.00**

Zorro, mask, whip & lariat, 1960s, MOC .............................**85.00**

Zorro, target set, litho tin, darts w/rifle, Cohn, EX .........**100.00**

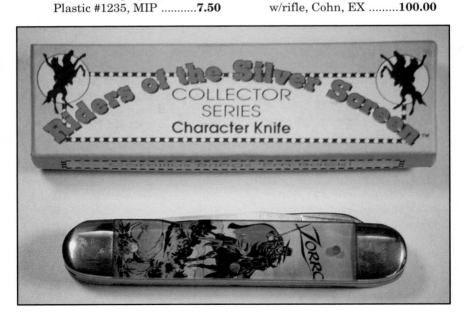

**Zorro knife, Riders of the Silver Screen, Camillus, 2-blade, 4½", with papers, MIB, new, $50.00.**

# Westmoreland

Originally an Ohio company, Westmoreland relocated in Grapesville, Pennsylvania, where by the 1920s they had became known as one of the country's largest manufactures of carnival glass. They are best known today for the high-quality milk glass which accounted for 90% of their production. For further information we recommend contacting the Westmoreland Glass Society, Inc., listed in Clubs and Newsletters. See also Glass Animals and Figures.

Bonbon, Waterford, ruby stain, heart form, handle, 6" ...**37.50**
Bowl, Beaded Grape, milk glass, footed, 4" ......................**25.00**
Bowl, Della Robbia, heart shape, dark stain, w/handle, 8" .**50.00**
Bowl, Doric #18, milk glass, footed, 10" ......................**25.00**
Bowl, Paneled Grape, cupped, 8" ................................**45.00**
Bud vase, Roses & Bows, milk glass, footed, 9½" ..........**32.50**
Candle holders, Old Quilt, milk glass, single, pr .............**22.50**
Candlesticks, Ring & Petal, milk glass, pr .........................**22.00**
Candlesticks, Waterford, ruby stain, pr .........................**55.00**
Candy dish, Beaded Grape, milk glass, footed, 9" .............**50.00**
Celery tray, Old Quilt, milk glass, flat, 10" .........................**40.00**
Cocktail, Paneled Grape, crystal .................................**17.50**
Creamer & sugar bowl, Della Robbia, light stain ...............**27.50**
Creamer & sugar bowl, Della Robbia, milk glass ...............**15.00**
Cup & saucer, Beaded Edge, milk glass ...............................**12.50**
Cup & saucer, Paneled Grape, milk glass ......................**22.50**
Goblet, Della Robbia, milk glass ...........................**12.50**

**Paneled Grape open-handle basket, pink and blue floral decoration, 6½" long, $45.00.**

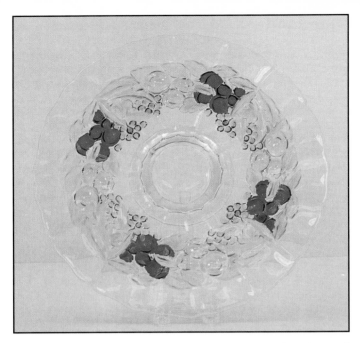

**Della Robbia footed plate, crystal with colored fruit, 13½"
diameter, $28.00.**

Goblet, water; Paneled Grape,
milk glass .......................**18.50**

Plate, Beaded Edge, enameled strawberry, milk glass, 7" ...........**15.00**

Salt & pepper shakers, Paneled
Grape, milk glass, footed,
pr .................................**18.00**

Sugar bowl, Paneled Grape, milk
glass, lacy edge, w/lid ...**35.00**

Tumbler, Beaded Edge, milk
glass, footed, 8-oz ..........**12.50**

Tumbler, Paneled Grape, milk
glass, flat, 8-oz ..............**25.00**

Vase, Old Quilt, milk glass, fan
form .............................**20.00**

## Willow Ware

Inspired by the lovely blue and
white Chinese exports, the Willow
pattern has been made by many
English, American, and Japanese
firms from 1750 until the present.
Many variations of the pattern have
been noted; mauve, black, green, and
multicolor Willow ware can be found
in limited amounts. The design has
been applied to tinware, linens, glassware, and paper goods, all of which
are treasured by today's collectors.
Refer to *Blue Willow* by Mary Frank
Gaston (Collector Books) for more
information. See also Royal China.

Bowl, cereal; Japan, 6¼" ......**10.00**

Bowl, fruit; England, 5" .........**6.00**

Bowl, soup; Ridgway, 8¾" ....**24.00**

Butter dish, Allerton ..........**190.00**

Butter pat, Allerton, 3⅛" .....**25.00**

Creamer, Japan, 3½" ............**16.00**

Creamer & sugar bowl, w/lid,
Japan, oval ....................**30.00**

Cup, USA, stacking ...............**4.00**

**Bowl, marked Japan, 10½" long, $29.00.**

Cup & saucer, Japan, inside decal ..............................**14.00**

Cup & saucer, red, Made in Japan, inside decal .......**18.00**

Glass, decal on clear, American, ca 1940s, 4", from $10 to ....**15.00**

Mug, farmer's cup, heavy, Japan, 4" ....................................**25.00**

Plate, dinner; Buffalo, 1907, 9½" ..............................**40.00**

Plate, dinner; Ridgway, 10½" .**22.00**

Plate, dinner; Shenango ......**20.00**

Plate, grill; Japan, 10¾" ......**15.00**

Plate, Maastricht, 6" ............**10.00**

Plate, Ridgway, dinner size .**22.00**

Plate, unmarked American, 9" .**7.00**

Salt & pepper shakers, England, pr ....................................**55.00**

Salt & pepper shakers, short or tall, Japan, pr, from $20 to .....**40.00**

Salt & pepper shakers, wood & ceramic, unmarked, 6", pr ..............................**20.00**

Teakettle, enamelled metal, brass trim, wood handle, Heritage/Taiwan ..................**15.00**

Teapot, North Staffordshire Pottery Co, 1940s, 4-cup ....**65.00**

Teapot, unmarked, Japan, musical ................................**100.00**

Toothpick, Marked Wedgwood, English, 2¼" ..................**50.00**

Toothpick holder, unmarked **85.00**

Trivet, decal on porcelain, handled wrought-iron frame, Japan ............................**30.00**

Tumbler, fat, short ..............**10.00**

Tumbler, flat, 5" ..................**12.00**

# DIRECTORY

The editors and staff take this opportunity to express our sincere gratitude and appreciation to each person who has in any way contributed to the preparation of this guide. We believe the credibility of our book is greatly enhanced through their efforts. Check these listings for information concerning their specific areas of expertise.

You will notice that at the conclusion of some of the narratives, the advisor's name is given. This is optional and up to the discretion of each individual. We hope to add more advisors with each new edition to provide further resources to you, our readers. If you care to correspond with anyone listed here in our Directory, you must send a SASE with your letter.

**Arizona**
Lund, O.B.
13009 S. 42nd St.
Phoenix, 85044
602-893-3567
Specializing in milk bottles

**Arkansas**
Antiques of Law and Order
Tony Perrin
1401 N Pierce #6
Little Rock, 72207
501-868-5005 or
501-666-6493 after 5 pm
Specializing in law enforcement and crime-related antiques and memorabilia

**California**
Ales, Beverly L.
4046 Graham St.
Pleasanton, 94566-5619
Specializing in knife rests and editor of *Knife Rests of Yesterday and Today*

Begin, David H.
4901 Cabrillo Pt.
Byron, 94514
Specializing in the buying and selling of comic strip art

Brooks, Mike
7335 Skyline Blvd.
Oakland, 94611
510-339-1751
Specializing in typewritters, early televisions & the Statue of Liberty

Carter, Tina M.
882 S Mollison Ave.
El Cajon, 92020
619-440-5043
Author of *Teapots* (available post-paid by sending $15.50 or $16.41 California residents); specializing in teapots and tea-related items

Cox, Susan
Main Street Antique Mall
237 East Main St.
El Cajon, 92020
619-447-0800 or FAX 619-447-0185
Author of *Frankoma Pottery, Value Guide and More*; also specializing in American pottery (California pottery in particular), Horlick's advertising, matchbooks, and advertising pencils

Escoe, Adrienne
P.O. Box 342
Los Alamitos, 90720

Specializing in glass knives; Editor of *Cutting Edge,* newsletter; SASE required for information concerning club or newsletter

Friedman, Barry
22725 Garzotta Dr.
Valencia, 91355
805-296-2318
Specializing in Western memorabilia with interests in Skookum dolls

George, Tony
22431-B 160 Antonio Pky., #252
Rancho Santa Margarita, 92688
714-589-6075
Specializing in sports pins and watch fobs

Hughes, Martha
4128 Ingalls St.
San Diego, 92103
619-296-1866
Specializing in advertising and figural pencil sharpeners

Inouye, Roger
765 E Franklin Ave.
Pomona, 91766
909-623-1368
Specializing in trolls

Kingsbury Productions & Antiques
Katherine Kreider
4555 N Pershing Ave. Ste. 33-138
Stockton, 95207
209-467-8438
Specializing in valentines

Lewis, Kathy and Don
Chatty Cathy's Haven
187 N Marcello Ave.

Thousand Oaks, 91360
Authors of *Chatty Cathy Dolls, an Identification and Value Guide*

Mallette, Leo A.
2309 S Santa Anita Ave.
Arcadia, 91006-5154
Specializing in Betty Boop

Mantz, John
1023 Baldwin Rd.
Bakersfield, 93304
805-397-9572
Specializing in barb wire

Santi, Steve
19626 Ricardo Ave.
Hayward, 94541
510-481-2586
Specializing in Little Golden Books and look-alikes; author of *Collecting Little Golden Books*, (Books Americana) and available from the author; information requires SASE

Utley, Bill, Editor
*Flashlight Collectors of America*
P.O. Box 4095
Tustin, 92681
714-730-1250 or FAX 714-505-4067
Specializing in flashlight and collector newsletter on the subject

Van Ausdall, Marci
P.O. Box 946
Quincy, 95971
Specializing in Betsey McCall dolls and accessories

W.B.S. Marketing
P.O. Box 1663
Palm Springs, 92263

Author of *W.B.S. Collector's Guide for Swatch Watches*; specializing in Swatch watches

## Connecticut
MacSorley, Earl E.
823 Indian Hill Rd.
Orange, 06477
Specializing in figural nutcrackers

Sabulis, Cindy
3 Stowe Dr., #1S
Shelton, 06484
203-926-1076
Specializing in Tammy, Tressie, Liddle Kiddles, and other dolls of the 1970s through 1980s

## Colorado
Diehl, Richard
5965 W Colgate Pl.
Denver, 80227
303-985-7481
Specializing in license plates

Tvorak, April
P.O. Box 126
Canon City, 81215-0126
719-269-7230
Specializing in Kitchen Independence, Kitchen Prayer Ladies, Pyrex, Fire-King (guides available), Holt Howard, and researcher of other import lines as well as post-war glass companies

## District of Columbia
Kolodny-Nagy, David
3701 Connecticut Ave. NW
Apt. #500
Washington DC, 20008

202-364-8753 or FAX 202-244-7098
Specializing in transformers, Robotech, and any other robots or Japanese animated items

McMichael, Nancy
P.O. Box 53262
Washington DC, 20009
Author of the first illustrated book on the subject, *Snowdomes* (Abbeville Press); editor of *Snow Biz*, a quarterly newsletter on snowdomes

## Florida
Donnelly, Donna and Ron
P.O. Box 7047
Panama City Beach, 32413
Specializing in Big Little Books and Western heroes

Neuschafer, Charles R.
New World Maps, Inc.
1123 S Broadway
Lantana, 33462-4522
407-586-8723
Specializing in maps and National Geographic Society map supplements

Poe-Pourri Bill and Pat Poe
220 Dominica Cir. E
Niceville, 32578-4068
904-897-4163 or FAX 904-897-2606
Specializing in buy-sell-trade fast-food collectibles, cartoon character glasses, PEZ, Smurfs, and California Raisins; for a 70-page catalog (published twice a year in January and July) send $3 US delivery ($4 Canadian or $6 overseas)

## Idaho

McVey, Jeff
1810 W State St. #427
Boise, 83702
Specializing tire ashtrays; *Tire Ashtray Collector's Guide* available for $12.95 postpaid; or if you have items for sale, send complete descriptions of your items along with SASE for my 300+ sale item catalog

## Illinois

Capell, Peter
1838 W Grace
Chicago, 60613-2724
Specializing in automobilia, gas station collectibles, and figural gas pump salt and pepper shakers

Garmon, Lee
Glass Animals
1529 Whittier St.
Springfield, 62704
217-789-9574
Co-author of *Glass Animals and Figural Flower Frogs of the Depression Era*; specializing in glass animals, Royal Haeger, Royal Hickman, Roselane Sparklers, Borden's Elsie, Reddy Kilowatt, Elvis Presley, and Marilyn Monroe

Hoffman, Pat and Don Sr.
1291 N Elmwood Dr.
Aurora, 60506
708-859-3435
Specializing in Warwick

Klompus, Eugene R.
The National Cuff Link Society
P.O. Box 346

Prospect Hts., 60070
708-816-0035
Specializing in cuff links and men's accessories

Rodrick, Tammy
Stacey's Treasures
R.R. 2, Box 163
Sumner, 62466
618-947-2240
Specializing in Avon, antiques, and collectibles

Rosie Wells Enterprises Inc.
R.R. #1
Canton, 61520
309-668-2565
Author of *The Ornament Collector's Price Guide Hallmark's Ornaments and Merry Miniatures* and *Precious Moments® Collectibles*. Specializing in Enesco ornaments, David Winter, Carlton ornaments, Lowell Davis Collection 'All God's Children,' and Coca-Cola ornaments

Ross, Harry
Soitenly Stooges Inc.
P.O. Box 72
Skokie, IL 60076
708-432-9270
Specializing in Three Stooges collectibles

Stifter, Craig and Donna
511 Aurora Ave, #117
Naperville, 60540
708-717-7949
Specializing in soda memorabilia such as Coca-Cola, Hires, Pepsi, 7-Up, etc.

TV Guide Specialists
Jeff Kadet
P.O. Box 20
Macomb, 61455
309-833-1809
Specializing in buying and selling
of *TV Guide* from 1948 through
1993

**Indiana**
Hoover, Dave
1023 Skyview Dr.
New Albany, 47150
Specializing in fishing tackle and
equipment

**Iowa**
Addy, Geneva D.
P.O. Box 124
Winterset, 50273
515-462-3027
Specializing in Imperial Porce-
lain, Pink Pigs, and Strawberry
Shortcake collectibles

De Lozier, Loretta
1101 Polk St.
Bedford, 50833
712-523-2289
Author of *Collector's Encyclopedia of Lefton China, Identification and Values* (Collector Books);
specializing in Lefton China and
research

Devine, Joe
D&D Antique Mall
1411 3rd St.
Council Bluffs, 51503
712-232-5233 or 712-328-7305
Specializing in Royal Copley

**Kansas**
Anthony, Dorothy Malone
World of Bells Publications
802 S Eddy
Ft. Scott, 66701
Specializing in bell research and
publication; author of *World of
Bells*, #5 ($8.95); *Bell Tidings*
($9.95); *Lure of Bells* ($9.95); *Collectible Bells* ($10.95); and *More
Bell Lore* ($11.95); autographed
copies available from the author;
please enclose $2.00 for postage

Fountain, Melvin
201 Alvena St.
Wichita, 67203
316-943-1925
Specializing in Swanky Swigs

**Kentucky**
Betty's Antiques
Betty Hornback
707 Sunrise Ln.
Elizabethtown, 42701
502-765-2441
Specializing in Kentucky Derby
and horse racing memorabilia

Courter, J.W.
3935 Kelley Rd.
Kevil, 42053
502-488-2116
Author of *Aladdin — The Magic
Name in Lamps, Aladdin Collectors
Manual and Price Guide #15,
Aladdin Electric Lamps*, and
*Aladdin Electric Lamps Price Guide
#2*; also publishes newsletter for
Aladdin collectors; information
requires SASE

Don Smith's National Geographic
Magazine
3930 Rankin St.
Louisville, KY 40214
502-366-7504
Specializing in *National Geographic* magazines and related
material

## Maryland

Gordon, Steve
G&G Pawnbrokers
1325 University Blvd. E
Langley Park, 20783
FAX 301-439-7296
Specializing in beer cans and
breweriana

Losonsky, Joyce and Terry
7506 Summer Leave Lane
Columbia, 21046-2455
Their book, *The Illustrated Collector's Guide to McDonald's®
Happy Meal® Boxes, Premiums,
and Promotions©*, is available
from the authors for $9.50 plus $2
postage and handling

The Shoe Lady
Libby Yalom
P.O. Box 7146
Adelphi, 20783
301-422-2026
Specializing in glass and china
shoes and boots. Author of *Shoes
of Glass* (with updated values)
available from the author by
sending $15.95 plus $2 to above
address

Welch, Randy
1100 Hambrooks Blvd.

Cambridge, 21613
410-228-5390
Specializing in walkers, rampwalking figures, and tin wind-up
toys

## Massachusetts

Bruce, Scott; Mr. Cereal Box
P.O. Box 481
Cambridge, 02140
617-492-5004
Publisher of *Flake* magazine;
author of *Complete Cereal Boxography, Cerealizing America*
(Faber and Faber), and *Cereal
Box Bonanza — the 1950s* (Collector Books). Specializing in
buying, selling, trading cereal
boxes, cereal displays, and
cereal premiums; free appraisals
given

Jones, Gen
294 Park St.
Medford, 02155
617-395-8598
Author of *Shirley in the Magazines*; available by sending $45
with $4.50 for shipping

Rodolfos, Jimmy
Dionne Quints Collectors Club
P.O. Box 2527
Woburn, 01888
617-933-2219
Specializing in Dionne quintuplets

Schmuhl, Marian H.
7 Revolutionary Ridge Rd.
Bedford, 01730-2057
617-275-2156
Specializing in dollhouse furnishings

TVC Enterprises
P.O. Box 1088
Easton, 02334
508-238-1179
Specializing in TV, movie, and rock 'n roll memorabilia; sample catalog available for $2

Wellman, BA
88 State Rd. W
Homestead Farms #2
Westminster, 01473-1435
Specializing in all areas of American ceramics with video book; identification and price guides available on Ceramic Arts Studio; researcher on Royal China with interest in metal accessories

## Michigan
Bruner, Mike
6980 Walnut Lake Rd.
W Bloomfield, 48323
810-661-2359
Specializing in telegraph and express memorabilia, insulators, exit globes, railroad lanterns, lightning rod balls, target balls, and porcelain advertising

Gilbert, Carol Karbowiak
2193 14 Mile Rd. 206
Sterling Heights, 48310
Specializing in Breyer horses & animals

Pickvet, Mark
P.O. Box 90404
Flint, 48509
Specializing in shot glasses (SASE required for information);

Author of *Shot Glasses: An American Tradition*, (167 pages of information, over 1,000 illustrations, current values) available for $12.95 plus $2.50 postage and handling from Antique Publications, P.O. Box 553, Marietta, OH 45750

## Minnesota
Flynn, Patrick
MinneMemories
108 Warren St.
Mankato, 56001
Specializing in Bobbin' Head Dolls; send SASE for information about price guide

## Missouri
Allen, Col. Bob
P.O. Box 85
St. James, 65559
Author of *A Guide to Collecting Cookbooks*; specializing in cookbooks, leaflets, and Jello memorabilia

*Holly Hobbie Collectibles of America*
Helen L. McCale
Box 397
Butler, 64730-0397
816-679-3690
Specializing in Holly Hobbie; newsletter available

Van Hoozer, Gary
Publisher/Editor
*Farm Antiques News*
812 N Third St.
Tarkio, 64491
816-736-4528
Specializing in old farm items, tractors to smaller collectibles

## New Hampshire

Chris Russell & The Halloween Queen
4 Lawrance St. & Rt. 10
Winchester, 03470
Specializing in Halloween collectibles and postcards

## New Jersey

Cole, Lillian M.
14 Harmony School Rd.
Flemington, 08822
908-782-3198
Specializing in collecting pie birds, pie vents, and pie funnels; also pie bird research

Dezso, Doug
864 Paterson Ave.
Maywood, 07607
Specializing in candy containers, nodders, Kellogg's Pep pinback buttons, Shafford cats, and Tonka toys

*Eggcup Collectors Corner*
Dr. Joan M. George, Editor
67 Stevens Ave.
Old Bridge, 08857
Specializing in eggcups and collector information

McClane, Jim
232 Butternut Dr.
Wayne, 07470
201-616-1538
Specializing in MAD collectibles

Sigg, Walter
3-D Entertainment
P.O. Box 208
Swartswood, 07877

Specializing in View-Master and Tru-View reels and packets

Sparacio, George
P.O. Box 791
Malaga, 08328
609-694-4167
Specializing in match safes

Vintage Cocktail Shakers
Stephen Visakay
P.O. Box 1517
W Caldwell, 07007-1517
Specializing in vintage cocktail shakers; by mail & appointment only

## New Mexico

Mace, Shirley
Shadow Enterprises
P.O. Box 1602
Mesilla Park, 88047
505-524-6717
Author of *Encyclopedia of Silhouette Collectibles on Glass* (available from the author), and specializing in silhouette collectibles

## New York

Arlene Lederman Antiques
150 Main St.
Nyack, 10960
914-358-8616
Specializing in vintage cocktail shakers, 18th through 20th-century antiques, American, European, furniture, glass, decorative accessories, and collectibles

Brenner, Howard S.
106 Woodgate Terrace
Rochester, 14625
716-482-3641

Author of *Comic Character Clocks and Watches* (Books Americana); specializing in character and comic timepieces

Dinner, Craig
Box 4399
Sunnyside, 11104
718-729-3850
Specializing in figural cast iron items (door knockers, lawn sprinklers, doorstops, windmill weights, etc.)

Doucet, Larry
Dick Tracy Collectibles
2351 Sultana Dr.
Yorktown Hgts., 10598
Specializing in Dick Tracy memorabilia; for free appprasials, send photos, detailed descriptions, and SASE; also an active buyer

Eisenstadt, Robert
P.O. Box 020767
Brooklyn, 11202-0017
718-625-3553 or FAX 718-522-1087
Specializing in gambling chips and other gambling-related items

Gerson, Roselyn
P.O. Box 40
Lynbrook, 11563
516-593-8746
Collector specializing in unusual, gadgertry, figural compacts and vanity bags and purses; author of *Ladies' Compacts of the 19th and 20th Centuries*, a 240-page, 8½" x 11" hardcover book, available from the author for $34.95 plus $2 postage and handling, and *Vintage Vanity Bags and Purses* (Collector Books), the first book devoted solely to bags and purses that incorporate compacts

Luchsinger, Paul P.
1126 Wishart St.
Hermitage, 16148
412-962-5747
Specializing in antique and unusual corkscrews

Margolin, Freddi
P.O. Box 5124P
Bay Shore, 11706
Specializing in *Peanuts* and Charles Schulz collectibles

Romano, Pat
32 Sterling Dr.
Lake Grove, 11202-0017
718-625-3553
Specializing in golf collectibles

**North Carolina**
Kaifer, Carole S.
P.O. Box 232
Bethania, 27010
Specializing in novelty animated and non-animated clocks

Retskin, Bill
P.O. Box 18481
Asheville, 28814
704-254-4487 or FAX 704-254-1066
Author of *The Matchcover Collector's Price Guide, 1st Edition* (available for $16.95 plus $3.25 shipping and handling), and editor of *The Front Striker Bulletin*; specializing in matchcovers

Sayers, Rolland J.
Southwestern Antiques and Appraisals
P.O. Box 629
Brevard, 28712
Specializing in Boy Scout Collectibles. Author of *Guide to Scouting Collectibles*, available from the author for $19.95 plus $3.50 postage

**North Dakota**
Farnsworth, Bryce L.
1334 14½ St.
S Fargo, 58103
Specializing in Rosemeade

**Ohio**
Bruegman, Bill
137 Casterton Ave.
Akron, 44303
216-836-0668 or FAX 216-869-8668
Author of *Toys of the Sixties; Aurora History and Price Guide*; and *Cartoon Friends of the Baby Boom Era*. Write for information about his magazine and mail order catalog. Specializing in Aurora figure kits and toys from the baby boom era

Dutt, Gordy
*Gordy's/KitBuilders Magazine*
Box 201
Sharon Center, 44274-0201
216-239-1657 or FAX 216-239-2991
Author of *Collectible Figure Kits of the '50s, '60s, and '70s* ($24 US postpaid or $25 Canadian), containing over 400 photographs with information and values; specializing in models other than Aurora, Weirdos, and Rat Finks

Kaduck, Margaret and John
P.O. Box 26076
Cleveland, 44126
216-333-2958
Specializing in watch fobs, postcards, and advertising items. For more information on their many books or monthly mail auctions call or send SASE

Kerr, Ann
P.O. Box 437
Sidney, 45365
513 492-6369
Author of *Collector's Encyclopedia of Russel Wright Designs* (Collector Books); Specializing in work of Russel Wright with interests in 20th-century decorative arts

Marsh, Thomas
914 Franklin Ave.
Youngstown, 44502
216-743-8600 or 800-845-7930
Publisher and author of *The Official Guide to Collecting Applied Color Label Soda Bottles* Volumes I and II (available for $24.95 each plus $4 for postage and handling); specializing in applied colored label soda bottles and related items

Norris, M.G. 'Bud'
1324 N Hague Ave.
Columbus, 43204
Author of *The Tom Mix Book*; available by sending $27.95 for autographed edition

**Oklahoma**
Phillips Archives of Western Memorabilia

1703 N Aster Pl.
Broken Arrow, 74012
918-254-8205 or FAX 918-252-9363
Author of *Roy Rogers, a Biography,*
*Singing Cowboy Stars, Silver*
*Screen Cowboys, 'King of the Coy-*
*boys' and Dale Evans, 'Queen of the*
*West'* — among others; authority on
Classic Western comics, TV west-
erns, character collectibles, coun-
try-western music; ardent western
researcher and guest columnist

Terri's Toys and Nostalgia
Terri Mardis-Ivers
419 S First St.
Ponca City, 74601
405-762-8697
Specializing in buying/selling character
collectibles, lunch boxes, advertising
items, Breyer & Hartland figures, etc.

## Oregon
Brady, Glen
P.O. Box 3933
Central Point, 97502
503-772-0350
Sepcializing in Smokey Bear

Morris, Tom
Prize Publishers
P.O. Box 8307
Medford, 97504
503-779-3164
Author of *The Carnival Chalk*
*Prize*, a pictorial price guide on
carnival chalkware figures with
brief histories and values for each

## Pennsylvania
BOJO/Bob Gottuso
P.O. Box 1203

Cranberry Twp., 163033-2203
Phone/FAX 412-776-0621
Specializing in the Beatles and
rock 'n roll memorabilia

Foley, Edward
P.O. Box 572
Adamstown, 19501-0572
Specializing in advertising porce-
lain door push plates.

Greenfield, Jeannie
310 Parker Rd.
Stoneboro, 16153
Specializing in egg timers, cake
toppers, and Jasco bells

Homestead Collectibles
Art and Judy Turner
P.O. Box 173
Mill Hall, 17751
717-726-3597
Specializing in Jim Beam decanters
and Ertl die-cast metal banks

Huegel, Joan L.
1002 W 25th
St. Erie, 16502
Specializing in bookmarks

McEntee, Phil
Where the Toys Are
45 W Pike St.
Canonsburg, 15317
412-745-4599
Open 7 days 10:30 am - 5:00 pm
Specializing in antique and col-
lectible toys and games

Posner, Judy
R.D. 1, Box 273
Effort, 18330

717-629-6583
Specializing in figural pottery, cookie jars, salt and pepper shakers, Black memorabilia, and Disneyana; sale lists available

## South Carolina
Roerig, Fred and Joyce
R.R. 2, Box 504
Walterboro, 29488
Authors of *The Collector's Encyclopedia of Cookie Jars, Book I and II* (Collector Books)

## Texas
Cooper, Marilyn M.
P.O. Box 55174
Houston, 77255
Author of *The Pictorial Guide to Toothbrush Holders* ($22.95 postpaid)

Docks, L.R. 'Les'
Shellac Shack
Box 691035
San Antonio, 78269-1035
Send $2 for a 72-page catalog of thousands of 78 rpm records that he wants to buy, the prices he will pay, and shipping instructions

Nossaman, Darlene
5419 Lake Charles
Waco, 76710
817-772-3969
Specializing in Homer Laughlin china information

Pringle, Joyce
Chip and Dale Collectibles
3500 S Cooper
Arlington, 76015
817-467-7030

Specializing in Boyd art glass, Summit, and Moser

Woodard, Dannie
P.O. Box 1346
Weatherford, 76086
Author of *Hammered Aluminum, Hand Wrought Collectibles,* and publisher of *The Aluminist* newsletter (6 issues, $12)

## Utah
Barnes, Richard D.
1520 W 800
N Salt Lake City, 84116
801-521-4400
Specializing in I Dream of Jeannie and Barbara Eden; editor of *PR News.* Subscription: $20 for next 8 issues; send $3 for sample copy

Rick Spencer
3953 S Renault Cir.
West Valley, 84119
801-973-0805
Specializing in Shawnee, Roseville, Weller, Van Telligan, Regal, Bendel, Coors, Rookwood, Watt; also salt and pepper shakers, cookie jars, etc., cut glass, radios, and silver flatware

## Virginia
Cranor, Rosalind
P.O. Box 859
Blacksburg, 24063
Author of *Elvis Collectibles* and *Best of Elvis Collectibles* (each at $19.95 with $2 postage and handling), available from the author

De Angelo, Larry
516 King Arthur Dr.
Virginia Beach, 23464
804-424-1691
Specializing in California Raisin
collectibles

Giese, David
1410 Aquia Dr.
Stafford, 22554
703-569-5984
Specializing in character shaving
mugs and razor blade banks

Henry, Rosemary
9610 Greenview Ln.
Manassas, 22100
Specializing in cookie cutters,
stamps, & molds; send SASE for
info about *The Cookie Shaper's
Bible* & *Cookies* newsletter

Reynolds, Charlie
Reynolds Toys
2836 Monroe St.
Falls Church, 22042
703-533-1322
Specializing in banks, figural bottle openers, toys, etc.

**Washington**
Eclectic Antiques and Collectibles
Jim and Kaye Whitaker
P.O. Box 475, Dept. FM
Lynnwood, 98046
206-774-8571
Authors of *Motion Lamps,
1920s to the Present*; specializ-
ing in *Josef Originals* and
motion lamps

Klepey, Terry and Kay
P.O. Box 553
Forks, 98331
360-327-3726
Specializing in Lone Ranger mem-
orabilia and publishers of *The
Silver Bullet Newsletter*

Palmer, Donna
Our Favorite Things
3020 Issaquah Pine Lake Rd. #557
Issaquah, 98027
206-392-7636
General line but specializing in
Scottie dog collectibles

Thompson, Walt
Box 2541
Yakima, 98907-2451
Specializing in charge cards and
credit-related items

**Wisconsin**
Helley, Phil
Old Kilbourn Antiques
629 Indiana Ave.
Wisconsin Dells, 53965
608-254-8659
Specializing in Cracker Jack
items, radio premiums, toys
(especially Japanese wind-up
toys), banks, and old Dells souvenir items marked Kilbourn

**Canada**
Warner, Ian
P.O. Box 93022 499 Main St.
S Brampton Ontario L6Y 4V8
905-453-9074 or FAX 905-453-2931
Specializing in Wade pottery

# CLUBS AND NEWSLETTERS

*Abingdon Pottery Collectors Club*
Elaine Westover,
Membership and Treasurer
210 Knox Hwy. 5
Abington, IL 61410
309-462-3267

*Action Toys Newsletter*
P.O. Box 31551
Billings, MT 59107
406-248-4121

Akro Agate Collectors Club and
*Clarksburg Crow* quarterly
newsletter
Roger Hardy
10 Bailey St.
Clarksburg, WV 26301-2524
304-624-4523
Annual membership fee: $20

*The Aluminist*
Dannie Woodard
P.O. Box 1347
Weatherford, TX 76086
817-594-4680
6 issues per year; back issues or
sample copy available for $2
each

American Barb Wire Collectors
Society (ABWCS)
John Mantz
1023 Baldwin Rd.
Bakersfield, CA 93304
805-397-9572
Bi-monthly newsletter, $10.00 per
year, includes membership for
entire family and discount buying
privileges. Sample copy free.
Inquiries invited

The American Matchcover Collecting Club
P.O. Box 18481
Asheville, NC 28814
704-254-4487 or FAX 704-254-1066

American Quilter's Society
P.O. Box 3290
Paducah, KY 42002-3290
$18 annual membership includes
4 issues of the *American Quilter*
magazine

*Antique and Collector Reproduc-
tion News*
Mark Cherenka, Circulation Dept.
P.O. Box 71174
Des Moines, IA 50325
800-227-5531
Monthly newsletter showing differences between old originals
and new reproductions; subscription: $32 per year

*Antique Souvenir Collectors News*
Gary Leveille
P.O. Box 562
Great Barrington, MA 01230
413-528-5490

*The Antique Trader Weekly*
P.O. Box 1050
Dubuque, IA 52004
Subscription: $32 (52 issues) per
year; Sample: $1

*Ashtray Journal*
Chuck Thompson,
Editor/Publisher
Box 11652
Houston, TX 77293

Subscription: $14.95 (6 issues) per year or send $3.95 for sample copy; send SASE for free list of publications

Association of Map Memorabilia Collectors
8 Amherst Rd.
Pelham, MA 01002
413-253-3155

*Avon Times*
(National Newsletter Club)
c/o Dwight or Vera Young
P.O. Box 9868, Dept. P.
Kansas City, MO 64134
Send SASE for information

Barbara Eden's Official Fan Club
P.O. Box 556
Sherman Oaks, CA 91403
818-761-0267

*The Bell Tower*
Official publication of the American Bell Association International, Inc.
P.O. Box 19443
Indianapolis, IN 46219

*Bookmark Collector*
Joan L. Huegel
1002 W 25th St.
Erie, PA 16502
Quarterly newsletter, $5.50 per year ($6.50 in Canada); sample copy: $1 plus stamp or LSASE

The BotCon Transformer Convention
Jon Hartman
209 W Rush St.
Kendalville, IN 46755

or David Kolodny-Nagy
3701 Connecticut Ave. NW, #500
Washington, DC 20008

Boyd's Art Glass Collectors Guild
P.O. Box 52
Hatboro, PA 19040-0052

Candy Container Collectors of America
P.O. Box 352
Chelmsord, MA 10824-0352

CAS Collectors Association
(Ceramic Arts Studio)
P.O. Box 46
Madison, WI 53701
608-241-9138

Compact Collectors
P.O. Box 40
Lynbrook, NY 11563
516-593-8746

*The Cookie Jar Collectors Express*
Paradise Publications
Box 221 Mayview, MO 64071
816-584-6309

*Cookies* Newsletter
Rosemary Henry
9610 Greenview Ln.
Manassas, VA 22110
Request information about *The Cookie Shaper's Bible*

*The Copley Courier*
1639 N Catalina St.
Burbank, CA 91505

Cowboy Museum & Gallery
Jack Glover

209 Alamo Plaza
San Antonio, TX 78025
512-229-1257
Author of *Bobbed Wire VIII*

*The Cutting Edge*
Newsletter of glass knife collectors
Wilbur Peterson
711 Kelly Dr.
Lebanon, TN 37087
615-444-4303
Subscription: $5 per year, sample:
$1.25

*The Daze*
Teri Steel, Editor/Publisher
Box 57
Otisville, MI 48463
313-631-4593
The nation's market place for
glass, china, and pottery

*Eggcup Collectors' Corner*
c/o Joan George, Ed.D.
67 Stevens Ave.
Old Bridge, NJ 08857
Published 4 times a year ($18
United States and Canada, other
$22). Sample copies available at
$5 each

*Farm Antique News*
Gary Van Hoozer,
Publisher/Editor
812 N Third St.
Tarkio, MO 64491
816-736-4528
A bimonthy magazine available
by sending $14 per year which
includes one free classified ad;
actively sells, trades, and welcomes inquires

Fenton Art Glass Collectors
of America, Inc.
Williamstown, WV 26187

*FBOC*
(Figural Bottle Opener Collectors)
Donna Kitzmiller
117 Basin Hill Rd.
Duncannon, PA 17020
717-834-4867
Please send SASE for information

*Fiesta Club of America*
P.O. Box 15383
Loves Park, IL 61132-5383
send $20 for 1 year's membership
and newsletter

*Fiesta Collector's Quarterly*
China Specialties Inc.
19238 Dorchester Cir.
Strongville, OH 44136
$12 (four issues) per year

Fisher-Price Collector's Club
Jeanne Kennedy
1442 N Ogden
Mesa, AZ 85205
Monthly newsletter with information and ads; send SASE for more
information

*FLAKE, The Breakfast Nostalgia
Magazine*
P.O. Box 481
Cambridge, MA 02140
617-492-5004
Bimonthly illustrated issue
devoted to one hot collecting area
such as Disney, etc.; plus letters,
discoveries, new releases, and
ads; single issue: $4 ($6 foreign),

annual: $20 ($28 foreign); free 25-word ad with new subscription

*Flashlight Collectors of America Newsletter*
Bill Utley
P.O. Box 4095
Tustin, CA 92680
714-730-1250 or FAX 714-505-4067
$12 for four issues per year; single copies and back issues are $3 each

*Frankoma Family Collectors Association*
c/o Nancy Littrell
P.O. box 32571
Oklahoma City, OK 73123-0771
Membership dues: $20 (includes quarterly newsletter and annual convention)

*The Front Striker Bulletin*
Bill Retskin
P.O. Box 18481
Asheville, NC 28814
704-254-4487 or FAX 704-254-1066
Quarterly newsletter for match-cover collectors $17.50 per year for 1st class mailing + $2 for new member registration

The Glass Press
P.O. Box 205
Iowa City, IA 52319-0205
FAX 319-626-3216
Monthly publication for buying, selling, & trading all kinds of glassware; free monthly ads w/$25 yearly subscription

*Gordy's / KitBuilders*
Gordy Dutt

P.O. Box 201
Sharon Center, OH 44256
216-239-1657 or FAX 216-239-2991

*Grandma's Trunk*
The Millards
P.O. Box 404
Northport, MI 49670
616-386-5351
Auction and set price lists in newspaper format for all types of paper ephemera; subscription: $5 yearly bulk rate or $8 for 1st class

Grandpa's Depot & Caboose
John 'Grandpa' White
Denver Union Station 1616 17th St.
Denver, CO 80202
303-892-1177 or FAX 303-573-5505
Publishes catalogs on railroad-related collectibles

Hall China Collectors Newsletters
P.O. Box 360488
Cleveland, OH 44136

*Hartland Newsletter*
Gail Fitch
1733 N Cambridge Ave. #109
Milwaukee, WI 53202
Send $8 for six issues or $4.50 for 3 issues of monthly newsletter. Classified ads are $2 for 50 words. Please send SASE for information and order form for book, *Hartland Horses and Riders*, which covers horses and western heroes made from 1947 to present day

*Holly Hobbie Collectibles*
c/o Helen McCale

P.O. Box 397
Butler, MO 64730-0397

International Nippon Collectors Club
c/o Phil Fernkes
112 Oak Ave
N. Owatonna, MN 55060
Publishes newsletter 6 times per year

*Just for Openers*
John Stanley
3712 Sunningdale Way
Durham, NC 27707-5684
919-419-1546

*Kitchen Antiques & Collectibles News* Newsletter
Kana & Darlene DeMore, Editors
4645 Laurel Ridge Dr.
Harrisburg, PA 17110
717-545-7320
Subscription: $24 per year for 6 issues

*Knife Rests of Yesterday and Today*
Beverly L. Ales
4046 Graham St.
Pleasanton, CA 94566-5619
Subscription of $20 per year for 6 issues

*The Laughlin Eagle*
c/o Richard G. Racheter
1270 63rd Terrace South
St. Petersburg, FL 33705

Line Jewels-Insulators
3557 Nicklaus Dr.
Titusville, FL 32780

Marble Collectors' Society of America P.O. Box 222
Trumbull, CT 06611

*McDonald's® Collecting Tips Newsletter*
Meredith Williams
Box 633 Joplin, MO 64802
Send SASE for information

McDonald's® Collector Club
c/o Joyce and Terry Losonsky
7506 Summer Leave Lane
Columbia, MD 21046-2455
301-381-3358

Sunshine Chapter, McDonald's® Collector's Club
c/o Bill and Pat Poe
220 Dominica Circle E.
Niceville, FL 32578-4068
904-897-4163 or FAX 904-897-2606
Annual membership is $10 per individual or $15 per family and includes 6 newsletters and 2 McDonald's® Only shows for the year

*Model & Toy Collector Magazine*
Toy Scouts, Inc.
Bill Bruegman
137 Casterton Ave.
Akron, OH 44303-1552
216-836-0668 or FAX 216-869-8668

*The Mystic Lights of the Aladdin Knights*
J.W. Courter
3935 Kelley Rd.
Kevil, KY 42053
502-488-2116
Subscription: $20 per year for

bimonthly issues with current buy-sell-trade information; post-paid first class

National Association of Avon Collectors
c/o Connie Clark
6100 Walnut, Dept. P
Kansas City, MO 64113
Send large SASE for information

The National Association of Paper and Advertising Collectors
P.O. Box 500
Mount Joy, PA 17552

*National Blue Ridge Newsletter*
Norma Lilly
144 Highland Dr.
Bloutville, TN 37617
Subscription: $15 per year (6 issues)

The National Cuff Link Society
Eugene R. Klompus, President
P.O. Box 346
Prospect Hts., IL 60070
708-816-0035

National Graniteware Society
P.O. Box 10013
Cedar Rapids, IA 52410

National Imperial Glass Collectors' Society, Inc.
P.O. Box 534
Bellaire, OH 43906
Dues: $12 per year (+$1 for each additional member of household), quarterly newsletter, convention every June

National Insulator Association
1315 Old Mill Path
Broadview Hgts., OH 44147

National Milk Glass Collectors' Society & *Opaque News* quarterly newsletter
c/o Helen D. Storey
46 Almond Dr.
Cocoa Townes Hershey, PA 17033
Please send SASE for information

National Reamer Association
c/o Larry Branstad
R.R. 3, Box 67
Frederic, WI 54837

National Toothpick Holder Collectors' Society
Joyce Ender, Treasurer
Box 246 Sawyer, MI 49125
Dues: $15 (single) or $20 (couple) per year; includes montly *Tooth-pick Bulletin* newsletter. Annual convention in August

National Valentine Collectors Assoc.
Evalene Pulati
P.O. Box 1404
Santa Ana, CA 92702
714-547-1355

*The Nelson McCoy Express*
Jean Bushnell, Editor
3801 Rock Creek Dr.
Broomfield, CO 80020
303-468-8309

Nutcracker Collectors' Club & Newsletter
Susan Otto, Editor
12204 Fox Run Dr.

Chesterland, OH 44026
216-729-2686
$10 annual dues for quarterly newsletter and free classified ads

The Occupied Japan Club
c/o Florence Archambault
29 Freeborn St.
Newport, RI 02840-1821
Publishes *The Upside Down World of an O.J. Collector*, a bimonthly newsletter. Information requires SASE

*On the Lighter Side* International Lighter Collectors
Judith Sanders, Editor
136 Circle Dr.
Quitman, TX 75783
903-763-2795 or FAX 703-763-4953
Annual convention held in different cities in the US; send SASE when requesting information

*Our McCoy Matters*
Kathy Lynch, Editor
P.O. Box 14255
Parkville, MO 64152
816-587-9179 or FAX 816-746-6924

*Paper Collectors' Marketplace*
Doug Watson, Publisher/Editor
470 Main St.
Scandinavia, WI 54977-0128
715-467-2379 or FAX 715-467-2243
(8 am to 8 pm, Mon-Sat); subscription of 12 issues per year is $17.95. Add $15 for first class delivery per year

*Paper Pile Quarterly*
Ada Fitzsimmons, Publisher/Editor

P.O. Box 337
San Anselmo, CA 94979-0337
Subscription: $12.50 per year in USA and Canada

Phillips Archives
Robert W. Phillips
1703 N Aster Place
Broken Arrow, OK 74012
918-254-8205 or FAX 918-252-9362
Author and leading authority on western genre and Roy Rogers. Current books include: *Roy Rogers, a Biography*, *Western Comics Journal*, *Bob Willis Journals*, and *Singing Cowboy Stars*

*Pie Birds Unlimited Newsletter*
Lillian M. Cole
14 Harmony School Rd.
Flemington, NJ 08822
908-782-3198

*The Pokey Gazette*
Steve Santi
19626 Ricardo Ave.
Hayward, CA 94541
510-481-2586
A *Little Golden Book* collector newsletter

*Police Collector News*
Mike Bondarenko, Publisher
R.R. 1, Box 14
Baldwin, WI 54002

*The Political Bandwagon*
M. Jeannine Coup, Editor
P.O. Box 348
Leola, PA 17540
Subscription: $15 per year

The Political Gallery
Thomas D. Slater, Director
5335 N Tacoma Ave., Ste. 24
Indianapolis, IN 46220
317-257-0863 or FAX 317-254-9167
Auctioneers and dealers in vintage
political campaign and sports memorabilia; subscriptions available

*Pottery Lovers Newsletter*
Pottery Lovers Reunion
Pat Sallaz
4969 Hudson Dr.
Stow, OH 44224

*Powder Puff* Newsletter
P.O. Box 40
Lynbrook, NY 11563
Contains information covering
all aspects of compact collecting, restoration, vintage ads,
patents, history, and articles by
members and prominent guest
writers. A 'Seekers and Sellers'
column and dealer listing is
offered free to members

*Quint News*
Dionne Quint Collectors
P.O. Box 2527
Woburn, MA 01888
617-933-2219

*Red Wing Collectors Newsletter*
Red Wing Collectors Society, Inc.
Doug Podpeskar,
membership information
624 Jones St.
Eveleth, MN 55734-1631
218-744-4845
Please include SASE when
requesting information

*Rosevilles of the Past* Newsletter
Jack Bomm, Editor
P.O. Box 656
Clarcona, FL 32710-0656
407-294-3980
Send $19.95 per year for 6 to 12
newsletters

Salt & Pepper Novelty Shakers Club
Irene Thornburg
581 Joy Rd.
Battlecreek, MI 49017
616-963-7953

*Scottie Sampler*
Donna Newton, Editor
P.O. Box 1512
Columbus, IN 47202

Shawnee Pottery Collectors' Club
c/o Pamela Curran
P.O. Box 713
New Smyrna Beach, FL 32170-0713
Monthly nation-wide newsletter.
Send SASE for more information;
sample newsletter available for $3

The Shot Glass Club of America
Mark Pickvet, Editor
P.O. Box 90404 Flint, MI 48509
$6 yearly membership includes a
monthly 3-page newsletter

*The Silver Bullet*
Terry & Kay Klepey
P.O. Box 553 Forks, WA 98331
Yearly subscription for Lone
Ranger enthusiasts and collectors
is $12 for USA or $20 Canadian
or foreign; sample copy available
for $4. Please allow 2 to 4 weeks
to process a new subscription

Smurf Collectors' Club
24 Cabot Road West, Dept. P
Massapequa, NY 11758
Specializing in Smurf memorabilia, 1957-1990

*Snow Biz*
c/o Nancy McMichael
P.O. Box 53262
Washington, D.C. 20009
Quarterly newsletter (subscription: $10 per year) and collector's club, annual meeting/swap meet

*Tea Talk*
Diana Rosen
419 N Larchmont Blvd., #225
Los Angeles, CA 90004
213-871-6901 or FAX 213-828-2444

*TeaTimes Newsletter*
P.O. Box 841
Langley, WA 98260
$18 yearly subscription; a newsletter on the pleasures of afternoon tea

*Vernon Views*
Newsletter for Vernon Kilns collectors

P.O. Box 945
Scottsdale, AZ 85252
Quarterly issue available by sending $10 for a year's subscription

View-Master Reel Collector
Roger Nazeley
4921 Castor Ave.
Philadelphia, PA 19124
215-743-8999

*Vintage Fashion & Costume Jewelry* Newsletter/Club
P.O. Box 265
Glen Oaks, NY 11004
718-969-2320 or 718-939-3095
Yearly subscription: $15 (U.S.) for 4 issues; sample copy available by sending $5

Westmoreland Glass Society
Steve Jensen, President
4809 420 St.
SE Iowa City, IA 52240
319-337-9647
Publishes 6 newsletters per year; meets in March and August

# INDEX